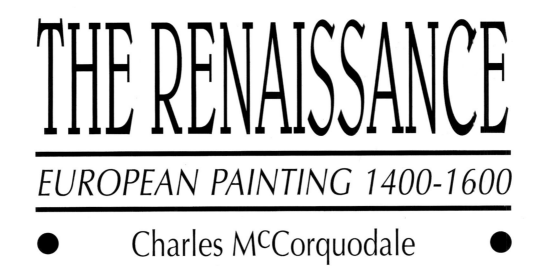

THE RENAISSANCE

EUROPEAN PAINTING 1400-1600

● Charles McCorquodale ●

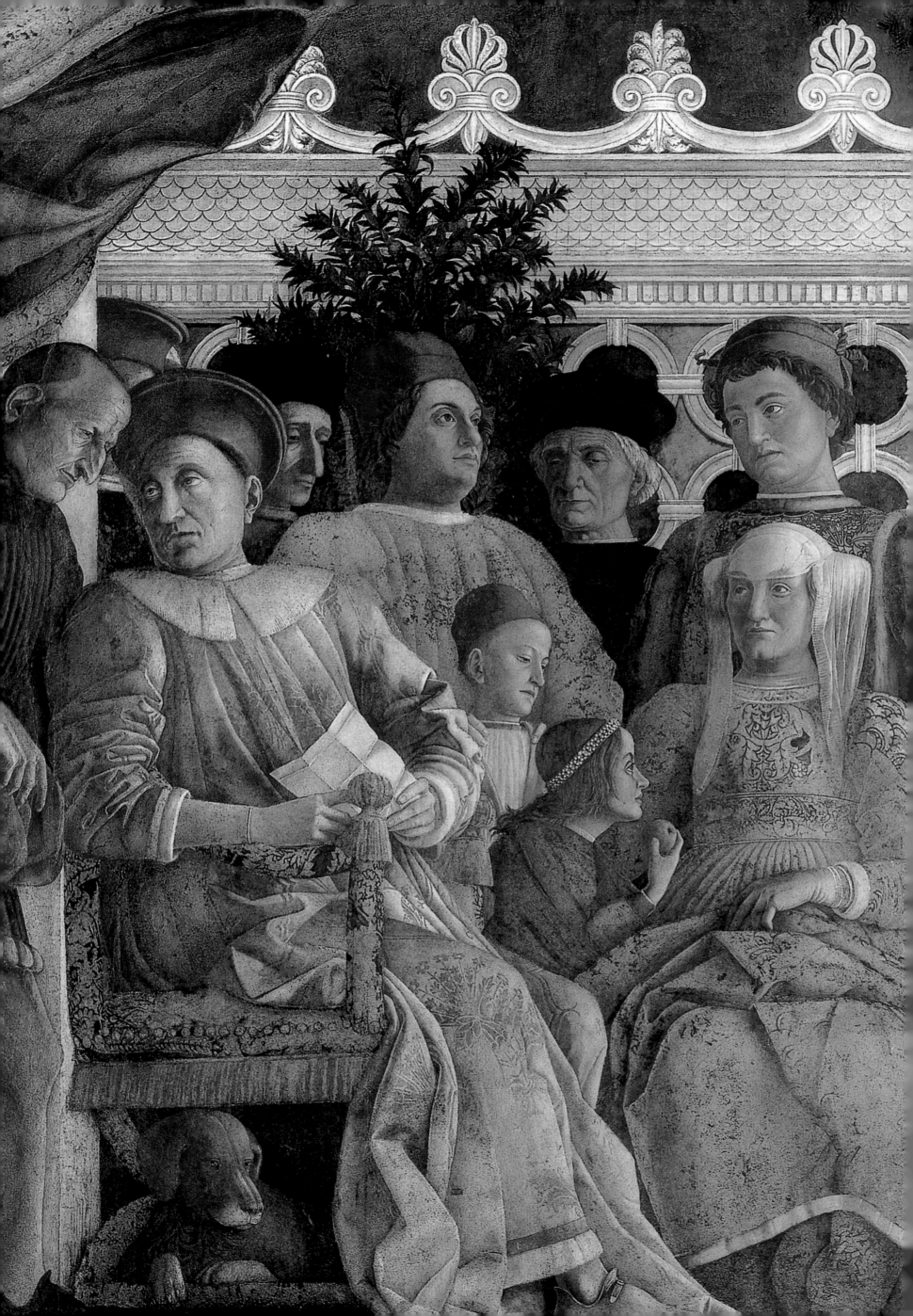

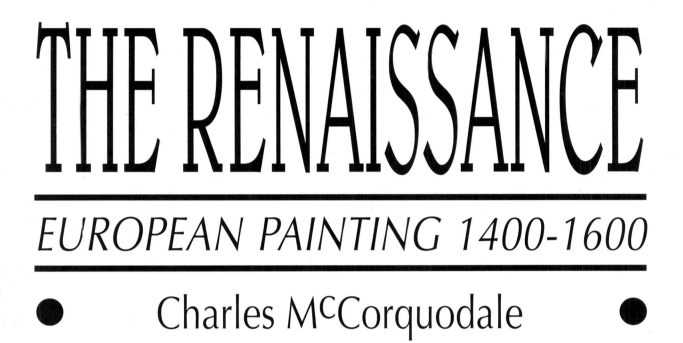

THE RENAISSANCE

EUROPEAN PAINTING 1400-1600

● Charles McCorquodale ●

N D E
PUBLISHING

This edition is published for
North America
in 1999 by

**NDE
Publishing**

300 Empress Avenue, Toronto,
ON, Canada ,M2N 3V4

————

Copyright © The Gallery Publishing

————

An exclusive design for the jacket and the slipcase
for this 1999 edition
is made by NDE Publishing.

————

————

ISBN 0-9684749-8-5

————

This book was written by Charles Mc Corquodale
Edited by Caroline Bugler, Alice Peebles and Robyn Ayers.
Designed by Joy FitzSimmons, Simon Bell and Paul Griffin
Picture Researcher Julia Brown

————

Frontispiece   : Detail showing the *Gonzaga Family* from the *Camera Degli Sposi* in the Palazzo Ducale, Mantua, by ANDREA MANTEGNA (*see also plate 105*).
Facing Forword : Detail from *Madonna of the Rose Bower* by STEPHAN LOCHNER (*see also plate 156*).

Contents

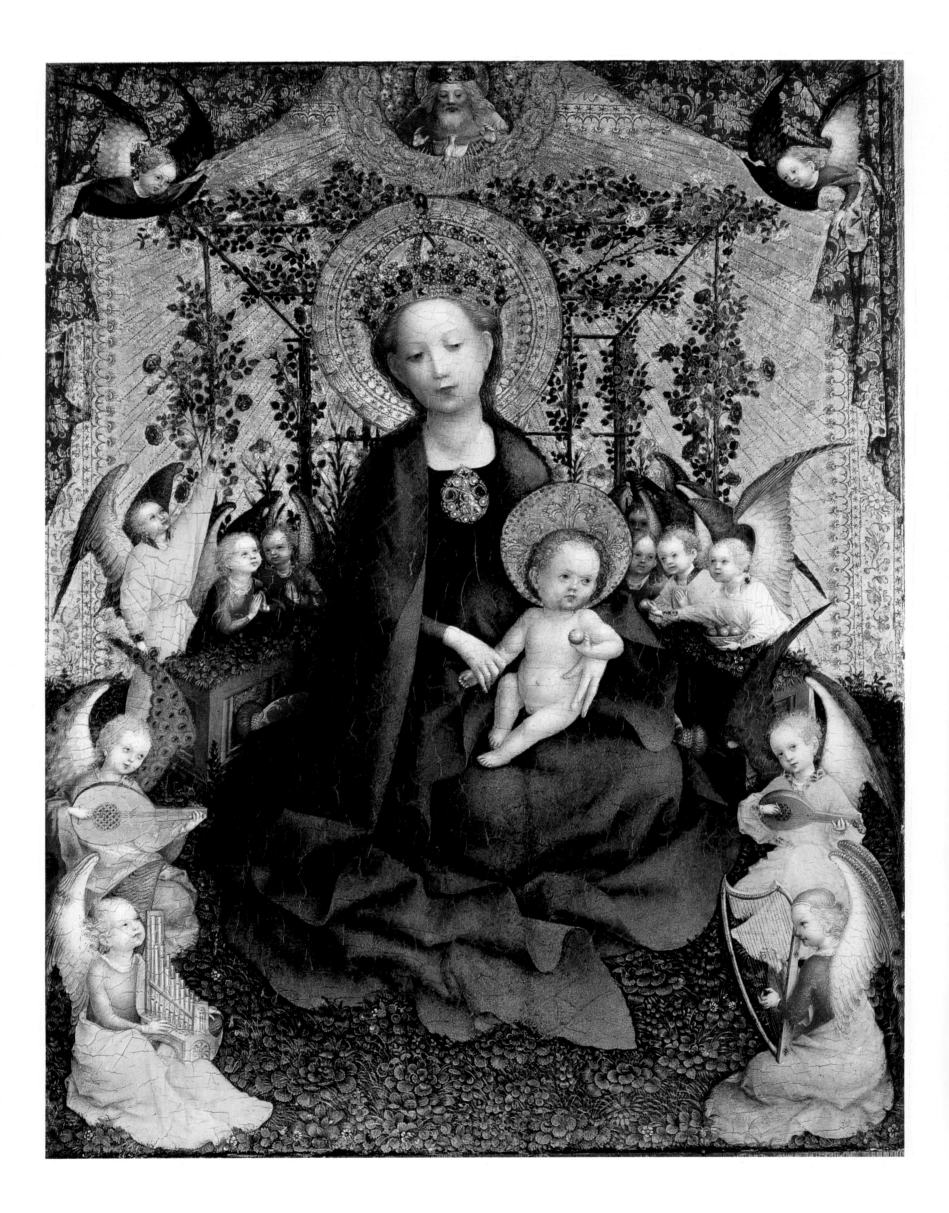

Foreword

When I was asked to write this book, my reaction was one of disbelief that a market already flooded with books on every aspect of Renaissance art could sustain yet another. I quickly realized, however, that there was no single large-scale survey of Renaissance painting across Europe, from which to obtain a wide and comprehensive view. I hope this book will fill that gap. It is intended to make comparisons between the aims, ideals and styles of the Renaissance as they evolved in the different regions of Europe.

For a book of this kind to achieve its purpose, the selection of paintings to be illustrated should be as comprehensive and balanced as possible. This presents two problems. Those who already know something of Renaissance art will expect to see many important, well-known pictures, despite the frequency with which these are reproduced elsewhere. On the other hand, the beginner's lack of preconceived ideas allows for a greater flexibility in the picture selection. I have tried to satisfy both kinds of reader, including many of the best-known paintings alongside a range of less familiar ones. Some have been selected for their art historical importance, some for the light they shed on an artist's range, and others, unashamedly, for their beauty.

This book is the result of the compilation of material from an enormous variety of sources, and its creation has been largely a solitary process. I would, however, like to record my deep gratitude to my editor, Caroline Bugler, whose infinite skill, patience and tact have been of inestimable importance in weaving together the many complicated strands of text, captions and illustrations. The same goes for the expertise and persistence of my picture editor Julia Brown in assembling illustrations from a bewildering range of sources: her informed taste was invaluable in the painful process of final selection. Without their combined professional aptitude and continuous support the book would never have reached completion. I should also like to record my gratitude to the staff of the Courtauld Institute and Witt Libraries for their help with last minute problems, and to the staff of the Villa I Tatti and the Kunsthistorisches Institut in Florence, who have sustained my love of Renaissance painting over many years.

Charles McCorquodale

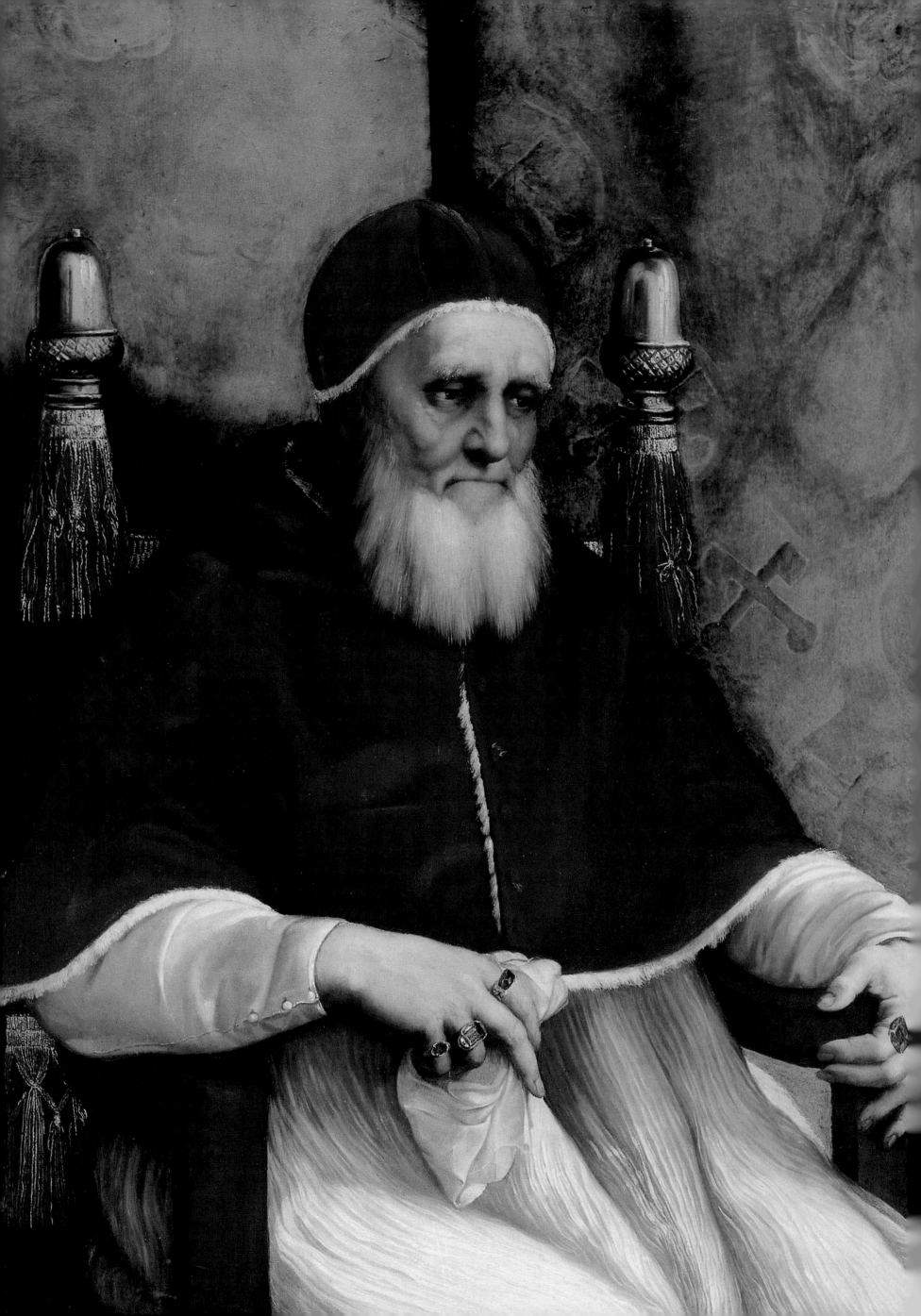

CHAPTER I

The Historical Background to the Renaissance

This book deals with the art of more than two centuries over a wide geographical area, extending from Sicily to Spain, from Edinburgh to Antwerp and Brussels to Vienna and Prague. During the period, the map of power in Europe underwent almost continuous change, and the national boundaries we know today had little relevance. Present-day Germany and Italy then consisted of city-states, duchies and principalities, often with allegiance to a larger power, most notably the Holy Roman Empire.

The empire dated from the coronation of Charlemagne in 800, but the term 'Holy Roman Empire' was first applied only in the mid-thirteenth century. At various times, much of Italy fell under German domination, a fact always at the back of the Holy Roman Emperors' minds in their manipulation of Italian politics. The ideal for the Emperors of the fifteenth and sixteenth centuries would have been to rule the whole of Europe from Germany, and this was virtually attained by Charles V, who reigned from 1519 to 1556. The highest international attainment of any artist in the Renaissance was to work for the reigning Emperor – a patron equalled only by the Papacy.

Imperial power mirrored, on a larger scale, the political aspirations of many great families. This was particularly evident in France and Italy, where dynasties such as the Valois and Medici manipulated local and international affairs for their own gain. It was to their advantage to

1 RAPHAEL Pope Julius II *c.*1512

Raphael, like Titian, painted many of the foremost personalities of his day, among them Pope Julius II of the Della Rovere family. Julius initiated the tradition of Papal patronage which continued into the Baroque age, and left Rome its incomparable legacy of ecclesiastical architecture and painting. This is one of the most perceptive portraits of the Italian Renaissance, at the same time grandiose and informal, respectful but offering compassionate insight.

maintain friendly relations with the Emperor, who could give military support, as well as grants of lands and titles. Such power could, however, prove double-edged, as when Imperial troops sacked Rome in 1527.

It is easy, in front of most Renaissance painting, to forget the disasters such as war and outbreaks of plague and famine, that recurred throughout the Renaissance period. During the fourteenth century, social unrest at every level had ravaged Europe, from peasant uprisings to the activities of an aspirant bourgeoisie. In addition various terrifying forms of the Black Death spread rapidly through Europe from late 1347, and almost one third of the population of Western Europe died, with catastrophic social effects. The poet Boccaccio, in the preface of his *Decameron* (*c.*1350), describes the full horror of the plague, and underlines its social nature, since his upper-class *dramatis personae* escaped from the deadly cities to the country. During the last years of the fourteenth century the whole of Europe was in crisis, with particular unrest in France and Italy. The 'revolt of the Ciompi' or day-labourers in Florence in 1378 furthered Florence's move to an oligarchy first under the Albizzi, then the Medici. In 1380, there were revolts in Bruges and Ghent and the following year there was massive unrest in southern England. In retrospect, however, these disastrous events scarcely seem to have diminished the remarkable flourishing of court life with its attendant benefits for the arts.

One of the most dramatic changes that occurred during the Renaissance was the radical improvement in the status of the artist. This was due to the growth of wealth, to a decreased dependence on ecclesiastical patronage and to the spread of humanistic ideas. This process originated in Italy. Although Giotto achieved high social status, it was not until the last years of the fifteenth century that artists such as Leonardo and Raphael began to be welcomed not as useful craftsmen but as courtiers.

As in the medieval era, art was the greatest luxury available to the rich, and Renaissance princes indulged to the full. Throughout Europe, they surrounded themselves with the finest architects, sculptors, painters and craftsmen money could buy, and if native talent was thin on the ground, they imported artists – mainly from Italy. This practice occurred with greater frequency during the sixteenth century. For example, Titian worked for the Emperor Charles V, Holbein moved to London and a group of Italian artists was established at Fontainebleau. Many works of art served as diplomatic gifts, and the exchange of portraits between intended spouses ensured work for portraitists in addition to their normal activities.

2 AGNOLO BRONZINO Duke Cosimo I de' Medici in Armour
c. 1545
This shows the young Duke of Florence virtually in the form of an icon, and is one of the most striking examples of International Mannerist court portraiture. One of the longest ruling dictators of the Renaissance, Cosimo united Tuscany, maintained excellent international relations with Emperor Charles V and established the type of virtual state monopoly of the arts that was later to culminate in the patronage of Louis XIV of France. The portrait's distant, inhuman coldness appears to have been regarded by Cosimo as the perfect representation for his rigid regime.

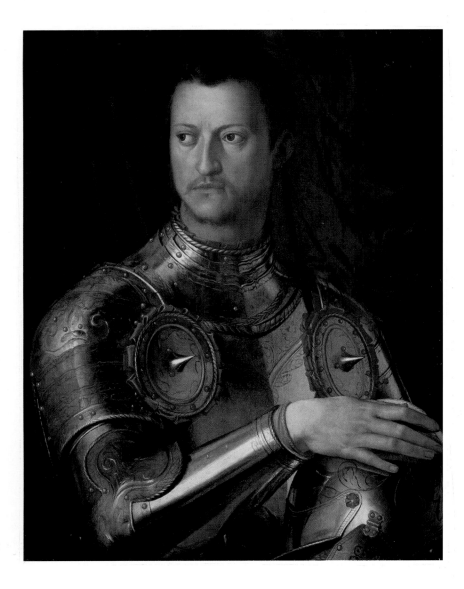

Italy

'Italy', said the nineteenth-century Austrian chancellor Klemens Metternich, 'is a geographical expression'. In dismissing the idea of an Italian nation he was correct; since the Middle Ages Italy had been made up of disparate city-states, which proved both a weakness and a strength, but was particularly beneficial in cultural terms. The diversity of the Italian regions accounts in part for the richness of its culture. At no time was this more true than during the Renaissance.

Because Florence appears in retrospect to have been the most significant artistic centre during the fifteenth and sixteenth centuries, it is easy to lose sight of the effect of political events elsewhere in Italy. Northern Italy, because of its proximity to France, Germany and Austria, was subject to constant upheaval, which only Venice resisted. Naples and Sicily were first under Aragonese then Habsburg rule, both of which had an important effect on their cultures. The ambitions of the Papacy resulted in the changing borders of its states: and within Tuscany itself, cities such as Siena and Lucca were gradually absorbed into the Medici super-state of Tuscany, led by the first Grand Duke of Tuscany, Cosimo I (see plate 2), with the help of the Holy Roman Emperor.

The reasons for Florence's primacy in the development of fifteenth-century Italian culture are complex. During the thirteenth and fourteenth centuries, the Florentines established a major European trading position, resulting in economic expansion. Florence was therefore ripe for development, and this openness was fundamental to the city's acceptance of new intellectual and cultural phenomena. The city's continuous objective assessment of Papal power and the ecclesiastical establishment was also important. This already existed in the mid-1370s when Florence was engaged in open warfare with the Papacy; mistrust continued sporadically into the later period of the Medici Grand Dukes.

Scepticism about ecclesiastical matters was inherent in the Florentine temperament, a fact signalled as early as the eleventh century by Giovanni Gualberto's concern with reforms. Florence's major churches (except the Cathedral) were all reform churches, whose independence from Papal jurisdiction was a distinctive feature of Florentine life. The Franciscan legacy from the early thirteenth century, of many large, impressive churches (with their fresco cycles and altarpieces) and other buildings in Florence, Pisa, Lucca, Arezzo, Siena and Assisi, was very important in the development and spread of painting.

Florence's wealth was based on trade in articles manufactured there from imported wool and silk. This was one

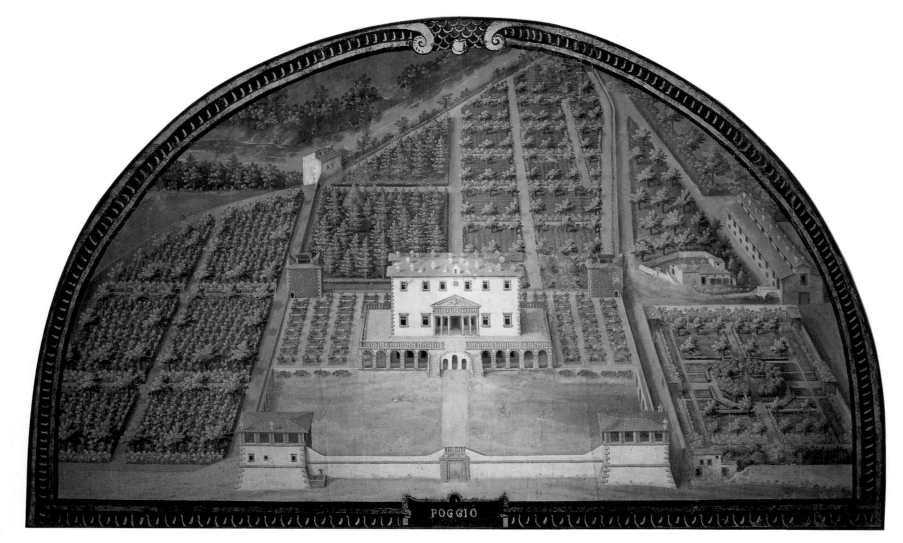

POGGIO

3 JUSTUS VAN UTENS *The Villa Medici at Poggio a Caiano after 1598*

Lorenzo the Magnificent bought the villa near Florence around 1480 and commissioned its reconstruction on a H-plan in the Tuscan Renaissance style from Giuliano da Sangallo in the 1480s. The villa, which was conceived as the setting for the ideal humanistic country life, became the protoype for the increasing numbers of country houses and gardens in the later Quattrocento and Cinquecento, culminating in the Veneto villas of Andrea Palladio. It remained a favourite Medici residence, and its splendid salone *houses major frescoes by Andrea del Sarto, Franciabigio, Pontormo and Alessandro Allori. This is one of a group of fresco lunettes which Utens painted for the nearby villa of Artimino.*

of the main reasons for its contact with the Netherlands, which had important artistic repercussions for both areas. To create independence in financial dealings, the city rapidly established its own sophisticated financial system. Florentine banks had branches as far afield as London, Paris, Bruges and Jerusalem. The basis of the currency, which the Florentines coined themselves, became the *fiorino*, which at certain moments was the principal European currency of its day. On this wealth the conspicuous and lasting visual achievements of the Florentine Renaissance were built.

At the turn of the fourteenth century, many new families came to prominence through their financial prowess. They began to replace the old feudal aristocracy, and one family slowly gained pre-eminence: the Medici. Their political and financial star waxed first with Giovanni di Bicci (1360–1429), whose son, Cosimo, *Pater Patriae* (father of the fatherland), became Florence's first citizen in 1434 on his return from exile. Cosimo's many skills were overshadowed by his genius as a financier, aided by his family bank's international connections. He was, however, the first of his line to have an extensive and active involvement in the intellectual and artistic life of his day. He launched the scholar Marsilio Ficino, employed the architect Michelozzo and the sculptor Donatello, and founded the great libraries of San Marco, the Badia Fiesolana and the Laurenziana.

This balance between the man of commerce and the statesmen created the prototype for all the later Medici, and made the name synonymous with unstinting and discriminating art patronage. At least among the family's earliest members, it distinguished them clearly from grander patrons, who were not involved with commerce. This stigma never really left the Medici, in spite of their later aspirations and rise to become Grand Dukes.

It was Cosimo's grandson Lorenzo (1449–92) called *il magnifico* ('the Magnificent' a courtesy title), who fulfilled the family's artistic ambitions in the fifteenth century. He succeeded Piero de' Medici in 1469, and was one of the major catalysts in European civilization. The period of his dominance saw the flowering of the Renaissance with the great age of Tuscan fresco decoration, the art of Botticelli, Filippino Lippi, Ghirlandaio, Verrocchio and the young Leonardo da Vinci and Michelangelo. Lorenzo's private taste tended more to the collecting of precious objects: cameos, gems, precious stones and gold or silver vessels set with jewels, a fashion which lasted until the end of the Medici dynasty and forms the core of the great collections still in Florence today.

Indicative of his love of country life was one of Tuscany's most serene villas at Poggio a Caiano (see plate 3), which Lorenzo commissioned from Giuliano da Sangallo. This was the setting for major works by the Della Robbias, and later, Del Sarto, Pontormo and Alessandro Allori. *Villeggiatura*, or the summer escape to a country estate, became increasingly popular with the rich in this period, resulting in the creation of the great Renaissance and Baroque villas and gardens. The effect in painting of this liberation from the dominance of urban life, which had been characteristic of the Middle Ages, may be seen throughout the fifteenth century, culminating in Botticelli's *Primavera* (see plate 115).

Lorenzo was a gifted poet, and surrounded himself with philosophers and poets: Marsilio Ficino (1432–9), Pico della Mirandola (1469–1533), Luigi Pulci (1432–84) and Angelo Poliziano (1454–94). Ficino was the most important in founding Renaissance Neoplatonism, and the intellectuals around Lorenzo played a crucial part in his and the period's approach to visual arts. Such men as these mastered the ideals of humanism, which set man, not God at the centre of the world, and escalated individualism and the full development of human potential. From this arose the passion for the ancient liberal arts: rhetoric, poetry painting, sculpture, architecture and music.

Lorenzo was the last of the Medici to enjoy a period of relative peace, and this is often reflected in subsequent nostalgia for his 'golden age'. The hedonistic aspects of Lorenzo's world, however, drew bitter attacks from the Dominican friar, Girolamo Savonarola (1452–98). His moral crusade against contemporary degeneracy briefly diverted Florentine attention from the pursuit of luxury, and had a strong impact on the visual arts. After Lorenzo's death, Florence was in turmoil, terrified by Savonarola's preaching, and on the brink of civil war. Lorenzo's heirs were expelled, and Savonarola, who had been excommunicated by the Pope, gained support from the invading French but was finally condemned to death (see plate 4). After periods of exile, the Medici made their definitive return with Alessandro in 1530 and then Cosimo I (1519–74) (later first Grand Duke of Tuscany), who was the last of the great Florentine Renaissance patrons (see plate 2). The importance of the two Medici popes, Leo X and Clement XII, in their family's fortunes as in the arts was also considerable.

While the Medici dominate the Italian scene throughout the Renaissance, the importance of several other families cannot be underestimated. Intermarriage between members established strong links between the courts, which were often consolidated by artists and scholars working for related patrons in different cities. The Italian aristocracy set the standard for Europe in their lavish patronage of the arts, and their involvement in every aspect of court life.

Aided by Cosimo de' Medici the Sforza dynasty came to prominence through Francesco, Duke of Milan from 1450 to 1466. He was a prime example of an adventurer-*condottiere* rising to the position of a respected prince. His second son, Lodovico 'il Moro' (1451–1508), described by Burckhardt as 'the perfect type of despot' was a considerable patron of all the arts, including music and theatre. Much admired by Baldassare Castiglione, author of the *Book of the Courtier* (see plate 12), he was wily enough to marry his niece Bianca to his protector, the Emperor Maximilian. It was during Lodovico's region that Leonardo painted the *Last Supper* (see plate 41) and Bramante began his ascendancy in architecture before moving to Rome.

Castiglione's inspiration for the book came from his intimate knowledge of the refined court life of Urbino in the early sixteenth century. Urbino's ruling family, the Montefeltro, had enjoyed particular cultural prominence under Duke Federico (1444–82) and his Sforza wife, Battista (see plates 101 and 102). Their beautiful hilltop palace, designed by the architect Luciano Laurana, was also the setting for the artistic activities of Piero della Francesca, Melozzo da Forlì and Francesco di Giorgio Martini (1439–1502), and it had a formative influence on the youthful Raphael.

The Gonzaga dynasty of Mantua was one of the grandest of the Renaissance, and among the most important patrons of the arts (see plate 105). The family had ruled Mantua since 1328, were raised to the title of marquess by Imperial concession, and made dukes in 1530. The most notable family member was Lodovico (1412–78), one of the finest Renaissance ruler-statesmen, who ruled from 1444. He had an informed interest in art and architecture, and invited Mantegna and Leon Battista Alberti to Mantua, where he surrounded himself with humanistic scholars. An ally of Duke Francesco Sforza and of the Medici, he sponsored building in the great Florentine church of the Santissima Annunziata, where Alberti experimented with the centralized plan.

The celebrated Isabella d'Este (1474–1539) married Francesco Gonzaga and made the court at Mantua a cultural showplace. In contrast to the Sforzas and many other Italian ruling families, the Este family maintained their power over an exceptionally long period, principally by sound statecraft and by making advantageous marriages in the sixteenth century with noble Italian, French and German families. Established from 1267 as rulers of Ferrara and its hinterland, they extended their power to Modena and Reggio, and Rovigo in the north.

4 UNKNOWN TUSCAN PAINTER The Martyrdom of Savonarola 1498

Seen here is the execution of the Dominican friar Girolamo Savonarola in the Piazza in front of the Palazzo Vecchio (or della Signoria, as it was then). His vitriolic attacks on Medici materialism and abuse of power led to his own downfall and death. The Piazza was later the setting for many important sculptures.

Isabella's brother, Alfonso I (born 1476), was Duke of Ferrara from 1505 to 1534 and his second marriage was to Lucrezia Borgia, daughter of Pope Alexander VI. She did much to civilize the court of Ferrara. Alfonso and his brother, Cardinal Ippolito, both employed Lodovico Ariosto (1474-1533), best-known as the author of the epic poem *Orlando Furioso*. Celebrating the Este family and the particular splendour of their court, this was the inspiration for countless later works of art and music.

Outside these city-states ruled by dynasties lay Venice and the Papal States. Papal power centred in Rome remained largely constant during the fifteenth and sixteenth centuries, and in addition to the large part of Italy in Papal control, a vast bureaucracy maintained its contacts throughout Catholic Europe. The Protestant Reformation and the resultant loss of support particularly from England, came as a great blow. The Papacy rallied its forces with immense vigour during the Counter-Reformation of the mid-sixteenth century, re-affirming

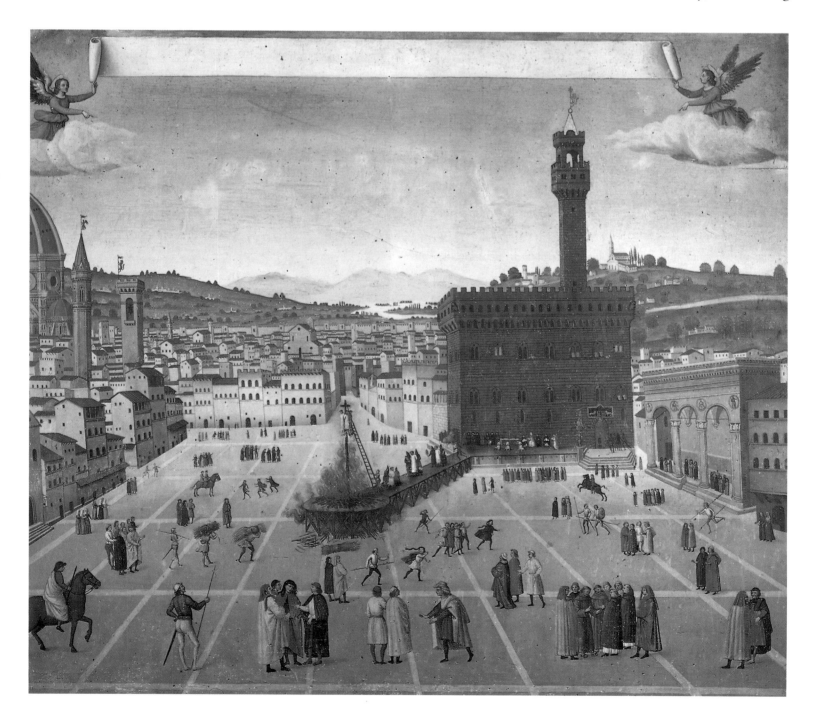

included Nicolas Rolin (see plate 142), David, Bishop of Utrecht, Anthony of Burgundy and Philip of Cleves.

In addition to collecting art, the court (like most in Europe) also provided major commissions for temporary decorations. These must have occupied many artists, but little evidence of them remains. They were expected at almost any major event such as ducal weddings, state entries to towns and funerals, and included elaborate triumphal arches and street decorations, and *tableaux vivants* which were probably related to contemporary sculpture groups. The most celebrated of such displays were Philip the Good's 'Banquet of the Pheasant' held in Lille in 1454 and the state entry of Charles the Bold and Margaret of York into Bruges in 1468.

During the fifteenth century, the Catholic Church also continued to be a leading patron of the arts, commissioning not only altarpieces large and small, but also a wealth of illuminated pages and initials contained within many different types of book for use in the Mass. Private devotional images increased greatly in importance in the north at this time, and the very rich could afford the services of leading painters. Thus, donors appear on the wings of their altarpieces in adoration of the Virgin or saints, fulfilling both a sacred function, and a secular one in recording their pious magnanimity for posterity. Many such pictures are named after their donors.

The guilds were of great importance in Flemish art and civic life. Part of their work was charitable, ensuring that their members and dependents were cared for in widowhood or old age. By demanding long periods of apprenticeship, and controlling the quality of all work produced by their members, they ensured very high standards. Through protective legislation, they monitored the quality and amount of imported work from other places.

In about 1430, the 'state' of Burgundy was formed of parts of the principalities making up the boundaries between the kingdom of France and the Holy Roman Empire. The Duchy of Brabant was the leading principality, whose main centres were Brussels and Louvain. Ghent was the central town of the area of Flanders, which was smaller in extent than its modern counterpart. Philip the Good inherited the area by the sheer chance that a very large number of his relatives were childless. By one stroke, he was made the richest Western ruler, richer even than the Holy Roman Emperor himself.

Philip the Good spent much time travelling between the numerous residences which he had inherited in Brussels, Ghent, Arras, Bruges, The Hague and Lille, but Brussels was gradually made the capital of his new 'state'. A court formed itself, with the nobility buying estates in north Brabant, not too distant from Brussels, and establishing town houses or *hôtels* in the city. In order to unify his disparate aristocracy, Philip created an order of chivalry, the Golden Fleece, and a court etiquette for the old nobility, 'national' coinage and assemblies where representatives from the various lands could meet. Thus a Burgundian nobility was formed out of diverse peoples, and through education at the University of Louvain the second generation evolved with a Renaissance not a medieval outlook. This was of enormous importance in the patronage of painting.

Philip was a man of immense energy, and in his devotion to the arts created a golden age like that of Lorenzo the Magnificent in Florence. He built up the most important library of his time and collected, much in the manner of the Medici, paintings, sculpture, plate, tapestries, jewels and manuscripts. He also had a great love of music.

At the beginning of the fifteenth century, the population of many towns, whose autonomy during the Middle Ages had been so important, began to fall. The celebrated textile trades of Bruges, Ypres, Douai, Arras and Rouen all experienced competition from the Italian towns of Florence, Siena, Lucca and Arezzo, notably in the production of luxury goods. The protectionism current in the urban production of lower level textiles led merchants to use smaller towns and rural bases which sometimes caused economic crisis in the older centres.

The wealth necessary for the lavish life at the Burgundian court and among the nobility derived from the sale of woollen cloth of every quality, urban rent-rolls from industrial and commercial tenants and rent-rolls from agricultural tenants. Bruges was the principal port for the entry of foreign goods (for customers as far distant as Germany) and the exit of exports and became enormously rich. Its luxury imports included coveted Italian velvets, silks, damasks and satins. Linen fabric was also important, as were the various productions in metal, especially brass, which were extensively in demand throughout late medieval and Renaissance Europe. Fifteenth-century Burgundy saw the rise in what was to become one of its most celebrated products – tapestry. It was mainly woven in the southern Netherlands at Arras, after which the tapestries and related cloth were named. The best-known sets were commissioned by Philip the Good himself and his son Charles the Rash, who reigned from 1467 to 1477. Tapestry was in demand at courts everywhere, and it was only much later that Netherlandish production was rivalled, for example at Cosimo I's court in Florence.

Killed in battle at Nancy, Charles the Rash left a female heir, his daughter Mary. Louis XI of France seized the opportunity to invade, but although he took Lorraine and

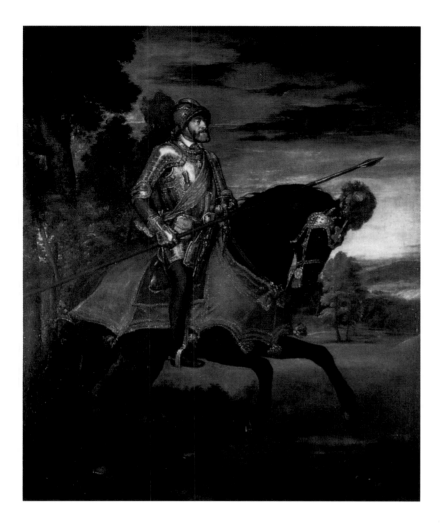

7 TITIAN Emperor Charles V at Muhlberg 1548

Charles V (1500–58) became ruler of Austria, Germany, the Netherlands, Naples and Sicily, Spain and her American possessions. Painted to commemorate the Emperor's victory over the German Protestants in 1547, this portrait created the prototype for equestrian state portraits thereafter. As a deeply pious Catholic, this victory was of immense importance for Charles, who is seen with an image of the Madonna on his breastplate and the rose-coloured sash that was the symbol of the Holy Roman Empire, Spain and the Catholic parties in the religious wars.

Alsace, the Netherlands stood firm in Mary's defence. Louis died in 1483 leaving France with immense debts. Although Mary died at the age of twenty-five, she and her step-mother, Margaret of York, were notable patrons of the arts. Mary had married Maximilian, son of Emperor Frederick III, whom he succeeded in 1508. Ruinous civil war resulted from Maximilian trying to force his claim to the Netherlands. In 1493, however, his son by Mary, Philip the Handsome, managed to obtain power, and was supported by the old Burgundian families.

Maximilian had arranged Philip's marriage to Joanna, the daughter of Ferdinand and Isabella of Aragon and Castile, to ensure an anti-French alliance, and in 1506, on Isabella's death, Philip laid claim to the throne of Castile. After his death, however, his nephew became king of Castile and Aragon, thus ruling Spain and its vastly rich American dominions.

In 1506, Charles also inherited Franche-Comté and much of the Netherlands, and in 1519, the Habsburg lands in Germany and Austria on Maximilian's death, followed by Bohemia and Hungary through the marriages of his brother and sister. His kingdom thus extended from Sicily and Spain to the North sea, bringing with it an immense burden visible in his face and pose in Titian's portraits of him (see plate 7), and expressed in his eventual abdication in 1556.

The map of European power had been redrawn, with a Burgundian court installed in Spain. By the end of Charles's reign however the roles had been reversed and the Netherlands was ruled by a now virtually Spanish monarch. Burgundy, so carefully created from the fourteenth century onwards, no longer had any autonomy and was merely part of a vast empire.

France

While the Renaissance was emerging in Italy, France was intermittently involved in the Hundred Years War (1377–1453) between the partisans of the Valois dynasty and those of the English Kings.

The reign of Charles VII (1422–61) was fundamental in the formation of modern France, although his kingdom at that date consisted only of the central region of the present country. The Duke of Burgundy, Philip the Good, continually encroached on new territory, while north of the Loire was under English rule.

The Peace of Arras in 1435 united Charles VII and the Duke of Burgundy and their troops took Paris from the English the following year. Charles made his solemn regal entry into the city, and gradually the Ile-de-France was reclaimed from the English, who remained mainly in Normandy. By 1453, only Calais remained in English control, and the Hundred Years War was ended, confirming Charles's power over most of present-day France. Charles VII's 'Grand Argentier' and councillor, Jacques Coeur, symbolized the rising newly rich bourgeoisie, and changes in society.

Louis XI (1423–83), who reigned from 1461, married Margaret of Scotland, thus initiating Franco-Scottish relations which were to have a lasting impact on Scottish culture. In 1465, the so-called 'Ligue du Bien Public' was formed, uniting the royal dukes of Burgundy, Bourbon and Berry in an early attempt to control the power of the various aristocratic factions. Louis XI was in advance of his time, and France prospered, attracting foreign trade, opening the English market to French production (in spite of renewed war with England) and trying to set up

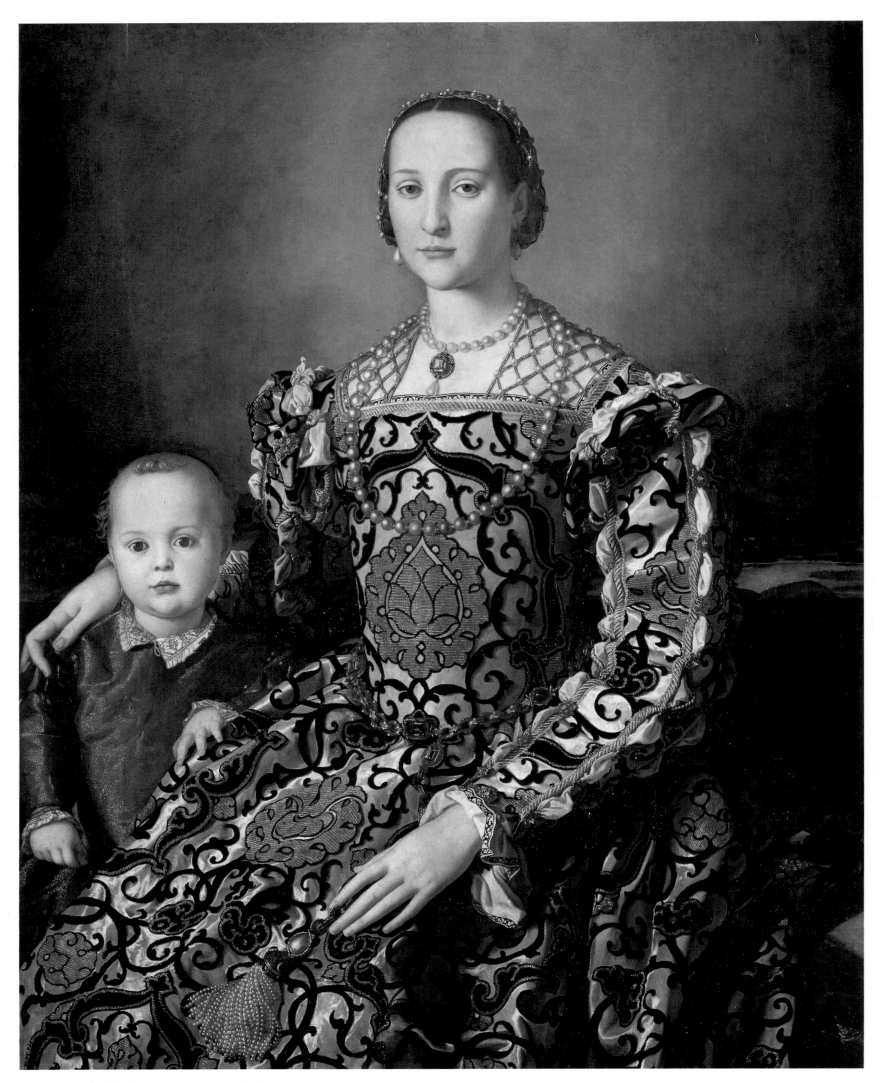

11 AGNOLO BRONZINO Eleonora of Toledo c. 1545

Although not a pair to the portrait of her husband, this portrait of Eleonora forms an excellent counterpart. Bronzino has deliberately rendered Eleonora's lavish costume and jewels as rigidly as her husband's armour. Her dynastic importance is emphasized by her *loving gesture to her son, Giovanni. The Duchess belonged to a tradition of strong-willed, intelligent and active women of the period. Intensely pious and involved in ecclesiastical affairs, she also contributed positively to her husband's financial arrangements.*

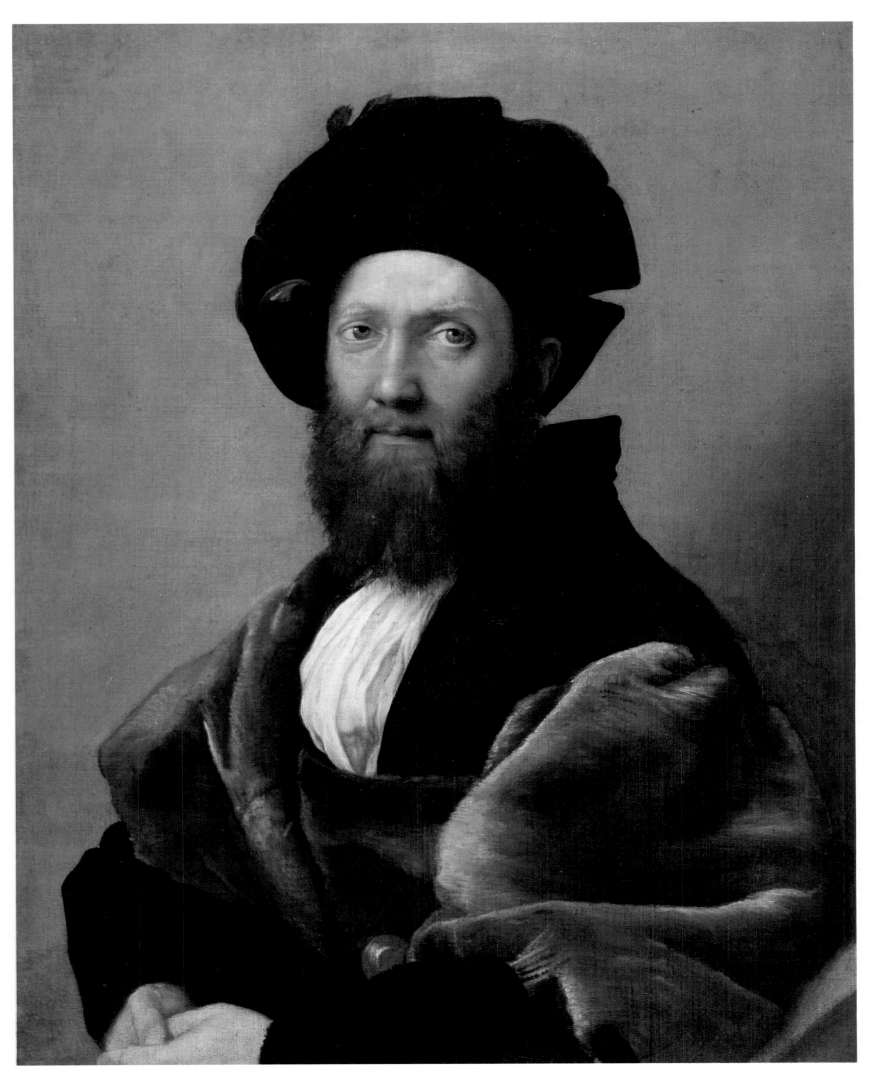

12 RAPHAEL Baldassare Castiglione 1514–15

Count Baldassare Castiglione (1478–1529) was one of the most celebrated poets and men of letters of the later Renaissance, and a friend and advisor to Raphael. Sent to Milan to enter the court of Lodovico Sforza, he rapidly gained a reputation for military and political astuteness, and enjoyed important positions at the courts of Mantua and Urbino. In 1528 his Book of the Courtier *was published in Venice. It was conceived as a portrait of the court of Urbino and a guide to the education of a courtier.*

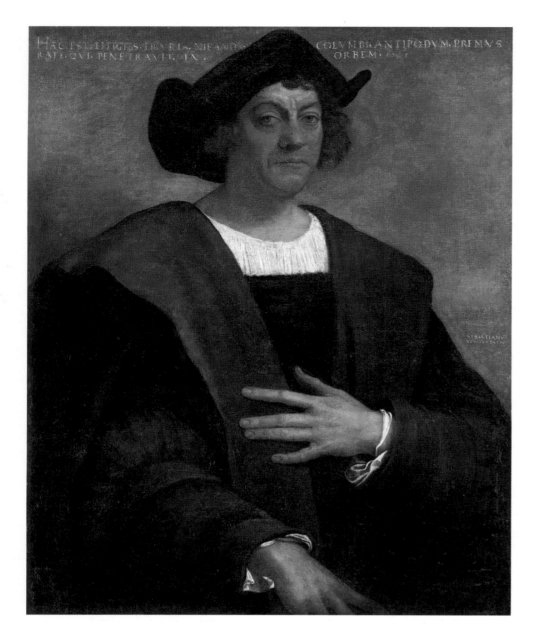

15 PEDRO BERRUGUETE Federico da Montefeltro and his Son Guidobaldo, undated

Federico (1422–82) was signore of Urbino in 1444 and Duke of Urbino from 1474, and was the first member of his family to create a stable state. Guidobaldo died without an heir in 1508, leaving the Duchy to Francesco Maria della Rovere. Federico's studiolo in the Ducal Palace at Urbino was one of the most significant humanist decorative schemes, uniting paganism and Christianity in its iconography, which encompassed theological virtues and a series of illustrious men chosen from scientists, literary figures and the law. It may have been conceived by the architect Bramante, and it included trompe l'oeil wooden inlays probably designed by Botticelli and Francesco di Giorgio Martini.

13 SEBASTIANO DEL PIOMBO Christopher Columbus 1519

This posthumous portrait of the greatest Renaissance navigator, who died in 1506, was probably painted from a lost portrait drawing. It shows Sebastiano's early mature style, and typifies the sixteenth century's nascent taste for portraits, often posthumous, of notable historical figures. Sometimes these were produced in series to point moral lessons, as in the Illustrious Men *formerly in Federico da Montefeltro's studiolo, or* Titian's Roman Emperors *series for Mantua.*

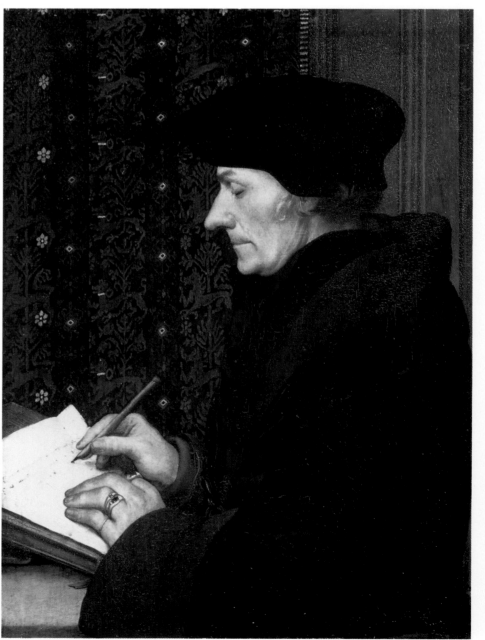

14 HANS HOLBEIN THE YOUNGER Erasmus of Rotterdam 1523

The simultaneous emergence of Holbein and Erasmus was symptomatic of the effect of humanism on German culture, and each man admired the other. Erasmus settled in Basle largely on account of its pre-eminence in European printing, which enabled him to maintain his intellectual power throughout Europe. Our image of Erasmus is formed almost entirely by Holbein's portraits of him, which are intensely penetrating likenesses revealing the innermost soul. When Holbein left the troubled city of Basle in 1526 for England, he was armed with a letter of introduction from Erasmus to Sir Thomas More.

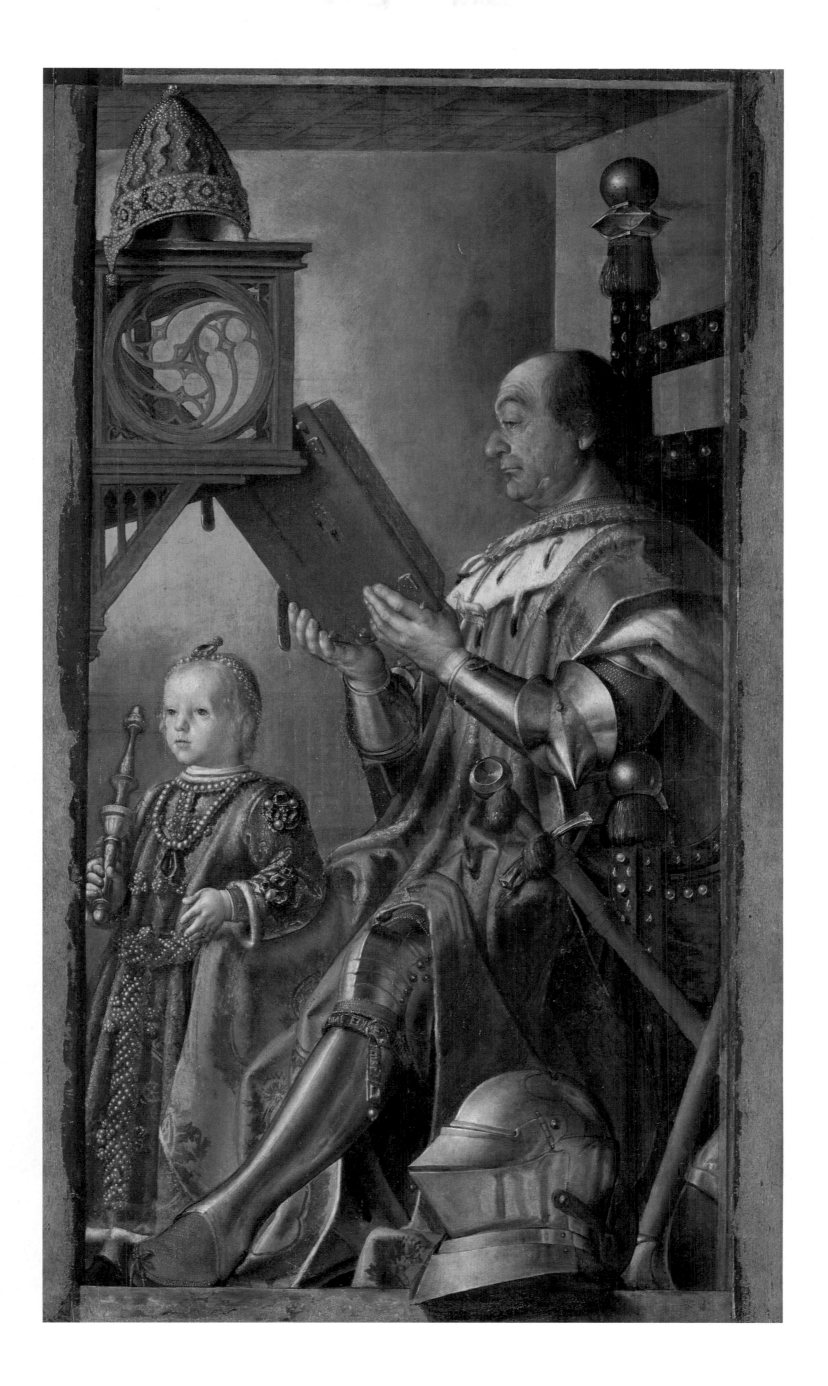

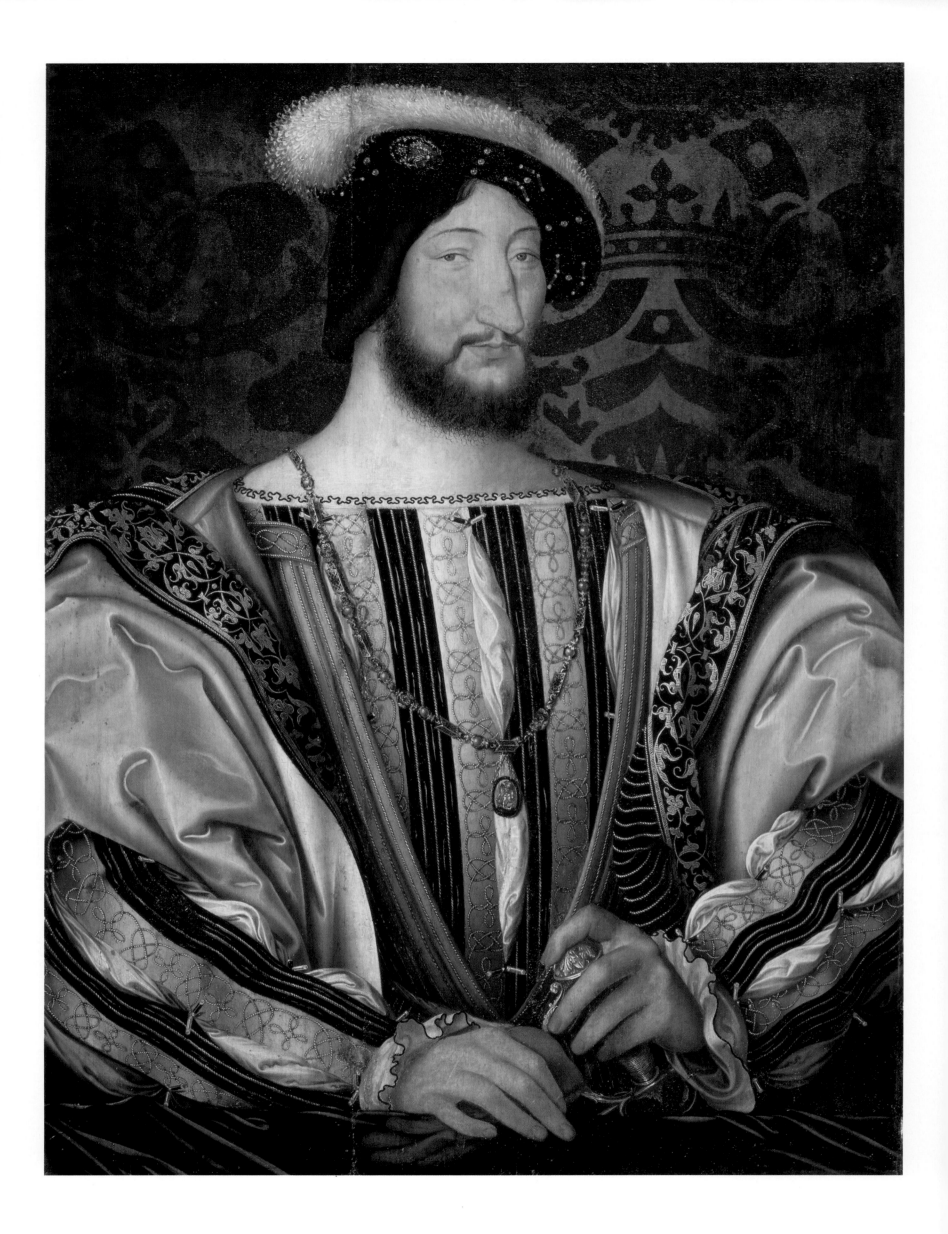

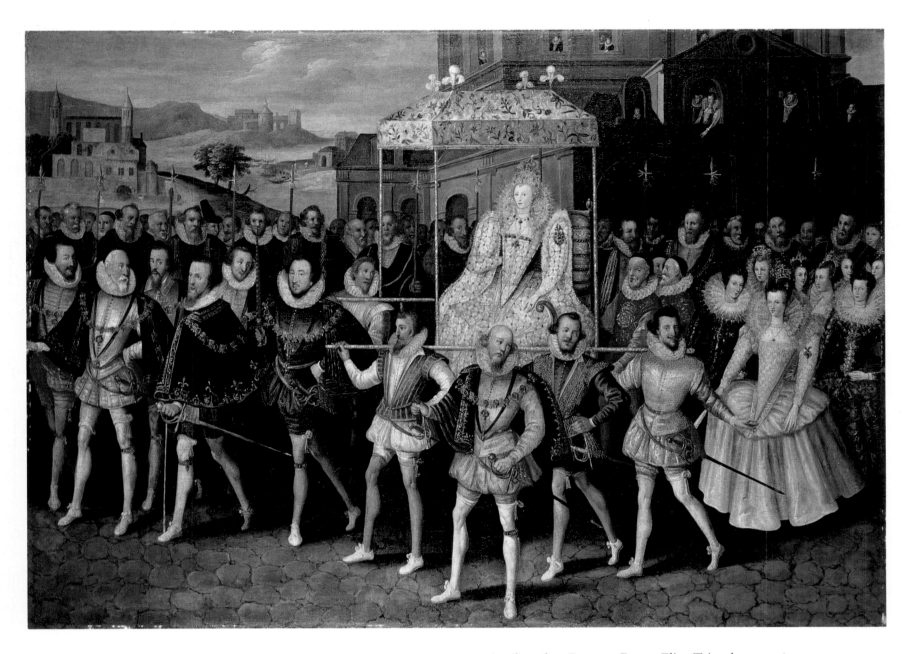

16 JEAN CLOUET Francis I, undated

This portrait and its sitter epitomize the spread of Italian Renaissance ideas throughout the courts of Europe. Francis I's obsession with Italy and things Italian opened the way for the importation of Italian art and artists into France, and the rise of native French painters like Jean Clouet who could rival them. His creation of a new Franco-Italian school of painting at his great Renaissance palace of Fontainebleau launched French art on the international level which it subsequently maintained. Clouet, listed among the king's artists in 1516, was also an exceptional portrait draughtsman, and his son François succeeded him as King's Painter in 1540.

17 Attributed to ROBERT PEAKE Eliza Trimphans *c.* 1600

During the reign of Queen Elizabeth I the Renaissance in England was fully consolidated. Robert Peake (c.1557–1619) was influenced by Nicholas Hilliard, and this picture corresponds to his pale palette and linear approach to form. It represents a celebration of the Queen by her last Master of the Horse, Edward Somerset, 4th Earl of Worcester, who appears immediately in front of the Queen holding a pair of gloves in his right hand. The painting seems to echo a Roman Imperial triumph (the Queen is in a chair with wheels, rather than a litter) in which Worcester is her escort.

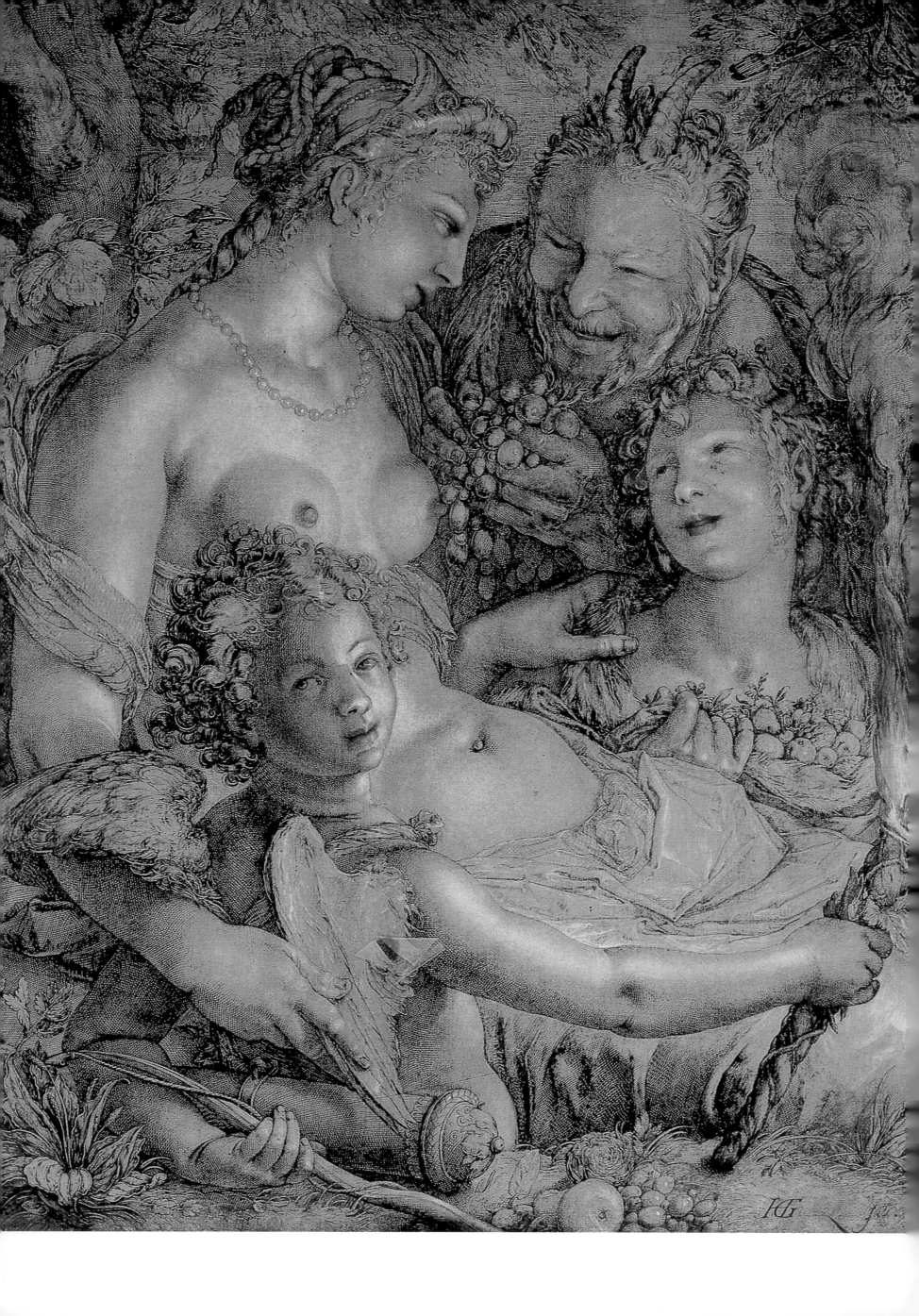

CHAPTER II

Painting and Drawing Techniques
in the Renaissance

Drawing

The advance toward mastery of linear representation in drawing lies at the heart of Renaissance art. Its progress and increase in status was rapid during the fifteenth century, as painters grasped not only the new techniques but also the liberating effects of drawing. By the High Renaissance period, drawing had been freed from its exclusively functional, preparatory role to become an end in itself, a process which gained momentum throughout successive centuries. By the mid-sixteenth century, Vasari felt able to define drawing as 'the father of all the arts'.

Many of the greatest painters of the Renaissance were also its greatest draughtsmen. Outstanding examples of the art of drawing are Botticelli's magical illustrations to Dante, Leonardo da Vinci's vast corpus of studies of all kinds, the unrivalled perfection and variety of Raphael and Michelangelo's drawings, the riches of Correggio and, notably, the Tuscan and Roman schools.

Outside Italy, some of the finest draughtsmanship is to be found in the highly finished portrait drawings of painters such as François Clouet (see plate 20) and Hans Holbein the Younger (see plate 29). Dürer's draughtsmanship (see plate 19) ranks with his painting and engraving, and along with his German contemporaries, he used drawings in many new ways. In England, only a fine distinction exists between draughtsmanship and painting in

18 HENDRICK GOLTZIUS Without Ceres and Bacchus, Venus is a-Chill 1599–1602

The subject is taken from a maxim in the comedy The Eunuch *by the Roman dramatist Terence. Venus is seen awakening from a deep sleep in response to the symbolic presence of Ceres and Bacchus, while Cupid turns towards us and illuminates the scene with his torch. Such virtuoso drawings in pen and brown ink and brush and oils on blue-grey canvas won Goltzius widespread acclaim.*

that most characteristic of contemporary English productions, the portrait miniature (see plate 169).

The increase in the number and uses of drawings after 1400 is matched only by the new diversity of subject matter for draughtsmen. The Middle Ages' fear of, and even revulsion from, the nude human form was being replaced by the study of living models and by an understanding of the intentions and achievements of ancient sculptors. With the reassessment and rediscovery of Classical writers, it was inevitable that one of the most tangible elements in the legacy of ancient Rome – sculpture – should become a rich source of reference in the Renaissance. Contemporary developments in sculpture also exercised considerable influence on painting, especially with a major innovator such as Donatello. The human body was no longer simply the temple of the Christian soul, but, as in ancient times, an object of beauty in its own right.

The potential released by the emergence and development during the fifteenth century of new techniques came at a time of intellectual probing, which led artists to investigate every aspect of the visible world. Drawing became one of the main outlets for the enquiring artistic mind. It permitted exploration and experiment which could be carried over to other media only with the greatest difficulty, as in Leonardo's attempts to create diagrammatic drawings of storms and deluges. The sum total of these experiments greatly enriched the art of painting.

Initially the property of painters, drawing soon exerted its fascination throughout the visual arts, and became the common factor in painting, sculpture and architecture. Its role in liberating the artistic mind cannot be overemphasized. It formed the basis of linear perspective, which revolutionized pictorial representation from the 1420s, and received much attention in writings as diverse as Ghiberti's *Commentaries* and Alberti's treatises. Piero della Francesca's

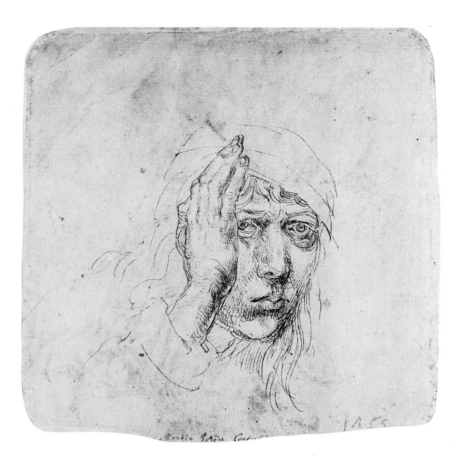

studios and artists is known to have had considerable impact on the spread of new ideas.

In about 1400, most studios had model books, normally on high quality parchment (vellum) for durability, containing drawings to set formulae for use in various permutations in the creation of new paintings. But

21 LEONARDO DA VINCI The Anatomy of a Shoulder *c.1510 (Right) Leonardo's almost fanatically meticulous anatomical studies represent the highest point of the Quattrocento artist's examination of the body's underlying structures, particularly as he considered them in a much broader context than any of his contemporaries.*

20 FRANÇOIS CLOUET Francis II *c.1553*
This drawing was executed prior to Francis's marriage at fourteen to Mary Stuart. He became King of France at sixteen, dying the following year. Clouet's portrait drawings enjoy an unusual place in European draughtsmanship, since they were made entirely as works of art in their own right. His technique aimed for the finest and most detailed modulations of line and tone in fused combinations of coloured chalks, simply taking the place of painted portraits as a more intimate record kept, like English miniatures, for private contemplation.

19 ALBRECHT DÜRER Self Portrait as a Journeyman 1491–2
Dürer's self portraits stand apart in Renaissance imagery for their astonishing individuality and for the artist's determination to record not only the details of external reality but also many aspects of his innermost nature. This drawing reveals most clearly how novel his approach was, and that its insights come not from the assimilation of Italian ideas but from a strong German tradition of seeking to penetrate reality.

perspective treatise, *De Prospettiva Pingendi*, was illustrated with engravings based on his own drawings. But the late fifteenth century's most exhaustive work on painting and drawing, combining theory and practice, was Leonardo's uncompleted *Trattato della Pittura (Treatise on Painting)*, which indicates the importance which drawing had by then assumed in workshop methods.

Drawing offered a far quicker way of exploring forms and ideas than painting. Its spontaneity (which increased during the fifteenth century as drawing media developed) permitted the artist to test his ideas in note form. Drawing was also fundamental to the control which a painter kept over his pupils. Imposing a studio style on the countless copies basic to every apprenticeship ensured that homogeneity which enabled works by many hands to bear a single name – the master's own. It suffices to think of the early work of great Renaissance masters, such as Masaccio or Raphael, to realize that it was only exceptional talent which liberated them from spending their lives as accomplished purveyors of the style in which they had been trained. The exchange of drawings between

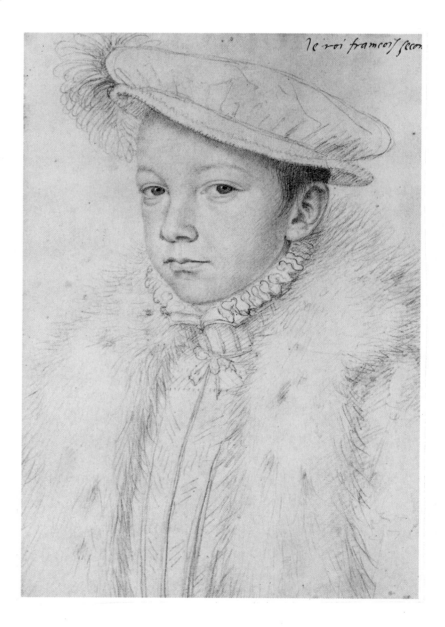

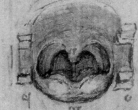

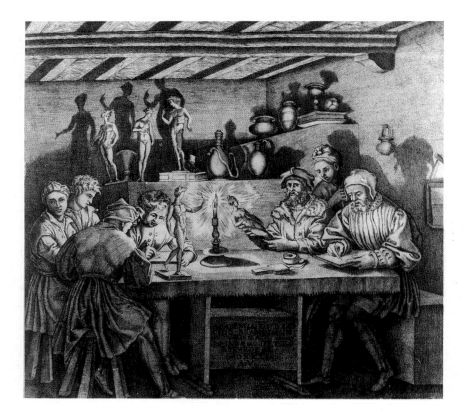

*The interest of this drawing lies in the fact that it shows compositions
related to different periods in Antonello's career. The drawing itself is
not by him, but is probably the work of an artist working in his
studio or circle. The sketches relate to the San Cassiano
Altarpiece, the destroyed Disputà di San Tommaso and another
lost picture. The sheet is almost certainly a page from a sketchbook,
and it is known to have been used and re-used by the artist at
different times and for different purposes; the rapid pen technique
visible in these studies enhances the informality of the sketches, which
may have been drawn from memory and would have been used for
reference.*

22 AGOSTINO VENEZIANO Baccio Bandinelli's Studio *c.*1531
*The engraving shows a group of artists working by candlelight around
a table. Two are drawing, while another examines what appears to
be a bronze statuette of Venus. Further statuettes, apparently after
the Antique, stand behind. Bandinelli himself made excellent
variations of Classical prototypes, working extensively for the Medici.
In 1531 he named his small art school an 'Academy', and here he
illustrates the fundamental role played by the study of sculpture in an
artist's training.*

the ideas propounded by Cennino Cennini (c.1370–
c.1440) in his *Libro dell'Arte*, the earliest craftsman's handbook of the Renaissance, written in about 1390–1400,
began to break the stranglehold of manual, and often
mindless, copying. Cennini favoured considered, inventive and original design and, in doing so, harked back to
Giotto's workshop practices, not those of the 1380s and
1390s. This is particularly significant, as it reveals Giotto's
continuing importance at a time when many painters had
turned away from his revolutionary innovations.

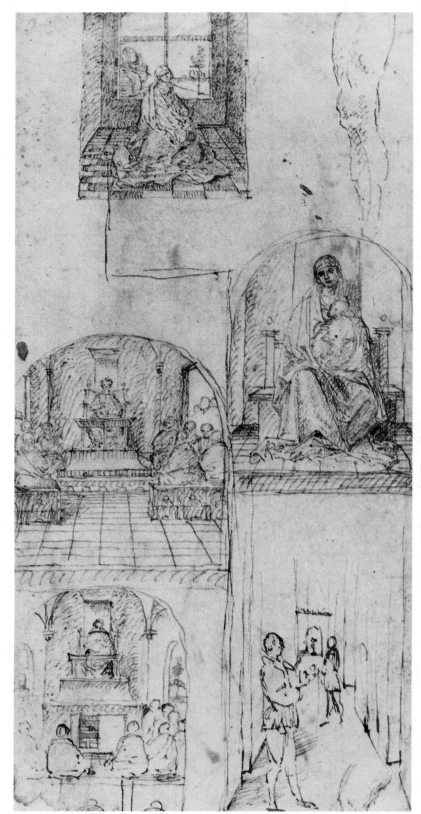

The result was the evolution of the sketchbook to
replace the studio model book. In one of the most original
and striking passages in his *Libro*, Cennini states that
'Painting . . . calls for imagination, and skill of hand, in
order to discover things not seen, hiding themselves under
the shadow of natural objects'. This anticipates Leonardo's
tenets on the potential of painting.

With such liberation came an increasingly obvious
pleasure that fifteenth-century painters took in revealing
their personal vision of the material and spiritual worlds.
One of the best examples of the new approach is the
Codex Vallardi in the Musée du Louvre in Paris, which is

partly an amalgam of Pisanello's sketchbooks. Pisanello (Antonio Pisano, *c.*1395–1455) had a restless career which took him to the courts of Ferrara, Mantua, Milan, Naples and Rimini. His enlightened patrons must have been surprised and intrigued by his drawings of the nude, landscape, birds, animals, costume, ornament and portrait likenesses, which anticipate many later developments.

Technical Advances

During the fifteenth century in Italy, drawing techniques advanced dramatically. Until as late as the mid-century, vellum or parchment were the preferred supports. Yet vellum was costly, being made from the skins of kids or young calves, which were elaborately prepared to provide a perfect surface for drawing, especially with pen and ink. The increasing availability of paper benefited not only the production of books and therefore the spread of learning in the Renaissance, but also the development of drawing. Once they grew accustomed to it, artists felt less constraint in their use of paper, and drawings multiplied, although the use of vellum continued, particularly in areas of northern Italy.

Silverpoint, considered the prime drawing medium by Cennini, was executed with a silver stylus. When dragged over the surface of prepared vellum, a delicate residue of silver remains and oxidizes in various grey or grey-yellow tones. Gold, lead and copper were also used in the same way. Sureness of touch was essential, which was partly why Cennini regarded the medium as the first test of a young artist's ability, and advocated practice on prepared wooden tablets. Rogier van der Weyden, Jan van Eyck and Gerard David were among the Northern artists of the fifteenth century who used silverpoint, and it continued to find greater favour outside Italy during the sixteenth century in the virtuoso performances of Dürer and the Holbeins. In Italy its use declined rapidly.

Pen and Wash Drawing

Gradually, ink applied with a quill pen replaced silverpoint. Pen drawing revealed the character of the artist much more immediately than the uniform line of metalpoint. Further elaboration could be done with the brush, although fluidity in this technique was rarely achieved in Italy, where artists remained largely hidebound by the need to establish a clear outline and shading.

A great advantage of paper was that it did not require elaborate surface preparation prior to drawing, but often

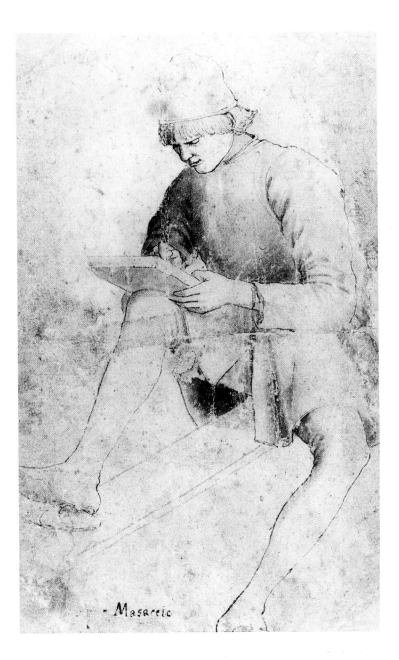

24 WORKSHOP OF MASO FINIGUERRA Seated Youth Drawing *c.*1450?

This probably shows a young artist drawing with silverpoint on a prepared wooden tablet, possibly of boxwood, which Cennino Cennini had recommended as the craftsman's most rigorous training. All Florentine painters of the Quattrocento would have studied in this way while they were garzoni *or studio assistants at the outset of their career. Maso's name was particularly associated in Florence with the development of engraving, to which this draughtsman's way of holding his pen may relate. Maso was very concerned with the creative process, which is particularly evident in the beautiful study attributed to him of a draughtsman's hands at work, now in the Uffizi, Florence.*

a coloured wash, usually either pink or blue, was applied first. The effects achieved with the pen could be enhanced by white heightening, which became one of the devices increasingly favoured from the sixteenth century onwards. During the first part of the sixteenth century in Germany, its greatest achievements were seen in the highly detailed drawings of Hans Baldung Grien, Urs Graf and Albrecht Altdorfer, whose fantastic landscapes using extensive white heightening are among the most striking of their kind.

The importance of grey washes of Indian ink in Renaissance draughtsmanship was considerable. They appeared in Italy in the second half of the fifteenth century applied to a fine linen. Vasari describes Leonardo using this medium for his studies of drapery on clay figurines. Sometimes the dividing line with painting becomes unclear. Mantegna laid such washes over a coloured *camaieu* or monochrome underpainting, and a similar underlying structure is visible in Cima da Conegliano's *Virgin and Child with Saints Andrew and Peter* (see plate 25).

Colour washes in drawing involving diluted inks and the brush were favoured by the Mannerists, notably Bernardo Buontalenti, Parmigianino and Perino del Vaga in Italy, Jacques Bellange in France, and among the Dutch and Flemings Joachim Wtewael, Bernaert van Orley and Bartholomaeus Spranger. Although brown ink washes only entered widespread use from the Baroque period, certain Italian Mannerists favoured them, such as Niccolò dell'Abbate and Parmigianino.

25 CIMA DA CONEGLIANO Virgin and Child with Saint Andrew and Saint Peter 1490s

Cima's first name derived from his father's occupation as a cimatore di panni, or cloth trimmer, and his surname from his place of birth north of Venice. He painted mainly altarpieces, of which this is probably a small example for private devotion. Although Venetian painters were increasingly using canvas as a support for their pictures at this time, Cima used poplar wood here. The white gesso ground common to Venetian painters even after the introduction of canvas remains clearly visible in the unfinished parts of the picture. After making preparatory studies for each figure, Cima drew his composition on the gesso with a fine brush, using black iron gall ink, now faded to brown; this is best seen in the tree and figure of St Peter. Tight parallel hatching was used to give the forms solidity and colour was then applied in oil.

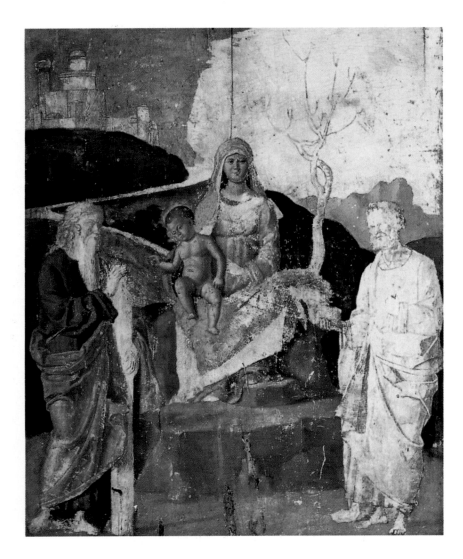

Chalks

Cennini discusses chalks, but it is clear that their use was severely limited in his period, only coming into their own in the sixteenth century. Black chalk is really a close-grained slate and first gained favour in the later fifteenth century, particularly in Florence, where one of its most extensive uses was for large-scale work such as cartoons for frescoes and other works of art. Major artists of the High Renaissance used it relentlessly. Black chalk does not permit great subtlety in drawing, which is the preserve of red chalk, deriving from an iron oxide called haematite. Its delicacy accords with the increasing sophistication of imagery sought in High Renaissance and Mannerist art, and in combination with other media, such as pen and brown ink, or with black and white chalk ('three crayon') results in great refinement. Possibly no other drawing medium allows such delicacy and softness of modulation, from firm, broad strokes to almost transparent parallel hatching and 'rubbed' modelling. Its highest achievements were in Tuscan drawings, notably by Leonardo, Michelangelo, Fra Bartolommeo, Andrea del Sarto and Pontormo. Correggio was also especially gifted in the use of red chalk. Significantly, these were painters who prepared for painting with the aid of innumerable drawings.

Coloured chalks used in combination enjoyed particular favour among Northern portraitists, notably the Holbeins and the Clouets, who were all noted for the fineness of their application. The potential sumptuousness of different chalks applied together appealed also to Mannerists like Hendrick Goltzius and, in Italy, the brothers Federico and Taddeo Zuccaro and Federico Barocci, who achieved exceptionally suave effects.

Charcoal, whose preparation from willow-sticks is described by Cennini, tended by its nature to require bold application, although its principal advantage was that it could be easily erased if required. It was thus perfect for large-scale cartoons, and in the preparation of fresco.

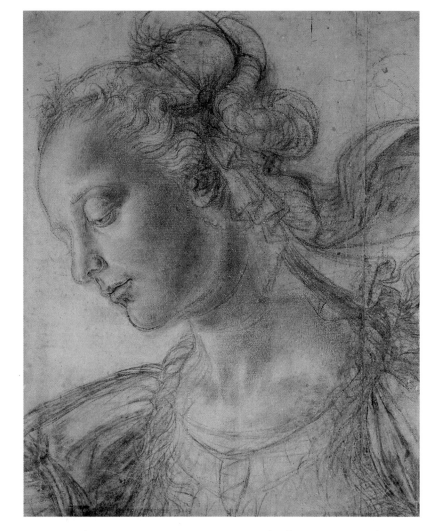

26 ANDREA DEL VERROCCHIO Head of a Woman, undated
This is among the finest surviving chalk drawings of the
Quattrocento period; the pen retouchings were added later. It belongs
to a group of Verrocchio black chalk cartoons for transferring forms
directly to a panel for painting: this is shown by the pricking of the
outline. The drawing illustrates perfectly the freedom given by the use
of chalk in combining fluid lines (hair and drapery), rubbed areas (the
cheeks) and precise modelling (eyes, nose and lips). The somewhat
distorting reworking is by a left-handed artist in Verrocchio's studio,
possibly Leonardo, and the subtle modelling recalls Verrocchio's major
role as a sculptor.

Watercolour and Gouache

The remaining principal techniques related to advances in
drawing which evolved during the latter part of the
Renaissance were watercolour and gouache. These were
closely linked to the expansion in the range of subject
matter around 1500, particularly in the painting Northern
Europe.

Watercolour consists of coloured pigments mixed with
gum arabic (from the Latin *arabicus*) and applied in a water
solution in varying degrees of intensity to white paper.
The brilliance of the paper as seen through the transparent wash constitutes one of the principal effects of the
medium. Its most widespread use in the Renaissance

occurs in the Mannerist period, in theatrical and decorative designs (such as Buontalenti's famous drawings for
Medici court entertainments).

Its most creative applications were, however, seen in
still lifes and landscapes in late fifteenth-century Germany.
One example is the remarkably precocious set of about
fifteen views combining watercolour and gouache, made
by Dürer in the Tyrolean Alps on his return from Venice
to Nuremburg in 1495 (see plate 35). Watercolour later
became one of the principal media preferred by landscape
painters, since it was easily transportable and could be used
out of doors in preference to oil or tempera. Its capacity
for the precise rendering of colour and light is best seen
in Lucas Cranach the Elder's still lifes, which also sometimes include gouache.

When an exceptionally velvety finish was required,
watercolour was used on vellum, which permitted the
most refined detailing possible, in addition to jewel-like
colour. Because of the depth possible in this medium, an
almost *trompe-l'oeil* effect was achieved, which perfectly
suited the late Renaissance artists who perpetuated the
great tradition of miniature painting. Of these, Giulio
Clovio was a consummate artist (see plate 259) and in
Northern Europe, the Hoefnagel and de Gheyn dynasties,
and the Frenchman Jacques Lemoyne de Morgues. The
sixteenth century, with its love of preciosity, took particular delight in these miniaturists' exquisite renderings
of plants, insects and animals, a fascination also linked with
great advances in natural science in that century.

Gouache (from the Italian *guazzo*, distemper), also
known as body colour, is rendered opaque by the addition
of white pigment, and was extensively used by miniature
painters and manuscript illuminators. Drying much
lighter than when applied, it requires great skill in judg-
ing its effects in advance. Its use in conjunction with
watercolour produces rich effects of depth and surface
contrast.

The interaction of these media with the evolution of
painting itself was crucial. From the new applications of
drawing came much of the naturalism of the fifteenth
century, the precise balance achieved in High
Renaissance art, the genius for elaboration in the
Mannerist period and, at the end of the sixteenth century,
the emergence of landscape in its own right.

From Drawing to Painting

The evolution of a painting may be studied by various
means. The first method is to examine the picture with
the naked eye. Sometimes, the changes made during

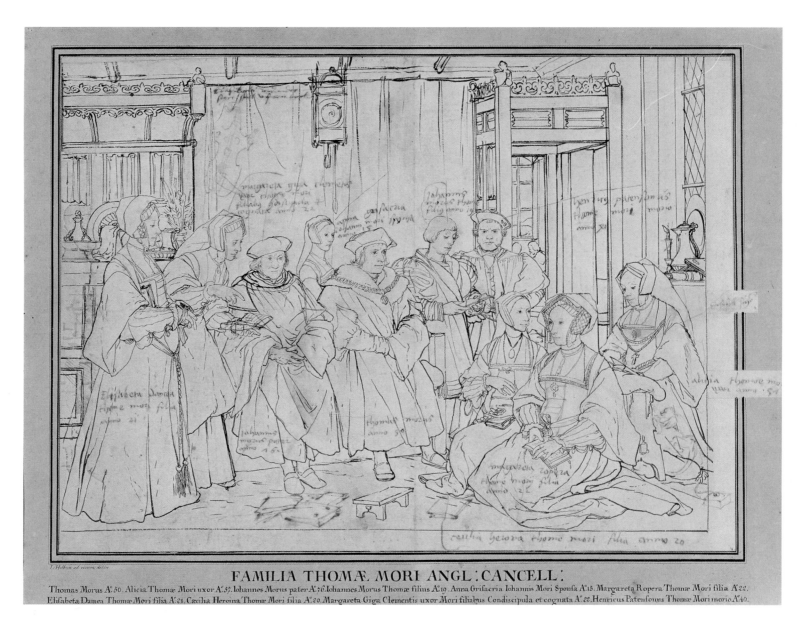

FAMILIA THOMÆ. MORI ANGL : CANCELL :

Thomas Morus A.º 50. Alicia Thomæ Mori uxor A.º 57. Iohannes Morus pater A.º 76. Iohannes Morus Thomæ filius A.º 19. Anna Grisacria Iohannis Mori Sponsa A.º 15. Margareta Ropera Thomæ Mori filia A.º 22. Elisabeta Damea Thomæ Mori filia A.º 21. Cæcilia Hereina Thomæ Mori filia A.º 20. Margareta Giga Clementis uxor Mori filiabus Condiscipula et cognata A.º 22. Henricus Patensouus Thomæ Mori morio A.º 40.

27 HANS HOLBEIN THE YOUNGER Sir Thomas More, his Father and his Household 1527–8

This particularly interesting drawing reveals the method adopted by Holbein for what seems to have been the first group portrait of the Northern Renaissance. Two notes on the drawing, probably made by Holbein after consulting with More, indicate that Dame Alice should sit instead of kneel, and that the viol hanging on the wall should be changed to musical instruments placed on the buffet. This is clearly not Holbein's first drawing for the picture, but having reached this stage of perfection he probably followed it with chalk studies of individual heads, seven of which are now at Windsor Castle. The lost picture for which it was a study may have been in tempera on canvas, and was probably commissioned by More to celebrate his fiftieth birthday. The English painter Rowland Lockey made three copies of the picture (see plate 165).

composition may become visible over time, as the top layers of paint become more transparent. These are called *pentimenti*. The second process involves the scientific examination, with X-rays, chemical analysis and so on, of the various components of paint and support (the canvas or wooden panel). A third process involves the examination of the artist's drawings. This often makes it possible to follow the artist's mind at work from the first germ of an idea to the final stage when he is ready to realize the composition in paint.

Significantly, it was only during the later Renaissance that the value of drawings in revealing the creative process began to be appreciated. It was at that time also that the idea of collecting drawings for their own sake emerged. Vasari (see Chapters III, VIII) was probably the first to do so, and by the year of his death (1574) had amassed Old Master drawings spanning three centuries. Collected into his *Libro de'Disegni*, they form an important part of his study of the development of Italian art (see plate 37). The artistic value that such drawings acquired is also illustrated in a letter from the poet Pietro Aretino to Michelangelo, which says that two charcoal strokes of his on a scrap of paper meant more than royal gifts of precious jewels.

The dimensions of a painting or the number of figures it contains may bear no relation to the extensiveness of the artist's preparations through drawings. This is the case with a particularly well documented work, Barocci's *Visitation* of the 1580s in Rome's Chiesa Nuova, containing only five principal figures. Extensive drawing was also a hallmark of Andrea del Sarto, Raphael and the

Florentines, and was consciously revived in the later years of the century by the Carracci family as a means of restoring the equilibrium lost in Mannerist studio practice.

Fresco

The art of fresco painting is primarily associated with Italy during the Renaissance, Baroque and Rococo periods, although other, isolated periods of greatness in the medium occur, for example in Rococo Germany. These geographical locations bear a direct relationship to the nature and limitations of the medium, since it is not suited to the humidity of the Northern European climate. Because of its foundations in water and its salty air, Venice was never suited to fresco. This, however, did not prevent the Venetians using it, even on exteriors, as in the case of Giorgione's now vanished Fondaco dei Tedeschi decorations. A special *intonaco*, or smooth plaster base, was even evolved to counteract the effects of damp.

Because of the difficulties involved in fresco, and the impossibility of last minute alterations, it came to be regarded by Vasari and others as the supreme test of any artist's assurance. Cennini, who reflects the thinking of the 1390s, calls mural painting 'the most agreeable and impressive kind of work'. *Fresco* is the Italian for 'fresh', and the finest variety known as *buon fresco* or 'true fresco', consists of colour dissolved in water and applied to wet areas of freshly mixed and applied *intonaco*. This is a very smooth blend of lime, fine sand and sometimes marble dust, and as it dries so the painting is integrated with its base. True fresco is surprisingly rare, the two most perfect examples to survive being Giotto's cycle in the Arena Chapel in Padua (see plate 56) and Masaccio's in the Brancacci Chapel, Florence (see plate 70) – coincidentally two of the highest achievements in Western painting.

Intonaco was applied thinly over a rough plaster layer normally called the *arriccio*, on to which a broadly conceived drawing was often made with a pigment such as red haematite or iron oxide, called *sinopia* after Sinope in Asia Minor (see plate 38). Techniques known as *stacco* or *strappo* are now refined enough to detach frescoes from walls, sometimes revealing the delicate *sinopia* underpainting. Simone Martini's *Madonna of Humility* at Avignon reveals up to four layers of *sinopie* in certain parts of the composition. *Sinopie* often reveal a painter's initial ideas.

Because the *intonaco* layer dries rapidly (Cennini recommends certain months only in which to paint frescoes), the fresco would be built up in a series of daily applications or *giornate*, depending on the artist's speed of working. Occasionally, two or more sections of *intonaco* could be applied and worked on each day. The overlapping joints between *giornate* often permit a precise reconstruction of the time involved in a fresco, and its starting and finishing point. Major examples clearly revealing the *giornate* are Masaccio's *Trinity* (see plate 93), Raphael's *Stanze* frescoes (see plate 196) and Michelangelo's Sistine Ceiling (see plate 40).

A complete understanding of the problems involved in tackling the difficult art of fresco was essential. For example, ignorance of the properties of certain pigments could be disastrous, as in the case of lead white, which oxidizes and turns black (as happened in Cimabue's transept frescoes in San Francesco at Assisi). Cennini warns against using lead white in fresco, along with vermilion, azurite, verdigris, minium and orpiment.

Additions and minor alterations such as decorative accessories could be made to *buon fresco* with *fresco a secco* or 'dry' fresco. This is a confusing term for colour mixed with an organic binding medium, using animal or vegetable glues, and painted over areas of fresco that have dried. Certain colours, in particular azurite (the deep blue often seen in the Virgin's garments) could only be applied *a secco*. Sometimes especially lavish decorative detail could

28 GIOVANNI DA MILANO Detail from the Rinuccini Chapel in Santa Croce, Florence *c.*1365
The Rinuccini Chapel is one of the best-preserved examples of a Trecento frescoed chapel. In buon fresco *or* true fresco, *the* intonaco, *or plaster base, consists of lime, very fine sand and sometimes marble dust mixed to a very smooth consistency and applied to the wall surface in* giornate. *In this example the* intonaco *is particularly smooth, giving the paint applications a very fine finish.*

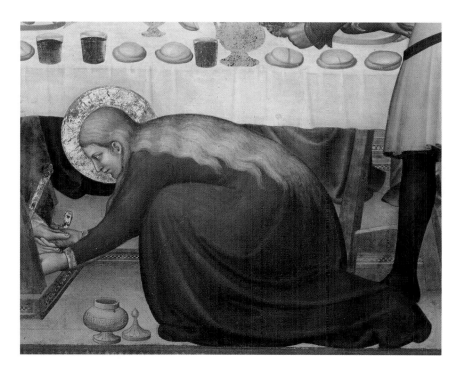

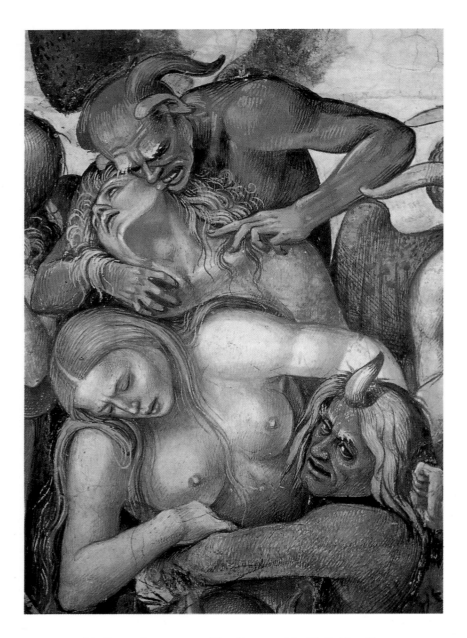

29 Luca Signorelli The Damned in Hell (detail)
1499–1504
This shows the importance, particularly in large-scale frescoes meant to be viewed from a distance, of modelling a secco by means of hatching and cross-hatching to accentuate the figures' relief. In view of the rapidity with which fresco dries in warm weather, such a technique permitted the painter to reconsider the contrasts he required and to build up a more strikingly three-dimensional effect. Signorelli in particular valued this sculptural approach to the human figure, a factor which drew Michelangelo to study these frescoes.

be added in gold leaf. Mantegna appears to have added a considerable amount of detail in *fresco a secco* to his decorations in the Camera degli Sposi at Mantua, much of which has disintegrated (see plate 105). Restorations to Renaissance frescoes were frequently carried out in *fresco a secco*, sometimes with disastrous results. One such case was Carlo Maratti's 'restoration' of Raphael's frescoes in the Loggia of Psyche at the Villa Farnesina, Rome. Leonardo appears to have experimented with a variety of *a secco* means in the *Last Supper* in order to speed up the process of execution, which led to its almost immediate disintegration (see plate 41).

Cartoons

Preparation for fresco painting involved drawings and possibly a *modello* leading to the execution of a cartoon (from the Italian, *cartone*, a large sheet of paper). By the late fifteenth century, cartoons were widely used for frescoes, panel paintings and even embroideries.

Early *modelli* were usually small drawings showing the full composition, the earliest unquestionable examples of which date from about 1400. During the later Renaissance and particularly in the Baroque period, the word is generally associated with small oil sketches of a finished composition. The cartoon, on parchment or fairly thin paper, carried the completed design, which was usually executed full-scale in black chalk or charcoal. This was often realized on a large scale by squaring – transferring the design from a grid of lines traced over the smaller drawings and simply recreating the layout of squares and their content on the cartoon. Smaller cartoons were executed in pen and ink, brush and wash or even metalpoint. The drawn outlines on the finished cartoon were then 'pricked for transfer' with a sharp instrument, the cartoon placed against the wall or other surface to be painted, and powdered charcoal 'pounced' or rubbed thorough the holes to leave dark outlines on the plaster or other surface beneath (see plate 30).

The cartoon preserved one stage in the creative process of frescoes which had previously been lost when the *intonaco* was painted on. It not only enabled the painter (or his assistants) to check the composition continually, but also, as in the case of Michelangelo's celebrated *Battle of Cascina* cartoon (see plate 208) preserved the original conception for the education of other artists, if only temporarily. The nature of the transfer process increased the cartoon's fragility, particularly when it consisted of many joined sheets of paper. As the average sheet size, called *reale*, measured roughly 445 × 615 mm, it was necessary to glue sheets together with overlapping edges for very large commissions, and the resultant weakening has led to the destruction of most large cartoons of this period. An exception is Raphael's series for the Sistine tapestries (see plate 205).

From about 1470–1520, changes took place in the technique of cartoon transfer, and stylus-tracing came into greater use. After 1520, pouncing was considered old-fashioned, and was mainly reserved for the creation of decorative detail and repeat patterns. Stylus-tracing or incising involved tracing or indenting the drawing outline on to the painting surface from the cartoon, using a sharp instrument or even the end of a paintbrush. In fresco, this was done by digging sometimes quite deep lines into the moist plaster, leaving an incision drawing for the painter to follow. These lines are often clearly visible on the surface of frescoes (for example, Raphael's *School of Athens*). In the case of the dry, primed surfaces used in panel or canvas painting, black chalk or pouncing dust was rubbed on to the verso (back) of the cartoon itself or the verso of a separate sheet of paper laid underneath, which left dark, somewhat hard lines with minimal indentation.

Painting on Panel and Canvas

Until the fifteenth century, the most commonly used medium for panel painting was tempera. Powdered pigments were mixed with a binder, usually egg white, to make them workable before they were applied to the prepared wood. The paint dried quickly, but several degrees lighter than when wet. The innovation of mixing the pigments with oil meant that far greater richness of colour and depth of tone could be obtained. Although the technique of painting in oils was first developed in Flanders in the early fifteenth century, it gradually spread throughout Italy. It was adopted with particular enthusiasm in Venice, where the new possibilities it offered painters were exploited to the full. The preparation necessary for applying tempera or oil paint to panel or canvas was, in the Renaissance, infinitely more painstaking than the preparation for fresco. The result, however, is the astonishing degree of preservation of many paintings of the period, with many of their colour balances intact enough for us to see or envisage their original splendour.

Most European painting of the fifteenth century was executed on wooden panels, a support which continued in popularity in Northern Europe in particular, but also found favour with certain painters in Italy well into the sixteenth century. In Tuscany, the support (often referred to simply as *albero* or tree) was usually of wood, most commonly poplar. There were, of course, exceptions to this. Mantegna, for example, sometimes painted on fine linen or canvas, using tempera or distemper, sometimes varnishing this to achieve a vitreous finish.

Cennini remains the prime source of knowledge on how artists approached panel painting. He outlines in meticulous detail the prerequisites for working with 'tree', be it poplar, lime or willow. Properly seasoned, the panel should be without knots, 'or other faults', but if these exist, they should be filled with sawdust softened by boiling in glue. Tin foil should be used to prevent rust from any protruding nails or rivets from penetrating the paint layer. A size (glue) is then prepared from boiled clippings of parchment:

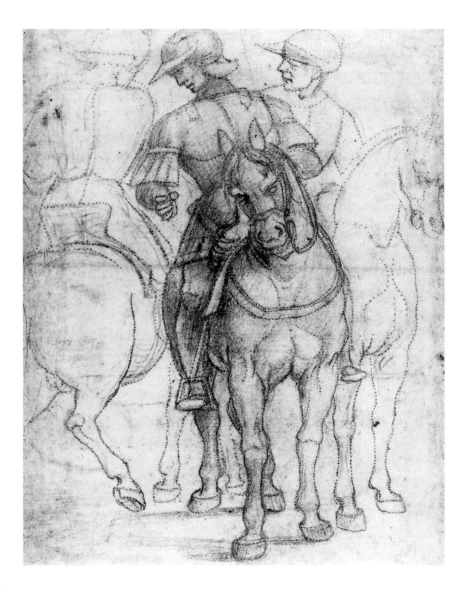

30 Luca Signorelli Three Horsemen, undated
This is a superb example of a preparatory cartoon for a fresco, showing the artist, Luca Signorelli, using 'pouncing' holes through which coloured dust or charcoal could be dusted on to the plaster surface, in order to provide the outline for later painting. The cartoon is particularly interesting since Signorelli has not only followed the pre-existing chalk outline with his pouncing, but also, in the right-hand horse, has virtually created the figure with the pounced holes themselves. The technique appears to have been introduced originally by embroiderers and manuscript illustrators. Signorelli's Orvieto Cathedral frescoes show his command of the technique.

'Test it with the palms of your hands, and when you find that one palm sticks to the other, it will be right. Strain it two or three times. Then take a pot half full of this size, one third water and let it all boil well. Then apply this size to your panel . . . using a large, soft brush. Then take more of the original strong size and make a further two applications, always letting it dry in between. The size will then adhere excellently. And do you know what the first size, with water, accomplishes? Not being so strong, it is just as if you were fasting, and ate a handful of sweetmeats, and drank a glass of good wine, which is an inducement for you to eat your dinner. Thus it is with this size: it is a means of giving the wood a taste for receiving the coats of size and gesso.'

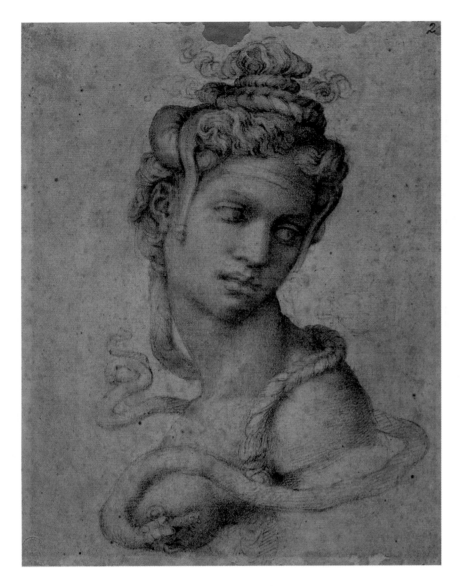

34 JAN VAN EYCK Saint Barbara 1437
(Right) This may be the underdrawing for a finished painting, although some critics believe it is too finished for that role. Artists would usually make preparatory brush drawings in monochrome, over which colours would be laid in a series of glazes to achieve the depth and transparency peculiar to oil painting. Although the faux marbre frame bears the inscription 'JOHES DE EYCK ME FECIT. 1437' this may have been completed before the picture was finished, a common practice at the time. Saint Barbara, holding her palm of martyrdom, is placed before the construction of the tower in which she is to be imprisoned, which recalls the great Gothic cathedrals of Germany.

32 MICHELANGELO Divine Head 1533–4
In his account of the life of Properzia di Rossi, Vasari says that in 1562 Tommaso de' Cavalieri made a gift to Duke Cosimo de' Medici of a drawing by 'the divine Michelangelo, showing Cleopatra'. This is generally identified with this drawing of the theme. The Egyptian queen is shown in an idealized form with the facial features typical of Michelangelo. A complex arrangement of plaits of hair winding and falling around the head makes an ambiguous play with the large asp, whose bite killed Cleopatra.

33 JAN VAN EYCK Cardinal Niccolò Albergati c.1431
(Below) When Cardinal Albergati visited Bruges in December 1431, Van Eyck made this silverpoint portrait of him. In spite of its high finish and technical command, this superb drawing was clearly conceived by the artist as a form of shorthand note for a painted portrait of the Cardinal now in the Kunsthistorisches Museum, Vienna: Van Eyck even made notes about colour and other points on the silverpoint to remind him of the details. The silverpoint is strikingly realistic when compared to the painting, showing how assured a great master could be even with such a demanding medium.

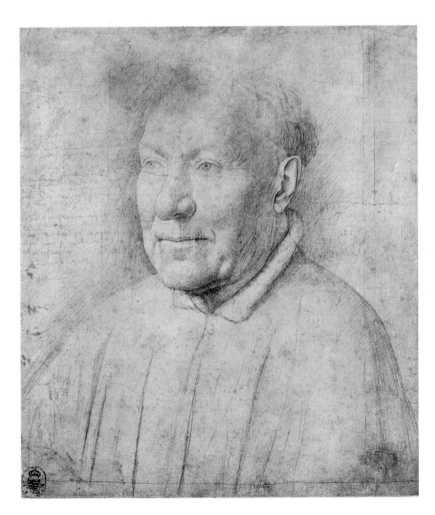

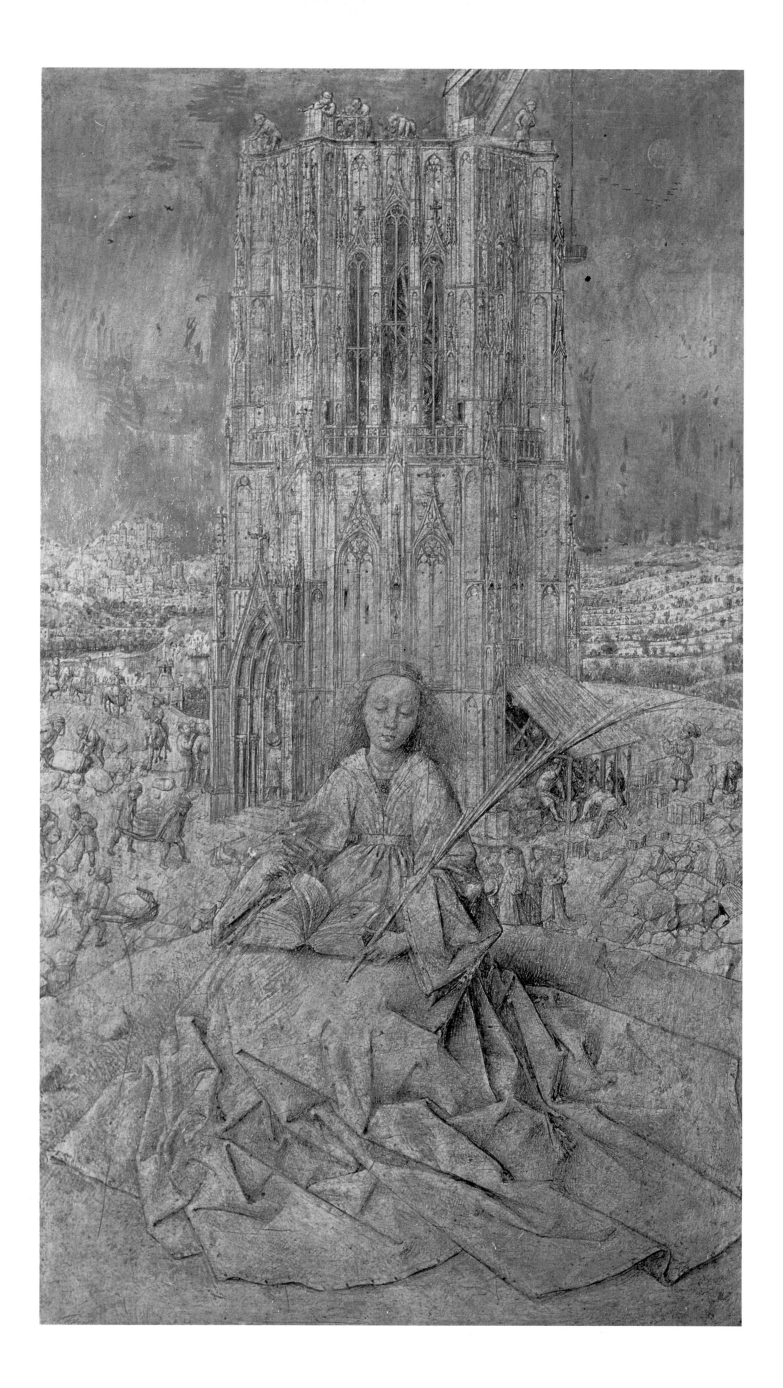

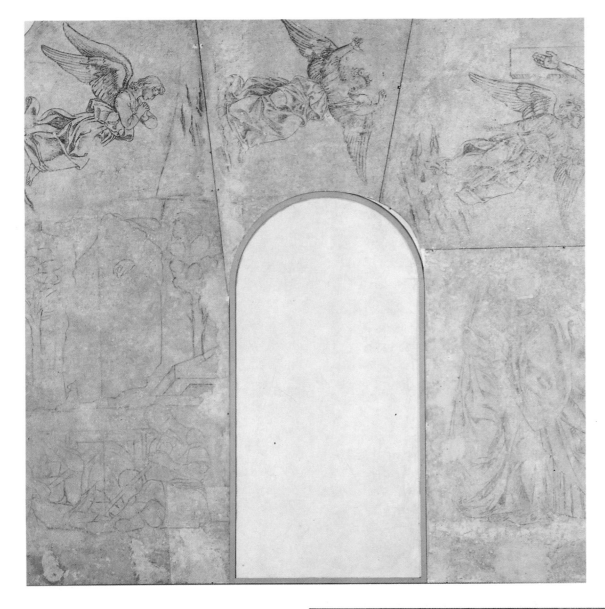

38 and 39 ANDREA DEL
CASTAGNO Resurrection
1445–50
(Above and right) Castagno's
Resurrection *is one of three scenes*
from the Passion, which the artist
painted on the north wall of the
refectory of Sant'Apollonia, above
his fresco of the Last Supper: *these*
were recovered in 1890 from beneath
a layer of whitewash, and the
sinopie found and removed in 1953.
The sinopia for the Resurrection
is the only one in the cycle
containing figures corresponding
exactly to the fresco, and offers a
particularly firmly drawn example of
the method underlying the creation
of the major frescoes.

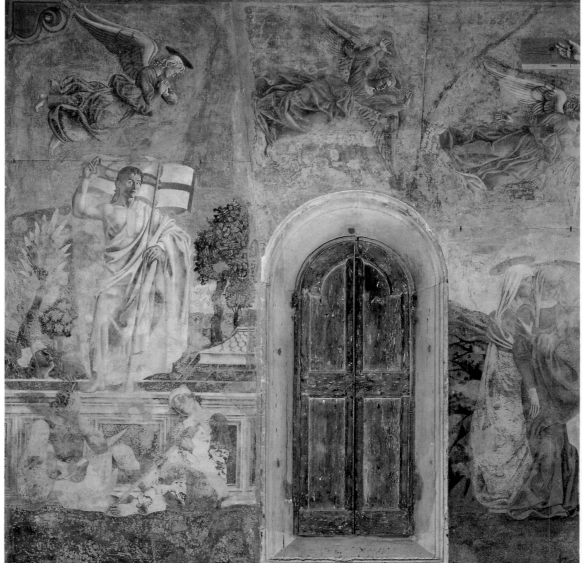

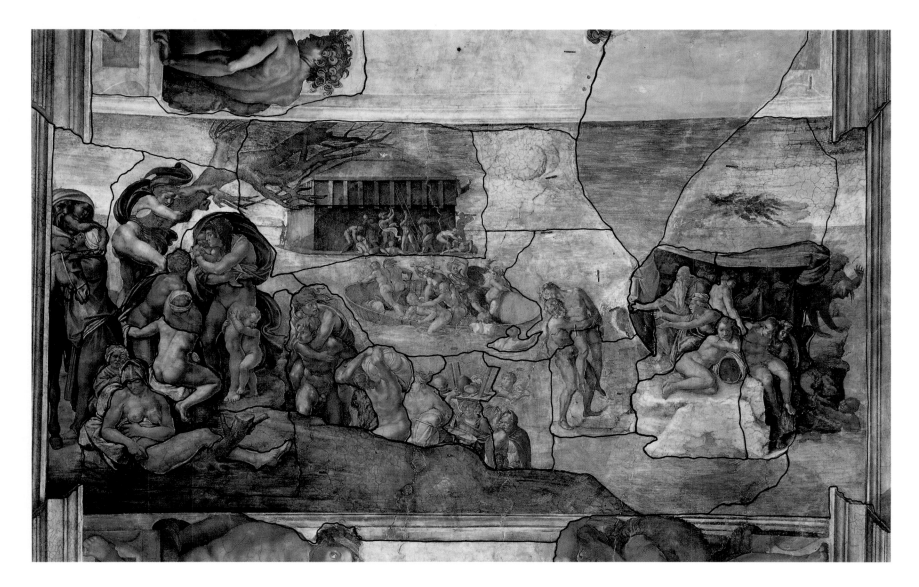

40 MICHELANGELO The Deluge 1508

(Above) This was apparently the first of the Sistine ceiling scenes painted by Michelangelo. The individual giornate, or sections painted each day, are outlined in black. The scene of the Fall and Expulsion from the Garden of Eden was carried out in eight or nine days. The architect Giuliano da Sangallo had to be consulted about dealing with the mould which grew because the fresco's lime base had not dried quickly enough.

41 LEONARDO DA VINCI Last Supper 1495–7

(Below) Leonardo's Last Supper has always been recorded as one of the greatest technical failures in Western art. Leonardo used oil paint rather than fresco, a serious misjudgement because of subsequent deterioration. Little of the original paintwork remains, and it is only really possible to understand the impact the work had from copies and preparatory drawings. As early as 1517–18 it was noted that it was disintegrating, possibly due to humidity.

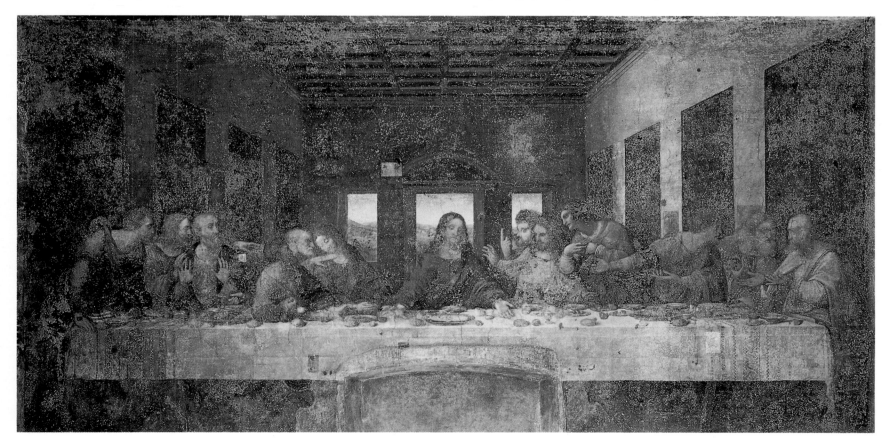

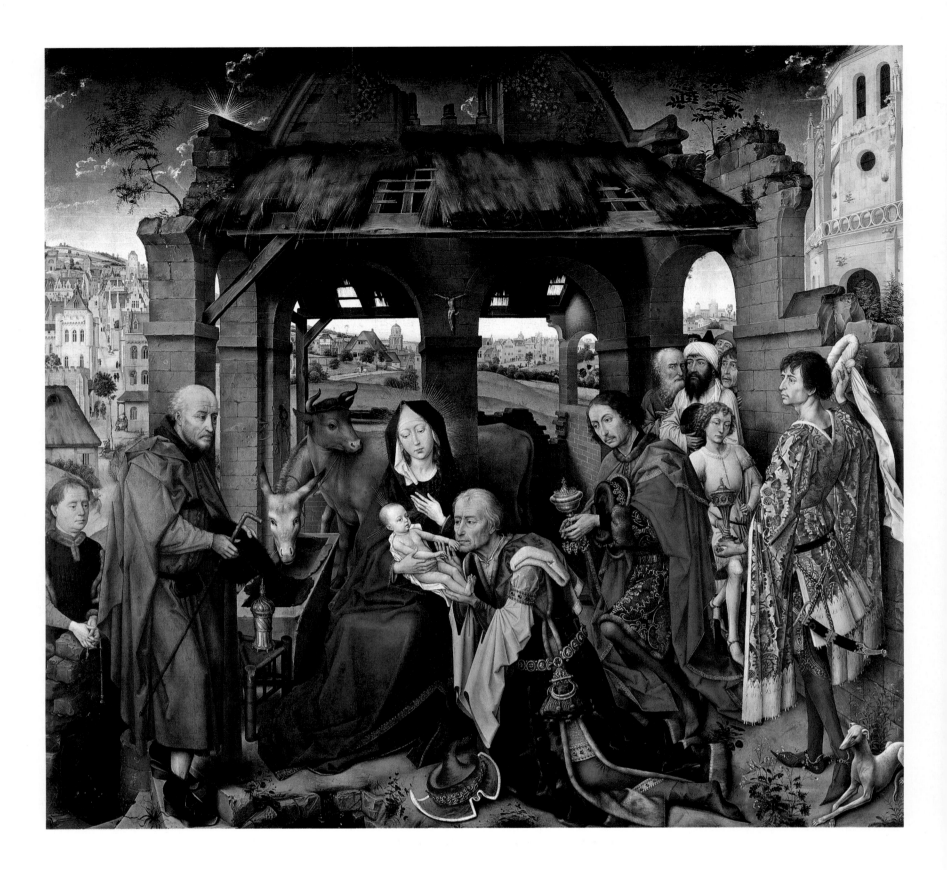

42 ROGIER VAN DER WEYDEN The Saint Columba Altarpiece
*c.*1435
Coming from the church of St Columba in Cologne, this is a major
work of the painter's late period, and shows his fully evolved style
and technique. Rogier van der Weyden painted it on an oak panel,
and it is remarkable for showing the range of brilliant colour available
to Flemish painters. Van Eyck had perfected the technique of
applying countless layers of oil-based paint over a white chalk
ground applied to the panel. This gave an astonishing transparency
to the final colours, particularly when compared to tempera, which
was inevitably more opaque. It also permitted the depiction of fine
detail, as in the jewellery, costume and landscape, the transparency
contributing greatly to the effect of light on distant buildings. An
ever-increasing level of technical expertise was required by the guilds,
who maintained control over artistic production in the Netherlands.

43 ALBRECHT DÜRER Knight, Death and the Devil 1513-14
This is not only one of the artist's most celebrated copperplate
engravings, but also among his most striking images. Along with
Saint Jerome in his Study and Melancholia, both of the same
years, this is one of Dürer's most ambitious plates. Death stares the
Knight in the face and the Devil waits to catch him if he falls, but he
rides on undaunted. In these plates, Dürer follows directly in
Schongauer's wake in achieving rich effects of light, shade and volume
within the limitations of line. His interpretation of forms in such
dense juxtapositions exercised an incalculable influence on painting
both north of the Alps and in Italy, Dürer himself having been
greatly influenced by Mantegna's prints.

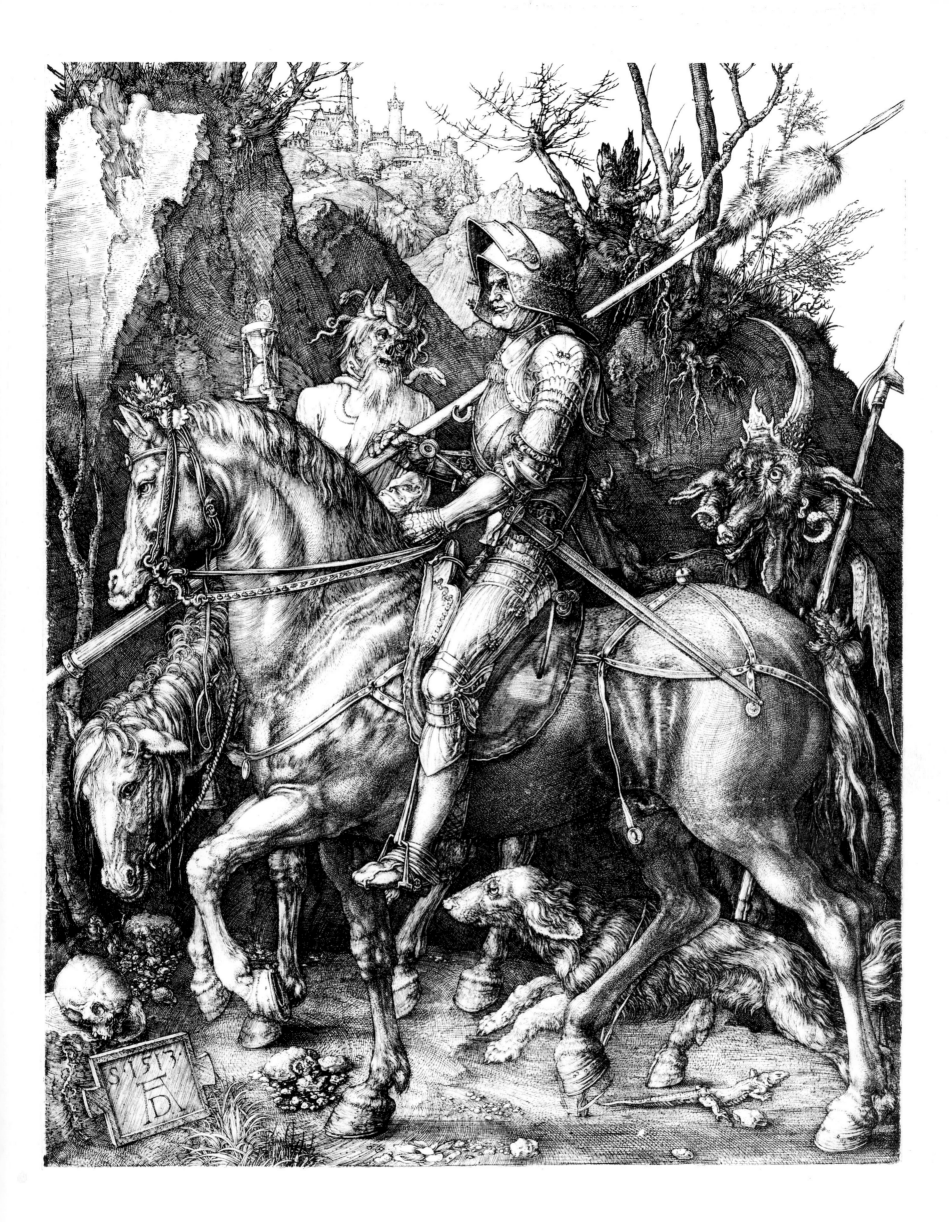

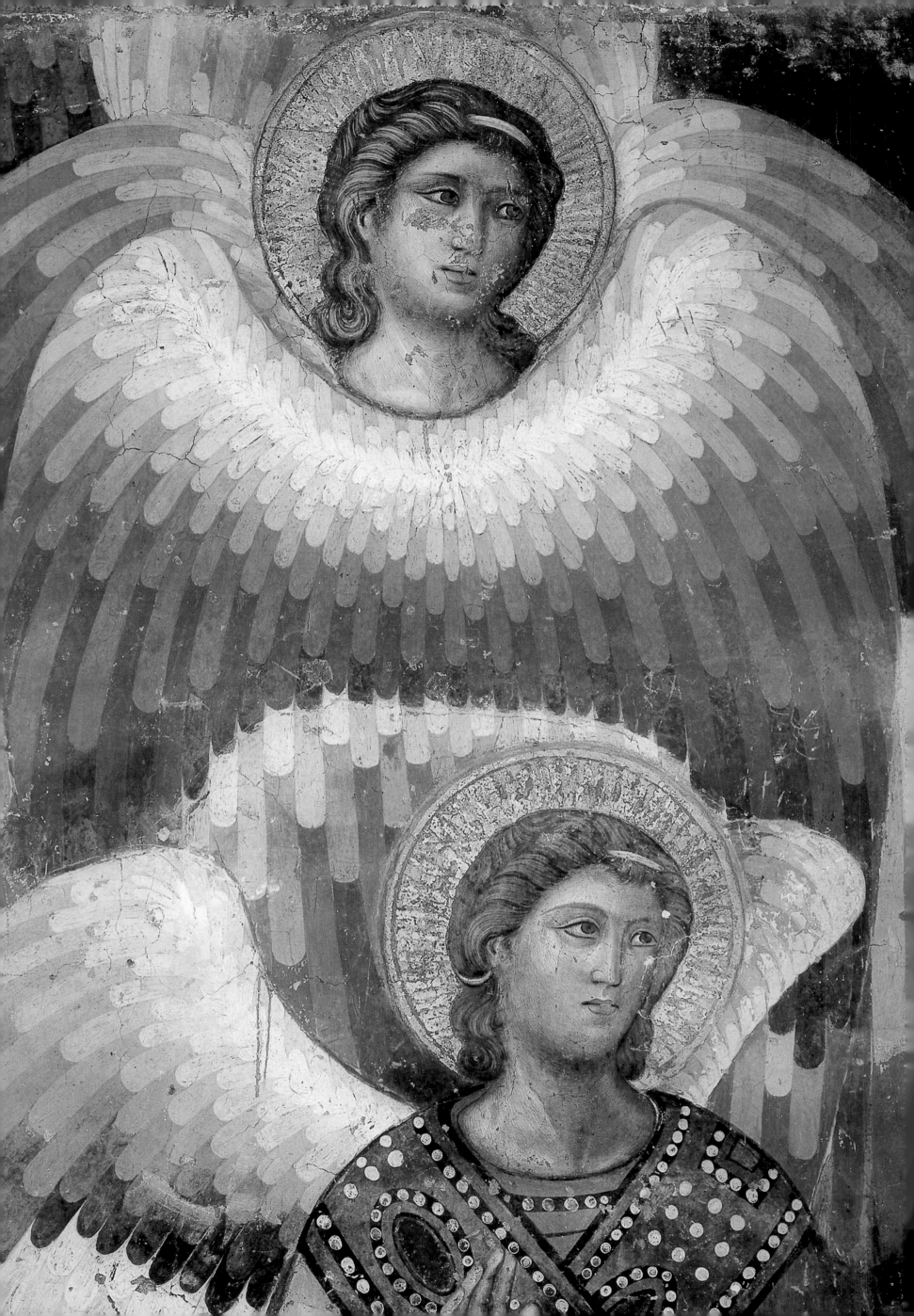

CHAPTER III

The Rebirth of Painting in Italy and the Prelude to the Renaissance 1250–1400

Rediscovering the Primitives

The art of the 'primitives' – the Italian painters of the thirteenth and fourteenth centuries (the Dugento and Trecento) was virtually rediscovered by the Victorians, unlike the art of the Renaissance, which enjoyed almost unbroken favour with connoisseurs and collectors. Indeed, it is a miracle that any painting from these two centuries has survived, given the attitude of the post-Renaissance period. Fresco cycles were white-washed or destroyed, panel paintings jettisoned and all forms of 'primitive' art were obliterated by later decoration and architecture. Had it not been for an enlightened Paduan historian, the Marchese Pietro Selvatico, even Giotto's Arena Chapel (see plate 56) – the fourteenth century's equivalent of the Sistine Chapel – would have been razed to the ground.

The ideals of the Dugento and early Trecento can seem very remote from the Renaissance, but it was the influential art historian Giorgio Vasari (1511–74) who first perceived the connection between the work of Giotto and Fra Angelico, for example, and rightly dated his examination of the rebirth of art in his native land from this period. Compared with his writing on his own period, however, the reliability of much of his information and many of his conclusions about earlier artists are questionable, and often completely unreliable. But there

44 PIETRO CAVALLINI Angels, before 1308

This is a detail from Cavallini's partly destroyed fresco of the Last Judgement *in Santa Cecilia in Trastevere. The clarity of figure modelling and the characterization of the faces are typical of Cavallini's attractive style. They indicate that he was almost certainly the leading Roman painter/mosaicist of his day, and they provide the background from which Giotto drew many elements of his new style.*

are other contemporary sources of information and attributions, particularly the wealth of documents recording commissions and payments, and the *Commentaries* of the Florentine sculptor, Lorenzo Ghiberti (1378–1455). This large incomplete manuscript comprises an autobiography, a survey of ancient art and notes on optics, together with much detail about Italian Trecento painters and sculptors.

The Church: Patron and Inspiration

Painting in the later Middle Ages in Italy, as throughout Europe, was almost exclusively religious, since the artist's first allegiance was to the Church. With the exception of rarities like Ambrogio Lorenzetti's *Good and Bad Government* (see plate 64), large public fresco cycles were entirely devoted to religious themes, or at the very least semi-religious allegories. The other principal type of commission was the altarpiece, and in the late Gothic and early Renaissance, frame and picture were virtually (and sometimes literally) inseparable. In early painting, the frame often served as a physical support for more than one panel, hinged to form a diptych, triptych or polyptych. Italian altarpiece frames of this date are often made to resemble cross-sections of Gothic churches, with pointed arches, small buttresses and florid pinnacles. They were frequently elaborately painted and gilded and this could be considered an act of veneration to the images they contained: as Cennini says, 'God and Our Lady will reward you for it, body and soul'.

The main source of patronage in Italy was indeed to remain the Church throughout the Renaissance and Baroque periods. Moreover, during the fifteenth and sixteenth centuries, much of the necessary finance for important private decorations stemmed from church funds through newly enriched members of Papal families.

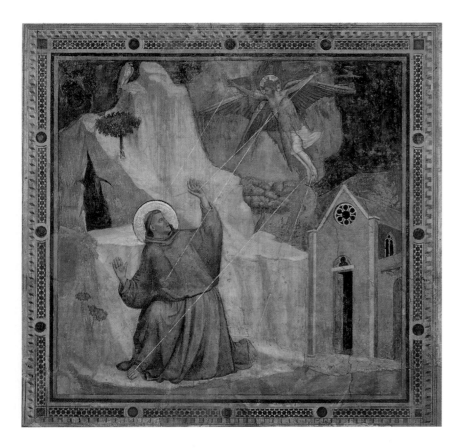

45 GIOTTO The Stigmatisation of Saint Francis *c.*1325
*Giotto frescoed at least three chapels in the great Franciscan church of
Santa Croce in Florence, of which two survive. Those in the Peruzzi
Chapel depict the lives of St John the Evangelist and St John the
Baptist, while seven pictures in the Bardi Chapel are devoted to the
life of St Francis of Assisi. These are approximately contemporary
with the Ognissanti Madonna. This scene shows the kneeling saint
receiving the stigmata from a seraph.*

The religious revivals of the later Middle Ages were of
incalculable importance in nurturing the growth of an
Italian school of painting. A prime influence in this
respect was St Francis of Assisi (c.1181–1226), founder of
the Franciscan Order, who was canonized in 1228.
St Francis may be said to have given a human face to late
medieval Catholicism, which is directly reflected in the
aims of Trecento painting in Italy. Second only to
him was his contemporary, St Dominic (1170–1221),
founder of the Dominican Order, who was canonized in
1234 and established his order in France and England.
St Francis's spirituality and his particular devotion to the
Holy Cross and to the Virgin gave rise to many new
images, and his own life inspired two of Giotto's greatest
works: *The Legend of Saint Francis* (Upper Church, Assisi),
and the Bardi Chapel frescoes in the church of Santa
Croce, Florence (see plate 45). Painted images assumed
rapidly increasing importance, not only as an inspiration
for prayer to the faithful, but also as an accredited source
of miraculous powers. A crucifix had supposedly spoken
to St Francis himself, commanding him to go forth and
found his order.

New writings began to exercise an immense influence
before the Renaissance, notably the *Meditations on the Life
of Christ*, probably written by John de Caulibus of San
Gimignano towards the end of the thirteenth century.
This book features the process of visualization which culminates in the *Spiritual Exercises* of St Ignatius Loyola
(published in 1548). Their aim was to enable the reader,
while meditating, to form mental pictures of biblical
scenes, so that their symbolism and inner meaning would
leave a deeper impression on the mind. Art was the natural expression of such processes, both before and during
the Renaissance. Another devotional work written in the
thirteenth century that was to prove immensely influential was *The Golden Legend* by Jacopo da Voragine. A compilation of the lives of saints, it became an important
source book for Renaissance artists.

The stylized forms and expressions of earlier Byzantine
painting must have exasperated painters struggling to render the new spirituality. At the same time, it was probably
difficult for them to shake off their predecessors' belief in
the power of a generalized image, with few if any individual features indicating character. New ideas first made
their appearance in sculpture, in the cities of Pisa, Siena
and Pistoia, where interest in Classical prototypes came to
be united with a limited degree of naturalism. The leaders
of this movement were Nicola Pisano (c.1220/5–84?) and
his son, Giovanni (c.1245–50 – after 1314). Nicola's first
known work is a pulpit in the Baptistery at Pisa, signed
and dated 1260, which, together with the three later pul-
pits by the Pisani, clearly takes inspiration from Late
Roman sculpture.

Elements such as facial expression, the rendering of
depth, and the use of drapery as an indication of underlying form all depart from the stylized approach prevalent
in European Romanesque sculpture at the time. This synthesis of antique art with Christian iconography looked
forward to the achievements of Giotto and his contemporaries in painting, and indeed announced some of the
aims of Renaissance art.

It was in the Tuscan cities of Florence, Siena, Lucca and
Pisa that the first signs of a new and distinctive style of
Italian painting made their appearance, edging away from
the hard conventions of Byzantine art. The mosaics in the
vault of the Baptistery of Florence Cathedral sum up the
artistic background to this period. Vasari claims that these
were the work of a Greek mosaicist called Apollonio, and
Andrea Taffi (who is mentioned by the poet Boccaccio),
who have been identified with the so-called 'Bardi St
Francis Master' and the 'Magdalen Master'. The mosaics
are arranged in tiers in the manner which was to be continued right up to the late Quattrocento, and the vault is

dominated by the gigantic figure of Christ. Although strongly Byzantine in feeling, the expressiveness of the figures is characteristically Tuscan and their grandeur undoubtedly influenced later artists, not least of all Giotto himself. It is tempting to see a reflection of the Baptistery Christ in Giotto's Arena Chapel *Last Judgement*.

Cimabue

The Byzantine manner of Cimabue (Cenni di Peppi, *c*.1240–1302) in the later Dugento was the foundation from which some of the subsequent developments of the Renaissance were to grow. Cimabue, whose nickname means 'Ox-head', enjoys a reputation built partly by his

46 CIMABUE Crucifix *c*.1288–98
The attribution of this monumental work to Cimabue is now generally accepted: it is shown here as it looked before the severe damaged sustained in the Florence flood of 1966. The work's greatness lies in Cimabue's decision to create a human and approachable image of a God suffering on the cross rather than triumphantly alive. This new approach to the human incarnation of Christ, which is also visible in Cimabue's huge Crucifixion *fresco in the Upper Church of San Francesco at Assisi, looks forward to the fifteenth century's thinking on religious imagery.*

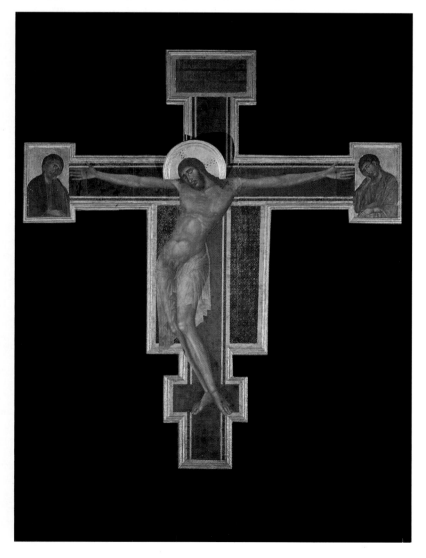

contemporary, the poet Dante, who refers to him in *The Divine Comedy*: 'Cimabue thought to hold the field in painting, but now Giotto's name is on everyone's lips'. Although Dante intended this as an allusion to the vanity of all earthly ambitions, the phrase was always regarded as a quasi-historical statement about Cimabue. Later writers from Ghiberti to Vasari continued to assert that Giotto was Cimabue's pupil, and Vasari used this to confirm his belief in the traceable rise of Italian art from the 'Greek' (i.e. Byzantine) to the superior art of his own day, by way of Giotto, Masaccio and Michelangelo. Vasari was correct in sensing that Cimabue was the last representative of many trends clinging to late Byzantine traditions, and his importance lay in his example to the next, reforming generation of Giotto. There remains only one work securely by Cimabue (the figure of St John in a mosaic in Pisa Cathedral dating from 1301), but his present day reputation is based on a combination of traditional attributions and modern connoisseurship.

The three principal pieces traditionally accepted as Cimabue's manifest an impressive artistic talent. These are the famous *Crucifix* in Santa Croce, Florence (see plate 46), the *Santa Trinità Madonna* (see plate 58) and a *Crucifixion*, part of a fresco cycle in the Upper Church of San Francesco at Assisi. The white lead employed by Cimabue in the lights of his Assisi fresco has oxidized and turned black, with the result that their original brilliance and most of their detail has vanished. Remarkably, the original dramatic impact of the scene is still hauntingly present, however, and from it one can deduce what Cimabue passed on to his pupils.

Pietro Cavallini

The importance of mosaic decoration in the Dugento and early Trecento (during the Renaissance itself its use survived mainly in Venice) is seen in the work of a Roman painter-mosaicist, who also opened the way to Giotto's developments: Pietro Cavallini (active 1273–1308). He was the most important painter active in Rome, and later Naples (where Giotto was to work in 1329–33). His style united Classical inspiration with the new ideas introduced into sculpture in Rome by Nicola Pisano's pupil, Arnolfo di Cambio (died 1302). Arnolfo worked in Bologna, Siena, Orvieto and Rome and in his role as an architect-sculptor was responsible for the design of both Santa Croce and the Cathedral in Florence. The peripatetic lives of these leading artists gave them much more than merely local renown, and ensured the spread of new ideas so important in later Renaissance art.

Cavallini's career was greatly helped by Pope Nicholas III, who commissioned great fresco cycles in Old St Peter's and the churches of San Paolo fuori le Mura and San Lorenzo in Rome. Sadly, our only knowledge of these lost cycles is through later drawings and paintings, but we know from Ghiberti's *Second Commentary* that Cavallini was responsible for them. The surviving fragments of his frescoes in Santa Cecilia in Trastevere (see plate 44) show that Cavallini was mastering the techniques of modelling with light and shade and architectural foreshortening – features which Giotto later made so much his own. Cimabue visited Rome in 1272, and may also have been influenced by Cavallini.

47 GIOTTO Enrico Scrovegni Offering his Chapel to the Virgin 1306
This is a detail of the Last Judgement *on the entrance wall of the Arena Chapel, Padua. It contains one of Giotto's most memorable profile portraits, showing the donor who paid for the entire chapel in the expiatory act intended to compensate for his father's usury, the source of his great wealth. The same scene shows the usurers hung by their purse strings in Hell. Although Giotto probably entrusted the execution of much of the* Last Judgement *to assistants, this is certainly by him.*

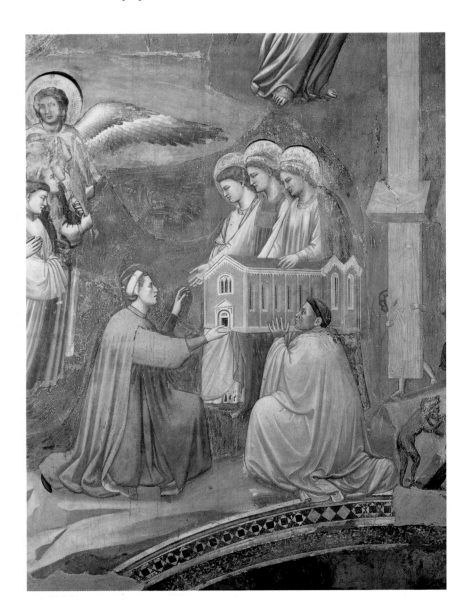

Giotto

It is perhaps indicative of the difficulty for Vasari in understanding this period, that he thought Cavallini was Giotto's pupil. On one thing, however, Vasari was clear – that Giotto (Giotto di Bondone, 1266/7–1337) was the most important artist of his age, having abandoned 'that clumsy Greek manner of painting and arrived at the modern and good way of painting, introducing the likenesses of living people'. Giotto's contemporaries had known this, from Dante and Boccaccio onwards, and their opinion was firmly backed by Cennini ('Giotto translated the art of painting from Greek to Latin'), the poet Angelo Poliziano and Leonardo da Vinci. The poet Petrarch (1303–74) owned a *Virgin and Child* by Giotto, and said that the ignorant would never appreciate its beauty, which would, however, amaze those who understood art. Giotto was even listed by the mid-century as the only artist among Florence's renowned citizens.

It is significant that Giotto attained considerable wealth through his work. Unlike Cimabue, whose status never seems to have risen much above that of a labourer, he owned houses in Florence and Rome as well as country estates. Giotto came into direct contact with Roman art in all its forms shortly after 1300, when he was employed in Old St Peter's to design the *Navicella* or Ship-of-the-Church mosaic above the cathedral entrance. Of this nothing remains.

Giotto was first documented in Florence in 1301, and his first securely dateable work is also his greatest – the frescoes of 1303–6 in the Arena (or Scrovegni) Chapel in Padua (see plates 47, 56). Fortunately, these are among the best preserved frescoes of the Trecento, and had they been the only example of Giotto's work to survive, would have ensured him a prime position in European painting. They are also clearly the work of a mature and self-confident artist, which assures us that Giotto had had considerable previous experience as a frescoist. Their whole approach is startlingly revolutionary, and their individual parts unrivalled for originality in their period.

Whatever Giotto's previous fresco experience may have been, it probably included work on some of the frescoes in the Upper Church of San Francesco at Assisi (see plate 48). Giotto's precise contribution there is much debated. Many critics insist that certain scenes reveal his beginnings, while others maintain that none of the painting is his. The chronicler Riccobaldo Ferrarese stated in 1312 that he painted there without specifying what, and by the mid-fifteenth century Ghiberti was asserting that he had painted almost all of the lower sections in the Upper Church. In any case, he would have

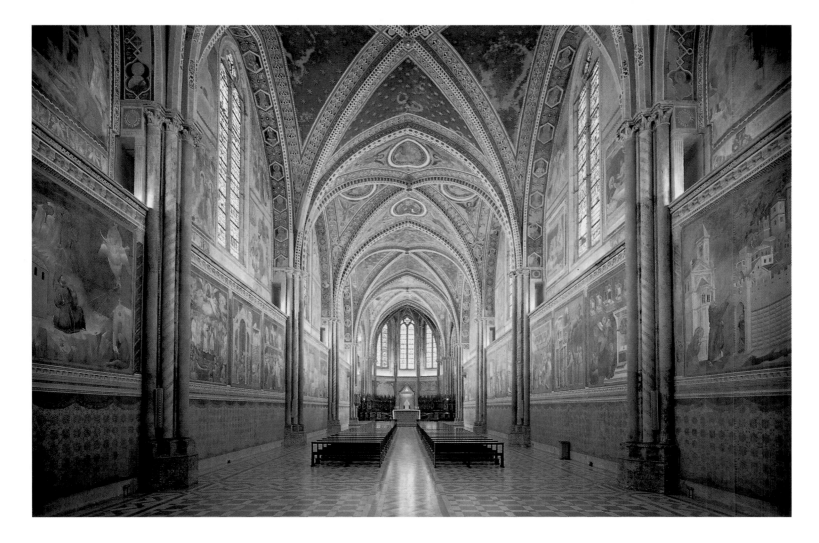

48 ASSISI General view of the Upper Church *c.*1290–1307
The decoration of the single nave was begun c.1290. Vasari initially attributed the twenty-eight scenes from the life of St Francis on the first register to Giotto, and these were probably complete by 1307. It is likely that the decorations were a collaborative effort in which Giotto's naturalism was the most important influence. Four main artists have been suggested, including the St Francis Master and the St Cecilia Master. The saint's life is explored through his relationship with God, Man and Nature as illustrated by episodes from the Legend of Saint Francis *by St Bonaventura.*

been following directly in the footsteps of Cimabue, who probably worked there around 1280.

If Giotto's hand is still visible, it is in the *Stories from the Old Testament* on the right wall; *The Doctors of the Church* and *Saints* in a vault and arch; and *Stories of the New Testament* on the left wall and the entrance wall. More securely attributable are the *Scenes from the Life of Saint Francis*, twenty-eight episodes divided into groups of three corresponding with the church's bays. These contain in embryo much that Giotto later perfected in the Arena Chapel at Padua – individualized portraits, skilful use of space, careful architectural perspective and brilliant dramatic sense in figure composition and in the relationship of figures to their surroundings.

The most striking quality of Giotto's figures in the Arena Chapel in Padua is their convincing solidity – they are subject to gravity, unlike the flattened, weightless forms of Byzantine painting. Giotto's gift for pictorial narrative in mural decoration is best seen in the Padua frescoes, which are set in sumptuous borders of *trompe-l'oeil* inlays of marble and semi-precious stones. Although Giotto retains some of the influences of Byzantine art, both in form and iconography, his new realism permeates each scene. His ability to reduce certain of the stories to the barest essentials, as in the *Pietà* with its chilling, rocky setting, arises from his genius for abstraction and from his study of Roman relief sculpture. Indeed, throughout the Trecento painters, like their sculptor colleagues, often turned to Roman statuary for direct inspiration.

Giotto's preoccupations were to be taken up by most representational painters in the West, and in this respect his work marks a major turning point. He was the first European painter to exploit the drama inherent in the three-dimensional human form. Examples in the Arena Chapel, such as the seated Saint Anne in the *Annunciation to St Anne*, are worthy of Masaccio. *The Flight into Egypt*, a masterpiece of composition uniting figures (and a donkey) in elegant motion against the landscape, forecasts the magical world of Fra Angelico by more than a century. He recreates the beauty of a Classical frieze in *The Virgin's Return Home*, while *The Kiss of Judas* concentrates dramatically on the central event through surrounding gesture and movement. Throughout the cycle, the subtly

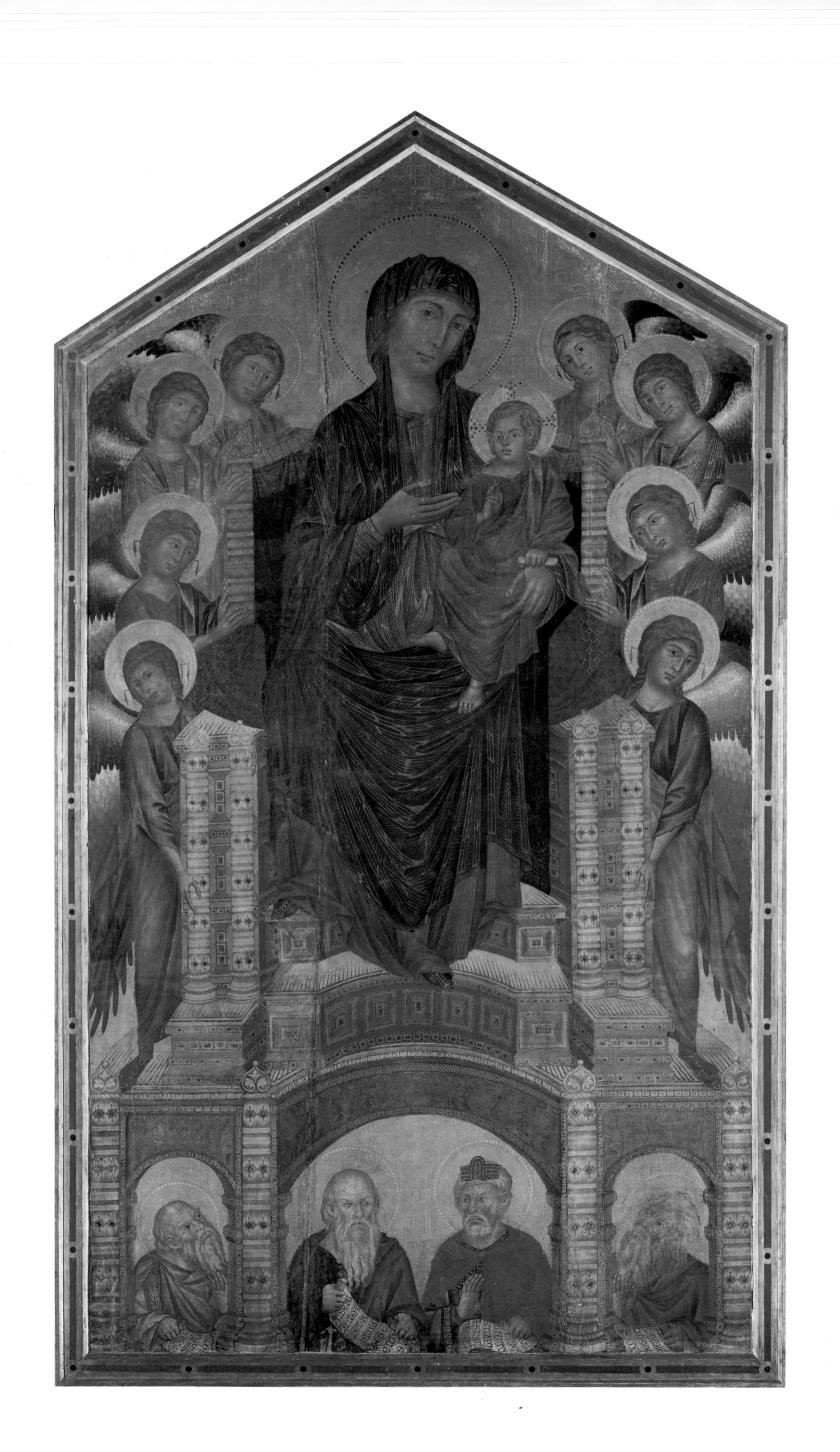

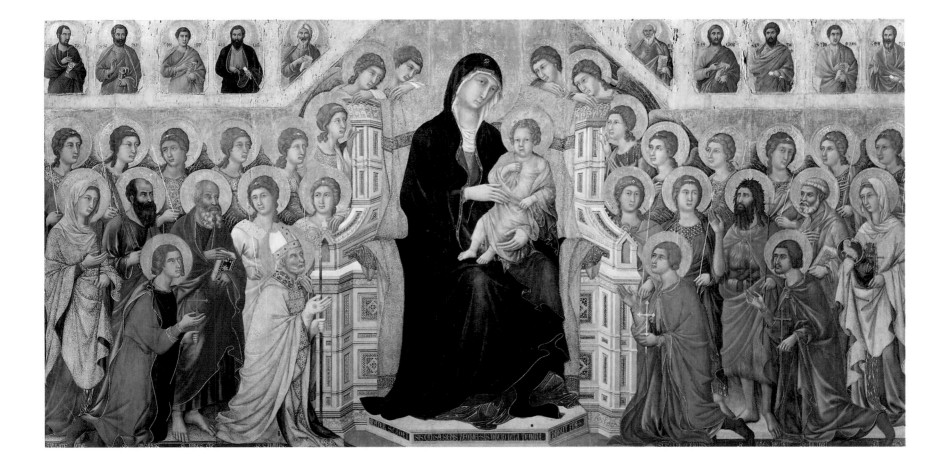

58 CIMABUE Santa Trinità Madonna early 1280s
(Left) This was painted for the high altar of the Florentine church of Santa Trinità. With its elaborate gilt throne and stylized drapery folds, it conforms to the traditional Byzantine Madonna type and its composition strongly resembles Duccio's Rucellai Madonna. *Below the throne are the prophets Jeremiah, Abraham, David and Isaiah.*

59 DUCCIO Madonna and Child with Saints and Angels 1308–11
(Above) This is the front of Duccio's Maestà, *commissioned in October 1308 for the high altar of Siena Cathedral. After the Sienese victory over the Florentines at the Battle of Montaperti, Siena had been placed under the Virgin's protection, with the implication that as 'Queen of Heaven' she was also Queen of Siena. The* Maestà *celebrates the Virgin in this role. As originally painted, the whole altarpiece included seven scenes from Christ's early life, flanked by the prophets who had foretold the events. In the pinnacles above were scenes of the Virgin's last days, probably culminating in her coronation. The scenes at the back of the altarpiece showed the* Life of Christ *in many panels.*

60 BERNARDO DADDI Madonna and Child 1346–7
(Right) Set in Andrea Orcagna's famous tabernacle of 1359, this eventually replaced a renowned miraculous image of the Virgin destroyed by fire in 1304. This Madonna, with her exquisite elegance and intimacy, is the finest example of Daddi's mature style. The painting rejects the grandeur of Giotto, and it shows that Daddi catered for the increasing demand for the private devotional paintings introduced by Duccio, in which details like the playful child play an important part.

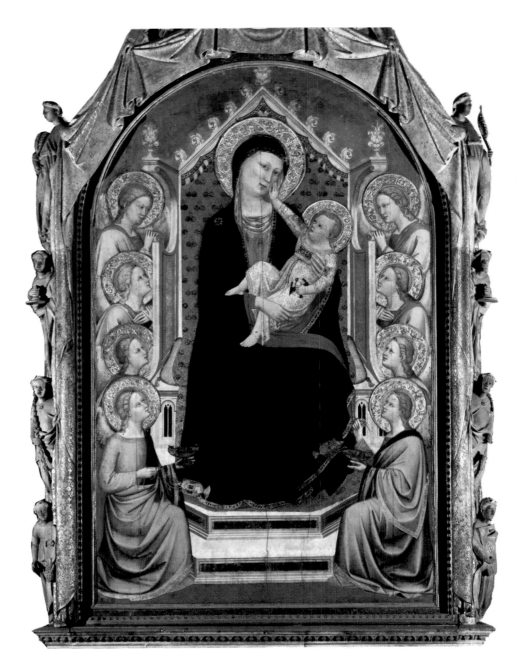

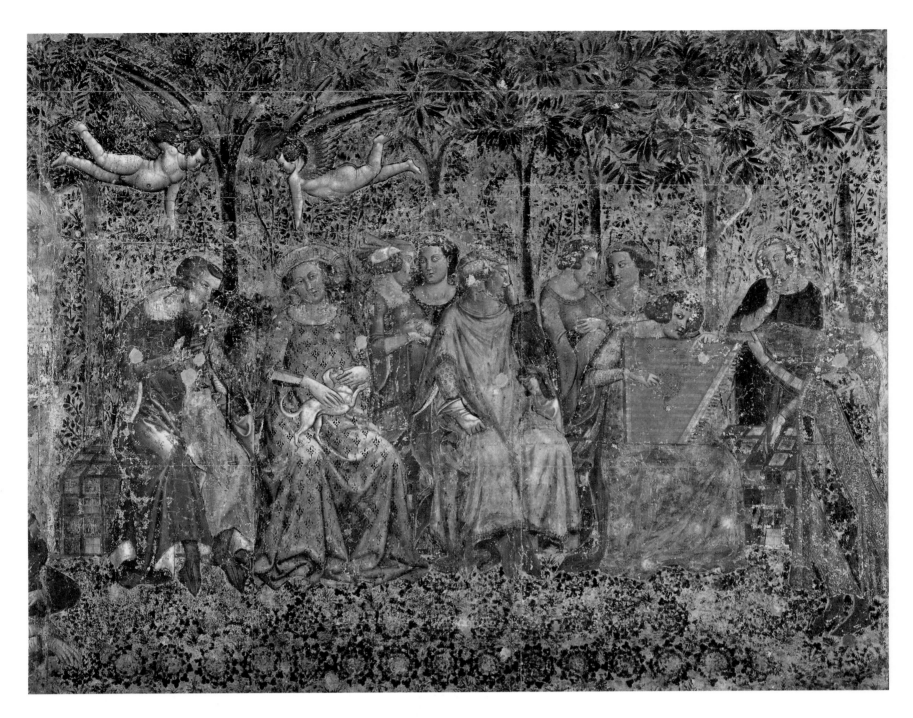

63 MASTER OF THE TRIUMPH OF DEATH Music-making in a
Garden, pre-1348
The attribution of the Triumph of Death *and its related frescoes
remains uncertain, and its iconography is novel, particularly in the
attention devoted to the scene of Hell. Once thought to refer to the
major plague outbreak of 1348, the frescoes are now considered earlier.
Here, a group of elegant young people evoking the atmosphere of the*
Decameron *enjoy themselves in a garden, oblivious to the hideous
fate awaiting them close at hand. Two flying* amorini *deriving from
antique examples may allude to the transience of earthly love. The
brevity of life at this time renders the scene all the more poignant.*

64 AMBROGIO LORENZETTI The Effects of Good
Government in the City 1338–9
*This view occupies the left-hand side of the composition, and the
contrast with the famous view of the countryside around Siena could
not be greater. The city and the country are also contrasted in the
ruined frescoes on the facing wall showing an Allegory of Tyranny
and Bad Government. The programme of the cycle is based on
Thomist and Aristotelian theory, and several direct quotations from
antique sculptures in Siena are included. Based on closely observed
reality, the view shows a typically Italian combination of the towers
which dominated medieval cityscapes and added wooden structures.*

65 ALTICHIERO The Crucifixion *c.*1379
*This forms the central panel of a tripartite Crucifixion scene. In
works such as this Altichiero forms a link between the innovation of
Giotto and the powerful drama of Masaccio: expression and gesture
are rendered by drawing of a very high standard and the figure
composition is among the most advanced of its period.*

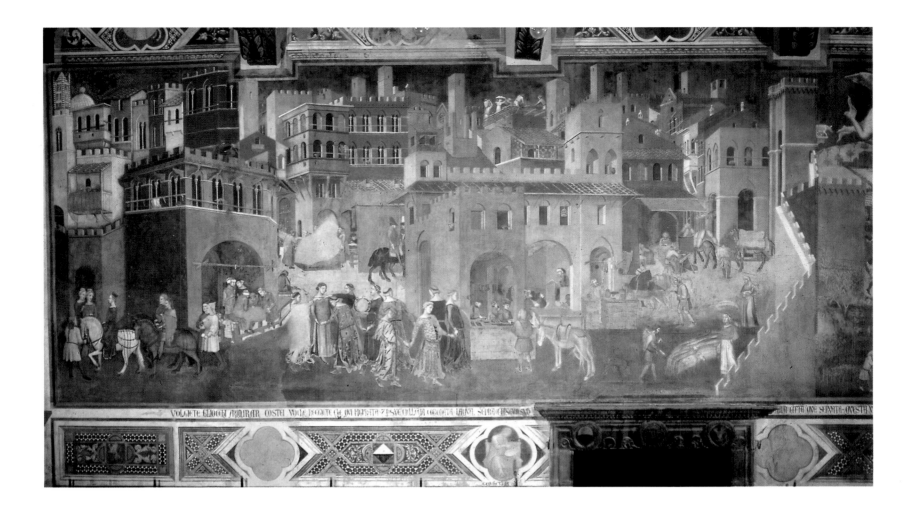

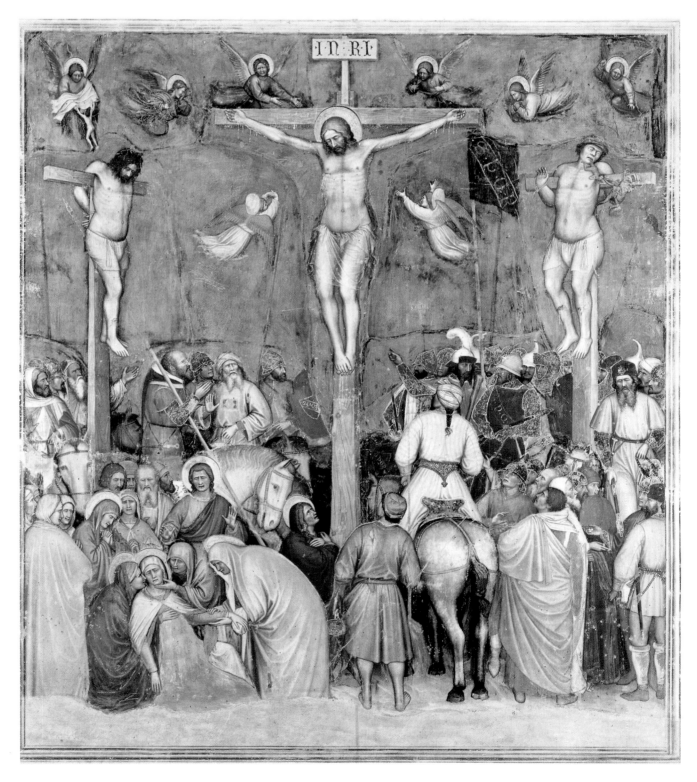

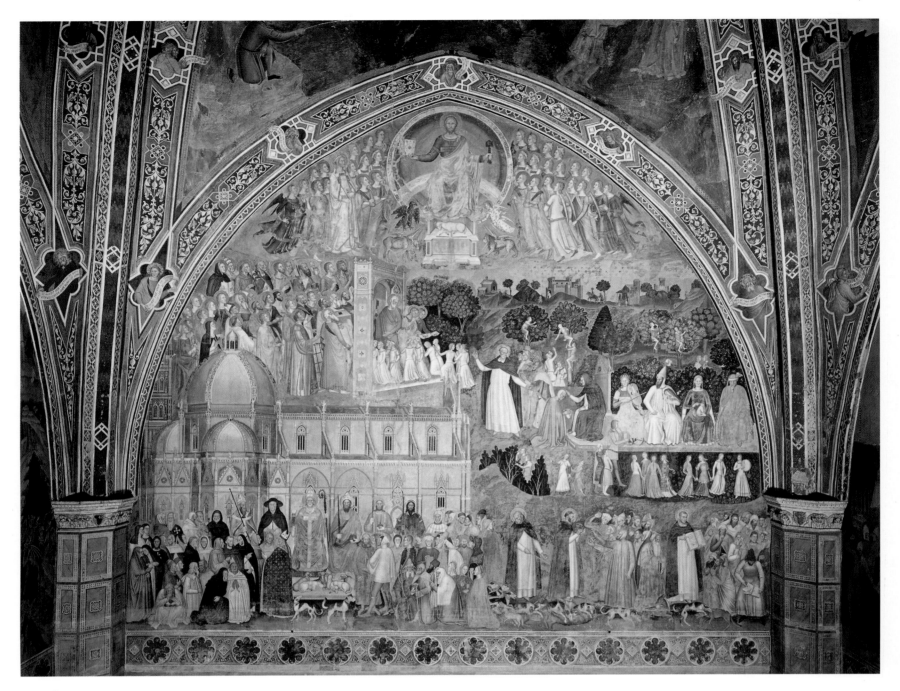

66 ANDREA BONAIUTI (ANDREA DA FIRENZE) Triumph of
the Church 1365–7
*Of all the frescoes in the Spanish Chapel in Santa Maria Novella
this is the best-known; the chapel served as the council chamber for
all the Dominicans of the province. The Church is represented by
Florence Cathedral complete with a dome before Brunelleschi actually
built it. The Pope and other ecclesiastics and laymen appear before
the Cathedral, while before them black and white domini canes (a
punning reference to the Dominicans as 'hounds of God') rescue lost
sheep from wolves, while actual members of the Dominican Order
dressed in black and white preach and lead people to the Gates of
Paradise. The Redeemer appears above amid the heavenly host.*

67 PAOLO VENEZIANO Saint Mark's Body Carried to Venice,
undated
*One of the panels making up the cover of the Pala d'Oro, the
precious gold and enamel altarpiece which is still preserved on the
high altar of San Marco in Venice, it was made during the reign of
the learned humanist Doge Andrea Dandolo, and it may incorporate
Classical references. This scene shows one of the most popular parts
of the St Mark legend, when the saint's body was transported by sea
to Venice. Veneziano has used warm colours richly combined with
figures which recall Venice's Byzantine past.*

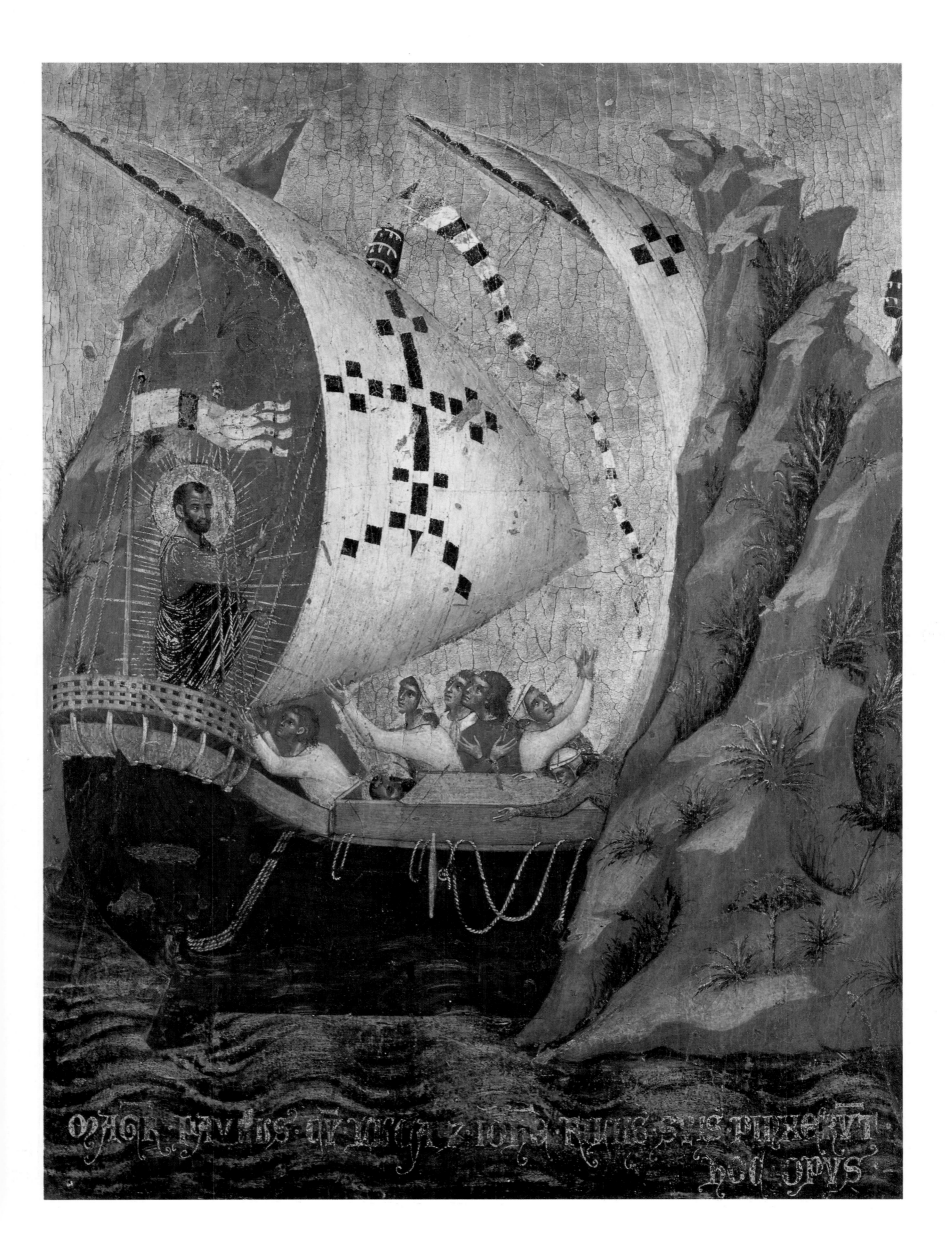

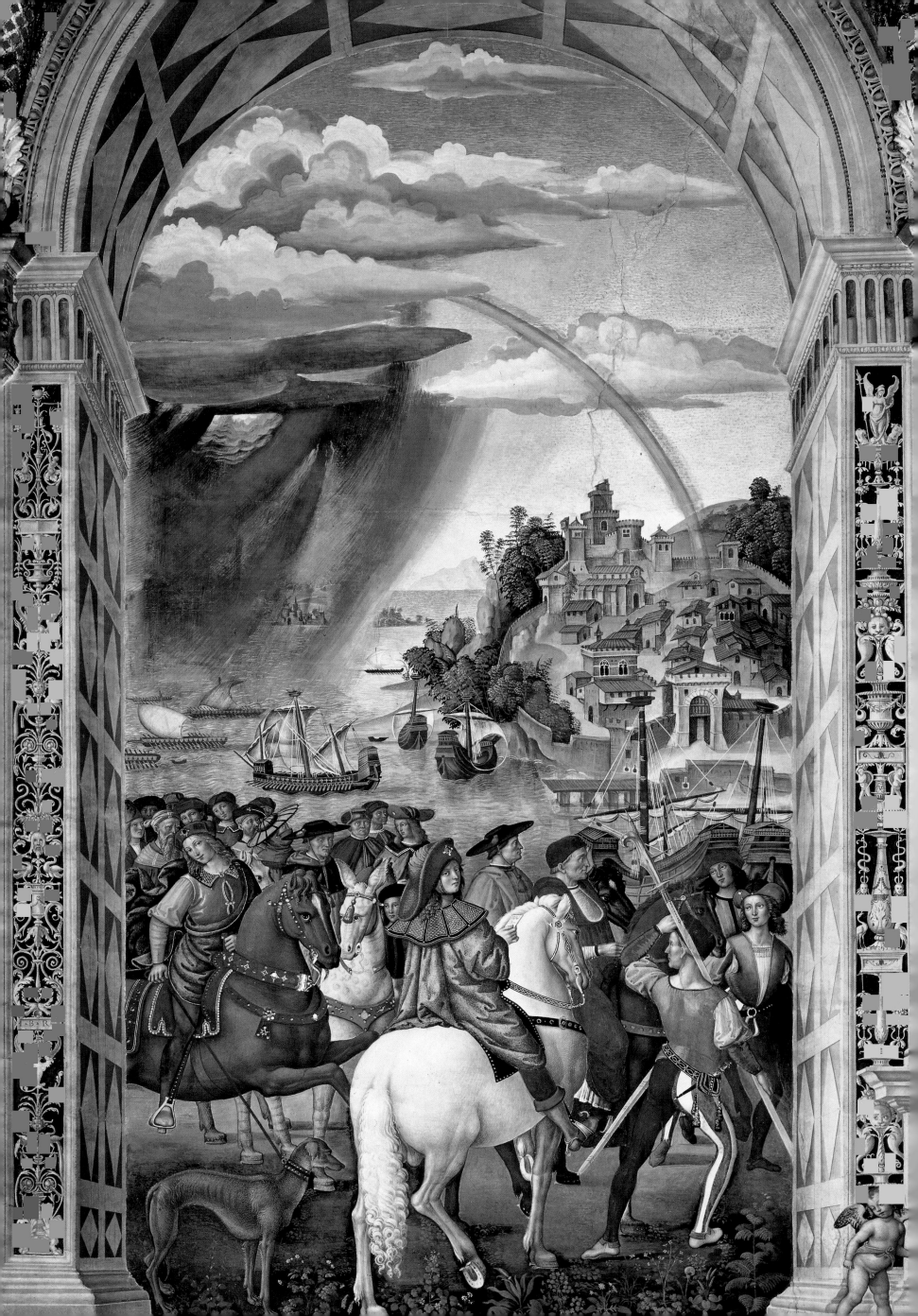

CHAPTER IV

Fifteenth-Century Italian Painting

The Italian fifteenth century – the Quattrocento – has come to be synonymous with the first achievement of the ideals of the Renaissance period. There have been many attempts in the history of European culture to revive the impetus which gave the ancient world and its art such force, but the Quattrocento's was the most complete and arguably the most successful. The major names in painting alone evoke its richness – Masaccio, Fra Angelico, Botticelli, Mantegna, Piero della Francesca, Giovanni Bellini and Leonardo da Vinci.

The Classical Legacy

Although Classical architecture and sculpture had never been wholly forgotten in Italy (it was impossible to ignore the visible evidence of Rome's past in its monuments and sculptural fragments) they began to exert the strongest fascination for fifteenth-century artists. This was true for painters as well as sculptors. During the High Renaissance in Rome, more knowledge of Roman painted decoration was acquired but at the beginning of the Quattrocento, ideas of ancient figurative depiction were based almost entirely on surviving sculptures. Indeed, the great archaeological rediscoveries, including Roman wall paintings (often by Greek artists), were not made until well into the

68 Bernardo Pintoricchio Scenes from the Life of Pius II
1502–9
The Piccolomini Library of Siena Cathedral was built in the 1490s by Francesco Todeschini Piccolomini, later Pope Pius III. It housed the manuscripts collected by Aeneas Sylvius Piccolomini (1405–64), Pope Pius II. Pintoricchio frescoed the ten compartments with scenes from his life both before and after his election as Pope. Vivid in incident, detail and colour, they continue the Quattrocento tradition of multi-figure scenes set in an extensive landscape.

eighteenth century: Herculaneum and Pompei were excavated in 1738 and 1748 respectively.

This period's understanding of antique painting was therefore vague and highly idealized, and produced results as widely different as Mantegna's *Pallas* (see plate 87) and Botticelli's *Primavera* (see plate 115). It derived much from the literary accounts of Classical writers, such as Pliny the Elder (AD 23–79) His 'breathtaking proto-encyclopedia', the *Historia Naturis* included, in his own words, '20,000 matters worthy of consideration', among them painting. The section devoted to art was translated into Italian in 1473. Quattrocento painters and theorists paid great attention to Pliny, while architects turned to Marcus Vitruvius's book *De Architectura*, which had been rediscovered during the first part of the century. Pliny summed up the basic requirement for a painter: to create an illusion of reality with the aid of proportion, harmony and above all, mathematics, without which 'art could not attain perfection'. Mathematics included that science intrinsic to Renaissance art, perspective.

Leon Battista Alberti (1404–72) may be said to have inherited the mantle of Pliny and Vitruvius, along with the practical approach of a more recent Italian, Cennino Cennini. This diversity, coupled with a highly enquiring mind, made Alberti the precursor of Leonardo da Vinci as a 'universal man' typical of this period. 'In what category of learned men shall I place him?' pondered one contemporary. Alberti's importance in the Quattrocento cannot be over-estimated, in terms of his architecture, his theories on art and the influence of his reliance on reason. His writings differ from Leonardo's in that they were published, circulated and discussed. Alberti was Genoese by birth, but his natural father belonged to a rich, exiled Florentine family. His education in classics, canon law and mathematics led him naturally to a career, from 1432–64, at the Papal Court in Rome, which enabled him to follow his preferred intellectual and architectural aims. In 1428 he accompanied Pope Eugenius IV to Florence, a visit which enhanced his interest in the revival of Classical principles. After direct contact with the works of the Florentine architect Filippo Brunelleschi (1377–1446), Donatello and Masaccio, he wrote *De pictura* ('On Painting') in 1435, translating it from Latin into Italian (*Della pittura*) the following year.

Alberti's writings are important because they abandon the theological basis current in the Middle Ages for approaching questions of art. He defines painting as a window on the world, and proposes that man's highest aspiration should be for the public good. This early humanistic approach is fundamental to understanding the links between art and civic pride in the Quattrocento. For Alberti, the artist was no longer a craftsman in the service of the Church, but an independent and creative being free to depict the world as he saw it, whether in religious or secular terms. Alberti believed man's will could enable him to achieve anything he wished. Although links between such idealism and the breadth of Quattrocento painting are tenuous, the sense of liberation inherent in these new ideas spreads like oxygen through all aspects of the period's civilization. Alberti's other two principal treatises on the arts, *De re aedificatoria* (On Architecture) and *De statua* (On Sculpture), are also concerned with man's place in a perfect social structure. This rationality ultimately distinguishes him from the mystical aspects of contemporary Neoplatonism.

The question of Neoplatonism has puzzled many people in relation to Quattrocento art, and its impact must be accepted but not over-emphasized. The rebirth of Italian interest in the Greek philosopher, Plato, occurred in about 1400 with the arrival from Constantinople of manuscripts of his writings. By 1484 a complete Italian translation by Marsilio Ficino (1433–99) was available.

As one of the most important philosophers of ancient times, and the author of more than thirty works, Plato would naturally have interested any Classical revival. However, there was one aspect of his philosophy which drew the Renaissance to him, and which found ready reflection in the arts: his emphasis on the spiritual. In Plato, themes such as harmony and poetic inspiration are constantly present, and for him mathematics are the key to understanding nature. The latter struck a resonant chord with Quattrocento artists, with their love of perspective and proportion. It brings to mind at once a habit of thought dominant in Masaccio, Donatello and Brunelleschi.

The essence of Florentine Neoplatonism was its linking of Plato's philosophy with Christian thought, and in

this Ficino led the way, founding the Platonic Academy in the beautiful Medici villa at Careggi, above Florence. After 1462 he was helped in this by Cosimo de' Medici's generous patronage, followed by that of Lorenzo the Magnificent. In 1469–74 he produced *Platonic Theology Concerning the Immortality of the Soul*, in which he described the purpose of human life as freeing the soul from the constrictions of the body and bringing it as close as possible to God. His philosophies and those of his followers, notably Giovanni Pico della Mirandola (1469–1533), filtered into works of art through specially devised literary 'programmes' and through symbols which became pictorial currency in the second half of the century. The resulting marriage of such philosophies with Classical forms and imagery in painting could not have been more opportune or appropriate, and often enriched even traditional Christian themes with new possibilities.

Painting in Tuscany

In 1396 the Paduan humanist Pier Paolo Vergerio (1370–1444) noted that the only great example for his contemporaries among painters was Giotto, who had died about sixty years previously. Agnolo Gaddi died in 1396, leaving as a final heritage his famous frescoes in the Chapel of the Sacra Cintola in Prato Cathedral. Impressive as they are, they reveal that Florentine painting needed an injection of new vitality. It must have seemed impossible that any modern artist would ever equal or surpass Giotto, and indeed almost every painter of the intervening period owed him a debt, directly or indirectly. Many painters, however, turned away from Giotto's monumental example (see Chapter III).

The Quattrocento was, nevertheless, to prove the great age of fresco painting, with Masaccio, Uccello, Gozzoli, Castagno, Fra Filippo and Filippino Lippi, Piero della Francesca, Ghirlandaio and many others leaving an incomparable legacy in this field. Although not an age of technical innovation – Leonardo's attempts to emulate the secrets of antique mural painting in the *Last Supper* (see plate 41) failed dramatically – experiments in fresco occurred, notably in Tuscany. Thus, two of the most original works of art of the century, Masaccio's Brancacci Chapel and his *Trinity* (see plates 70, 93) are both frescoes. As fresco was notoriously difficult, it was regarded as the supreme proof of a painter's abilities.

Vasari has been accused of 'Tuscocentricity' (placing too much emphasis on developments in Tuscany), but it is undeniable that the greatest concentration of achievement is found in Florence and nearby towns and cities like

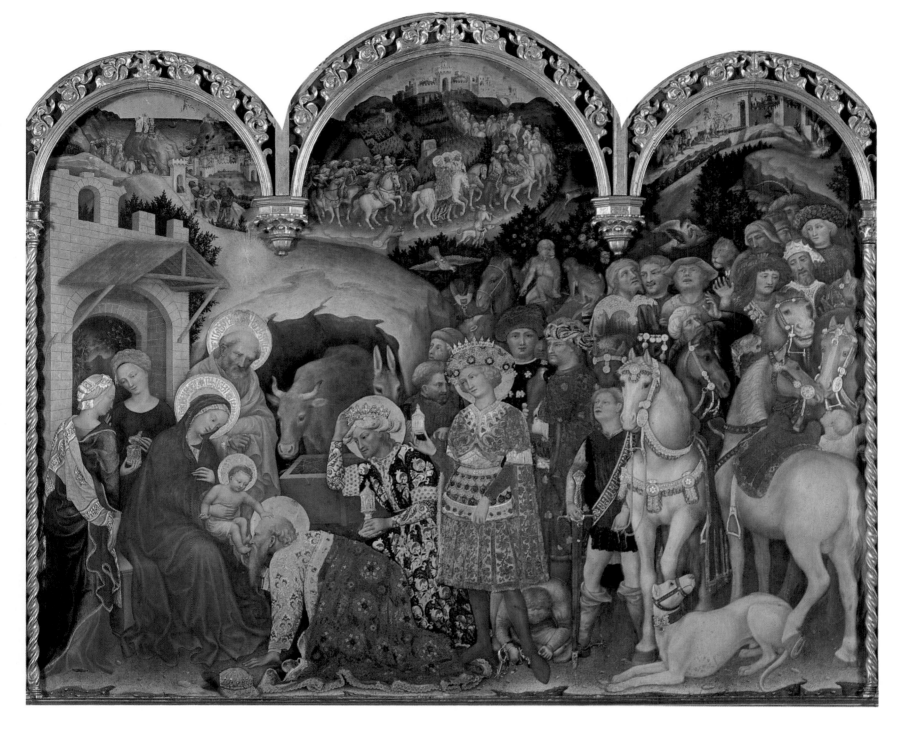

69 GENTILE DA FABRIANO Adoration of the Magi 1423
*Painted for the Strozzi Chapel in Santa Trinità during Gentile's
Florentine stay of 1420/22–5, this is the artist's major panel
painting, and provides the main key to his style. Gentile's love of
rich textures and decorative accessories derives from Venetian and
Sienese art and harks back to the International Gothic style. The
rich landscape here shows none of the contemporary Florentine
rational approach, and is predominantly decorative.*

Siena, Pisa and Arezzo. Florentine painters travelled regularly between these and other centres such as Rome,
Venice and Urbino, resulting in a constant interchange of
ideas which it is difficult to chart accurately. More accomplished painters were in demand for work in provincial
centres, whose native artists eagerly adopted the latest
fashion from Florence as best they could. Thus an isolated
altarpiece by Masaccio or Fra Angelico in a provincial
town could have the greatest effect on local style.

The same applies to the arrival in Florence of the paint-
ings of contemporary Netherlandish and other artists.
Sometimes foreign painters came in person, as did the
Portuguese Alvaro Pirez, active in Pisa, Lucca and
Volterra in 1410–35, and the Catalan painter Jacomart
Baço, called to Naples by the King, Alfonso of Aragon.
Flemish art quickly found its way into Italy. In 1437
Michele Giustiniani, a member of a leading Genoese fam-
ily, commissioned a small triptych from Jan van Eyck. In
Venice and the Veneto, the connoisseur Marcantonio
Michiel recorded the presence of such Flemish pictures as
the influential *Crucifixion* in the Ca d'Oro. Many com-
missions and purchases were made as a direct result of the
intensive trading between the Netherlands and Italy, and
the presence of Italian bankers in the North. Zanetto
Bugatto was sent by Bianca Maria Sforza of Milan to the
Brussels studio of Rogier van der Weyden from 1460 to
1463. It is probable that Van der Weyden visited the court

of Ferrara in 1450 during his Italian journey of the Holy Year, and the French artist Jean Fouquet may have painted his delightful *Gonella* there (see plate 176).

Although the Renaissance in sculpture is usually dated from 1401, when the open competition for the bronze doors of the Florence Baptistery was announced, in paint-

70 MASACCIO, MASOLINO AND FILIPPINO LIPPI The Brancacci Chapel general view, 1425–7 and 1481–3
The Brancacci Chapel occupies the right transept of the Church of the Carmine, and was mainly frescoed by Masaccio in collaboration with Masolino. Filippino Lippi completed the frescoes in 1481–3. On the entrance arch, Masolino's Fall of Man *faces Masaccio's* Expulsion from Eden, *clearly showing their different styles. The stories of St Peter symbolize salvation after The Fall. Centrally placed on the left wall is the famous* Tribute Money, *emphasizing Christ's delegation of the Church to St Peter (relegating the actual miracle of the money in the fish's mouth to the background).*

ing the situation is less clear. In effect, Florentine painting did not begin its Quattrocento renewal until the 1420s. Siena produced a livelier painter in this period than Florence: Taddeo di Bartolo (1362/3–1422). Among those Florentines who were active in the intervening years before Masaccio's appearance were Antonio Veneziano whom we now believe may have lived until 1419; Lorenzo Monaco (1370/2–*c*.1425); Starnina (active *c*.1390–*c*.1314); and Giovanni del Ponte (*c*.1385–1437). Of these Lorenzo Monaco is possibly the most appealing.

Gentile da Fabriano

One of the most significant and attractive artists of his day, Gentile da Fabriano (*c*.1370–1427) probably arrived in Florence in 1420. He had already received extensive prestigious commissions elsewhere, including the Doge's

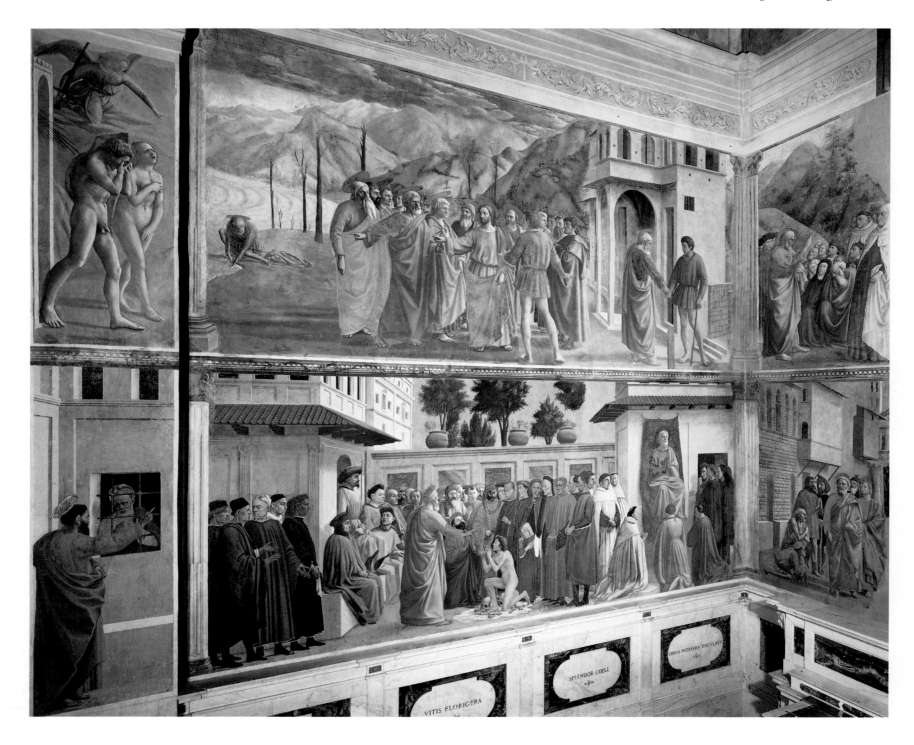

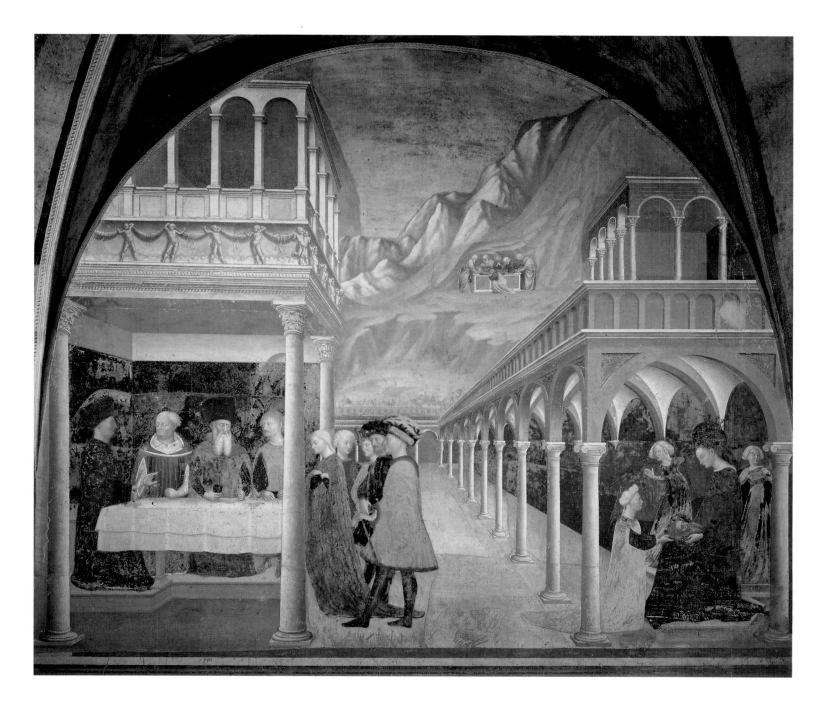

71 MASOLINO DA PANICALE   Feast of Herod 1435

This forms part of Masolino's extensive fresco cycle showing The
Life of the Baptist, *which he painted for Cardinal Branda in the
Baptistery at Castiglione Olona. It shows the moment when Salome
demands St John the Baptist's head. Many portraits have supposedly
been identified through the scene. Herod has been identified variously
as Cardinal Branda himself, the Emperor Sigismund or Niccolò
d'Este, with the young man on the right as Pippo Spano,
Masolino's Italian patron in Hungary. Masolino derived the
composition from Andrea Pisano's bronze relief version in the
Florence Baptistery.*

Palace, Venice, in 1408 and was later to work at St John
Lateran in Rome. He had worked in and around Venice
after a training in the Marches, and his concerns overshadowed those of the Florentine painters he encoun-
tered. His love of magnificently textured fabric, striking
effects of light on all surfaces and his romantic approach
to nature contributed to his widespread contemporary
influence. Gentile was one of the earliest Italian painters
to make a virtue of cast shadows, a seemingly obvious
step, but one of great importance in the quest for natural
representation. His masterpiece, the *Adoration of the Magi*
(see plate 69), dates from his Florentine period, and shows
why many artists there were more attracted to his
sophisticated and decorative manner than to Masaccio's
less approachable monumentality. Gentile's naturalism
was developed after his death by his follower, Antonio Pisanello (*c.*1395–*c.*1455/6), who continued his
work in Rome. Pisanello was an excellent portrait
painter, and achieved great fame as a portrait medallist
(see plate 92).

Gentile's style formed a precise parallel with the sculpture of Lorenzo Ghiberti (1378–1455). Just as the Trecento
painters looked at sculpture, so the sculptor Lorenzo
Ghiberti turned for inspiration to Northern art, which he
discussed in his *Treatise*, through the work of one Cologne
goldsmith, Master Gusmin. Ghiberti's new approach to
voluminous draperies in his relief sculpture had a considerable impact on contemporary painters. This feature

remains constant in Florentine painting, along with Gentile's delicate traceries of decoration, well into the Quattrocento. Of much more fundamental importance, however, was the sculpture of Donatello (Donato di Niccolò, 1386–1466) and Nanni di Banco (c.1386–1421). Donatello's astonishing naturalism (he was accused of using casts), and the vitality and portrait realism he learned from Roman sculpture, proved irresistible to painters. In his incomparable marble relief, *Saint George and the Dragon* of 1417–20 (Museo Nazionale del Bargello, Florence), Donatello furthered the advances made by Brunelleschi, who had already discovered perspective. This relief is a milestone in art, for in it Donatello used orthogonals and a vanishing point to create the illusion that the figures exist in real depth. Masaccio was the first painter who followed in its footsteps.

Masolino and Masaccio

The lives of Tommaso di Cristofano called Masolino (c.1383–1447) and Masaccio (Tomasso di Ser Giovanni di Mone, 1401–c.1428) are closely linked, but Masaccio is credited with having left the more momentous impact on the art of painting. Masolino has long taken a poor second place to Masaccio, but was a painter of considerable merit. No document links their names or connects them with the patrons of their major works, but there is no doubt that they collaborated. Masolino may have been a pupil of Agnolo Gaddi, and Vasari says that he excelled in chasing and modelling in Ghiberti's workshop – an instance of the interdisciplinary training of many young artists in the Renaissance.

Vasari was confused by Masolino's collaborations with Masaccio, and believed paintings we now think are Masaccio's to have been his. The *Saint Anna Meterza* (Galleria degli Uffizi, Florence) of about 1424 is a good example of this joint authorship. Masolino spent just over one year in Hungary, working there for the Florentine soldier Pippo Spano, and returning to Florence late in 1427. The two painters then probably went together to Rome in May 1428, and it appears that Masaccio died there. On hearing of this, Brunelleschi supposedly said, 'We have sustained a great loss'.

Masaccio was probably already active as a painter by the age of seventeen. At twenty, in April 1422, when he dated the San Giovenale a Cascia Triptych (Pieve di San Pietro, Cascia di Regello), he was already an accomplished artist. On the basis of this, Masaccio's early career can be partly understood, since there is no proof of his having trained with Masolino as Vasari believed. He telescoped into a period of about eight years one of the most innovative careers in European painting. Amazingly, there is little surviving documentation on his art, and even the great *Trinity* (see plate 93) and the Brancacci Chapel frescoes (see plate 70) are shrouded in mystery. He does not appear to have made much money, and may have allied himself with Masolino in late 1422 or early 1423 to further his career in Florence.

It is therefore possible that Masaccio was employed by Masolino, who, as an older, established painter received important commissions. Their first collaboration seems to have been on an altarpiece of 1423, once in Santa Maria Maggiore, Florence, now dismembered. The last was the great Brancacci Chapel. It was Masolino who received the Brancacci commission in 1424, but Masaccio who gave most of the scenes their monumental and heroic form, brilliant perspective and impressive humanity. For example, *The Fall* by Masolino has none of the dynamism of Masaccio's famous *Expulsion from Paradise*. Masolino may simply have lacked Masaccio's receptiveness to the great examples of contemporary sculpture, notably Donatello's *John the Evangelist* and *Jeremiah*. He may also have remained almost impervious to Masaccio's innovations, adjusting his style when they worked together in order to achieve visual unity, but reverting to his own more delicate manner elsewhere, notably after Masaccio's untimely death (see plate 71).

Fra Angelico

Had Masaccio lived, there can be no question that his influence would have been more immediate and lasting, but Gentile's highly ornate style of surface patterning found more eager followers in Florence. Among these, Fra Angelico was the greatest example in the Italian Renaissance of a painter uniting intensely personal religious feeling with the highest degree of artistic accomplishment. Angelico (Guido di Pietro, c.1400–55) entered the Observant Dominican convent of Fiesole, outside Florence, in 1418–21, and was elected prior in 1449. Vasari describes Angelico as 'a simple and most holy man' while John Ruskin went as far as to call him 'not an artist properly so-called but an inspired saint'. Although long known as 'Beato' (Blessed, one level below sainthood) he was only officially beatified in 1984.

From his beginnings in about 1417 in the studio of Lorenzo Monaco, Angelico's artistic life was extraordinarily productive. His earliest painting is likely to have been manuscript illustration, nurtured by the great influx into Florence of European manuscripts (of which the

Medici family were leading collectors). The International Gothic style of Gentile da Fabriano must have seemed simply a grand development of such minute work, and thus compatible with the Dominican desire to put art to the service of religion.

In addition to his work as a painter, Fra Angelico maintained an active involvement in the religious politics, movements and debates of his day. The two activities were probably related, as is suggested by the fact that he painted a chapel in the Vatican for Pope Nicholas V, whom he knew personally. In Florence, his closest involvement was with the much-revered Dominican, Saint Antonino, who in 1436 took over the friary of San Marco, which was remodelled by the architect Michelozzo (1396–1472), with financial assistance from Cosimo de' Medici.

At San Marco, Angelico and his assistants (particularly Zanobi Strozzi) created a group of forty-five frescoes (c.1438–45) and other paintings (see plates 72, 94, 95) unrivalled in the Renaissance for their devotional homogeneity. San Marco became a leading centre for the new humanism, which Angelico succeeded in reconciling with the intensity of residual medieval piety. This may be seen in his great *Last Judgement* of around 1431 (Museo di San Marco, Florence), showing the division between the elect and the damned. Here he imposed the most recent ideas about light, perspective and form on the iconographic tradition approved by his Order.

Angelico heads Vasari's long list of the painters who studied with Masaccio in the Santa Maria del Carmine in Florence. This became increasingly important in his later work, notably his fresco scenes from the *Lives of Saints Stephen and Lawrence* (1447–50) in the Vatican. These show his mature style, with solid, large-scale figures and a more dramatic intent, accentuated by a new realism of detail, more in tune with contemporary ideals than much of his earlier work. However, the innate sweetness of his art remained, and was to exert a considerable influence on painters such as Perugino.

The combined influence of Masaccio and Angelico on Italian Quattrocento painting was immense, and was immediately seen in the latter's pupil Benozzo Gozzoli (Benozzo di Lese, c.1421–97), who assisted Angelico in Orvieto and Rome. His most important undertaking was the 1459 fresco cycle in the Medici Palace Chapel showing the *Journey of the Magi* (see plate 114), where the two traditions are harmoniously united with his experience of the Franco-Flemish art of Jean Fouquet and Rogier van der Weyden. This cycle is noted for its inclusion of contemporary portraiture in the guise of religious imagery, and its wealth of minutely observed detail.

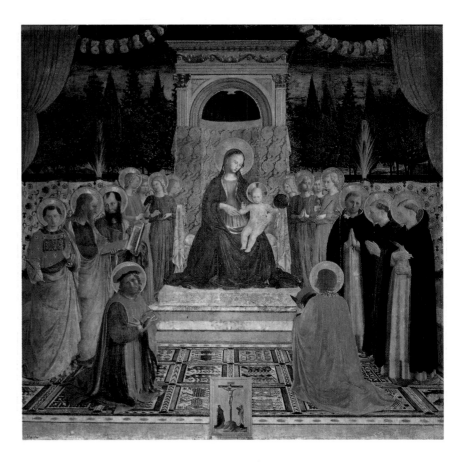

72 FRA ANGELICO   The San Marco Altarpiece 1438–40
One of the grandest altarpieces of the Quattrocento, this was painted for the high altar of the conventual church of San Marco in Florence, dedicated to Sts Cosmas and Damian. It is the Virgin and Child Enthroned with Angels and Sts Cosmas and Damian, Lawrence, John the Evangelist, Mark, Dominic, Francis and Peter Martyr. It was always considered one of Angelico's masterpieces, and Vasari, noting its unique beauty, says that the Madonna 'moves to devotion those who look at her, by her simplicity . . . it is impossible to imagine ever being able to see anything more diligently made.' The predella was nonetheless dismantled and dispersed, and the altarpiece subject to drastic overcleaning. Cosimo de' Medici decided in 1438 to send a triptych by Lorenzo di Niccolo which was previously on the high altar, to Cortona, to be replaced by Angelico's picture; no record remains of the picture's commission.

The grandeur of its composition reflects Angelico's study of Masaccio, with the enthroned Virgin raised at the centre of a figure group of great solemnity against a simple background of cypress trees. The cypresses, palms and garlands of roses refer to the biblical passage comparing the Virgin to the cedar of Lebanon, the cypress of Mount Sion, the palm of Cades and the rose of Jericho. St Mark holds open the book at the passage from his Gospel describing Christ's teaching in the synagogue. The kneeling St Cosmas on the left may be a portrait of Cosimo de' Medici, and the kneeling St Damian may be a portrait of Lorenzo de' Medici, who died in September 1440.

Filippo Lippi

In contrast to the exemplary life of Fra Angelico, that of Fra Filippo Lippi (*c*.1406–69), as depicted so colourfully by Vasari, has intrigued posterity for its sheer irregularity. In 1421, he took his vows as a Carmelite friar at the Carmine convent where he had been raised as a foundling. This did not prevent him from conducting a celebrated affair (much to the mirth of his contemporaries) with the nun who was also his model, Lucrezia Buti. She bore him his painter son Filippino (see plate 73), and a daughter. Both were released from their vows and permitted to marry. Lippi was also tortured for embezzling money from an assistant, and made a rope from sheets to escape 'protective custody' in the Medici Palace! This waywardness is perhaps reflected in his paintings, produced over a career of more than thirty years, which glow with a spontaneity not too restricted by rules of perspective or humanist 'programmes', and it has been said that he undertook more complex and original subjects than any of his contemporaries.

Lippi's first dateable work is from the mid-late 1420s, the fresco of a *Scene from Carmelite History* in his own Carmine convent. Vasari tells us that Lippi had been inspired by watching Masaccio paint in the adjacent Brancacci Chapel. Of the same period, his *Madonna of Humility* (Fitzwilliam Museum, Cambridge) already shows the elements which he derived from Masaccio (particularly the sheer volume of the main figures) but with facial types which were to become very much his own, exemplified in the infant Christ with his chubby features and enquiring expression. By the time of the *Barbadori Altarpiece* (Musée du Louvre, Paris) about 1437, most of Lippi's characteristics were fully formed, and his preferred settings, amid marbled niches and arcades, well established.

His interest in architecture is also reflected in his love of Donatello, from whose Cavalcanti *Annunciation* in Santa Croce Lippi derived his own painting on the theme now in the National Gallery, Rome. It was ultimately his Madonnas, often in tondo form, which created posterity's image of him. Of these possibly the finest is the *Madonna and Child with the Birth of the Virgin and the Meeting of Joachim and Anna* dating from the 1460s (Pitti Palace, Florence).

In both of his great fresco cycles, in Spoleto Cathedral and Prato Cathedral (see plate 97), Lippi demonstrated his ability for subtle figure composition within grand architecture, and an agility of linear design different from the more solid approach of his pre-1440 works. This sinuous line was the mainspring of the art of Botticelli, who was

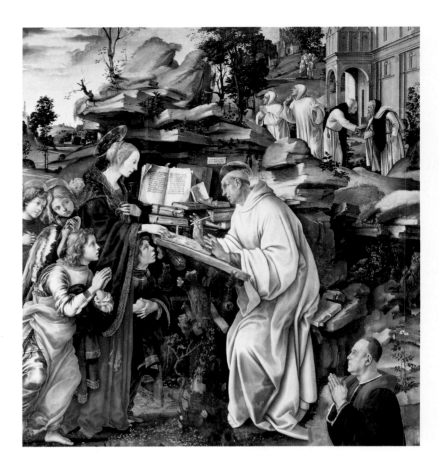

73 FILIPPINO LIPPI The Virgin Appearing to Saint Bernardo *c*.1482–6

Possibly Filippino Lippi's finest painting, this was commissioned by Piero di Francesco del Pugliese, and the donor is shown in profile with joined hands in the lower right, while tradition has it that the Virgin and angels portray his wife and children. Lippi unites an extraordinary chromatic richness with the most detailed description of every part of the picture, from the minute portraiture of the background friars to the striking still life of books, all of which are recognizable texts referring to the Mother of Christ.

probably Lippi's pupil and inherited much of the intensity of his last paintings, such as the *Dead Christ* (Musée Thomas Henry, Cherbourg). The critic Bernard Berenson once thought that this was by the young Botticelli. Overall, it is possible to follow his creative processes through the remarkable number of his surviving drawings, many of which are connected directly with known paintings.

Paolo Uccello

If Lippi represented a rational development from Masaccio, Paolo Uccello (Paolo di Dono, 1397–1475) was, like many great experimentalists, limited by his very adventurousness. 'He had no greater pleasure than to investigate certain areas of difficult and (indeed) impossible perspective,' says Vasari, while Ruskin concluded that 'he went off his head' with this obsession. Vasari also tells the story of his wife urging him to come to bed when he was working late into the night, and Uccello's supposed reply, 'What a sweet mistress is this perspective'.

First documented as working in Ghiberti's studio in 1407, Uccello naturally learnt there the latest ideas on perspective. In 1425, he went to Venice and worked as a mosaicist (although none of his mosaics has been identified), returning to Florence in 1430. His first surviving dated work there is the immense fresco in Florence Cathedral of the English *condottiere* Sir John Hawkwood (see plate 75).

Uccello's major work in fresco was the series of Old Testament scenes in the Chiostro Verde ('Green Cloister') of Santa Maria Novella in Florence. Here, he adopted the 'perspective naturalis' advocated in ancient treatises, such as Euclid's. Like most painters of his day, Uccello would have turned to Ghiberti's Florence Cathedral's Baptistery doors for inspiration, and Ghiberti himself advocates this Classical type of perspective in his *Treatise*.

The cloister frescoes culminate in the famous *Flood* (see plate 74), where Uccello (as in the *Hawkwood*) reveals his flexible approach to perspective, and his desire to use it not merely for increased spatial realism but to exploit the inherent drama of the scene. In the *Flood*, for example, he selects two vanishing points whose lines cross, to maximize an impression of chaos appropriate to the subject.

From one point of view, Uccello's art could be regarded as a regression from Masaccio's in that, until his later years, he shows no interest in the evocation of atmosphere. Masaccio excelled at this, placing his figures in such a way that they seem to inhabit real space; and Masolino's broad treatment of colour also created such an impression, in a more contained manner. Uccello's figures are suspended unrealistically in space, and colour is often dissonant. However, it was precisely their atmosphere of unreality, coupled with their sense of volume, which must have attracted the young Piero della Francesca to Uccello's paintings.

Uccello's art found favour briefly with the Medici, and in the mid-1450s Cosimo de' Medici commissioned three panels from him showing *The Battle of San Romano*, to decorate a room in the Medici Palace. The *Battle* sequence has now been separated and distributed among London's National Gallery, the Louvre and the Uffizi. Drastic overcleaning has reduced the London picture to its bare bones, but has revealed Uccello's magnificent concept of large-scale form, which he blocked in prior to achieving his finish with careful paint glazes. From the London picture in particular, it is clear that Vasari did not exaggerate, and for Uccello, even round forms such as the horses' flanks, could be subjected to linear perspective.

The subtlety of such thinking is in contrast to the almost naive manner in which broken lances and corpses are somewhat startlingly foreshortened.

Uccello was one of the first Italian painters to use canvas as a support, in his later paintings such as *Saint George and the Dragon* (National Gallery, London). Among the most magical of his panels is *The Hunt in the Forest* (Ashmolean Museum, Oxford). This was painted in the 1470s, about the time of his enchanting *Profanation of the Host* (Galleria Nazionale, Urbino), which is also a wonderful record of a simple room of the period. The *Hunt's* night setting and the delicacy of its components show that Uccello was abandoning the strongly didactic use of perspective in his last years. Vasari's account of the artist's mental condition is touching, his obsession with perspective comparable in its effects to Parmigianino's with alchemy much later: 'Solitary, strange and melancholy. . . he came to live the life of a hermit, scarcely knowing anyone and shut away in his house for weeks and months at a time.' In a late tax return he claimed he was destitute.

Andrea del Castagno

In contrast to Uccello, Andrea del Castagno (Andrea di Bartolo di Bargilla, *c*.1421–57) achieved a monumental figure style with greater economy of means, and fits the mainstream of Florentine art in his period. Donatello's single sculpted figures are never far away, and the classical nobility of Castagno's figures looks forward to Mantegna. Like Uccello, Castagno visited Venice, returning to Florence in 1444 to create a pendant for Uccello's Hawkwood fresco, the equestrian figure of *Niccolò da Tolentino*. Castagno's masterpiece, the fresco cycle in Sant'Apollonia, Florence, notably the *Last Supper* (see plate 76), is at once more prosaic and less disturbing than Uccello's work, but more subtle in its use of perspective. Using a unified perspective system, he linked the *Resurrection*, *Crucifixion* and *Deposition* with the *Last Supper*, and coupled with a fine sense of colour, achieved a unique grandeur.

It may have been the convincing 'presence' of his figures which gained him the macabre commission to paint the rebels who rose up against Cosimo de' Medici. Their punishment was to be hanged by the heels, and Castagno rendered this in a fresco on the façade of the Palazzo del Podestà, as a grim warning to others. The painting no longer exists, but its startling realism may be imagined from the magnificent figures of *Famous Men and Women* in the Villa Carducci near Florence. The theme of exemplary historical figures (here including contemporary

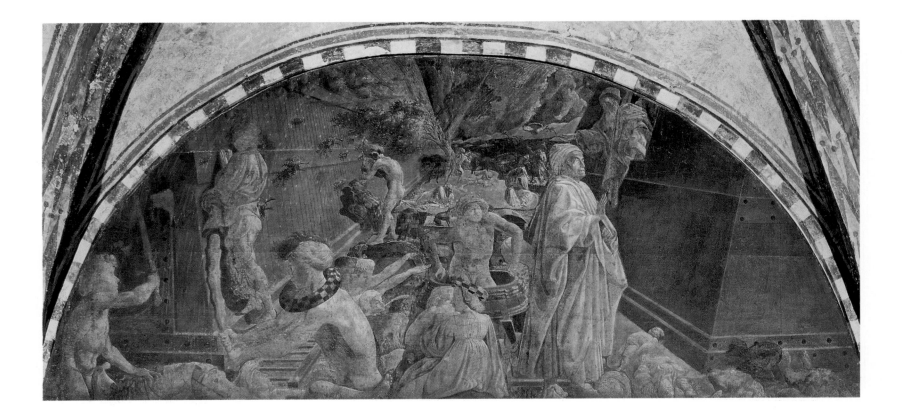

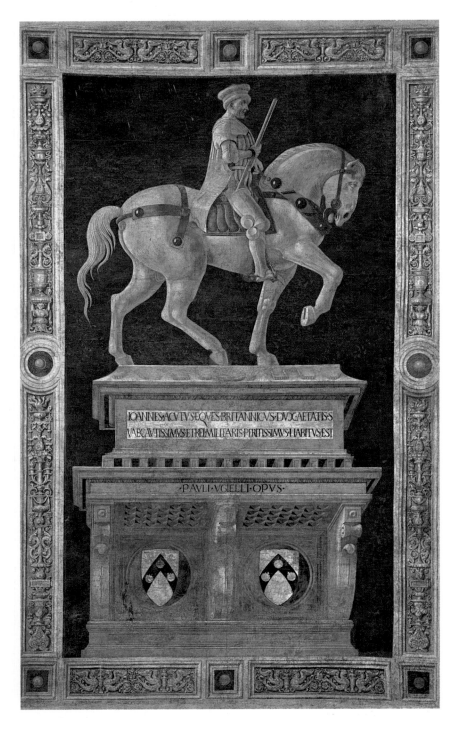

74 PAOLO UCCELLO The Flood and the Recession of the
Waters 1446–8
*One of the great undocumented works of Uccello's maturity, this
comes from the Chiostro Verde of Santa Maria Novella, so-called
because of the* terra verde *or predominant green used in the frescoes.
Vasari's famous eulogy of the frescoes praises the rendering of the
storm and its manifestations, and the fear shown by the figures.
There is disagreement about the type of perspective employed by
Uccello, but it is clear that he was deeply influenced by his friend
Donatello's Paduan works which he saw on a visit sometime between
1443 and 1453. Thus he probably included different vanishing points
to accentuate the scene's inherent drama, and may have been aware of
earlier theories concerning the visual distortion experienced during
violent storms. The* Flood *may have been painted on a single*
intonaco *patch.*

75 PAOLO UCCELLO Cenotaph to Sir John Hawkwood 1436
*(Left) Hawkwood was an English mercenary who fought for the Pope
and the Milanese and became Captain-General of the Florentine
Republic. In the year before his death the Florentine Signoria voted
to give him a memorial in the cathedral with no expense spared. The
influences of the horses of St Mark's in Venice, Ghiberti and Luca
della Robbia are combined to create one of the greatest equestrian
images of the Quattrocento. Uccello's choice of simulated bronze
influenced Donatello and later sculptors.*

Florentines, thus linking past and present) was popular in Quattrocento Italy and seen as setting an elevated example. Vasari noted that Castagno 'excels in depicting movement in his figures and the disquieting expression of their faces. . .', emphasizing their gravity with vigorous drawing. Vasari believed that Castagno murdered the painter Domenico Veneziano (died 1461), but we now know that Castagno pre-deceased him, a victim to plague.

Antonio Pollaiuolo

Vasari also praised Castagno's interest in *scorti* (usually referred to by the French term *écorchés*) or dissections of corpses, and this links Castagno directly with one of the

76 ANDREA DEL CASTAGNO Last Supper *c*.1447–50

The Last Supper *had been the usual choice of subject for a refectory mural in Florence since the early fourteenth century and the theme is known as a* cenacolo. *Castagno painted this dramatic fresco as though it were illuminated by the real windows of the refectory, but apparently taking place in a separate spatial unit. The command of perspective is flawless.*

Above the Last Supper *he painted the* Crucifixion, Entombment *and* Resurrection, *the latter striking an optimistic note. Castagno has adopted vaguely Roman details in the fresco, such as pilasters and sphinxes, to harmonize with the period of the scene. Sphinxes, which usually guard the mysteries of religion, are probably included here as guardians of the mystery of the Institution of the Eucharist with the Last Supper. Castagno has used colour symbolically throughout, notably in the placing of the different coloured marble slabs behind the figures. It appears that each figure or small group had its own cartoon.*

most influential figures active in the later decades of the century, Pollaiuolo (Antonio di Jacopo Benci, *c*.1432–98). Vasari says that he studied many dissections 'to see their underlying anatomy', which became for him what perspective had been for Uccello. Throughout Pollaiuolo's work, a new consciousness of the expressive force of the nude body in movement prevails, particularly in his most famous work, the *Battle of the Nude Men* (see plate 77). Pollaiuolo was equally gifted as a sculptor on a small scale, and as goldsmith, engraver and draughtsman and he frequently collaborated on projects with his less talented brother Piero.

Together with Piero, Antonio was commissioned by Piero de' Medici in about 1460 to paint *The Labours of Hercules* for the young Lorenzo de' Medici's bedchamber in the Medici Palace. Although lost, these are known from replicas by Pollaiuolo and other artists, and the almost frenzied vigour of the original can easily be imagined from the *Martyrdom of Saint Sebastian* (National Gallery, London). Its examination of the male figure both nude and dressed in a wide variety of poses (like the *Battle of the Nude Men*) prefigures Leonardo's and Michelangelo's battle scenes for the Palazzo Vecchio (see plate 208). Its Arno landscape background is equally forward-looking.

Like Castagno at Sant'Apollonia, Pollaiuolo exploited the painted illusion of space as an extension of 'real' space, in his altarpiece for the Chapel of the Cardinal of Portugal in San Miniato, Florence (the original is now in the Galleria degli Uffizi, a copy in the Chapel). In it, three saints are placed on a 'terrace' of coloured marble extending the lavish sculpture of the actual Chapel space and leading the eye on to a sweeping background landscape.

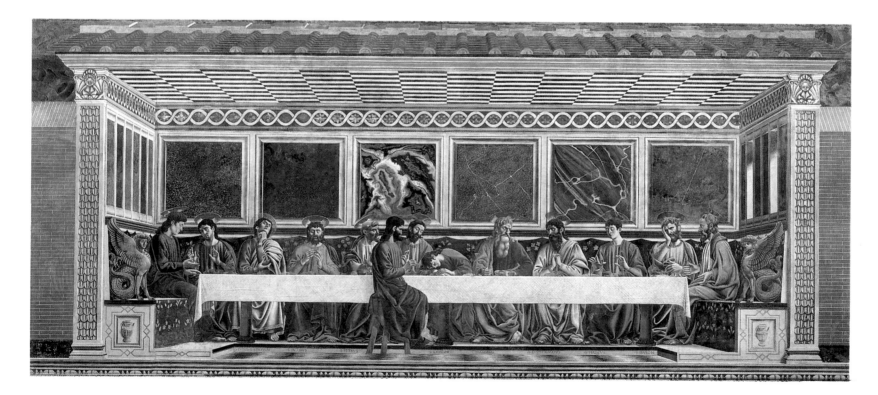

116) and *Minerva and the Centaur* (see plate 117). It is particularly apparent in the *Primavera* and *Birth of Venus* that Botticelli's treatment of outline owes rather more to Gothic art (such as miniatures or small sculptures) than it does to the Classical art which was to inspire Michelangelo.

Vasari says that Botticelli came under the influence of Savonarola (whom he probably knew well) and that, inspired by the priest's message of purification, he abandoned painting to atone for having depicted 'pagan' subjects. We know this to be untrue, as some of his finest paintings were made after Savonarola was burned at the stake. These include the much-discussed *Mystic Nativity* of 1500 (National Gallery, London), with its message referring to the end of the world and the dawn of the millenium, and the very late, intensely tragic *Lamentation of Christ* (see plate 79). It is clear, however, when these late

80 Vittore Carpaccio The Arrival of the Ambassadors 1490–4
This is the first picture of nine in the Saint Ursula *cycle. In the scene at the left, the English ambassadors arrive at the Breton court. In the centre they present Prince Ereus's request for the hand of Ursula, and at the extreme right Ursula and her father discuss the matter. The* Arrival *is the most elaborate picture in the cycle, and many of the faces are probably portraits of members or patrons of the Scuola. Carpaccio's usual wealth of detail fills the scene, from the Perugino-inspired architectural background to the unforgettable seated figure of Ursula's nurse in the bottom right-hand corner. The gap at the bottom of the canvas corresponds to where a door was placed in the early sixteenth century.*

81 Piero di Cosimo Cleopatra (so-called 'Simonetta Vespucci') *c.*1485–90
The identification of the sitter as Simonetta Vespucci, a celebrated beauty loved by Giuliano de' Medici, depends on the later inscription, and is only partly accepted. Simonetta died of tuberculosis at twenty three, and the snake could thus be a symbol of immortality or eternity. However, the contrast of the elaborate hairstyle with the exposed breasts creates an eroticism at variance with Simonetta's chaste reputation. Vasari's description of the picture as 'a very beautiful Cleopatra with an asp round her neck' seems to fit better than the traditional title.

paintings are compared with the decorative qualities of his earlier Madonnas, that Botticelli did undergo some profound spiritual maturing.

His large studio was very active (Lippi was his best pupil (see plate 97), and it seems clear that many assistants were trained specifically to repeat and vary his own successful compositions *ad infinitum*.

The Early Careers of Leonardo and Michelangelo

For Leonardo da Vinci (1452–1519), paintings pertained to philosophy, 'because they deal with the movement of bodies in the promptness of their actions just as philosophy extends itself into the world of movement'. This is conspicuous in every aspect of his intense and varied output, whether as painter, draughtsman, architect, sculptor, scientist, musician or philosopher.

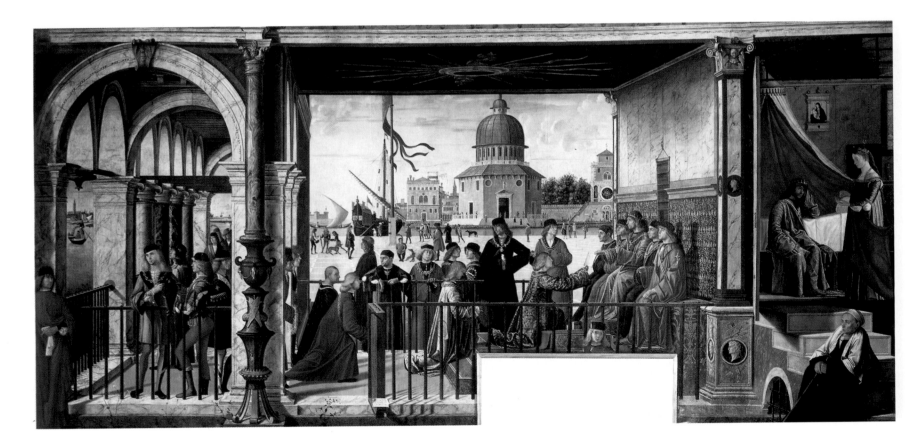

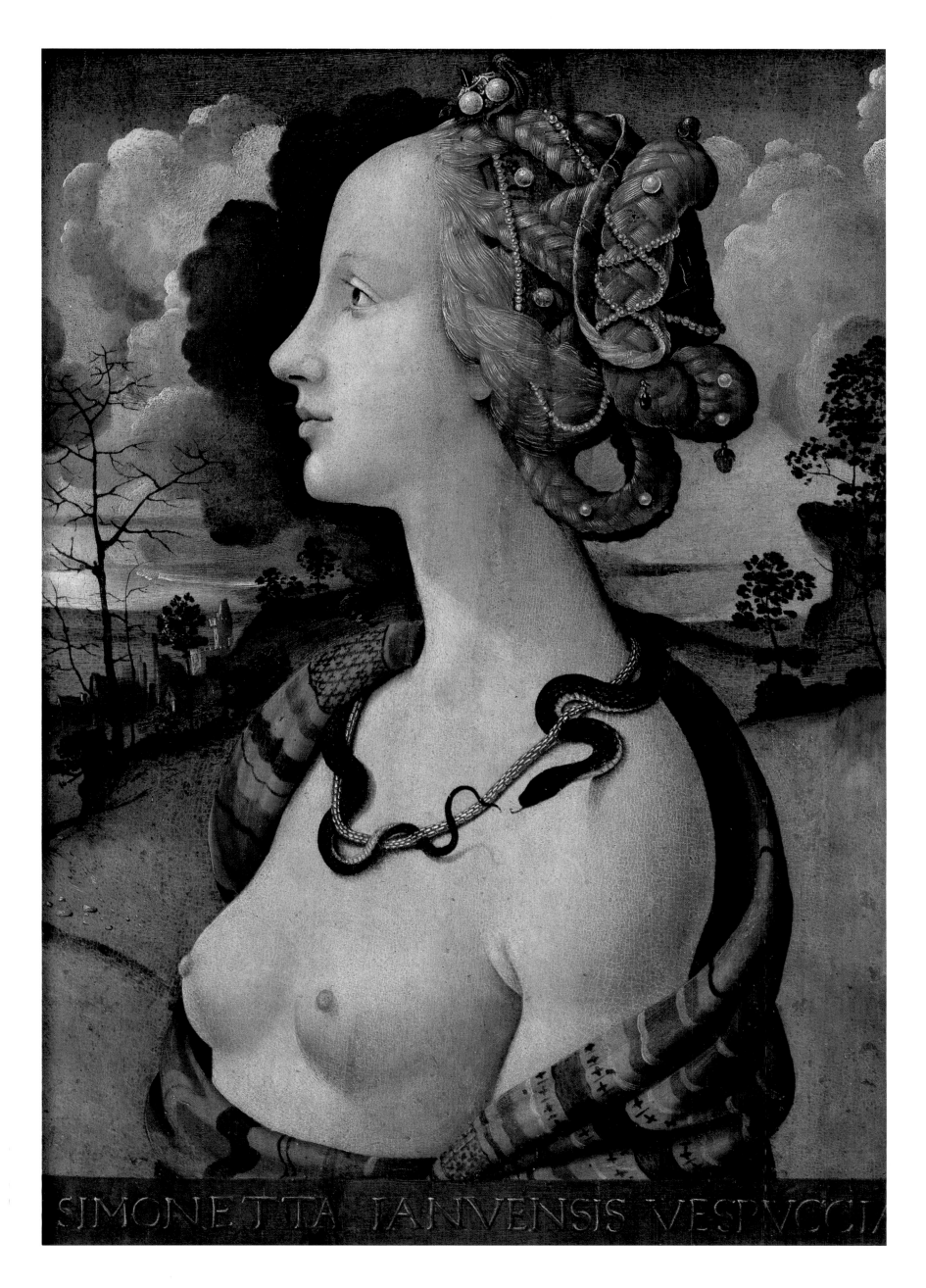

SIMONETTA IANVENSIS VESPVCCIA

89

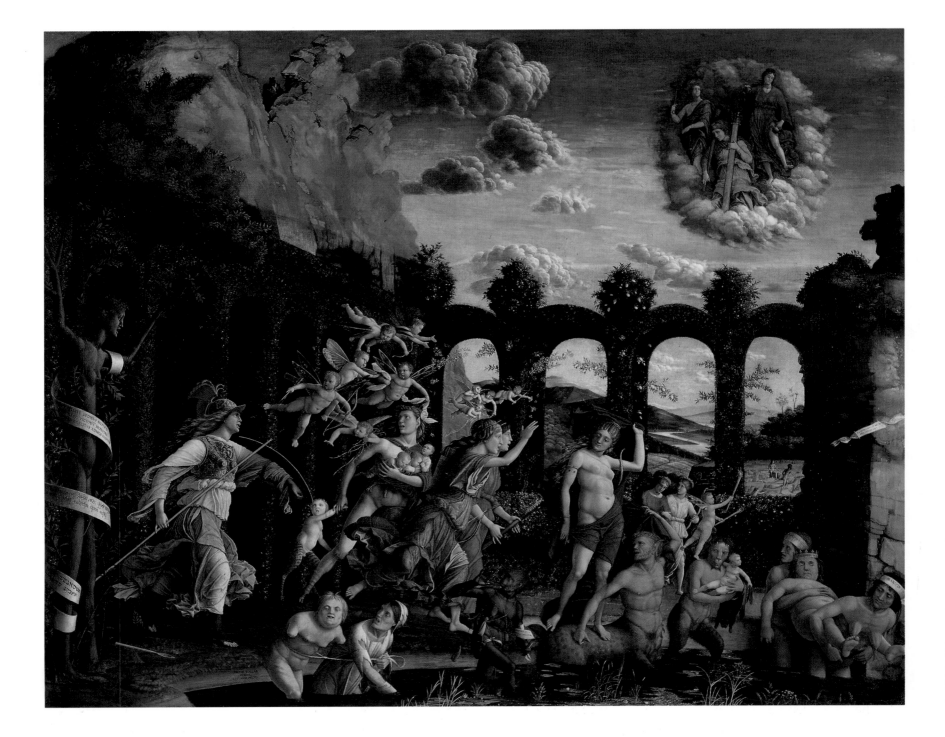

87 ANDREA MANTEGNA Pallas Expelling the Vices from the
Garden of Virtue *c.*1499–1502

*This is the second of two pictures which Mantegna painted for the
Studiolo of Isabella d'Este in the Ducal Palace in Mantua, the other
being* Parnassus *(also in the Louvre). The programme was probably
provided by Paride da Ceresara, Isabella's advisor, and is the major
instance in Mantegna's work of his painting a complete illustration of
a philosophical idea. The long inscription wound round the tree was
to enable Isabella's visitors to read the picture like a narrative. Pallas
Athene rushes into the Garden of Virtue from the left, raising her
hand against a swarm of armed cupids; she scatters the other figures.
The figure on the left being transformed into a bay tree symbolizes one
of the four Cardinal Virtues deserting the garden. The Vices escape
through the swamp, led by the figure of Avarice helped by Ingratitude
to carry the fat Ignorance. They are followed by a grotesque satyr
signifying Lust. The armless Idleness is led by the rope by Sloth. A
hermaphrodite monkey stands for Immortal Hatred, Fraud and
Malice, and has bags containing evil, worse evil and worst evil.*

money'. By 1481, after studying with Verrocchio in
Florence, and possibly with Piero della Francesca, he was
sufficiently esteemed to join the team in the Sistine
Chapel (see plate 114). The style he evolved there was to
change little, and at its best combined elegant, simplified
figures in rather conventional poses, occasionally reaching
real pathos as in his *Pietà* (Palazzo Pitti, Florence).

Perugino's earliest style appears to combine the influences of Piero with Flemish art, as in the superb *Adoration
of the Magi* (Galleria Nazionale dell' Umbria, Perugia).
Considered of local importance in 1475, he was commissioned to fresco a room in the Palazzo de' Priori in
Perugia (lost), and after his Sistine work he moved continuously between Perugia, Florence and Rome receiving prestigious commissions. The high point of his
painting in these years is *The Vision of Saint Bernard* of
1489–90 (Alte Pinakothek, Munich), which achieves a
purism resembling that of contemporary architecture in

Florence, totally at variance with the deliberate sophistication of Botticelli. In 1493, he settled in Florence on his marriage to the daughter of the architect, Luca Fancelli.

His decline in reputation was signalled in 1505 by Isabella d'Este's dissatisfaction with his *Love and Charity* (Musée du Louvre, Paris) painted for her *studiolo* (study), and in 1508 Julius II dismissed him from work on the Vatican *Stanze* (Papal Rooms). His last years were spent mainly working in Umbria, where he died of plague.

Pintoricchio (Bernadino di Betto, *c.*1454–1513) was probably Perugino's pupil, and evolved from him a decorative and alluring style with a profusion of colourful detail and costume. In 1492–5 he was employed in the Borgia Apartments of the Vatican, but his greatest achievement is the fresco cycle in the Libreria Piccolomini of Siena Cathedral (1503) showing the *Life of Aeneas Sylvius Piccolomini* (Pope Pius II)(see plate 68).

Mantegna in Padua and Mantua

Andrea Mantegna (1431–1506) grew up in Padua, which had a crucial influence on his art, not least in his obsessive love of sculpture and archaeology. With Giotto's Arena Chapel frescoes and Donatello's Paduan work in the background, Mantegna was trained by his adopted father Francesco Squarcione, whom he took to court for exploitation when he was seventeen. Squarcione's studio was the only one in Northern Italy claiming to teach 'in the modern manner', but Mantegna, who quickly developed a personal style, was the only major name to emerge from it. When he composed a shortlist of the leading artists of his day, the Urbino court painter Giovanni Santi (Raphael's father), put Mantegna in first place, even ahead of Leonardo. Vasari says of his first commission (at the age of sixteen) for an altarpiece (now destroyed), 'it seemed painted, not by a youth, but by an old man of long practice'.

Mantegna's first major commission was in 1448, for

88 ANDREA MANTEGNA   Man of Sorrows with Two Angels *c.*1500

This is the major religious work of Mantegna's last years, and is unusual in depicting Christ full length. It also includes some of Mantegna's most subtle observations of landscape. Christ is shown seated against a sarcophagus 'in the antique style' supported by two angels, one of whom has red wings and the robe of a seraph, the other of whom wears the blue associated with a cherub. On the left are two holy women walking towards the tomb on Easter morning, and Jerusalem appears in the background. The sarcophagus symbolizes the altar, with Christ as the Eucharist, while the left-hand landscape refers to Christ's death, the right to His Resurrection.

frescoes showing the lives of St Christopher and St James in the Ovetari Chapel in Padua's Eremitani Church. These were virtually destroyed in the Second World War, but are recorded in photographs. It remains clear that perspective, one of Mantegna's lifelong passions, was fully in his control, since the two lower scenes of the life of St James were realistically foreshortened as if viewed from beneath. Such perspectival realism was rare in the Quattrocento, and relates to his later work in Mantua (see plate 104), which in turn looks forward to Correggio's domes (see plate 222) and the dramatic foreshortenings, known as *sotto in sù* (from below upwards), of Baroque ceilings. Mantegna was one of the strongest influences on the young Correggio.

Many other features of his style were already present in the Eremitani frescoes. These include rigidly drawn outlines and a sculptural treatment of the human figure,

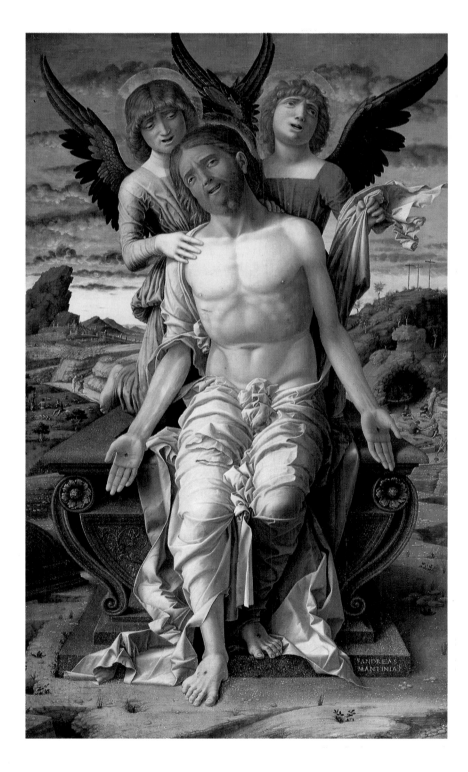

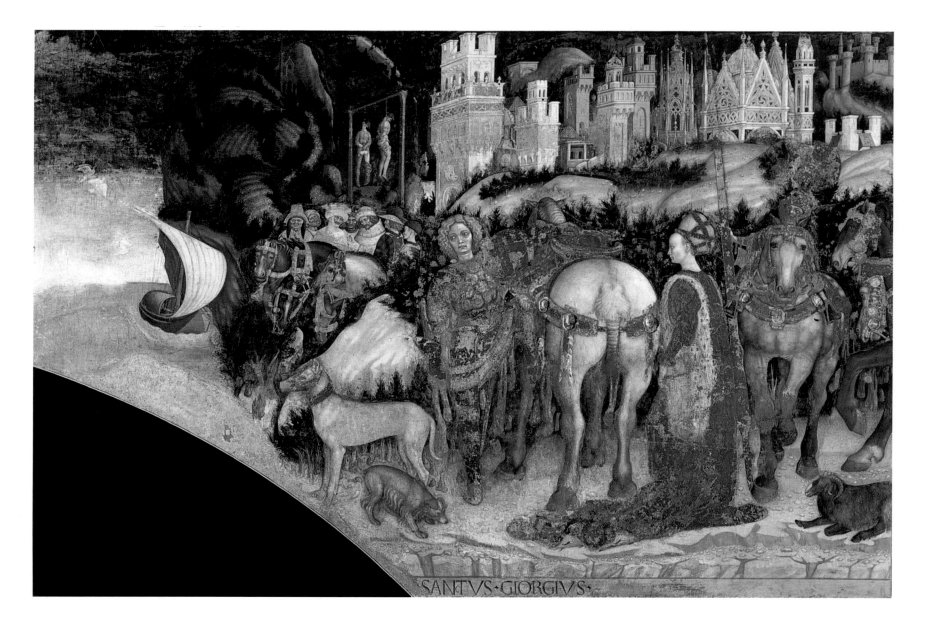

SANTVS·GIORGIVS·

92 ANTONIO PISANELLO Saint George and the Princess
1437–8
*This is the only remaining fresco by Pisanello in the Pellegrini
Chapel of Sant-Anastasia in Verona, and it documents his style after
his Roman visit. The prevailing delicacy retains much of the
International Gothic style as transmitted in the work of Pisanello's
master, Gentile da Fabriano. The carefully observed horses and dogs
and the towers and pinnacles of the city in the background create a
masterpiece of north Italian naturalism.*

93 MASACCIO Trinity 1425–8
*Masaccio's great fresco survives as only a shadow of its former self. It
is very thinly painted; Vasari says that it was painted over other
frescoes, which may have been partly visible from the beginning, and
successive restorations have almost ruined it. The patron is uncertain,
as is the identity of the donors in the fresco, and the iconography is
unusual to the point of remaining a mystery. Masaccio merges the
image of the Trinity with the idea of a Calvary indicated by the
presence of Virgin and St John the Evangelist. Behind, the chapel
painted in perspective may be a symbol of the Church as in
Netherlandish paintings. Below, a skeleton lies on a sarcophagus;
this may refer to Adam, whose skull is often placed below the cross in
Crucifixion scenes, and this may be a reference to the hope of
resurrection.*

*The fictive architecture is strongly influenced by Brunelleschi and
Donatello, and reconstructions of the chapel's 'plan' suggest that the
space would be square. The command of drawing, perspective and the
depiction of the figures strongly suggest that Masaccio painted the
Trinity after he had completed the Brancacci Chapel frescoes (see
plate 70).*

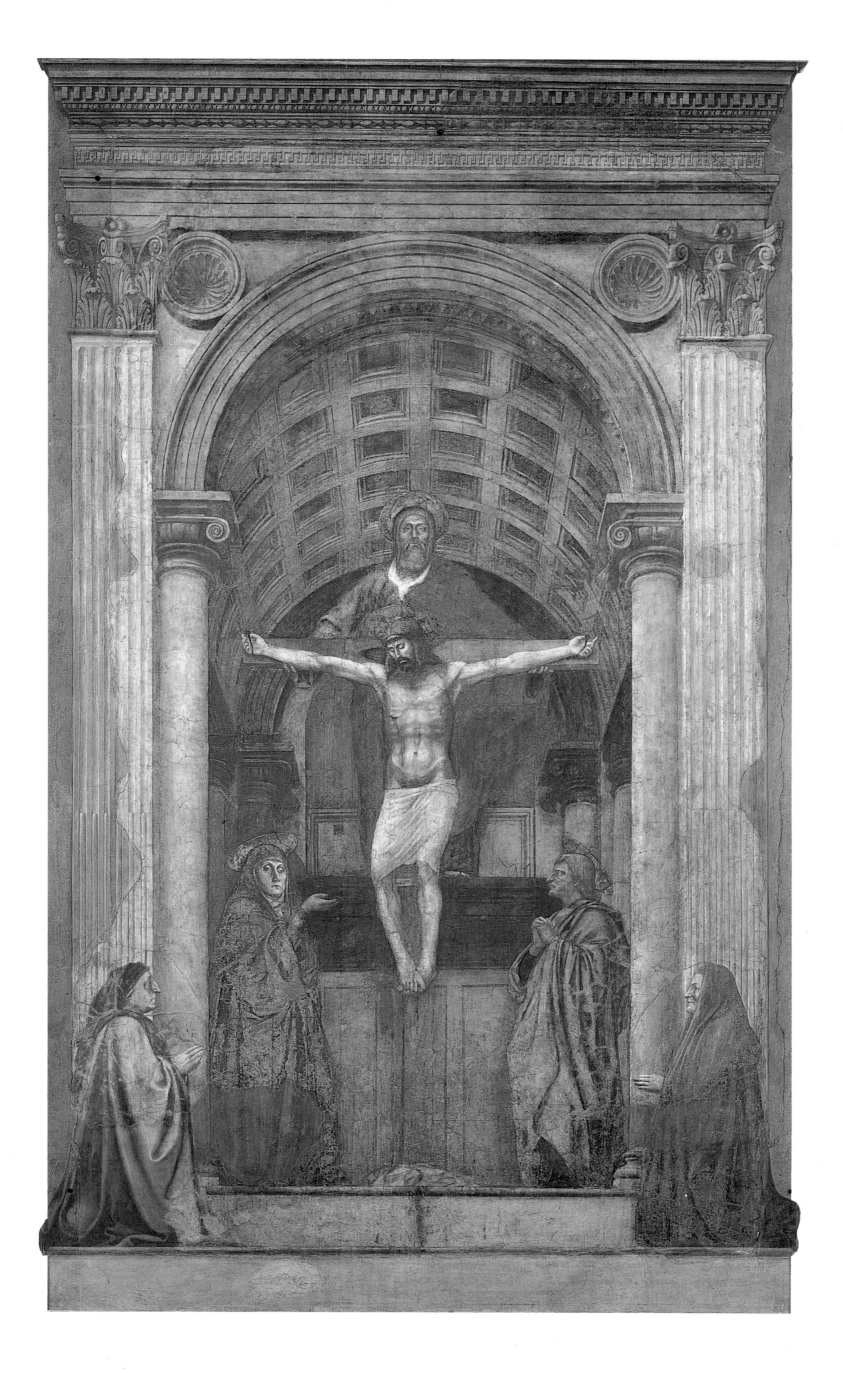

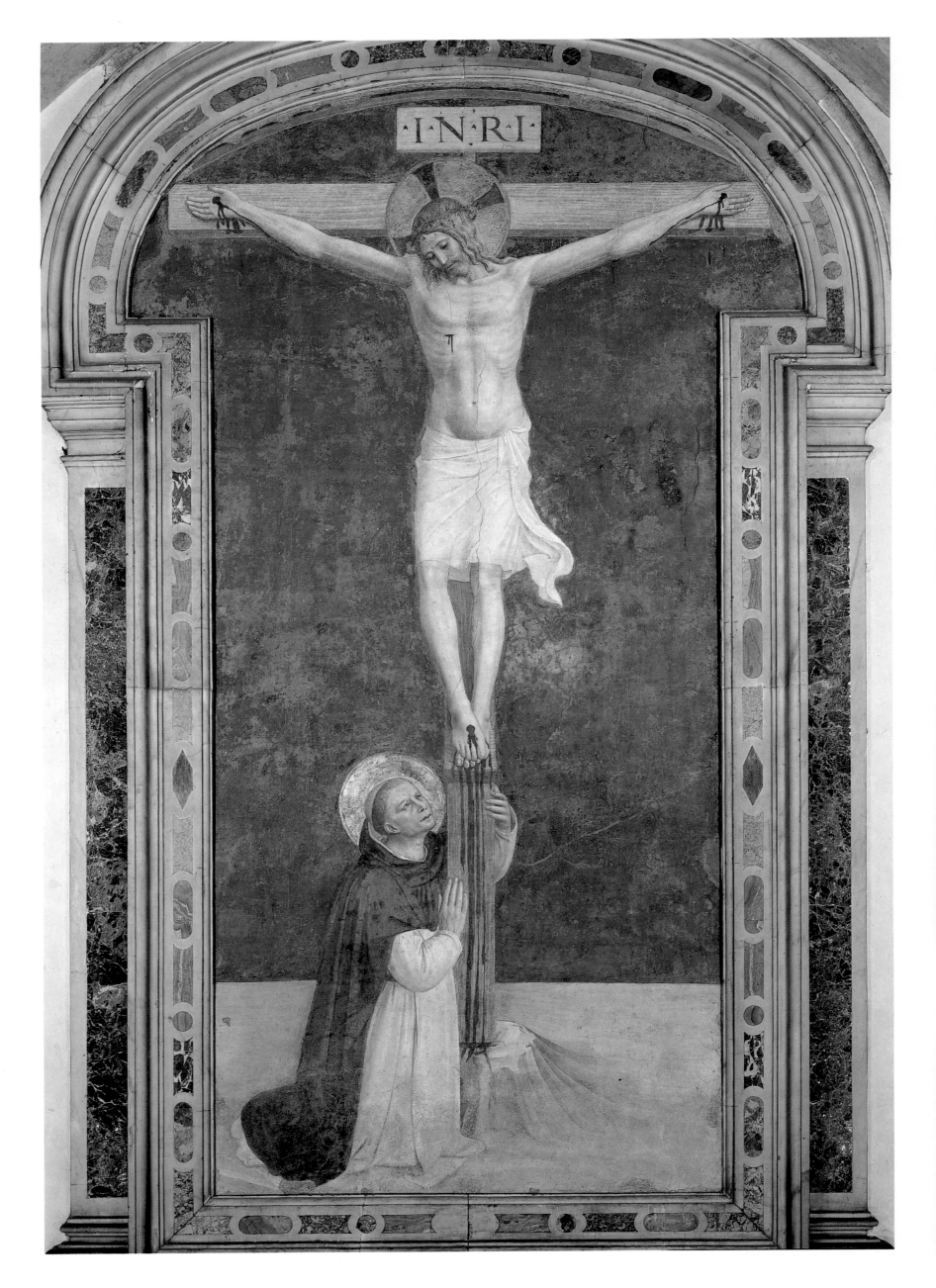

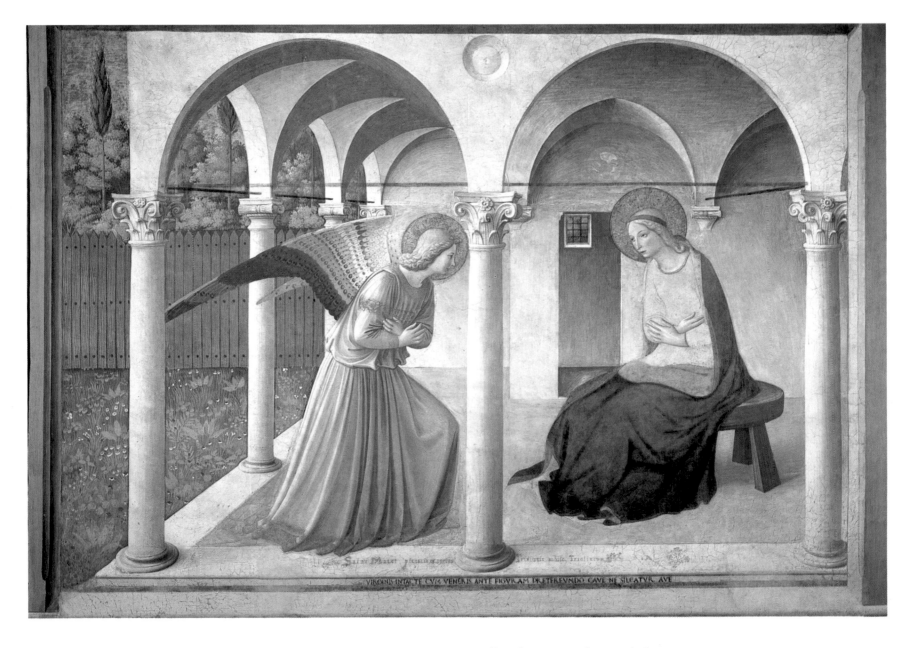

95 FRA ANGELICO Annunciation c.1450

This scene is set on the inner wall of the upper corridor facing the staircase in the convent of San Marco. It is set in a Classical loggia, clearly reflecting the architecture of Michelozzo's new convent of San Marco, and the Ionic and Corinthian capitals are derived from capitals by Michelozzo in the cloisters of the SS Annunziata and San Marco. One of the most satisfying of Angelico's compositions, the scene is flooded with miraculous light. Although the figures are still Gothic in their elongation, their simplicity and solidity reflect Masaccio's lesson. The brilliant colouring of the angel's wings strikes the main note in a harmony of soft pinks, beige, browns and greens.

94 FRA ANGELICO Saint Dominic Adoring the Crucifix, after 1442

This fresco greets the visitor on entering the cloister of the convent of San Marco, and is one of the most moving scenes in its simplicity and concentration. Although Angelico was assisted throughout the extensive work at San Marco, no documentary record of the artists involved is known. Certain scenes, such as this, have a good claim to being largely by his hand, but the attribution of the frescoes in the monks' cells remains the subject of debate.

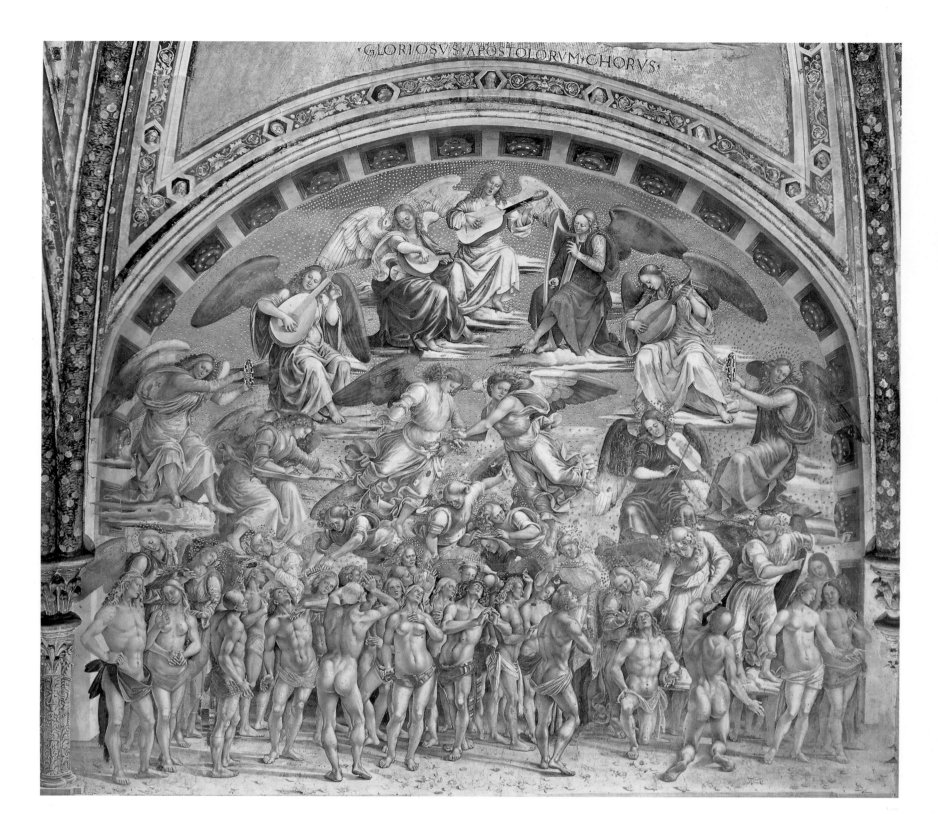

GLORIOSVS·APOSTOLORVM·CHORVS

96 LUCA SIGNORELLI Calling of the Elect 1500–4
(Above) In 1447 Fra Angelico and Benozzo Gozzoli started the
frescoes in Orvieto Cathedral, but only in 1499 was the completion of
the chapel entrusted to Signorelli. In this scene of the Calling of the
Elect the elect are crowned by angels while other angels scatter roses
and make music. Throughout these frescoes, the dominant feature is
the presence of many nude figures. This was without precedent in
Italian painting, and it looks forward to Michelangelo, who admired
these frescoes intensely.

98 DOMENICO GHIRLANDAIO The Birth of Saint John the
Baptist 1485–90
(Right) Ghirlandaio's famous frescoes for the chancel of Santa Maria
Novella in Florence were commissioned by Giovanni Tornabuoni.
They were executed in collaboration with the painter's brother
Davide, Sebastiano Mainardi and the youthful Michelangelo. On
the left wall are scenes of the Life of the Virgin, and on the right is
the Life of the Baptist. One of the highest achievements of
Renaissance narrative painting, these frescoes combine a serene
equilibrium with many contemporary portraits and other details from
Florentine daily life, including costume and interiors.

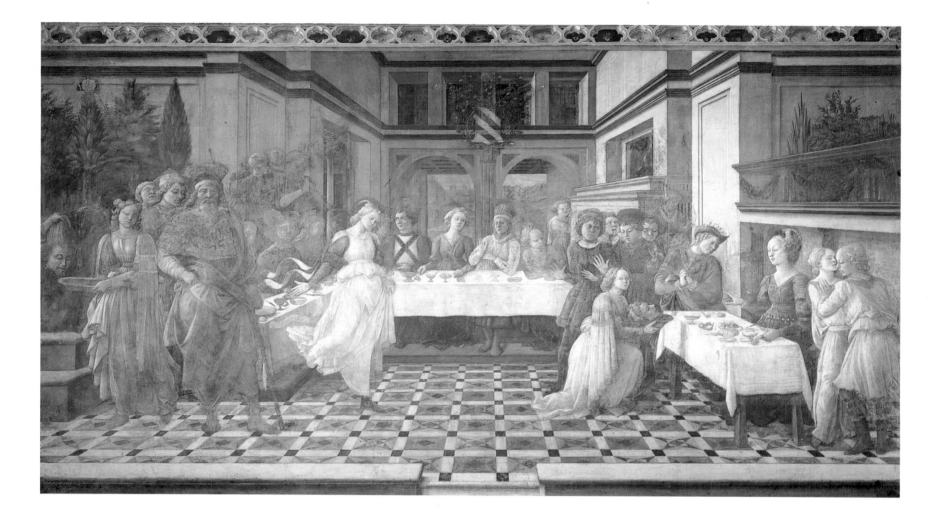

97 FILIPPO LIPPI Dance of Salome (Herod's Feast) 1452–66

(Above) This forms part of Lippi's fresco cycle in the main chapel of Prato Cathedral, which shows the lives of St John the Baptist and St Stephen, the patron saints of Prato. As many problems delayed the work, it took Lippi almost thirteen years to complete with the help of various assistants. Because Lippi worked over the fresco surface with tempera, adding an incalculable wealth of detail and nuance, he achieved the elaboration and richness of surface normally associated with panel painting. Three events are included in one scene – Salome's dance, her reception of the Baptist's head, and her presentation of it to her mother, Herodias.

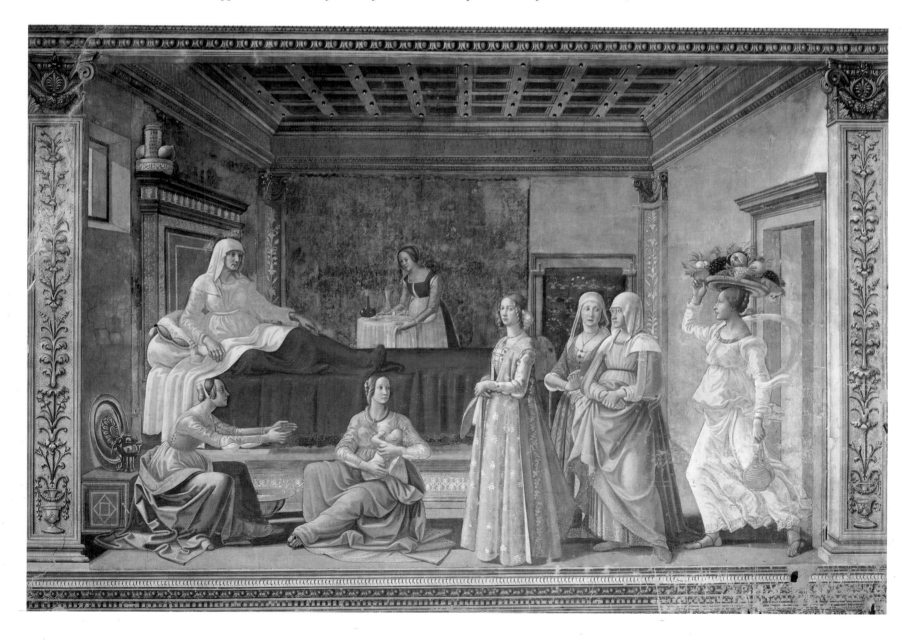

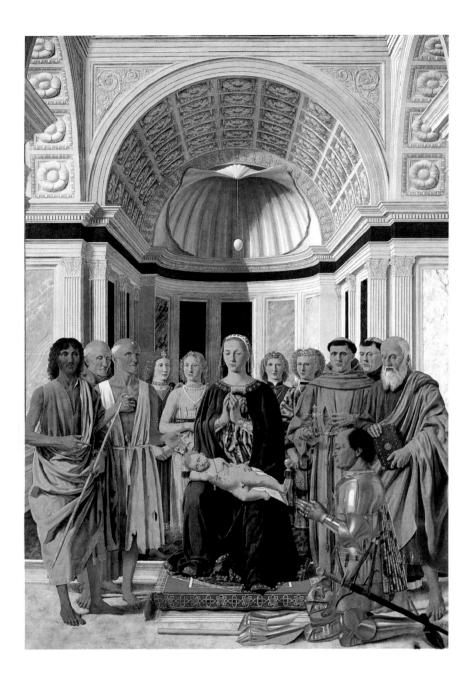

99 PIERO DELLA FRANCESCA The Brera Altarpiece
1472–4
(Left) This Madonna and Child with Six Saints, Angels
and Duke Federico II da Montefeltro *came from the
church of San Bernardino in Urbino. It undoubtedly has a
votive character, and may have been commissioned on the birth
of Guidobaldo da Montefeltro in 1472. The suspended ostrich
egg may be a Christian symbol for the four elements or a
symbol of the creation – possibly a reference to Guidobaldo.
The architecture was no doubt intended to relate to the original
setting, and shows not merely an apse but also transepts and
part of the walls of a nave. Like Van Eyck's painting of the
Madonna in a Church (see plate 125), Piero's Madonna
figure is disproportionately large, and a similar symbolic
presentation of Mary as a temple may have been intended.*

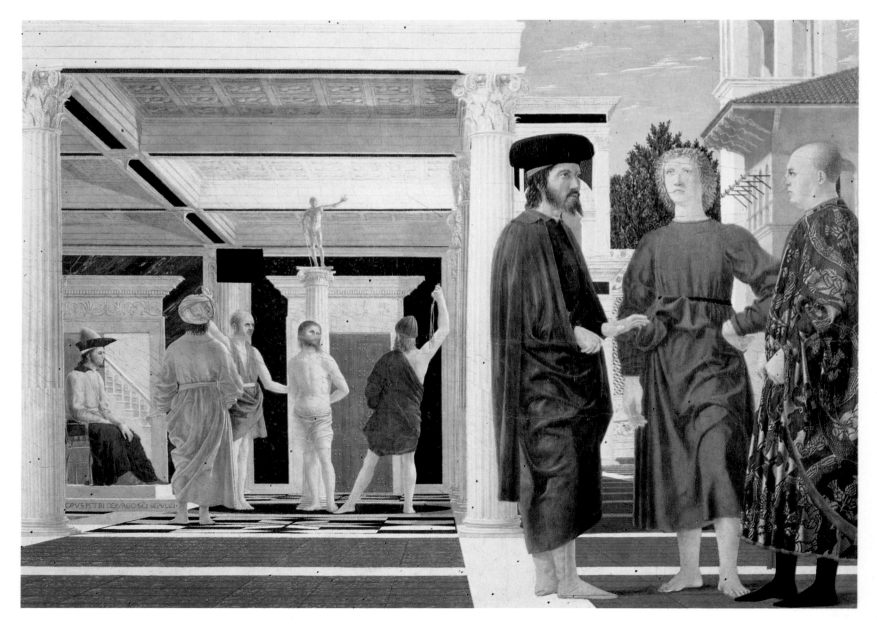

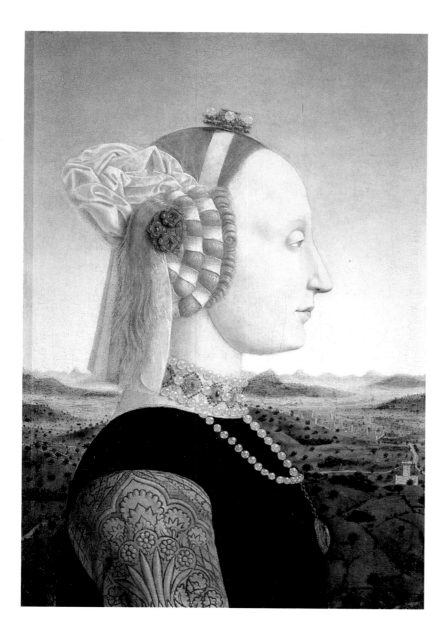 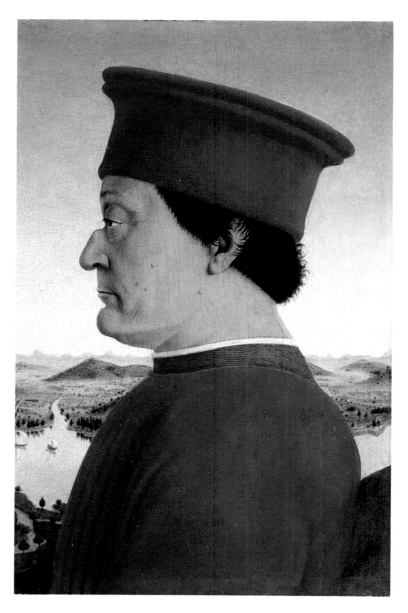

101 and 102 PIERO DELLA FRANCESCA Federico II da
Montefeltro and Battista Sforza 1465
(Above left and Above) This diptych was probably originally in the
audience chamber of the Ducal Palace at Urbino, moving to Florence
in 1631 with the Della Rovere inheritance. Federico's nose was
broken in a tournament, and Piero contrasts his hard outline with the
soft one of his wife. The striking feature of the portraits is their close
involvement with the background landscape, whose appearance recalls
contemporary Florentine experiments by Pollaiuolo and others: there
also appears to be a strong Flemish influence. On the reverse of the
paintings is an allegorical triumph of the couple.

100 PIERO DELLA FRANCESCA Flagellation of Christ 1455
(Left) Traditionally the central figure of the right-hand group
represents Oddantonio da Montefeltro with his ministers Manfredo
dei Pio and Tommaso dell'Agnelo, ultimately responsible for the
death of the young prince in 1444. Some critics have interpreted the
picture as an allegory of the crisis in the Church which culminated in
the Fall of Constantinople in 1453. The painting offers one of the
most astonishing examples of 'pure' Renaissance architecture for its
date, and the layout of the figures on the ground plan may have a
precise mathematical symbolism.

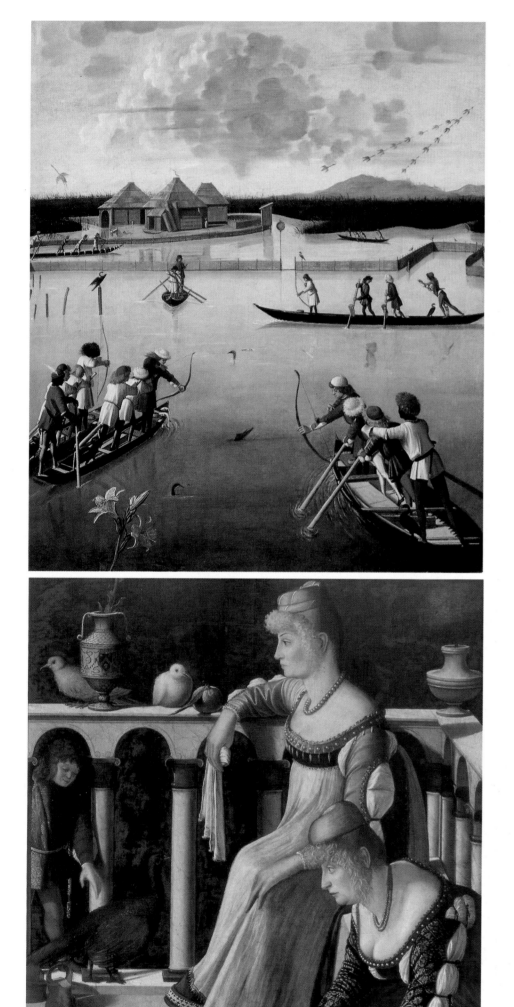

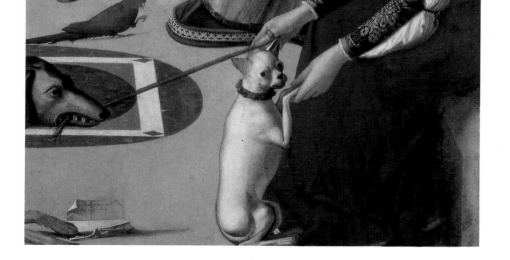

109 and 110 VITTORE CARPACCIO A Shooting Party on the Lagoon *and* Two Women Seated on a Balcony 1490–6 *(Left and Below Left) These two fragments clearly belong together. The lilies at the lower left of the* Shooting Party *correspond exactly with the vase on the lower balustrade. On the vase itself is the coat of arms of the noble Venetian Torella family, so it seems likely that the painting shows two ladies of the Torella family watching the hunt from their palace terrace, rather than two courtesans as was previously thought. It has been suggested that the painting might contain some reference to Circe, who had the power to transform men into animals, but it is not unlikely that it is simply a genre scene including two portraits.*

111 VITTORE CARPACCIO Young Knight in a Landscape (Francesco Maria della Rovere, Duke of Urbino) 1510 *(Right) The subject is almost certainly the young Duke of Urbino (1490–1538), the son of Giuliano della Rovere and nephew of Pope Julius II. It once carried a false monogram to suggest that it was by Dürer, whose engraving of* A Knight, Death and the Devil *of 1504 (see plate 43) appears to be the source of the equestrian figure. Dürer's Venetian visit of 1505–7 did not go unnoticed by the city's artists. Full of direct and indirect references to the sitter and his family, this portrait typifies the Renaissance love of symbol and allegory. It is probably a knightly allegory of the Christian soul's struggle between good and evil, identifying the sitter with the characteristic strengths and weaknesses of the oak tree (rovere=oak). In the foreground are an ermine and a Latin inscription ('die painfully rather than be sullied'), both pertaining to the Neapolitan Order of the Ermine and also to the Dukes of Urbino. The mounted knight bears the black and gold colours of the Duke of Urbino. The foreground stump of oak and the background oak tree may suggest a gradual process of regeneration, probably referring to Francesco Maria's role in the family. He was christened Maria after his birth on the feast of the Annunciation, and the lilies and irises associated with the Virgin Annunciate are a further dual reference.*

The picture's air of unreality is emphasized by the lack of aerial perspective and real shadows, and the way in which depth is arbitrarily suggested as if with stage wings. Detail is given equal scrutiny throughout the picture, contributing to the timeless, frozen atmosphere.

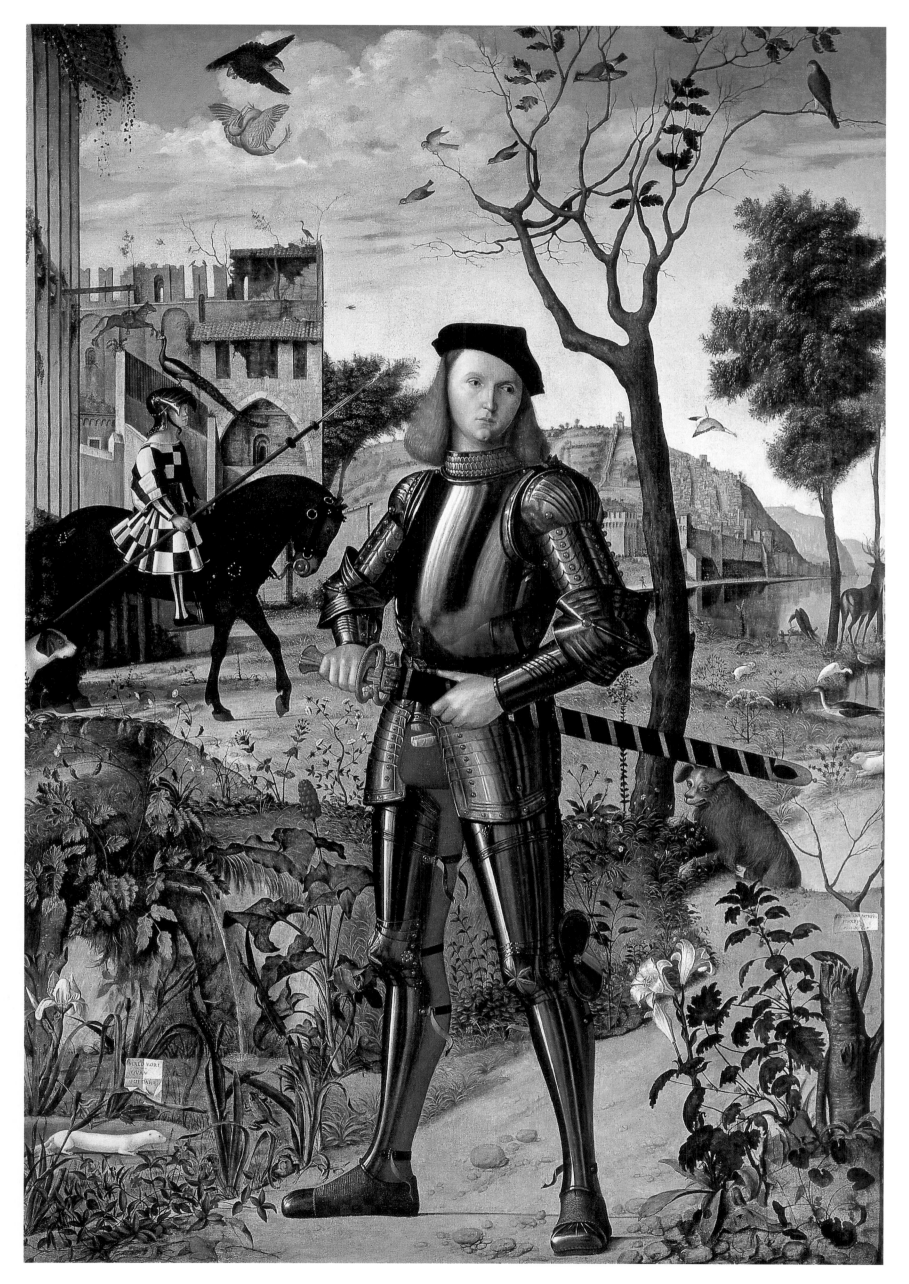

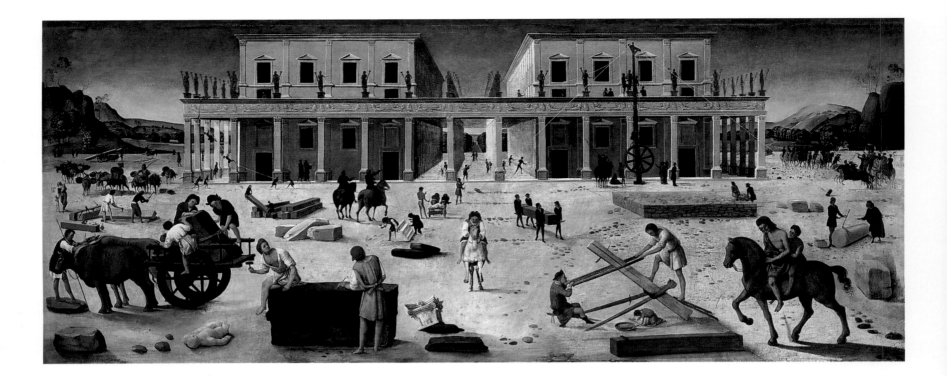

112 PIERO DI COSIMO The Building of a Palace *c.*1515–20
(*Above*) *Although there is no specific key to this picture's meaning, it may be an allegory of The Triumph of Architecture, possibly partly in memoriam for the Sangallo family of architects. Piero knew the family, and painted a memorable portrait of Giuliano da Sangallo in c.1500–4 (Rijksmuseum, Amsterdam). The building is clearly in Giuliano's style, and its bipartite structure recalls the plan of the Villa Medici at Poggio a Caiano.*

113 PIETRO PERUGINO Christ Handing the Keys to Saint Peter 1482
(*Below*) *This fresco is part of the Sistine Chapel cycle commissioned in 1481. Its background architecture and formal disposition of the figures in a vast piazza give it a dignified monumentality. Many portraits of contemporaries are included.*

114 BENOZZO GOZZOLI Journey of the Magi 1459
(*Right*) *These frescoes were commissioned by Piero de'Medici, son of Cosimo, for the tiny chapel of the family palace by Michelozzo in Florence. Piero's taste is important in understanding the fresco's dazzling display of colour and decorative detail; he was a highly refined collector of antique gems, tapestries, goldsmith's work and Flemish pictures in the tradition of the Duc de Berry and, among his contemporaries, Borso d'Este. Following a tradition dear to the Medici, the procession includes portraits of the family and their court set against a magnificent landscape. Recalling the glittering detail of Gentile da Fabriano's* Strozzi Altarpiece, *the procession is, however, rendered with the realism of an historic event to which it makes reference, the 1439 Council held in Florence. One of the three kings is Constantine XI Palaeologus, the last Roman Emperor, who died in 1453 defending Constantinople against the Turks.*

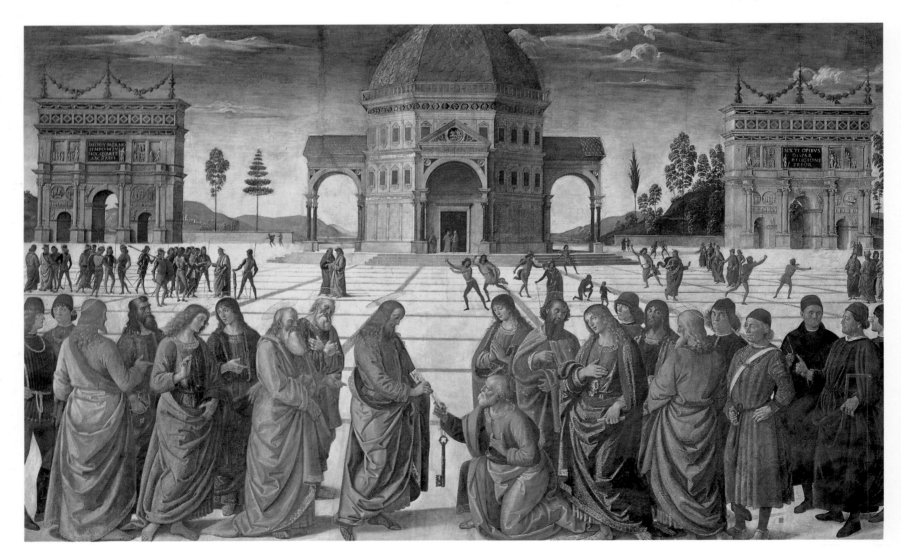

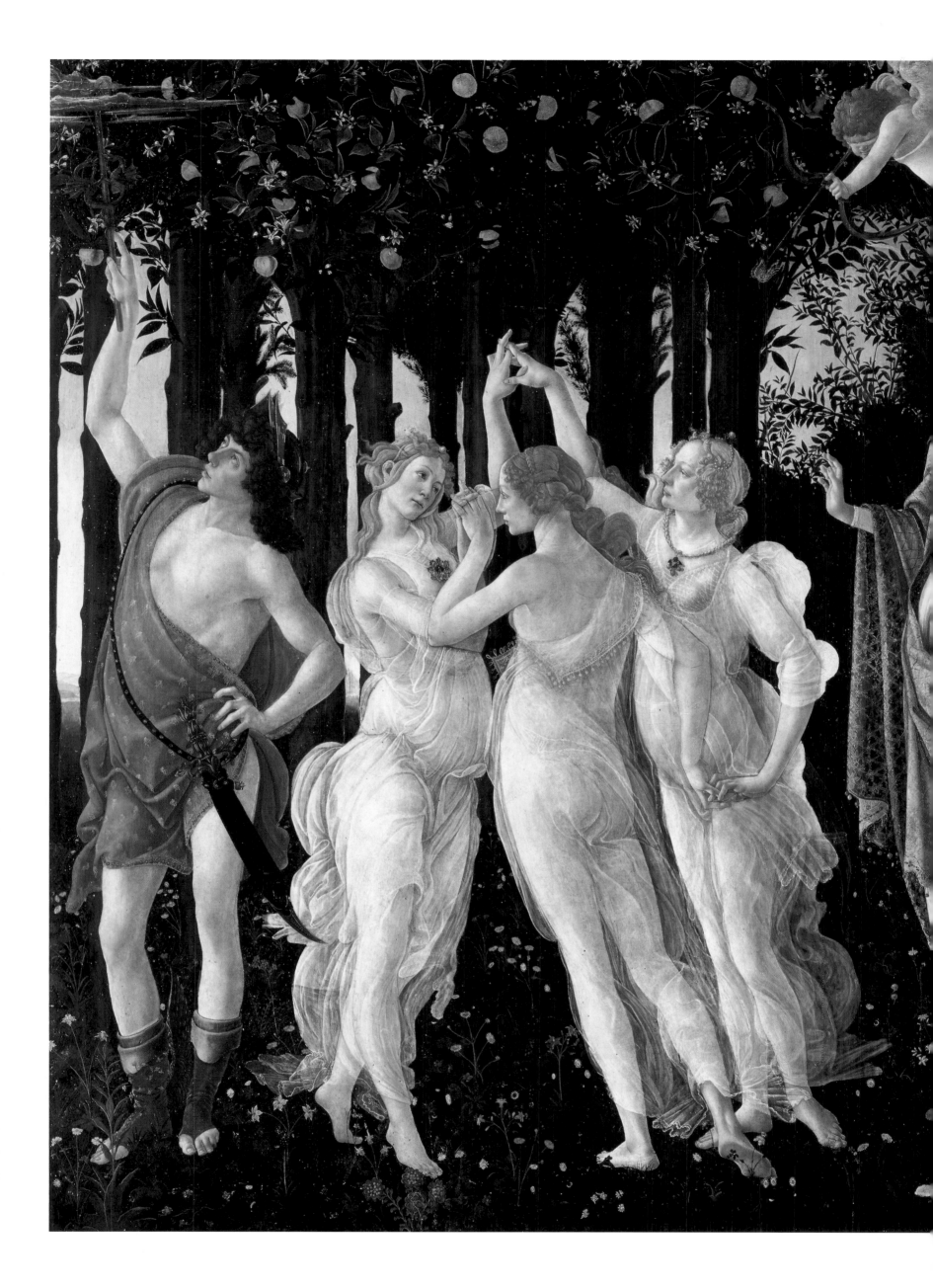

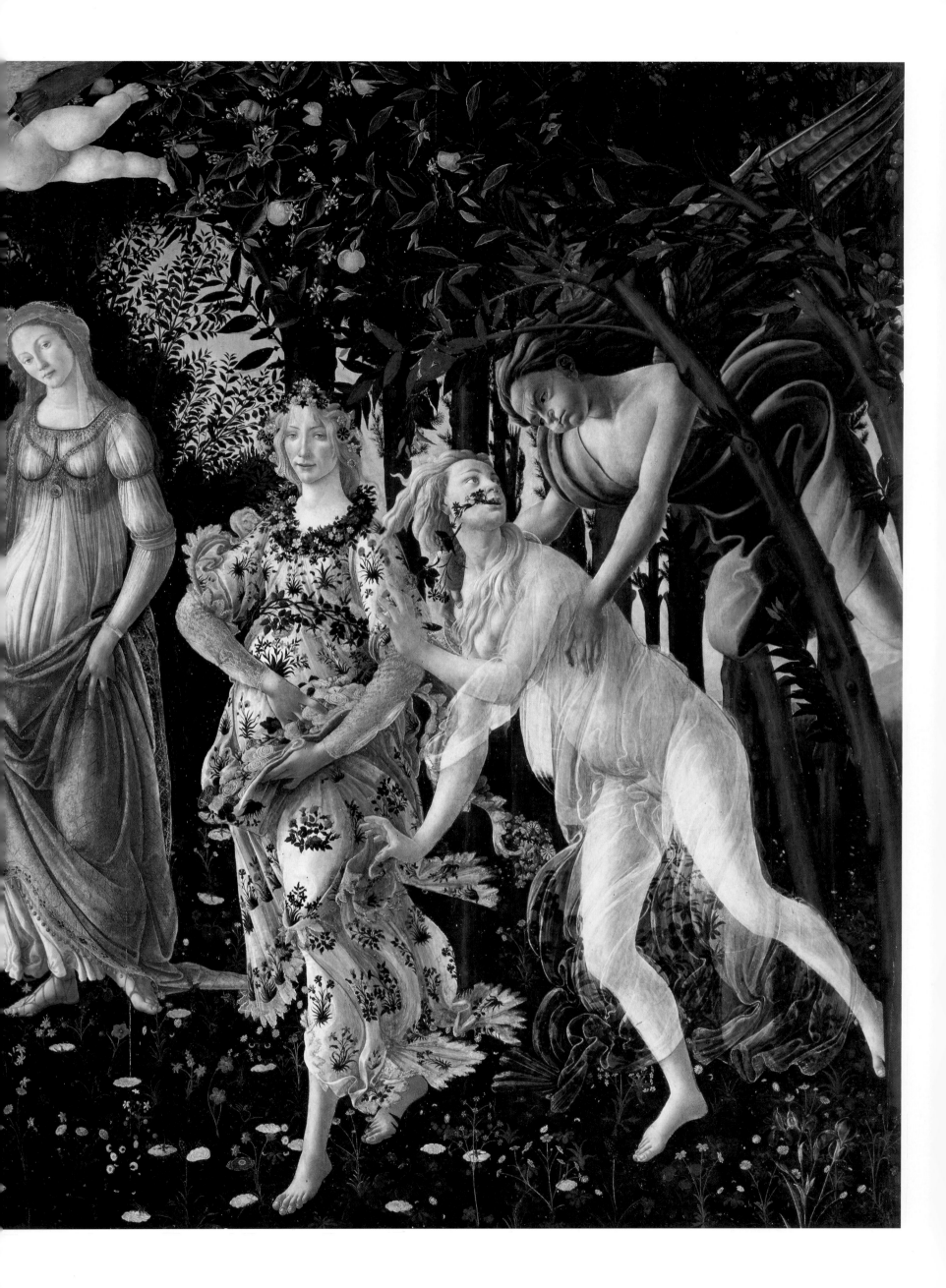

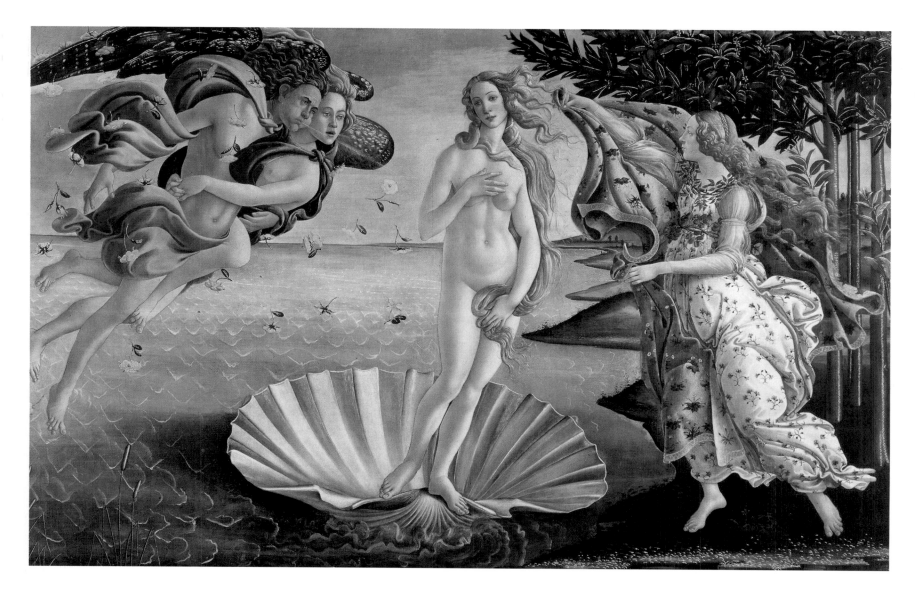

115 SANDRO BOTTICELLI Primavera *c.*1478
(Left) This painting forms part of a cycle including the
Birth of Venus *and* Minerva and the Centaur, *and*
all have a complex iconography. They offer a synthesis of
Neo-Platonic doctrines. Zephyr (extreme right)
personifies human love and nature's life-giving power.
He seizes the nymph Chloris, who is transformed into
Flora. Above, Cupid helps Venus to arouse this
passionate love, but also to sublimate it through the
intellect (the three Graces) towards an ideal
contemplation of worlds beyond through the figure of
Mercury (extreme left).

116 SANDRO BOTTICELLI Birth of Venus 1484–6
(Above) This picture was painted for Lorenzo de'
Pierfrancesco de' Medici as the companion piece to
Primavera, *but has probably been cut at the top. The*
sources include Hesiod's Genealogy and Homer, as
interpreted by the Neoplatonists.

117 SANDRO BOTTICELLI Minerva and the
Centaur *c.*1480
(Right) Wrongly identified as Pallas and the Centaur
on the basis of a misidentification with a painting
described by Vasari, this picture shows Minerva as
goddess of wisdom triumphing over the baser instincts
symbolized by the satyr.

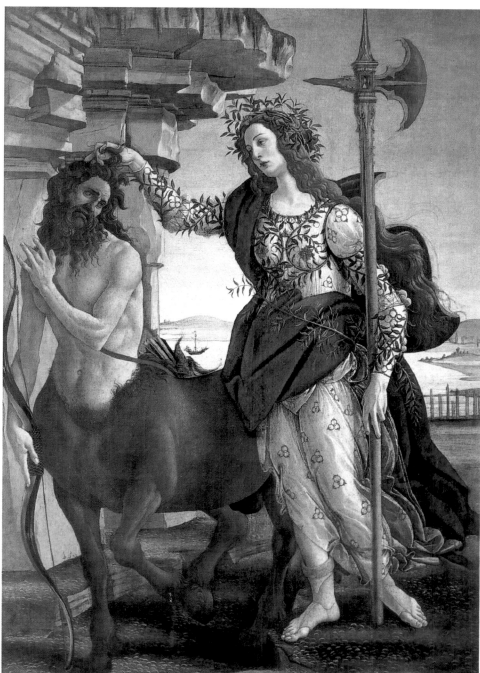

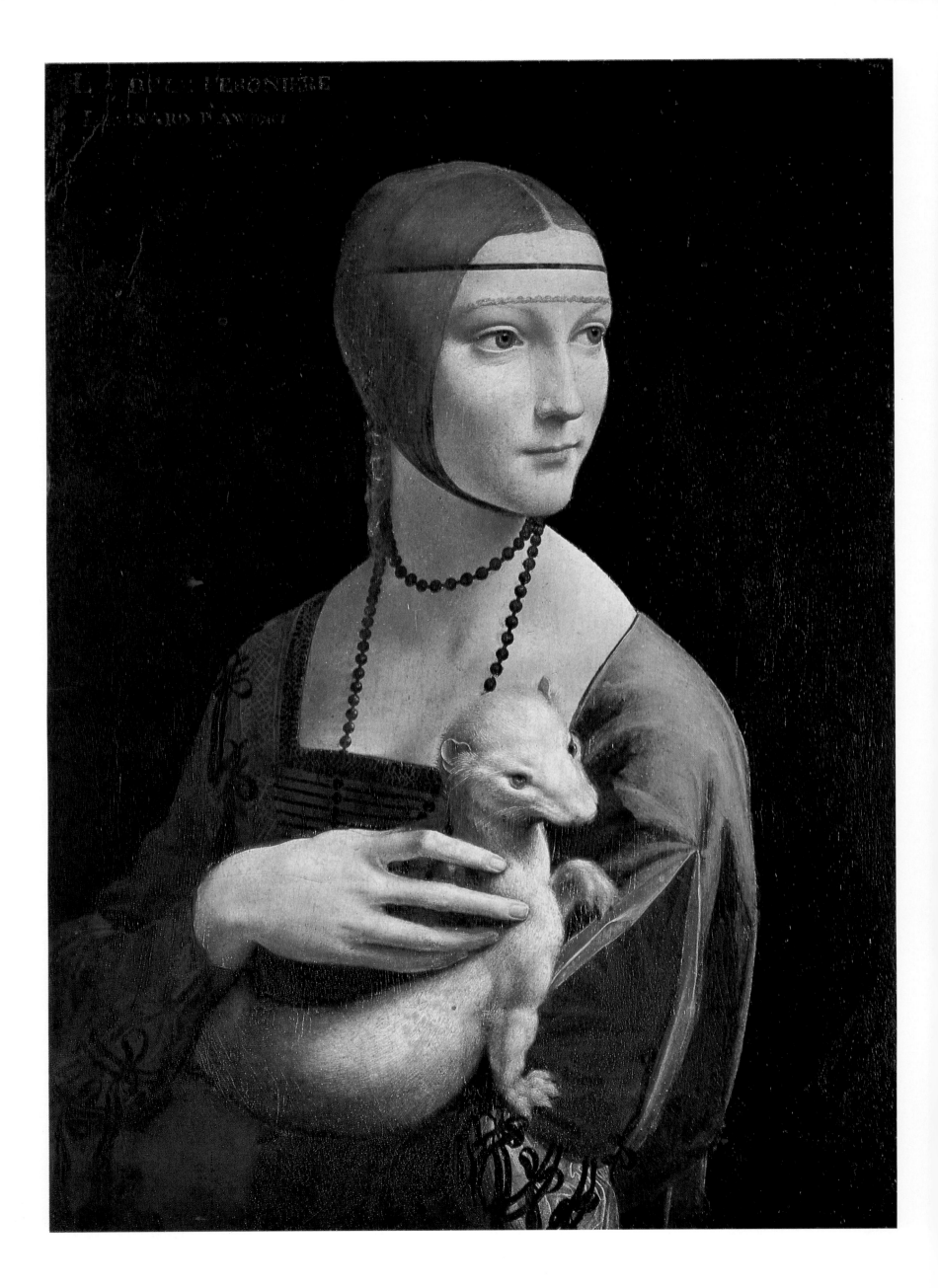

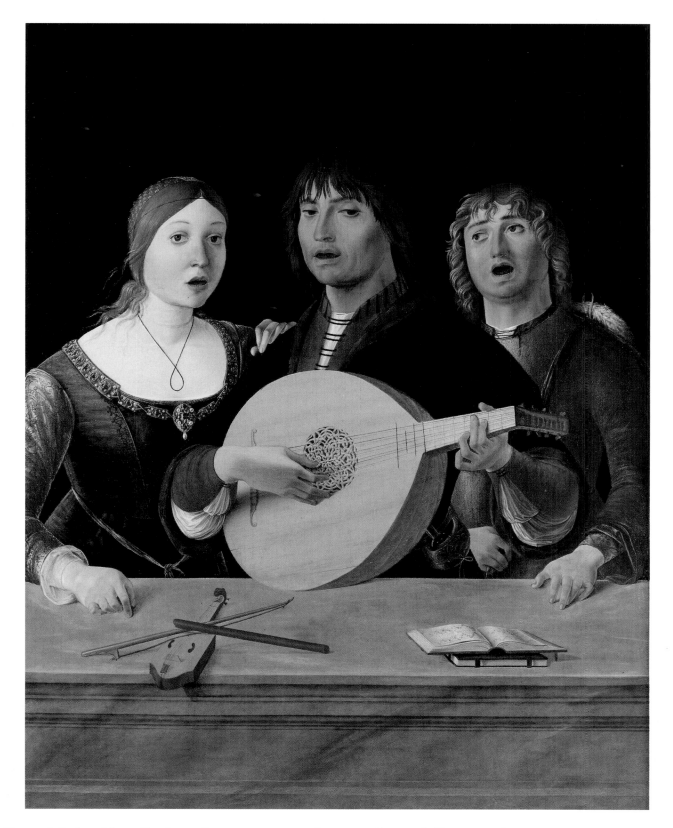

118 LEONARDO DA VINCI A Lady with an Ermine 1485–90
(Left) *It is now generally agreed that this portrait shows Lodovico Sforza's mistress, Cecelia Gallerani, and is the one praised in a sonnet by the court poet Bellincioni, who described it as a listening rather than a speaking likeness. The portrait is discussed in a correspondence between its sitter and Isabella d'Este, who had asked for her likeness by Leonardo to be sent. The lady holds an ermine, Lodovico's emblem: the word ermine in Greek includes a punning reference to her own name. Although damaged, the important parts of this painting are clearly among Leonardo's finest work, notably the modelling of the face and the ermine's head, making nonsense of suggestions that it is the work of a follower. While still in the Florentine tradition, its extremely subtle pose and atmosphere set it in advance of any contemporary work.*

119 LORENZO COSTA A Concert 1487–1500
(Above) *Formerly ascribed to Ercole de'Roberti, this is one of Costa's most pleasing pictures. It is also one of the earliest examples of a genre painting of this kind with, apparently, no allegorical meaning. As such, it looks forward to the work of Giorgione.*

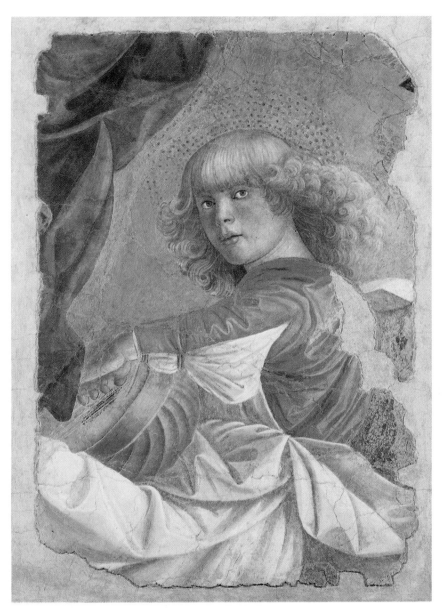

120 MELOZZO DA FORLÌ Musical Angel 1478–80
(Left) This is one of the many fragments from Melozzo's Ascension fresco for the dome of Santi Apostoli in Rome, which are now divided between the Vatican and the Quirinal Palace. It shows the influence of Piero della Francesca, but this is coupled with an idiosyncratic sweetness and sense of movement.

122 CARLO CRIVELLI The Annunciation with Saint Emidius 1486
(Right) The Angel Gabriel kneels in the street with St Emidius. He holds a model of the town of Ascoli, of which he is patron. The picture was painted to commemorate the papal grant of 1482 to Ascoli's citizens of certain rights of self-government. The announcement of this privilege was made in Ascoli on 25 March, the Feast of the Annunciation, and each year a procession was made to the church of Santissima Annunziata, for which the picture was painted. Typical of Crivelli is the fastidious attention to architectural, sculptural and other details, including the birds, the carpet, flowers and the interior.

121 GENTILE BELLINI A Procession in Piazza San Marco 1496
(Below) This picture belongs to the Miracle of the Cross cycle, formerly in the Scuola di San Giovanni Evangelista in Venice. Originally the cycle comprised ten paintings by Carpaccio, Mansueti, Bellini and others. The cartouche in the lower centre reads '1496/the work of Gentile Bellini of Venice, knight, afire with the love of the cross.' The painting shows the St Mark's Day procession in which each scuola participated carrying its relics. The event shown took place on 25 April 1444, when a Brescian merchant, Jacopo de' Salis, obtained miraculous help for his injured son. It also records the Piazza's appearance before later changes, including the pink pavement (later replaced with grey) comparable with that in Florence's Piazza della Signoria (see plate 4). It also shows the original mosaics on the basilica, of which only one now survives.

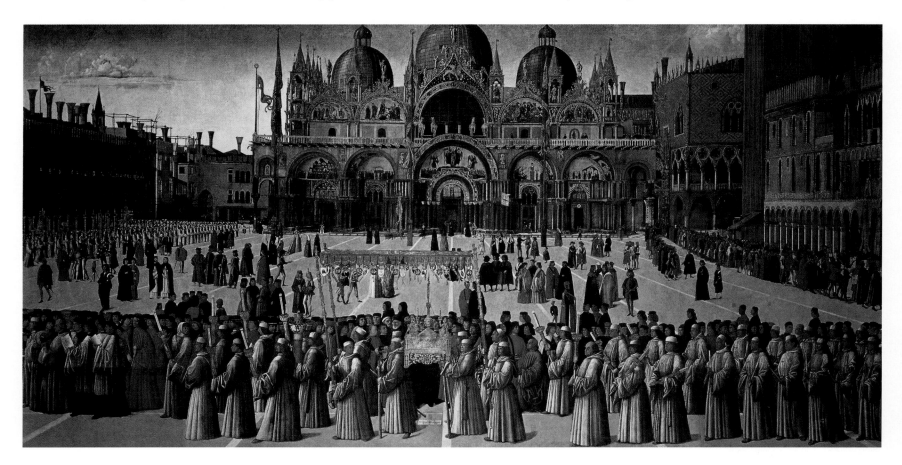

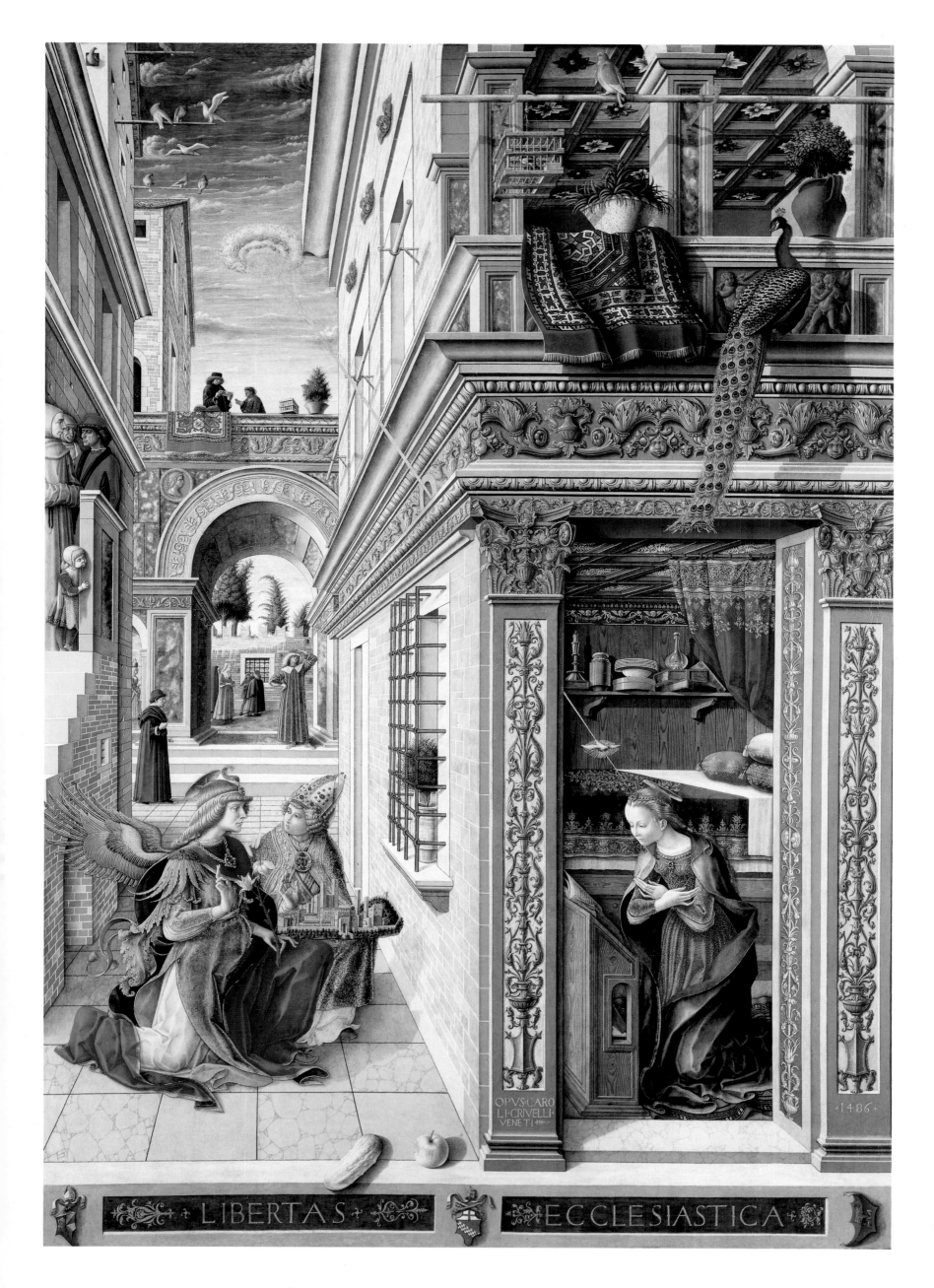

OPVS CARO
LI CRIVELLI
VENETI

·1486·

LIBERTAS · ECCLESIASTICA ·

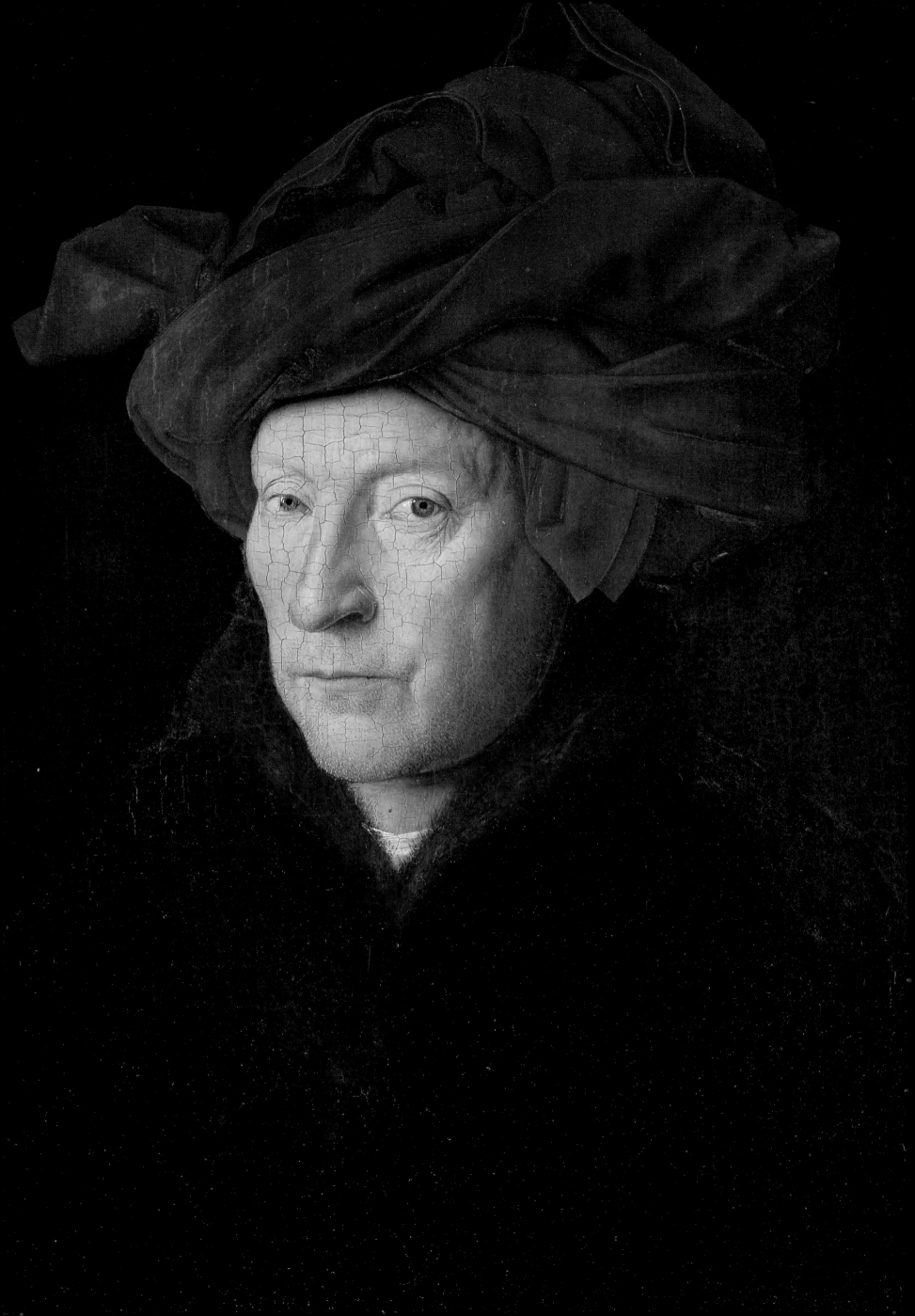

CHAPTER V

Fifteenth-Century Painting
in the Netherlands

Fifteenth-century Flanders was primarily an urban culture, nurtured by three important sources of patronage: the Burgundian court, which shared a passion for the arts with an aspiring bourgeoisie; the Church, which commissioned a wealth of paintings and illuminated manuscripts; and the guilds, who enjoyed considerable status in civic and religious affairs, and often endowed their own chapels with altarpieces.

In addition to collecting art, the court (like others in Europe) also provided important commissions for temporary decorations. These must have occupied many artists, although little evidence of them remains. They formed part of any major event, such as ducal weddings, funerals and state entries into towns, and included elaborate triumphal arches and street decorations, as well as *tableaux vivants* which were probably related to contemporary sculpture groups. The most celebrated of such displays was Philip the Good's 'Banquet of the Pheasant' held in Lille in 1454, and the state entry of Charles the Bold and Margaret of York into Bruges in 1468.

The Dukes of Burgundy adopted the Chartreuse de Champmol, a Carthusian monastery near Dijon (destroyed in the French Revolution) as the focus of their artistic patronage and as their dynastic burial place. A number of highly important artists gathered here, led by the sculptor Claus Sluter (died 1405/6), and the International Gothic painter Melchior Broederlam (*c.* 1378–1409).

Sluter's tomb of Philip the Bold was his last work, and

123 JAN VAN EYCK Man in a Turban 1433

One of Van Eyck's most detailed portraits, this picture is notable for its light effects and the way in which the head turns suddenly to look at the spectator. It has been suggested that it may be a self portrait, but an alternative suggestion of the artist's father-in-law has also been proposed for the sitter.

along with his other surviving sculpture exercised an immeasurable influence on Netherlandish painting. Just as the sculptor Ghiberti's ideas at the same moment in Florence were instrumental in the evolution of painted form, new ideas in the Netherlands were also first explored in three dimensions. Sluter's expressive use of drapery folds and monumental forms transformed the approach of painters, notably that of Robert Campin (*c.* 1375–1444), the Master of Flémalle, the founder of fifteenth-century Netherlandish painting.

Until the Hundred Years' War (1337–1453), the school of Paris had dominated painting in the Netherlands, but the situation then reversed and the ideas of the emerging Flemish school spread throughout Europe. The French called the style Franco-Flemish, which, at least until the dawn of the fifteenth century, was certainly true in part. During the first quarter of the fifteenth century, the International Gothic style (see Chapter III) began to lose favour as painters pursued a new realism. Besides the Master of Flémalle, these included the Van Eyck brothers and their followers: Petrus Christus, Rogier van der Weyden, Dieric Bouts, Hans Memlinc and Gerard David.

The complicating element for the study of painting in fifteenth-century Netherlands is the lack of documented facts, so that some artists' identities and even existence are questioned. Attribution by means of connoisseurship has always been much more important in early Netherlandish than in contemporary Italian art, with resulting uncertainties and diversities of opinion.

This also leads to a much greater reliance on the works of art themselves for indications of the development of schools and individuals – even of the stature of Van Eyck and Van der Weyden. Hieronymus Bosch is a case in point, with the most unfathomable development and chronology in fifteenth-century Netherlandish painting. A further complication is the fact that Protestant iconoclasm obliterated much pictorial evidence in the northern Netherlands.

The depiction of popular Flemish saints helps to give the original location of many pictures, since a cult was often connected with one particular place. Many are saints who rarely occur in art outside the Netherlands. Thus, at Tournai St Piat enjoyed special favour, while Sts Bavo, Amelberga and Donatian are often seen in paintings along with the English saints, Hugh of Lincoln, Edmund, Mildred and Oswald.

The Master of Flémalle

Of all the painters designated 'Master of' because their precise identity was long unknown, the Master of Flémalle is the most celebrated because of his great importance for fifteenth-century painting. He is generally regarded as its principal catalyst. His most significant immediate predecessors, who can likewise only be discussed as 'Masters', were both active in Hamburg. Master Francke painted in the International Gothic Style in the early fifteenth century and had exceptionally close links with Burgundy; and Master Bertram (active 1367–1414/15) was a German painter from Westphalia who attained a considerable reputation in his adopted city. Both painters reveal the movement of new ideas in Northern Europe which plays such an important role in the development of Netherlandish art.

In the world of these two masters can be seen the earliest impetus in Northern painting to progress from Late Gothic principles. Master Bertram's *Grabow Altar* (Kunsthalle, Hamburg) dates from 1379, and shows an understanding of the Bohemian painting favoured in Prague at the court of Charles IV (1316–78). He was King of Bohemia from 1346, and Holy Roman Emperor from 1355, and his cultivated court attracted artists from as far afield as France and Siena.

Master Francke's main surviving work is an altarpiece also in the Kunsthalle, Hamburg, and known as the *Englandfahrer Altarpiece* because it was painted for the guild of merchants who traded with England. Its refined, delicate style and colour and various iconographical features indicate that the artist knew both Byzantine art and Netherlandish painting, and this establishes him on more than a local stage. It is surmised that his latest known painting, the *Man of Sorrows* (Kunsthalle, Hamburg), must date from about 1430, and its use of light and shade and carefully controlled outline mark a distinct progression in the rendering of nature.

The Master of Flémalle takes over where Master Francke's stylishness and tentative attempts at naturalism leave off. His name derives from three pictures (notably the very beautiful *Saint Veronica* – see plate 124), which were once wrongly believed to have come from Flémalle, near Liège. There is now almost unanimous agreement that this 'master' was in fact the painter Robert Campin, who was active in Tournai 1406–44, but from whom there is no documented work. Few now adhere to the idea that the Master of Flémalle was the young Rogier van der Weyden. Campin's style leads directly to that of his pupil, Jacques Daret (1406–68 or later), and Van der Weyden himself (1399/1400–64), who was almost certainly another of his pupils.

Campin was born possibly in Valenciennes, in about 1375, and obtained citizenship in Tournai in 1410, where he began taking pupils some five years later. Significantly, Tournai was better known for its sculpture than its painting at this time. In 1423, Campin was elected dean of the painters' guild. He was a member of one of the three city councils, and his civic importance is shown by the intervention of the Count of Holland's daughter on his behalf, when he was charged with a dissolute relationship with one Laurent Polette. Many of our suppositions about the development of early fifteenth-century Netherlandish painting depend on documents connected with Robert Campin.

The Master of Flémalle's principal aims seem to have appeared early, and to have been dominated by an urge to render the Christian stories with tangible figures in credible natural settings and space. This matches the aspirations of artists of his generation in Italy, but may also derive from the experiences of Northern painters who had visited Italy in the post-Giotto period. It also has direct parallels in the incomparable work of the Limbourg Brothers, who all died in 1416 (see Chapter VI).

Shortly after 1421 (just as Masaccio was emerging in Florence), the Master painted his first masterpiece in an independent style, the *Entombment* (Courtauld Institute Galleries, London). This has distinctly plebeian figures and retains the decorated gold background of medieval painting, but has a formal grandeur which might lead one to believe that its painter had studied Sluter, the only Northern sculptor capable of such monumentality at this time. Its realism is startling (notably in the angels' expression of grief) compared with its predecessors, as are all the components soon to be characteristic of Flemish painting – expressive gesture, individualized facial expression and, most importantly, a full sense of the event's innate drama and tragedy. In the wings, a new feeling for depth is evident, and the landscape setting of the Crucifixion almost suggests the direct observation of nature. Hebrew inscriptions add a further touch of authenticity, and were extremely rare in Flemish painting at this date.

In the *Betrothal of the Virgin* (Museo del Prado, Madrid), now assumed to be the Master's next painting, the crowd scene in the great Gothic church is memorable for its rendering of jostling people anxious not be excluded from the ceremony. In this painting, a major step forward has been taken from the Courtauld *Entombment*, since the artist seems not to accept the limitation of a gold background, but wants to give the viewer the pleasurable illusion of participating in the event as if seen in real space. Two grisaille panels on the outside of the altarpiece show *Saint Clare* and *Saint James the Greater* and again vividly evoke the work of Claus Sluter. The *Nativity* (Musée des Beaux Arts, Dijon) perfects these tendencies, particularly in the very deep landscape, which prefigures much later Netherlandish painting. In all of these paintings, the artist is extending his use of visual symbols with increasing confidence.

The Master's experiments culminate in the great *Mérode Altarpiece* (see plate 150) which centres on the indoor *Annunciation*, is filled with symbolism, and carries the promise of the great Netherlandish art to come. In spite of its uncomfortable raked perspective and the awkward relationship of the two principal figures to their setting, the altarpiece excels in its rendering of many delightful details.

The Master's work then follows two divergent trends, one leading to the homely intimacy of the *Virgin and Child before a Fire Screen* (National Gallery, London) normally dated about 1428, the other moving in a more grandiose direction. The latter is first seen in the *Virgin in Glory* of 1428–30 (Musée Granet, Aix-en-Provence) with its miraculously elevated throne set against a superb and distant landscape, and culminates in the three pivotal and large-scaled Frankfurt pictures, the *Virgin and Child, Saint Veronica* (see plate 124) and the grisaille *Trinity* in its *trompe-l'oeil* niche. *Saint Veronica* in particular is more difficult to associate with Campin's style, since the saturated richness of the saint's garments and her statuesque remoteness might suggest a later dating. What is certain, however, is that the tentativeness of the Courtauld *Entombment*

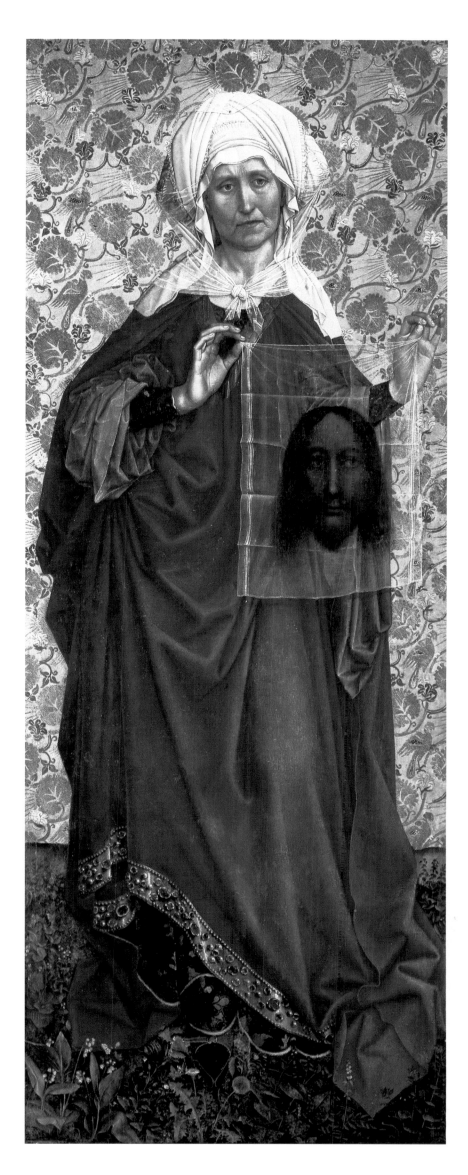

124 THE MASTER OF FLÉMALLE Saint Veronica c.1430–34
This is the most beautiful of the three large panels in Frankfurt from which the master takes his name, since they supposedly come from Flémalle, near Liège. The others are the Virgin and Child *and a grisaille* Trinity*, which originally formed the back of* Saint Veronica*. The intense expression and statuesque form of the saint make this picture one of the most impressive of the painter's inventions.*

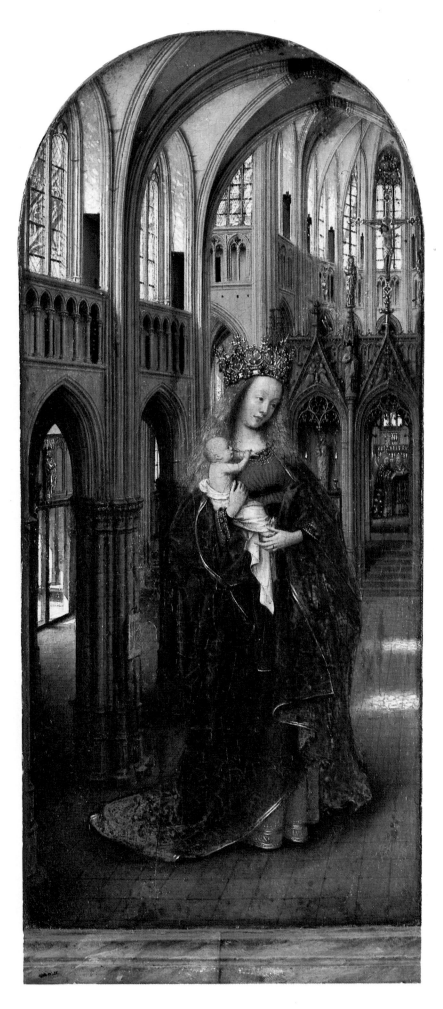

125 JAN VAN EYCK *The Madonna in the Church c.1425 Originally this was the left half of a diptych, and it is the culminating point of the painter's early period prior to the Ghent Altarpiece. The Virgin's crown identifies her as the Queen of Heaven, the pearls and precious stones are symbols of her royal dignity and chosen state. On her gown the damaged inscription comes from Solomon 7.29, which praises the Virgin as 'more beautiful than the sun', and the sunlight streaming through glass refers to her virginity. Since early Christian times the Mother of God was identified with a temple and the house of God, since at Christ's incarnation he dwelt in her as a temple. This may be echoed in the Virgin's over-large dimensions within the Gothic church setting. Among many other Marian symbols are the statue between two burning candles, referring to the Virgin as an altar of Christ. Two angels in liturgical vestments refer to Mary's priestly role.*

Jan and Hubert van Eyck

If the painting of the Master of Flémalle provides an opening fanfare for fifteenth-century Netherlandish art, the Van Eyck brothers created the art which we associate with the fullest manifestation of its highest qualities. Controversy surrounds the contribution of Hubert (died 1426?), but Jan (*c.*1390–1441) today reigns supreme as the greatest artist of his age – a prince among court painters. He even adopted a princely motto, '*Als ick Kan*' – as best I can – in accord with the improving status of painters.

His reputation was established in the Netherlands during his lifetime, and after his death it spread south of the Alps. Within a decade the Italian antiquarian collector, Ciriaco Pizzicoli d'Ancona, noted his fame, and he received lavish praise from Antonio Filarete in the 1460s. Twenty years later Van Eyck was singled out by Raphael's father, Giovanni Santi. His name became a by-word for perfection in the oil technique, and he was even credited by early writers, including Vasari, with its invention.

The *Ghent Altarpiece* (see plate 149) became an object of pilgrimage for painters such as Dürer, and for the Dutch writer on art, Karel van Mander, Van Eyck stood at the head of Netherlandish art. The luminous perfection he achieved through applying pigment layers with numerous glazes, which have retained their brilliance, is unrivalled. His use of colour is, however, unemotional. This, coupled with his astonishing virtuosity in the rendering of detail and differentiation of texture, makes him the supreme technician in European painting. His late grisaille *Saint Barbara* (see plate 34), although probably a finished work, provides a key to Van Eyck's methods.

Surprisingly, we do not know where he trained and his first recorded appearance is in 1422 at The Hague, on

has been replaced by an absolute assurance. This assurance is also seen in the beautiful *Portrait of Woman* in the National Gallery, London, which is normally associated with the Master, and compared unfavourably with *A Man* (also National Gallery, London), whose weakness of handling is attributed to his workshop.

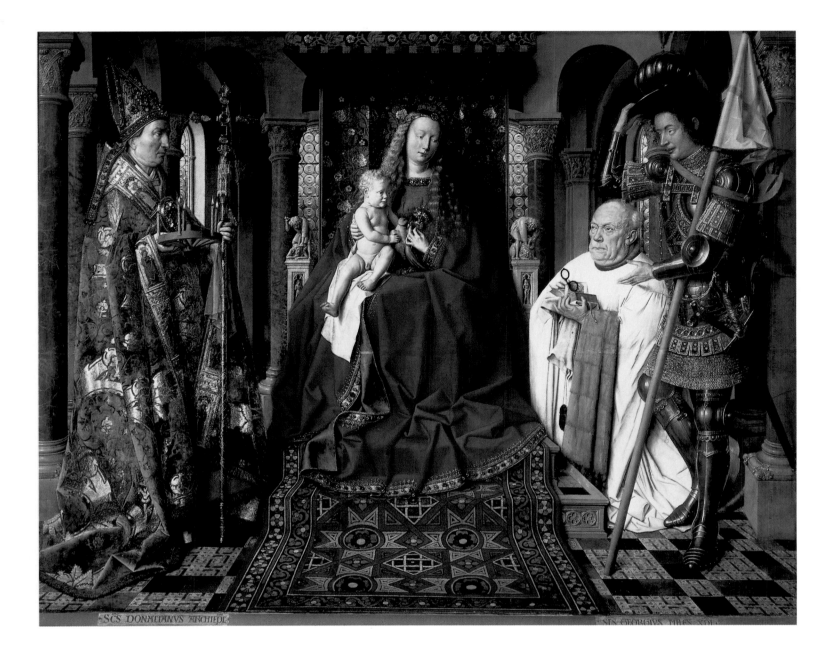

126 JAN VAN EYCK Madonna and Child with Canon van der
Paele 1434–6
One of the most richly detailed Flemish paintings of its period, this
was commissioned by Canon van der Paele for the former St
Donatian church in Bruges. The Virgin is seated in the choir of a
church which is decorated with sculptures showing Cain Killing
Abel *and* Samson and the Lion. *On the throne are two tiny*
statues of Adam and Eve. St Donatian is at the left in a sumptuous
blue brocade cope, while Van der Paele kneels at the right behind his
patron, St George, who presents him to the Virgin. The painter is
shown kneeling, on the saint's buckler. An inscription on the frame
says it was commissioned in 1434.

entering the service of the Count of Holland, John of
Bavaria. By this time he already had apprentices. After the
Count's death, Van Eyck found a new patron in Philip the
Good, Duke of Burgundy, who appointed him official
painter on 19 May 1425. He was also the Duke's *varlet de
chambre* or equerry, and thus occupied a position comparable with that of Rubens two centuries later, as a great
painter-diplomat who held the confidence of kings. He
settled in Bruges, where he spent the rest of his life apart

from secret diplomatic missions to Spain and Portugal
between 1526 and 1536. On his two Tournai visits, it is
likely that he studied and benefited from Campin's work.
After Philip's marriage to Isabella of Portugal in 1430,
there are few mentions of Van Eyck, except that he
acquired a house in Bruges in 1432, had ten children, and
painted and gilded six statues on the façade of Bruges
Town Hall in 1535.

Jan van Eyck's artistic personality is established by the
existence of nine pictures which he signed and dated. In
all, about twenty-five pictures are traditionally accepted as
his. The first painting ascribed to him is one of the most
delightful renderings of the Madonna and Child in fifteenth-century art, the *Madonna in the Church*, painted
about 1425 (see plate 125). A spectacular debut, albeit still
in the International Gothic style, this already transcends
all its medieval details with a richness and vitality which
he was rarely to surpass. The immense sculptural Virgin is
completely out of scale with the magnificent Gothic
church in which she stands like a miraculous apparition
(which she is no doubt intended to suggest). Everything
contributes to a sense of mystical beauty – light, colour,

the ethereal Virgin and the various Marian symbols, which already form part of Van Eyck's pictorial language. The astonishing realism of the architecture, permeated by memorable atmospheric effects, makes this an emotional as much as a devotional experience. Although the same effects are present in his *Annunciation* of some three years later (National Gallery of Art, Washington), the peculiar magic of the earlier painting is greatly diluted.

The *Ghent Altarpiece* centres on *The Adoration of the Lamb*. Its frame carries an inscription which states that it was begun by 'the painter Hubert van Eyck, than whom none was greater' and completed by 'Jan, second in art' on 6 May 1432. If this were accepted, it could throw all attributions to Jan into confusion, were not the few works associated with Hubert of inferior inspiration and technical quality. These include two panels forming a diptych

127 PETRUS CHRISTUS Portrait of a Young Woman c.1460–73 *The sitter's clothing seems to correspond with that of Maria Baroncelli-Portinari in a Memlinc portrait of the early 1470s in the Metropolitan Museum, New York, but some critics assert that the clothing is French, not Burgundian, and that this was the painting listed in the 1492 inventory of Lorenzo de'Medici's collection as by 'Pietro Cresti da Bruggia'.*

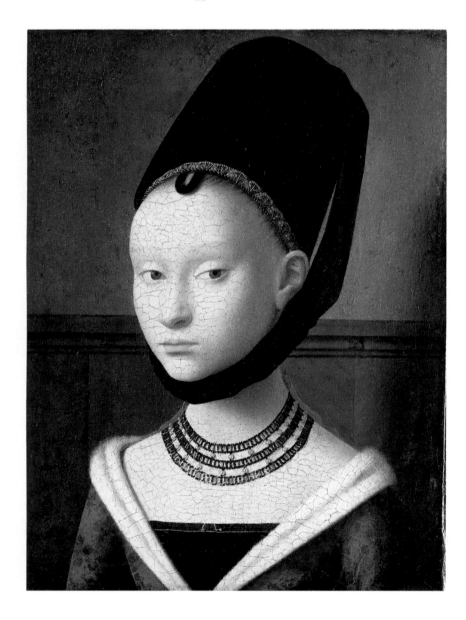

showing the *Crucifixion*, the *Last Judgement* and an unconnected *Annunciation* (all Metropolitan Museum of Art, New York). Even if we accept that Hubert (and others) had a hand in its conception and execution, the *Ghent Altarpiece* forms the basis for the study of all Jan's works.

His next signed and dated work after the altarpiece is the *Ince Hall Madonna* of 1433 (National Gallery of Victoria, Melbourne) which appears to be a copy of his own original. He used this type with even greater monumentality in the near-contemporary *Lucca Madonna* (Städelsches Kunstinstitut, Frankfurt). The *Madonna of the Chancellor Nicolas Rolin* (see plate 142) probably followed close on its heels. This, like the background of the *Ghent Altarpiece*, is a monument to the development of landscape. The human figure seems to have fascinated him increasingly, and the greatest achievements of his last decade (with the exception of the *Dresden Triptych* in the Dresden Gemäldegalerie) were in portraiture.

Although Van Eyck is known to have painted a bathing female nude (possibly reflected in Memlinc's *Bathsheba*, see plate 154), his remaining work is either religious or portraiture. The *Rolin* and *The Madonna with Canon van der Paele* of 1436 (see plate 126) lie midway between the two, as they include portraits of donors. Just as the *Ghent Altarpiece* is unrivalled in religious art of the time, so *The Marriage of Giovanni Arnolfini and Giovanna Cenami* (see plate 144) remains the quintessential portrait, and sums up Van Eyck's love of form explained by light, detail, human physiognomy and symbolism. The London *Portrait of a Man in a Turban* (see plate 123) may be a self portrait and must have provided the model for any subsequent likeness of its kind. Van Eyck also became involved in illuminated miniature painting in the *Turin-Milan Book of Hours*.

Petrus Christus

Van Eyck is thought to have collaborated with Petrus Christus (died 1472/3), who was probably his pupil. Christus clearly absorbed the externals of Van Eyck's style more than any other painter, and was possibly responsible for the studio work which spread his master's ideas and imagery. The intimate *Saint Jerome in his Study* (Institute of Arts, Detroit) may be a collaborative work of the early 1440s, and a version of the painting which belonged to Lorenzo the Magnificent and inspired both Botticelli and Ghirlandaio. Its type was extremely popular in Central and Northern Italy from the mid-fifteenth century onwards, and Christus may have had more impact than has been thought on the growing interest in interior views.

Not many facts are known about Christus, although he may be the 'Piero from Bruges' who was recorded in Milan, at the court of the Sforzas in 1457. He seems to have been born in one of the two towns called Baerlehe and the first mention of him is in July 1444. It was then that he was granted citizenship of Bruges with specific mention of his being permitted to work as a painter there. Although Van Eyck had then been dead for three years, there is no reason to suppose that Christus had not already been active in his studio, which he probably inherited. He is the painter most likely to have completed some of Van Eyck's works unfinished at his death, such as the Detroit *Saint Jerome.*

In 1462, Christus and his wife were admitted to the 'Confraternity of the Dry Tree' and the next year he painted what was probably a banner for a religious procession. Christus perpetuated the principles that Van Eyck and Campin had established, and evolved new elements. He quoted several of Van Eyck's works directly in his own *Exeter Madonna* (Gemäldegalerie, Berlin) which probably closes his first phase in about 1444.

In the *Lamentation* of the later 1440s (Musées Royaux des Beaux-Arts, Brussels) and *Nativity* of the mid-1450s (National Gallery of Art, Washington) the influence of Rogier van der Weyden is felt, and it becomes clear to what extent Christus was an eclectic. One area in which he achieved a high degree of originality was portraiture, and it is perhaps here that any trace of his supposed Italian journey might be sought. In 1446 Christus signed and dated two portraits, the *Carthusian Saint* (Metropolitan Museum of Art, New York) and *Edward Grimston* (Gorhambury Collection, St Albans). Three years later, he signed and dated one of his most original ideas, *Saint Eligius and the Lovers* (see plate 145). This shows clearly the absorption in detail which distinguishes many of his later interior scenes, such as the *Virgin and Child in a Gothic Interior* (Nelson Gallery-Atkins Museum, Kansas City). The *Virgin and Child with Saints Jerome and Francis* of 1457 (Stadelsches Kunstinstitut, Frankfurt) seems to be the earliest dated Northern painting using geometric perspective and a single vanishing point, while his famous *Portrait of a Young Woman* (see plate 127) provides his most stylish final statement.

Rogier van der Weyden

Like Van Eyck, Rogier van der Weyden (1399/1400–64) enjoyed contemporary fame in his own country, and also south of the Alps. Financially, he was very successful, and ran a large, productive studio, which spread versions of his

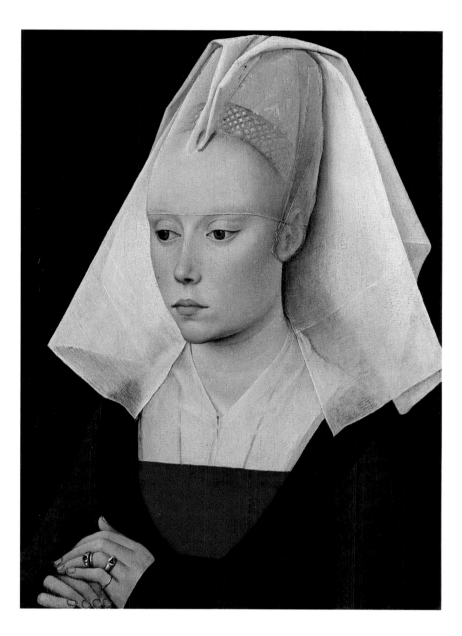

128 ROGIER VAN DER WEYDEN Portrait of a Lady *c.*1450–60
This extremely beautiful painting has on its reverse a frontal image of Christ Crowned with Thorns, *which is of poor quality. On the front, the sitter's expression suggests that she is lost in contemplation. Her pose and gaze suggest that the portrait – one of Rogier's finest – did not form half of a diptych, and from the costume it can be deduced that he painted her after 1440. A similar portrait by the same artist is in the National Gallery, Washington.*

work far and wide. His paintings reached Germany, France, Italy and Spain within his lifetime, and his immediate influence was greater than Van Eyck's. Little definite knowledge of his career has come down to us, and the body of his work has been reconstructed on the basis of style and a few known facts. There are no signed or dated paintings and most of those cited in contemporary sources remain unknown. Those that are known, however, show a homogeneity of style from which our attempt to understand his art must start.

His early years are a matter of conjecture. In 1427, a painter called Rogelet de la Pâture was admitted to Campin's workshop in Tournai, and is recorded as leaving five years later under the title 'Maistre Rogier'. Since

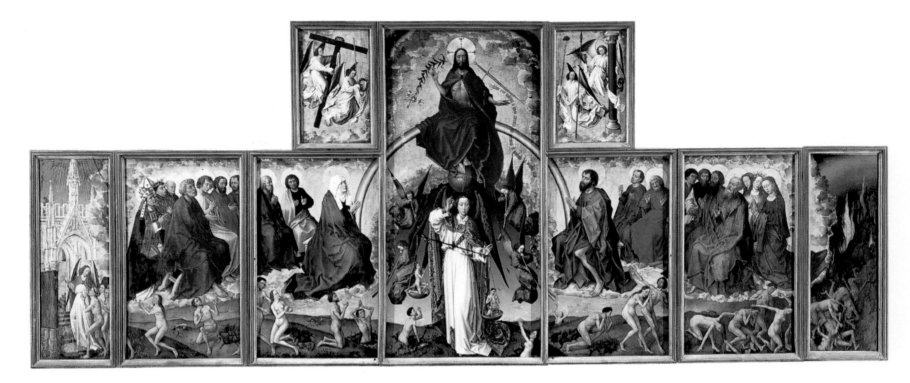

129 ROGIER VAN DER WEYDEN Last Judgement Altarpiece
*c.*1444–8

*Rogier's most important painting, this was created in collaboration
with his studio in the mid to late 1440s for the Hôtel-Dieu in
Beaune, although it is no longer in its original position there. It is
conceived on a huge scale, and is about eighteen feet wide when
opened. It was commissioned by Nicholas Rolin, and the patron and
his third wife Guigonne de Salins are shown kneeling on prie-dieux
and adoring the grisaille figures of Sts Sebastian and Anthony, with
the Annunciation above. The interior is dominated by the grandiose*
Christ in Judgement with the Archangel Michael adored by
the Virgin and Saint John the Baptist. *Resurrected figures judged
by St Michael in the centre are condemned either to Hell at the right
or Heaven at the left, and various other figures including possibly
Rolin's confessor also appear.*

both the Flemish (Weyden) and French form (Pâture) of
his name mean 'Rogier of the Meadow', is seems reasonable to assume that the two names relate to the same person. He then moved to Brussels, where he became city
painter in 1436, receiving prestigious official commissions. Like Van Eyck's, Van der Weyden's surviving
paintings comprise religious themes and aristocratic
portraiture, although he never became a court painter.
Throughout his life, he maintained contact with Tournai,
and masses were said there for him after his death.

Throughout Van der Weyden's later work, there are
indications of his knowledge of Southern art, as in the
Pietà forming the central panel of the *Miraflores Altarpiece*
of the mid-1440s (Staatliche Museen, Berlin), where the
Virgin's last kiss to her son derives from Italian iconography. Although Van der Weyden cannot be called
'Italianate', his painting reflects Quattrocento ideas more
than any of his contemporaries.

In 1450, the Holy Year, he made a pilgrimage to
Rome and painted the *Entombment* (Uffizi, Florence),
once in the Medici collections, catalogued as a Dürer. Its
iconography and composition derive from Fra Angelico
and led some critics to attribute it to Van der Weyden's
Lombard pupil, Zanetto Bugatto. Even more 'Florentine'
is his *Madonna with Four Saints* (Städelsches Kunstinstitut,
Frankfurt) which bears the Medici arms, depicts four
saints connected with the Medici, and follows a *sacra con-
versazione* prototype deriving from painters such as
Domenico Veneziano, in which the Madonna and Child
and saints are all shown together in one scene.

Van der Weyden received commissions from many
members of the Burgundian court, including the Bishop
of Tournai, Jean Chevrot, and Peter Bladelin, Duke
Philip's controller of finance and founder of Middelburg.
The latter's *Nativity* triptych of 1452–5 (Gemäldegalerie,
Berlin) is among Van der Weyden's more monumental
later works. The cultivated Chancellor Nicholas Rolin
commissioned from him a huge altarpiece centred on the
Last Judgement for the hospital foundation under his
patronage, the Hospice de Beaune, or Hôtel-Dieu (see
plate 129).

Van der Weyden's style does not show dramatic developments. His earliest manner, dating from 1432, reflects
Van Eyck and is represented by the delightful, tiny
panel (18.5 × 12 cm) of the *Virgin and Child* enthroned
under a delicate Gothic canopy (Kunsthistorisches
Museum, Vienna). Van Eyckian elements are further
explored in the much grander *Annunciation* of two or
three years later (see plate 140) but this picture is perhaps
the first where Van der Weyden begins to find a personal
manner. He is more linear than Van Eyck and incorpo-
rates a greater love of circumstantial detail, particularly of

domestic interiors which reflect the luxury (if not the comfort) prevalent in rich Burgundian homes.

Apart from the famous *Deposition* (see plate 141), Van der Weyden's major painting of the later 1430s is also one of his best-loved: *Saint Luke Painting the Virgin* (see plate 143). It is based on Van Eyck's *Rolin Madonna* (see plate 142) but offers a much more intimate interpretation of St Luke's encounter with the Virgin. A comparison of the Prado *Deposition* with the work of Campin clarifies the changes in Netherlandish painters' aims during this period. Compositions become much more sophisticated and fluid, and the more rustic Gothic elements in Campin are transformed into rhythmic patterns of great beauty. Perhaps most notable is the quality of portrait heads in Van der Weyden's religious painting, which immediately focuses attention on moving facial expressions. Such concentration on the human impact of a tragic scene is also one of Van der Weyden's major contributions, and must have been a reason for his international success. The

function of colour, too, has changed and its potential for unifying a multi-figure composition is increasingly exploited. All of this culminates in his magnificent late *Saint Columba Altarpiece* (see plate 42) with its splendid Romanesque architecture and lavish, courtly costume.

Van der Weyden's portraits, in addition to those included in his religious works, are among the most appealing in Netherlandish art, and include an impressive range of sitters, such as *Charles the Bold* (Gemäldegalerie, Berlin), and *Francesco d'Este* (Metropolitan Museum of Art, New York) who was educated in Brussels. Others form (or formed) part of small diptychs for private devotion, where the sitter is portrayed adoring the Virgin as in *Laurent Froiment* (Musées Royaux des Beaux-Arts, Brussels) and *Philippe de Croy* (Musée Royal des Beaux-Arts, Antwerp).

Dirk Bouts

Whereas the Master of Flémalle was an innovator in several spheres, and Van Eyck and Van der Weyden were great figure painters and portraitists, the achievement of Dirk (or Dieric) Bouts (Theodorik Romboutszoon, 1420s–1475) lay in other areas. His beautiful landscape

130 DIERIC BOUTS Deposition Altarpiece *c.*1450–55
Rogier van der Weyden's influence is clearly felt in this altarpiece, notably in the expressive female figures. Its Crucifixion, Deposition *and* Resurrection *borrow extensively from Rogier's compositions. The central scene is given great presence and monumentality by its placing within a fictive sculpted arch.*

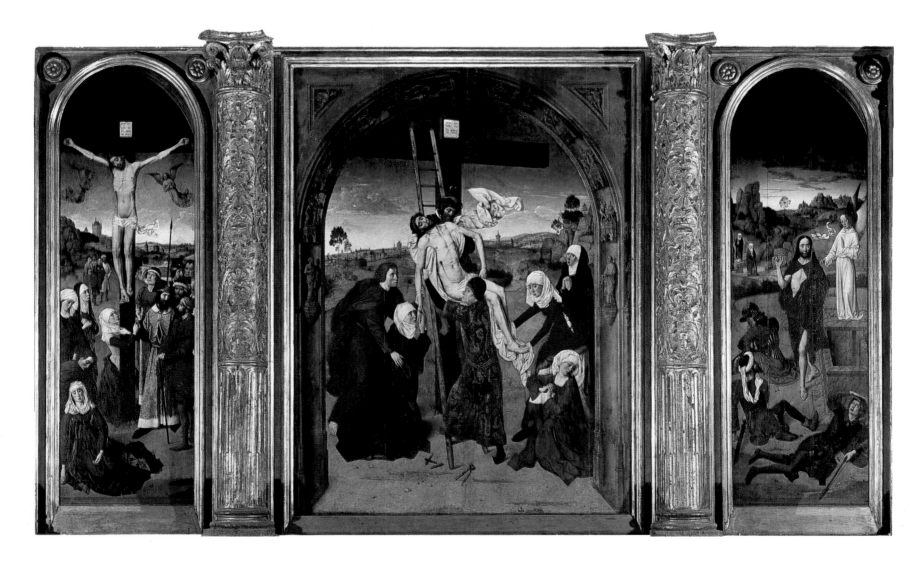

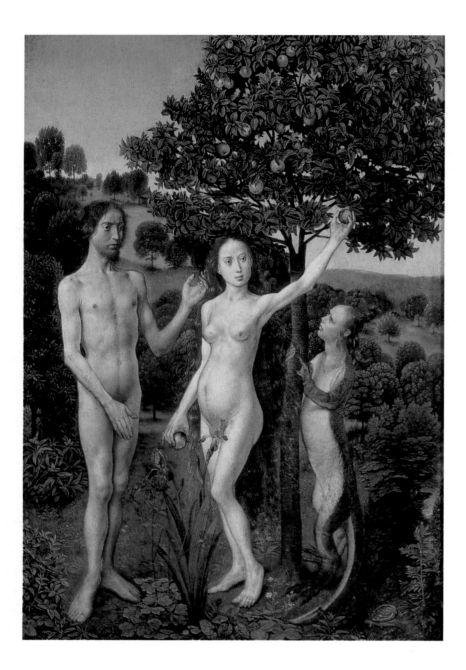

131 HUGO VAN DER GOES *Adam and Eve (The Fall of Man)*
*c.*1468–70
This forms half of a tiny divided diptych, the other part showing the
Lamentation. *The stories complement each other, as Christ's death*
was a direct consequence of man's Fall. The style echoes the Ghent
Altarpiece, *and the panel includes one of Hugo's most luxuriant*
landscapes, whose verdant flowing lines contrast with the painful
angularity of the two figures.

backgrounds and his perception of light were of great
importance for the development of Netherlandish and
German painting. His painting probably appealed to a
wider and less cultivated audience than that of his great
contemporaries.

His early style derives from Petrus Christus whom he
probably met in Bruges. He was born in Haarlem, but
from 1468 he was city painter at Louvain, having probably settled there between 1445 and 1448. About that
time he married Katharina van der Brugghen, whose
nickname Metten Gelde means 'with the money'. It was
there that he painted his most important commissions

(and only secure works), the *Last Supper Altarpiece* of
1464–7 (see plate 148) and two large panels showing
the *Justice of the Emperor Otto* which he painted for the
Hôtel de Ville in 1470–75 (Musées Royaux des Beaux-
Arts, Brussels).

The developments which Bouts brought to landscape
are already apparent in his earliest paintings, such as the
Infancy Altarpiece of the mid-1440s (Museo del Prado,
Madrid). One panel of this shows the *Visitation*, which
includes one of the most convincing landscapes
in Netherlandish painting up to that time. By means of
various devices, Bouts succeeds in painting the Virgin
and St Anne as if they are actually standing in the
countryside framed in a Gothic arch, and not against a
backdrop. These devices include a forward-curving patch
of lighter ground where the two figures are standing,
which seems to break into our space, and the skilful contrast of a steep nearby hill with the distant landscape.
Although Bouts later used further variations on this
scheme, he never again succeeded so well as in the effect
of this landscape. The balance of figures and landscape is
also very satisfying, making the whole a thoroughly
remarkable composition.

In the *Visitation*, the two women convey a remarkable
sense of volume, another rarity in Bouts' work, for his
figures are often awkward. This is particularly noticeable
in the two *Emperor Otto* panels in Brussels, where not only
are the figures grotesquely elongated, but the background
suggests a reversion to the type of landscape found in
earlier miniatures. It is almost tempting to think that a
conscious reference to some earlier prototypes was
intended. The *Deposition Altarpiece* (see plate 130) has a
supreme beauty of light and atmosphere which transcends
the somewhat inexpressive figures. Bouts' light effects are
perfected in the small private altarpiece known as the *Pearl
of Brabant* of the early 1460s (Alte Pinakothek, Munich).
In it the left panel, showing St John the Baptist, is bathed
in morning light, while St Christopher in the right-hand
panel is seen at sunset in a threatening landscape.
Unusually full of Marian symbols, this may have been
painted for a convent.

Individual heads in the *Emperor Otto* panels reveal the
mastery of portraiture attained by Bouts during his last
years, and the gently introspective *Portrait of a Man*
(National Gallery, London) painted in 1462, revitalizes a
device favoured by Christus, of placing the best-length
figure in the angle of a room. Unlike Van Eyck and Van
der Weyden, who painted some of the most memorable
likenesses of women, Bouts seems to have felt more at
home with male portraits. The great scene of the *Last
Supper Altarpiece* (see plate 148), which is so memorable

for its interior and atmosphere, makes it Bouts' undoubted masterpiece.

To Albert van Ouwater, active in the middle years of the century, Van Mander ambitiously credits the foundation of the Haarlem school of painters. The only painting accepted as his, however, is *The Raising of Lazarus* (Gemäldegalerie, Berlin), a charming scene set in a Romanesque church apse.

Hugo van der Goes

First documented in 1467, when he became a master in the Ghent painters' guild, Hugo van der Goes remains the great painter of the second half of the century. By the time of his death in about 1482, Italian painting had gained considerable importance for the North, and this increased as the Netherlands moved towards unification within the Holy Roman Empire in 1519. Van der Goes painted one of the most important Netherlandish paintings to enter Italy, the immense *Portinari Altarpiece* (see plate 151), on which other attributions to him are based.

What we know of Van der Goes presents him as a much more rounded 'personality' than any of his immediate predecessors, and one who captures the imagination. He became dean of the Ghent painters' guild in 1474, but entered the monastery of the Red Cloister near Brussels as a lay brother four years later. It is tempting to think that this was prompted by his tendency to religious melancholia, but he actively pursued his painting career and maintained contact outside the monastery. He was certainly not isolated, as he was visited by the future Emperor Maximilian, he received the Portinari commission there, and he travelled to Louvain in 1480 (appraising Bout's *Emperor Otto* panels) and to Cologne in 1481. During this journey he appears to have succumbed to acute depression which led to a fit of insanity. A year later he was dead.

The grandeur of the *Portinari Altarpiece* alone would have guaranteed Van der Goes a prominent place in art history, but his reputation rests on about fifteen paintings, none of which is signed or dated. Although there are arguments for the diptych showing the *Fall of Man* (see plate 131) and a *Lamentation* (Kunsthistorisches Museum, Vienna) being his earliest work it has been suggested that this is predated by the *Virgin and Child with Saint Anne and a Franciscan Donor* (Musées Royaux des Beaux-Arts, Brussels), possibly of about 1468. This does not fit with the style of any contemporary painter, and has much of the massive form which is a feature of Hugo's mature manner. It also includes a rolling landscape of great beauty such as he was to repeat many times.

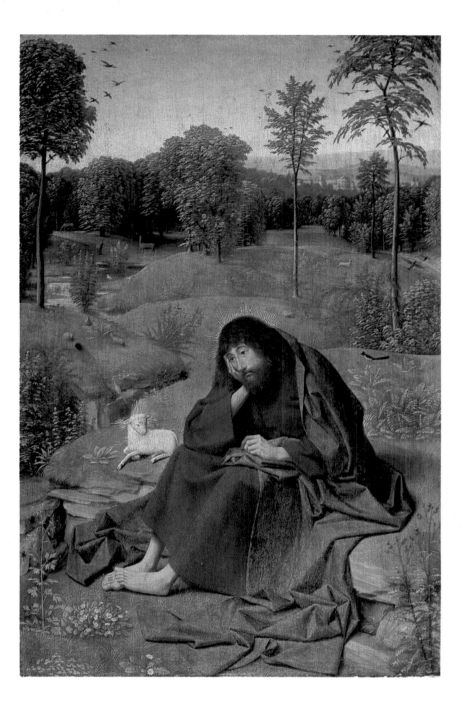

132 GEERTGEN TOT SINT JANS The Baptist in the Wilderness *c.*1490–95

St John is depicted lost in the contemplation of Christ's Passion and the grace of forgiveness of sins. The Lamb, a symbol of Christ, is seen next to him, according with St John's words, 'Behold the Lamb of God, which taketh away the sins of the world'. The saint is the patron of the Knights of St John, and this was probably painted as a devotional picture for a member of the Haarlem Order of St John, of which the artist was a lay member until his death at the age of twenty-eight. The desert is seen as a verdant landscape, and is one of the earliest in Netherlandish art to deal so confidently with space. Colour and textures are particularly well balanced.

The *Adoration of the Magi* panel (Gemäldegalerie, Berlin) was bought from the Monforte de Lemos monastery in Spain in 1914, and is all that survives of the Monforte triptych. Dates between 1472 and 1475 are given for this painting of extraordinary beauty, which makes sudden and immense strides in its realistic treatment of the visual world. The illusion of reality it gives is enhanced by rich colour, and its dramatic unity and large scale figures suggest that Van der Goes had either visited Italy or knew Italian painting very well. It was precisely these qualities in the *Portinari Altarpiece* which made such an impression on the Italians. No other Netherlandish painter could have tackled its huge scale.

The *Portinari Altarpiece* offers every facet of Van der Goes' style at its finest – remarkable portraiture, landscape, architecture, outstanding still life, delightful depictions of animals and richly varied colours. Above all, it gives a clear insight into the oil painting technique which was widely used by then in Northern painting. The one pure example of portraiture almost certainly by Van der Goes is the *Portrait of a Man* (Metropolitan Museum of Art, New York).

Another of Hugo's masterpieces (at least of design, since there is extensive overpainting), the so-called *Bonkil Panels* or 'Trinity Altarpiece' of the late 1470s, was destined for a foreign setting (see plates 133 and 134). The panels were probably the wings of a triptych whose central painting is lost, and show the *Holy Trinity Adored by Sir Edward Bonkil with Musical Angels* and *King James III and his Son presented by Saint Andrew* and *Queen Margaret presented by Saint George*.

In his last painting, the *Death of the Virgin* (Groeningemuseum, Bruges), Hugo attained a remarkable pathos. Its largely original composition and Christ's dramatic appearance in the light above the Virgin's bed indeed suggest a disturbed mind and convey an intensity that belies the Virgin's expression.

Geertgen Tot Sint Jans

A creator of particular individuality, Geertgen Tot Sint Jans (*c.*1460–*c.*1490) painted charming figures with smooth faces, dot-like eyes and squat, dolls' bodies. The best-known example of his work is the small *Nativity* in the National Gallery, London, with its magical lighting. Geertgen's name means 'Little Gerald of the Brethren of St John' since like Hugo van der Goes he was a lay brother, in his case at Haarlem. According to Van Mander (who says that he died at the age of twenty-eight), Dürer was an admirer of his painting. His sole documented work is a triptych of the *Crucifixion* which he painted for his monastery church. Of this only two parts survive (Kunsthistorisches Museum, Vienna). They show the *Burning of the Bones of Saint John the Baptist* and the *Lamentation of Christ*, and are fairly large, unlike most of the other pictures (about twelve or thirteen) attributed to him (see plate 132). The *Burning* (after 1484?) is a

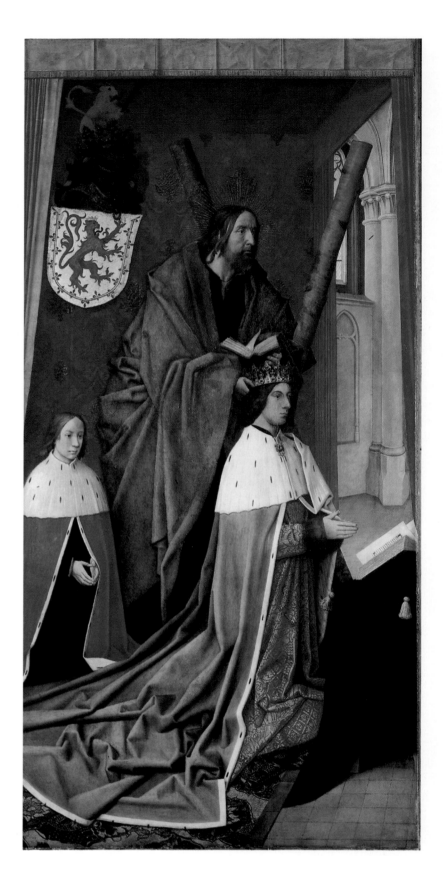

133 and 134 HUGO VAN DER GOES The Trinity Altarpiece *c.*1478–9

Links between Scotland and the Netherlands were strong due to commerce, and the Trinity Altarpiece is the most important survival of fifteenth-century painting in Scotland. It seems likely that it was commissioned by Edward Bonkil, first Provost of the Collegiate Church of the Holy Trinity in Edinburgh, whose brother was a successful Scottish merchant who settled in Bruges. Hugo van der Goes spent his last years in an Augustinian monastery near Brussels, and this foundation also controlled the royal Abbey of Holyrood in Edinburgh, which may account for the commission of this painting. On the reverse is the Holy Trinity Adored *by Sir Edward Bonkil.*

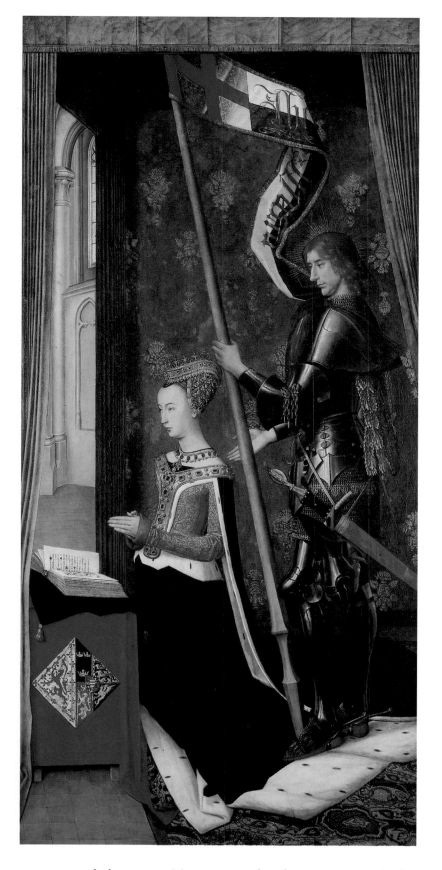

Hans Memlinc

More distinguished as a portraitist than as a painter of religious themes, Hans Memlinc (or Memling, *c.*1430–94) ran a large studio which perpetuated his ideas in this field. Although born near Frankfurt, he must have moved early in his life to the Netherlands since there is no indication of a German training. He was traditionally a pupil of Rogier van der Weyden, whose style appears in his precocious early work along with traces of Bouts' and Van der Goes' influences. The *Donne Triptych* of the early 1470s in the National Gallery, London, also quotes from Van Eyck.

Memlinc became the leading painter in Bruges, and according to tax records was among its richest citizens – so rich indeed that he had to pay the Emperor Maximilian's wealth tax levied as a result of the war with France. He seems to have moved from Brussels to Bruges after 1464, the year of Van der Weyden's death, and simply continued where his master had left off, but in a softer and less demonstrative style. Once evolved, this style showed little change, which complicates the dating of his work. Much has been made of Memlinc's apparent lack of strong religious convictions, but in effect the gentle melancholy of his work (particularly evident in the face of *Bathsheba* – see plate 154) may appear as restraint, and was probably one of the reasons for his immense success.

Like Bouts, Memlinc was fascinated by landscape, and his views, with their clever placing of architecture in the middle distance, are sometimes highly original. His landscape suggests tranquillity much as Perugino's simplified backgrounds did at the same time in Italy. Memlinc's, however, perhaps deliberately, do not relate to the mood of the subject, however intense that may be. In his *Scenes of the Passion* of about 1470 (Galleria Sabauda, Turin) fantastic architecture runs riot, rendering the figures subsidiary to a surreal forest of towers, turrets, windows and doorways. Something of this fantasy is also seen in the background of the *Martyrdom of Saint Sebastian* probably painted at the same period (Musées Royaux des Beaux-Arts, Brussels). *Saint Sebastian* illustrates the reticence with which the nude was still regarded in the North, whereas in Italy it had already become a proper and expressive subject. One major exception is his own extraordinary *Bathsheba* (see plate 154) – a rarity in this period.

Fantasy and reality meet in Memlinc's famous *Chasse of Saint Ursula* of 1489 (Hospital of St John, Bruges) – a richly carved and gilded wooden Gothic reliquary framing painted panels. The small size of these panels inspired in Memlinc a particularly concentrated version of his usual style, with generously scaled figures, colour in keeping

crowded composition not related to any particular Netherlands tradition. The possibility that he was a pupil of the Haarlem painter, Albert Van Ouwater, tells us little except that the latter's style also seems to belong to a semi-naive tradition.

Related to Geertgen Tot Sint Jans is the 'Master of the Virgo inter Virgines' (active *c.*1470–*c.*1500) who is called after the picture on this theme in the Rijksmuseum, Amsterdam. He is known to have worked in Delft, and was also active as a designer of woodcuts for books. His other major work is the *Entombment* (Walker Art Gallery, Liverpool).

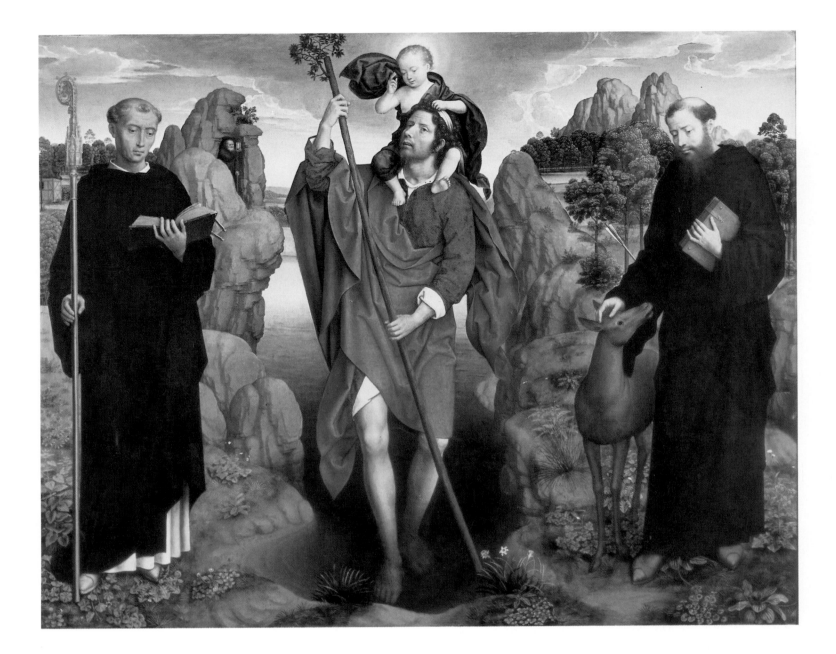

135 HANS MEMLINC Saint Christopher Altarpiece 1484
The left wing of this triptych shows the donor, William Moreel, with
his sons, presented by his patron saint William of Maleval. On the
right wing his wife Barbara van Vlaenderberghe appears with her
patron saint and daughters. In the central panel, St Christopher is
flanked by St Giles and St Maurus.

with the jewel-like object itself, and inventive background views. The palette used is unlike what Friedländer characterized as Memlinc's 'cool, opaque colouring', and the style recalls miniature painting rather than Memlinc's grander panels. In its combination of sculpture with painting of the highest quality, the *Chasse* is one of the most beautiful objects of its kind to survive from this period. It is also one of the finest works in the Memlinc Museum, in the Hospital of St John in Bruges, one of the few places where sufficient work by a single painter of this period is collected, allowing a rounded view of his style.

The *Portinari Altarpiece* must have been well-known prior to its departure for Italy, but a comparison with Memlinc's *Floreins Triptych* (Hospital of St John, Bruges) reveals a common tendency of the end of the century, for painters to hark back to Van Eyck and Van der Weyden; similarly the *Saint Christopher Altarpiece* (see plate 135) pays homage to Bouts.

The sheer number of portraits (around thirty) attributed to Memlinc indicates his popularity in this sphere, although there is no record of his reputation as a portraitist. He was probably much more inventive in portraiture than his contemporaries, and his range included the three-quarter length *Martin van Niuwenhove* (St John's Hospital, Bruges), a textural *tour-de-force* with evocative background details of windows, stained glass and shutters. The *Portrait of a Man with a Medal* (see plate 153), on the other hand, is Italianate in influence.

Memlinc is one of the most appealing artists of his age, and his style largely discards Late Gothic elements in favour of a contemplative art with, as one critic put it, 'the gift of inducing serene contemplation'. For the nineteenth century, he was the most important Netherlandish painter after Jan van Eyck. This judgement may have been based on the survival of a greater number of attributed paintings than is usual with his contemporaries. His lack of fanaticism also endeared him to the Victorians.

Gerard David

Like his contemporary Bosch, Gerard David, who died in 1523, was a transitional painter who carried fifteenth-century developments into the next century. David, however, remained much closer to those earlier traditions. He filled Memlinc's place in Bruges on his death, having probably arrived from Oudewater, near Gouda, between 1480 and 1484. David's career there saw the final decline of the city as an innovative centre, but he probably played a significant role in the developing export trade in pictures. And although Antwerp was already assuming its new importance through Metsys (see plate 275), in some ways David also achieved many of the aims of the northern High Renaissance in his later work. It is possible that he painted the first pure landscapes in Flemish painting, in his altarpiece wings in the Mauritshuis at The Hague.

With the exception of a possible visit to Genoa between 1510 and 1515 (where he may have painted the simple and extraordinary *Crucifixion* in the Palazzo Bianco), he remained in Bruges until a recorded visit of unknown duration to Antwerp in 1515. However, instead of becoming merely a provincial painter he evolved a highly personal style in which Late Gothic elaboration is completely replaced by a human element of warm naturalism.

It seems likely that David arrived in Bruges as a master with an established reputation, since he obtained an important commission, now lost, from the city's magistrates in 1488 – the year he was elected a member of the painters' guild council. Three years later, he became its dean. *Christ Nailed to the Cross* (see plate 136) is probably one of his earliest works, painted on his arrival in Bruges, and it already indicates the essential elements of his style. Its realism is striking, and above all, he attempts to imbue the composition with its full drama by filling the entire centre stage with the cross, and focusing attention on Christ's subtly observed expression of fear. David's model at this point must have been Hugo van der Goes.

He reached his first maturity in the *Judgement of Cambyses* of 1498 (Groeningemuseum, Bruges), which is full of colourful incident, but also reveals a new energy in the composition of figure groups. This tendency is perfected in the early years of the new century with *Canon Bernardinus de Salviatis and Three Saints* (National Gallery, London). During that first decade he worked in a more grandiose manner than at any other time. Perhaps the most important example of this style is the *Madonna and Child with Saints and Musical Angels* of 1509 (Musée des Beaux-Arts, Rouen). The painting is unique in David's work for its combination of elegance and calm grandeur, and was important to the painter himself. It includes his own and his wife's portraits, and was given by him to the Carmelite Convent in Bruges.

136 GERARD DAVID Christ Nailed to the Cross *c.*1480–5
This central panel from a triptych shows three separate scenes, and is unusual in its tightly packed and uptilted composition, which attempts to introduce a novel sense of immediacy and drama. Hugo van der Goes' influence can be seen in the realism of Christ's terrified expression. The wing panels, which are now in Antwerp, show mourning women and Roman soldiers with Jewish judges.

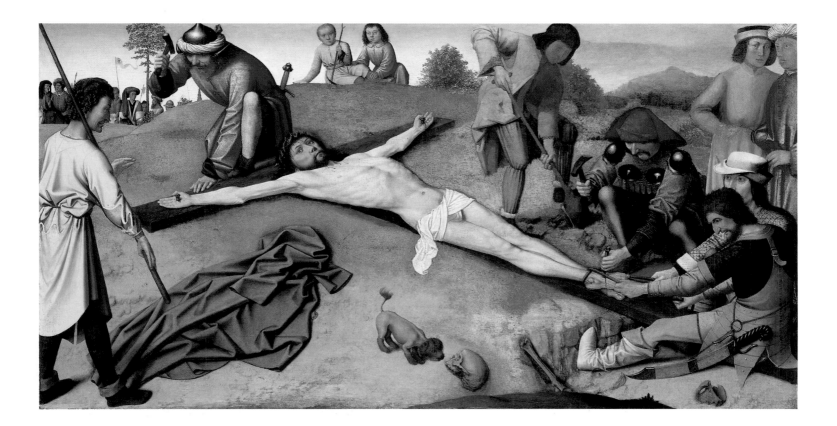

Contrary to what might be expected, David did not pursue this style, possibly because of the prevailing taste in Bruges rather than his own. The works of his last decade are marked by the intimate and simplified manner which many consider most characteristic of him. This style is ushered in, about 1510, by the delightful *Rest on the Flight into Egypt* (National Gallery of Art, Washington). Its lovingly depicted details of the donkey and the Virgin's basket, and the tiny figure of St Joseph knocking nuts from a tree, have a deeply appealing simplicity unequalled at this time. If his Genoese visit did occur, it would

137 HIERONYMUS BOSCH Christ Carrying the Cross *c.*1501–2
Among the cruellest images of human persecution in Western art, this panel compresses nineteen heads into an airless, spaceless setting, which concentrates on their nightmarish appearance. It may illustrate a Middle Dutch text of a verse from the Psalms: 'And in their fury they raged against you and gnashed their teeth like angry dogs.'

explain the Italianate character of David's various late renderings of the *Virgin and Child with a Bowl of Milk* (one version of which is in the Musées Royaux des Beaux-Arts, Brussels). Here the prototype may be Leonardo or his followers, but the feeling of intimacy and silvery light is entirely David's.

Hieronymus Bosch

The most enigmatic of all Netherlandish painters is Hieronymus Bosch (1453–1516). The contrast between his quiet provincial life and the bizarre imagery he painted could not be greater, while mainstream religious painting of the fifteenth century appears completely conventional beside Bosch's peculiar nightmare vision. He could conform when necessary however, as is demonstrated by his mundane *Crucifixion* of the later 1480s (Musées Royaux

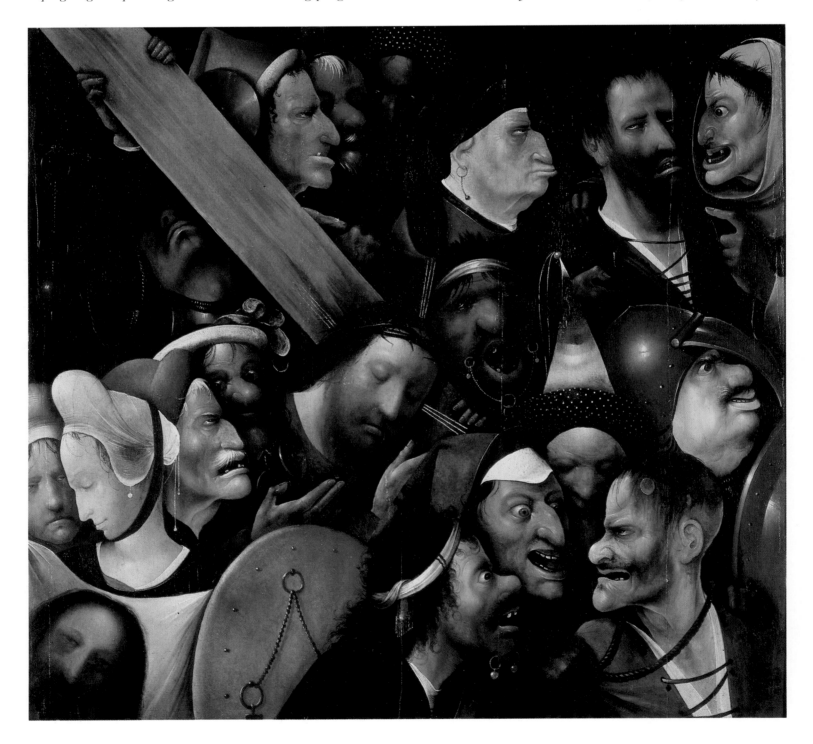

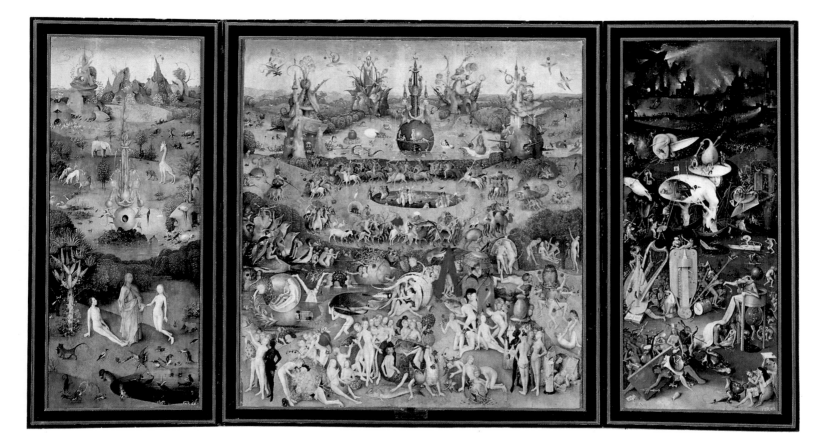

138 HIERONYMUS BOSCH Garden of Earthly Delights *c.*1505
That Bosch's pictures were accepted in orthodox Catholic circles in the
sixteenth century seems to discount implications of his heretical
leanings. This triptych is probably Bosch's most complex image,
offering for some a symbolic vision of man's sinfulness, for others an
earthly paradise. The newly created world appears on the altarpiece's
exterior, with the Garden of Eden in the left wing and Hell on the
right. In the centre appears man's folly after the Fall. Astrological
references are included, and there appear to be countless plays on
words. Throughout the picture balance is always at risk, and souls
are tortured by the ways in which they have sinned. It has also been
suggested that there are references to the Inquisition. The text from
Isaiah 40:6 – 'All flesh is grass, and all the goodliness thereof is as
the flower of the fields' has been applied to this painting.

de Beaux-Arts, Brussels). But he also was capable of rendering ostensibly straightforward scenes with a macabre
genius for the unexpected, as in his *Death of a Miser* of
about 1500 (see plate 147). Bosch's iconography has
inspired more conjecture than any other Netherlandish
painter's. His orthodoxy as a Catholic is undoubted, however, and he worked for a local religious confraternity of
which he was a member. The answer to his fantastic cre-
ations may simply lie in Bosch's overwhelming mission,
as a didactic moral artist, to warn of the torments of Hell
awaiting a sinful mankind.

How his style evolved is unclear, but Bosch came from
a dynasty of painters. His grandfather had moved in the
last years of the previous century from Aachen to
s'Hertogenbosch in northern Brabant, now part of modern Holland. s'Hertogenbosch was a prosperous provin-

cial town of little artistic importance, yet Bosch seems to
have evinced no desire to move to any of the more active
cultural centres. The immediacy of his technique – applying paint directly in glazes over underdrawing on a white
ground – owed little to the complicated methods perfected by his predecessors. In his early twenties, Bosch
painted a circular table top with the *Seven Deadly Sins*
(Museo del Prado, Madrid) and a lost pendant showing
the *Seven Sacraments*. These are thought to be his earliest
works. The form used recalls the Wheel of Fortune, and
most of the symbols conform to well-established Christian
iconographies for death and its aftermath. Its claustropho-
bic scenes, in which figures exist in a vacuum, introduce
that aspect of his art where even his extensive landscapes
are hermetically sealed.

The novelty of Bosch's art, however, lies in the obvious delight he takes in inventing figures which best represent both human and non-human creatures, and in his
complete disregard for fashionable style. Many of his
paintings show subjects unique to him, such as his
Temptations and allegories of the Last Things – Heaven,
Hell, Death and Judgement.

Perhaps the most distinguishing feature of his art is its
rejection of the importance of large-scale human figures
in contemporary work. In Bosch, the human figure is
nothing more than a formula for expressing his concepts
in a recognizable way, and the kind of contemporary studies of anatomy that were undertaken in Italy were irrele-
vant to his perception of the nude. Thus his human
figures belong to the same species as all the natural forms
in his pictorial world. They are angular, uncomfortable,

sharp and suggestive not of the dignity sought by the High Renaissance but of the degradation of the flesh through inevitable suffering. This prevented him from producing that most admired of Flemish art forms, the portrait, since his interest in humanity is always general, not particular.

From his early pictures – such as *Saint John on Patmos* of the later 1480s (Gemäldegalerie, Berlin), to the famous *Haywain* triptych (see plate 146) of the following decade – the period of his first maturity – landscape is merely the means by which Bosch anchors events in this world. In the *Haywain*'s right wing, Hell is made all too tangible by the graphic depiction of fire, while in subsequent paintings it is manifested in less obvious ways.

In his multi-figure paintings (such as the *Garden of Earthly Delights*, see plate 138), aesthetic considerations are subjected almost entirely to meaning and content. In this respect, such scenes represent the fullest expression of his didactic mission, and show his roots in the medieval rather than the Renaissance approach to imagery.

Christ Carrying the Cross (see plate 137) is now believed to be Bosch's last painting. He also portrayed himself in old age in the so-called 'Arras Sketchbook'. The Ghent painting is as cruel a testament as any from an artist's old age. Only a few years previously, Bosch had returned to a conventional pattern with his *Epiphany Triptych* (Museo del Prado, Madrid), which accentuates the horror of *Christ Carrying the Cross*. With the exception of Christ and Saint Veronica (both of whom have their eyes closed), all the figures have stepped out of nightmares, toothless, grimacing and wholly malevolent. Strikingly modern in concept, only the heads and a few shoulders appear, pressing in on Christ and suggesting little hope for humanity.

It is uncertain how Bosch's contemporaries received his anarchic style, although its popularity is shown by the engravings of his work made locally by Alart du Hameel, and the many copies of his paintings. His work was collected by Philip the Handsome and Margaret of Austria, and the fanatical Catholic, Philip II of Spain, attracted by Bosch's elaboration of simple themes with complex layers of meaning. Bosch's moralistic and ultimately pessimistic vision of man's inevitable sin and damnation may have conformed to Counter-Reformation taste in Spain.

Painting in Germany

Germany in the fifteenth century had little resemblance to the geographical area bearing that name today, being made up of many individual city states among which none dominated. The absence of aristocratic and court patronage and the presence of a rich mercantile class produced a specific provincial bourgeois art. A small number of painters attained more than merely local importance, preparing the way for major artists in the future like Schongauer and Dürer.

While Italian and Flemish painters explored many facets of the visible world, creating a modern art in which innovations such as perspective, atmospheric effects and an individualized portrayal of human physiognomy achieved a greater approximation to reality, artists in Germany remained more closely linked with miniature paintings and the International style. In interpreting such influences in their panel paintings however, a greater breadth and expression inevitably developed. The innovations of Flemish art were apparently known by the third or fourth decade, while advanced Italian ideas only became accepted in Germany much later in the century.

One of the most delightful German representatives of style was the Cologne 'Master of St Veronica', whose love of pale pastel colour and delicate figures was taken up by the leading master of the Cologne school, Stephan Lochner. Lochner, who seems to have been active from about the mid-1430s until 1451, came to Cologne from Meersberg near Lake Constance. He may have been trained in the Netherlands, or at least under a Netherlandish artist, since his work shows a much richer power of detailed observation than that of his German contemporaries. His career in Cologne was distinguished: he received a commission in 1442 on the Emperor Frederick III's visit to the city and served in the painters' guild.

His miniaturistic delicacy is best expressed in his female figures, such as the *Madonna with the Violets* of the mid-1430s (Erzbischöfliches Diözesan-Museum, Cologne) and the famous *Madonna of the Rose Bower* (see plate 156). He also painted multi-figure altarpieces like the *Last Judgement Altarpiece* (Wallraf-Richartz-Museum, Cologne) and the great *Adoration of the Magi* now in Cologne Cathedral but painted for the town hall; this was later much admired by Dürer. In it, although the figures are still miniaturistic, a feeling of monumentality is nonetheless present, and it seems clear that Lochner increasingly attempted the conscious inclusion of modern Flemish ideas while sometimes retaining an old-fashioned gold background. The so-called 'Cologne school' which was highly influenced by Netherlandish art, produced a surprisingly large number of painters during the second half of the fifteenth century, but many are not precisely identified.

Although he was born in Swabia, and was thus technically German, Konrad Witz (*c.*1400–44/6) is usually

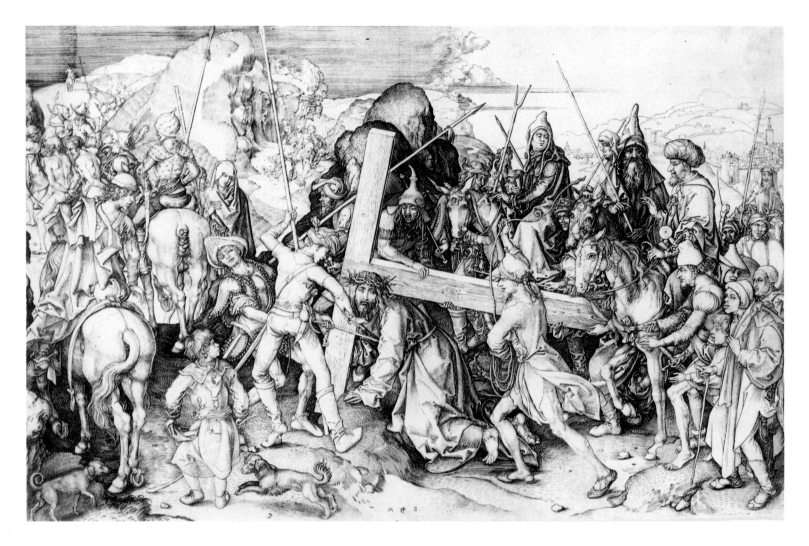

139 MARTIN SCHONGAUER Christ Carrying the Cross *c*.1480
This rare engraving was Martin Schongauer's masterpiece, and among the largest and most impressive engravings ever made. Schongauer may have based the composition on a lost painting by Jan van Eyck, which is known from a copy in Budapest. Its rich texture results from its deliberate emulation of the complexity of oil painting, transcending the limitations of engraving. This novel feature and its combination of an elaborate composition with an extraordinary wealth of detail and landscape background must have particularly impressed Dürer.

associated with the Swiss school, as he became a citizen of Basle in 1435. He may have travelled in the Netherlands prior to this, as he seems to have known the style of Van Eyck and other Flemings. Although we know few pictures by him, these original works indicate his abilities. His figures are often rigid, as in the panels from his *Saint Peter Altarpiece* for Geneva Cathedral (Musée d'Art et d'Histoire, Geneva). This altarpiece also incorporated his famous *The Miraculous Draft of Fishes* (see plate 155), a masterpiece of landscape observation.

The work of one other artist of this time working in Ulm, Hans Multscher (documented 1427, died before 1467) should be mentioned. He typifies the German sculptor-painter, whose main activity was the production of the often immense multi-panelled altarpieces combining sculpted scenes with paintings, all set in elaborately carved and gilded Gothic frames. Another artist of this type was Michael Pacher (active 1465?–98) who worked in the Tyrol.

It was in Colmar that the most important artist of the period prior to Dürer was active – Martin Schongauer, who died in 1491. Only one secure painting by him is known, the *Madonna in the Rose Garden* of 1473 (St Martin's, Colmar), although others are attributed to him. It was as the masterly engraver of about 115 plates that he earned his place in German art. He alone among his German contemporaries received favourable attention, and he exercised considerable influence outside his chosen workplace. What he was able to realize in his engravings was of profound importance to many other artists of all kinds, including Dürer.

Schongauer appears to have been in the Netherlands and certainly visited Leipzig, and the allure of his prints derives from their painterly approach, which gives them a higher degree of atmospheric expressiveness than those of his predecessors. From early works influenced by Rogier van der Weyden, he rapidly found his personal manner in images like the *Temptation of Saint Anthony* of *c*.1470–75. The immense variety of his style is impressive, ranging from individual figures such as his *Saint Michael* of the 1480s and the moving study of a *Censor* with all its elaborate Gothic metalwork detail, to the dramatic late multi-figure *Christ Carrying the Cross* (see plate 139).

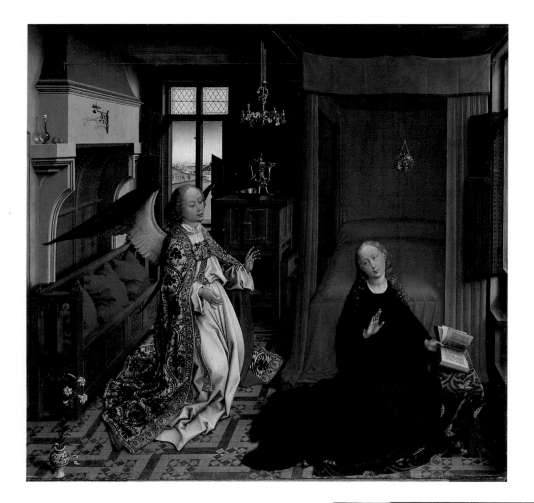

140 ROGIER VAN DER WEYDEN Annunciation
*c.*1435
Now separated from its wings in the Galleria Sabauda in Turin, this panel clearly reveals the impact on Rogier's style of Van Eyck, both in form and colour. The vibrant scarlet bed, borrowed from Van Eyck's Arnolfini Marriage, *the cupboard and the wooden settle, serve to compress the main scene on to a narrow foreground stage, where the earthbound figure of the Virgin accentuates the floating movement of the angel. This shows the relative discomfort of even a moderately grand room at this period. Of particular interest are the lavish floor tiles and hinged and bolted window shutters.*

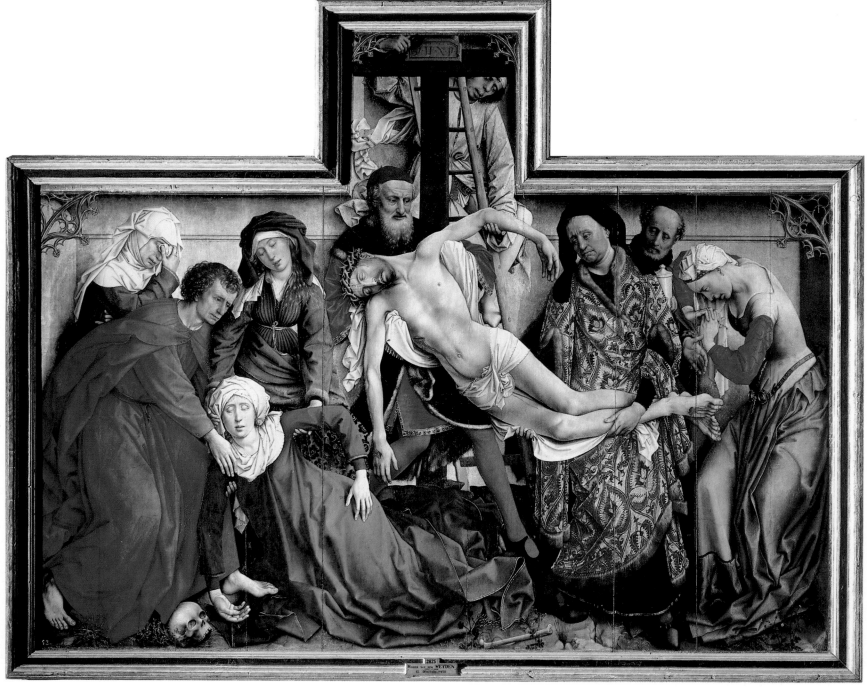

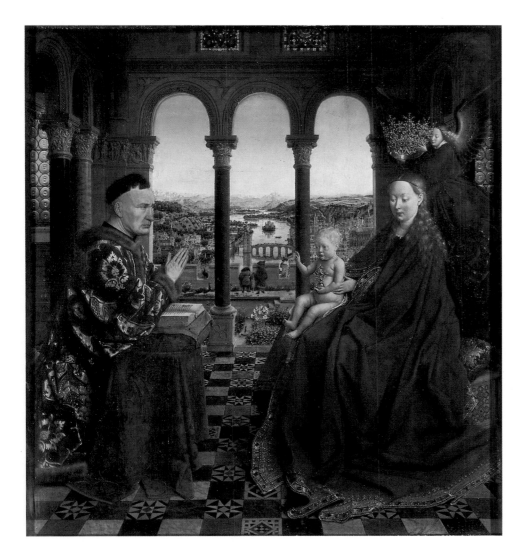

142 JAN VAN EYCK Madonna of the Chancellor
Nicholas Rolin ('The Virgin of Autun') c.1432
*This painting was probably presented to Autun
Cathedral in 1437 by the unscrupulous Chancellor of
Burgundy, Nicholas Rolin, when his son Jean was made
Bishop there. The idea of showing the donor in the
Virgin's presence without mediating saints was
innovative, and the sweeping background view enjoyed
by two tiny figures on the balcony outside is also novel.
Many suggested identifications for the town have been
made, including Bruges, Brussels and even Prague. The
triple Romanesque arched openings refer to the Trinity,
while in the garden are symbols of the Virgin - lilies,
irises and birds. Even the carved capitals to the left
contain symbolic Old Testament scenes.*

141 ROGIER VAN DER WEYDEN Deposition
c.1438
*(Left) Possibly Rogier's best-known painting, this once
formed the central panel of a triptych, and was
commissioned by the Archers' Guild at Louvain for the
church of Notre Dame hors-les-murs. Filling the entire
picture space to bursting point, its unique combination of
high drama with intensely wrought decorative surfaces
and brilliant portraiture make it one of the most
appealing Flemish paintings of its age. The swooning
Magdalene is much more naturalistic than most of
Rogier's figures, and the deliberate proximity of the
figures to the picture surface renders the scene's pathos
unavoidable.*

143 ROGIER VAN DER WEYDEN Saint Luke
Drawing the Virgin c.1435–7
*(Right) This is probably the original of four versions of
this picture. St Luke, patron saint of artists, is making a
silverpoint drawing of the Virgin and Child, while
glimpsed beyond in his tiny study is his symbol, the ox.
The setting and much detail are borrowed from Van
Eyck's* Madonna of the Chancellor Rolin, *but
Rogier's originality lies in his splendid characterization of
St Luke and the playful Christ child; his smaller-scale
figures also lend greater intimacy.*

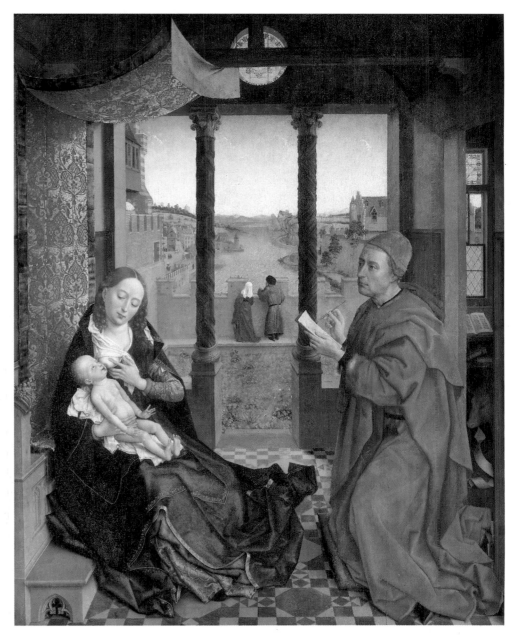

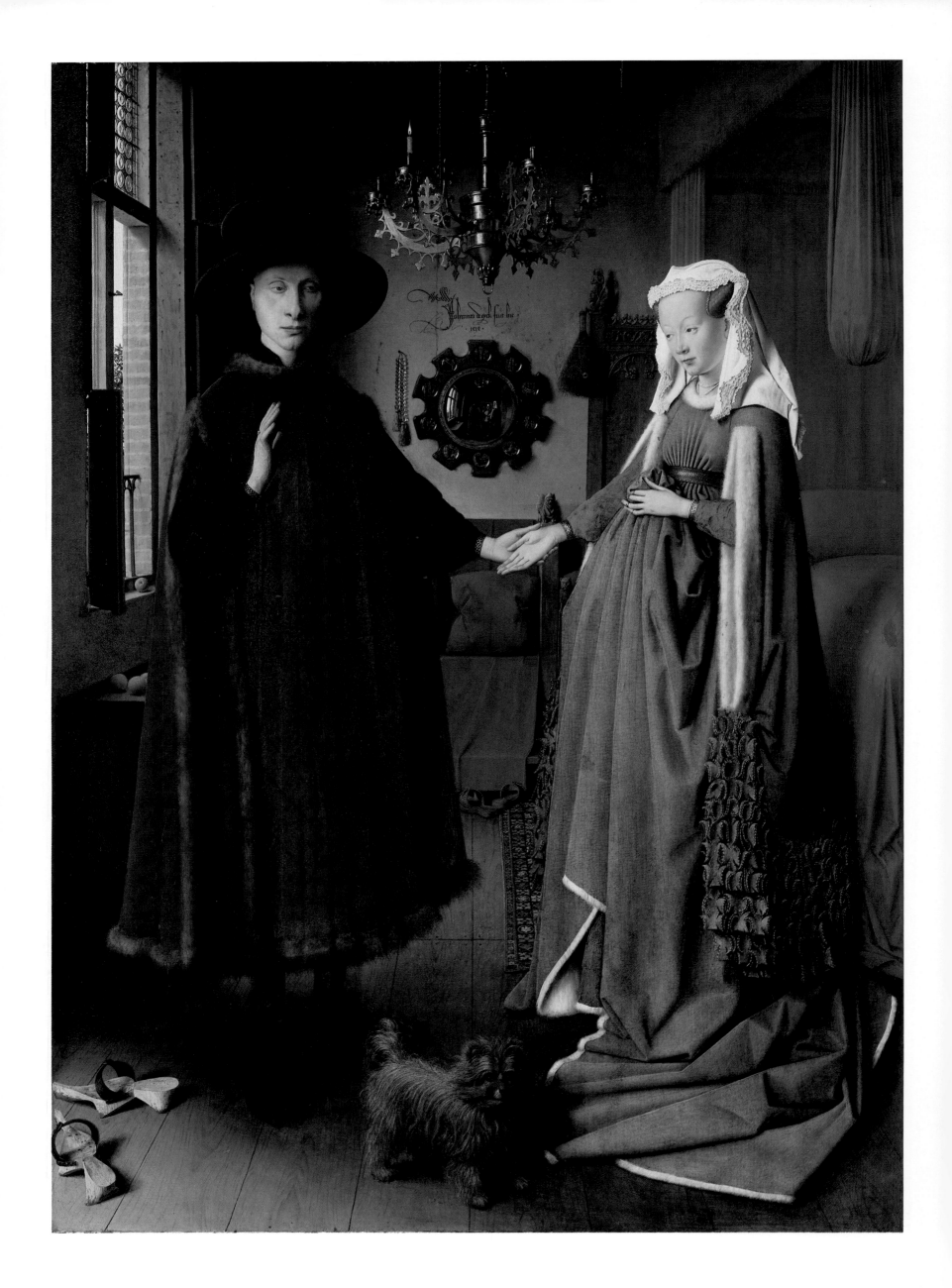

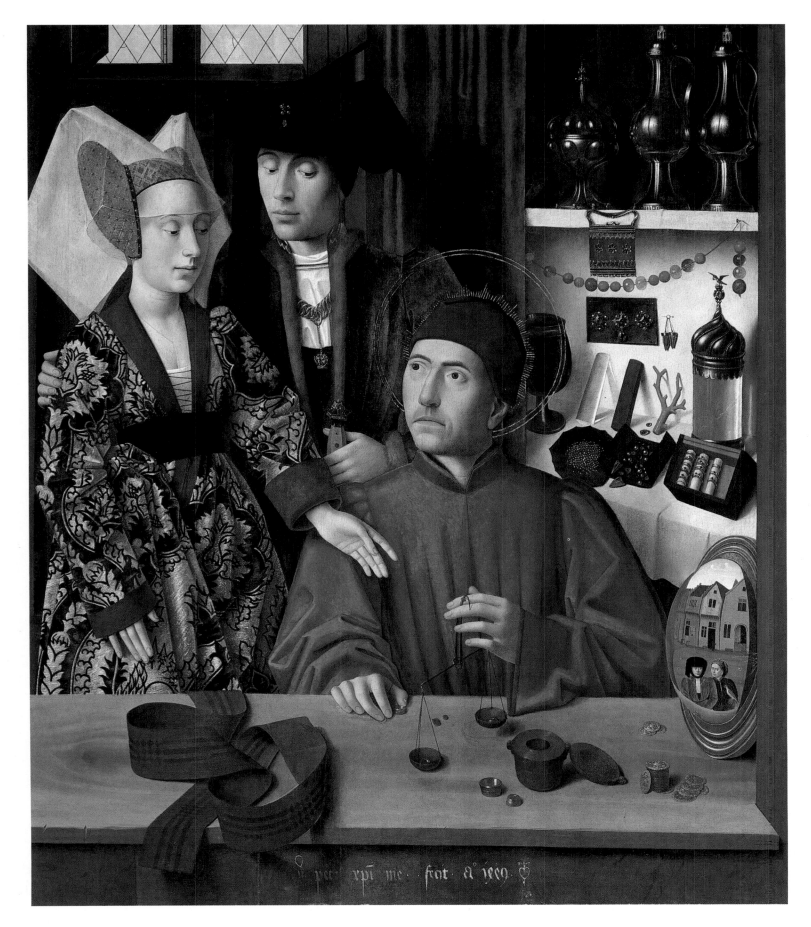

144 JAN VAN EYCK The Marriage of Giovanni Arnolfini and Giovanna Cenami 1434
(Left) Arnolfini was a merchant from Lucca who settled in Bruges. He and his wife here appear in a public bedroom to solemnize their marriage vows before two witnesses, one of whom is Van Eyck. The dog symbolizes marital fidelity, and the single burning candle which sometimes represents the all-seeing Christ was used when an oath was taken and also as the marriage candle of newly-weds. St Margaret is the patron saint of childbirth, while the crystal beads and the 'spotless mirror' are symbols of Marian purity. The fruit refers to man's innocence before the Fall. The painting thus symbolizes the state of marriage, referring through symbols to an ideal.

145 PETRUS CHRISTUS Saint Eligius and the Lovers 1449
St Eligius is the patron saint of gold and silversmiths. Here he is shown in his workshop weighing a wedding ring for the young couple and surrounded by precious metals, crystal and coral. Christus succeeded Jan van Eyck as Bruges' leading painter, and he adopts Van Eyck's use of light on precious objects and textures: the convex mirror may even be a quotation from the Arnolfini Marriage. Much of the picture's charm derives from its awkward placing of the figures, in direct contrast to Van Eyck's sophisticated poses.

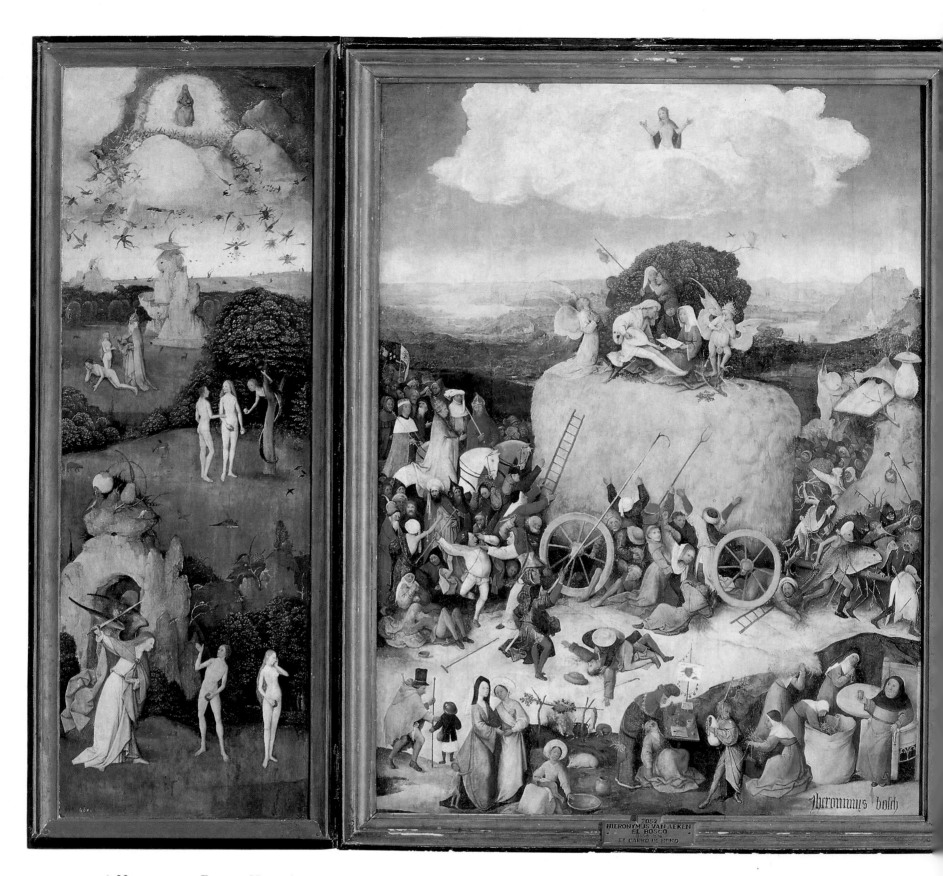

146 HIERONYMUS BOSCH Haywain 1495–1500

*There seems to be greater agreement as to the possible meaning of this
picture than many others by Bosch. It probably represents worldly
vanity with overtones of the uselessness of human aspirations and
greed for worthless values. It may illustrate a Flemish proverb about
the haywain with the rabble snatching the hay, but it is also a moral
lesson on the eternal curse of original sin, with Luxuria present as
the principal sin. In the left panel there is a deliberate parallel drawn
between the Fall of Adam and Eve and the Fall of the Rebel
Angels.*

147 HIERONYMUS BOSCH Death and the Miser
*c.*1485–90

*The shape of this panel indicates that it was a wing, possibly of a
Seven Deadly Sins triptych. The dying man hesitates between the
choice of a crucifix and the moneybag, but the certainty of death is
indicated by his fixed gaze on Death's figure entering the room. It is
probable that the picture illustrates medieval texts such as 'When the
evil miser lies in his deathbed, he does not wish to be separated from
his dishonest possessions. This is a true sign that he loves those
possessions more than God, and more than his own soul.'*

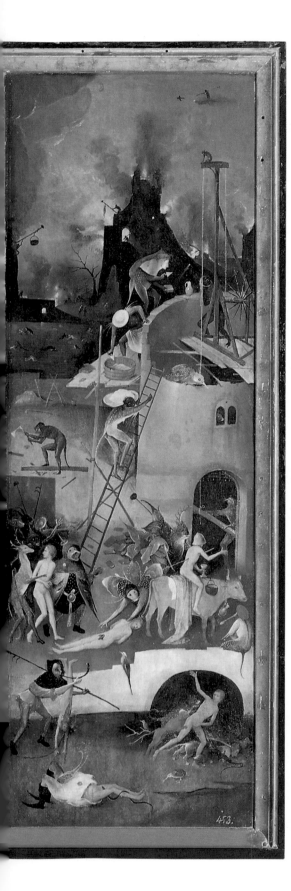

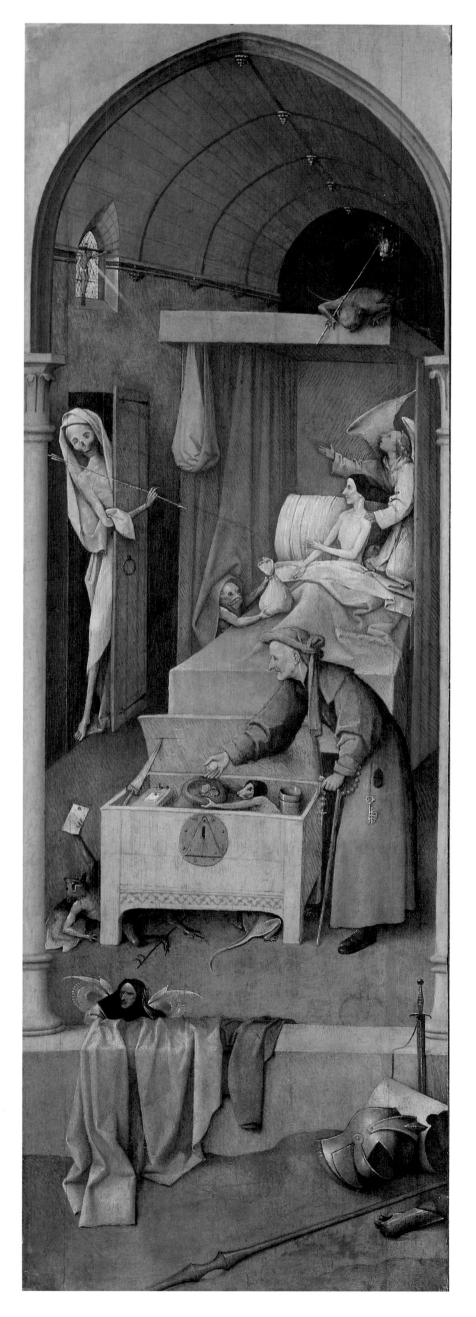

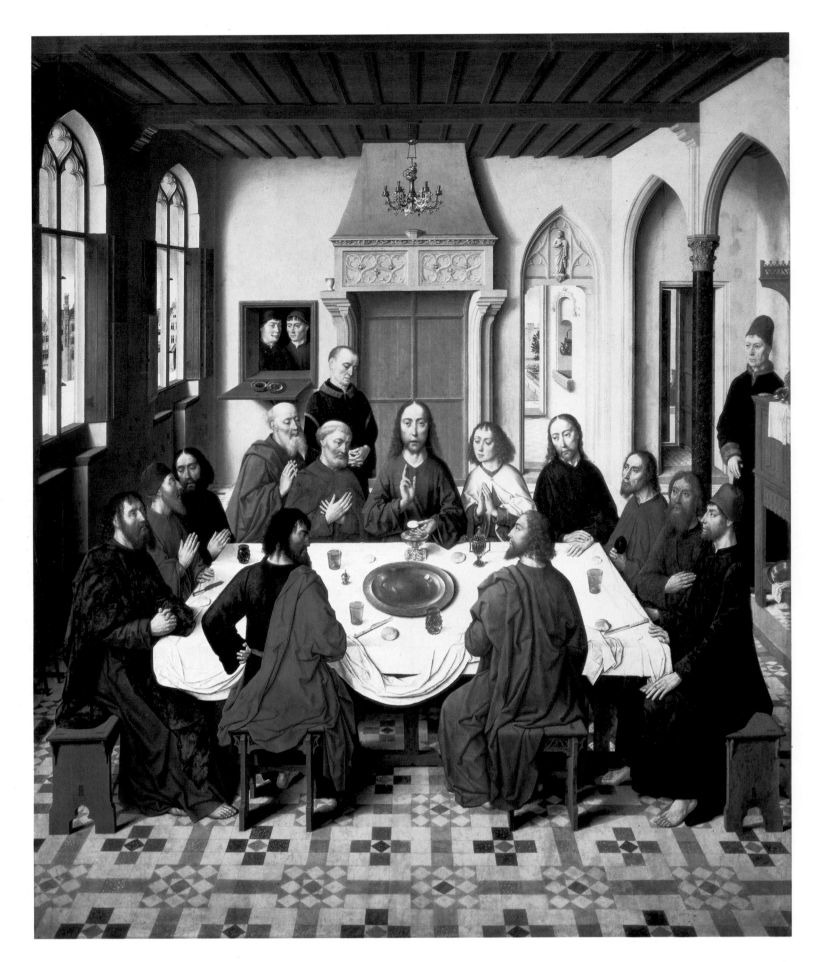

148 DIERIC BOUTS Last Supper Altarpiece 1464–7
*The wings include four prefigurations of the main theme (*The
Institution of the Eucharist*):* Abraham's Meeting with
Melchizedeck, The Sacrifice of the Pascal Lamb, The
Gathering of Manna *and* Elijah and the Angel. *The theme was
prepared for the painter by two theology professors at Louvain
University, and most of the participants appear to be portraits of
known contemporaries. Following an established medieval tradition,
the figure of Christ is disproportionately large.*

149 JAN VAN EYCK The Ghent Altarpiece, completed 1432
*(Right) This important painting has been extensively repainted, and
the precise contributions of Jan and Hubert Van Eyck and their
studio are still debated. A figure in a papal tiara (God the Father,
Christ and the Holy Ghost) is the focus of the upper register, flanked
by the Virgin and St John the Evangelist, musical angels and Adam
and Eve. The outer right panels show holy hermits led by Sts Paul,
Anthony Abbot, Mary Magdalene and Mary of Egypt, while the
outermost panel shows St Christopher leading the pilgrims. On the
left are the knights of Christ with Sts Martin, George and
Sebastian, and the outermost panel shows the 'just judges'.*

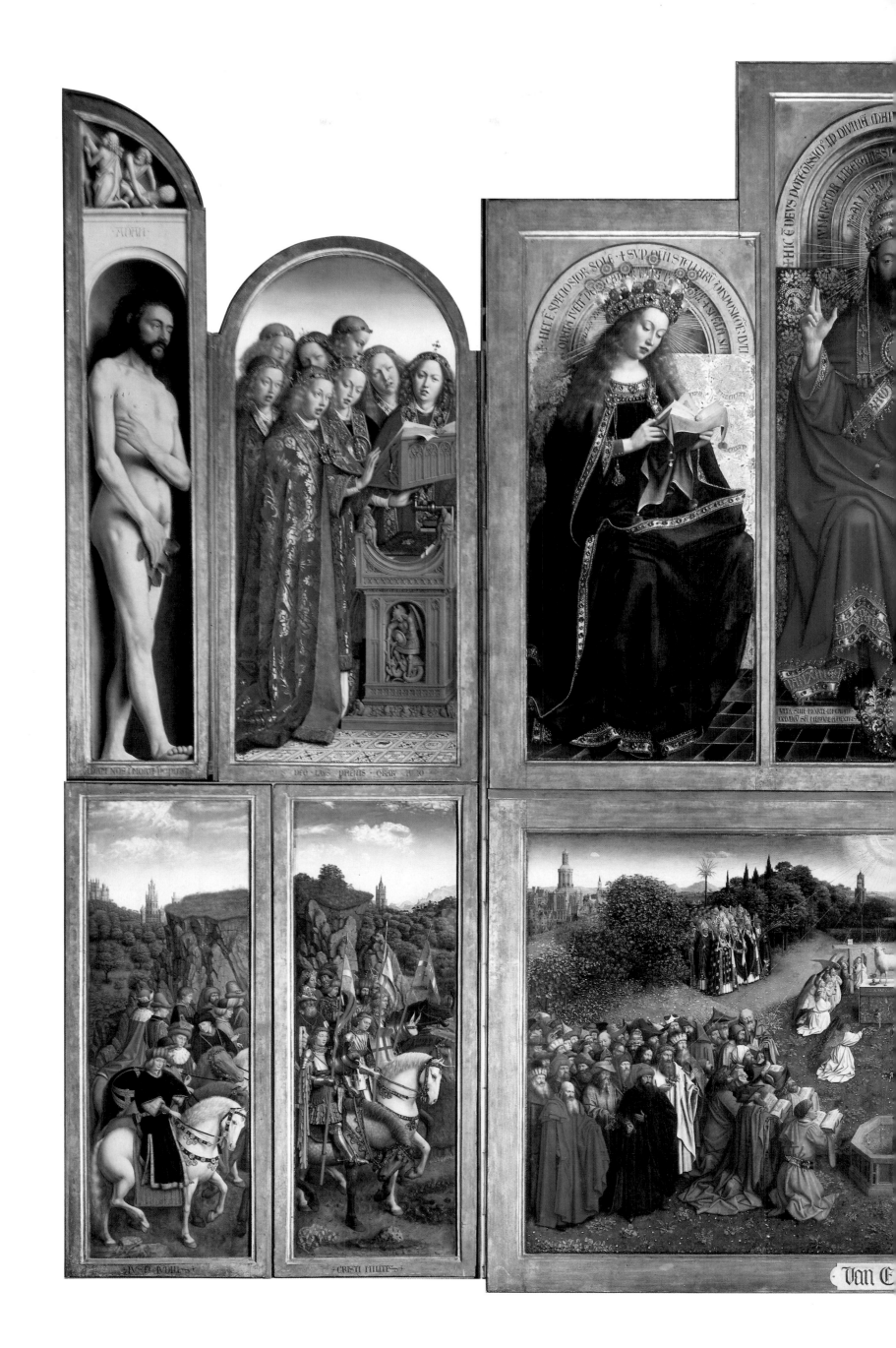

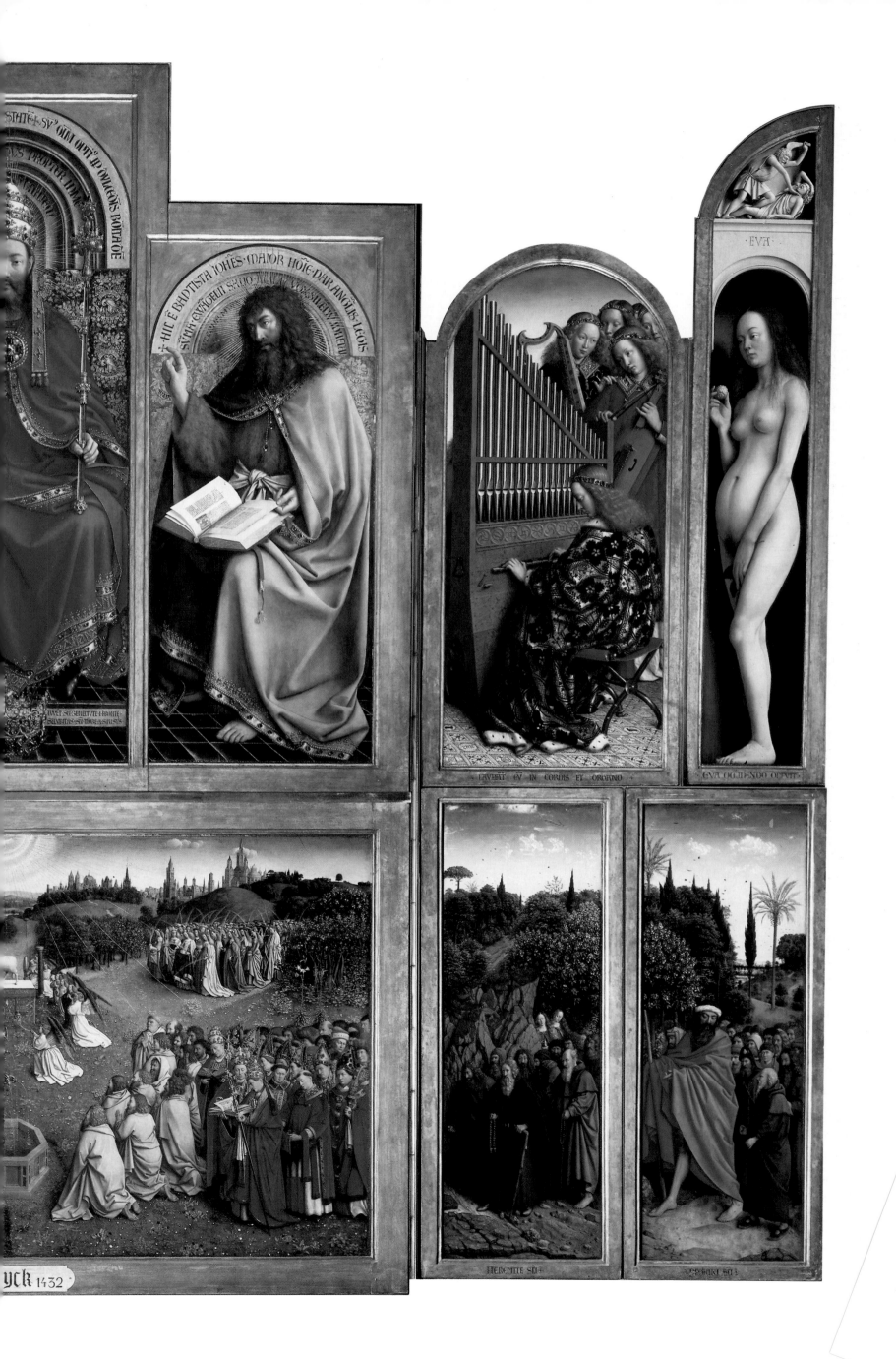

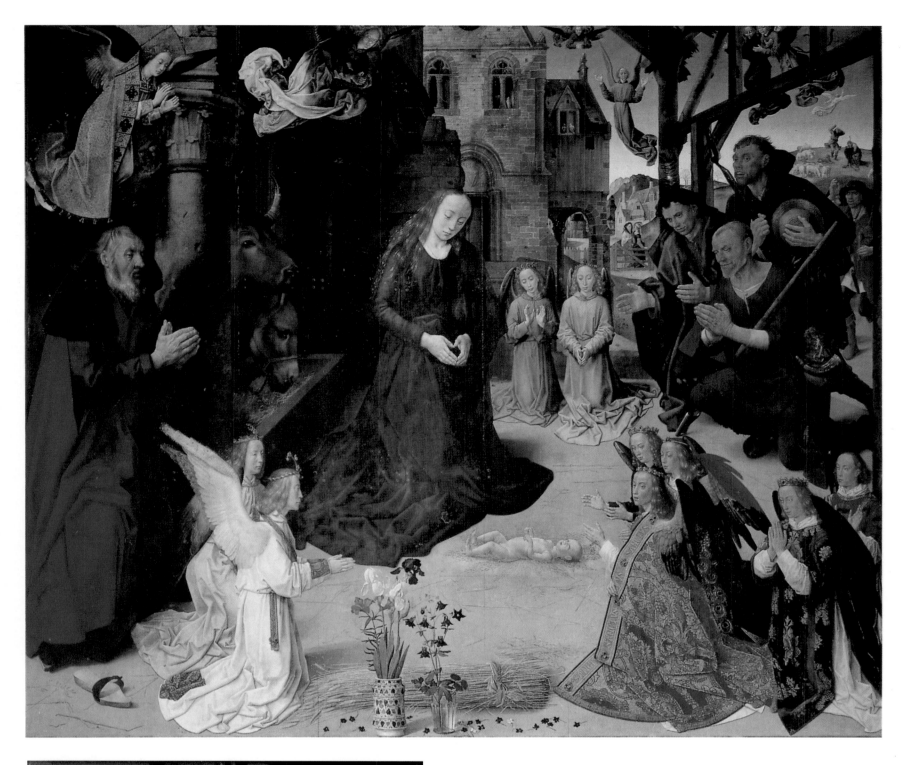

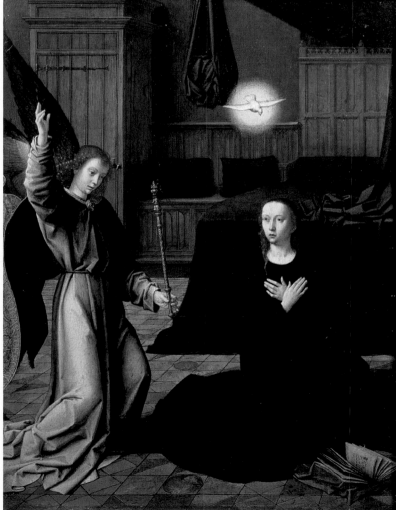

151 HUGO VAN DER GOES The Portinari Altarpiece 1474–6
(Above) This immense triptych was painted in Bruges for the Medici
representative there, Tommaso Portinari, who appears in the wings
with his family. On the left is Tommaso with his sons Antonio and
Pigello, with Sts Anthony and Thomas, and on the right is his wife
Maria Bonciani and their daughter Margherita with Sts Margaret
and Mary Magdalene. In this central panel are both the Nativity
and the Adoration of the Shepherds. The altarpiece was sent from
Bruges to Italy, and installed on the altar of Sant' Egidio, under
Portinari patronage, on 28 May 1483. In 1567 the altarpiece was
dismembered, and following the destruction at the same time of
frescoes by Domenico Veneziano and Andrea del Castagno, its
panels were for a time thought to be by these two Italian painters. Its
variations in scale and the high viewpoint were unusual, and the
striking portraits not only of the Portinari but also of the shepherds
profoundly appealed to Florentine painters.

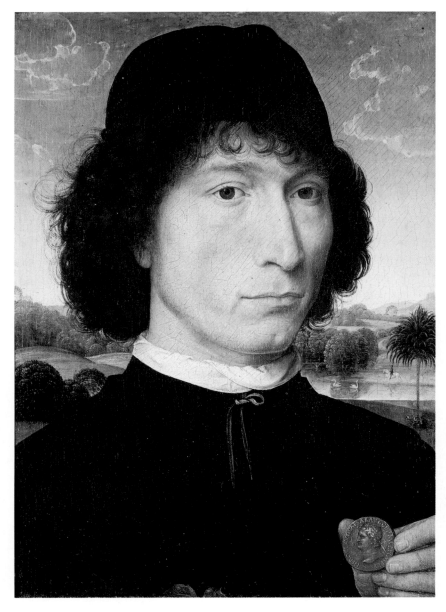

153 HANS MEMLINC Portrait of a Man with a Medal
c.1475–80
(Above) Memlinc appears to have been a prolific portraitist, and
many of his portraits survive. It has been suggested that the sitter was
one of the Italian medallists active in the Netherlands, Niccolò
Spinelli or Giovanni di Candida, or he may be one of the many
Italian merchants in Bruges who was also a collector. The medal
shows the Emperor Nero, and the portrait evokes Italian prototypes.

154 HANS MEMLINC Bathsheba 1484
(Below) One of the finest examples of Memlinc's mature style, this
may have been a diptych; a fragment in Chicago shows the figure of
King David watching. This treatment of the nude is something of a
rarity in Flemish art, and it may reflect a lost composition by Jan van
Eyck. Devoid of erotic content, it concentrates on the moral aspects of
the theme. As much attention is paid to the magnificent background
architecture and still life details as to the main figure.

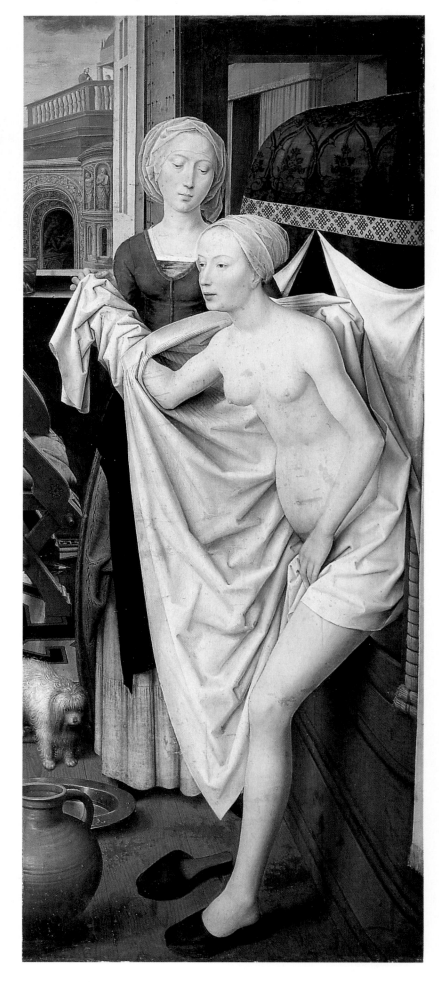

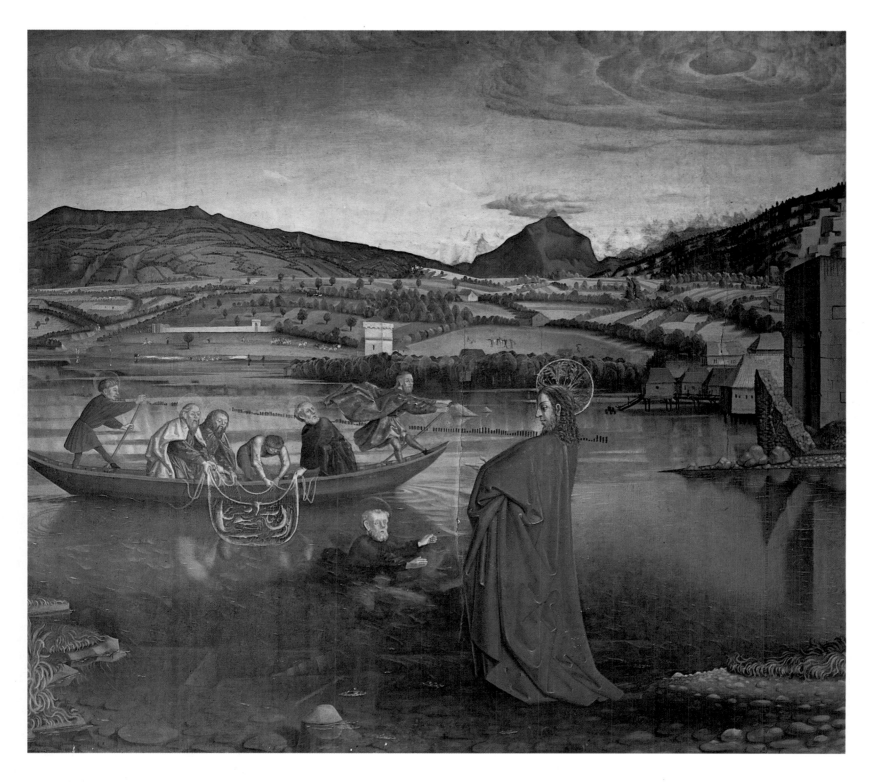

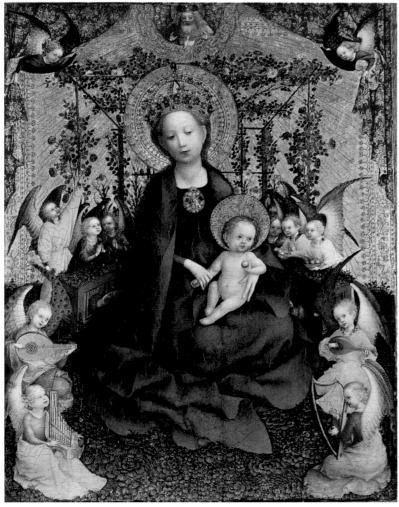

155 KONRAD WITZ Miraculous Draft of Fishes 1444
(Above) This forms part of Witz's last known painting,
commissioned by Bishop François de Mies for the Chapel of
Notre Dame des Maccabees in the Cathedral of Saint-Pierre in
Geneva. It forms the rear of the left wing of the altar, whose
central panel is lost; on its reverse is the Adoration of the
Magi. The effects of light, both reflected and refracted, and the
appearance of underwater phenomena make this one of the first
real observations of water in European painting, and lends the
figures a remarkable spatial realism.

156 STEPHAN LOCHNER Madonna of the Rose Bower
c.1450
(Left) One of the most appealing paintings of the Cologne
School, this picture relies on its contrasts of glowing, brilliantly
coloured detail rendered with almost sculptural precision, and
its flat gold background, accentuating the preciousness of the
image. Its delicacy is still reminiscent of International Gothic,
but it is coupled with more naturalistic expression.

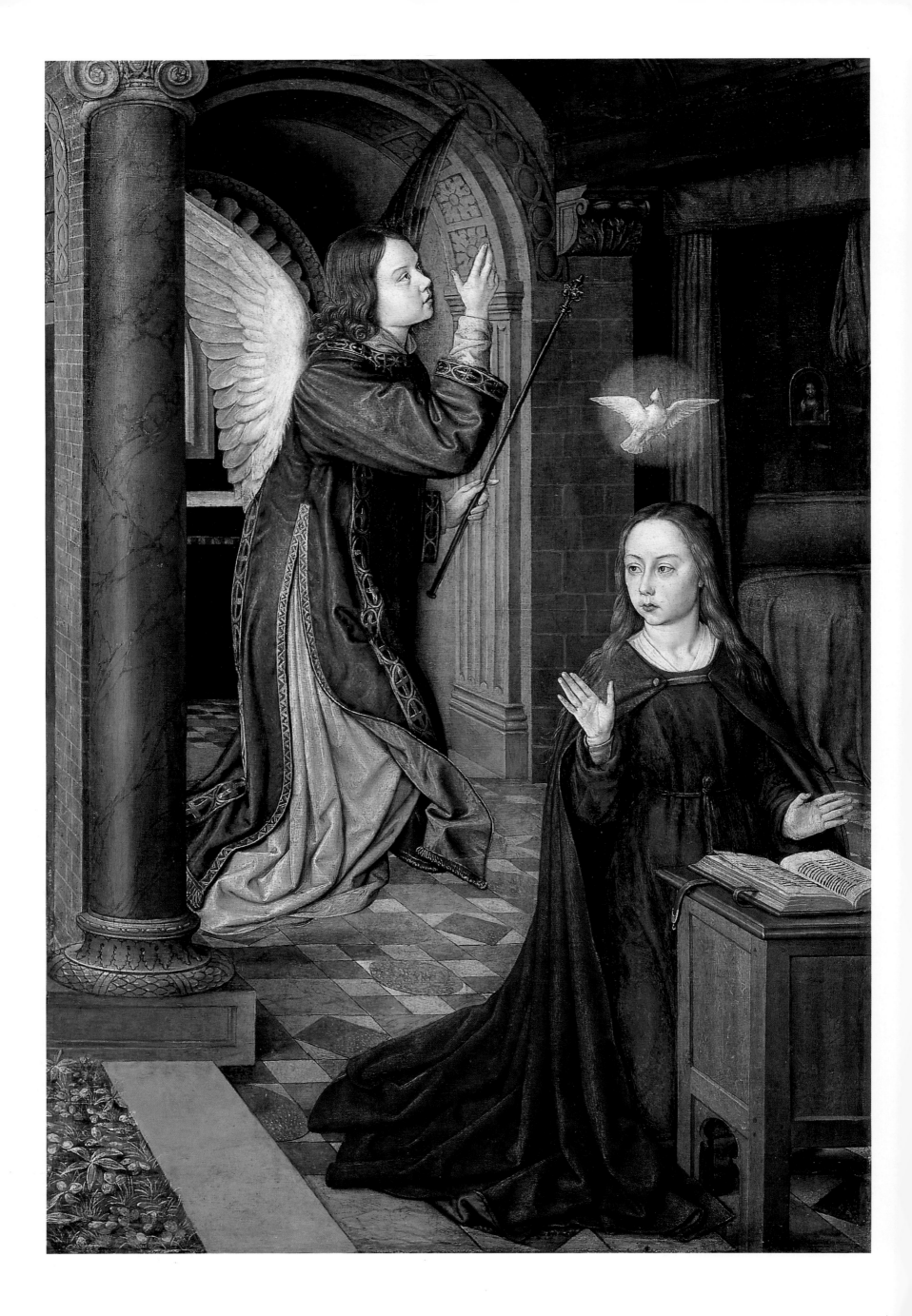

CHAPTER VI

The Renaissance
Elsewhere in Europe

The degree to which Italian and Northern Renaissance principles were accepted or even known in other countries depended on a variety of conditions. France's proximity to Italy did not hasten her adoption of the Renaissance, which only reached maturity there in the sixteenth century. However, the presence of Masolino in Hungary for some time before 1422, and of other Florentine painters there during the 1420s – thanks to the encouragement of the Florentine *condottiere* Pippo Spano – shows a remarkable receptivity to new ideas in that country. And by about 1360, Tommaso da Modena had painted two Madonnas for Charles IV in Prague. Throughout the Renaissance works of art made the finest ambassadors, changing not only political destinies but also the course of local art.

Spain's close connections with Italy and Flanders resulted in somewhat confusing reactions to their different impetuses, while in England the Reformation scotched any real developments from the latest Italian ideas. Styles and fashions in painting also depended on political and religious movements, the presence of a court, and the strength of previous prevailing artistic movements, particularly the International Gothic style. The clear motivations and progression of the Italian Quattrocento provide the yardstick by which the spread of humanist and artistic ideas must be gauged.

157 THE MASTER OF MOULINS Annunciation *c.*1510
Probably originally part of a diptych, the interior in this painting is particularly satisfying, and shows an awareness of Italian architectural ideas in the Ionic column and coffered arch with a fluted pilaster. Light effects are also notably subtle, and notwithstanding the over-large angel, perspective is well handled in relation to the Virgin and the contents of the room. The Virgin's portrait-like appearance links the picture with others by the Master, notably the late Saint Maurice with a Donor *and* A Princess *(see plate 175).*

France

French art and architecture had reached a pitch of unrivalled perfection during the Middle Ages, and the transition to the Renaissance was slow and difficult in France. Even as late as the early sixteenth century, the French preferred the complex architectural decoration of Lombardy to Tuscan examples, possibly because of its resemblance to the most elaborate patterning of Flamboyant Gothic.

The immense production of illuminated manuscripts in France was one of the principal manifestations of International Gothic, with its overtones of courtly magnificence. Two of the greatest early manuscript illuminators were Master Honoré (probably died before 1318) and Jean (or Jehan) Pucelle (*c.*1300–*c.*1355). Appropriately named, the style flourished in most of Europe *c.*1375–1425. The artists it attracted travelled throughout western Europe, and it spread to Italy, Flanders, Brabant, the Rhineland, northern Germany and Spain.

The Wilton Diptych (see plate 186) is one of the most perfect but most problematic works of International Gothic. It was probably painted in Paris by an artist with a remarkable knowledge of international developments, not only in France, but in Italy and even Hungary. Although painted in the first years of the fifteenth century, it sums up all the characteristics of the preceding period in the most sumptuous manner, and shows the background against which Renaissance ideas were to filter into French art from Italy.

The Avignon papacy (1309–77) – during which all the popes and most of the cardinals were French – imported Italian painters, such as Simone Martini (who lived there from about 1335 until his death in 1344), to its rich court. A key figure in stimulating interest in the ancient Classical world, the Italian poet Petrarch (1304–74), lived for

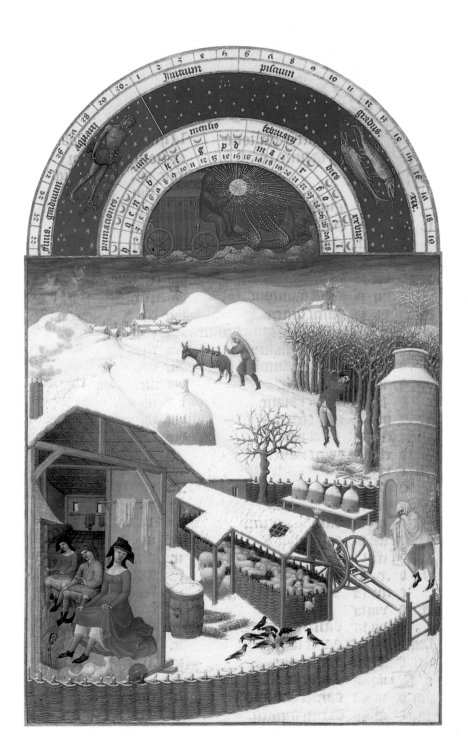

158 LIMBOURG BROTHERS Month of February *from the* Très
Riches Heures du Duc de Berry, begun *c*.1413
*The Netherlandish illuminators Herman, Jean and Paul were among
the most gifted of their age. When they died these* Heures *were
completed by Jean Colombe. The atmosphere of deepest winter is
captured in the details, such as the people by the fire.*

fourteen years at Fontaine de Vaucluze, near Avignon,
and owned work by Simone.

Avignon then belonged to the Angevin princes of
Naples. Petrarch's contacts with the Papal court were very
important in the growth of Humanism outside Italy, as
visitors came from all over Europe. From Avignon the
latest Sienese ideas travelled into France, the Netherlands,
Austria and Bohemia. In addition to frescoes, panel paintings were produced by the Italianate painters at Avignon,
and while their style remained Gothic, the contacts with
Italy were of great importance.

The Valois dynasty ruled from 1328 until 1498, and
included Charles V (1364–80) and his brothers, the dukes
of Anjou, Berry, Burgundy and Orléans. Along with
members of the court, they were important artistic
patrons and particularly favoured luxurious and costly
illuminated manuscripts. Of these brothers John, Duke of
Berry, was the most important collector (see plate 158).
This period firmly established the rich tradition of French
royal patronage of painting which endured until the
Revolution. Paris became the centre of the International
Gothic style during the first quarter of the fifteenth century. The earliest independent easel paintings by Parisian
artists were produced during the reign of Charles VI
(1386–1422). These could not have been more at variance
with contemporary developments in Florence, which
appear to have had no impact whatever on French art.

The 'Second School of Avignon' produced the masterpiece which signals the real end of medieval principles in
French art: the *Pietà of Villeneuve-les-Avignons* (see plate
185) now attributed to Enguerrand Quarton or
Charonton (*c*.1410–66). Under the Papal Legates,
Cardinal della Rovere and Cardinal de Foix, patronage
flourished in Provence. It emerges that a peculiarly
intense religiosity prevailed among the painters of this
school, seen in the anonymous, harrowing *Christ in the
Tomb*, also known as the Boulbon altarpiece (Musée du
Louvre, Paris).

Jean Fouquet

Although the seeds were sewn during the fourteenth century, and Italian ideas continued to filter into France, the
Renaissance did not come to fruition there until the sixteenth century. Unlike Italy and the Netherlands, fifteenth-century France produced remarkably little talent
in painting. The major exceptions were Jean Fouquet
(*c*.1420–*c*.1481), who worked as a painter of easel pictures
and miniatures, and the mysterious Master of Moulins.

Born in Tours, Fouquet, of whom we know little,
appears to have had a more international vision than any
of his contemporaries. Between 1443 and 1447 he was in
Rome, where his prestige secured him a commission to
paint Pope Eugenius IV's portrait, which is no longer
traceable. It is tempting to think that he passed through
Florence, since one of the principal effects of his Italian
journey is a combined interest in Classical architecture
and perspective. There are also indications that he knew
the work of Florentine painters, including Fra Angelico.

The main surviving legacy of his journey is his remarkable portrait of *The Court Jester Gonella* (see plate 176) and

the extensive Italianate detail in his *Hours of Etienne Chevalier* (Musée Condé, Chantilly) painted between 1450 and 1460 for one of his most important French patrons. Fouquet may first have trained with miniature painters in Paris, such as the Boucicaut and Bedford Masters, and he perpetuated the miniature tradition through his influence on Jean Bourdichon and Jean Colombe.

His experience in Rome may have been instrumental in securing him court patronage on his return to Tours, although he was not made Painter to King Louis XI until 1475. Fouquet's memorable likeness of *Charles VII* (Musée du Louvre, Paris) typifies his combination of Northern and Italian styles, with his own sense of the monumental. This even informs his later work, exemplified by the superb illustrations to the *Antiquités Judaïques* manuscript (see plate 159), and his *Descent from the Cross* (Parish Church, Nouans). Throughout his career, Fouquet exhibited a gravity which gives his paintings a unique dignity, and imbues his incisive portraits with a strong sense of introspection and remoteness unparalleled in Europe at this time.

Nicolas Froment (active *c*.1450–*c*.1490) from Uzès in Languedoc was instrumental together with Quarton (see plate 185) in introducing Flemish ideas of naturalism into French painting of the time. His masterpiece is the *Altarpiece of the Burning Bush* of 1476 (Cathedral of Saint-Saveur, Aix-en-Provence).

The Master of Moulins

All that is securely known of this anonymous, elusive but gifted painter is that, in about 1498, he painted a triptych showing the *Virgin and Child in Glory with Donors* in Moulins Cathedral. Its central panel is of an exquisite delicacy which has been compared to Ingres, with remarkable effects of light, and on the basis of its clear style a body of other works has been established. Since its commission came from the Bourbons (the donors are Pierre, Duc de Bourbon, his wife, Anne de Beaujeu, daughter of Louis XI, and their daughter Suzanne) it is clear that the Master of Moulins was favoured by an important circle of aristocratic patrons (see plate 175). It has also been suggested that he was another artist of the Bourbon court, Jean Hay from Brussels.

It is now believed that the Master was probably active from about 1480 to about 1520, not 1500 as has been previously thought. The earliest works attributed to him, such as *Cardinal Charles II of Bourbon* (Alte Pinakothek, Munich) and a *Nativity* of about 1480 (Musée Rolin, Autun) show Flemish influence, particularly that of Hugo van der Goes' *Portinari Altarpiece* (see plate 151). This seems to have been replaced by Fouquet's manner, and supposed later works show an elegant restraint still informed by his feeling for texture and light (see plate 157). Particularly reminiscent of Fouquet's grand conception of form is the Master's latest presumed work, the magnificent *Saint Maurice with a Donor* (Art Gallery and Museum, Glasgow) possibly dated about 1516. The handling of paint is, however, quite different from Fouquet's, as is the dynamic relationship between the two figures.

The Sixteenth Century

The Renaissance developed with astonishing suddenness in France during the first part of the sixteenth century. At this time, many vestiges of the Middle Ages were discarded and French politics and culture developed significantly towards the modern world. However, the

159 JEAN FOUQUET Fall of Jericho *from the* Antiquités Judaïques 1470–6

Dating from the later years of Fouquet's career, these miniatures illustrate a Josephus manuscript. Even on this scale, Fouquet achieves an astonishing monumentality comparable with the latest Italian achievements, and shows an ability to organise many-figure compositions that distinguishes him from his Northern contemporaries.

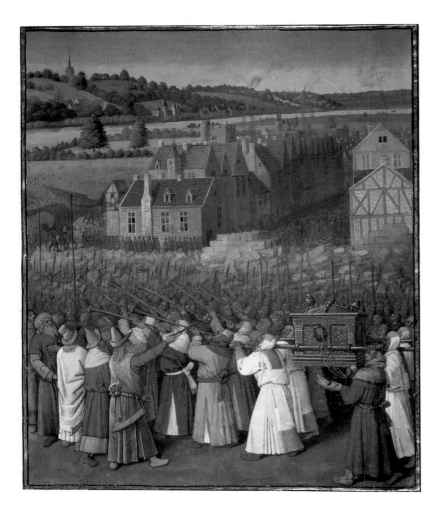

importance of miniature painting appears to have been perpetuated. The two principal active painters of this period seem to have been Jean Perréal (died 1530) and Jean Bourdichon (c.1457–1521), but little is known of their careers.

Bourdichon was Fouquet's leading pupil, serving both Charles VIII and Louis XII at Tours. He certainly produced larger paintings, and may have visited Italy, but his principal known works are the miniatures in the *Hours of Anne of Brittany*, completed in 1508 (Bibliothèque Nationale, Paris). These show the influence of Italian decorative designs and an acquaintance with Italian painters, including Perugino. Such borrowings include little personal innovation, however.

Perréal appears to have been better known (Leonardo even mentions him) yet no paintings are securely attributed to him. Working as a sculptor, painter and court designer, he certainly made three Italian journeys, once in the company of Charles VIII and again with Louis XII. The portrait of *Louis XII* of about 1514 attributed to Perréal (Royal Collection, Windsor), shows why certain critics attempted to identify him with the Master of Moulins. It was against this background, where even important painters failed to make their mark on history as their Italian peers did, that the innovations of the reign of Francis I should be seen. At the same time, the status of the artist in French culture rose, and became an intrinsic part of court activity, as was the situation in Italy.

Francis I and the First School of Fontainebleau

Under Louis XII (1462–1515) taste had been led by a minister, Cardinal Amboise, but already Italian art was regarded as the measure for real developments. From the start of his reign in 1515, Francis I (1494–1547) made it clear that he intended to create a court to rival those of Italy. However, he was perhaps more attracted by the superficial glitter of Italian court life than by its underlying Humanism. To this end, he surrounded himself with men of learning and artists. He failed to bring Michelangelo to France, but obtained the services of Leonardo (1516–19) and Andrea del Sarto (1518–19), during which time the latter painted his magnificent *Charity* (Musée du Louvre, Paris), and Benvenuto Cellini (1540–45). The new style in French art inspired by the King was the work of a colony of imported Italian artists, but it soon evolved into a specifically French manner.

Francis' new building works at Blois and Chambord exemplified the grand scale of his ambitions, and his rebuilding and redecoration of the palace of Fontainebleau after 1528 led Vasari to praise it as a 'new Rome'. The aristocracy and newly rich were also patrons of the arts, although cultural life was centred more in the châteaux of the Loire than in Paris at this time, initially because of the good hunting there.

Francis himself had visited Milan, Pavia and Bologna, and probably had a clear idea of what he wanted for his favourite residence, Fontainebleau. He was fortunate in attracting two of the leading Italian painters of the day, Rosso Fiorentino (see Chapter VIII) and Francesco Primaticcio (1504/5–70), who arrived in France in 1530 and 1532 respectively, together with their Italian assistants. The third member of the group, Niccolò dell'Abate (c.1512–71), arrived in about 1552, and it is revealing that Primaticcio admitted that his sole reason for inviting him was that 'in Paris . . . there was no one capable'.

Primaticcio came from Bologna and his painting, used in conjunction with elaborate plasterwork, proved of immense importance. He had been Giulio Romano's assistant in the complex decorations of the Palazzo del Tè in Mantua, and through Giulio knew Raphael's style. Vasari credited Primaticcio with introducing stucco decoration into France, and he travelled to Rome twice to buy antiquities and casts for the King. On Rosso's death in 1540, he assumed an unchallenged position of power. French assistants absorbed the new Italianate style, but few of their names are known and little of their work can be identified.

160 FRANCESCO PRIMATICCIO Ulysses shooting through the Rings *c.*1555–9
This is a highly finished preliminary study for the thirty-ninth of Primaticcio's fifty-eight fresco decorations in the Galerie d'Ulysse of the Palace of Fontainebleau. In the Iliad, Penelope had agreed to wed the suitor capable of bending Ulysses's great bow to shoot through twelve rings.

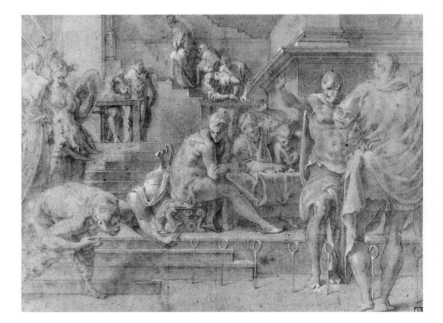

Rosso's cultivated tastes led Francis to appoint him his First Painter and canon of the Sainte-Chapelle, granting him many special privileges by letters patent. Mysteriously, little survives of Rosso's extensive French work, which included easel pictures, masquerade designs, goldsmiths' models and miniatures. Of his Fontainebleau decorations in the Pavillon de Pomone (with Primaticcio), the Pavillon des Poêles and the Galerie Basse almost nothing remains, and his major French pictures, including the *Saint Michael* and *Leda*, have vanished, leaving only his great *Ecouen Pietà*, now in the Musée du Louvre, Paris. The *Pietà*'s dramatic and highly stylized pathos must have run somewhat contrary to French tastes, which tended to a more decorative manner. The most impressive interior in the palace initiated by Rosso was the Galerie François I (see plate 161). After his death in 1540, Charles Dorigny, Luca Penni and Antoine Caron carried the Rosso manner to Paris.

Primaticcio's more refined, less demanding style is best seen in the superb Chamber of the Duchesse d'Etampes and the somewhat unwieldy ballroom (1554). Sadly, Primaticcio's Galerie d'Ulysse (after 1556) was dismantled in the eighteenth century (see plate 160). Beneath the Galerie François I was the Appartement des Bains, with its decorations of a 'delicious indecency' summing up so much of the tone of the handsome King's court and private life. It is significant that a copy of Michelangelo's notorious *Leda* also hung there, and this picture, with Bronzino's *Allegory of Venus* (see plate 228), exercised considerable influence on the French approach to the nude. Francis's collection of contemporary Italian works was unequalled outside Italy, and included Leonardo's *Virgin of the Rocks* among other paintings by him, Raphael's *La Belle Jardinière*, a Titian *Magdalen* and the Bronzino *Allegory*. Cellini's superb sculpted Porte Dorée was among the palace's principal ornaments.

In spite of Primaticcio's apparent reservations, Niccolò dell'Abbate was already a highly talented and esteemed painter and frescoist in Italy. Vasari describes his synthesis of drawing and colour as *unione*, a term the critic also applied to Giorgione's 'fused' manner. Niccolò had had direct contact with two Italian artists of immense stature, Correggio and Parmigianino, and the latter's *Conversion of Saint Paul* (see plate 265) has sometimes been attributed to Niccolò. He thus introduced another phase of Italian Mannerist ideas to the court of Henry II (1519–59) who reigned from 1547, and whose marriage to Catherine de' Medici in 1533 increased the influx of Italian artistic ideas. Niccolò also received many commissions in Paris, Ecouen and elsewhere. He is one of the few Fontainebleau painters whose works survive in any quantity. His princi-

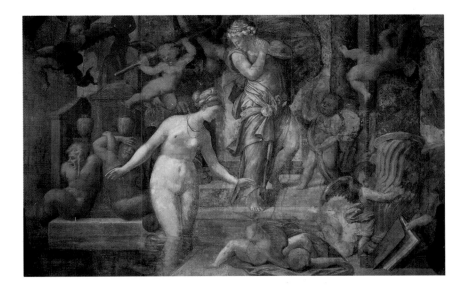

161 ROSSO FIORENTINO Venus *c.*1534–40
The twelve frescoes in the Galerie François I are dedicated to Francis I and are set amid a wealth of richly ornamented stuccoes which relate to the fresco themes. Scibec de Carpi executed the elaborate carved wooden panelling below. The cuir or strapwork cartouche motif derived from leatherwork is often repeated in the decorative surrounds, and exercised international influence through adaptations in decorative engravings. The fresco subjects are taken from classical literature and mythology, but their precise iconography is unclear, some making general references, others precise ones to the King.

pal contribution to French painting lay in his exquisite landscapes, in which he specialized after 1556 (see plate 178). Despite their Mannerist artificiality, these introduced the taste for romantic, far-reaching views which culminated in the work of Claude Lorraine in the following century.

Because of the anonymity of many painters at Fontainebleau, a large number of works from there are regularly described as 'School of Fontainebleau' (see plate 189). This in no way denigrates their quality, and indeed many may be included among the finest artistic productions of the period.

Cousin and the Clouets

Fontainebleau did not exclusively dominate French painting at this time, although its influence was irresistible because of its prestige. Jean Cousin the Elder (*c.*1490–1560/61) moved to Paris from his native Sens in 1538, where he evidently enjoyed a successful career as a painter and a designer of stained glass. In Paris, he would have seen prints of Italian art, and even original paintings which developed his style. His *Eva Prima Pandora* (see plate 179) indicates how independent Cousin was from developments at Fontainebleau, but his only documented work is his designs for three tapestries showing the *Life of Saint*

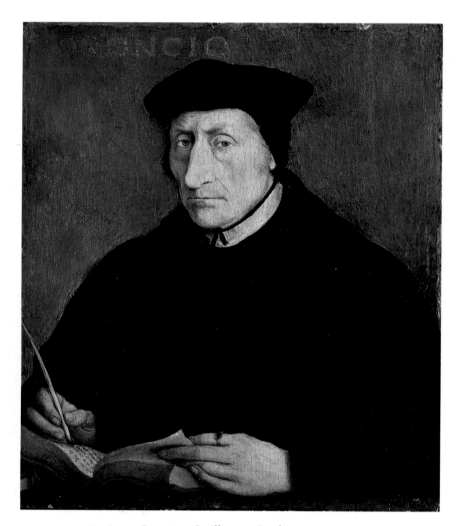

162 JEAN CLOUET Guillaume Budé *c.*1535
Guillaume Budé (1467–1540) was the finest scholar of Greek in Northern Europe. Erasmus called him the 'marvel of France'. Painted in tempera and oil, the finishing glazes on the face have vanished, leaving a false impression of unusually thin paintwork. But the original intensity of the likeness remains, together with an austerity very different from the richly wrought surfaces of Holbein. The inscription was added later.

Mammès for the Cathedral of Langres. Two of the tapestries still hang in the Cathedral. His son, Jean the Younger (*c.*1522–*c.*1594), had a successful career between Sens and Paris mainly as a book illustrator.

The portraiture of the mid-century is dominated by Corneille de Lyon (active 1533–74) and François Clouet (*c.*1510–72). Confusingly, the latter often shared the nickname 'Janet' with his father, Jean Clouet (died 1540/1), who was probably the son of a Flemish painter, another Jean Clouet (or Jan Cloet), who arrived in France around 1460. François' father was an exceptionally gifted portrait draughtsman, whose softly hatched work suggests Italian influence. Although portraits can rarely be securely attributed to him, his appointment as court painter to Francis I and examples such as *Francis I* (see plate 16), *Mme de Canaples* (National Gallery of Scotland, Edinburgh) and *Guillaume Budé* (see plate 162) seem to justify a comparison with Holbein.

François succeeded him as court painter and *valet de*

chambre in 1541, and introduced a more superficially Italianate feeling to some of his portraits, notably in the superb *Pierre Quthe* of 1562 (see plate 163), one of the finest but less characteristic likenesses of the French Renaissance. He remains, however, quintessentially French in the character analysis of his portraits and in the mixture of Italianate and Northern inspiration in his approach to the female nude (see plate 181). Both tendencies appear in the *Bath of Diana* (Musée des Beaux-Arts, Rouen). Clouet's portraits belong to a sort of 'International Mannerist' style, represented by Jacob Seisenegger (1504/5–67) in Austria, Bronzino in Italy and Sanchez Coello in Spain (see plate 184).

His portrait drawings (mainly in the Musée Condé at Chantilly) are firmer and more meticulous in outline than his father's, and include such august sitters as Francis II (see plate 20) and his young widow, *Mary, Queen of Scots, in*

163 FRANÇOIS CLOUET Pierre Quthe 1562
Possibly the best example of the Mannerist portrait style in mid-century France, this is also one of the finest French portraits of the Renaissance. Quthe or Cutte was a noted apothecary, as is indicated by the open book of herbs. The combination of restrained dignity in the figure and sumptuous detail in the glowing green curtain and book indicates that Clouet was probably aware of the style of Bronzino.

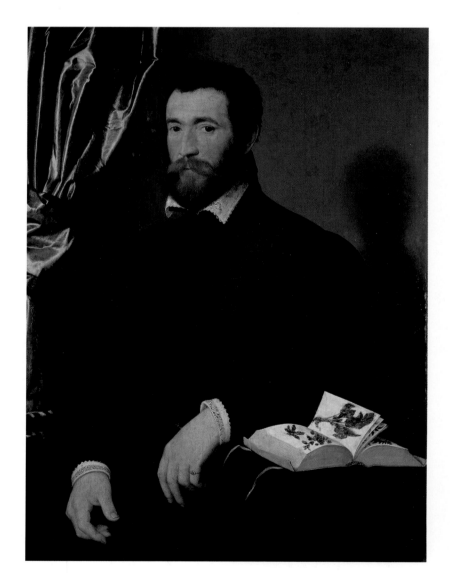

White Mourning (Bibliothèque Nationale, Paris). In keeping with the striking attention to character in *Pierre Quthe*, these drawings reveal much more concern for surface realism than Jean's, and are among the highest achievements in French draughtsmanship.

In France, this was the period of 'portrait albums', in which were collected groups of portraits, usually executed in chalk, for reference for paintings, or records of important contemporary figures or families. It is thanks to these albums that numerous French drawings of this type have survived.

Corneille de Lyon came to Lyons from The Hague some time before 1534, and became a French citizen in 1547. He became Painter to the Dauphin (subsequently Henry II) in 1540, and later, to King Charles IX. He had a highly successful career, and was described by a contemporary as an 'incomparable' portraitist. Although his only secure portrait is that of *Pierre Aymeric* of 1553 (Musée du Louvre, Paris), his style is recognisably individual because of his preference for a small format, into which the bust-length portrait is fitted quite tightly, and for a highly characteristic green (occasionally blue) background (see plate 164). Corneille's was a gentle talent, often probing a sitter's character with great sensitivity and sympathy.

Henry IV and the Second School of Fontainebleau

Henry IV (1553–1610) was the first Bourbon king of France, and his second marriage, to Marie de' Medici in 1600, was the second of the century with a member of that powerful family. The artistic traditions established by Francis I, Henry II and Charles IX were largely perpetuated by Henry IV, through the so-called 'Second School of Fontainebleau'. Although the painters of the 'Second School' based their style on the innovations of Rosso, Primaticcio and dell'Abate, additional influences, especially from Northern painting, led them to evolve distinctive new contributions. The more important painters were Toussaint Dubreuil (1561–1602), Ambroise Dubois (1542/3–1614) and Martin Fréminet (1567–1619), followed by Guillaume Dumée and Gabriel Honnet, but little is known of their personalities. Antoine Caron (*c.*1520–*c.*1600) typifies one strand of French Mannerist fantasy painting. He was made court painter to Catherine de' Medici after studying with Primaticcio, and he specialized in brightly coloured many-figured scenes set against elaborate architecture, often drawn directly from ancient Roman examples.

The fascination with courtly, mythological and 'gallant'

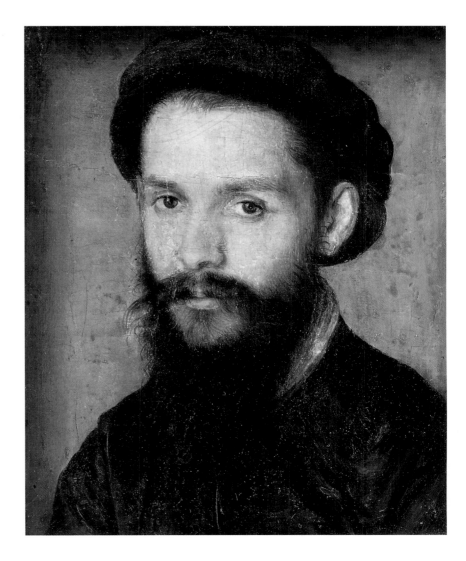

164 CORNEILLE DE LYON Clement Marot, undated
This sensitively observed portrait shows Corneille de Lyon's almost miniaturistic style at its most refined. The artist has used thin paint and set a dark figure against the pale green background so favoured by many Mannerist painters. The picture shows strong affinities with the work of Netherlandish painters like Joos van Cleve, but its softness and delicacy is more typical of French portraiture at this time.

themes current among the First School painters continued with the Second School. Likewise, Henry IV perpetuated his predecessors' tradition of publicly flaunting his mistresses, including the most celebrated, Gabrielle d'Estrées (see plate 187).

The painters of Nancy, then the capital of the Duchy of Lorraine, maintained a flourishing school that lasted well beyond the sixteenth century. Mannerism found unreserved support there, although the two artists who best represent it lie somewhat outside the scope of this study. They are Jacques Callot (1592–1635) and Jacques Bellange (active 1600–17), both of whom had a genius for engraving. Callot's series, *Grandes Misères de la Guerre*, was inspired by the French invasion of Lorraine, and its brilliant detail and dramatic use of light and shade give it a unique place in the history of the art. Bellange's figures are among the most sophisticated, exaggerated and elegant of late Mannerism.

England

The Renaissance arrived late, abruptly and hesitantly in England, and the evolution of painting there offered no parallels with France's continual interest in Italian art and its gradual assimilation of Northern and Southern Renaissance ideas. It was conditioned and severely limited by the secularization of the church under Henry VIII (1491–1547). At a time when Italian Renaissance ideas might well have found fertile ground there were only intermittent signs of its arrival, such as the few works left

165 ROWLAND LOCKEY Sir Thomas More, his Household and Descendants *c.*1595–1600

Rowland Lockey made three versions of the great More family portrait, which is now lost. This miniature was probably commissioned from him by Thomas More II after Lockey's 1593 version in the National Portrait Gallery, London. The impact of this composition showing a great intellectual 'at the centre of a family united in the common pursuit of piety and learning' must have been immense on English artists.

by the Florentine sculptor Pietro Torrigiano during his stay of *c.*1511–22. The major exponents of the new style in painting were all initially foreign immigrants, such as Hans Holbein and Hans Eworth.

The English Reformation involved devastating iconoclasm, thereby eradicating a long and rich artistic tradition. In 1559 (one year after the respite given by the Catholic reign of Mary Tudor), two particularly horrifying acts of barbaric destruction took place in London. These bonfires were recorded by a contemporary: 'of Mares (Virgin Maries) and Johns and odur images, there they wher bornyd (burned) with gret wondur'.

By such means, any expression of religion through art, particularly after 1535, was prevented. This spelt disaster for painting in all but the most limited secular forms. It was thus that portraiture began to assume an importance in England unparalleled elsewhere in Europe, mainly because of its propaganda possibilities. Allegory also came into its own under the Tudors, partly as a result of Italian Renaissance influence, and was to constitute an important part of painting in the Elizabethan era.

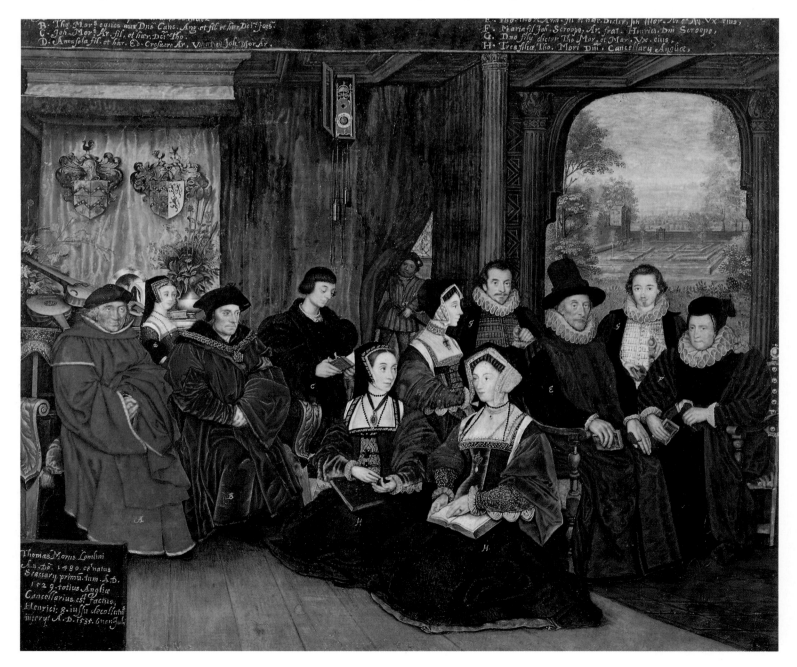

Henry VIII was quick to grasp the possibilities of Holbein's genius for portraiture, and the German artist remains the only painter of real importance in this period. The only likeness of Henry certainly by Holbein (Thyssen Collection, Madrid) depicts the cruel monarch with steely precision. From originals such as this, it was common practice throughout Europe for a painter or his studio to make any number of copies for use as diplomatic gifts, or reminders of the monarch's existence and power. Holbein's output in England was immense, with ninety portraits known from this period alone.

Hans Holbein the Younger in England

In spite of the efforts of Basle Town Council to deter their leading artist from leaving, Hans Holbein the Younger (1497/8–1543) moved to England after a visit in 1526, prompted by the loss of commissions in Basle as a result of the Reformation, when he had stayed for two years as the guest of Sir Thomas More. In 1527, he painted More's portrait (Frick Collection, New York) with a surface realism and grandeur which must have been astonishing in England. Even Erasmus continued to be amazed by Holbein's genius for creating a likeness and wrote of his *Sir Thomas More and his Family* (see plate 165), that it was 'so completely successful that I should scarcely be able to see you better if I were with you'. The highest compliment paid to portraitists during the Renaissance was to say that their likenesses were mistaken for real figures.

In 1532 Holbein settled in England, where he died of the plague in 1543. His first London contacts came through his association with the German Steelyard Merchants, whereby he probably met Thomas Cromwell. Cromwell may have commissioned the celebrated *Ambassadors* of 1533 (see plate 180) with its atmosphere of intense intellectual life and international grandeur, its anamorphic image of a skull and complex symbolism. It has been interpreted as part of a conscious revival of Van Eyck's painting style, which in part explains the combination of austere outline with rich textures and glowing colour, characteristic of Holbein's finest work.

This combination endeared Holbein to the English aristocracy and intelligentsia (see plate 166), and led to his appointment as court painter in 1536. In the manner of his contemporaries elsewhere, Holbein was employed in a range of court activities, including portraiture (see plate 167), designs for costume, textiles, jewellery and court masques. The latter were to gain in importance under Elizabeth I. Holbein was also an engraver, exemplified in the *Dance of Death* published in 1538.

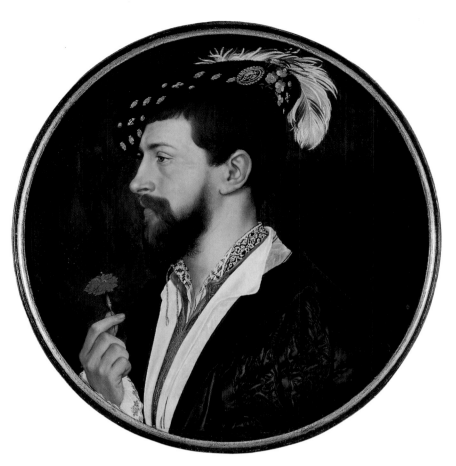

166 HANS HOLBEIN THE YOUNGER Simon George of Cornwall 1535
The sitter is Simon George of Quocote, who became part of the Lanyon family of Cornwall by marriage. A strikingly modern preparatory drawing at Windsor shows him with a moustache and beard stubble, probably indicative of Henry VIII's order of 8 May 1535 that courtiers should cut their hair and no longer wear beards; radiographs reveal that originally the painting showed him with a shorter beard. The circular format and reflective pose reflect Holbein's activity as a miniaturist.

His major work for the court was a large mural portrait in the Privy Chamber of the New Palace of Whitehall. Henry, his third wife, Jane Seymour, and his parents, Henry VII and Elizabeth of York, were depicted against the background of the latest Italianate Renaissance architecture. Although later destroyed by fire, its appearance is recorded in Holbein's cartoon (National Portrait Gallery, London). Such a forcefully realistic celebration of a monarch was previously unknown in England, and exercised a strong fascination for successive artists.

Holbein transformed English art, and some native masters succeeded in emulating at least his style's externals, as in the fine, anonymous *Elizabeth I as a Princess* of the mid-1540s (Royal Collection, Windsor). Few European artists succeeded in achieving Holbein's balance of extreme sensitivity to his sitter and to his superb technique. His drawing technique was as refined as his painting, and the portraits in this medium (see plate 167) attain a perfection without contemporary equal.

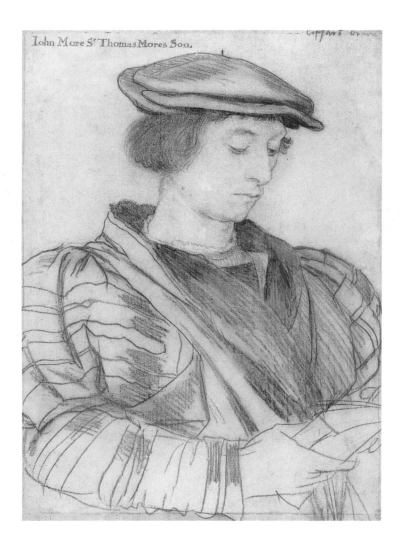

167 HANS HOLBEIN THE YOUNGER John More the Younger
c.1527–8
*John More (c.1509–47) was the fourth child and only son of Sir
Thomas More. This is the largest study made for the More family
group (see plate 165). It was made at the time of the sitter's betrothal
to his father's ward, Anne Cresacre, whom he married two years
later. The variety of chalk strokes indicates the breadth of expression
the medium permits, from the delicacy of the facial treatment to the
vigorous directness of the lower parts.*

Almost every painter active in England between 1540
and 1570 hoped to emulate Holbein's style. His immediate followers included John Bettes the Elder (active
*c.*1531–before 1576) and the Antwerp painter Hans
Eworth (*c.*1520–after 1573), who worked in England
from 1549 to 1573. Eworth's early travels resulted in a
fusion of ideas from Netherlandish art and the
Fointainbleau School with Holbein's style, as in his striking *Mary Neville, Baroness Dacre* of around 1555 (National
Gallery of Canada, Ottawa). Its complex surface patterns
contrast with Holbein's particular genius for simplified,
large-scale figures against very simple backgrounds.
Holbein's tendency to flatten his images was also reflected in the work of later followers like William Segar and
George Gower (died 1596), who was appointed Serjeant-
Painter to Elizabeth I (1533–1601) in 1581, and may have
been the most significant English painter of the later

century. Holbein's methods were carried on into the next
century by William Larkin (died 1619?) and Robert Peake.

Prior to Hilliard's emergence in the later 1560s, the most
important artists were mainly Netherlandish or German,
such as Gerlach Flick (died 1558) from Osnabruck.
William Scrots (active 1537–53) painted in the
International Mannerist style and became court painter to
the Regent of the Netherlands, Mary of Hungary, in 1537,
and to Henry VIII in 1546. He may have brought the fashion for full-length portraits to England, modelling them on
the Austrian work of Jacob Seisenegger and the German
Christoph Amberger, and he helped bring a more international outlook to English portraiture.

168 SIMON BENNINCK Self Portrait aged 75, 1558
*With the replacement of the illustrated book by the woodcut,
illuminators turned to other outlets, including miniature painting.
Benninck was already painting detailed portrait miniatures in the
1520s. Here, he has begun the painting of a Virgin and Child on his
easel, which is interesting for having racks for colours and brushes.
Although a Netherlandish painting, its importance lies in the fact
that it shows the style developed by Benninck's daughter, Lavinia
Teerlinc (1510/20–76), who entered the service of Henry VIII in
1546, and it links the Ghent-Bruges school with Nicholas Hilliard.*

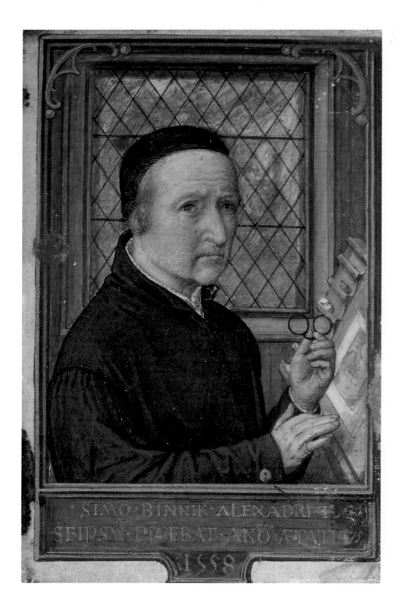

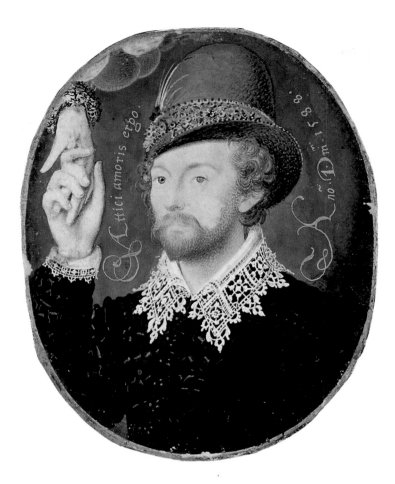

169 NICHOLAS HILLIARD Man Clasping a Hand from a
Cloud, perhaps Lord Thomas Howard 1588
*Howard served in the fleet sent against the Armada, and was a
distinguished naval commander. Clasped hands were a common
emblem of Concord and plighted faith in Elizabethan art and
literature, but the motto remains untranslated and unexplained,
suggesting a recondite complexity of meaning and purpose for the
portrait typical of such miniatures. Since Howard was a courtier, he
may have been involved in theatrical performances, and the miniature
may refer to one of these.*

Nicholas Hilliard and the 'Art of Limning'

England's greatest miniaturist or 'limner', Nicholas
Hilliard (1547–1619) was the first English-born painter
whose talent was recognized by his contemporaries, and
indeed the first native artist of the English Renaissance.

His immediate predecessor was Lucas Hornebolte
(*c.*1490/5–1544) from Ghent, active at Henry VIII's court
along with Holbein, and an exceptionally gifted miniaturist. Hilliard's training as a goldsmith with his father led
to his continued activity in this sphere, and he probably
made the *Armada Jewel* (Victoria and Albert Museum,
London). In 1570 Elizabeth I made him her Court
Miniaturist and Goldsmith, and he clearly enjoyed her
favour since she later decreed that no painter should paint
her portrait 'excepting only one Nicholas Hilliard'.
Hilliard's miniature of the Queen painted in 1572
(National Portrait Gallery, London) assumed a status

comparable to Holbein's *Henry VIII*, and was reproduced
on different scales. Hilliard expressed his debt to Holbein
as follows: 'Holbeans maner of limning I have ever
imitated and howld it for the best' (regard it as the finest).

Hilliard was known in France, which he visited about
1577 and where he probably saw the lavish art of the
Valois court, including François Clouet's miniatures. His
Treatise Concerning the Art of Limning was not published
in his lifetime. In spite of his talent and success, he was
frequently in financial difficulty, and was even involved in
speculative gold mining in Scotland!

170 NICHOLAS HILLIARD Young Man Leaning against a Tree
1588
*Hilliard's most famous miniature seems to show a young lover
encouraged by the roses of love but pricked by their thorns, but the
motto* Dat poenas laudata fides *comes from Lucan's* Pharsalia,
*urging the assassination of Pompey. This does not tally with a
proposed identification as Robert Devereux, Earl of Essex.*

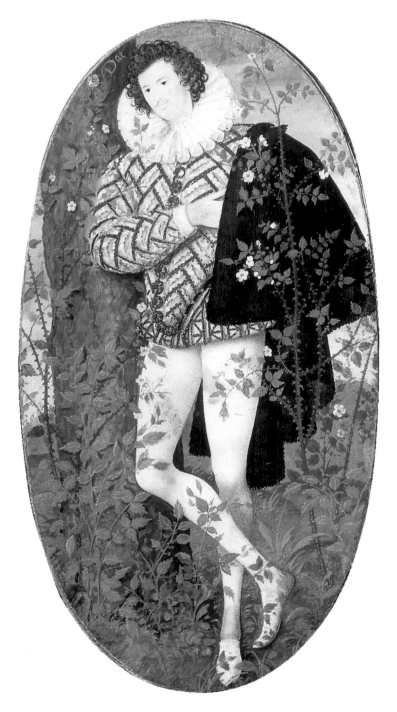

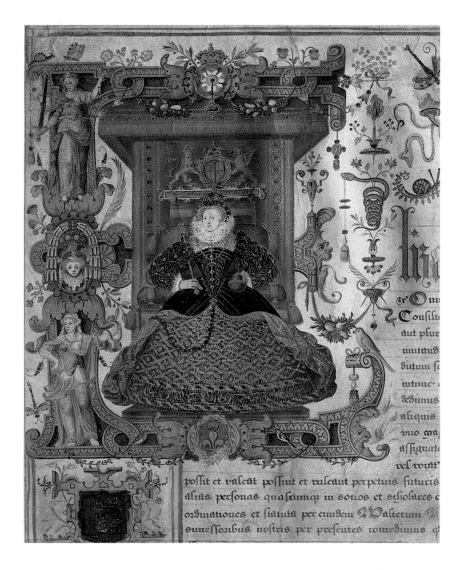

171 NICHOLAS HILLIARD AND ASSISTANTS The Mildmay
Charter 1584

*This is the charter authorizing Sir Walter Mildmay to found
Emmanuel College, Cambridge. Hilliard designed the whole
composition, painted the figure of the Queen, and then presumably
delegated the border to an assistant. The grotesques reflect Italian
prototypes, and probably derive from those decorating Nonesuch
Palace, by Toto del Nunziata. The charter is basic to any
understanding of Hilliard's work as a graphic artist, and shows how
he tried to keep up with the latest Italian ideas.*

The close relationship between miniature painting and
precious metalworking are obvious, although Hilliard's
freedom of technique and command of brilliant colour
within his chosen limitations of scale are never finicking.
Elizabeth I kept her miniatures in her bedroom, individ-
ually wrapped and labelled with the sitter's name, and in
general miniatures were carefully hidden from light and
dust in boxes of ivory or other valuable materials.

The intensely private nature of the portrait miniature
lent it a unique position in European Renaissance art, a
position somewhat comparable to the portrait drawings of
Clouet and his circle in France. Like these, miniature
portraiture was quintessentially a royal art, and remained
exclusive for the first half-century of its existence. Its evolution resulted directly from the removal of Italianate

inspirations with the Reformation, a fact proven by the
changes which affected the miniature when strong links
were again forged with Italian culture under Charles I.

One of the aspects of Renaissance thinking which
directly influenced the miniature from the 1580s was the
employment of emblems and *imprese* (mottoes). Thus
symbols began to play an increasing part in miniature
imagery. Flames could symbolize the passion of love,
while a black background could indicate constancy. As
they were often gifts between lovers (or a highly prized
gift from the Queen herself), these hidden meanings sat-
isfied the Tudor and Jacobean love of the esoteric. As
Elizabeth's reign closed, her miniaturists delighted in portraying her as eternally young and beautiful, embellished
with luxurious jewellery and clothes, while clearly his
next patron, James I, failed to inspire Hilliard or indeed
any of the other painters who had produced such images
of the Virgin Queen.

Hilliard's studio was probably extensive (see plate 171).
Rowland Lockey (*c.*1565–1616) became his apprentice in
1581, working for Bess of Hardwick and learning from
Hilliard the crafts of goldsmith, miniaturist and painter on
canvas. His record copy of Holbein's *Sir Thomas More and
his Family* (see plate 165) is an important document. In the
hands of the mysterious Isaac Oliver (1560–1617), late
Elizabethan and Jacobean miniature painting entered a
new and different phase, with the inclusion of intensely
religious works like the *Lamentation over the Dead Christ* of
1586 (Fitzwilliam Museum, Cambridge). Most closely
related to European Renaissance ideas are his portraits of
sitters in masque costume (see plate 304).

Renaissance Painting in Spain

The immense *Retable of Saint George* begun by Marzal de
Sax (active 1394–1405) about 1400 (Victoria and Albert
Museum, London) typifies Spanish painting at the dawn
of the fifteenth century. It consists of principal scenes and
over thirty subsidiary scenes and figures, contained in a
carved and gilded Gothic framework. Astonishingly, two
thousand retables have survived in varying degrees from
the fourteenth and fifteenth centuries, and constitute a
heritage we associate particularly with Spain. Luis
Borrassá (*c.*1360–*c.*1425) who was active in Barcelona
probably painted a large number of these complex and
demanding works, in a combination of French and
Sienese styles. About twenty have survived.

It is impossible to present a simplified picture of
the complex changes in Spanish late medieval art under the
impact of Flemish, French and Italian ideas. The character

of Spanish paintings was always different from the rest of Europe, often dominated by fervent religiosity which evolved and intensified through El Greco into the Baroque era. The International Gothic style survived in Spain well into the fifteenth century. Gradually, however, the influence of Sienese painting displaced the Gothic idiom, and religious imagery of sometimes shocking directness was combined with strong narrative. Illumination remained one of the principal areas of production. The Florentine Gherardo di Jacopo called Starnina (active *c*.1390–died *c*.1413) had a long stay in Spain until 1403, and his delightful version of late International Gothic must have been influential. No other Italian painter is recorded there in the fourteenth century.

Bernardo Martorell (active 1427–52) was the leading Barcelona painter after Borrassá, although only his *Altarpiece of Saint Peter of Púbol* of 1437 (Gerona Museum) is documented. He combined Flemish and French ideas in a uniquely forceful version of International Gothic. Within his lifetime, however, the so-called Hispano-Flemish style, with its strong echoes of Jan van Eyck, made its appearance in Barcelona and rapidly began to replace International Gothic. This must have been directly reinforced by Van Eyck's presence in Spain on a diplomatic mission in 1427 and 1428. The direct result of his visit was a superb painting by Luis Dalmau (active 1428–60): the *Virgin of the Councillors* of 1445 (Museo de Arte the Cataluña, Barcelona). Jaime Huguet (active *c*.1448–92) became the leading Catalan painter of the later fifteenth century, although his influence extended to Aragon, where the Gothic style was strongly entrenched.

Fernando Gallego (*c*.1440–after 1507) is the first relatively well-documented Castilian painter, and may have visited the Netherlands. He evolved a recognizably personal style, with distinctive slim figures rather different from any other contemporary work. This greatly facilitates attributions to him in a period when these are often problematic. One of the principal sources for his life is the book *Museo Pictórico y Escala Optica* by Antonio Palomino y Velasco (1655–1726), 'the Spanish Vasari', which provides invaluable biographies of sixteenth-century artists. Gallego's first dated painting is the *Retable of Saint Ildefonso* (Zamora Cathedral), which shows the influence of German prints but also considerable expressiveness in the figures.

Gallego's major contemporary was the Master of Ildefonso (active 1470s). This generic name derives from his key work, the *Investiture of Saint Ildefonso* (see plate 182) of the later 1470s, a colourful work which is evidence not only of Flemish influences, but of a growing knowledge and understanding of Italian painting. Gallego is at the centre of a group of painters whose work illustrates the

sudden flowering of the last years of the century, also seen in the highly independent painter Bartolomé Bermejo, born in Cordova but active in Aragon and Barcelona between 1474 and 1498. His *Saint Michael* of 1468 (see plate 172) and his haunting *Pietà* of 1490 (Barcelona Cathedral) both mark him as an original master, and show

172 Bartolomé Bermejo Saint Michael and the Dragon 1468

This, probably an early painting by the master, suggests he may have experienced Flemish painting at first hand. Its combination of Flemish and Spanish elements resulted in an intense, personal style. Characteristic is the highly stylized tight drapery.

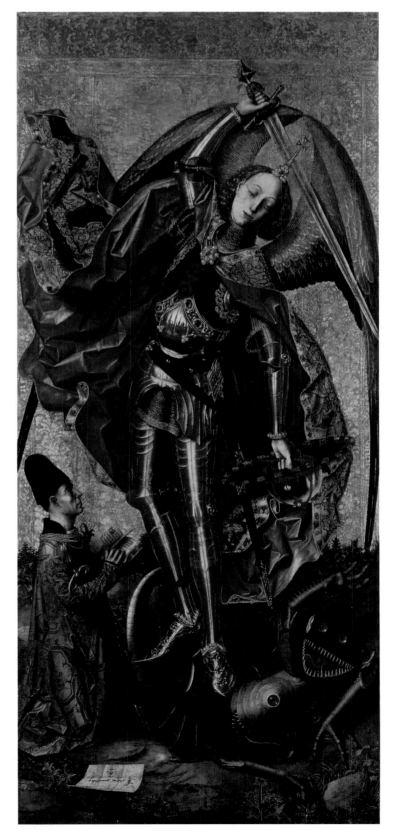

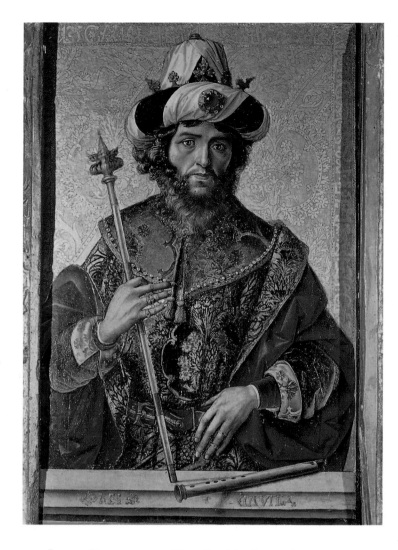

173 PEDRO BERRUGUETE King David, after 1483
This is one of the six predella paintings of Kings and Prophets of Israel from the Retable of St Eulalia, and it shows Berruguete's Italian experience, notably at the court of Urbino in 1477 under Joos van Ghent. It was he who introduced the larger concept of form, gesture, colour and pattern into Spanish painting.

the progression from an angular Flemish imagery to an Italianate manner in which atmospheric landscape plays an important role.

Ferdinand and Isabella expressed considerable favour for Italianate painters. The Flemish Juan de Flandes (died *c.*1519) was Isabella's court painter from 1496 until her death in 1504. Although he worked on a smaller scale than the major retable painters, his refined painting grafts Italianate detail on to the style he had learnt in Antwerp. The Castilian Pedro Berruguete, who also died in 1504, was court painter to both monarchs, and he demonstrates the fullest understanding of Italian Quattrocento ideas. Within Spain he was probably unique in his direct experience of the finest Italian art of the day. He seems to have worked for Federico da Montefeltro at the Court of Urbino, in the company of Melozzo da Forlì and Joos van Ghent. Although his early work was probably influenced by Gallego, he evolved a grandeur based on large forms, rich detail and colour, and expressive faces and gesture (see plate 173).

The Sixteenth Century in Spain

Towards the end of the sixteenth century, Spanish art was dominated by El Greco, who settled in Toledo in 1577. Although painting flourished between the two powerful polarities of court and Church, a distinct lack of fine painters is evident at this time particularly when compared with the seventeenth century. The High Renaissance produced as its leading painter the somewhat dull Fernando Yáñez de la Almedina (active 1506–*c.*1531), who may have assisted Leonardo in Florence on the *Battle of Anghiari* in 1505. Alonso Burruguete (*c.*1488–1561) also spent time in Florence from 1504 to 1518, after which Charles V made him court painter.

Philip II imported a group of significant Italian artists to decorate his Escorial Palace, including the painters Pellegrino Tibaldi (1527–96), Luca Cambiaso (1527–85) and Federico Zuccaro (1540/41–1609). They introduced Spain to the latest developments in Italian Mannerist painting, leaving many important examples of the style in the Escorial. Philip's tastes were eclectic, and in addition to commissioning some of Titian's most sumptuous later works, he included in his collections many paintings by Hieronymus Bosch.

Two other painters can be said to have achieved much more than local status: Alonso Sánchez Coello (1531/2–1588) and Luis de Morales (*c.*1520/25–86). Coello was, with Titian and Anthonis Mor (see plate 297), Philip II's court portraitist. He was sent as a child to Portugal, whose king, John III, made him study under Mor in Flanders. By about 1550 he had returned to Portugal and five years later was in Philip II's court, a royal favourite. The king was godfather to his daughters, and Coello evolved the perfect painted equivalent to the rigid etiquette of the time. Within the confines of the International Mannerist portrait style, his balanced, restrained likenesses allow no elaborate detail to dominate, but sumptuousness is everywhere implied (see plate 184).

Morales was Spain's greatest native Mannerist painter, principally of religious themes. He owed his occasional use of monumental scale to Portuguese art (he lived in Badajoz, a border town), and after 1558 he painted numerous large altars. Leonardo inspired his compositions, and his love of romantic, rocky scenes and mysterious *sfumato* effects, which were also practised in Spain by the Dutch painter Hernando Sturmio. Best known for his small, half-length Madonnas (see plate 183) and Pietàs, which earned him the nickname '*El Divino*', Morales sums up one side of Spanish Counter-Reformation provincial piety – sweet, intimate and introspective.

Painting in Spanish America was by definition colonial

and usually provincial, dependent on prints or imported paintings from Europe. But it included many examples of interest and beauty. In Bolivia, paintings from the workshop of Quentin Metsys and others were known, and before 1550 the influence of Antwerp combined with that of Italian Mannerism. The latter prevailed from the mid-sixteenth century, lasting well into the eighteenth century throughout Spanish America. Under Philip II, painting in Mexico suffered a setback when many Flemish, French and even Italian artists were imprisoned, falsely accused of Lutheranism. The Inquisition was even more rigid in Spanish America, thereby limiting subject matter.

Prague Mannerism

One of the last and greatest outposts of Renaissance ideals was at the Prague court of the Emperor Rudolph II (1552–1612). He modelled it on the refined style of the later Medici, such as Cosimo I and his son Francesco I, who favoured an opulent mixture of the fine and decorative arts, mingled with the extravagant and bizarre. Elsewhere it was matched by the courts of Francis I at Fontainebleau, Philip II at Madrid and Albrecht V in Munich. While Bronzino and Vasari dominated a host of lesser artists in Florence, and Frederick Sustris and Pieter Candid excelled in Munich, the leading painters in Prague were Bartholomeus Spranger (1552–1615), Hans von Aachen (1552–1615) and Josef Heintz (1564–1609). Of these, Spranger was certainly supreme.

Spranger was born in Antwerp, trained there, and was strongly influenced by Franz Floris (c.1517–70). He achieved a sophisticated international style thanks to his travels. In 1565 he visited Paris and then Italy, at a time when Italian Mannerism had created its major masterpieces. His involvement in the great fresco cycles by the Zuccari at the Villa Farnese in Caprarola was fundamental to his development, as was the art of Parmigianino. After a stay in Vienna, Spranger settled in Prague to become court painter to Rudolph in 1581. As at Fontainebleau, the taste of Rudolph's court tended to a strong interest in the erotic, including its most perverse forms. All subjects, whether religious or mythological, were permeated with this eroticism, so that both *Susanna and the Elders* (Schleissheim Schloss) and the magnificent *Triumph of Wisdom* (see plate 189) have a similarity of intent. This, together with extrovert distortions of the human figure (and face), enamel-like paint surface and the rich vocabulary of jewels, armour and complex dress, which Spranger had learned in Italy, resulted in one of the last great examples of true court art before the advent of the Rococo.

174 Attributed to ALONSO SANCHEZ COELLO View of Seville, undated
The rarity of urban views in European painting of the sixteenth century makes this particularly interesting: the best-known example is El Greco's famous if more idiosyncratic View of Toledo. *Carefully observed landscapes appear in the backgrounds of some Coello portraits.*

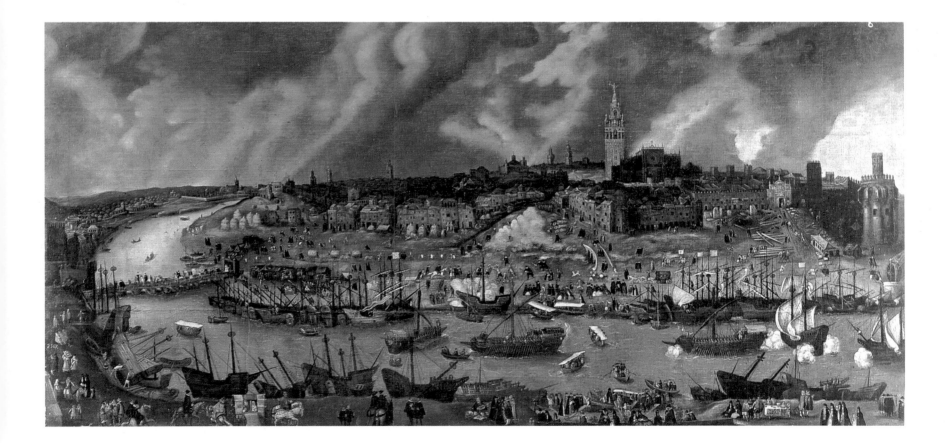

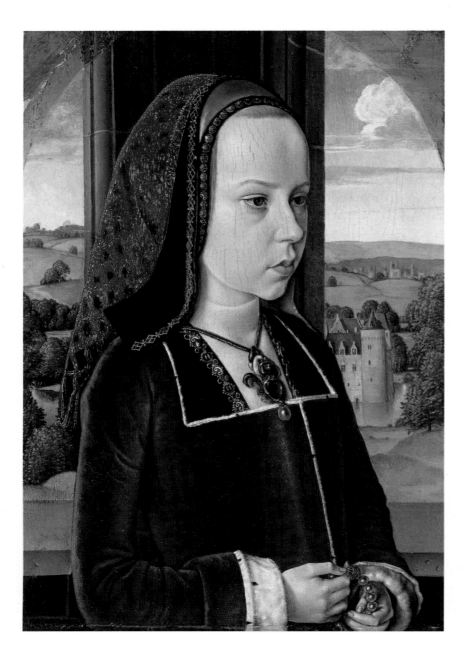

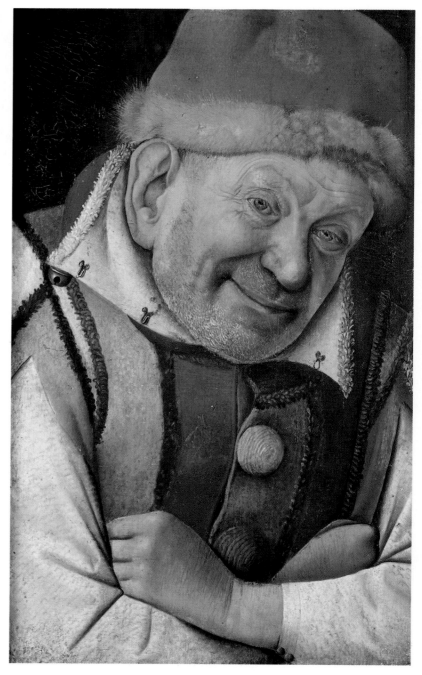

175 THE MASTER OF MOULINS Young Princess c.1498
(Left) Two possible identifications for this unusual portrait have been
proposed; Suzanne of Bourbon and Marguerite of Austria. Its jewel-
like colour and intensely concentrated expression, together with the
positioning of the figure apparently on a high columned terrace, lend
it a remoteness at variance with the sitter's proximity to the viewer.
The luminous landscape and jewels are beautifully painted.

176 JEAN FOUQUET The Court Jester Gonella c.1445
Once attributed to Bruegel the Elder, then to Jan van Eyck (whose
treatment of physiognomy it recalls), this unique portrait is almost
certainly Fouquet's work. It shows the famous court jester of the court
of Niccolò III d'Este. It is likely that the portrait was painted for
Niccolò's son, Lionello d'Este, a well-known amateur of Flemish
art. The device of representing figures tightly enclosed in the frame
with their arms folded in this way appears in miniatures by Fouquet
and his successor Jean Colombe. Particularly striking is the direct
gaze, engaging the sitter with irresistible intimacy. Compared with
Fouquet's portrait of Charles VII (see plate 8) this shows a complete
liberation from late medieval conventions, and may have been
painted in France after the artist's return.

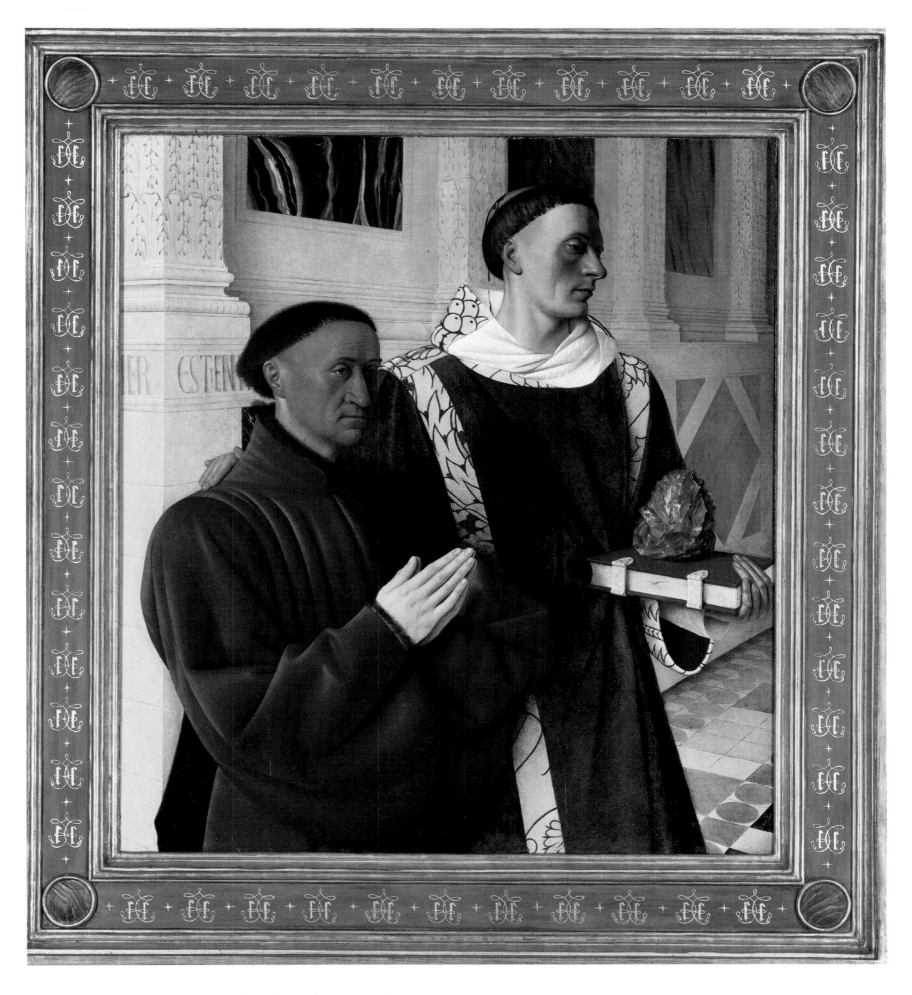

177 JEAN FOUQUET Etienne Chevalier with Saint Stephen, 1477

The diptych of which this is half was located above the tomb of Etienne Chevalier in Melun Cathedral until 1775. Its right wing, showing the Madonna and Child with Angels, *is in the Musée Royal des Beaux-Arts, Antwerp. Here, the saint wears a deacon's robe and carries a book and stone referring to his martyrdom. Chevalier's name is repeated several times along the base moulding of the background architecture. Chevalier, who died in 1474, was the son of a secretary to Charles VII, and became Treasurer of France in 1451. Fouquet also made other portraits of Chevalier in* Chevalier's Book of Hours: *most of these miniatures are in the Musée Condé at Chantilly. The crystalline clarity of form and colour in both figures and background, and the intensely observed character of the two faces, mark this out as Fouquet's masterpiece.*

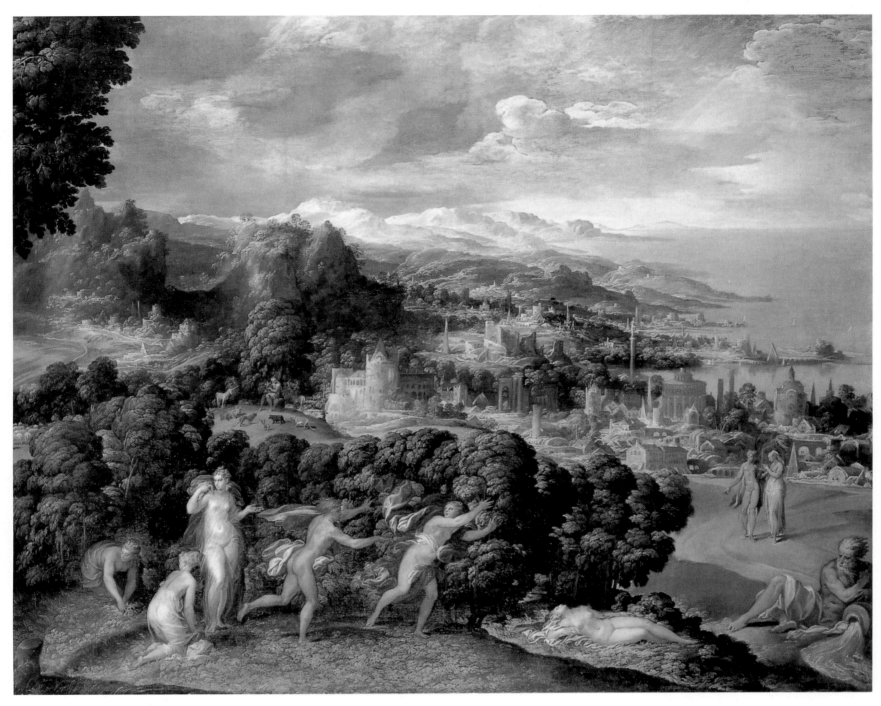

178 Attributed to Niccolò dell'Abate Landscape with
Euridice and Aristarchus c.1558–59
*Drawing on a variety of sources, this landscape typifies dell'Abate's
approach to the romanticized landscape which he introduced at
Fontainebleau. Its high viewpoint, permitting the depiction of
foreground, middle ground and horizon in equal detail, is typical of
Northern Mannerist art and was used by Bruegel the Elder, among
many others. The elegant figures, notably the broad-hipped, small-
headed women, recall the painter's Bolognese training.*

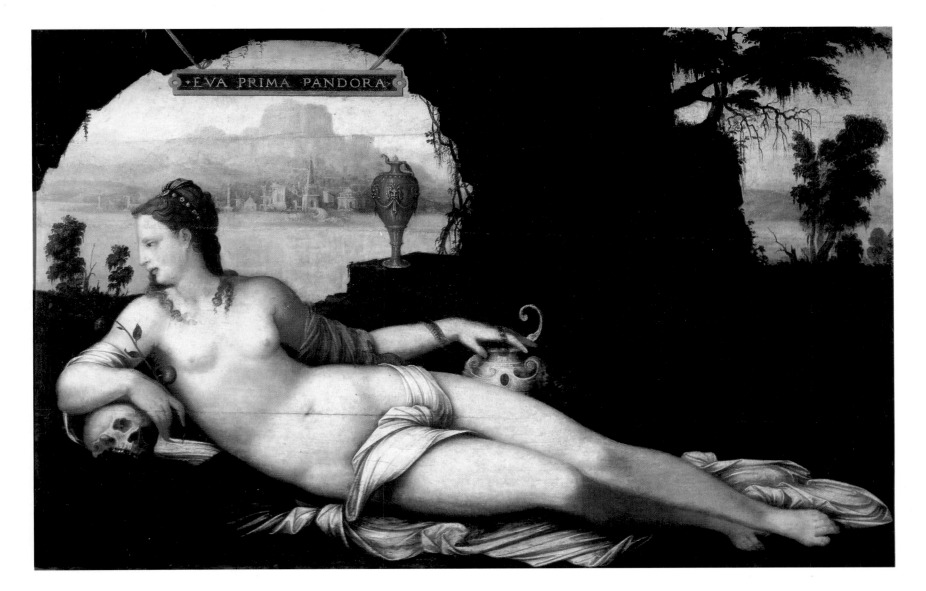

179 JEAN COUSIN THE ELDER Eva Prima Pandora, undated

*In Greek myth Pandora was created with earth and water by
Prometheus, and originated illness and vice on earth by opening a
forbidden box. This painting was already attributed to Cousin
within his lifetime, and is the best-known interpretation from the
French Renaissance of Pandora as a pagan Eve who, like Pandora,
released evil by biting the forbidden apple. Vasari much admired
Cousin, and his Italianate rendering of the nude reflects the concerns
with idealized Mannerist form of the artists active at Fontainebleau,
notably Niccolò dell'Abate and Francesco Primaticcio.*

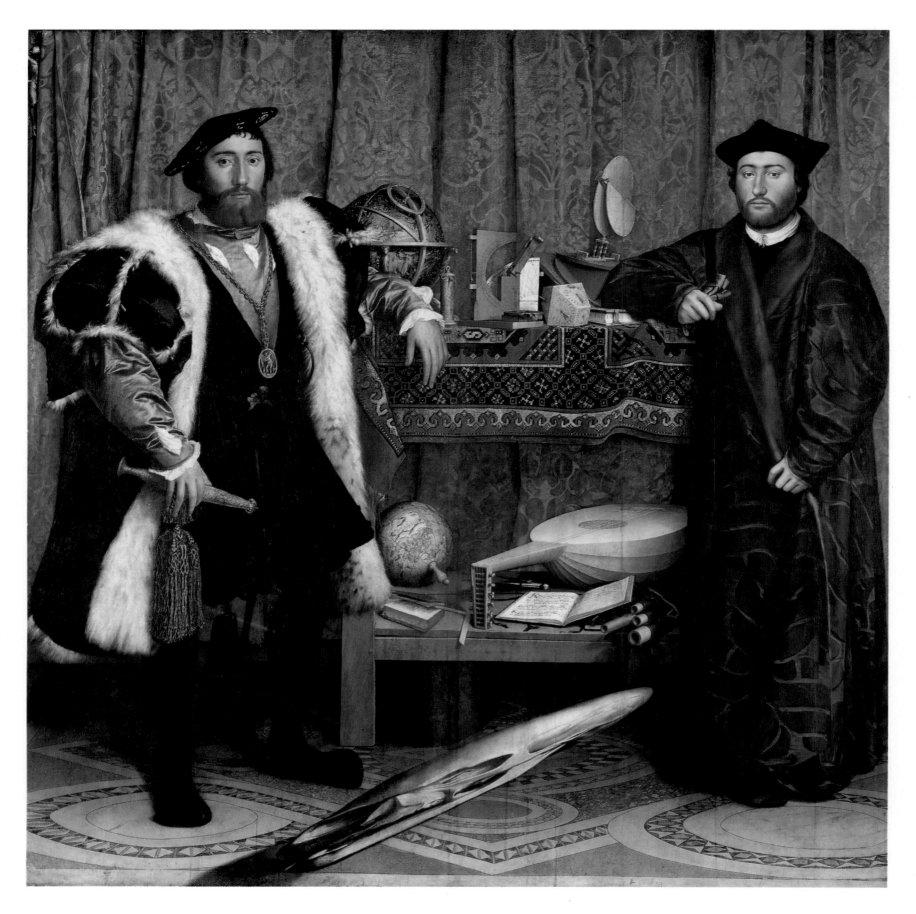

180 HANS HOLBEIN THE YOUNGER The Ambassadors 1533
*At the left is Jean de Dinteville, who was ambassador or diplomatic
envoy to England on five occasions. He is shown wearing the Order
of St Michael. At the left is his friend George de Selve, who visited
him in London April–May 1533, and who was several times
ambassador to the Emperor, the Venetian Republic and the Holy
See. This picture's extremely complex symbolism still eludes complete
explanation. A skull appears on de Dinteville's cap and in
perspective across the mosaic floor, which is an almost exact copy of
Abbot Ware's in Westminster Abbey. The skull seems to indicate
that the picture is a sort of* memento mori*: the broken lute signifies
a vanitas theme. The inclusion of so much still life is unique in
Holbein's painting.*

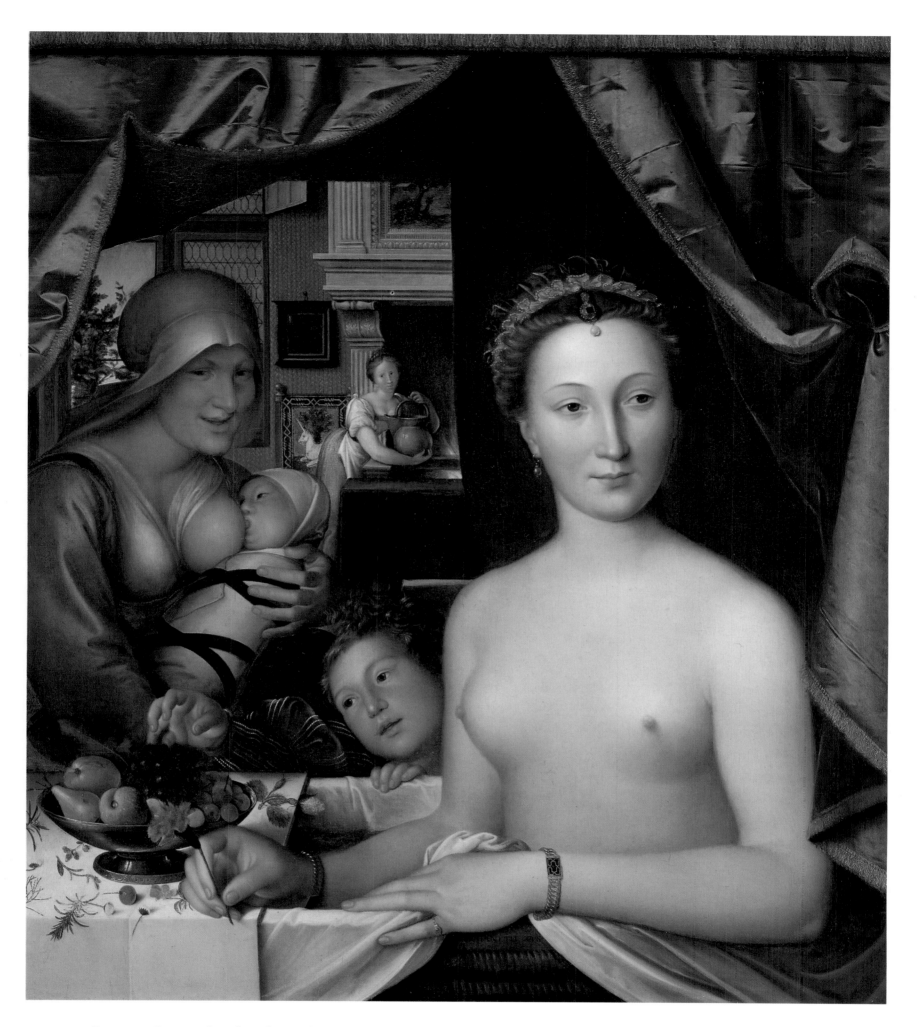

181 FRANÇOIS CLOUET A Lady in her Bath c.1571

Clouet signed two paintings, this and Pierre Quthe (see plate 163).
This portrait has sometimes been identified as Henry II's mistress,
Diane de Poitiers. It is a remarkable amalgam of influences, notably
that of Leonardo da Vinci's lost nude Mona Lisa – which exercised
a considerable fascination for French painters – and undeniably
Flemish features, notably in the nurse and the child in the middle
distance. With the exception of the nude, the rest of the painting

suggests the influence of Peter Aertsen in its combination of realistic
figures, closely observed interior and still life. The nude's artificiality
is typical of refined court taste, probably created in part by the
presence there of Bronzino's Allegory of Venus (see plate 228).
Many variants on this half-length type were produced in France at
the time.

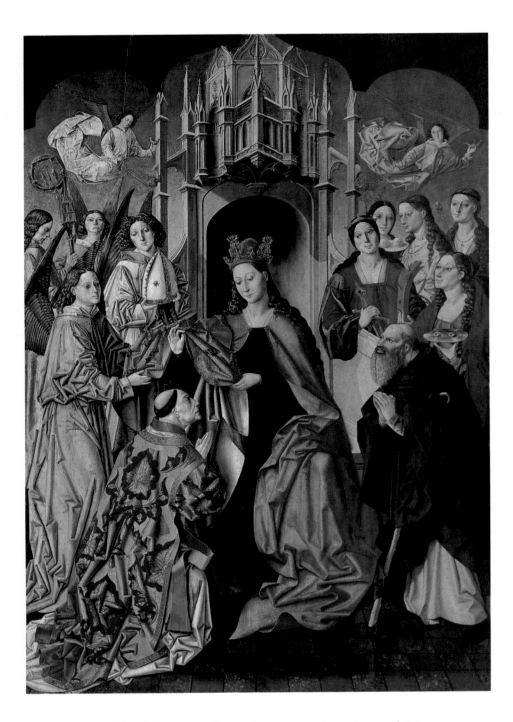

182 THE MASTER OF SAINT ILDEFONSO Investiture of Saint
Ildefonso *c*.1475–80
The master gained his name from this painting, which indicates the
main trends in painting in Castile in the last years of the fifteenth
century, when an increased grandeur of figure style was moving away
from Gothic linearity. It is probable that this master was strongly
influenced by German prints and by the Master of Flémalle.

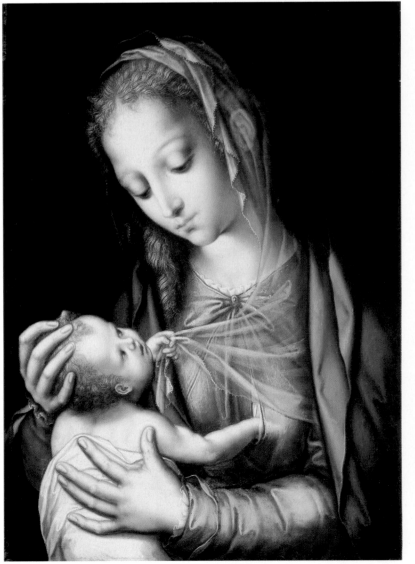

183 LUIS DE MORALES Virgin and Child, late 1560s
(Right) This is the first of several versions of this painting, indicating
its popularity, understandable in view of the image's simplicity and
the tender relationship between the mother and child. The
Madonna's face in particular typifies Morales' love of sfumato
technique, reminiscent of Leonardo's Lombard followers. His
knowledge and repeated use of Flemish, German and Italian
engravings may have been augmented by an Italian visit, since his
colour suggests a familiarity with Sienese artists such as Beccafumi.
However, the intensity of the image is essentially Iberian.

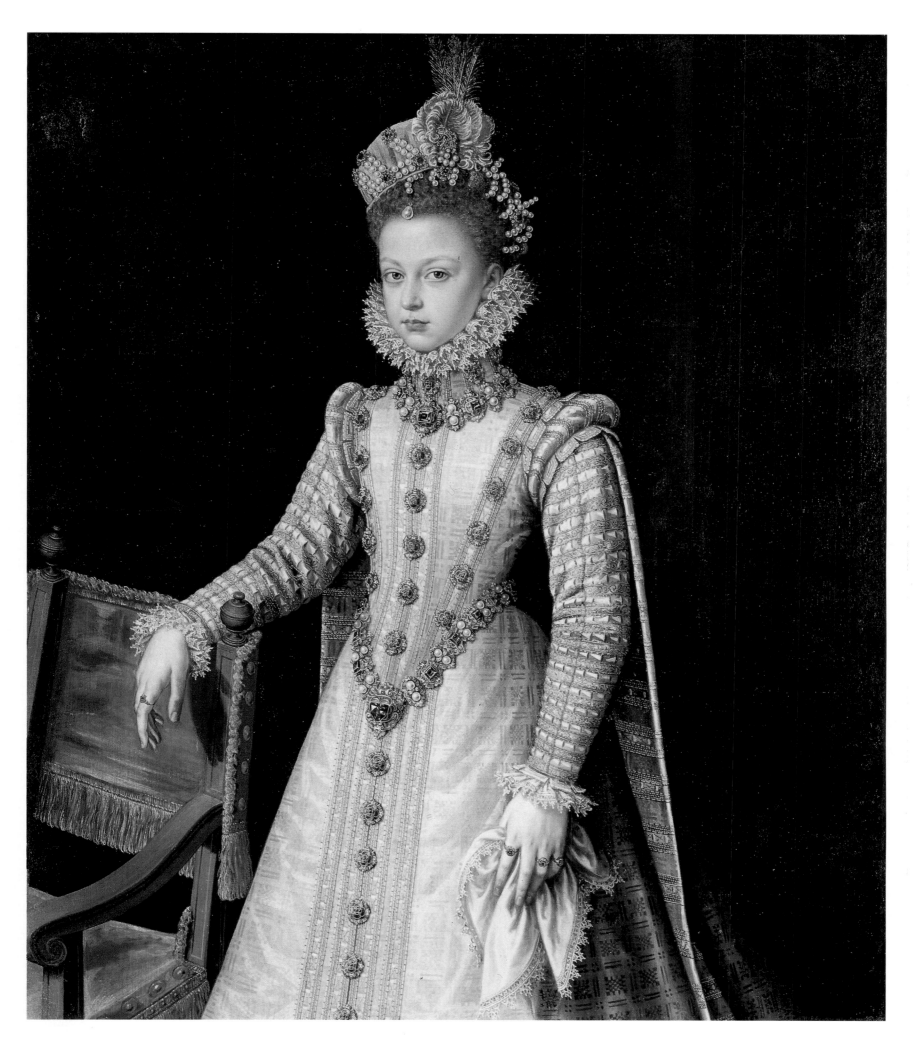

184 ALONSO SANCHEZ COELLO The Infanta Clara Eugenia
1579

*The sitter (1566–1633) was the daughter of Philip II of Spain and
Isabel de Valois. In 1599 she married the Archduke Albert of Austria
and was the Governor of the Low Countries. Coello's studies under
Anthonis Mor in Flanders in the early 1550s are reflected in the
precision of this strikingly stylish example of International Mannerist*
*court portraiture. Philip II's favourite portraitist, Coello also admired
Titian, and in portraits such as this introduced the relaxed formality
which characterizes subsequent Spanish portraiture. Its dazzling
display of jewellery is remarkable.*

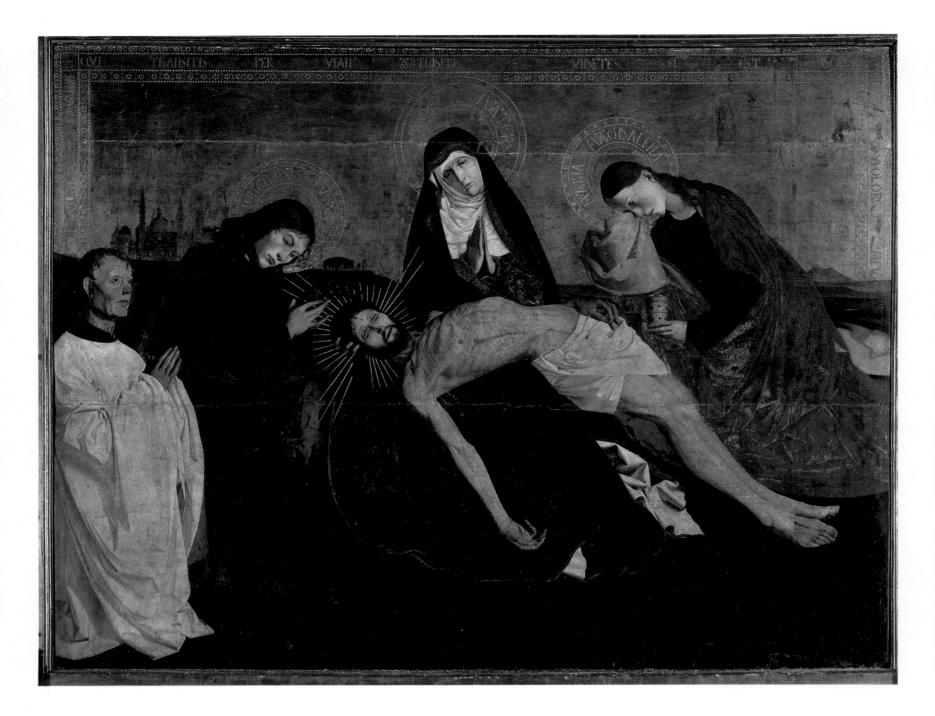

185 ENGUERRAND QUARTON The Pietà of Villeneuve-les-
Avignons, *c.*1460
*Quarton was active in Provence in the mid 1440s, and this
remarkable image is now accepted as by him, after continuous
reattribution to different provincial masters. Its grandeur remains
unique in French painting of its period, and it is coupled with a
pathos which has led some critics to think that it was Spanish. While
the conception is still late medieval, the intense characterization of the
faces and gestures reveals an awareness of Renaissance ideas.*

186 FRENCH SCHOOL (?) Wilton Diptych *c.*1395 or later
*The finest painting in England in the International Gothic style, its
authorship remains unknown, with various claims made for an
English, French, Italian or even Hungarian painter. Richard II
(1367–1400) is shown being presented to the Virgin and Child by his
patron saints John the Baptist, Edward the Confessor and Edmund,
king and martyr. Recent cleaning has revealed that the flag bears a
small map, apparently of an island which may be Britain. The
angels surrounding the Madonna wear collars made of broom cods
and white hart brooches – livery associated with Richard II.*

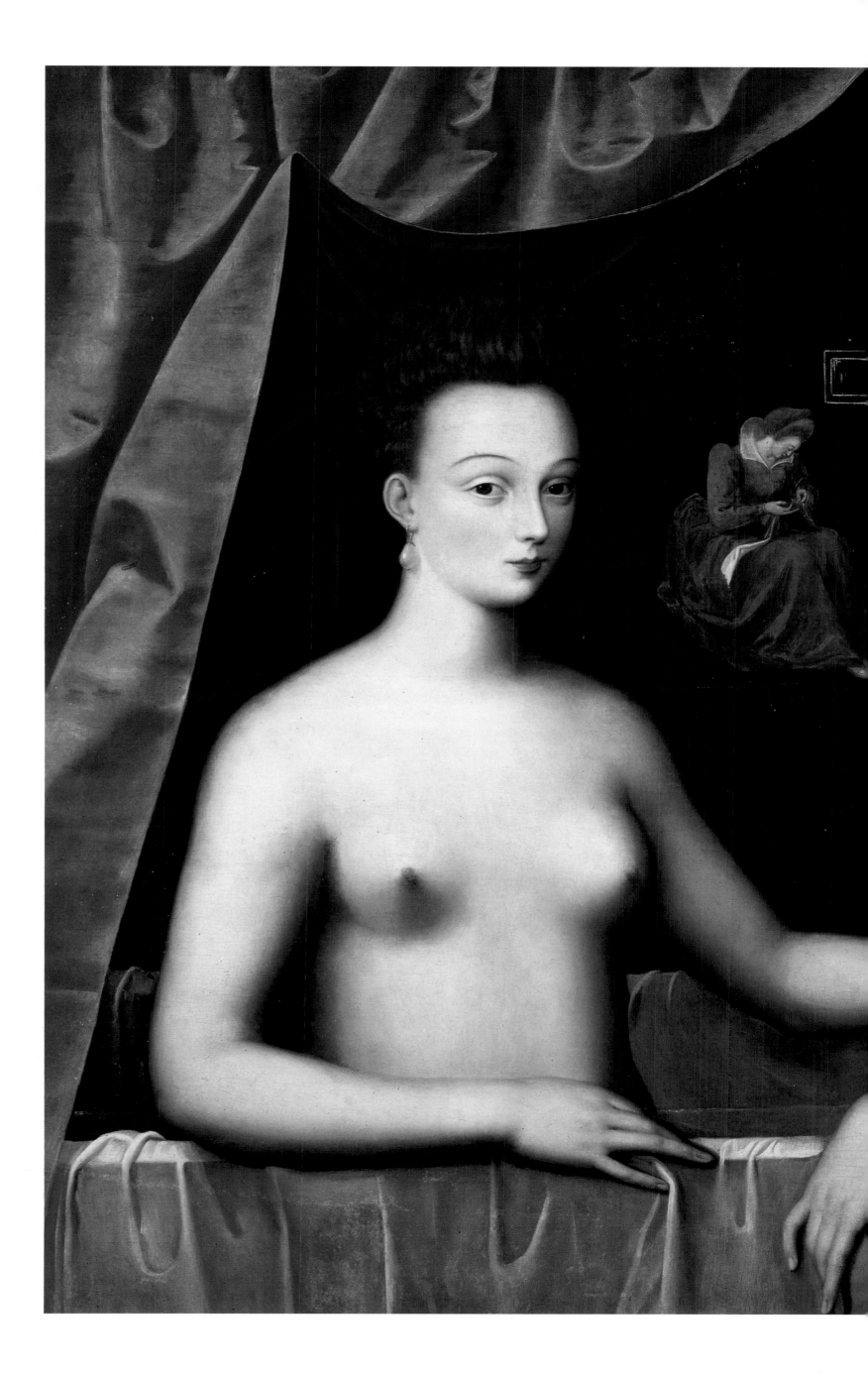

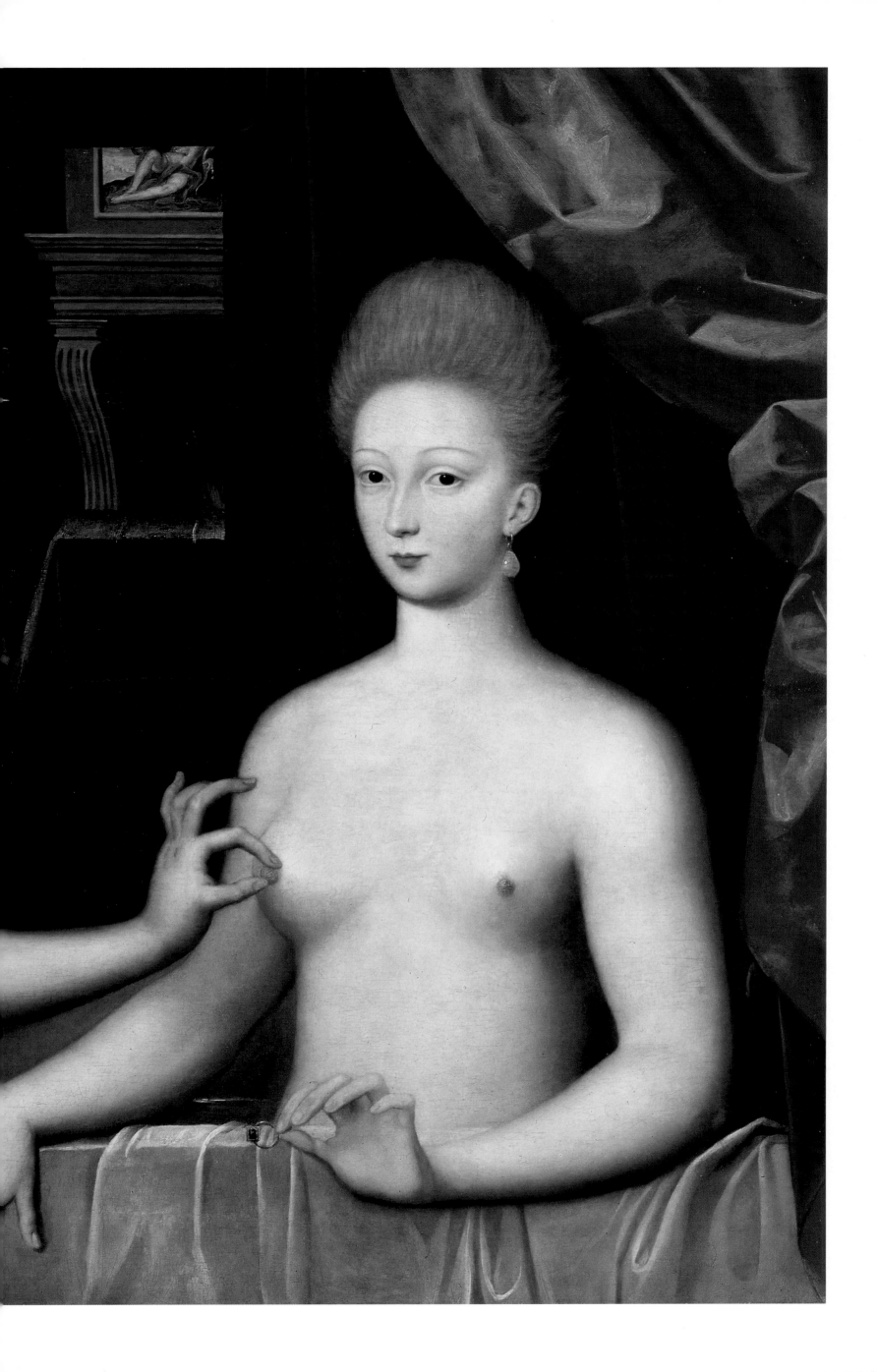

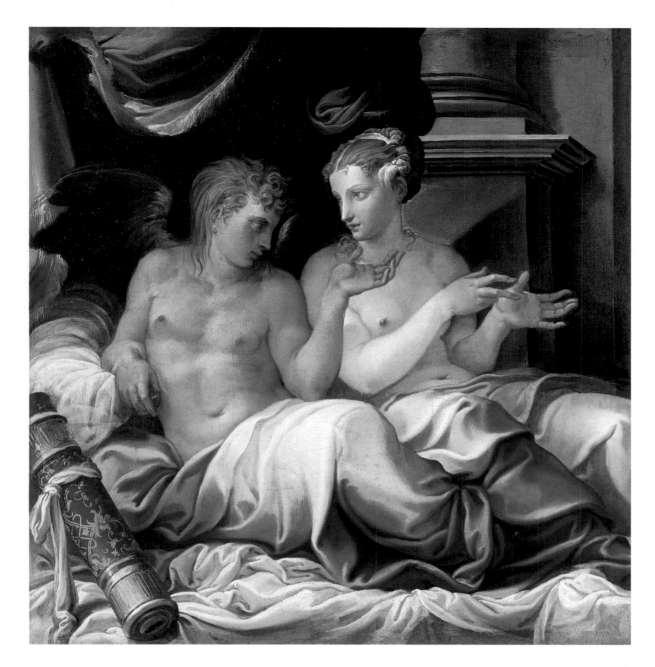

188 NICCOLÒ DELL'ABATE Eros and Psyche, undated
(Above) Very few paintings by Niccolò are known, although he
seems to have specialized in landscapes. The composition is based on
Primaticcio's painting Ulysses Recounting his Adventures to
Penelope in the Galerie d'Ulysse at Fontainebleau.

189 BARTHOLOMEUS SPRANGER Triumph of Wisdom c.1591
The composition centres on the Michelangelesque figure of Minerva,
goddess of Wisdom, presented in a thoroughly Mannerist pose. The
globe and compasses may indicate that this is an allegory of astrology,
the Emperor Rudolph II's favourite science. In the foreground is
Bellona holding Hercules' club, with the nine Muses at the sides.
Ignorance is shown with donkey's ears.

187 SCHOOL OF FONTAINEBLEAU Gabrielle d'Estrées and one
of her Sisters c.1591
(Left) Gabrielle d'Estrées (1571–99) was the only mistress of Henry
IV to wield political power. She urged the King to convert to
Catholicism in the hope of eventually marrying him, but her
premature death released him from the problem. The picture
illustrates the open eroticism prevalent at court, but also appears to
contain several symbols relevant to the sitter, such as the ring and the
sewing woman.

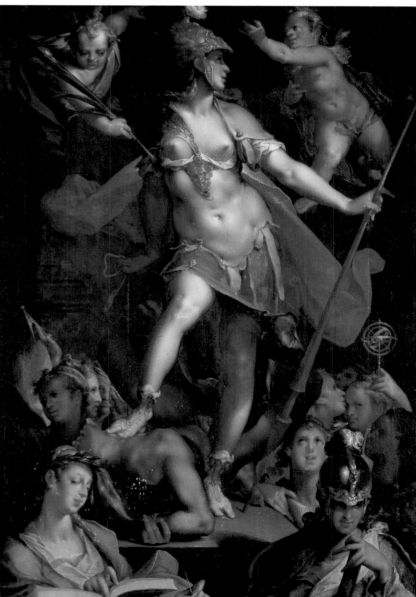

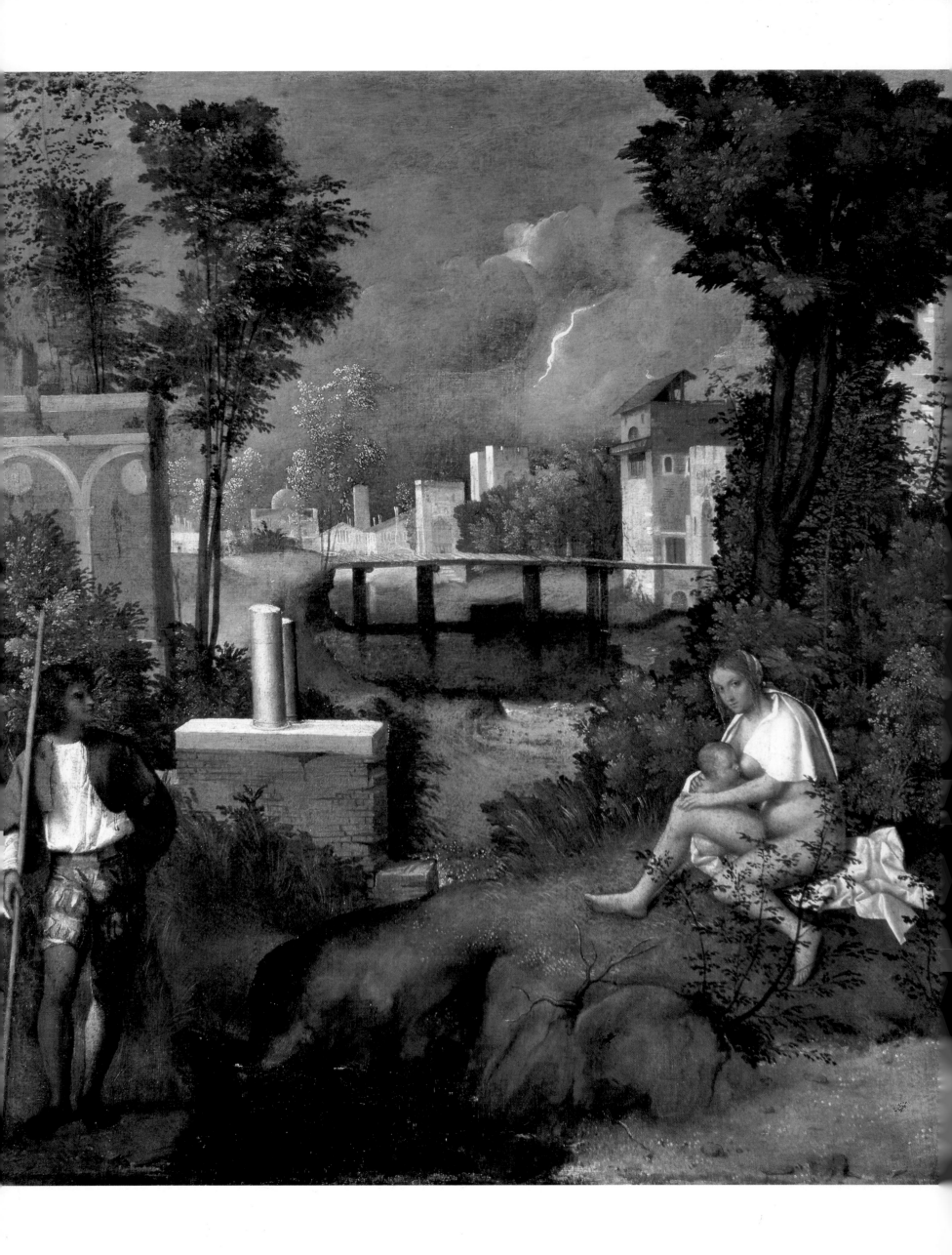

CHAPTER VII

The High Renaissance in Italy

The period we describe as the High Renaissance is generally accepted as the most complete flowering in Italy of Renaissance ideals in the visual arts. Any danger implicit in the use of the term lies in trying to define the High Renaissance in terms of specific dates, and the inherent suggestion that there was a decline after the period ended. For the purposes of this book, the term 'High Renaissance' defines a period in which specific aims were fully realized for the first time. Few nowadays would deny that these aims, once achieved, persisted even when they were elaborated to varying degrees into the style we call Mannerism. Thus, while the first explosion of genius which much later became defined as the High Renaissance was unquestionably muted by the time of Raphael's death in 1520, the principles evolved during his active lifetime continued to concern painters throughout the sixteenth century.

In painting, this unique creative concentration occurred in Italy alone, to encompass not only Leonardo, Michelangelo and Raphael, but artists as different as

190 GIORGIONE The Tempest 1505–10

Although this is one of the few paintings unanimously accepted as being by Giorgione, its significance remains much debated. The earliest description, made only two decades after Giorgione's death, describes it simply as a landscape with a gypsy and a soldier, and it is tempting to accept this straightforward interpretation. However, Giorgione originally painted another nude in the position of the present soldier, and so a simple explanation seems unlikely. The storm breaking in the background, the ugly object resembling a broken column, a gypsy woman and the possible identification of the youth as a mercenary soldier have led to its interpretation as an allegory of the transience of human fortune. This is the first picture of its kind in Western art to depict with such brilliance the passage of light and atmosphere over myriad different forms in nature, creating a visual magic unrivalled even by Giorgione himself.

Titian, Veronese and Correggio. Such a concentration had no equal elsewhere in Europe, and indeed few individual artists came anywhere near the stature of the greatest Italians. Rome, Florence and Venice were the three main centres of activity. Of these, only Venice continued to produce important artists and works of art throughout the sixteenth century, and in many ways perpetuated the achievements of the High Renaissance when these might be said to have been partly obscured elsewhere by Mannerism.

The term 'High Renaissance' was once used to refer only to the Classical art produced in Italy between 1500 and 1520, particularly by Leonardo, Michelangelo and Raphael. It is undeniable that within these two decades certain recognizable features covered by the term may be distinguished, characterized by Vasari as 'boldness of design, the subtlest imitation of all the details of nature, good rule, better order, correct proportions and divine grace'. Yet stylistic definitions are often blurred at the very heart of the period, when the artists destined to move away from High Renaissance principles were already active – notably among the first generation of Mannerists in Florence. Similarly, High Renaissance ideals continued parallel to Mannerism well into the second half of the sixteenth century; some might claim that its tenets never totally disappeared, since they were consciously revived by the Carracci as early as the 1580s.

The term is valid, however, since without it the transition from the ideals of the fifteenth century to those of the mid and later sixteenth century seems incomprehensible. The period brought the Renaissance to that 'sudden maturity' which Sir Joshua Reynolds, simplistically, attributed to Michelangelo's innovations alone. But to attempt to confine the High Renaissance to the first twenty or thirty years of the century is impossible, and it is undeniable that many of its salient features continue undiminished alongside the developments of the Mannerist style. This chapter examines the first period of High Renaissance impetus, when many of its ideals were already fully formed.

The Pre-eminence of Rome

Florence – its government, philosophy, art and architecture – had dominated the fifteenth century, and its emissaries spread its ideas throughout Italy and Europe. The invasion of Italy in 1494 by Charles VIII of France opened the floodgates for Italian culture to spread with greatly increased speed throughout the North. But a series of events saw a dramatic shift of emphasis to Rome, and by 1520 it had achieved the pre-eminence it was to maintain in the European artistic mind until the early nineteenth century. Only then was it replaced by Paris as capital of art. In spite of the devastation caused by the Sack of Rome in 1527 by German and Spanish troops, and the subsequent emphasis on other artistic centres, the city managed to retain its prominence.

There were clear reasons for the resurgence of Rome's supremacy. Firstly, it was the seat of the Roman Catholic church, whose power had recently been boosted by two strong popes, Julius II (1503–13) and Leo X (1513–21). It was soon to muster all its forces in the Counter-Reformation. Secondly, it was established as the focal point for any study of ancient Roman architecture and archaeology, then still in its infancy despite the fifteenth century's interest in all aspects of the Classical world. Lastly, it was the location of two of the most important and influential works of art in European history: Michelangelo's Sistine vault frescoes and Raphael's frescoes in the Vatican Stanze (see plates 218, 196).

Julius II succeeded that most corrupt of popes, Rodrigo Borgia, whose reign as Alexander VI had been characterized by nepotism and murder. So great was the loathing he engendered that Julius II felt obliged to move out of the first-floor Borgia apartments in the Vatican Palace, frescoed by Pintoriccio. Julius' reshaping of his chosen rooms in the Palace into the famous Stanze and the redesigning of St Peter's, under the direction of the architect Donato Bramante (1444–1514), were seminal in making Rome the new artistic centre of Italy. Indeed his entire reign as Pope, which spanned the core of the High Renaissance, had a crucial influence on the period. His patronage of Michelangelo and Raphael would alone have secured his place in history, and it is impossible not to see his forceful politics reflected in his artistic interests and ambitions for Papal Rome.

Leo X was the second son of Lorenzo the Magnificent. As a protégé of Julius II, he inherited many of his skills, as well as his artists and court intellectuals, including such men of letters as Cardinal Bibbiena and Pietro Bembo. Leo consolidated his predecessor's cultural activities in Rome, continuing the Stanze and the rebuilding of St Peter's, and commissioning the Sistine tapestries from Raphael.

Raphael's appointment as Superintendent of Antiquities is of great importance in understanding the atmosphere throughout the arts in the Papal city during these years. Raphael succeeded his uncle, Bramante, as architect of St Peter's in 1514, and the following year Cardinal Bembo declared that any ancient stones found within a mile radius of Rome had to be reported to Raphael within three days. Failure to do so would result in fines of 100 to 300 gold pieces, the latter being equal to Raphael's entire salary. Bembo also stated that in view of the possible destruction of important Roman inscriptions, no stone cutter could touch them without consulting Raphael. If one characteristic can be said to have dominated the High Renaissance in Italy, it was a greatly increased consciousness of the Classical world and of the need to preserve and study its artistic heritage.

The rediscovery in 1506 of the dramatic Hellenistic sculpture group, the *Laocoön* (considered by Pliny to be the greatest work of art) gave impetus to the dynamic and emotive elements emerging in Michelangelo's style. Along with the *Apollo Belvedere* and the *Belvedere Torso*, the *Laocoön* provided inspiration for sculptors and painters comparable to that of the Pantheon for architects. All three are now in the Vatican Museums.

Advances in Painting

Concurrent with this new awareness came a desire to record and analyse the progress of art towards the perfection seen in the art of Michelangelo. Of this trend, Vasari was the leading exponent (see Chapter VIII). His *Lives of the Most Excellent Painters, Sculptors and Architects*, written from the 1540s onwards, provides the most vital account of artists of the period, for Vasari was in a position not only to study the new work of his contemporaries, but to discuss much of it with them.

At this time, Renaissance ideals in painting matured at an unprecedented speed throughout Italy. Yet it is easy to overlook many developments in this period simply because the subject matter remained that of the Quattrocento. The didactic intention behind most religious art had not changed. The Blessed Giovanni

Dominici, in his 1503 treatise on family life, recommended to Florentine parents that they should have in their homes pious paintings or sculptures, which their children could easily understand. He stated that the most important images show holy children, most obviously the Virgin Mary with the Child, or images of childish obedience. These images proliferated, since every household of even moderate means aspired to own such works of art.

The means of conveying religious imagery began to alter much more dramatically than for Classical themes. A comparison of Botticelli's *Primavera* (see plate 115) with Raphael's *Galatea* (see plate 214) reveals many comparable sources of inspiration; but a comparison of Piero della Francesca's *Brera Altarpiece* (see plate 99) with Fra Bartolommeo's *Carondelet Altarpiece* (see plate 206) shows how far the interpretation of Christian art had travelled.

The three painters dominating the period – Leonardo, Michelangelo and Raphael – were Tuscan either by birth or by adoption and training, and it is therefore easy to see how Vasari's version of events emphasized Tuscany's supremacy. Yet their influence, even during their lifetimes, was national and international, rather than regional.

Leonardo's Later Career

The influence of Leonardo da Vinci (1452–1519) on northern and central Italian art and, later, on French painting was incalculable. Although his roots always remained in the Quattrocento, Leonardo was the undisputed pioneer of High Renaissance ideas, creating images twenty years in advance of their time, notably the *Adoration of the Magi*, begun in 1481, and the Louvre *Virgin of the Rocks*, begun shortly after (see plates 82, 191). The impact of his innovations reverberates throughout the work of Correggio, Giorgione and the Venetians and, to a less definable degree, Raphael. Leonardo's work also produced a school of Milanese imitators and followers in Bernardo Luini (*c.*1480–1532), Giovanni Antonio Boltraffio (1467–1516) (see plate 207), Ambrogio da Predis (*c.*1455–after 1508) and Andrea Solario (1450–1520). This strong following resulted directly from Leonardo's two stays in Milan, in 1482–99 and 1506/7–13. While there, he painted the *Virgin of the Rocks* and this would in itself have been enough to revolutionize Lombard art, even without the *Last Supper*. It is through the work of artists such as Cesare da Sesto (1477–1523) that we know lost pictures by Leonardo and others (see plate 192).

Leonardo returned to Florence from Milan in 1500 and exhibited his cartoon, the *Virgin and Child with Saint Anne*

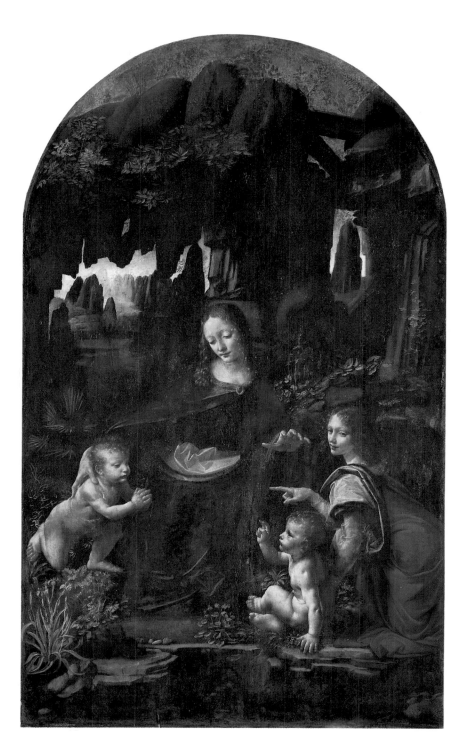

191 LEONARDO DA VINCI Virgin of the Rocks 1483–6
This is Leonardo's largest finished work and was commissioned in 1483 by the Confraternity of the Immaculate Conception for their altar in San Francesco Grande in Milan, although it was never delivered. The angel is pointing at the infant St John the Baptist, who in turn is praying to the infant Christ in the act of blessing. St John is receiving the special protection of the Virgin. This is the most extreme example of Leonardo's obsession with geological formations, flora and the mysterious capacities of light. It is possible that Lodovico il Moro offered Leonardo a high price for the picture as a gift for his niece in her marriage to the Emperor Maximilian. Leonardo's second version of this theme is in the National Gallery, London.

(see plate 208), in the church of the Santissima Annunziata the following year. Vasari describes the Florentines' enthusiastic response: it 'not only called forth the admiration of all creative spirits, but when completed, men and

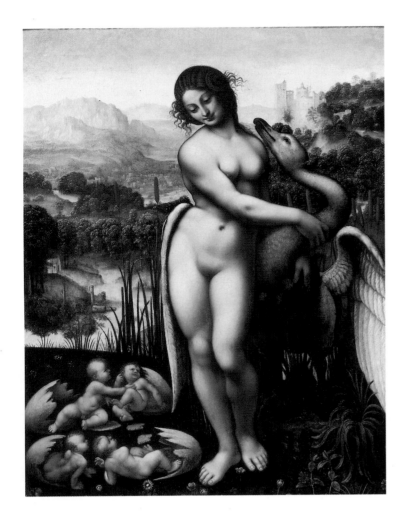

192 CESARE DA SESTO Leda and the Swan, after 1515

This is one of several copies with variations after the lost original by Leonardo dating from 1510–15, which Cassiano del Pozzo described with great precision at Fontainebleau in 1623. Leda is seen with her children Castor, Pollux, Helen and Clytemnestra by Jupiter, who is disguised as a swan. It is likely that Leonardo sketched the composition during his second Florentine period, possibly painting the picture in his second Milanese stay: most copies of the picture are by Lombard painters. Its overt eroticism would have appealed to the taste of the court of Fontainebleau and was certainly a novelty, even in the High Renaissance.

women, young and old, for two days, came to see it and to contemplate the marvels of Leonardo which were wondered at by all the people'. The cartoon may be seen as the starting point for changes in Florentine painting which matured through the Madonnas of Raphael, Michelangelo's *Doni Tondo* (see plate 210) and Andrea del Sarto (see plates 198, 213). Florentine painting of the High Renaissance might be said to aspire constantly to the achievements seen in this cartoon: its repose, supreme sense of balance, and its imitation of nature, as conveyed through a composition of deceptive simplicity and superb technical mastery.

In it, Leonardo perfected his celebrated *sfumato* technique, in which tones are blended to lose hard outlines. This now became one of the ideals of Florentine High Renaissance painting, continuing to some extent in the work of Andrea del Sarto and Pontormo. It contrasted with the 'dryness' of the Quattrocento which was so maligned by Vasari, but which persisted well into the new century in the work of many painters including Botticelli, who resisted the dramatic changes of the new style. Michelangelo also remained impervious to Leonardo's *sfumato*, as the sharp delineation of form in the *Doni Tondo* reveals. Indeed, this work shows the closeness of Michelangelo's sculpture to his painting. The forms are hard-edged and three-dimensional, the figures in twisted movement. For this painting, Michelangelo also designed the frame, which continued to be seen as an integral part of a work of art, especially in religious subjects.

The alternatives offered by Michelangelo when he returned to Florence in 1501, after over four years in Rome, impressed painters there for different reasons. The hostility between Michelangelo and Leonardo undoubtedly spurred on the younger artist to develop his own style in opposition to his rival. Michelangelo's adherence to the quintessentially Florentine ideal of *disegno* (strong, sculptural outline drawing) was to win the day, and it was his stylistic innovations rather than Leonardo's which increasingly dominated Tuscan painting from the middle of the second decade.

It was the aim of the new Florentine republic to enhance its status by commissioning major public works of art. This contrasted with the private patronage of the previous age of Lorenzo the Magnificent, and set the tone for the remainder of Medici rule throughout the sixteenth century. Much of this official art was placed around or inside the city's Palazzo della Signoria (later Palazzo Vecchio). In addition to Michelangelo's marble *David*, a potent and visible symbol of republican freedom which stood in front of the palace, the most important commission of this type came in 1503 for the mural decoration of its main hall, the Sala dei Cinquecento. In direct competition with each other, Leonardo was commissioned to provide a fresco showing the *Battle of Anghiari*, Michelangelo the *Battle of Cascina*, both historic Florentine victories.

It seems unlikely that these ever progressed beyond the preparatory stage, since Vasari and his school would surely never have obliterated even their traces when they frescoed the walls later in the century. Mystery surrounds them, but the surviving studies by both artists, together with the copy by Aristotile da Sangallo of Michelangelo's celebrated cartoon (see plate 209), clearly indicates how different they would have been. Leonardo speaks of the 'bestial madness' of war, and his fresco was to illustrate the heat of battle with all the energy of his drawn studies of storms. Leonardo's group was concentrated on a central explosion of inner forces, while Michelangelo's composition was more expansive. Michelangelo's choice was arguably more subtle, depicting a moment when bathing Florentine soldiers are surprised by imminent Pisan attack. This permitted the display not only of every conceivable anatomical contortion but also of differing psychological reactions. Michelangelo's conception was destined to exert far greater influence through his cartoon, described by Vasari as a 'school for artists' (among whom he lists many early Mannerists including Rosso Fiorentino, Pontormo and Perino del Vaga), and so much copied by leading painters of the day that it had already disintegrated by 1516. Its importance can be gauged by comparison with a contemporary painting by Botticelli, his *Mystic Nativity*, which already belongs to a past age.

Leonardo appears to have begun his most celebrated picture, the *Mona Lisa* or *La Gioconda* (see plate 194) at the same time as the *Battle of Anghiari*, and probably completed it about three years later. It is hard for us now to see the incalculable significance of this, the most overexposed painting in history. It represents the conclusion in Leonardo's portraiture of his attempts to explore the mysteries of sexuality, both male and female, a fact which has led to countless untenable interpretations of its meaning. The challenging yet withdrawn gaze of *La Belle Ferronnière* (Musée du Louvre, Paris), painted in 1490–95, already contains the germ of the *Mona Lisa*'s enigma. Michelangelo's attitude to women was also novel in Renaissance painting. Whereas Leonardo preferred to concentrate on the female characteristics of both sexes (as in his late *Saint John the Baptist* in the Louvre), Michelangelo invested his women with male physical characteristics. Such subtle nuances of psychology characterize much of Italian High Renaissance art, and appear in different ways in the contemporary Venetian works of Giorgione and his followers. It may be said that the tendency culminates in Correggio, but often assumes sinister implications in the work of Mannerists such as Rosso Fiorentino.

Leonardo returned to Milan in 1506 to complete the Louvre *Virgin of the Rocks*, and he later became Painter and Engineer to Francis I of France. The previous year Michelangelo had left Florence for Rome, in response to an offer from Julius II to create the architecture and sculpture for his immense mausoleum in St Peter's. But in the brief period they shared in Florence, both artists created work of outstanding importance, news of which lured other artists to the city.

Leonardo and Michelangelo both pushed the technical possibilities of art to the extreme in this period. Leonardo had opened the way, particularly in his private drawings,

which explored in great depth every conceivable facet of the world. Michelangelo continued the process later with his marble *Pietà* in St Peter's and accelerated it throughout the first decade of the new century. Their experiments were conceived to imbue art with a greater degree of naturalness, or at least the illusion of a closer approximation to the visible world. Vasari started his serious assessment of this period in the 1530s. He saw 'Nature' as the cornerstone of art, but knew that his contemporaries, and in particular his artistic god, Michelangelo, had done more than merely recreate it in paint or marble. He therefore perceived a definite change taking place about 1500, for although Quattrocento artists succeeded in rendering the external appearance of their world, they could not achieve the illusions given by such devices as the *sfumato* effects in Leonardo and Giorgione.

193 LEONARDO DA VINCI Saint John the Baptist 1513–16
This is Leonardo's last major work, and opinion has been sharply divided as to its intentions, quality and authorship. Leonardo has here carried to their conclusion his earlier experiments with sfumato *and the virtual exclusion of colour. The result can be interpreted either as a suave rendering of psychological ambiguity, or as a slightly ludicrous failure to capture a transient expression.*

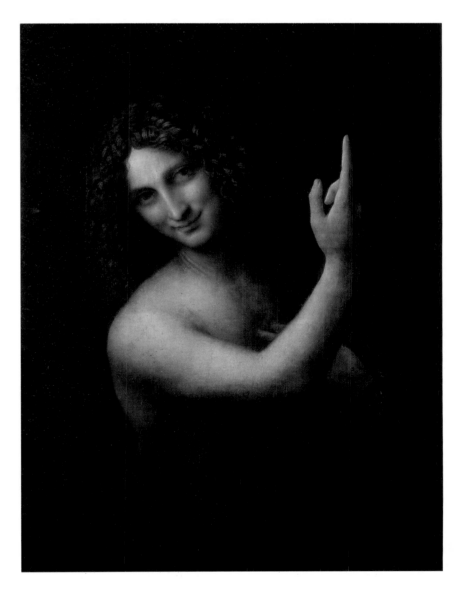

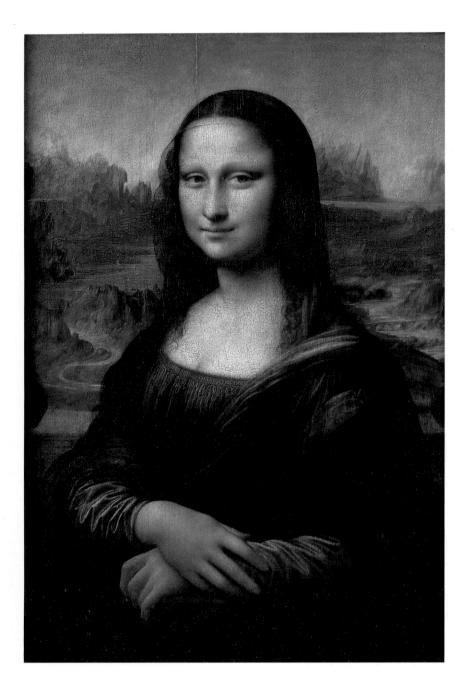

194 LEONARDO DA VINCI Mona Lisa 1503–5

This portrait shows Lisa Gherardini, who was born in 1479 and in 1495 married Francesco del Giocondo (which is why the picture is sometimes known as La Gioconda*). Vasari says that Leondardo painted 'for Francesco Giocondo the portrait of monna Lisa his wife . . . now in the possession of King Francis of France at Fontainebleau.' The picture is now one of the chief attractions of the Musée du Louvre in Paris.*

The mystery surrounding the painting's origins is accentuated by the sitter's ambiguous expression, the disparity of the two parts of the landscape background and the lack of any directly related preparatory drawings. Its greatest influence was, not surprisingly, on painting in France, where it is assumed Leonardo's original cartoon showing the model nude was widely known.

Vasari's description emphasizes the picture's naturalism, now difficult to assess under discoloured varnish. He commented that: 'the eyes had that lustre and watery sheen which is always seen in real life . . . the nose, with its beautiful nostrils, rosy and tender, seemed to be alive. The opening of the mouth . . . seemed not to be coloured but to be living flesh.'

Michelangelo and the Sistine Chapel

Michelangelo Buonarroti (1475–1564) contributed directly to High Renaissance painting through very few works, of which the ceiling of the Sistine Chapel overshadows all others. The impact of his sculpture on contemporary painting was, however, immeasurable. Having quarrelled with the Pope about his mausoleum project and fled to Florence, Michelangelo agreed to undertake the Sistine frescoes only under duress. The chapel, built by Sixtus IV from 1477 to 1481, already had wall frescoes illustrating the Old and New Testaments, by Ghirlandaio, Perugino, Botticelli, Signorelli and others.

Michelangelo conceived a novel form of illusionistic architectural framework for his combination of single figures and groups. 'Stone' ribs, like the supports for a gigantic vault, span the whole space, as if some of the infilling masonry has been removed to hold the important scenes. The ceiling is divided into three zones, with Man, before divine light penetrated his state of unconsciousness, placed symbolically in the lowest one. Moving upwards to the middle zone, we find the Seers (alternating prophets and Classical sybils), whose vision of the divine (the coming of Christ) foretells the awakening of Man to God. The culmination comes in the uppermost area of divine revelation, with God separating light from darkness, creating the world and Adam and Eve, until the three scenes depicting Noah show his continuation of the human race. Against the ribs are seated the *Ignudi* (nude youths), whose meaning has been ceaselessly debated. It seems remarkable that, in an age increasingly concerned with 'programmes' in art, no contemporary attempt at a written explanation of Michelangelo's intentions has been found. If it is accepted that Michelangelo was not required to work to pre-existing specifications, his freedom to create directly from the urgings of his spirit was unprecedented – and never equalled again.

The unimaginable task of painting more than 300 figures in an immense space exceeding 1000 square metres frequently led Michelangelo to despair. Apart from the physical toll, the artist's biographer, Ascanio Condivi, recounts technical difficulties such as the appearance of mould. Furthermore, there was no precedent for such a complex iconographic scheme on this scale, the technique of fresco was new to the artist, and the Pope was negligent in paying him. In 1509, Michelangelo wrote ' . . . I am uselessly wasting my time', and he lost a year's work through shortage of money.

When the ceiling was eventually completed in 1512, Michelangelo was hailed as the greatest artist of his age. The forms, colours and mood he had created were to transform Italian art. Since the vault's recent cleaning, we know that the sharp colours preferred by so many Mannerist painters derived directly from it, while its figure and facial types, anatomy and poses at once spoke a new and hypnotic language.

Michelangelo retreated to Florence, and with the exception of the unfinished *Entombment* (National Gallery, London), whose dating is uncertain, he concentrated almost entirely on sculpture and architecture. Only in his later years did he return to monumental fresco in the *Last Judgement* and the Cappella Paolina (see Chapter VIII).

Raphael

Raphael (Raffaello Sanzio, 1483–1520) remains one of the best-known but least understood of Renaissance artists. His importance is universally acknowledged, and his Madonnas have entered popular consciousness to a degree only paralleled by the *Mona Lisa*. But not even his secular paintings have made him a popular artist. Vasari's summing up of his art, full of unstinting praise as it is, contains the germ of an explanation. 'In truth, we have from him art, colouring, and invention harmonized and brought to such a pitch of perfection as could scarcely be hoped for.' It may be this perfection which has so alienated our age from the Madonnas and sweet-faced youths once so beloved of nineteenth-century *amateurs*: Somerset Maugham already saw in Raphael 'the vapidity of Bouguereau', the nineteenth-century French academic artist. It is easy to overlook the strength underlying Raphael's supremely controlled art, a strength not manifested with the shock effects of Michelangelo's *terribilità* (awesomeness), but in a refined sensibility, a highly developed sense of colour and flawless drawing.

Raphael was born in 1483 in Urbino. The town was far from provincial: Raphael's painter father, Giovanni, lived at the centre of the Montefeltro court's intellectual pursuits, and wrote a *Chronicle* of the reign of Federico, Duke of Urbino. The young Raphael spent eleven years in such an atmosphere – which was equivalent to the youthful Michelangelo's experiences in the intellectual circles of Lorenzo the Magnificent. He absorbed not only painting techniques from his father but also the love of literature and the arts which informs all his work, particularly after his move to Rome in 1508.

His early style depends entirely on Pietro Perugino (*c*.1445–1523), and there is no reason to doubt Vasari's claim that he was Raphael's master. Like Perugino, Raphael was peripatetic, travelling continuously throughout Tuscany and Umbria until he settled in Rome in 1508.

The year 1504 marks the turning point of his career, when he painted the Brera *Marriage of the Virgin*, taking Perugino's style to its conclusion. On 1 October, the Duke of Urbino's sister, Giovanna della Rovere, wrote to the Republic of Florence's *Gonfaloniere* (Governor) Piero Soderini, saying that Raphael has 'much talent in his vocation, and wishes to spend some time in Florence to study.' The youthful artist's sketchbooks reveal that he did study avidly, concentrating on two very Florentine preoccupations: the male nude and the Madonna. In addition to famous sculpture, such as Donatello's *Saint George*, he copied Pollaiuolo's engraving, the *Battle of the Ten Nudes* (see plate 77). It was clear from the beginning that his aspirations led him away from the static art of Perugino towards the dynamism of the Leonardo and Michelangelo *Battles* for the Palazzo della Signoria. The *Battle of Cascina's* grandiose nudes remained a formative influence on him throughout his career.

To his own gentle synthesis of Perugino, Raphael now added Leonardo and other Florentines, such as Ghirlandaio, whose earliest Madonnas, such as the *Madonna Terranuova* (Gemäldegalerie, Berlin), borrow exactly the Virgin's pose from Leonardo's *Virgin of the Rocks*. It also uses the favourite Florentine *tondo* or circular form, which Raphael was to perfect later in the *Madonna Alba* (see plate 211) and the *Madonna della Sedia* (Pitti Palace, Florence). While Leonardo and Michelangelo produced very few works in Florence, Raphael was prolific, each new painting charting his rapidly increasing originality, inventiveness and his evident excitement at his progress. From the uncertain steps of the early Madonnas, his increasing liberation is evident through the *Madonna del Granduca* (Palazzo Pitti, Florence), the *Small Cowper Madonna* (National Gallery of Art, Washington), the *Bridgewater* and *Colonna* Madonnas (Edinburgh, National Gallery of Scotland and Staatliche Museen, Berlin). By the time of one of the last Florentine Madonnas, the *Tempi* (Alte Pinakothek, Munich), he had achieved that illusion of naturalness coupled with the most subtle formal arrangement which characterized his subsequent Roman Madonnas. Another important aspect of Raphael's Florentine experiments in this area was his use of Leonardo's full-length seated Madonna compositions based on the pyramid form in *The Madonna and the Goldfinch* (Uffizi, Florence), *The Madonna of the Meadow* (Kunsthistorisches Museum, Vienna) and *La Belle Jardinière* (Musée du Louvre, Paris).

Raphael is recorded as being in Rome in the autumn of 1508, and his first documented payment followed in January 1509. This was for the room subsequently known as the Stanza della Segnatura, commissioned by Julius II as part of the redecoration of his Vatican apartment. There seems little doubt that Raphael had already visited Rome before he settled there, which, according to Vasari, was at the instigation of his uncle, Bramante. Elements of Classicism suggesting he already knew Roman art are evident in his works of the Florentine period, such as the *Madonna Esterhazy* (Szépmüvészeti Museum, Budapest) and the *Deposition* (Borghese Gallery, Rome). Bramante himself had arrived in Rome in 1499, escaping from Milan after the French invasion of Lombardy.

By the time Raphael settled in Rome, Bramante had already evolved his Roman Classical style, the effects of

195 RAPHAEL Detail of the mural grotesques from the Vatican Loggie 1518–19
The Loggie were erected by Bramante for Pope Julius II but completed under Leo X. Raphael decorated them in a mixture of stucco and fresco, in imitation of ancient Roman grotesques named after the grotte or underground chambers in which they were excavated. Raphael's designs inspired countless designers in the seventeenth and eighteenth centuries, and grotesques were metamorphosed into arabesques and other similar motifs. Their form is primarily vegetal and floral, but they also incorporate imaginative painted and stucco relief roundels, shields, lozenges and rectangles bearing figures, birds and animals, usually in tall, narrow vertical strips.

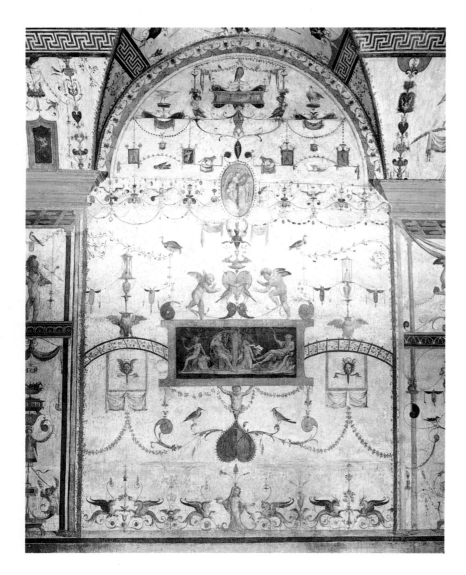

whose massive grandeur were to extend beyond the boundaries of architecture; Raphael worked daily in the shadow of Bramante's Vatican work, notably on the Cortile del Belvedere, and its innovations are reflected in his own architecture and paintings. His passion for the new domed, centralized architectural ideals is clear from the elegant background temple in his *Marriage of the Virgin* of 1504. Bramante gave Raphael a love for everything Roman, which not only helped to perfect his Classical figure style, but led to his epoch-making interior decoration using *grotesques* based on Roman mural designs in the Vatican Loggie and the Bathroom of Cardinal Bibbiena (see plate 195), and the Villa Madama in Rome.

The Stanze – Julius II's suite of personal, although not necessarily private, rooms – comprised his study (Segnatura), audience chamber (Eliodoro) and the meeting room of the Church's supreme court (Incendio). Only Perugino's ceiling in the Incendio remains of the earlier decorations, and by the end of 1508 Julius's select team of painters was ready to redecorate completely. The Segnatura's iconography reflects all aspects of intellectual exercise, its ceiling roundels in simulated mosaic showing Theology, Philosophy, Jurisprudence and Poetry.

Raphael's striking depiction of space in the first fresco in the Stanza della Segnatura (the *Disputà*) is already present in his lesser known fresco, in San Severo, Perugia, painted in 1505, the *Holy Trinity with Saints*. This stems directly from his experience in Florence of Fra Bartolommeo, who remained a close friend of Raphael's until the former's death in 1517.

The *Disputà's* composition shows the lingering influence of Fra Bartolommeo, but is filled with Raphael's new Roman *gravitas*, and his increasing awareness of the power of ancient art to transform his conception of the human form. This consciousness culminates in the same room in the celebrated *School of Athens* (see plate 196). The equilibrium achieved by Raphael in these works was, however, short-lived, as is seen from the rapid increase in visual drama, rich colour and other eye-catching effects found in the later frescoes of the Stanze. Already in the *Expulsion of Heliodorus* of 1513–14 (notwithstanding the thematic need for dramatic movement) the exquisite balance of the *School of Athens* has gone, to be replaced by something of that richness of surface pattern which evolved later in Mannerism. By the time of the *Fire in the Borgo* (1514) a new awareness of the possibilities of figure painting has swept away the freshness of the first frescoes in the series, replacing it with sophistication and the *grazia*, or gracefulness, so admired by Vasari. This *grazia* was already present in Fra Bartolommeo (see plate 206) but the addition of Classical Roman grandeur directs it

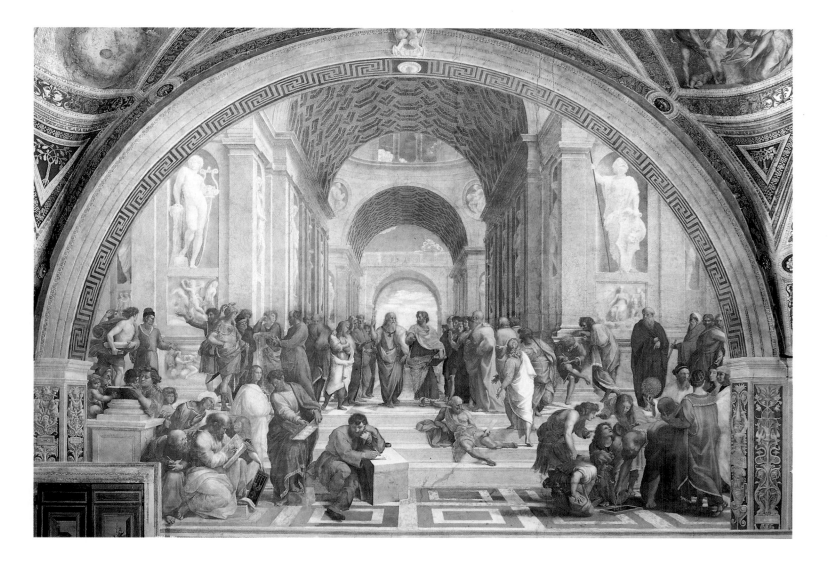

196 RAPHAEL School of Athens 1509–10

In this large fresco lunette in the Stanza della Segnatura of the Vatican, commissioned by Pope Julius II, Raphael achieved the total mastery of his individual style, not least in posing over fifty figures to create vitality and to relate each figure to its group, each group to the whole. With the Sistine ceiling it may be seen as the quintessential painting of the High Renaissance. Plato and Aristotle are dramatically placed at the centre of the composition, and every aspect of the philosophical life is represented, appropriate to a Pope's study-library.

While the Disputà *opposite still suggests a certain striving on Raphael's part for a classic solution, in the* School of Athens *his delight in placing his* dramatis personae *against sublime architecture, probably based on Bramante, renders a potentially pedantic theme human and approachable.*

towards magnificence. An increasingly dark palette already looks forward to Raphael's late work and Giulio Romano's version of it.

Raphael never experienced the psychological crises recurrent in Michelangelo's life, and which inspired the unique form of his art. As with all artists of his generation, however, he looked in awe at the external evidence of Michelangelo's style, already formed in the *Cascina* cartoon and brought to perfection on the Sistine vault. But Raphael did not become in any sense a 'Michelangelo

follower' and was gifted enough to assimilate the elements that attracted him. Thus, while his cartoons of 1515 for the Sistine Chapel's tapestries depicting the Acts of the Apostles (see plate 205) are inconceivable without Michelangelo's influence, they demonstrate how he pursued his own ends relentlessly.

The cartoons (now in the Victoria and Albert Museum, London), have been called the Parthenon sculptures of modern art. Raphael's portraiture during the reign of Leo X also reached new heights of individuality, and remains possibly the most accessible aspect of his later work. Under Venetian influence (and that of the *Mona Lisa*, brought by Leonardo to Rome in 1513), he evolved half-length portraits of men and women combining unique psychological insight with painterly sensuousness. From *La Donna Velata* (Pitti Palace, Florence) to *Baldassare Castiglione* (see plate 12) he rendered his sitters more approachable even than Titian's. His portraits of ecclesiastics such as *A Cardinal* (Museo del Prado, Madrid) or the celebrated *Leo X with Cardinals Giulio de' Medici and Luigi Rossi* (Uffizi, Florence) set the standard for unflattering likenesses nevertheless imbued with great dignity.

It is tempting to speculate how Raphael's style would have developed had he not died young (at the age of thirty-seven). Raphael was then at the height of his productivity,

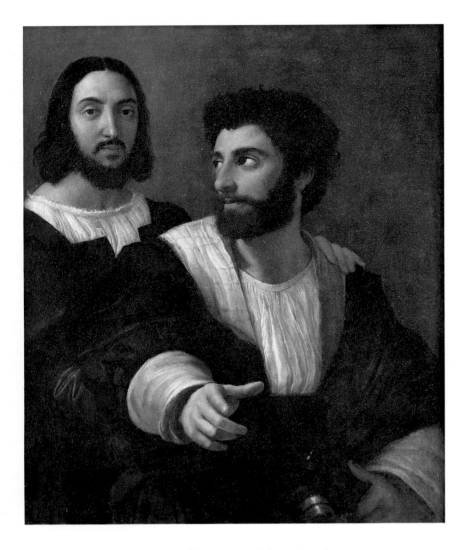

197 RAPHAEL Self Portrait with a Friend *c.*1518
Listed as being at Fontainebleau in the early seventeenth century,
this picture may have belonged to Francis I. The left-hand figure is
certainly Raphael, but the identity of his companion remains
uncertain. Among the many names suggested have been Pintoricchio,
Giulio Romano, Pietro Aretino and Giovanni Battista Branconio
dell'Acquila, a close friend of the artist during his last years and the
executor of his will. Raphael himself appears prematurely aged,
possibly by his heavy workload in this later period, as architect of St
Peter's and Director of Antiquities in Rome.

Along with Baldassare Castiglione *(see plate 12) and*
Navagero and de Beazzano *(Doria Gallery, Rome), this portrait*
reveals Raphael as the supreme master in the Renaissance of the
'speaking likeness', where sitters seem to communicate directly with
the viewer. There seems little doubt that a precise symbolism was
intended, and Raphael may have intended a veiled reference to
Christ with one of His disciples. More than any other of his
portraits, this painting recalls the sombre grandeur of the work of
Sebastiano del Piombo.

and with him, stylistic changes happened very rapidly. The
transformation from the three differing interpretations of
Classicism as seen in *Galatea* (see plate 214), the *Sistine
Madonna* of 1513–14 and *Saint Cecelia* of 1514 to the high
drama – both in content and form – of the *Transfiguration*
(see plate 248) indicate that Raphael would probably have
developed into a sophisticated Mannerist.

Painting in Rome and Florence

During his own lifetime, Raphael's fame and influence
spread through the engravings of his work made by
Marcantonio Raimondi. But it was from Raphael's late
style as seen in the *Transfiguration* that his pupils Giulio
Romano (1499–1546) and Gianfrancesco Penni (*c.*1488–
*c.*1528) developed. Romano was by far the more original.
Not only did he evolve aspects of Raphael's style in new
ways, but he also invented a rich new language in his
Mantuan frescoes (see plate 263).

An idea of how inimitable were the contributions of
Raphael and Michelangelo to Roman High Renaissance
painting may be seen in the Roman work of the
Piedmontese artist, Sodoma (Giovanni Antonio Bazzi,
1477–1549). He was influenced by Leonardo, and worked
in Siena before being commissioned by the Sienese
banker Agostino Chigi. In 1516 Sodoma decorated
Chigi's bedroom in the Villa Farnesina in Rome (see plate
227), alongside Baldassare Peruzzi (1491–1536), who was
then at work on the villa's Sala delle Prospettive. The
travels of such a painter as Sodoma (who returned to
Siena) were important in carrying the latest news of
Roman art to the provinces.

Meanwhile, Florence must have regretted the departure of the great triumvirate who had revitalized its painting. In spite of a handful of masterpieces from the second
decade, there is a provincial aura about its art until
Pontormo emerges as the Florentine genius of the 1520s.
However, Baccio della Porta, called Fra Bartolommeo
(1472/5–1517), not only painted some of the most memorable images of the period, but also exercised a wide
influence on his contemporaries and partly filled the place
left by Leonardo, Michelangelo and Raphael.

Like Fra Angelico before him, Fra Bartolommeo
became a monk in the convent of San Marco. His training with Cosimo Rosselli provides little clue to the peculiarly monumental style which he created after 1504,
when he painted his *Vision of Saint Bernard* (Galleria
dell'Accademia, Florence). His two versions of the
Marriage of Saint Catherine, 1511 and 1512 (Musée du
Louvre, Paris and Galleria dell'Accademia, Florence),
show the influence of his brief visit to Venice in 1508. In
them he evolved a static grandeur after seeing Venetian
altarpieces by Bellini and others. As with Andrea del
Sarto, there is a sense – for reasons which are not easy to
define – that his imagery falls short of the painters whom
he sought to emulate. Fra Bartolommeo's masterpiece is
the *Carondolet Altarpiece* (see plate 206); had he permitted
himself more of its effortless elegance in his other work,
his achievement might have been greater. His partner

from 1509 to 1512, Martiotta Albertinelli (1474–1515), used pronounced *chiaroscuro* to re-interpret Fra Bartolommeo's inventions.

If Fra Bartolommeo sometimes verges on the academic, this is never sensed in his countless beautiful drawings, including landscapes and urban scenes. Andrea del Sarto (Andrea d'Agnolo di Francesco, 1486–1530) was also a great draughtsman in the Florentine tradition, but his variety and inventiveness placed him in the avant-garde of the city's artists, at least during the second decade. While his colleague, Francesco Franciabigio (1482/3–1525) represented the Florentine attempt to emulate Raphael directly, Sarto absorbed much from Leonardo. It was to Leonardo's *sfumato* that Sarto owed the softness of his modelling, if not the models themselves.

198 RIDOLFO GHIRLANDAIO A Man of the Capponi Family, undated

Ghirlandaio is perhaps the most underestimated portraitist of the Florentine Cinquecento. His psychological insights were usually rendered in images of considerable restraint, but his innovations of form were of the greatest importance for artists such as Sarto, Pontormo and Bronzino. This portrait also shows Ghirlandaio's outstanding technical ability.

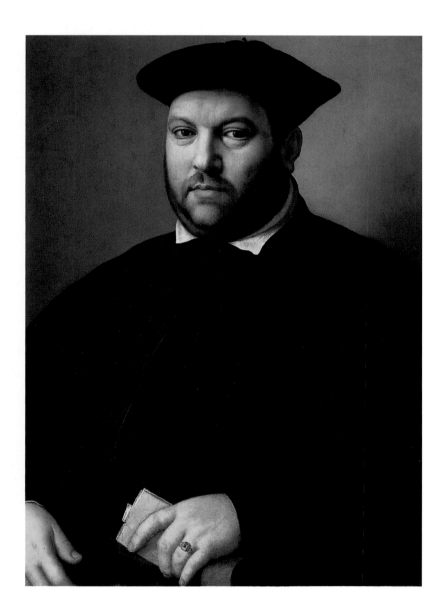

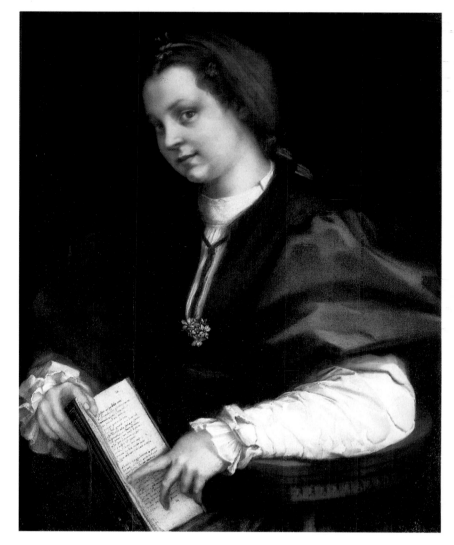

199 ANDREA DEL SARTO A Lady with Petrarch's Sonnets 1528–9

This is one of the most mysteriously fascinating portraits of its period. It seems safe to discount the old idea that it represents the artist's wife. The first sonnet refers to the lover's faith in Love's power in spite of uncertainties, while the second speaks of the sublimation of the baser desires to higher planes. The subject's glance at the painter is clearly not that of a distant aristocratic sitter. Recent cleaning has revealed the most subtle palette of colours and a delicate sfumato *technique, in which Sarto had few rivals at this time.*

His first important frescoes, completed in 1510 at the Santissima Annunziata, show the *Life of Saint Philip Benizzi* and recall Quattrocento art and his studies with Piero di Cosimo (*c.*1462–1521?). By 1514, when he completed another fresco in the same location, the *Birth of the Virgin*, he had fully entered the monumental spirit of the High Renaissance imported by Fra Bartolommeo. This grandiose scene is Florence's closest approximation to Raphael's Roman style of the same years, but is imbued with the late Quattrocento tradition of domestic intimacy best seen in Ghirlandaio.

In the steps of Leonardo, Sarto worked briefly for Francis I of France in 1518–19, having in the previous year completed his *Madonna of the Harpies* (Galleria degli Uffizi, Florence). This showed his closeness to the

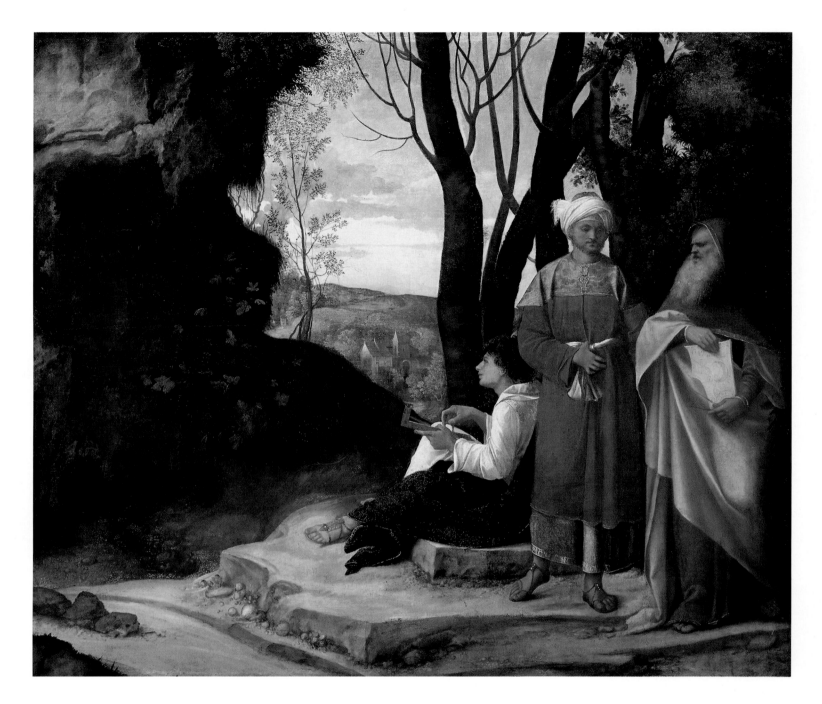

200 GIORGIONE The Three Philosophers *c.*1510
These figures have been variously interpreted as the three Magi,
symbols of the ancient, medieval and modern worlds, and
representatives of Arabic, medieval and Renaissance philosophies. A
copy by Teniers the Younger shows the picture was cut at the left and
originally gave greater emphasis to a cave there. It is clear that three
different ages of man and, probably, three nationalities, are
represented; this and their differing gestures clearly indicate a specific
meaning for each one, probably unified by their relationship with the
mysterious cave and the brilliantly painted sunset background.

Raphael of the *Sistine Madonna*. His French journey appears to have altered Sarto's approach, however, and on his return the first elements appeared which would soon lead to parallels with the early Mannerism of Pontormo, his former assistant.

The vigour of Raphael's classicism is absent from Sarto, whose imagery often appears passive, even in potentially dynamic themes. His real magic lies in the ethereal quality which his use of *sfumato* gives his faces. This works particularly well in his portraits, whose restraint lends them an elusive and enigmatic quality (see plate 199). Together with Ghirlandaio's underestimated likenesses (see plate 198), Sarto's original conception of portraiture was fundamental to the work of the Mannerist artists Pontormo and Bronzino.

Painting in Venice

Like Florence, and in contrast with Rome or Milan, High Renaissance Venice was to build on the achievements of its native painters during the Quattrocento. Giovanni Bellini, who may have been almost ninety at his death, retained his facility for adaptation, which enabled him even in later life to create novel imagery of startling beauty (see plates 212, 215). But in spite of his dominant presence at the turn of the century (and his importance as a teacher), the changes in Venetian art were almost entirely due to one remarkable painter, Giorgione.

In addition, the emergence of so great a genius as Titian from Giorgione's studio also created a situation unique to Venice, in that Giorgione's style was not merely continued by imitators, but evolved by a pupil of equal standing. No parallel exists for this in the High Renaissance, and it partly accounts for the undiminishing strength of Venetian art through almost an entire century. While there is a continuous ebb and flow of talent around Florence and Rome, Venice appears to go only from strength to strength: Titian, Veronese and Tintoretto were surrounded by a galaxy of lesser, but nevertheless talented painters.

The innovation of painting in oils on canvas proved crucial for Venice, and was generally adopted by the beginning of the sixteenth century. The new medium gave an infinitely greater richness of tone and depth of colour than tempera. Indeed, it is with sixteenth-century Venetian painting that we associate the first use of the canvas's texture to augment that of the paint laid on it. Giorgione's achievement is inconceivable without the aid of oil paint on canvas.

Painters in Venice generally used the same pigments as elsewhere, but its trade with the East led to the introduction of certain novelties. Orange, previously rare in Quattrocento painting, began to appear in the work of Carpaccio and his contemporaries, and was later adopted by Titian. The light effects, atmosphere and texture associated with Venetian art owe their existence to these artists' abilities to maximize the potential of canvas.

The impetus to employ such effects came from Giorgione (Giorgo Barbarelli or Giorgio del Castelfranco, 1476/8–1510), and the important innovations of early Venetian Cinquecento painting stem from the few pictures certainly by him. These are the *Castelfranco Altarpiece* (although even this has recently been doubted), *The Tempest* (see plate 190), *An Old Woman ('Col Tempo')* (see plate 201), *The Three Philosophers* (see plate 200), *Judith* (Hermitage Museum, Leningrad) *Laura* (Kunsthistorisches Museum, Vienna), and the Dresden *Sleeping Venus* (see plate 220). The attribution of others oscillates between Giorgione and his followers.

Giorgione was a nickname meaning 'great George', explained by Vasari as relating to 'the stature and the greatness of his mind'. Given that our knowledge of him comes from some contemporary references of 1506–10 and very few accepted paintings, his importance is all the more surprising. The uncertainty of attributions to him also indicates how great and immediate his influence was.

Vasari relates that Giorgione began his career as a purveyor of small devotional Madonnas. Cabinet pictures designed for private settings remained his preference and

the *Castelfranco Altarpiece* is in many ways unsatisfactory by comparison. Giorgione's fascination for us lies in the dichotomy between his surface realism and the indefinable magic of his images. A comparison with another sort of contemporary Venetian realism in Jacopo de' Barbari (active *c*.1497, died 1516?, see plate 202) shows how unfactual Giorgione was. Even his contemporaries seemed at a loss to ascertain the precise subject of many of his paintings. Michiel, the informed connoisseur, resorted to generalized descriptions of pictures such as *The Three Philosophers* (see plate 200), leaving their detailed interpretation to the twentieth century. However, none of his followers succeeded in capturing the intense, reflective and self-absorbed quality of his pictures. For example, Lorenzo Lotto and Dosso Dossi tended to create their individual styles from selected aspects of Giorgione's (see plates 246, 266).

Vasari attached great importance to Leonardo's Venetian visit of 1500. He saw Giorgione's *sfumato* as resulting from it, and placed him alongside Leonardo for his innovations. It is likely that Giorgione also studied in Giovanni Bellini's studio in the early or mid-1490s with

201 GIORGIONE An Old Woman 1508–10
The old woman holds a piece of paper bearing the motto 'col tempo' referring, together with her decrepitude, to the effects of time's passage. It is unlike any other painting attributed to Giorgione, particularly in the directness of its unambiguous message and its paint handling, although the figure's scale relative to the picture shape relates to several other works by or attributed to him.

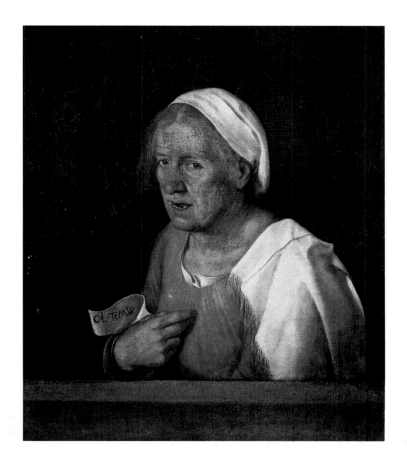

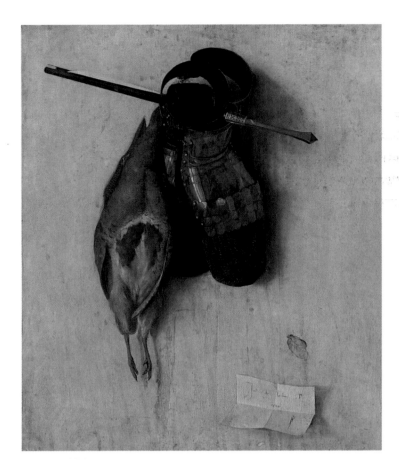

202 JACOPO DE' BARBARI *Still Life* 1504
*This may have formed the cover or reverse part of a portrait, in which
case it would have had less importance as an autonomous still life.
The influence of miniature painting is clear, probably along with that
of Dürer and Antonello da Messina.*

Lorenzo Lotto and Palma Vecchio. But unlike them he
appears to have had sufficient knowledge of central Italian
painting, including Perugino, to evolve in a very different way. If any development can be traced in Giorgione,
it is in the accelerated progress from slight hesitancy in
The Tempest of 1503/4, through a more classical assurance
in *Judith* (The Hermitage, St Petersburg) of 1504/5, to a
style comparable with High Renaissance monumentality
in *The Three Philosophers* of about 1506 (see plate 200). In
other hands, these paintings might well have been produced at intervals of ten years. In his last great image, the
Sleeping Venus of 1507–8, the sensuality which lightly surfaces in his earlier work triumphs completely (see plate
220). This quality, which Giorgione accentuated with
vibrating light and the liquid handling of paint, most
fascinated Titian and his other followers.

Giorgione's premature death from plague in 1510, followed by Bellini's in 1516, left the centre stage open for
Titian's all-conquering genius. The other major
Giorgione follower, Sebastiano del Piombo (*c.* 1485–
1547), made his career in Rome from 1511, and would
probably not have posed a serious threat to Titian.

Of Titian (Titiano Vecellio, *c.*1485–1576), Vasari says
that he '. . . imitated Giorgione so well that in a short time
his works were taken for Giorgione's'. For a long time
many eluded precise attribution (among them, the Louvre
Concert Champêtre, the Pitti *Concert* and the Glasgow
Woman taken in Adultery). His personal language was
formed by 1511 when he frescoed Padua's Scuola del
Santo. Already Titian showed more flexibility in his
handling of outline than his master, and this became one
of the important factors in his treatment of the human
form. By the 1550s, when he painted *Diana and Actaeon*
(see plate 238), the outlines had become absorbed into
their surroundings.

Titian's feeling for figure composition, and his increasingly rich colour, gained momentum after Giorgione's
death, and during the second decade of the sixteenth century he produced a number of innovative paintings,
including *The Three Ages of Man* (see plate 221) and *Sacred
and Profane Love* (see plate 219). His passion for brilliant,
saturated colour developed rapidly, culminating in the
series he painted in 1518–23 for his new patron, Alfonso
d'Este (see Chapter VIII).

Titian expanded his circle of patrons at this time, but
always resisted attempts to lure him away from his
beloved Venice. His status as the city's foremost artist was
crowned by one of the most important commissions of his
lifetime, and one of the major achievements of High
Renaissance art: the *Assumption of the Virgin* (see plate
254). Like the Vatican works of Raphael and Michelangelo, this transcended its period to express aspirations
which could only be fully realized during the Baroque
age. With the *Assumption*, and his other masterpiece in the
Frari Church in Venice, the *Pesaro Madonna* (1519–26),
Titian moved into a new dynamic phase in the 1520s.
Such wealth of inspiration and energy also characterizes
the Parmese dome frescoes of Correggio, which may be
indebted to his knowledge of the *Assumption* through
prints (see plate 222).

Like Raphael, Titian achieved social success equal to
his attainments in painting, and on an even greater international scale. Vasari speaks of his 'power of attaching
himself and making himself dear to men of quality'. His
connections with the Emperor Charles V (see plate 7) and
his son Philip II brought him a knighthood, and the
unbroken momentum of his career ensured him personal
wealth. Together with his friends, the sculptor Jacopo
Sansovino (1486–1570) and the poet Pietro Aretino
(1492–1556), Titian ruled the artistic life of Venice for
more than sixty years.

Titian's social mobility is clear from the immense range
of his portraits: of the Imperial family and European monarchs; of the Italian aristocracy, Venetian doges and popes,

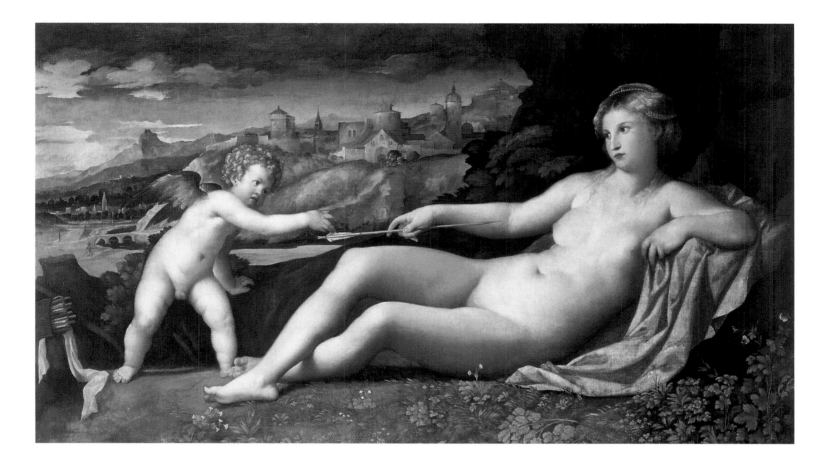

203 PALMA VECCHIO Venus and Cupid in a Landscape 1522–4
The subject appears to come from Ovid's Metamorphoses; *Venus was accidentally scratched by one of Cupid's arrows, leading to her tragic love for Adonis. Venus is surprisingly monumental, and her elongated limbs and Cupid's* contrapposto *are both Mannerist elements, but the effect is one of elegant naturalism.*

and of the leading intellectuals of the day. From his first portraits (such as the London *Ariosto*), to the last (such as the Vienna *Jacopo Strada*), he excelled in the half- and three-quarter-length formats, suggesting the status and character of his sitters with an economy of means which continued to influence portraiture long after his death. The portraits of Moretto da Brescia (Alessandro Bonvicino, *c.*1498–1554), who may have trained with Titian, are indebted to him. Another Brescian artist, Girolamo Savoldo (active 1508–after 1548) also came under his sway (see plate 226). The dividing line between Titian's female portraits and mythological paintings of women is often fine, as in the famous *Venus of Urbino* (Uffizi, Florence). With Palma Vecchio (see plate 203) and Paolo Veronese, Titian created absolutes for feminine beauty which far outlasted their period.

Correggio

The brief career of Correggio (Antonio Allegri, 1494–1534) overlaps the High Renaissance and early Mannerist periods. His development parallels that of

Raphael in his rapid absorption of Quattrocento influences before launching a new and unique style. That style remained faithful to High Renaissance ideals, never entering the realms of physical distortion which characterize his follower Parmigianino. Nonetheless, it contains many elements related to Mannerism.

The name of Correggio's master is unknown, but in the decade from 1510 he showed the influence of both Andrea Mantegna and Lorenzo Costa, who succeeded Mantegna as court painter at Mantua. These influences were rapidly superseded by Roman art and the work of Raphael. Maintaining that Correggio had never visited Rome (much of his early knowledge of Raphael came from Marcantonio Raimondi's prints), Vasari believed that it was '*La gran madre Natura*' rather than Classical influences which transformed the youthful painter's delicate, almost feminine manner, derived from Mantegna and Leonardo, into major art. The leap from Correggio's earliest paintings (such as the Detroit *Marriage of Saint Catherine*) to the grandeur of his two Parmese dome frescoes and the great altarpieces is, however, inconceivable without any experience of the avant-garde in Rome. The new spatial ideas found in Florentine and Roman painting around 1505–15, coupled with his inheritance of Mantegna's fascination with perspective, quickly changed Correggio's approach. It is now generally thought that he visited Rome in 1513, after Pope Leo X's election. Thus, not only could he have met Leonardo (and presumably have seen the *Mona Lisa*) but he also probably observed Raphael's latest style at first hand in the Stanza della

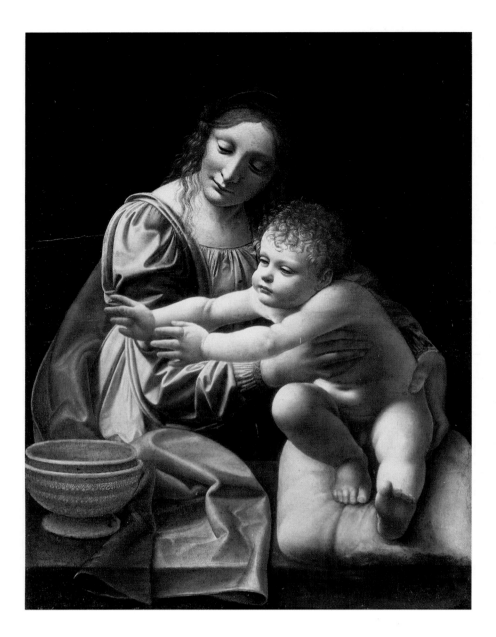

207 GIOVANNI ANTONIO BOLTRAFFIO Virgin and
Child, late 1490s
(Left) This picture is of such high quality that the
involvement of Leonardo has been suggested. Both facial
types show his influence, as does the meticulous handling of
the hair and other details. In this Boltraffio reveals himself a
greater master of composition, colour and psychology than
other Leonardo pupils, such as Luini.

208 LEONARDO DA VINCI Virgin and Child with Saint
Anne and Saint John the Baptist c.1498
(Right) The origin of this cartoon is unclear, although Louis
XII of France ordered a painting of the theme from Leonardo
in Milan before 1500. The grandeur of the composition led
Berenson to compare its drapery folds with those of the
goddesses of the Elgin Marbles. Its design had a considerable
influence on Milanese painters like Luini.

209 ARISTOTILE DA SANGALLO after MICHELANGELO
Battle of Cascina c.1542
Vasari described Michelangelo's conception thus: 'one saw
there muscles and nerves in their entirety . . . incredible
positions: standing, kneeling, bending, lying, getting up,
with skilful foreshortening' and it was at his instigation that
Sangallo made a partial copy of it. Michelangelo began the
cartoon in December 1504, making changes in 1506. It was
probably dismembered and destroyed by repeated copying.

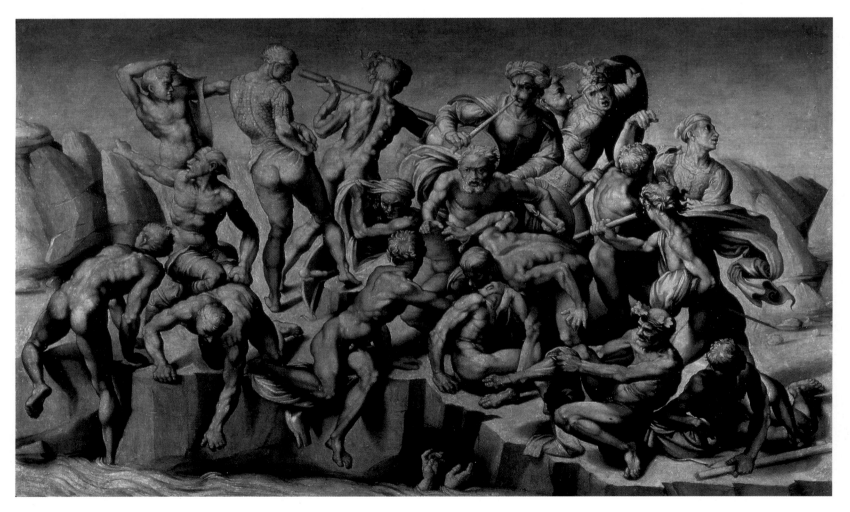

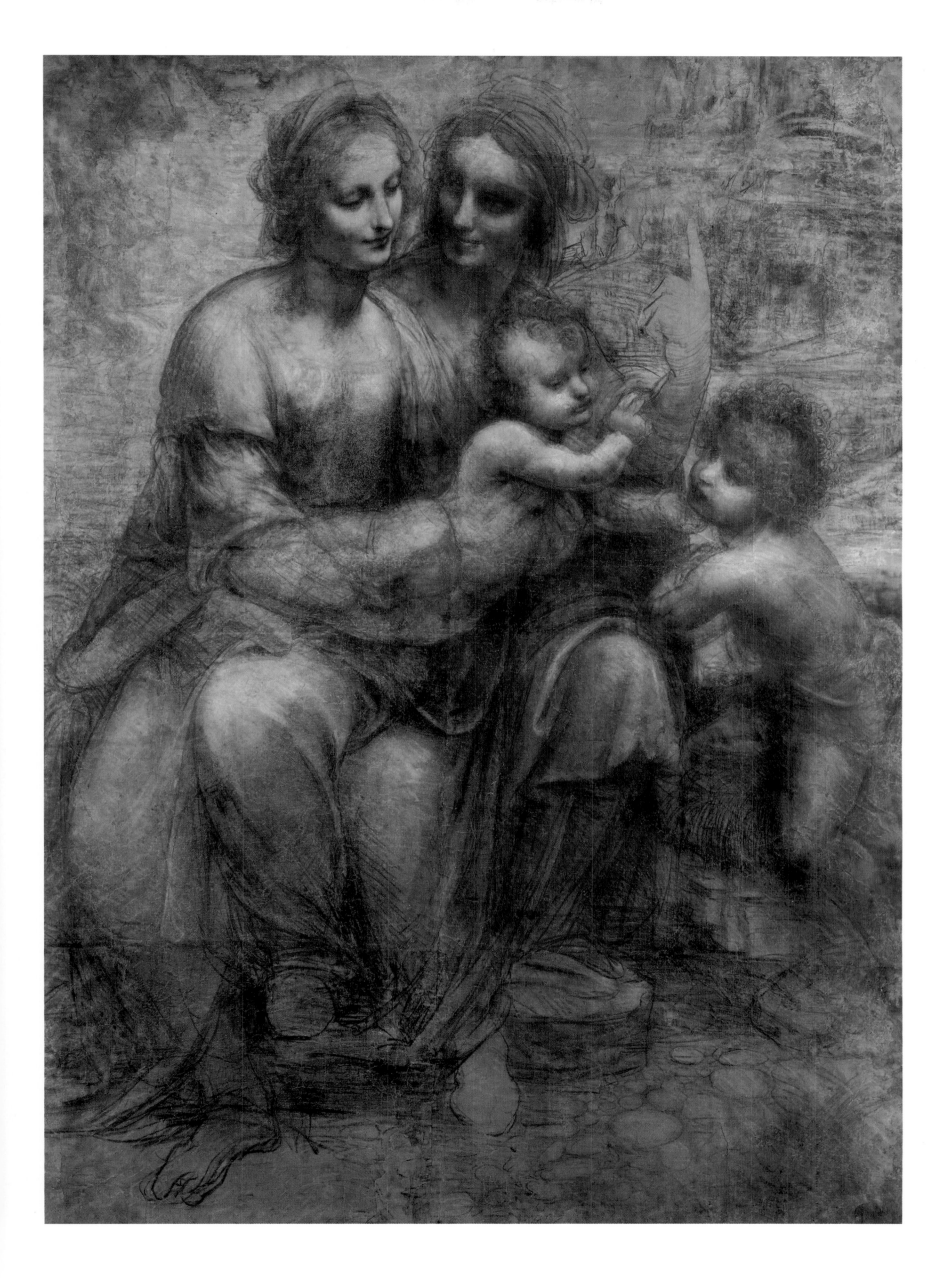

207

210 MICHELANGELO Holy Family with
Saint John the Baptist (Doni Tondo) 1504
*Vasari records the commissioning of this panel by
Michelangelo's friend Agnolo Doni for his
wedding to Maddalena Strozzi. The magnificent
carved and gilded frame bears her arms. This is
the only securely documented painting (as
opposed to fresco) by Michelangelo. The Virgin's
sculptural, monumental figure looks forward to
the Sistine sybils, and her* contrapposto *and
modelling of cool, acid colour without*
chiaroscuro *provide the starting point for the
Florentine Mannerists Pontormo and Bronzino.*

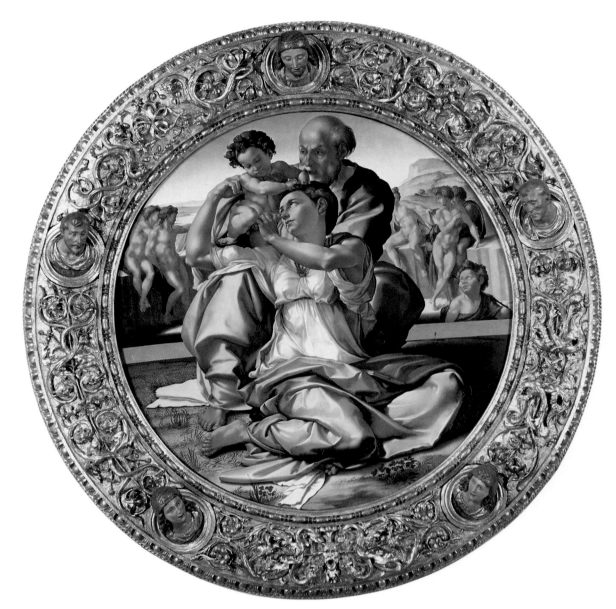

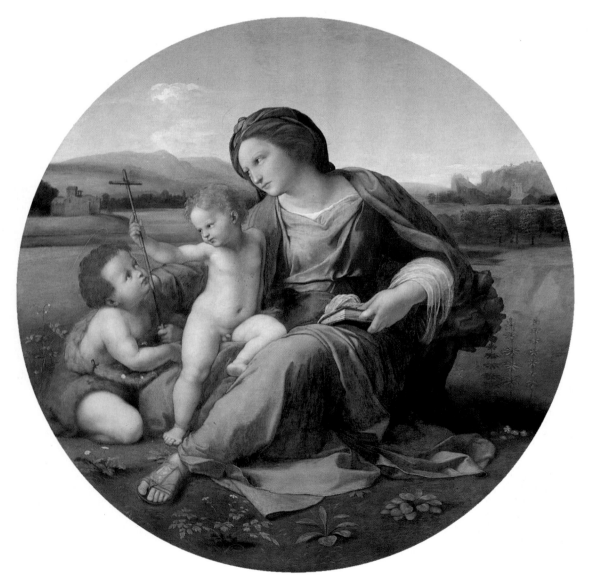

211 RAPHAEL Madonna Alba 1511
*Although the details of its commission are
unknown, this painting belonged among others to
the Duke of Alba and Czar Nicholas I of Russia.
It shows how rapidly Raphael evolved the tondo
form, with which he had experimented in Florence,
to the highest degree of sophistication. Basing the
Madonna's pose on a particularly beautiful red chalk
study of a male model, he achieved a sense of
natural movement, suggesting a deceptive simplicity
by the most complicated compositional means. The
subtle use of* contrapposto *is close to that in the
contemporary Triumph of Galatea (see plate 214),
and both reveal Raphael at the height of his powers
in integrating form with content.*

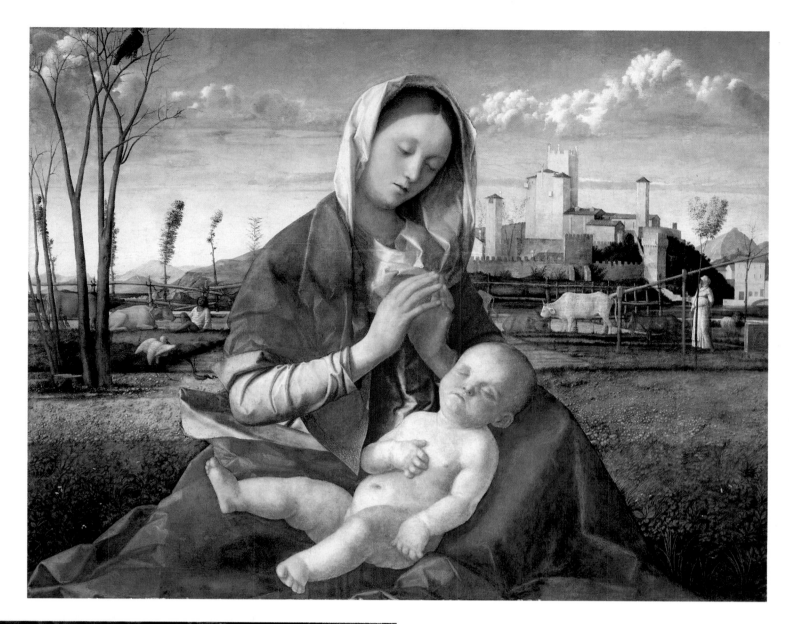

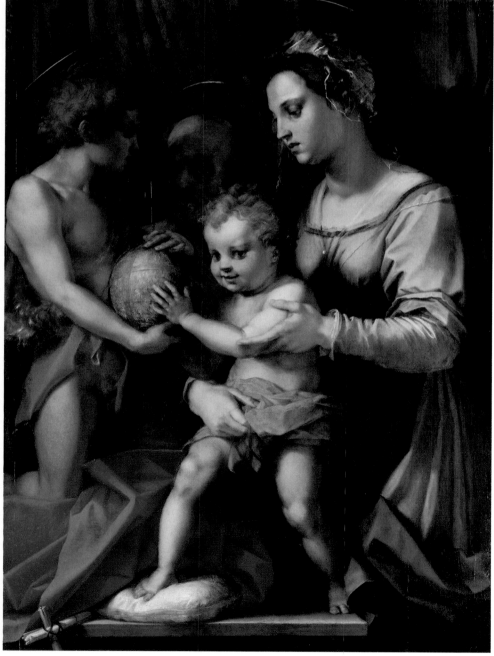

212 GIOVANNI BELLINI Madonna in the Meadow *c*.1505
*This painting is among Bellini's late masterpieces, achieving a
perfect synthesis of the figures with a sensitively observed
landscape background. The detail of the fighting snake and
white bird has been connected with Virgil's* Georgics.

213 ANDREA DEL SARTO Holy Family with the Youthful
Saint John *c*.1530
*This is among Sarto's latest works, and one of his most
monumental renderings of this theme. It is probably the version
recorded by Vasari as painted for Giovanni Borgherini. The
globe singles out Christ as Salvator Mundi, and the St Joseph
may be a modified self portrait. Less evidently mannered than
some other later works, it relies for its effect on magnificent
colour, crisp detail and the close proximity of the figures to the
framing edge.*

209

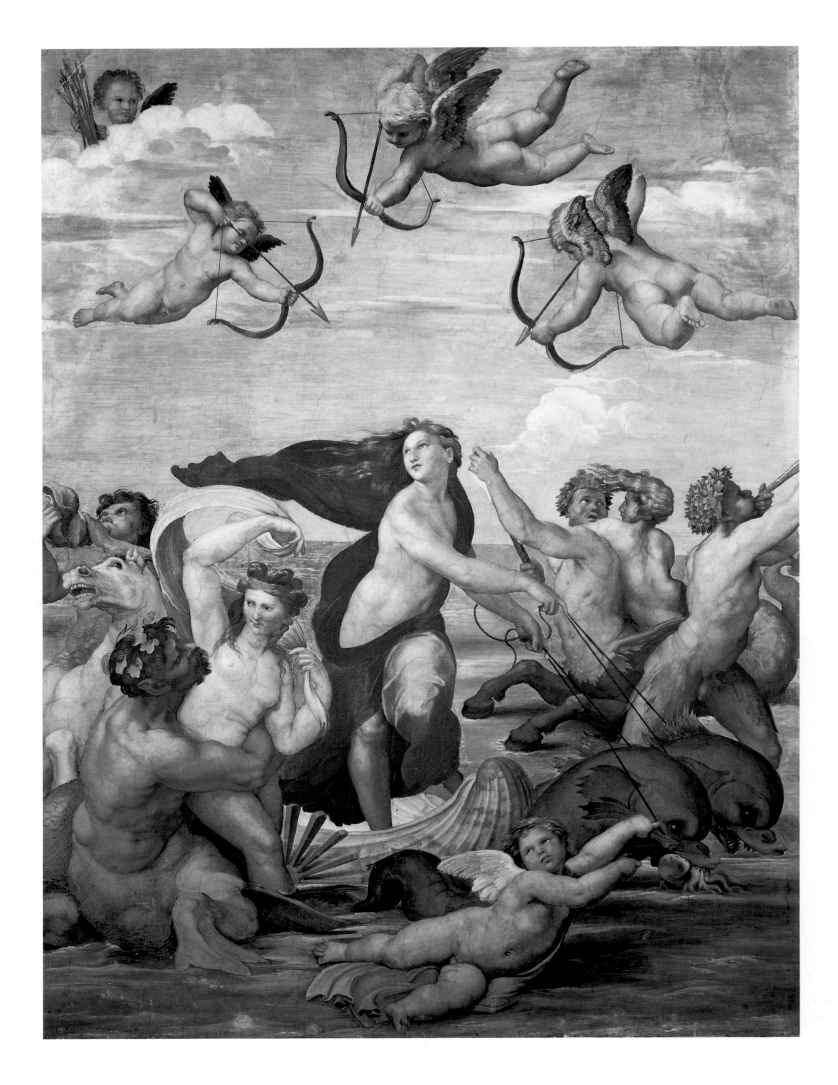

214 RAPHAEL Triumph of Galatea 1511

Raphael painted this fresco for the villa built by Baldassare Peruzzi for the Sienese Papal banker Agostini Chigi on the banks of the Tiber at the edge of Rome. The story of Galatea, a beautiful sea-nymph loved by the cyclops Polyphemus, comes from Ovid and Theocritus. Raphael shows her skimming over the water in a huge shell equipped with paddles and drawn by dolphins. This is Raphael's major tribute to Classical painting and sculpture.

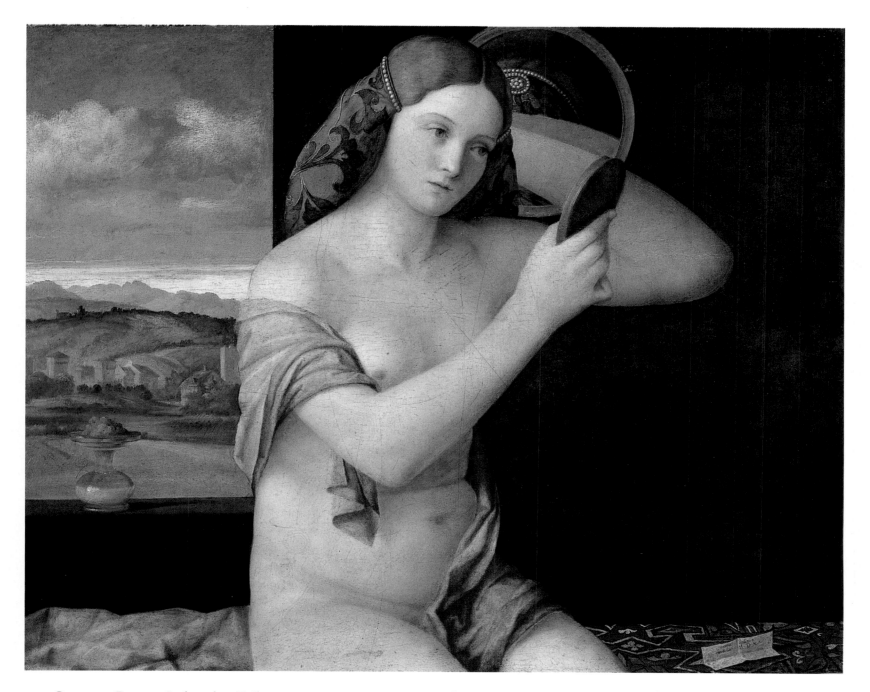

215 GIOVANNI BELLINI Lady at her Toilet 1515
One of Bellini's most lyrical paintings, this was made when he was
seventy-five and inspired by Giorgione and the young Titian. The
figure's silent self-absorption is accentuated by the translucency of her
pale skin, brilliantly offset by the dark background, the play on the
idea of reflections seen and unseen, and the delicate balance of
colours. The glass vase on the window sill against the Alpine foothill
landscape encapsulates the picture's clarity and purity.

216 SEBASTIANO DEL PIOMBO Death of Adonis c.1512
(Below) Although it was probably painted just after Sebastiano
transferred to Rome from Venice, this large picture clearly
demonstrates his debt to Giorgione and early Cinquecento painting
in Venice. The influence of Roman High Renaissance art is evident
in some of the poses, but there is none of the sharper outline and
forceful colour areas which Sebastiano was to adopt in Rome. The
background view of the Venetian Ducal Palace strikes an odd note.

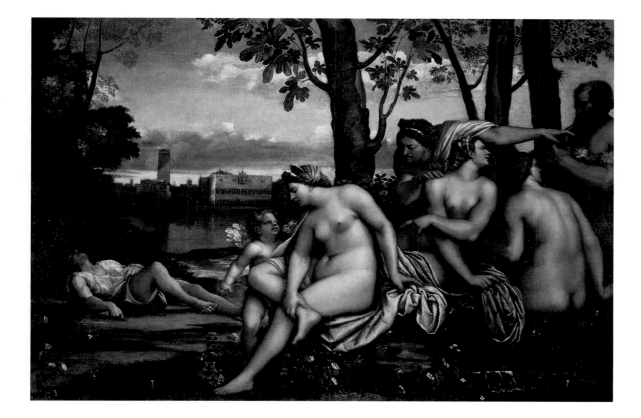

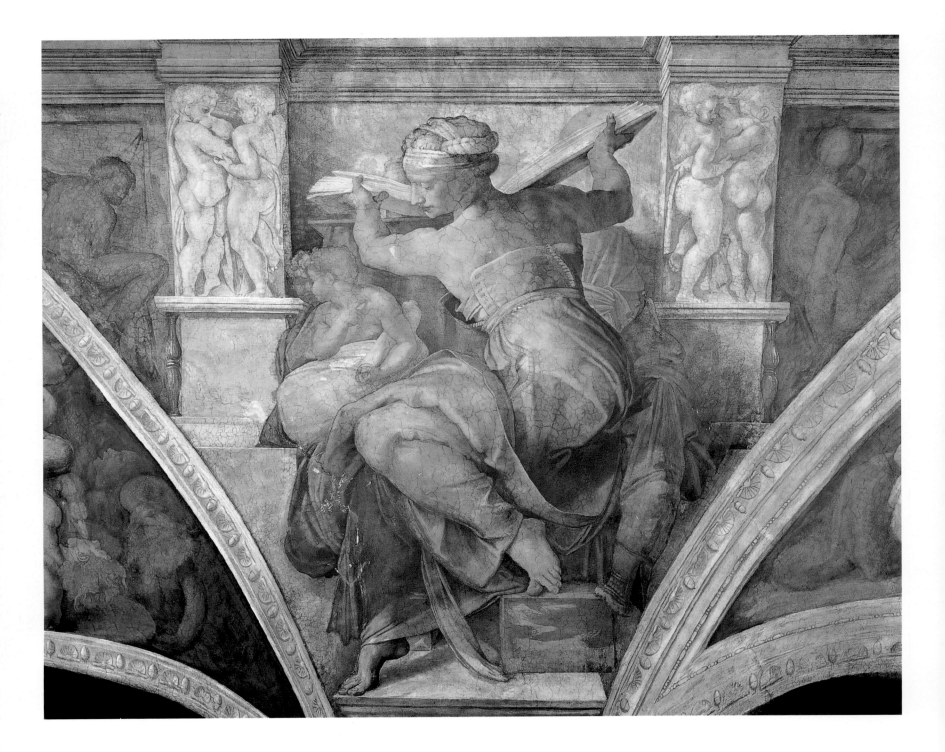

217 MICHELANGELO Lybian Sybil 1511

*This is one of the figures in the final section of the vault, and shows
Michelangelo's complete command of his medium by this point.
Particularly striking is the modelling of the flesh and face by very fine
hatched strokes. The precise meaning of the Sybil's gesture to the
book is unclear. Vasari believed she is symbolically closing it, but she
is probably simply taking hold of it to write in it. Her contrapposto
turning of the upper torso, elaborate headdress and the colours and
forms of her garments all had immense influence on later artists. The
fresco is shown here before its recent cleaning.*

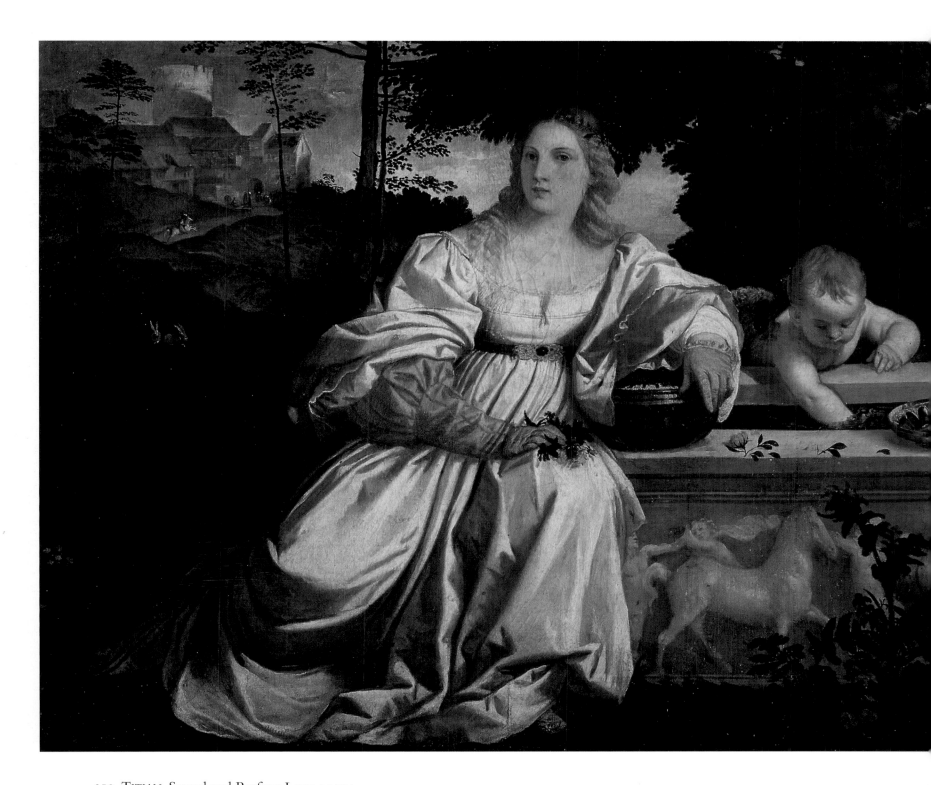

219 TITIAN Sacred and Profane Love *c.*1514
The precise meaning of this picture is uncertain. It was Titian's final
painting in the Giorgione manner, and is one of the most beautiful
allegories of the Renaissance. The only certain identifications are
those of Venus, seated at right, and Cupid, stirring the water in the
sarcophagus. It may represent the Neo-Platonic concept of the
Terrestrial Venus (clothed) and the Celestial Venus, or Polia
Recounting her Adventures to Venus *from the influential*
Hypnerotomachia Poliphili *published in Venice in 1499. The*
escutcheon on the frieze bears the arms of Niccolò Aurelio, one of
Venice's most important civil servants, and his wife appears on the
silver dish. It seems likely therefore that the painting's real subject
may be The Bride of Niccolò Aurelio at the Fountain of
Venus. *As deities were sometimes understood to be invisible to*
mortals, the bride seems unaware of Venus.

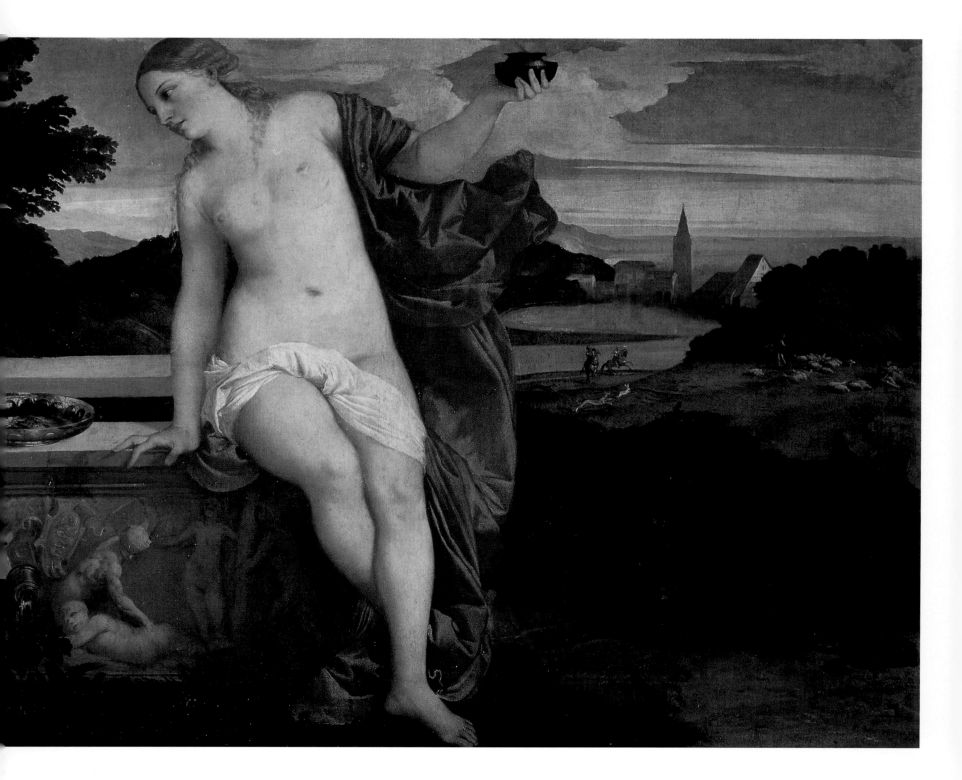

220 GIORGIONE Sleeping Venus *c.*1510
(Top right) A figure of Cupid was painted out at some time, almost certainly confirming that this was the picture described by the writer Michiel in 1525: he also stated that the landscape and Cupid had been painted by Titian. The contemplative, passive nature of the sleeping woman is wholly in character with Giorgione's vision of nature, totally transformed by Titian in his later variant, the Venus of Urbino, *into a sophisticated, worldly figure.*

221 TITIAN The Three Ages of Man 1516
(Bottom right) By the time he painted this, Titian had reached his first maturity and could combine restrained but potent allegory with images of unique poetic beauty and technical skill. In spite of an underlying melancholy (the inevitable passage of all living things towards decay and death), Titian's emphasis is optimistically on the youthful lovers. The girl is crowned with the flower associated with Venus, myrtle. The intensity of the lovers' gaze isolates them in space and time, suspends the girl's music-making and results in one of the most subtle and delicately erotic images in Western art. Only in the figures of the lovers is no obvious symbol of transience included: the putti *cluster around a dead tree and the old man contemplates two skulls, while the distant church symbolizes Christian hope beyond death.*

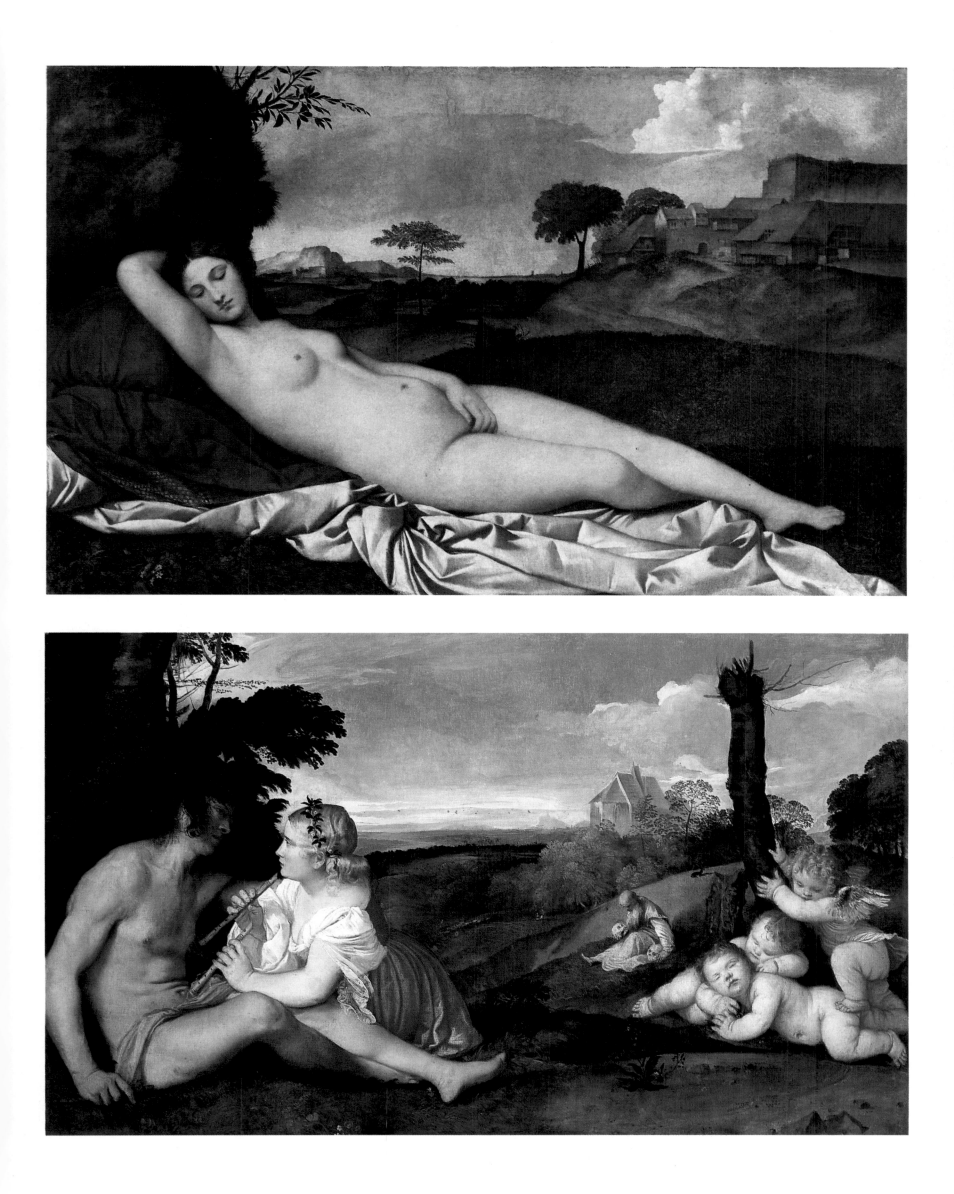

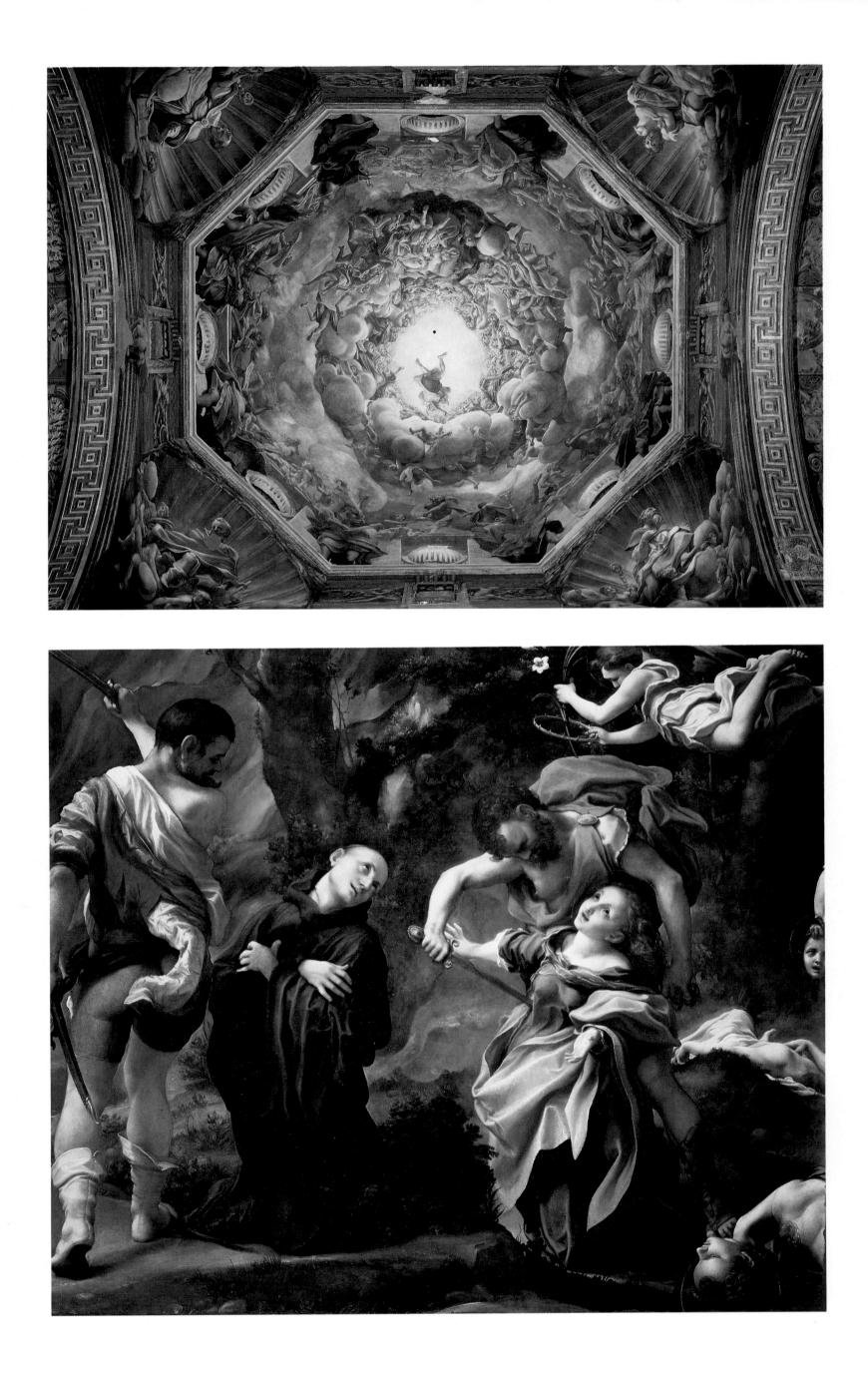

222 CORREGGIO Assumption of the Virgin 1526–8

(Top left) This dome fresco in Parma Cathedral is unusual in continuing down from the cupola area to surround the circular windows of the zone equivalent of the drum of the dome. At the centre of the composition is the figure of Christ surrounded by more than fifty heads of the blessed, with the Virgin below surrounded by thirty or forty angels. Further down are twenty-nine youths holding torches, and at the base huge figures of the Apostles. The perspective is so steep that in many cases the faces are invisible, and the effect was once compared to a 'hash of frogs' legs'. It is this daring exploitation of spatial effects which made this work so influential on Baroque ceiling decoration.

223 CORREGGIO Martyrdom of Four Saints 1524–6

(Bottom left) This martyrdom is somewhat obscure, and took place at Messina on the orders of a pirate in 541 or 542. Central to the drama are Sts Placido and Flavia, the others being the child martyrs Eutychius and Victorinus. Together with the Lamentation it was painted for the Del Bono Chapel in San Giovanni Evangelista in Parma. Correggio uses an intensity deriving from Beccafumi to create a novel type of religious painting, in which ecstatic expression plays a fundamental role. The central saints' raised eyes and hand gestures, the emotive use of drapery and the flying angel all introduce ideas later consciously adopted by the Baroque style. Such sweetness of expression was brought by Correggio to much of his religious painting.

224 CORREGGIO Io 1531

(Right) This small canvas belongs to a series of pictures illustrating the Loves of Jupiter, commissioned by Duke Federico II Gonzaga as a gift for the Emperor Charles V for his coronation in Bologna. The story is rare in Renaissance art. Jupiter embraced the nymph Io in the guise of a cloud and she was transformed into a white heifer. The extreme refinement of eroticism in this image makes it one of the most memorable nudes in Western painting. Its blond tonalities, Io's pose and her facial expression are all foretastes of the French Rococo style.

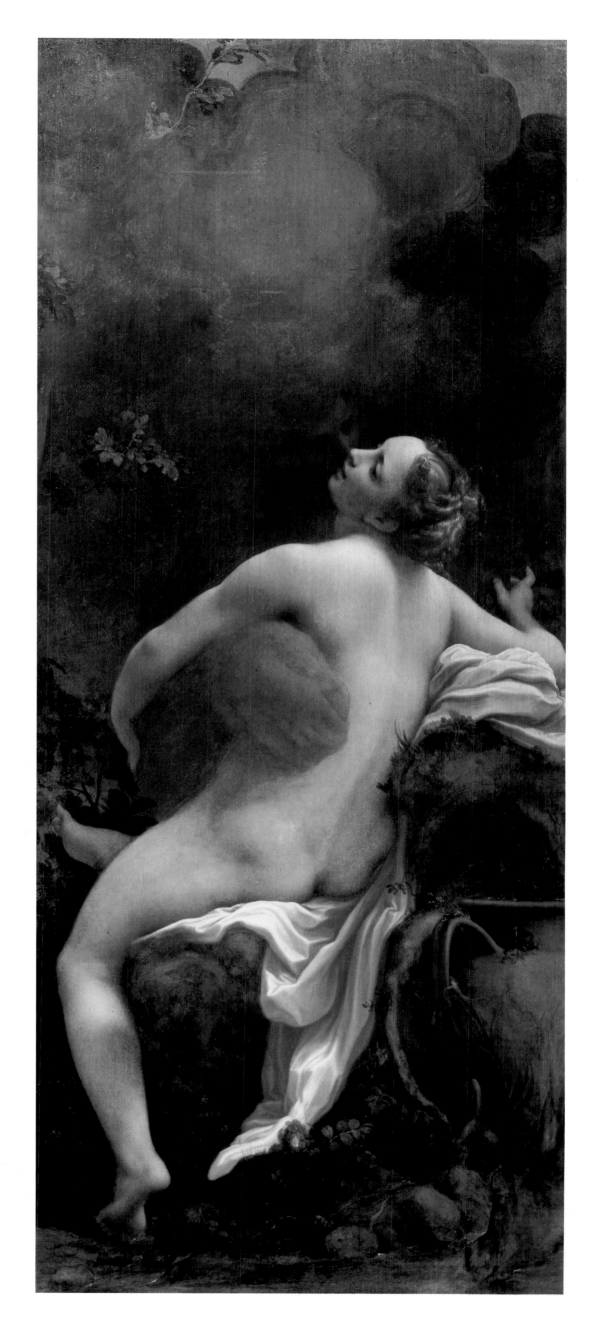

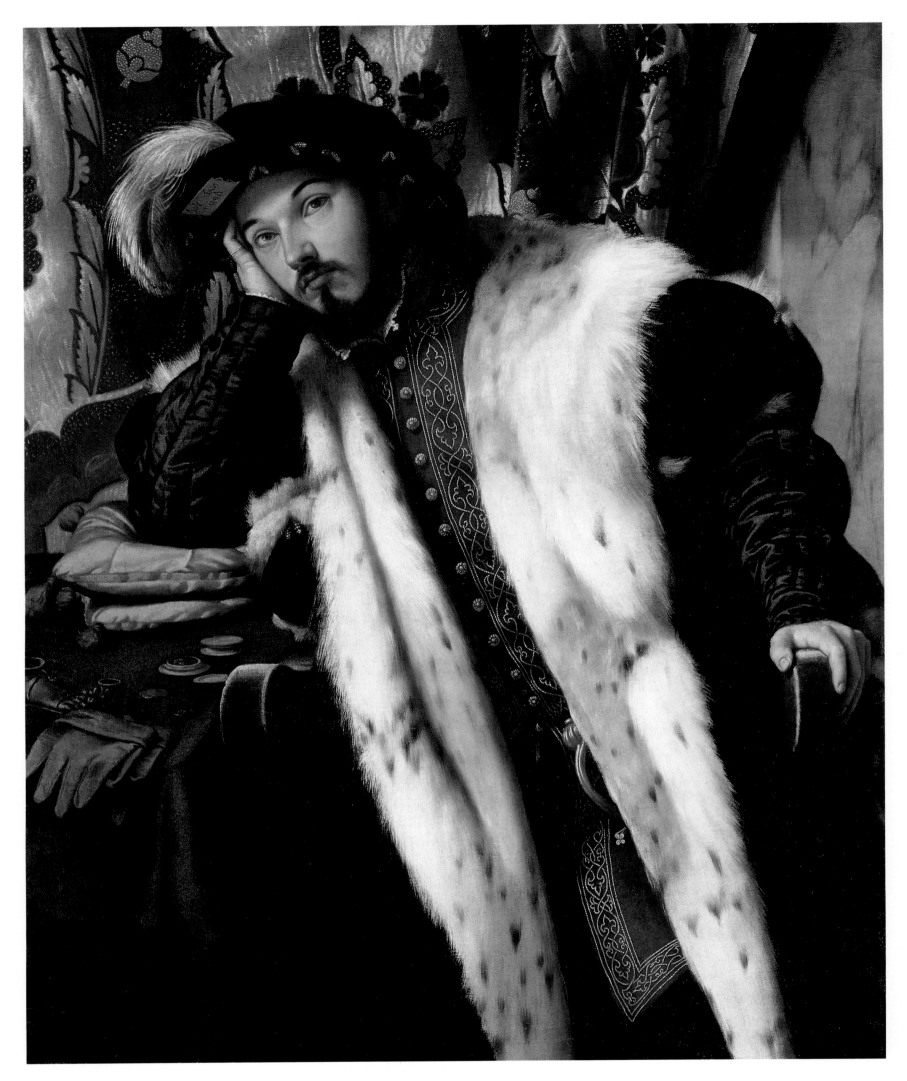

225 ALESSANDRO MORETTO, called MORETTO DA BRESCIA
Presumed Portrait of Count Sciarra Martinengo Cesaresco
*c.*1545–50

If the identification of the sitter is correct, he was page to Henry II of France, who created him a knight of St Michael at the age of eighteen. The precision of handling, vivid colour and the unusual pose combine to give the sitter striking presence, and suggest the influence of Lorenzo Lotto.

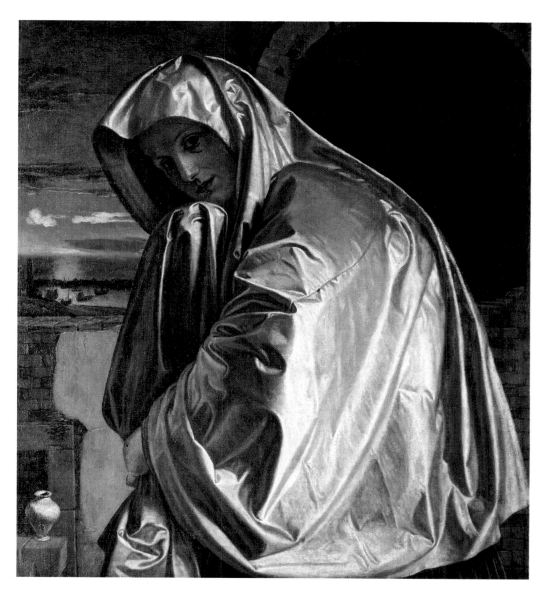

226 GIAN GIROLAMO SAVOLDO Saint Mary
Magdalene Approaching the Sepulchre
*c.*1528–30
*One of Savoldo's most striking images, this shows
his fascination with light effects and light on fabrics.
Although ultimately deriving from Giorgione,
Savoldo's intentions are more decorative. It seems
likely that the background shows a view of Venice.
Caravaggio was certainly influenced by Savoldo.*

227 SODOMA Marriage of Alexander with
Roxana 1516–17
*(Below) The little-known group of frescoes of which
this is the most appealing is among the most
delightful of the Roman High Renaissance period.
Sodoma painted them in the bedchamber of the
suburban Roman Villa Farnesina belonging to the
rich banker Agostino Chigi, where his compatriot
Baldassare Peruzzi was also painting. By
comparison with Raphael's suave classicism of these
years their style may seem old fashioned and fussy,
but they are full of delightful detail and incident.*

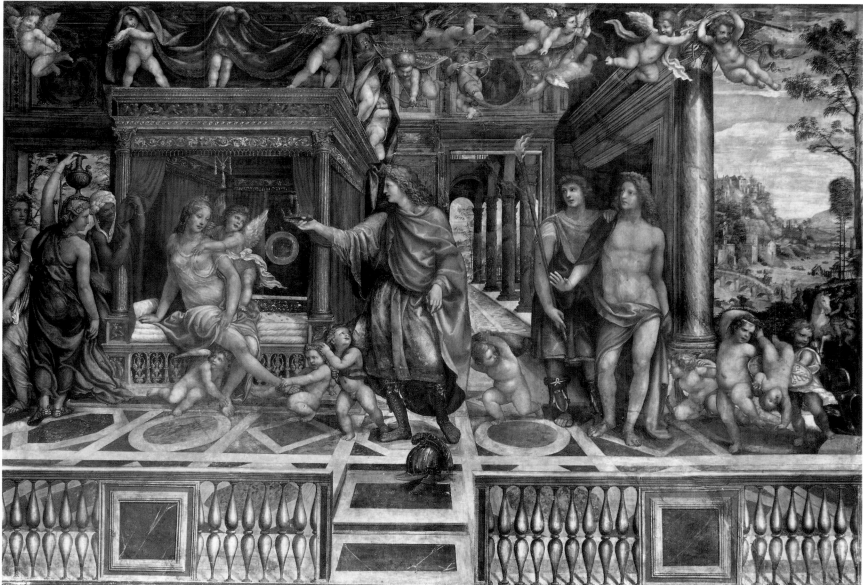

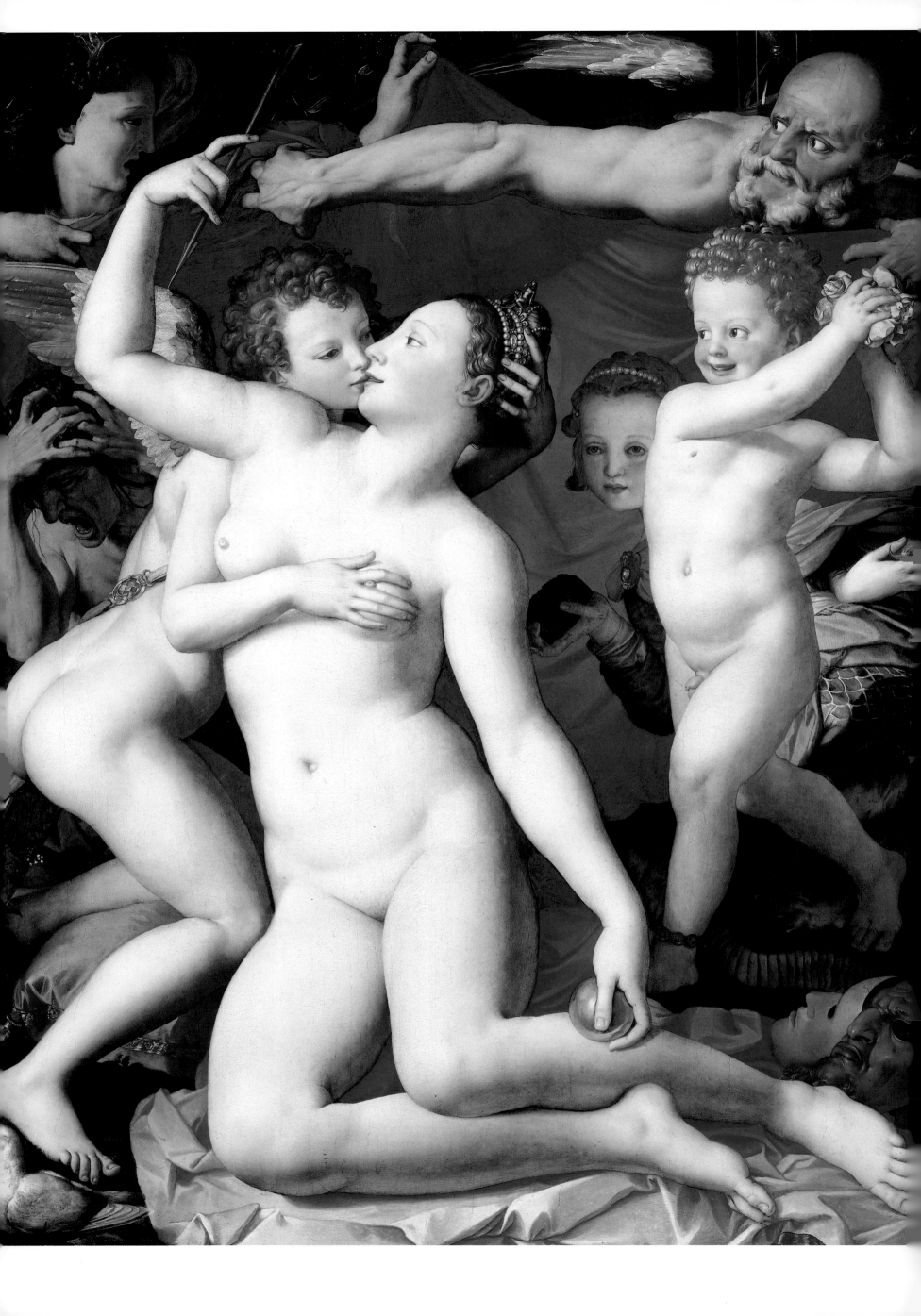

CHAPTER VIII

The Later Renaissance and Mannerism in Italy

The Counter-Reformation

After the richly creative and optimistic period leading up to the Sack of Rome in 1527, there followed a time of questioning in both society and the arts. The Papacy remained the most powerful single Italian state, but omnipresent in Rome at this time was the shadow of the Protestant threat to the Catholic Church. Pope Paul III was intent on introducing Catholic reformers in influential positions in Rome, to stamp out the heresies of the Protestant Reformation.

In 1540, the Society of Jesus (the Jesuits) was founded by the Spanish priest, Ignatius Loyola, with Paul III's approval. It was destined to be the strong right arm of the Counter-Reformation or 'Catholic Reformation'. Two years later, Giampetro Carafa (later Paul IV) had organized the Holy Office (the Inquisition) in Rome with Dominicans and Franciscans as Inquisitors. Only Venice was outside its jurisdiction, having set up its own tribunals in 1540. By 1547, the Jesuits' programme of education in universities and schools was launched, and their missionary activities began to spread through the world.

There was resistance to the Holy Office and the Jesuits in certain parts of Italy. But by 1551, in spite of Cosimo I de' Medici's opposition, they had founded a college in

228 AGNOLO BRONZINO Allegory of Venus, Folly and Time *c.*1545

This, one of the principal achievements of Italian Mannerist allegory, shows Bronzino's virtuoso technique in using startling colour to unique effect in creating icy eroticism. Venus engages in an incestuous embrace with her son Cupid, who tramples underfoot the doves of marital fidelity. Folly almost succeeds in concealing the fact that Pleasure not only offers a honeycomb but also has a hidden reptile's tail. Only Time, in drawing aside his curtain, will reveal what Folly hides from us, that illicit pleasure leads only to unhappiness.

Florence with the support of the Duchess, Eleonora of Toledo. Loyola's *Spiritual Exercises* was published in 1548; its rigorous self-examination, using every means to scrutinize the soul, had a great influence on the arts. Ignatius set an example of moderation and charity 'without hard words or contempt for people's errors'.

Meanwhile, the Holy Roman Emperor, Charles V, had been urging the Papacy since the late 1520s to call a council on Imperial territory, to placate the German cities and princes who had taken up the Reformation cause. Paul III promised this in 1536 – the year in which Michelangelo began work on his *Last Judgement*. The Council first met in Trent, an Italian city under the jurisdiction of the Emperor. Under the powerful leadership of the Pope, the Council dealt less with matters of reform (as Charles V wanted) and more with redefining Catholic orthodoxy. This made possible the enforcement of a new uniformity, and was summed up in one Act of the Council: 'No image shall be set up which is suggestive of false doctrine or which may furnish an occasion of dangerous error to the uneducated.' Although the atmosphere of religious change was already present in earlier painting, the effects of such explicit demands appeared increasingly in different ways as the century progressed. It was only a matter of time before the Church (like many Renaissance princes) saw art as a useful tool for propaganda.

Vasari and Contemporary Commentators

The key contemporary figure in understanding the art of the Cinquecento is Giorgio Vasari (1511–74), on whose writings we still depend for much information. More than any of his contemporaries, Vasari was in a position to know what he was talking about. Painter, architect, decorator, collector, historian, he was acquainted with most of the leading men of his day. In an age which saw a huge increase in writings about art and the world of art, he had no rivals. The peripatetic sculptor Benvenuto Cellini (1500–71) in his *Autobiography*, written in 1558–62, also provides a vivid picture of contemporary art and life. The Milanese painter, Giovanni Paolo Lomazzo (1538–1600), wrote two treatises on art, the *Trattato dell' Arte* (1584) and the *Idea del Tempio della Pittura* (1591). Cellini catches the romantic imagination, putting flesh (often ugly) on the bones of his period, while Lomazzo gives us real insight into the Mannerist point of view. A lengthy dialogue published in 1584, Raffaele Borghini's *Il Riposo*, provides our best account of the Florentine art scene in the Mannerist period, although its theorizing is borrowed directly from Vasari. In 1547, another Florentine intellectual, Benedetto Varchi, had the idea of asking various living artists for their ideas on the *paragone*, or relative merits of the arts, on which Leonardo had previously commented in his treatise. In Venice, Marcantonio Michiel's plans to write a history of art appear to have been scotched by Vasari's progress with his, but Michiel's notes survived and are particularly useful in their descriptions of collections and connoisseurship. Even Castiglione's *Book of the Courtier* (1518) offers a discussion of art. None matched Vasari's encyclopaedic vision, however, which formed posterity's image of the period and how to understand it.

Vasari began planning his *Lives of the Most Excellent Painters, Sculptors and Architects* about 1543, just as Italian Mannerism was reaching maturity. First published in 1550, a second and heavily revised edition appeared in 1568. It still strikes us as a remarkably modern work, with its sound introduction on the technical aspects of art followed by the biographical and analytical studies of past and present artists. Central to its aims was the desire to improve standards by example, a method fundamental to the practice of Florentine historians such as Guicciardini, and found in Machiavelli's *The Prince* (1513) and Castiglione's *Book of the Courtier* (1528). It also lay behind the academic ideal, best represented in the fine arts by the foundation under Cosimo I of the Accademia del Disegno in 1563 in Florence.

Vasari had gathered his material with a scientific method characteristic of the Renaissance, from interviews, correspondence and the works of art themselves. In spite of a much greater subjectivity than would be considered balanced today, we still return to the *Lives* not only for factual guidance on the period, but also for the general mood in the arts. This is qualified wherever possible by subsequent documentation and a greatly increased knowledge of the existence of works of art.

The sixteenth century's obsession with defining and writing about the perfection it sought in art and society has proved enormously helpful in seeing the period in its own terms. It also helps us to understand why certain artists adopted Mannerist styles while others (such as Veronese) remained almost impervious to them, in the same way that the French academic tradition continued to run in parallel with the development of Impressionism.

Vasari was born in Arezzo, which was then subject to Florence, where he was educated with Ippolito and Alessandro de' Medici, thanks to their guardian, Cardinal Silvio Passerini. Vasari therefore had the necessary contacts to launch his career on an Italian rather than a local scale. His artistic training was completed in the studio of Andrea del Sarto, but as a painter he was most influenced by early Florentine Mannerism and Michelangelo. With essential patronage from the Grand Duke of Tuscany, Cosimo I, Vasari built an enviable circle of patrons, including the Papacy and many religious bodies and private individuals. In order to respond adequately (and often little more than adequately) to his numerous commissions, he ran a large studio with exemplary efficiency. No one could claim that Vasari painted many pictures whose appeal lies outside a small circle of specialists, and his most attractive scheme was certainly the tiny studiolo of Francesco I de' Medici in Florence's Palazzo Vecchio (1570–73). His large decorative complexes, such as the Salone dei Cinquecento in the same palace (begun 1563), and the 'Room of a Hundred Days' in the Palazzo della Cancelleria, Rome, of the late 1540s contain admirable parts but are visually confusing and doctrinaire. Vasari is perhaps the proof that the gifted theorist may not be the finest practitioner.

Michelangelo's Later Years

Michelangelo (1475–1564) is the *eminence grise* behind all Italian Cinquecento painting and sculpture. During the last thirty years of his life, which he spent in voluntary exile from Medici Florence in Rome, he created three monolithic masterpieces of painting. One of these was the *Last Judgement* (see plate 229) in the Sistine Chapel. Pope Paul III, who succeeded Clement VII, appointed Michelangelo 'Supreme Architect, Sculptor and Painter to the Apostolic Palace', and this new commission took over from the tortured project of completing Julius II's tomb.

Begun in 1535, the *Last Judgement* occupied Michelangelo for the next six years. The decision to cover the entire altar wall of the Sistine Chapel with the fresco meant losing earlier work by Perugino, in addition to two

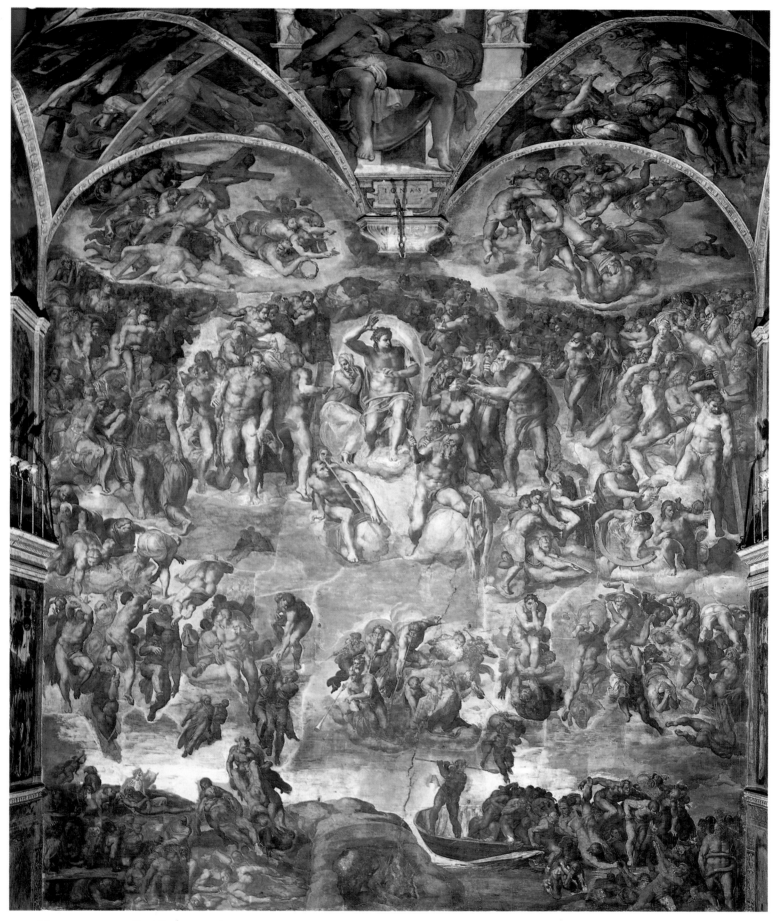

229 MICHELANGELO Last Judgement 1535–41

*Although originally commissioned by Pope Clement VII, it was
Pope Paul III who instigated the execution of this fresco in the
Sistine Chapel. An existing altarpiece and other decoration by
Perugino were removed to give Michelangelo the entire wall surface.
The immense scale and freedom of composition this allowed him were
unprecedented, and the resulting arrangement of figures was all the
more original. A gigantic Christ in an unforgettable attitude of
judgement is the focus of the whole, and His pose and gesture are*

*echoed throughout the movement of the entire figure group. The
Virgin as intercessor for the resurrected is pressed close to his side.
Michelangelo arranged the groups in a rotational pattern, with the
figures at the left ascending at the Resurrection, while those at the
right fall to damnation. Originally the nudity, which shocked many
at the unveiling, gave an impression of even greater vigour, recorded
in a copy made by Marcello Venusti in 1549. This photograph was
taken before the recent cleaning of the fresco.*

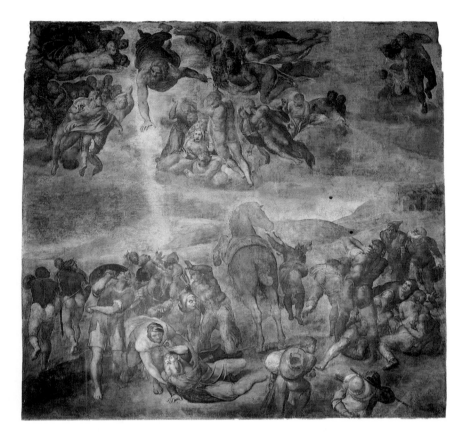

230 MICHELANGELO Conversion of Saint Paul 1542–5
On completion of the Last Judgement *Pope Paul III commissioned Michelangelo to paint two frescoes in the Vatican's Pauline Chapel. Their themes are complementary, as the other shows the crucifixion of St Peter, the other founder saint of the Catholic Church. The figures recall those of the* Last Judgement, *their grandeur and* contrapposto *accentuated by the up-tilted, simplified landscape setting.*

of his own *Ancestor* lunettes from the ceiling. This greatly extended the space, however, and permitted Michelangelo to create the most complex yet the most rational large-scale arrangement of figures in the Renaissance. In spite of the density and complexity of the groupings, all the figures are dependent on Christ's unforgettable gesture of condemnation, sending the Damned downwards while raising the Blessed upwards to Heaven.

The *Last Judgement* must have puzzled Michelangelo's artist contemporaries. In spite of its mass of writhing figures, it cannot be classified as a work of Mannerism, which it transcends by its sheer force. It does not display *grazia* and *maniera* – gracefulness and stylishness. The beautiful forms of the Sistine ceiling have been replaced by figures expressing a far greater urgency. Any sense of real space has been abandoned for an abstraction, and the muscularity of the ceiling's figures appears more self-conscious beside these massively formed creatures. More than the ceiling or any of Michelangelo's earlier works, it defies categorization. Like the later Cappella Paolina frescoes, it speaks a new language of total independence from all other current art trends. There can be no denying also that the mood of the *Last Judgement* stands for some of the dra-

matic changes which had occurred since the creation of the ceiling. Its completion in 1541 coincided with the arrival of the Counter-Reformation in Rome.

There was to be no respite for Michelangelo, as Paul III then ordered him to paint two frescoes in the Vatican's Pauline Chapel (see plate 230) recently built by Antonio da Sangallo the Younger. Only after the Pope had arranged for the ageing artist to be released from the contract for Julius II's tomb, could he start these frescoes in late 1542. They were finished in 1549 and unveiled the following year to little critical interest. Only Vasari and Condivi tried to understand them. 'These were his last paintings produced at the age of seventy-five', says Vasari, 'He spoke to me one day of fatigue: one discovers at a certain age that painting, particularly fresco, is not an art for old age.' These frescoes have never received the attention lavished on the artist's other works, and are certainly not easy to understand or appreciate. Vasari noted that Michelangelo '. . . dreamed only of perfection; he eliminated landscapes, trees, buildings, and all the various embellishments of art, refusing to stoop to them, to let his genius stoop to such things'. The style of these last frescoes provided no inspiration for contemporary painters chained to the *embarras de richesse* of Mannerist imagery, and remained largely without apologists until the present day.

Vasari's feeling that there could be no further progress in painting after the achievement of Michelangelo may well have been more prevalent in the mid-sixteenth century than is generally supposed. If so, it would have been another uncertainty added to those already perplexing many painters nearing the end of the Renaissance tradition. Indeed, self-confidence expressed in Vasari's historical and theoretical writing was probably based on what he hoped for his own age rather than what he actually saw in its art. It might have dismayed him to know that the twentieth-century art historian, Walter Friedlaender, would classify painting in his age as 'The Anticlassical Style'. Vasari saw contemporary painting (including his own) as the continuation of the Classical ideas of the High Renaissance period. But the very existence of Michelangelo's *Doni Tondo* and the Sistine vault at its heart suggests the tenuous nature of Classicism, even then.

The Mannerist Style

The Mannerist period in Italian art offers a bewildering assortment of styles. But the term 'Classical' does not describe the majority of painters included in this chapter – Giulio Romano, Pontormo, Rosso Fiorentino, Parmigianino, Perino del Vaga, Bronzino, Allori, Salviati or Vasari himself. The term does, however, have relevance for painters who made their debuts at the peak of the High Renaissance, such as Titian and Correggio, or those whose styles offer a late version of High Renaissance ideas, such as Veronese. Paradoxically, however, even in the most extreme manifestations of Mannerist physical distortion while the language may not appear Classical, the details and underlying inspiration often are. The sixteenth century's obsession with style blinds us to this fact. Even where it is least obvious, the moving force behind many Mannerist works of art remains the antique.

'Mannerism' is related to the word 'manners', implying an acquired code of behaviour which will bring its adherents close to a specific norm. More exactly, it derives from the Italian word *maniera* – manner or style – a word current with Vasari and his contemporaries. In an age like ours, which claims to value practicality and 'naturalness', something 'stylized' may tend to be dismissed as insincere, while something 'stylish' appears praiseworthy.

In its application to art, Mannerism may be said to incorporate both terms, since the later Renaissance valued any conspicuously stylized artefact (because it represented the triumph of art over nature). At the same time it demanded that art be stylish and polished, not *rozza* (coarse) as Vasari categorized the medieval period. Such stylishness depended on ceaseless refinement, whether in the deportment of a courtier, the turn of a literary or musical phrase, or the depiction of nature in art. The result, if successful, was seen as displaying *maniera* or being *manieroso* (mannered), or *artifizioso* (artificial, in a complimentary sense). All art is by definition artificial, but the Florentine man of letters, Benedetto Varchi, wrote in 1548 that it had to be 'an artificial imitation of nature'.

Two terms illustrate particularly well the source of much of the elegance achieved in Mannerist art – *contrapposto* and the *figura serpentinata*. While *contrapposto*, the turning of the different parts of the body to achieve compositional balance, had long been an essential constituent of variety, notably in sculpture, its exaggeration in Mannerism produced different results. Michelangelo's Doni Madonna is depicted in extreme and unnatural *contrapposto*, as are the men in the *Battle of Cascina* (see plates 210, 209). In his treatise, Lomazzo says that any figure with the form of a flame will be beautiful, going on to praise the '*Serpentinata*, like the twisting of a live snake in motion, which is also the form of a waving flame . . .'. The serpentine figure came to be increasingly regarded as the ideal of beauty, even in its most extreme and bizarre forms.

In spite of the elegance of much Mannerist painting, the style is often aggressive in a way whose only parallel

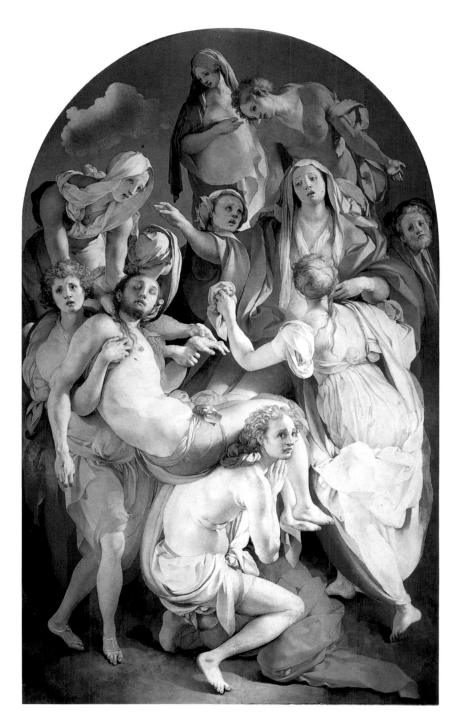

231 Jacopo Pontormo Pietà *c.*1526–8

This altarpiece is at the centre of the Capponi Chapel, which Vasari says Pontormo spent three years decorating in such secrecy that even the patron Lodovico Capponi could not follow its progress. Its now destroyed cuppola *contained a fresco of God the Father by Pontormo, who looked down past four* tondi *in oil of the Evangelists (two of which were by Bronzino) to the Deposition and the frescoed Annunciation, thus making a unified dramatic entity that looked forward to Baroque schemes. The chapel is Pontormo's only surviving decorative scheme.*

The Deposition was painted in Pontormo's first mature style. It is partly based on an antique sarcophagus, and comparison with the surviving modello *drawing shows that Pontormo pared the final composition down to its essentials. Its perspective, colour (deriving in part from Michelangelo) and costume are equally ambiguous, but all accentuate the intensity of feeling in the Virgin's gesture of farewell to the body of her son; the sense of frozen unreality and the illusion that the group is illuminated by a sudden flash of light underline the pathos of the theme.*

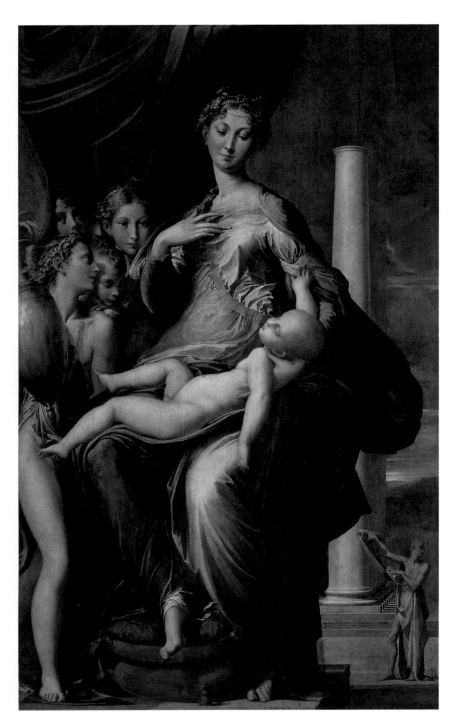

232 PARMIGIANINO Madonna of the Long Neck *c.*1535
This painting was commissioned by Elena Baiardi for her chapel in
Santa Maria dei Servi at Parma. Both the columns and the Virgin's
long neck may be references to a medieval hymn relating the Virgin
to a column, and not merely stylistic exaggerations like the elongated
limbs and small heads. Nonetheless, the painting remains one of the
highest points of Mannerist stylization, with an ideal of feminine
beauty refined from Correggio's.

in previous European art is late Gothic. Both present their
characteristic features in a way which appears to make
them the *raison d'être* of the work of art. Distortion appears
in every phase of Mannerism, with a preference for
attenuated limbs and extremities, small heads and
pronounced musculature. A rejection of the canons of
'realistic' space achieved with such effort during the
Quattrocento and High Renaissance is one of
Mannerism's most striking features, from Pontormo's
Pietà (see plate 231) to Parmigianino's *Madonna of the*

Long Neck (see plate 232) to Tintoretto in the Scuola di
San Rocco.

The theories of the mid-century bore out what had
already started to appear in painting thirty years earlier.
Raphael's real legacy to the next generation was not his
gentle Madonnas, but his darker, vigorous and assertively
stylish later work, such as *Saint Cecilia* (Pinacoteca,
Bologna), *Lo Spasimo di Sicilia* (see plate 250) and the
Transfiguration (see plate 248). Here, the composition of
the lower zone includes some of the most felicitous combinations of pose, gesture and facial expression in Western
art, while the foreground figure of the mother is one of
the clearest prototypes for Mannerist elegance.

Raphael was evolving towards *maniera* and *grazia*,
prime requirements of Vasari's and documented by
Raphael himself as vital to art. In his famous letter of 1519,
written with Castiglione to Pope Leo X, he condemns
Gothic architecture as *privi di ogni gratia, senza maniera alcu-*
na (devoid of all grace and entirely without style).

However, the assumption that all the seeds of
Mannerism are visible in one Raphael figure is of course
erroneous. Unlike High Renaissance style, most of whose
manifestations tend to share the desire for rational balance,
Mannerism divides into quite different currents. These
have been simplified, not misleadingly, as 'neurotic mannerism' and 'courtly mannerism', and the distinction is
borne out by an examination of many paintings made
between 1520 and 1550. The appearance of this greatly
heightened *grazia* in late Raphael coincides with an
intensely sybaritic period in Roman life which ended
abruptly with the Sack of Rome in 1527.

Raphael falls into the category of 'courtly', exemplified
in his *Transfiguration* figures, as do painters who turned to
his work for inspiration, particularly Perino del Vaga (see
plate 233) and Parmigianino (see plates 232, 245). It could
be argued that the *Ignudi* on the Sistine Ceiling, where
effortless beauty predominated, even belong to this category. Bronzino, as the supreme 'courtly' Mannerist, while
deriving from Pontormo, occupies a unique position.
Prime among the 'neurotic' mannerists are Pontormo (see
plates 231, 249) and Rosso Florentino (see plates 234,
251), neither of whom shows the ostensibly rational moti-
vation of their 'courtly' peers. The situation is further
complicated by the emergence in Vasari, late Bronzino
and others, of what might be termed 'academic
Mannerism'. Such a late permutation of the style
undoubtedly resulted from the exhaustion felt by many
painters in working and reworking a style fundamentally
based on formulae (i.e. Michelangelism). It was against
this that the reaction occurred in the Bolognese Carracci
family and Florentine painters like Santi di Tito.

Mannerism in Florence and Rome

There is disagreement as to whether the first real development of Mannerism occurred in Florence or Rome. Pontormo painted *Joseph in Egypt* (see plate 249) in Florence, probably in 1515, and while its figure style still belongs to the world of Sarto and Franciabigio, its bizarre conception of space and other unreal elements link it firmly to early Mannerism. But it still shows none of the distortions present in his fresco lunettes (1523–5) at the Certosa di Galluzzo (the Carthusian monastery outside Florence). These derive so much from Dürer's prints, which, according to Vasari, had flooded into Italy. Sarto, Pontormo and Bronzino were only a few of the Italians who studied them, along with those of Schongauer (see plate 139), Lucas van Leyden and others.

Incipient Florentine Mannerism, therefore, emerged in early Pontormo, and like much contemporary Tuscan work, required only the injection of Roman ideas to set it in independent motion. It seems reasonable to accept that the most direct current of influence did indeed come from Raphael to his Roman followers: Guilio Romano, Giovanni da Udine (1487–1564), Polidoro da Caravaggio (1500–43?) and Perino del Vaga. Without exception, their work was heavily influenced by Raphael's antique interests, whether in the extreme elegance of Polidoro's monochrome friezes on palace façades (such as Palazzo

233 PERINO DEL VAGA Martyrdom of the Ten Thousand 1522–3
This, the modello *for a lost cartoon for an unexecuted fresco, brought the latest Roman ideas to Tuscany. Its balletic movement and wealth of decorative detail had an immense influence on the next generation of Florentine painters, notably Bronzino.*

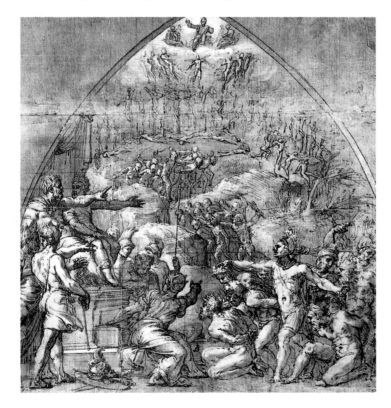

Ricci, Rome), da Udine's *grotesques* or Giulio's Classical themes at Mantua's Palazzo del Tè (see plate 263).

It was Perino del Vaga (1501–47) who created one of the first Tuscan monuments of the Roman Mannerist style, in his cartoon showing the *Martyrdom of the Ten Thousand* (see plate 233). Vasari describes the cartoon as 'a divine object' and praises Perino's success in expressing psychological states through pose and expression, thus relating directly back to Alberti's ideas of decorum in *Della Pittura*. It is significant that Vasari applauded the 'wealth of most beautiful ornament that one could possibly create, both imitating and supplanting the antique, drawn with that devotion and artifice which reaches the very heights of art'. He singles out precisely the type of decorative detail which proliferates in later Mannerism – '. . . cuirasses in the antique style and most ornate and bizarre costumes; and the leg-pieces, boots, helmets, shields and the rest of the armour . . .'. A similar, almost fetishistic interest in super-ornate costume, armour and hairstyles finds a direct expression in Michelangelo's drawings of *Divine Heads*, including the famous *Cleopatra* (see plate 32), which he may have based on Piero di Cosimo's *Cleopatra* or *Simonetta Vespucci* (see plate 81).

Leonardo, in his treatise on painting, cautions the artist: 'As far as possible avoid the costumes of your own day, unless they belong to the religious group. . . Costumes of our own period should not be depicted unless it is on tombstones in churches, so that we may be spared being laughed at by our successors for the mad fashions of men and leave behind only things that may be admired for their dignity and beauty'. The concept of achieving greater timelessness through idealized or fantastic dress distinguishes much Mannerist art, and the idea was everpresent in Michelangelo. Even cross-dressing was considered a means of removing figures from any toorecognizable context. In Pontormo's *Pietà* (see plate 231), for example, this is carried to the extent of creating deliberate ambiguity between flesh and clothing. In this fantasy world, Italy led the way, although Northern mannerists such as Spranger (see plate 189) and artists of the School of Fontainebleau eagerly borrowed such ideas.

Pontormo

The Florentine Pontormo (Jacopo Carucci, 1491–1557) moved rapidly from early work in the manner of Sarto, with whom he studied after a period with Piero di Cosimo and possibly Leonardo. The leap from his *Visitation* fresco, begun in 1514 (Santissima Annunziata, Florence), to the Pucci altarpiece of 1518 in San Michele

standing of his sitters. His faces already adopt that mask-like appearance which approaches surrealism in Rosso Fiorentino.

From the 1540s, Bronzino's new post as court painter resulted not only in the famous portraits of the Duke and his Duchess, Eleonora of Toledo, (see plates 2, 11), but in two major essays in interpreting the Michelangelesque nude: the London *Allegory of Venus* (see plate 228) and the frescoes in the Duchess's Chapel in the Palazzo Vecchio. The former has all the jewel-like colour and artificiality of high Mannerist ideals, and is based on the most elaborate use of extreme *contrapposto*, which also plays a large part in the chapel frescoes. In the altarpiece for the chapel Bronzino achieved a synthesis of all his mature ideals, and it is one of the key works of the period. His work for the Medici court included tapestry design (the late 1540s *Story of Joseph*, woven in Cosimo's tapestry manufactory, and now divided between Florence and Rome), and the large *Martyrdom of St Lawrence* fresco of 1569 in San Lorenzo. Notwithstanding the fact that it includes many fine portraits, this fresco illustrates with alarming clarity the vacuity of later Mannerism's narrative methods, and its impossibility of further evolution from Michelangelo's approach to anatomy and composition.

Bronzino's genius for portraiture only increased with age, and was particularly pronounced when he painted friends. As late as 1560, he created one of the most memorable 'homages' of one artist to another in his *Laura Battiferri* (see plate 253), where the figure is seen almost as a sculpted relief. Little of this picture's intensity occurs in his other late work. This may be partly explained by his sense of increasing isolation on the deaths of his closest friends and patrons, including Pontormo, Eleonora of Toledo and Michelangelo, all of which inspired tragic sonnets from the ageing painter.

The tired uncertainty evident in his late work was also partly occasioned by the confusion resulting from the impact of Counter-Reformation ideas on Florentine art, and the convulsive conscience-searching of artists, such as the sculptor Bartolommeo Ammanati (1511–92).

Venetian Painting After 1520

Whereas in Florence and Rome the linear preferences of the Quattrocento persisted, Venetian painting continued where Leonardo's experiments had left off. His *sfumato* approach was diametrically opposed to the method defined by Cennini and current through most of the Quattrocento, where vividly coloured areas of paint defined form. In exploring aerial perspective, which

requires the viewer's imagination to complete the relationship of forms to space, Leonardo prepared the way for the daring later experiments of Titian and Tintoretto. The rigid depiction of form through outline was being replaced already in Giorgione's work with the interaction of colour, light and atmosphere. In Giorgione's paintings, consequently, it is more often the impression of the whole canvas rather than individual detail that remains in the mind.

In Florentine and Roman painting, however, exactly the opposite prevailed, and the supremacy of traditional *disegno,* so much vaunted by Vasari, won the day. Even a thoroughly Venetian painter like Sebastiano del Piombo, trained in *Giorgionismo*, converted in Rome to local methods and Michelangelo's influence, as is seen in his *Raising of Lazarus* (National Gallery, London) painted with Michelangelo's help in direct competition with Raphael's *Transfiguration*. Ever since twentieth-century art history initiated the study of Italian Mannerism, the precise degree to which central Italian Mannerism influenced Venetian art has been much debated. From one point of view there can be little doubt that Venetian painting remained remarkably independent, since central Italian Mannerism depended on certain instantly recognizable features. These included a heightened concentration on individual human forms (even in making up the largest, most convoluted compositions) as vehicles for the display of anatomy and elaborate poses, costumes, accessories and colour. Mannerism's primary emphasis was on the artificial, often leading to accusations of its overriding concern with form at the expense of content.

Instances in Venetian painting where such criticisms can be made are rare. When the Holy Office accused Veronese in 1573 of introducing extraneous elements into a painting for a Venetian convent, the artist might well have cited any contemporary Florentine picture to demonstrate how ill-founded the accusation was. The work he actually used was Michelangelo's *Last Judgement*.

Opportunities for painters abounded in Cinquecento Venice more than any other Italian city, and both in quantity and quality their response was unique. Much importance was attached to working in the Palazzo Ducale (the Doge's Palace), where two disastrous fires in 1574 and 1577 led to considerable scope for redecoration. In addition, the city's unique *scuole* or religious societies were lavish patrons of the arts (see Chapter 1). There were two distinct groups, the *Scuole Grande* and the *Scuole Piccole.* The former had come into being to assert the pious, devotional life, but were predominantly lay, self-governing institutions which by the mid-sixteenth century wielded considerable power. The *Scuole Piccole* were smaller variations on this, and were often related to a trade or expatriate minority. Competition between the *scuole* for the most splendid buildings and works of art naturally benefited Venetian painters and architects.

Titian's Later Career

We rightly think of Titian (Tiziano Vecellio, died 1576) as a High Renaissance painter. It is thus sometimes easy to overlook the fact that most of his career coincides with Mannerism elsewhere. What Titian substituted for Mannerist tendencies was a unique dynamism, seen first in the awe-inspiring *Assumption of the Virgin* (see plate 254). He proved that huge scale was not necessary to achieve this, in his *Annunciation* in Treviso Cathedral completed in late 1522, and the contemporary polyptych with the *Resurrection, Annunciation and Saints* (Santi Nazaro e Celso, Brescia). In the first, drama is created by 'continuing' the real architecture of its setting, while the polyptych quoted directly from the *Laocoön* and two of Michelangelo's slaves for Julius II's tomb in Saint Peter's. Titian was not alone in the early 1520s in Venice in seeking a dynamic figure style, and even Palma Vecchio achieved an approximation to Roman grandeur and *grazia* with his *Saint Barbara* in Santa Maria Formosa.

The most sumptuous of Titian's paintings at this time were commissioned for the Camerino d'Alabastro (Alabaster Chamber) of his new patron, Alfonso d'Este of Ferrara. The room contained some of the best north Italian art of the day – Bellini's *Feast of the Gods*, (National Gallery of Art, Washington), Dosso Dossi's *Feast of Cybele* (National Gallery, London), Titian's the *Garden of Love* (Museo del Prado, Madrid), *Bacchus and Ariadne* (National Gallery, London), and *Bacchanal of the Andrians* (see plate 236). Titian's robustness must have made the Bellini and Dosso pictures appear very old fashioned. His paintings show his mastery of colour at its most seductive, exercising a spell on all subsequent colourists, notably Rubens.

It was also hoped that Michelangelo, Fra Bartolommeo and Raphael would contribute to the Camerino d'Alabastro scheme. Interiors of such lavishness were not common, and usually their cost could only be borne by public bodies, as in Venice. Its subsequent dismantling meant the disappearance of one of the greatest humanist painting schemes of the Renaissance.

The energy of these paintings culminated in an altarpiece whose commission Titian won in competition with Palma Vecchio and Pordenone (Giovanni Antonio de Sacchis, 1483/4–1539). This showed the *Death of Saint Peter Martyr*, and was completed in 1530 for Santi

Giovanni e Paolo, Venice. It was later destroyed but is known from engravings and copies. Contemporary with Correggio's largest dome fresco – the *Assumption* – in Parma Cathedral (see plate 222), it shared the same elements which were later utilized by Baroque artists. Although both works depend for their effect on dynamic figure poses (in Correggio's they are suspended in space, so enhancing their drama), that effect remains primarily natural. The three protagonists in the Titian are shown in *contrapposto*, but to heighten tension and not for stylistic reasons. Titian was aware of Michelangelo, Raphael and Roman prototypes but he deliberately chose an independent path. This allowed him to give colour, light and movement first place in his art, without attempting, as Sebastiano del Piombo was said to have done (unsuccessfully), 'to unite the drawing of Michelangelo with the colour of Giorgione'.

Only rarely did Titian later permit himself the drama of the early decades, most notably in the lost *Battle of Cadore* of 1537–8 for the Palazzo Ducale in Venice. In late works, such as *Tarquin and Lucretia* of 1571 (Fitzwilliam Museum, Cambridge), style has overtaken drama to create elegant surface pattern. Even in his last, intense *Pietà* (Accademia,

236 TITIAN Bacchanal of the Andrians, completed 1522
This formed part of a group of four paintings in the studiolo *of Alfonso I d'Este in the castle of Ferrara. The others were Titian's* Bacchus and Ariadne *and the* Worship of Venus, *and Bellini and Titian's* Feast of the Gods. *The theme of this picture comes from Philostratus the Elder's* Imagines, *and shows the inhabitants of the island of Andros drunk from the stream of wine created by Dionysus. Ariadne lies asleep at the right.*

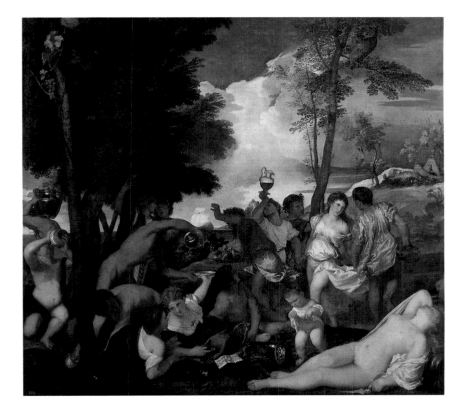

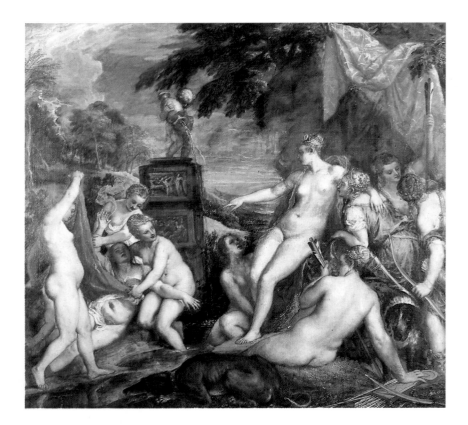

237 TITIAN Diana and Callisto 1556–9
As with its pendant, Diana and Callisto, *the source of the story is*
Ovid's Metamorphoses. *Diana discovers the pregnancy of her*
nymph Callisto, who has been seduced by Jupiter. Both pictures were
painted for King Philip II and despatched to Madrid in 1559.

Venice) there is a sense of the figures being frozen in their
dramatic poses.

Vasari defined Titian's position in Venice up until the
1540s and 1550s, saying that he 'had in Venice some competitors but not of much worth, so that he has surpassed
them easily with the excellence of his art'. This is
nowhere more evident than in his portraits (see plate 255).
Lavish dress (including armour) had to play a part in pre-
senting a sitter's character, and Titian had no equal in
achieving a perfect balance between the sitter's face and
his clothing, particularly during the 1530s. The portraits
of *Cardinal Ippolito de' Rovere* and his Duchess, *Eleonora
Gonzaga* (both Uffizi, Florence) exemplify the unique
combination, implied and visible, of richness with aristocratic restraint, which made Titian the model for so many
subsequent court portraits.

The measure of his genius was that he could transform
the prototype of Giorgione's Dresden *Venus* into the
Venus of Urbino of about 1538 (Uffizi, Florence) by giving
the generalized nude the particular quality of portraiture.
This painting is in many ways the artist's final farewell to
the quieter world of Giorgione and, in about 1540, he
experimented tentatively with central Italian Mannerism
introduced into Venice by Francesco Salviati (1510–63)
and others. Combined with the pose and scale of
Michelangelo's figure of *Dawn* in the New Sacristy of San

Lorenzo in Florence, the subtle Urbino *Venus* later
emerged as the majestic and voluptuous versions of *Danaë*
for Ottavio Farnese and King Philip II of Spain (Museo di
Capodimonte, Naples and Museo del Prado, Madrid).

In the decade between these two versions (Philip II's
painting dated from 1553–4), Titian's brushwork
progressed towards greater looseness and fluidity. This
is seen to perfection in two of his finest *poesie* (poems,
as Titian liked to describe them) for Philip II illustrating
the story of Diana (see plates 237, 238). It is also the secret
of *The Death of Actaeon* (National Gallery, London), where
colour is minimal and a total harmony is achieved
between the human figure and surrounding nature. Such
a feeling of resolution pervades many of Titian's late
paintings, from his moving *Self Portrait* (Staatliche
Museen, Berlin) of the early 1560s to his final testament,
the *Pietà* (see plate 256).

Titian's only real competition before 1550 in Venice
came from Palma Vecchio and Il Pordenone. After this,
the rise of Tintoretto, and then of Veronese, while in no
way diminishing Titian's stellar position in Europe, certainly provided viable alternatives.

238 TITIAN Diana and Actaeon 1556–9
Ovid describes how Prince Actaeon came across the pool where Diana
and her nymphs were bathing one day while he was out hunting in
the forest. Titian's painting is charged with mixed reactions to the
erotic encounter. He creates highly concentrated drama by the simplest
of means, using a V-like recession into depth and two monumental
figures (Diana and Actaeon) at either side, in a manner that
prefigures Baroque compositional methods. His colour is at its most
sumptuous, notably in the brilliant rose drapery set against a deep
blue sky and the powder blue cloth of the seated nymph.

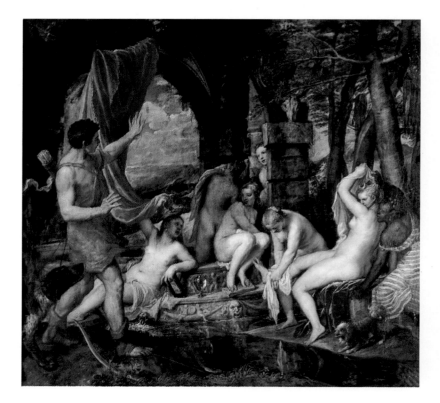

Tintoretto

Tintoretto (Jacopo Robusti, 1518–94) is already recorded as an independent painter in 1539, at which time he appears to have produced mainly *Sacre Conversazioni*. Even in these it is clear that Tintoretto, who was largely self-taught, was not content to purvey weak derivations of the established Titian style. Always original and immensely productive, Tintoretto possessed a boundless energy greater even than Titian's. His assimilation of ideas, from both outside Venice and within, meant that he was much more open to Mannerist concepts at a time when Titian continued largely to reject or ignore them. Tintoretto never became a Mannerist painter, although he made use of some Mannerist devices. It was left to lesser painters such as Andrea Schiavone (*c.* 1510/15–63) and Paris Bordone (1500–71) to attempt the style in Venice.

Among the central Italian and Emilian Mannerists he could have studied in Venice was Lorenzo Lotto (see plate 246, 247, 264), although Lotto's precise position is not easy to classify. It is possible that Tintoretto travelled to Florence and Rome in about 1540, when he would have seen Florentine Mannerism at its height and the work of Michelangelo. Throughout his life, Michelangelo's *terribilità* and dramatic distortion of the human figure seem to have remained in his mind, and different as the end results are, the explosive dynamism of Tintoretto's best pictures can have no other underlying inspiration. Tintoretto's excitement at the new narrative possibilities offered by many-figured, even slightly confused compositions, is evident in *Christ in the Temple* of the early 1540s (Museo del Duomo, Milan). Yet had Titian known these early efforts, he would rightly have detected little hint of a future rivalry, except perhaps in the untrammelled energy of the images.

Already by the mid-1540s, Tintoretto was experimenting with portraiture, which he later perfected with a unique sobriety very different from Titian's sparkling international manner. His late portraits are most memorable, including his haggard *Self Portrait* in the Louvre. He had also attracted sufficient attention for Pietro Aretino to commission two mythological ceilings from him. In 1548 he painted the *Miracle of the Slave* for the Scuola Grande di San Marco, which launched his reputation, and must have seemed to the Venetian public to offer a totally new alternative to Titian. In fact, when compared with a multi-figure Titian composition painted only five years earlier, *Ecce Homo* (Kunsthistorisches Museum, Vienna), it is clear that Tintoretto was giving a massive injection of new ideas to Venetian painting. Its colour is far from the suffused softness of Titian, using a colder and more metal-

lic glitter to highlight a palette of sharper greens, orange and steely blue. Its scale and exuberance, and the dramatic use of foreshortening and theatrical figure groupings also single it out as a turning point in Venetian art.

From the start, Tintoretto painted with what Aretino called his *prestezza del fatto* (immediacy), which the influential writer (who specifically favoured Titian and furthered his career) suggested might be replaced by *la pazienza del fare* (patient application). Tintoretto's 'immediacy' produced results very different from those of Titian's increasingly rapid working methods. Tintoretto exploited flickering light and tone, often with less colour, achieving a dryer effect for all his rich paint application. This is seen in *Saint Mary of Egypt in Meditation* in the Scuola di San Rocco and in the magical light effects in the *Last Supper*.

It was not only in visual dynamics, however, that Tintoretto now excelled. In *Susanna and the Elders* of the mid-1550s (see plate 262), Tintoretto avoids a classical grouping and, with characteristic invention, takes the viewer right to the core of the subject, bringing Susanna

239 JACOPO TINTORETTO Miracle of Saint Mark 1548
This story comes from Jacopo da Voragine's Golden Legend.
Tintoretto shows the moment when St Mark miraculously intervenes to save a servant who wished to venerate his relics, but was condemned to torture and death. Tintoretto chooses the high point of the drama, when the saint swoops down to save the servant surrounded by breaking instruments of torture, and accentuates the movement by extreme foreshortening. Serene Palladian architecture contrasts with the foreground violence. This picture launched Tintoretto with the Venetian public, demonstrating his ability to depict large crowds of figures in dramatic action. Portraits of the artist (with beard, at left), Aretino and others have supposedly been identified in the crowd.

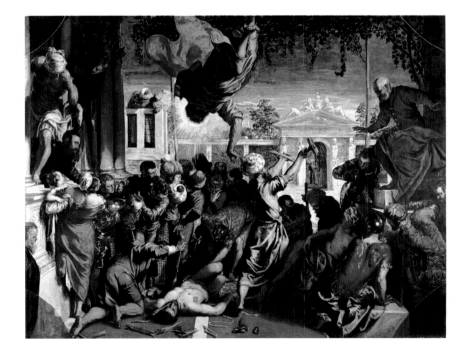

dramatically to the foreground and creating a screen of greenery in the centre which accentuates the tension of Susanna's surprise. Such devices and his brilliant ability to unify many figures in tightly-knit compositions distinguish his methods from those of central Italian Mannerists with their build-up of disparate units in a 'sum of the parts' approach.

In contrast to Titian's glamorous career; Tintoretto's was uneventfully confined to Venice, its principal milestones being his marriage and the births of his children. His major recognition outside the city came in 1566, when he was invited to join the Florentine Accademia di Pittura, together with Titian, Salviati and Andrea Palladio. This was the year that Vasari went to Venice, and noted that every visiting gentleman, man of letters or prince wished to meet Titian.

One year previously Tintoretto had initiated his lifelong involvement with the Scuola di San Rocco by painting the huge *Crucifixion* there, which remains one of his greatest achievements. It upsets all the perspective concepts established by previous Renaissance practice, using ladders, rising crosses and their complex interaction with elaborate figure groups to suggest the horror of the scene. Unity is imposed by Tintoretto's mastery of intensely dramatic lighting, difficult to control over so many figures and separate scenes. An illusion of our own presence at the scene is completed by the brilliant device of suggesting that we are not on the hill, but below it. The scale of Tintoretto's contribution to the Scuola decorations has no rival in European art.

Between 1581, when he completed the *Temptation of Christ* for the Sala Grande of the Scuola di San Rocco and his *Last Supper* of 1592–4 (San Giorgio Maggiore, Venice), Tintoretto was much more consistently a civic and ecclesiastical painter than Titian had ever been. His extensive works for the Palazzo Ducale and churches such as Santo Stefano and San Moisè, were undertaken simultaneously with major aristocratic commissions including the eight *Fasti Gonzagheschi* (scenes from the lives of the Gonzaga family of Mantua), now in the Alte Pinakothek, Munich. In these years, Tintoretto was tackling compositions on a scale equalled by few, such as the *Paradise* (1588) for the Sala del Gran Consiglio in the Doge's Palace. This was the result of a competition to redecorate some of the rooms after the fire of 1577: among other competitors were Veronese and Francesco Bassano, to whom the commission was originally given.

If Tintoretto cannot be termed a Mannerist, his expressive, sometimes even expressionistic, style generated an impulse among some of his Venetian contemporaries to experiment with Mannerism. Perhaps the most unexpected product of Tintoretto's influence was El Greco. Although supposedly a pupil of Titian's, he formed his style on the basis of Tintoretto's expressionism before moving to Rome in about 1570. There he painted the last great Italian miniaturist of the Renaissance, Guilio Clovio (see plate 258), and *Christ driving the Money-Changers from the Temple* (Institute of Art, Minneapolis), before settling in Toledo in 1577 for the remainder of his life.

Veronese

One painter who resolutely avoided any concessions to mainstream Mannerism after his tentative beginnings was Veronese (Paolo Caliari, 1528–88). He represents the serenity and resolution of an elegant and optimistic style which could well stand as a symbol for the close of the Italian Renaissance. While there are fleeting reflections of his contemporaries' influence, Veronese rapidly established his personal manner and varied it little throughout a career lasting more than forty years. Unlike Titian or Tintoretto, Veronese worked with equal success in oil and fresco, and two of his most beautiful decorative schemes, at the Villa Barbaro, Maser (see plate 240) and the Venetian church of San Sebastiano are in fresco. His early style reflected Giulio Romano, probably because Verona, his birthplace, was always more interested in Mantuan cultural developments than Venetian. Veronese also visited Mantua in 1552. Giulio's elaborate version of Raphaelesque Classicism with all its rich trappings must have opened Veronese's eyes to new and extravagant decorative possibilities. In many ways, it is through the sheer opulence of Veronese's paintings that we choose to visualize the Venice of the Cinquecento. This ability to reflect the ethos of an entire city's culture may come from a certain detachment from real drama which makes his pictures so easy on the eye.

In 1553 Veronese settled in Venice, where Titian dominated his attentions. With prestigious commissions from Cardinal Gonzaga and others behind him, he at once received work in the Palazzo Ducale. Veronese's interests must never have clashed with those of Titian, as may be deduced from ceiling panels showing the *Story of Esther* in San Sebastiano. In essence, these contain the germ of Veronese's subsequent work, and single him out as the most able illusionist ceiling decorator in the city. They show him breaking with the Giorgione traditions of fused outline and patches of colour, and substituting a vigorous clarity quite at variance with the prevailing taste in Venice. It is a mark of his sophistication that he chose paler colours than most Venetians, which ultimately led to

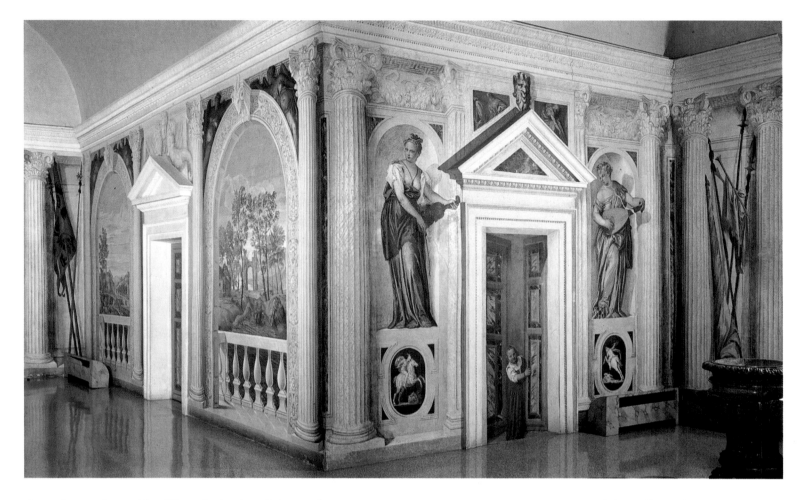

240 PAOLO VERONESE View of the Villa Barbaro, Maser 1561
Veronese frescoed the central block of Palladio's great villa in the
Veneto, built for the brothers Marcantonio and Daniele Barbaro.
The themes include Classical mythology, genre and landscape, and
the whole ensemble is Veronese's greatest single achievement in fresco.
Set in painted architecture are portraits, nudes, lavishly draped
figures, animals, statuary, garden pergolas and a wealth of visual
devices. Just visible on one wall is the famous scene of a carriage
approaching a villa in a landscape, and many other naturalistic
observations are included.

the palette adopted by Tiepolo in the eighteenth century.
The ceiling also affirms Veronese's love of illusionistic figure painting using the oblique perspective preferred in
Venice to Correggio's *sotto in sù*. Although he loved the
softness of Correggio's style, and the yielding allure of his
female models, none of their subtly implied sexuality
enlivens Veronese's women, for all their beauty.
Illusionism recurs throughout his work, perhaps most
successfully in the incomparable *Triumph of Venice* (see
plate 241) with its strong foretaste of Baroque ideas.

The fertility of Veronese's visual imagination exceeds
any of his contemporaries', and was praised by Vasari as
his *invenzione*. Inventive he certainly was, and there is
rarely any sense of the repetition of established formulae
in his painting. The superabundance of realistic detail
links him to the central Italian Mannerists, but his intention is to seduce the eye, rather than impress with erudi-
tion. This he achieved with a decorative use of colour,
and with models of an idealized beauty which nonetheless often give an impression of portraiture. But while
Titian or Tintoretto's figures suggest that their poses and
gestures spring from their emotions, Veronese's often
appear to offer only superbly elegant mime. This links
him with the intentions of Mannerists like Bronzino in his
greatest subject pictures. Veronese is at his most theatrical
– indeed operatic – in *Alexander and the Family of Darius*
(National Gallery, London).

According to Ridolfi's *Meraviglie dell'Arte* (Marvels of
Art), Veronese visited Rome in 1560, and the effect of this

journey can be seen in his superb frescoes at Maser (see
plate 240). He appears to have studied Raphael, not only
in the Stanze, but also the more sensuous moments in his
Farnesina *Story of Psyche*. Possibly more than any other
painter, Veronese transmits the mood of mid-century
Venice (without literally portraying it) in his unique
inclusion of grandiose Classical architecture, which
reflects the latest ideas of his younger contemporary,
Palladio (see plate 261).

Even Veronese, however, seems to have felt the new
currents of the Counter-Reformation's demands for
seriousness by the 1570s. This is particularly evident in
several renderings of the *Crucifixion* (Musée du Louvre,
Paris; Gemäldegalerie, Dresden and Szépmüvészeti
Muzeum, Budapest), where he can be seen struggling to
transcend the mere beauty of his technique. Depth of
feeling certainly increases during his last years, when
some of his religious themes almost assume the intensity

Parmigianino

One of the most fascinating figures of the period, Parmigianino (Girolamo Francesco Maria Mazzola, 1503–40) was also one of the most characteristic and original Mannerist painters. Vasari devotes much attention to his obsession with alchemy and eventual madness. He visited Rome in 1524–7 where he found favour with Pope Clement VII, who introduced him to Perino del Vaga and Rosso Fiorentino, and thereby Correggio's influence was transformed into one of Mannerism's most sensuous styles. While at work in Rome on the *Vision of Saint Jerome* (National Gallery, London) he was captured during the Sack of 1527, but he escaped to Bologna.

Parmigianino's use of elongated, curving forms and exceptionally elegant detail makes his work the finest example of *grazia* in Cinquecento art. This is undoubtedly

245 PARMIGIANINO A Lady 'The Turkish Slave' *c*.1522
This is one of the high points in Parmigianino's portraiture. The unusual headdress, assumed to be a turban, led to the mistaken identification 'the Turkish slave'. Although stylized to conform to Parmigianino's ideal of female beauty, it is definitely a likeness of an individual sitter. The suavity of its rounded forms, turn of the head and remarkable variety of textures accentuate her enigmatic beauty.

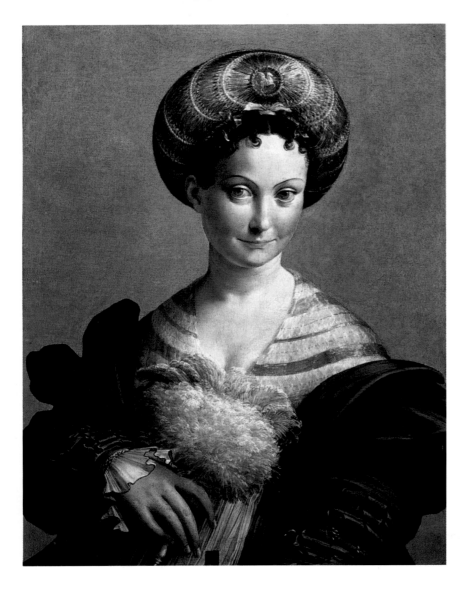

best expressed in the *Madonna of the Long Neck* (see plate 232). His influence was incalculable, mainly through his superb etchings which were imitated by Ugo de Carpi, and reached courts as disparate as Fontainebleau and Prague. His painting and drawing breathe a rarefied atmosphere of extreme refinement, which as much as Correggio's was to fascinate the painters of the Rococo style. In some ways, Parmigianino can be seen to have used decorative devices later found in Veronese, but instead of Veronese's ostensibly 'natural' approach to anatomy and composition, he achieved a highly romantic and perverse atmosphere. Apparently resolved and self-confident, his figures are really symptomatic of a profound unease, expressed in a way comparable to Bronzino's enamelled figures. Unlike Bronzino's portraits, however, Parmigianino's (such as *A Man with a Book*, in the City Art Gallery, York, or the mysterious *Antea* in the Museo di Capodimonte, Naples) suggest a deceptive intimacy with the spectator, while in fact being even more perversely withdrawn and inward-looking. In the late *Portrait of a Man* (Kunsthistorisches Museum, Vienna) – contemporary with his last great fresco work in Santa Maria della Steccata (completed 1539) – he adopts an architectural background device such as Bronzino exploited in the same years. The almost effete quality of some of these late works finds further expression in the work of Parmigianino's cousin by marriage, Girolamo Bedoli (*c*.1500?–69) who took the name Mazzola Bedoli.

Dosso Dossi

At Ferrara, Dosso Dossi (Giovanni di Niccolò de Lutero, 1490–1542) also created a very different, but equally romantic vision of both nature and man. Dosso was court painter under two successive Este dukes, Alfonso I (1503–34) and Ercole II (1534–59), who, at the apogee of the court's brilliance, aimed to employ painters of the stature of Raphael and Titian. Dosso's legacy was very rich, for he and his brother Battista worked in every facet of the luxury arts, including festival and theatre decorations in palaces and villas. Tragically, much of this vanished when the Papacy seized Ferrara at the end of the century and much of its culture was destroyed.

Dosso was in Mantua in 1512, after studying Giorgione and early Titian in Venice. He also visited Rome where Raphael most impressed him. It was his highly original distillations of such a variety of sources which produced his distinctive, vigorous style – at the very opposite polarity from an artist like Parmigianino. From the off-beat art of the Ferrarese court, with its interest in astrology and alchemy, may derive some of Dosso's highly unconventional iconography. Dosso's bucolic, earthy (and sometimes highly erotic) images are distinguished by their brilliant lighting, vivid colour and verdant landscape backgrounds. His *Melissa* of *c*.1523 (Galleria Borghese, Rome) shows his unique mixture of Classical grandeur, esoteric iconography, opulent texture and colour, landscape and even humour, all within a deceptively down-to-earth form. In his last years, he even permitted satire to appear, as in *A Scene of Witchcraft* (Uffizi, Florence).

Lorenzo Lotto

Like Dosso, Lorenzo Lotto (*c*.1480–1556/57) stands somewhat apart from mainstream trends. He worked mainly in the provinces (Treviso, Recanati and elsewhere) in spite of being Venetian by birth. His beginnings belong properly to the High Renaissance, since Vasari says that he studied alongside Giorgione and Titian in Bellini's studio. Lotto combined the clarity of Bellini and Antonello de Messina with an astonishing repertoire of sources including the Florentine High Renaissance masters and Leonardo. The results in his mature works are expected, both in his portraiture and religious and allegorical themes (see plates 246, 247 and 264). His dramatic sense is best seen in the *Annunciation* (Santa Maria sopra

246 LORENZO LOTTO Portrait of Andrea Odoni 1527
This picture perfectly illustrates the collector's passion in the later Renaissance. Odoni was a wealthy Venetian merchant, who clearly had a passion for the Antique. Titian, Parmigianino and Palma il Giovane were all influenced by the picture's original and pleasing composition.

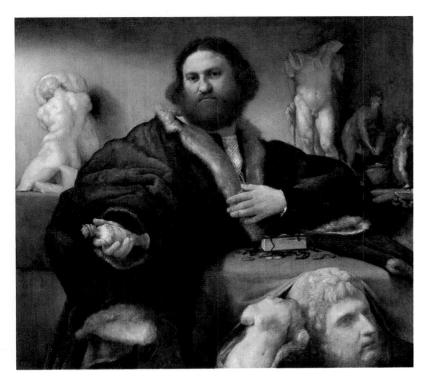

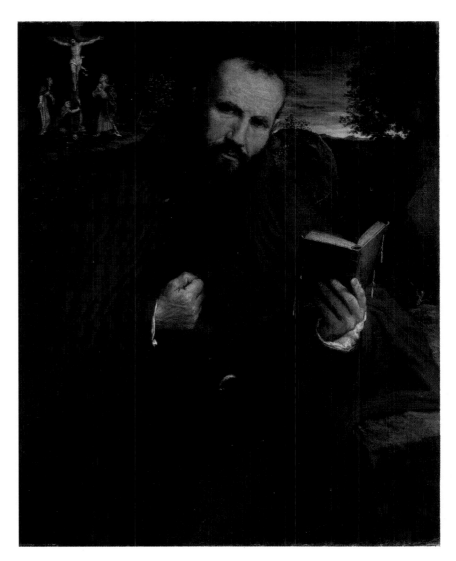

247 LORENZO LOTTO Brother Gregorio Belo of Vicenza 1547
This portrait shows early evidence of Counter-Reformation fanaticism, in the striking pose, with its clenched, almost threatening fist, the fierce expression and background Crucifixion. It is as though Belo were actually present. The fist evokes the iconography of the patron of the order of St Jerome, to which the friar belonged. Lotto painted another picture with comparable religious fervour in the same year – St Peter Martyr (Fogg Art Museum, Cambridge).

Minerva, Recanati) and the *Saint Lucy Altar* of 1532 (Biblioteca Communale, Jesi) where light and shade create an eerie world midway between reality and dream.

By the time of the deaths of Michelangelo, Titian and Veronese, a new spirit was emerging in Italian painting, partly under the influence of the Counter-Reformation, but also partly in reaction to the 'de-humanizing' elitist tendencies in Mannerist art. The ideals of Mannerism and its offshoots still belonged to the world of nostalgia for an imagined Classical and pagan past, which was the mainspring of the first Renaissance. The sixteenth century had contributed a new breadth of vision to the Quattrocento's dream of antiquity, aided by new concepts of scale and, in the case of such a painter as Titian, new technical means. Many of the painters discussed in this chapter represent the countless aspects of the end of this epoch.

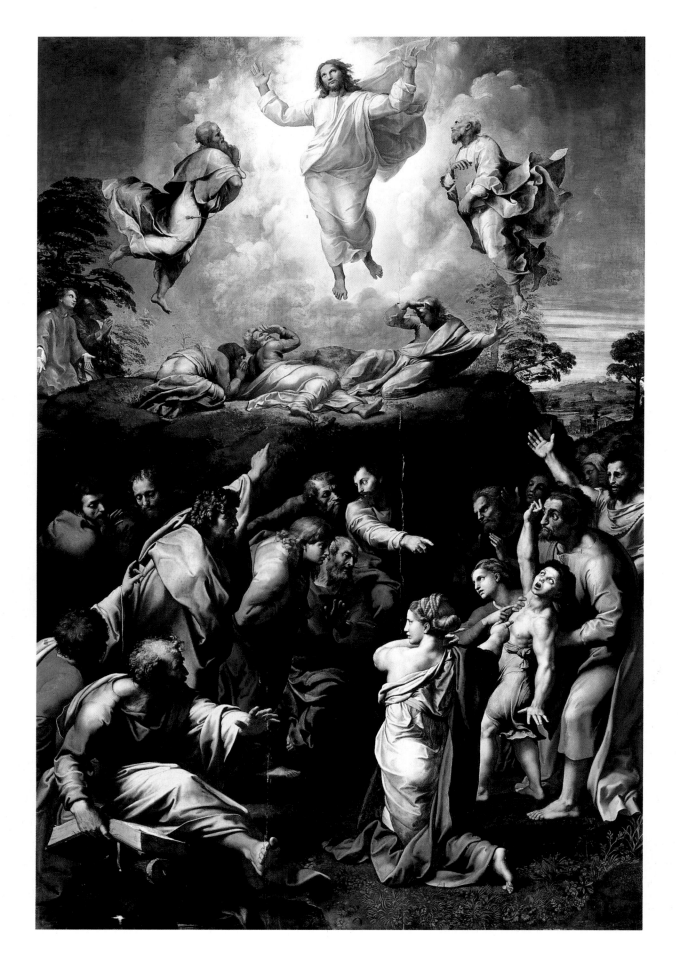

248 RAPHAEL Transfiguration 1518–20

The painting depicts the moment when Christ revealed His divine nature to His disciples on the top of a high mountain: Moses and Elijah appeared and Christ's face and garments became radiant with light, while the voice of God proclaimed: 'This is my son'. In the bottom half is the subsequent healing by Christ of a demoniac boy. In late 1516 Cardinal Giulio de'Medici ordered this altarpiece for the Cathedral of Narbonne; it was never sent. He then commissioned Sebastiano del Piombo to paint a Raising of Lazarus (National Gallery, London), to the design of Michelangelo, on the assumption that the competition between him and Raphael would stimulate

better results. In July 1518 Sebastiano wrote to Michelangelo suggesting that Raphael had still not begun the painting. By September 1519 he was devoting most of his time to it.

Both Sebastiano and Vasari were sure that Raphael had personally completed the altarpiece, and the suggestion that Giulio Romano or Penni finished it has been largely discredited. Battista Dossi, sent to Venice to obtain the necessary colours for the Transfiguration, saw Titian's newly unveiled Assumption in the Frari (see plate 254); its revolutionary composition may have led Raphael to alter his design.

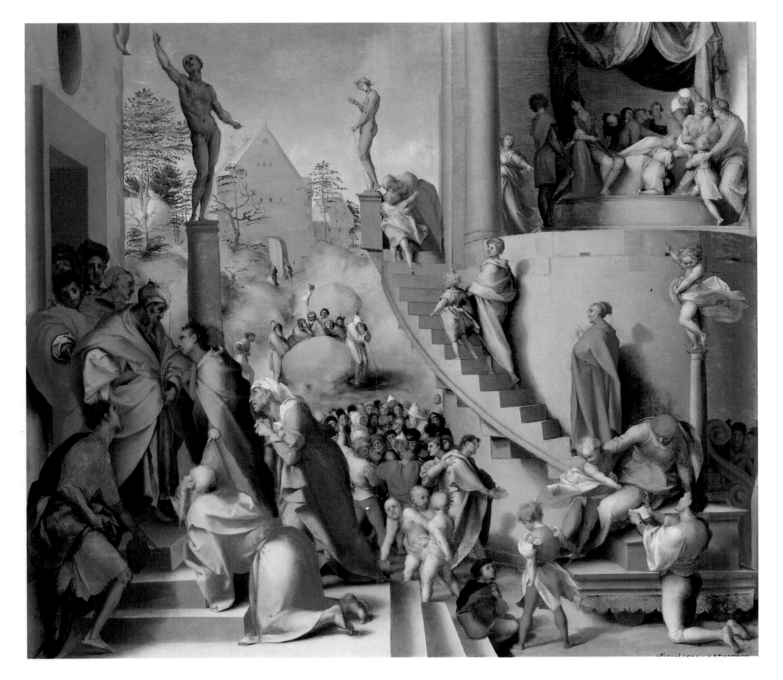

249 JACOPO PONTORMO Joseph in Egypt 1517–18
A number of Florence's leading painters – Andrea del Sarto,
Granacci, Bachiacca and Pontormo – collaborated on the decoration
of the nuptial chamber of Pier Francesco Borgherini's Florentine
palace. The theme chosen was the story of Joseph, and Pontormo's
Joseph in Egypt *is the most grand and complex of the paintings,*
notwithstanding its small scale, which recalls the small scenes in
predella panels and cassoni. Influenced by prints by Northern artists
such as Lucas van Leyden (notably in the landscape and background
architecture), it deliberately combines disparate chronological scenes in
one picture. The statuary seems ambigious as are various spatial
devices. Vasari says that the seated boy in the foreground represents
Bronzino, who had just entered Pontormo's studio as a pupil.

250 RAPHAEL The Road to Calvary (Lo Spasimo di Sicilia)
c.1517
Although much of the painting may be by Giulio Romano, the
design is Raphael's and shows his latest style at its most dramatic. A
vigour and a greatly increased forcefulness of gesture replace the
sweetness of his earlier style. The design is based on Dürer's woodcut
of Christ carrying the Cross, and in its turn Veneziano's
engraving after the Raphael exercised considerable influence.

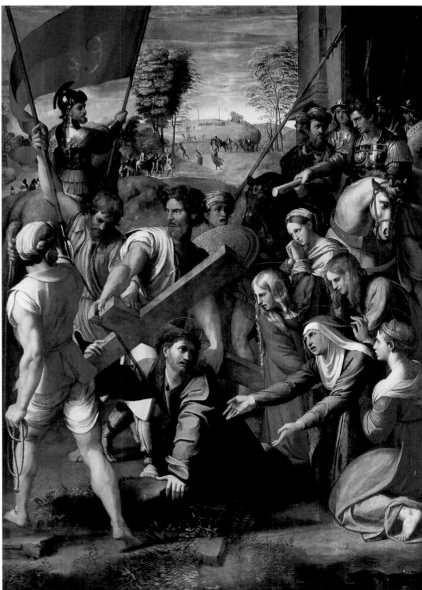

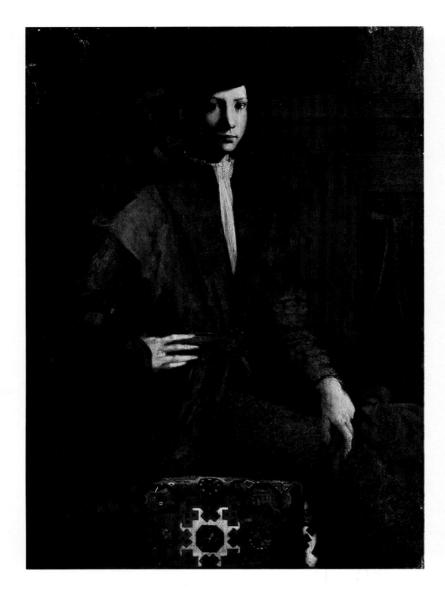

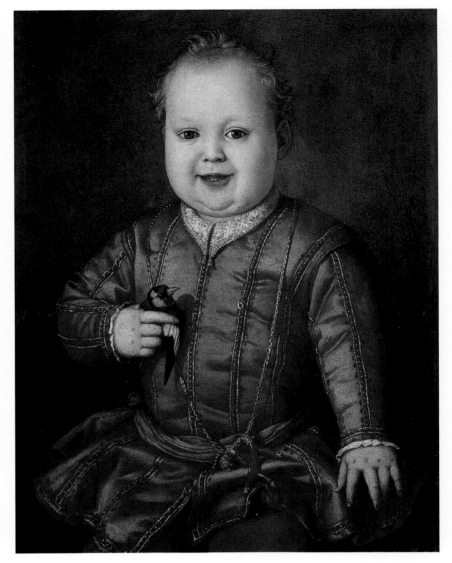

251 ROSSO FIORENTINO Portrait of a Young Man *c.*1528
*This is one of the classic portraits of Mannerism. The self-
conscious pose and remote gaze of the sitter recall effects sought by
Bronzino, but with a more elusive character. Its sharper features
and elongated forms are far from the courtly aims of Bronzino,
creating a more expressive and disturbing atmosphere.*

252 AGNOLO BRONZINO Portrait of Giovanni de'Medici as a
Baby 1545
*This was once thought to represent Garcia, son of Cosimo I and
Eleonora di Toledo, but is now known to depict his elder brother
Giovanni, aged eighteen months. Astonishingly vivacious, it shows a
very different side of Bronzino's portrait painting, reflecting his
recorded personal devotion to the Medici children.*

253 AGNOLO BRONZINO Portrait of Laura Battiferi, late 1550s
*(Right) One of the most original and striking portraits of the
Mannerist period, this shows Bronzino's close friend, the poetess
Laura Battiferi (1523–89), wife of the sculptor Ammanati. Her two
marriages were childless and she called herself 'a sterile tree'. She was
a close friend of Eleonora of Toledo and, like her, deeply religious
and involved with the Jesuits. She corresponded with many of the
leading men of her day, including Cellini and Torquato Tasso, and
published her first book of poems in 1560. Bronzino and she
exchanged Petrarchian sonnets (she is shown holding Petrarch's
Sonnets), and in Bronzino's sonnet dedicated to her, the artist
describes her as 'inside all iron, externally of ice.'*

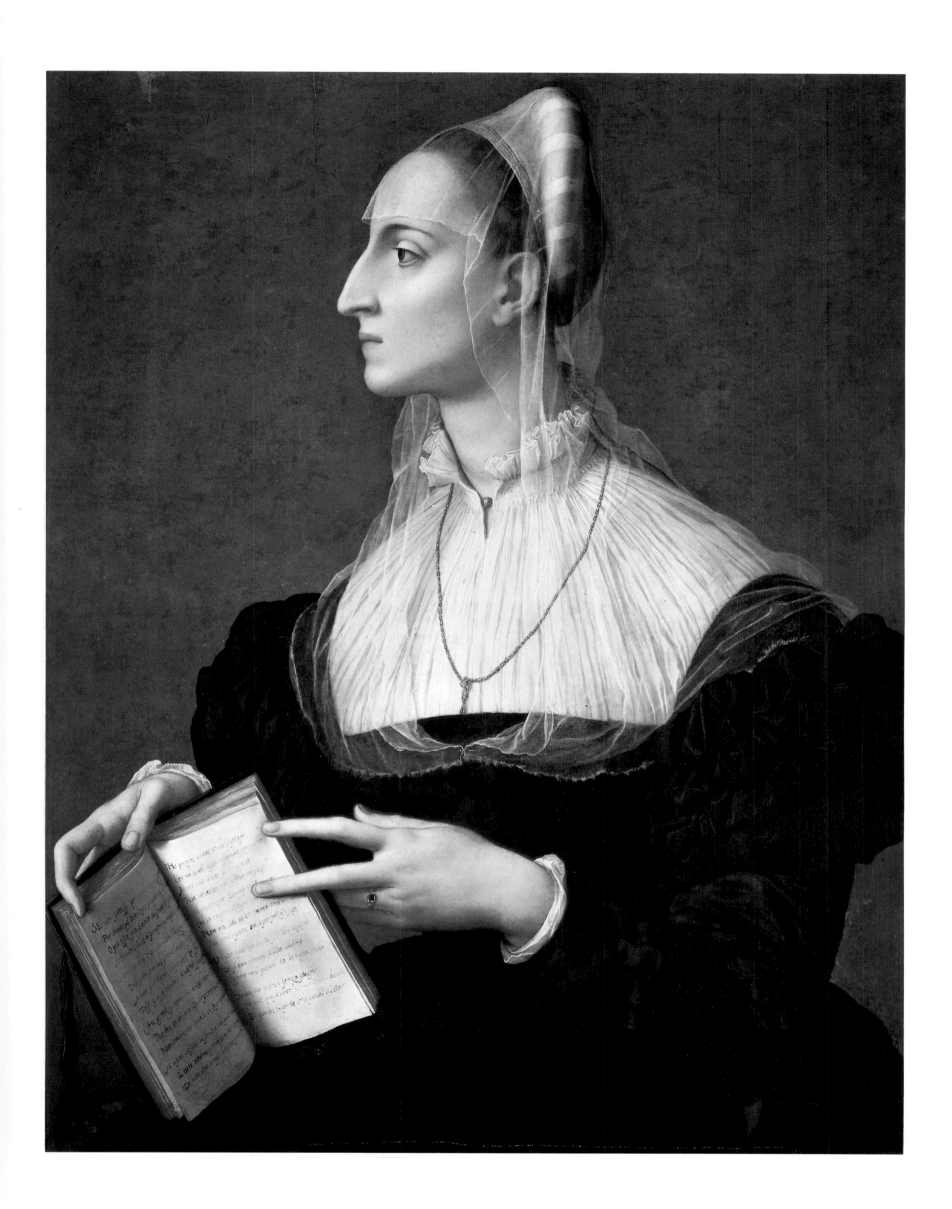

245

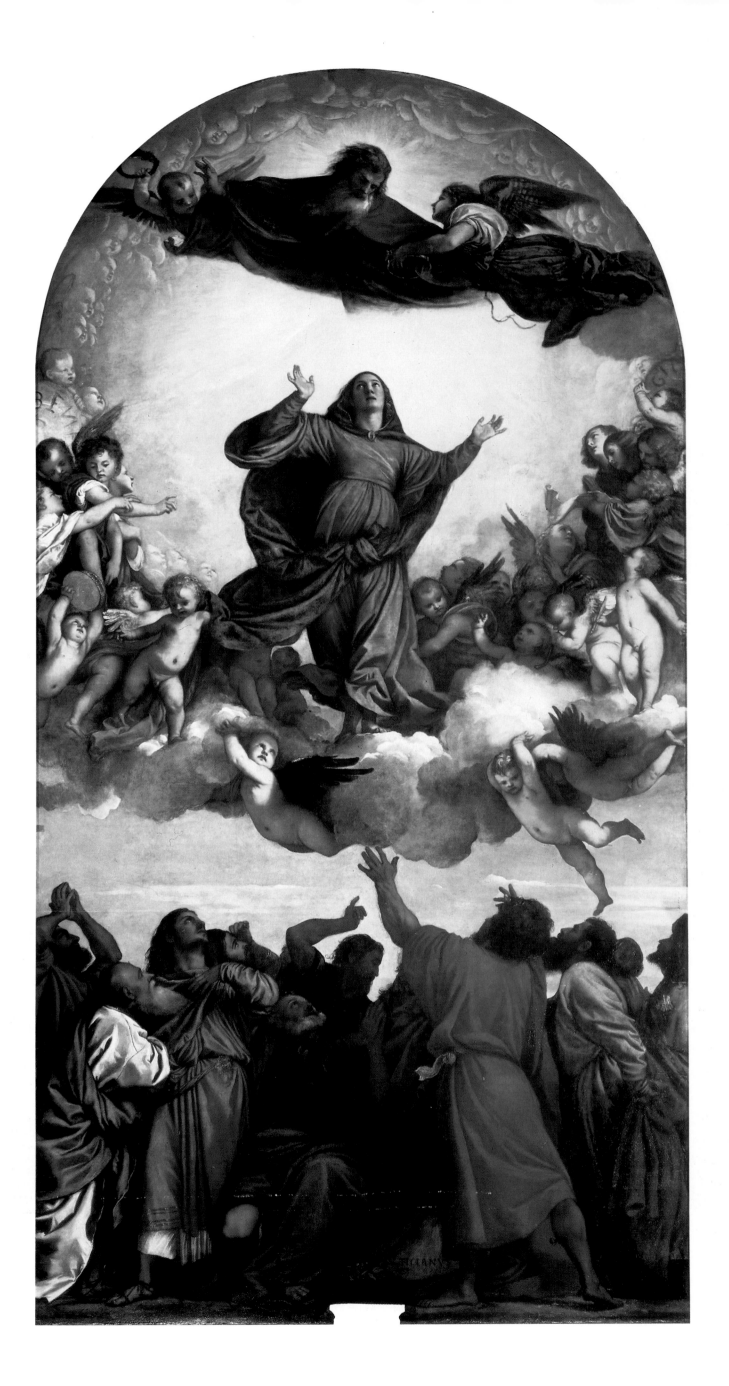

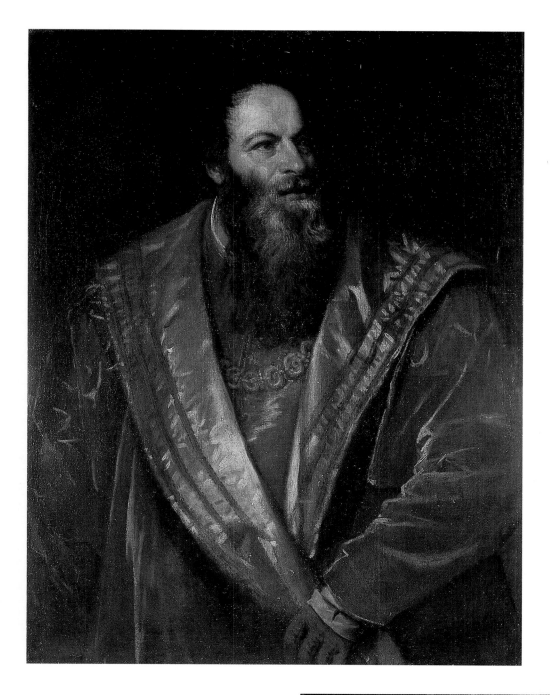

255 TITIAN Portrait of Pietro Aretino 1545
*Aretino from Arezzo was one of the leading
intellectuals of his period. After 1522 he was
active at several Italian courts, particularly
Mantua under Federigo II Gonzaga. Of humble
origins, his character was coarse and his sonnets
included the pornographic ones graphically
illustrated by Giulio Romano. Aretino thought
this portrait a mere sketch, but this did not
prevent him from giving it to Cosimo de'Medici.*

256 TITIAN Pietà 1576
*Palma il Giovane painted the inscription on the
central pedestal recording his completion of
Titian's unfinished picture. Titian had intended
this moving image to be placed over his own
tomb in the Cappella del Crocefisso in the church
of the Frari, Venice, but possibly on account of
its being incomplete at his death it was placed
elsewhere. Titian shows himself as St Jerome, at
right; the Hellespontic Sybil with cross and crown
of thorns prophesies Christ's death, while Moses
appears at left, with the Magdalene and the
Madonna. The setting reveals Titian's
familiarity with the architectural ideas of Serlio
and others, and the loose paint handling typifies
his own latest manner.*

254 TITIAN Assumption of the Virgin
1516–18
*(Left) This was Titian's first important
religious commission and the culmination of
his early career, and is one of the major
monuments of High Renaissance art. It was
conceived for its setting, so its strata
correspond with the great Gothic windows of
the Frari's apse. The painting's striking
novelty, in contrast to the prevailing taste of
Bellini's altarpieces, almost led to its refusal
by the church authorities. Titian probably
drew inspiration from Raphael's Disputà in
the Vatican, known to him through drawings
by other artists. An elongated triangle is
created against the predominantly gold
background by three dominant areas of red
drapery, accentuating the Virgin's upward
movement towards God the Father. The
painting's scale and drama exerted
considerable influence on Baroque painters.*

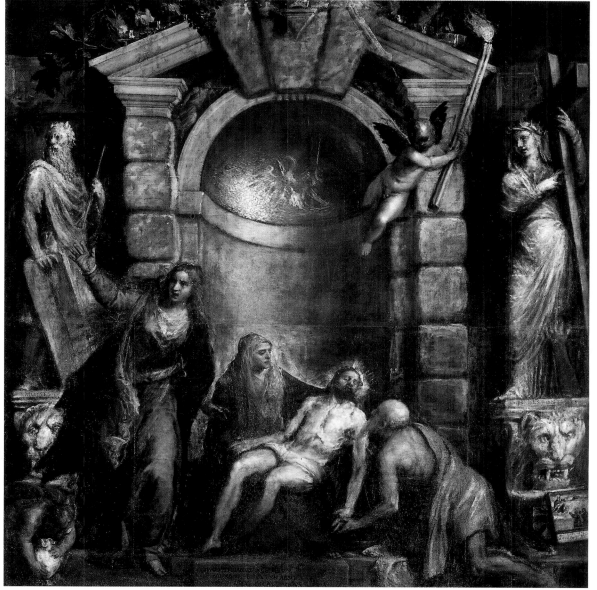

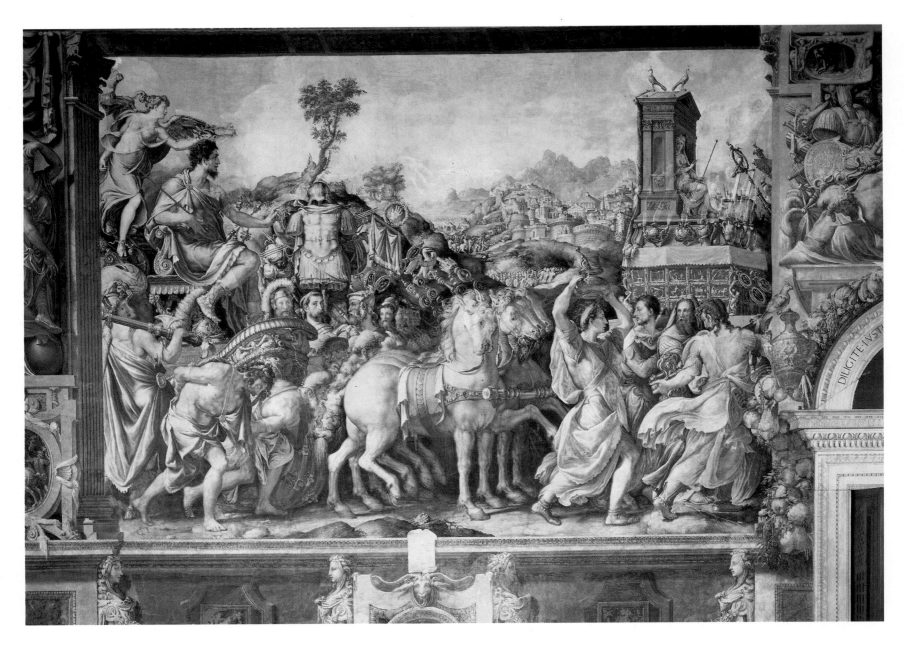

257 FRANCESCO SALVIATI Triumph of Camillus 1543–5
Salviati hoped for extensive Medici patronage while in Florence, but
although he worked for the court tapestry manufactory his failure to
obtain the San Lorenzo commission won by Pontormo and Bronzino
made him return to Rome. He was Bronzino's major rival at court
in the 1540s. These frescoes in the Audience Chamber of the
Palazzo Vecchio show the peculiarly Roman combination of elements
from both Raphael and Michelangelo found in mid-sixteenth century
painting there. Extensive Classical detail, vibrant colour and
elaborate compositions produce a somewhat overcrowded effect.

258 EL GRECO Giulio Clovio Holding the Farnese Hours
1570–2
(Top right) Clovio was a Croatian miniaturist, who worked
continuously for Cardinal Alessandro Farnese over some forty years
after he entered the Cardinal's service around 1537. The last great
European miniaturist, he lived first in the Cancelleria Palace, then
in the Farnese Palace after Alessandro inherited it in 1565, where he
died aged almost one hundred in 1578. He accompanied Alessandro
into exile at the Medici court 1551–c.1553. He also designed livery
for a carnival ball for the Cardinal, and acted as his artistic adviser.
Clovio and El Greco became close friends.

259 GIULIO CLOVIO Pages from the Farnese Hours,
completed 1546
(Bottom right) Clovio painted twenty-six paired miniatures, his
masterpiece, for Cardinal Alessandro Farnese, one of the greatest
patrons of the mid-century, over a nine year period. The Hours are
perhaps the finest production of Italian Renaissance miniature
painting, and by 1577 were included among the major sights of
Rome. Vasari thought they were 'something divine, not human'.
The whole set was given a silver-gilt binding by the master craftsman
Antonio Gentili. Clovio set the brilliantly coloured scenes in bronze
frames, including imitation antique cameos (Alessandro was an avid
collector of engraved rock crystals) and simulated marble figures,
possibly influenced by Salviati's work for the Farnese.

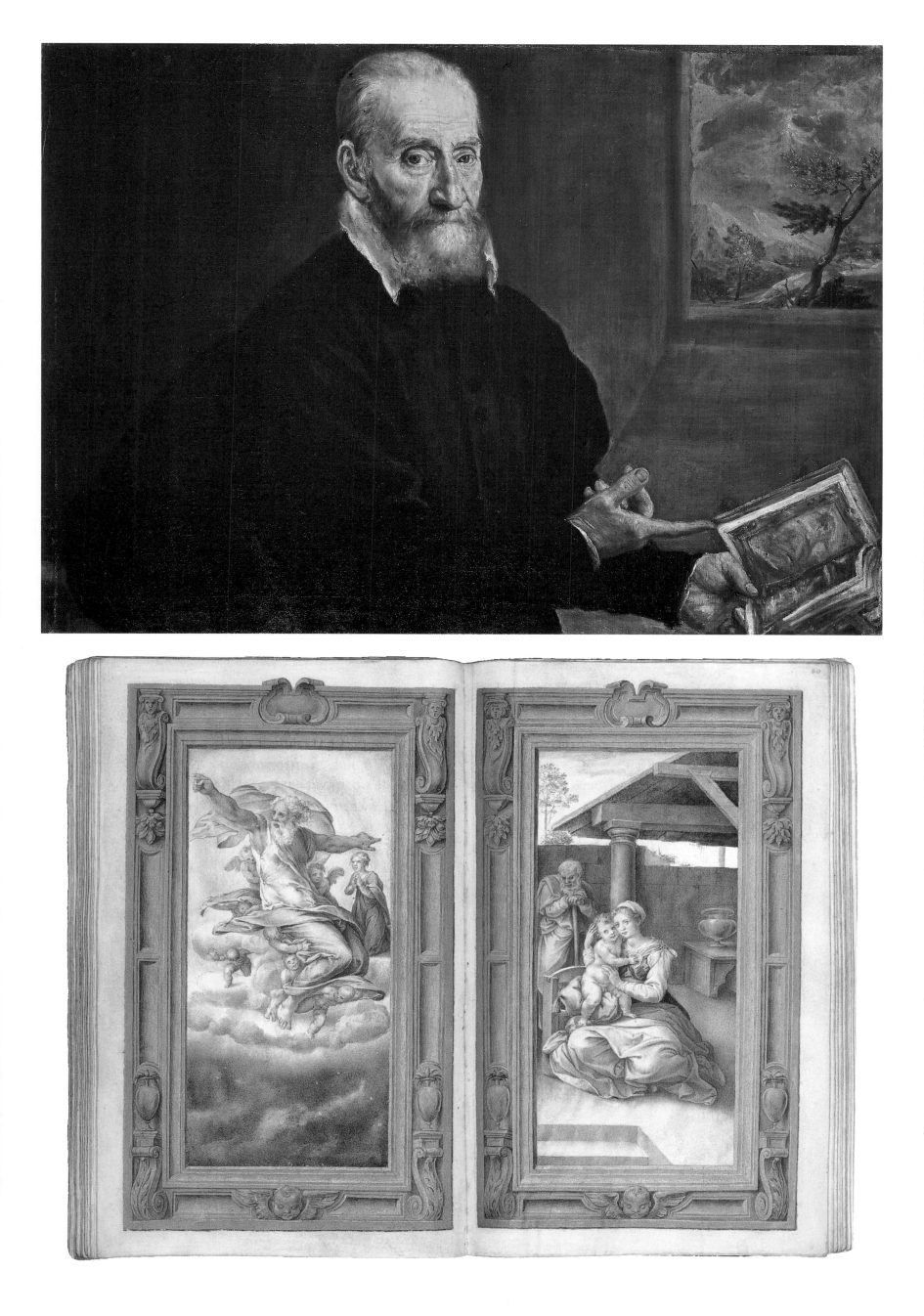

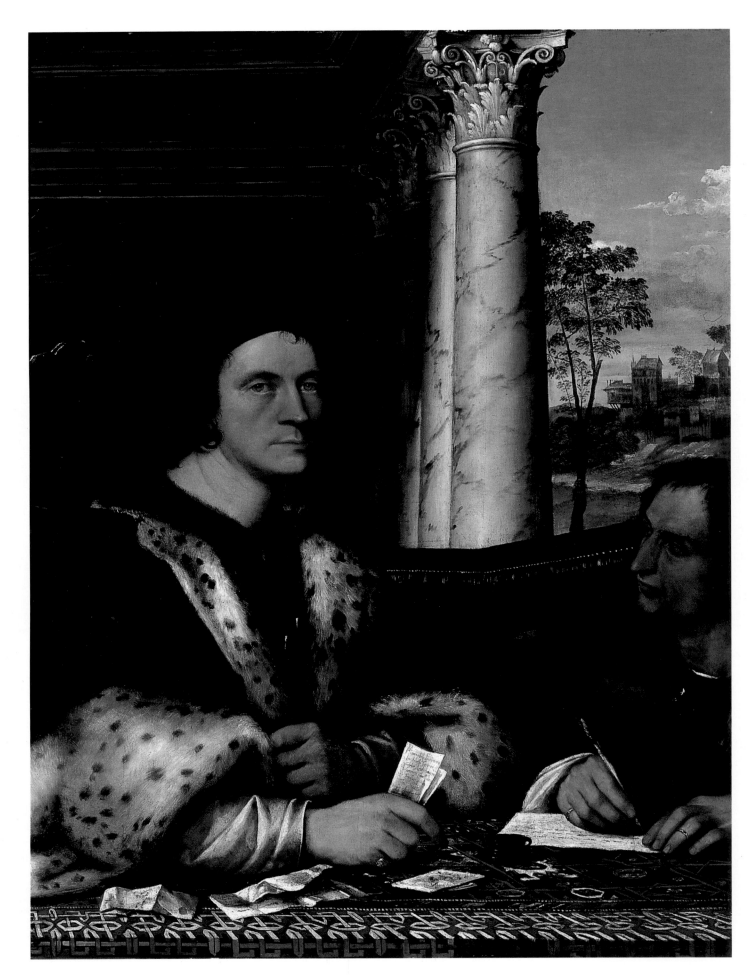

260 SEBASTIANO DEL PIOMBO Portrait of Ferry Carandolet
and his Secretaries 1511–12

Ferry Carandolet was a figure of great importance in his period,
Archdeacon of Besançon, adviser to the Emperor and Ambassador to
Rome. This portrait was painted in Rome: Sebastiano had arrived
from Venice in 1511 to fresco a room in the Villa Farnesina. Until
the nineteenth century it was believed to be by Raphael, the
intense characterization of whose Roman portraits it reflects. It is
certainly one of the most imposing portraits of the Roman High
Renaissance.

261 PAOLO VERONESE Marriage Feast at Cana 1562–3
(Right) This immense canvas was painted for the refectory of the
Benedictine convent of San Giorgio Maggiore, from where it was
looted by Napoleon. Its sense of space and grandeur have long been
praised, together with the variety and richness of the figures. This,
and its use of colour and lavish detail, contribute to a sense of
festivity without equal in Renaissance painting. There are many
portraits of notable contemporaries, including Titian (playing the
viol) and Veronese himself (playing the violin). The Palladian
architectural setting was painted by other specialist artists.

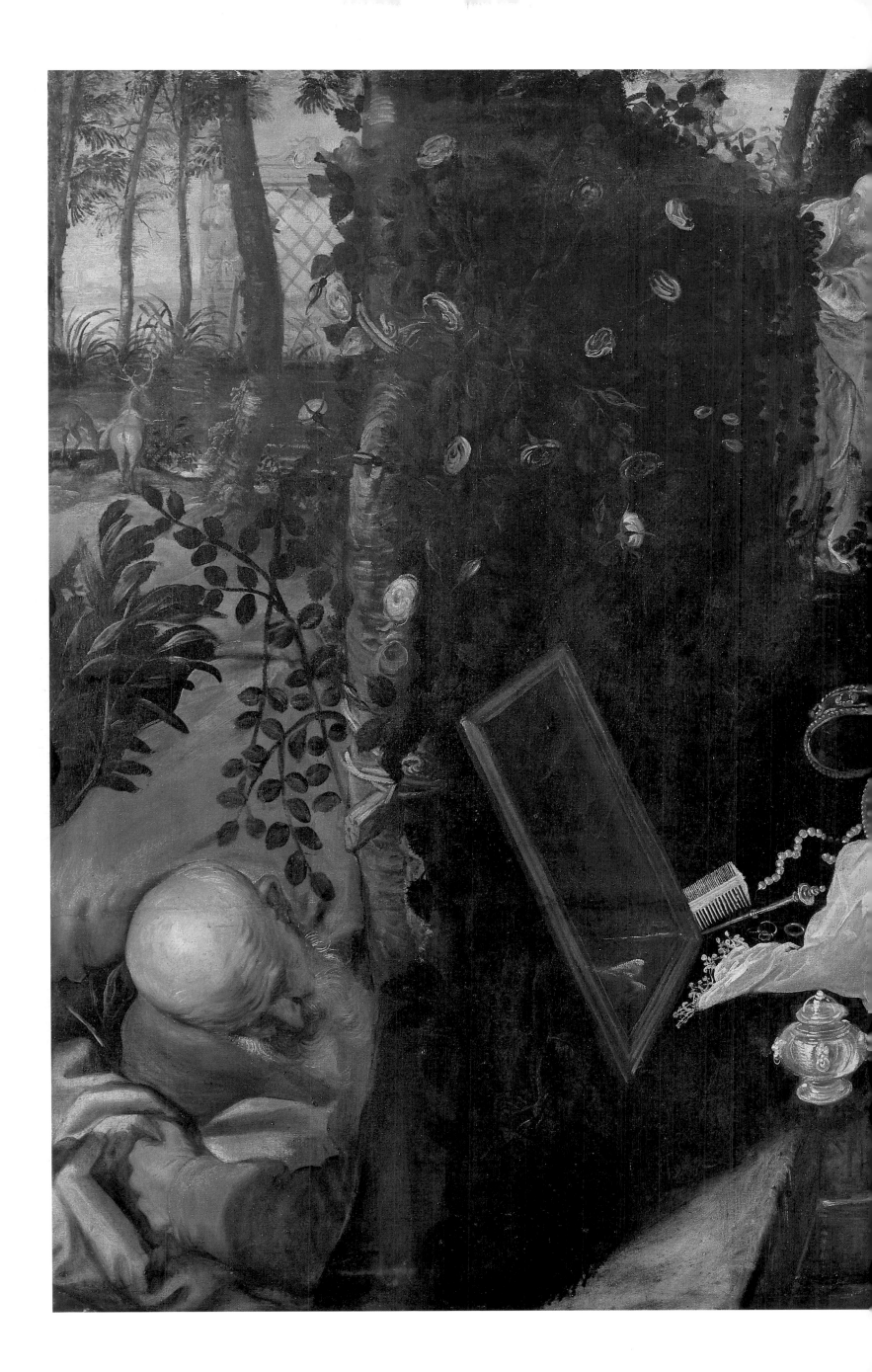

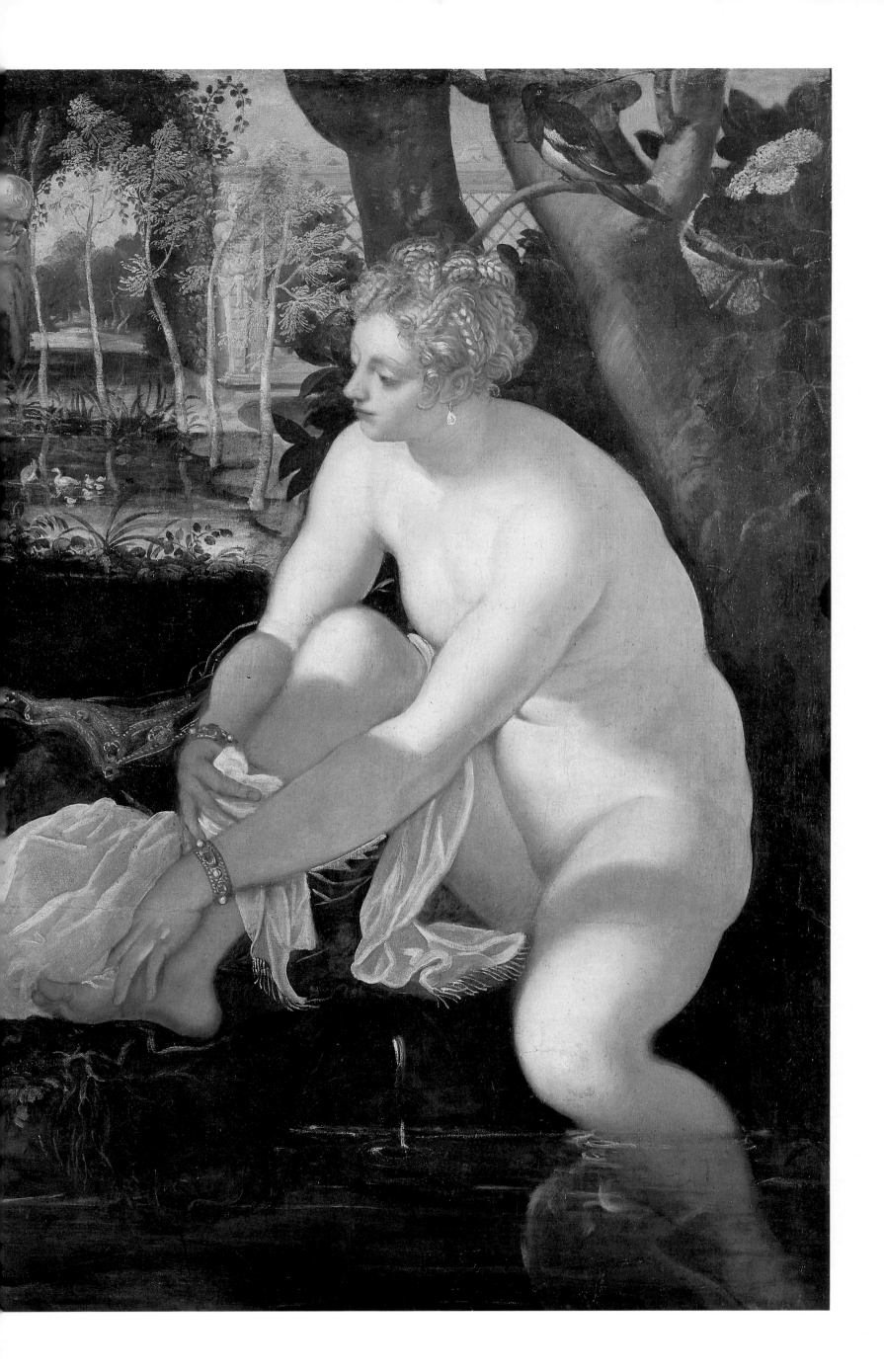

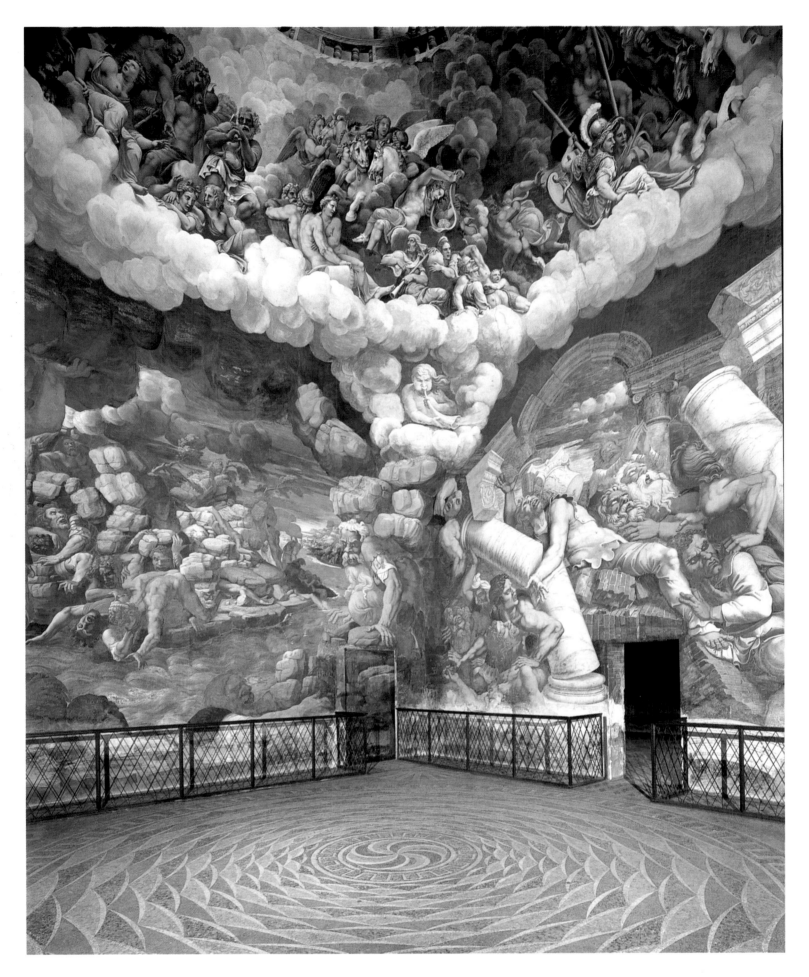

262 JACOPO TINTORETTO Susanna and the Elders 1557
(Left) Identified with the picture recorded by Ridolfi in the house of
the painter Niccolò Renieri, this is perhaps Tintoretto's most sensual
rendering of the female nude. Instead of the more usual episode when
the elders surprise Susanna, Tintoretto has chosen the much more
erotic, voyeuristic moment when she is still unconscious of their
presence, and gazes unperturbed at her reflection in the mirror.
Notable are the daring device of dividing the picture with the hedge,
which recalls Mannerist visual tricks, and the limpid painting of flesh
and the delicate still life and water.

263 GIULIO ROMANO The Sala dei Giganti, Palazzo del Tè,
Mantua 1532–4
(Above) Giulio Romano moved in 1524 from Rome to Mantua,
where he reinvigorated Mantuan painting under Marchese Federigo
Gonzaga and created some of the greatest interiors of the period. His
rooms in the Palazzo del Tè include vigorous frescoes and elaborate
stuccoes in a variety of styles. The Sala dei Giganti is unique there,
with its deliberately disturbing illusionism showing the destruction of
the Giants by the Gods, in a 'conceit' designed to disturb the viewer
in a witty fashion typical of Mannerist artifice.

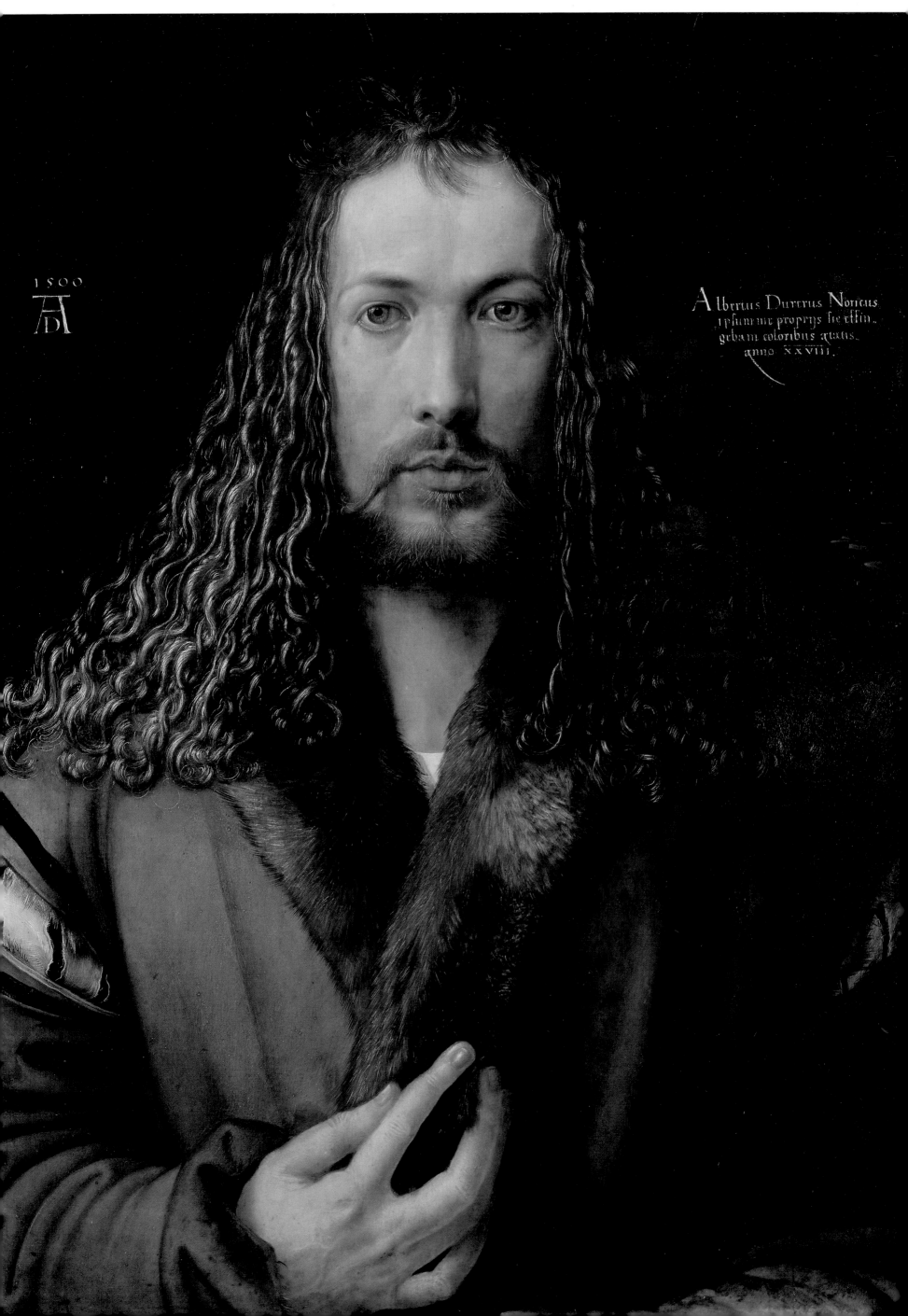

CHAPTER IX

Painting in Germany and the Netherlands in the Sixteenth Century

The sixteenth century in Northern Europe has left us some of the most memorable and diverse images in Western art, whether in Dürer's *Adoration of the Magi* (see plate 287), Altdorfer's *Battle of Issus* (see plate 289) or Bruegel's *Hunters in the Snow* (see plate 284). Each of these represents a different current in Northern European painting. While Dürer stands for the German equivalent of the Italian grand manner of the High Renaissance, Altdorfer represents the magical landscapes of the 'Danube School', and Bruegel's peasant scenes express one side of Netherlandish national feeling.

The first thirty years of the century saw an unprecedented flowering in German painting; Dürer, Altdorfer, Cranach, Grünewald and Hans Holbein the Younger were all active at this time, as were an unprecedented number of less well-known artists. Most of them worked at some time in the medium of engraving, and in Dürer's case this constituted much of his finest achievement.

Humanism in Italy had evolved during the early fifteenth century, and produced a very different sort of art from that of the Netherlands or Germany in the same years. With the achievements of the great Florentines of the 1420s, any remaining shadows of the Gothic world had been rapidly dispersed. Its vestiges lingered on much

longer in the North, however, and it was only towards the end of the fifteenth century that humanism filtered in; it was not fully embraced there, however, until the mid-sixteenth century.

Germany

While major centres such as Wittenburg, Regensburg, Ulm and Freiburg provided many ecclesiastical and court commissions, it was perhaps natural that painting flourished best in the wealthy city-republics of south Germany: Augsburg and Nuremberg. Munich grew into a great Catholic Renaissance city in this period, and Stuttgart and Landshut followed its example. The principal Protestant cities were Basle, Brunswick, Bern and Lübeck, while Catholic strongholds, such as Freiburg or Münster, remained within Protestant territories, and were sought out by painters for their lucrative altarpiece commissions. There can be no question that the Reformation dramatically reduced the possibilities for artists throughout the Protestant lands, making it necessary for them to travel in search of work.

Dürer and his Pupils

The greatest German artist of the period, Albrecht Dürer (1471–1528) was also the first to embody all the ideals of the Renaissance as expressed in Italian art and humanism. He and Raphael exchanged examples of their work, and Dürer was familiar with the writings of Vitruvius and Alberti, as well as the ideas of Leonardo (see Chapter VII). His travels and contacts were among the most stimulating of any painter in the Renaissance, and his sympathy for Luther's writings proved important in his spiritual

268 ALBRECHT DÜRER Self Portrait with a Fur-Trimmed Robe 1500

This is one of the greatest of Dürer's self portraits, and the culmination of his early development. Its rigid verticality seems almost medieval, with the hieratic feeling of a religious painting recalling Byzantine renderings of Christ. The intense expression and strong individuality of the face and hand gesture in addition to the virtuoso technique are, however, indicative of his complete confidence both as an artist and as a technician. The inscription reads 'Thus I painted myself, Albrecht Dürer of Nuremberg, using lasting colour, at the age of twenty-eight.'

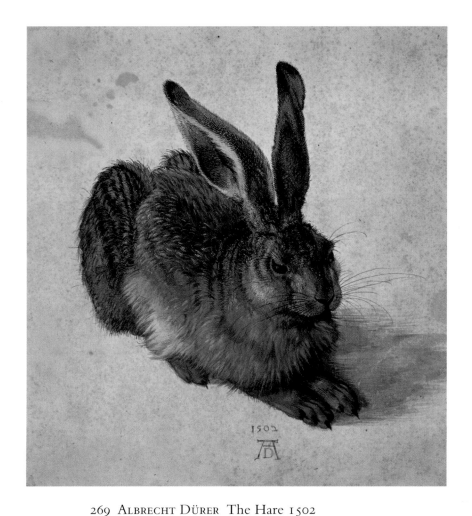

269 ALBRECHT DÜRER The Hare 1502

Always the most celebrated of Dürer's virtuoso watercolours, even good copies of it were treasured by other artists. The warmth of this study liberates it from the realm of pure scientific observation. It was painted entirely with the brush; the painter first outlined the general form with broad strokes, and then filled in the detail of the fur with a very fine brush, further highlighting this with white body colour. During Dürer's second Venetian visit, Giovanni Bellini asked him for one of the special brushes with which he obtained such miraculous effects, and was surprised to receive an ordinary brush.

growth. He towered above his northern contemporaries and, through his prints, exerted a remarkable influence in Germany, the Netherlands and Italy. Indeed, his contemporaries probably remembered him more as a printmaker than a painter (he collaborated on a triumphal arch for the Emperor Maximilian, which was made up of hundreds of separate woodcuts), and his genius with line is already visible in his silverpoint *Self Portrait* of 1484 (Albertina, Vienna). The great humanist Erasmus (1466–1536), whose portrait Dürer engraved, called him 'the Apelles of black lines'. (The Greek painter Apelles was considered the greatest in antiquity.)

The vigour of Dürer's personality and art still strike us as unique in his period, and the passion with which he pursued his ideals throughout his life, even in enfeebled old age, remains deeply moving. The new insight which he brought to his experiments in a wide range of themes from landscape watercolours to portraiture and religious

painting (see plate 270) compares with the breadth of vision we usually attribute only to Leonardo. His life could not have been more different from that of Leonardo, or any of his Italian contemporaries, and was intimately involved with the events of his time.

Dürer was born in Nuremberg, the son of a Hungarian goldsmith who had settled there in 1455. His education at a Latin school was enough to set him apart from most contemporary painters, and typified the beneficial effects of German humanism. Dürer was exceptionally fortunate in having as his godfather a leading printer and publisher, Anthony Koberger (c.1445–1513). This association shaped his enduring interest in graphic art and printing, which was furthered by his apprenticeship, at the age of fifteen, to the important Nuremberg painter and book illustrator Michael Wolgemut (1434–1519). It was he who gave the woodcut its independent status in German art. Dürer's lifelong friendship with the humanist poet, Willibald Pirckheimer (1470–1530), was only one of several associations with leading men of his day. It was Pirckheimer who opened the artist's mind to the idea of Italy, which he was to visit in 1494–5 and 1505–7.

In 1490, at the end of his apprenticeship, Dürer travelled by way of Mainz and Frankfurt to study with Martin Schongauer in Colmar on the Upper Rhine. Schongauer, then Germany's leading painter-engraver (see Chapter V), died before Dürer arrived in 1492, leaving a rich legacy of about 115 of his elegant and influential prints, but only one painting securely his, the *Madonna in the Rose Garden* (see plate 156).

In 1494 Dürer made an arranged marriage, having returned to Nuremberg after brief periods in Basle and Strasburg. Four years later, he produced his large woodcut series of the *Apocalypse*, to be followed by the *Great Passion* and the *Life of the Virgin* (1510), *The Knight, Death and the Devil* of 1513 (see plate 43) and the celebrated *Melancholia I* (1514). Through his engravings, Dürer developed the art to unforseen heights, achieving effects previously thought possible only in painting.

His *Paumgärtner Altar* of 1504 (Alte Pinakothek, Munich) and the *Adoration of the Magi* (see plate 287) show his early style in religious painting, before the crisis of the Reformation affected him. Soon after completing them, Dürer left for Italy – an unusual decision for a German artist at the time – and probably went to Venice, Padua, Mantua and Cremona. His next visit was to last two years, possibly taking in Florence and Rome as well as Venice and Bologna, where he hoped to learn perspective. The Venetian painter, Jacopo de'Barbari, seems to have shown him how to construct human figures on geometrical principles.

Giovanni Bellini's compositions and luminosity of colour influenced Dürer, who painted the *Feast of the Rose Garlands* (National Gallery, Prague) while in Venice, as both a tribute and a challenge to painters there. It was not until 1526, however, that Dürer made his most complete tribute to Italian High Renaissance ideals, with the monumentally conceived figures of the *Four Apostles*, (Alte Pinakothek, Munich). These reveal the artist's self-confessed obsession with proportion more than any of his other paintings, and relate to his two treatises on measurement and human proportions. His genius for portraiture (see plate 270) is an extension of his interest in every aspect of the natural world, as expressed in his famous watercolour *The Hare* (see plate 269), painted in 1502.

Profoundly influenced by Mantegna, Dürer was mainly active as an engraver in this period, but his paintings reveal his exceptional insight, as in the disturbingly penetrating gaze of his *Self Portrait* of 1500 (see plate 268). In publishing his own prints, Dürer was independent and invented a new form for the illustrated book – the album. This, together with his superiority over other artists in formal education and experience brought him many illustrious commissions, notably from the Emperor Maximilian, who became his most important patron after about 1512, and later from Charles V. During a journey to the Netherlands in 1520–21 Dürer met many important painters, recording events in his diary, and was hailed as the leading artist of the day. His influence can clearly be seen on the Flemish artist Marinus van Reymerswaele, whose *Saint Jerome* takes Dürer's 1521 version of the subject as its point of departure (see plate 298). German Renaissance art is inconceivable without Dürer's presence, but his universality is missing from his pupils and followers, who tended to concentrate rather on his style and detail. Altdorfer and, to a lesser extent, Baldung Grien are the only real exceptions.

Already during the 1490s Dürer's influence was producing a following among southern German painters. Among his most talented pupils were Hans Suss or Suess, known as Hans von Kulmbach (*c*.1480–1522), who was also influenced by Jacopo de'Barbari. Hans Schaufelein (1480/85–1538/40) studied with Dürer and worked in Augsburg and elsewhere, while the Beham brothers, Hans Sebald (1500–50) and Bartel (1502–40), were principally engravers, but worked in stained glass and other media. Bartel's painted portrait of 1529, *The Umpire* (Kunsthistorisches Museum, Vienna), reflects recent Italianate trends comparable with Amberger in Augsburg (see plate 9). The distinctive portraiture of Georg Pencz (*c*.1500–50) reflects his experience gained on two Italian

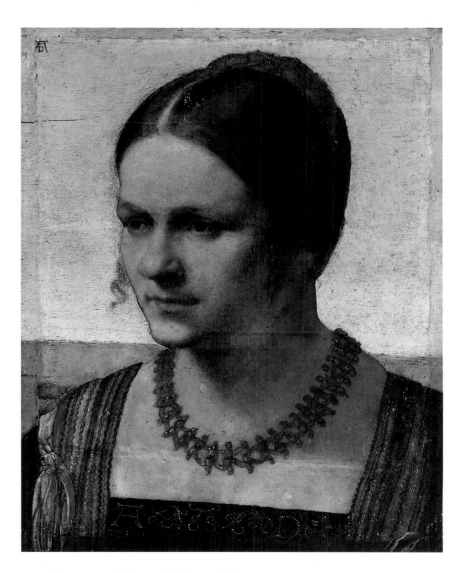

270 ALBRECHT DÜRER A Young Woman 1506
The sitter appears to be in Venetian costume, and its style indicates that it was painted during the artist's second Venetian journey, towards the end of 1506 when he would have seen Bellini's portraiture. This is not the painter's wife as was once thought.

The softness of outline and modelling strongly reflects what Dürer saw in Venetian painting, but he did not explore this new style after leaving Venice. The simplified background might suggest sky and sea.

visits, when Bronzino certainly influenced him. He was expelled from Nuremberg with the Beham brothers for holding extreme Protestant views.

Altdorfer and the Danube School

Dürer's near contemporary, Albrecht Altdorfer (*c*.1480–1538), a citizen of Regensburg from 1505, is best remembered for his remarkable landscapes (see plate 271), although he was primarily a painter of religious themes. His landscapes suggest a pantheistic belief in nature, whose exuberance he interprets with unique power. He also painted erotic works in the Cranach manner. Altdorfer was the leading painter of the so-called 'Danube School', a term which describes a number of artists

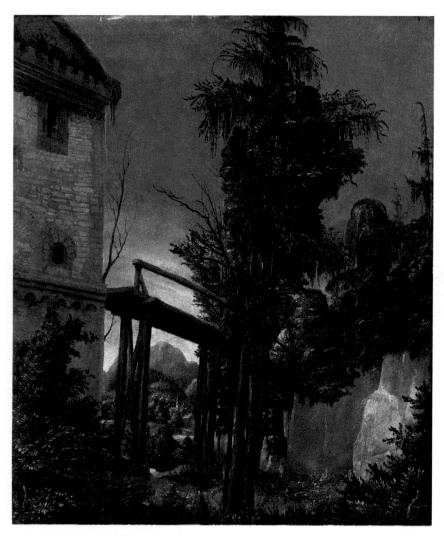

271 ALBRECHT ALTDORFER Landscape with a Footbridge
*c.*1518–20

This is among the earliest examples of pure landscape. It probably predates Altdorfer's only other landscape without figures, which is now in Munich.

Like Altdorfer's mature woodcuts, these landscapes derive much of their impact from the intensely concentrated forms, which crowd together to create the stifling effect observed in coniferous forests. They give the impression that they are closely based on natural observation. The same densely packed composition can be seen in the artist's Battle of Issus *(see plate 289) which depicts the battle between Alexander and Darius which took place in 333 B.C.*

working independently of each other in the Danube Valley. These included Lucas Cranach the Elder and Wolfgang (or Wolf) Huber (*c.*1490–1553), painter-architect to the prince-bishop of Passau. Huber possessed an inventive and spirited talent, and was innovative in the use of colour and light. The sources of his images are not easy to identify, but landscape dominates many of his paintings.

The origins of the Danube School lie in late Gothic painters such as Jan Polack in Munich and the Austrian painter and sculptor, Michael Pacher (active 1465?–98), whose masterpiece is his *Saint Wolfgang Altarpiece* of the 1470s (St Wolfgang, Abersee). Pacher introduced many Italian ideas into Germany, which were carried on by his follower Max Reichlich.

Until 1505, there is no documentation of Altdorfer's activity. After this, he appears to have been successful as a painter, and he died a moderately rich man, having refused to become mayor of Regensburg but accepted the post of city architect, apparently designing only somewhat mundane structures. Such an official image is perhaps difficult to reconcile with his sometimes eccentric art. Early graphic work by him is known, but his first signed painting is the tiny *Satyr Family* of 1507 (Gemäldegalerie, Dresden), an image full of nostalgic poetry which uses landscape to create a mood more intense than any others in contemporary painting. It is tempting to think that Altdorfer might have seen Venetian paintings such as Giorgione's, and he almost certainly knew Mantegna's work. It cannot be coincidence that such apparently Venetian elements also occur in Cranach the Elder's landscapes. Moreover, the Venetian Jacopo de'Barbari (see plate 202) worked for a series of Northern patrons including the Emperor Maximilian and Frederick the Wise of Saxony, to whom he was court painter prior to Cranach the Elder. Only in the 1520s did Altdorfer dare to eliminate figures completely from nature in his *Danube Landscape near Regensburg* (Alte Pinakothek, Munich), frequently achieving a pathos which was not recaptured in landscape painting until Caspar David Friedrich in the Romantic period.

The architecture in Altdorfer's pictures (such as *The Finding of the Body of Saint Florian* in the St Florian Monastery near Linz) is sometimes Italianate, and he explored architecture in his drawings of around 1520. Altdorfer remained unrivalled in his evocations of the grandeur of nature, and was often 'Gothick' in his effects (see plate 271). This experimental aspect was extended in his *Holy Night* of 1512 (Gemäldegalerie, Berlin) to include novel light experiments, which were to be a feature of much of his later painting.

Altdorfer worked for the Emperor Maximilian, and his connections with Austria appear to have been strong since his probably visited Vienna twice. In 1518 he worked at the monastery of St Florian, where he exploited astonishing colour and light effects in his *Christ on the Mount of Olives*, which echoes Dürer's *Passion* series. A quasi-Surrealism appears in the figures in other painting there. During the 1520s, Altdorfer perfected both an intimate landscape style and a monumental one, first seen in the delightful and highly original *Birth of the Virgin* (see plate 288) and culminating in the grandiloquent *Battle of Issus* painted for the Duke of Bavaria (see plate 289). Altdorfer's followers in landscape, however, failed to realize a comparable degree of high drama, preferring a less demanding form of imagery.

Lucas Cranach the Elder

Lucas Cranach the Elder (1472–1553), whose name derives from his birthplace Kronach, in southern Germany, appears to have lived in Vienna for about three years until 1504. He moved in the type of humanist circles to which Dürer was accustomed, and painted one of the most moving and sensitive images of that world (see plate 272). Perhaps the remarkable diversity of his work also comes from his Viennese experience. It ranges from landscapes – which relate him to Altdorfer and the Danube School – to magnificent altarpieces, celebrated nudes, forceful portraits and distinguished graphic work.

272 LUCAS CRANACH THE ELDER *Johannes Cuspinian c.*1502
This picture, together with its companion showing Cuspinian's wife Anna, is one of the most magnificent portraits of the German Renaissance. The pair are probably wedding portraits, as they include the couple's astrological birds, the owl and the parrot. Cuspinian, a noted and precocious humanist, was poet laureate to the Emperor, and his major work on the Roman Caesars and Emperors glorified the German Imperial ideal. Cuspinian is shown aged twenty-nine, as 'rector magnificus' of Vienna University. A typically rough Danube School landscape contrasts with the refined sitter.

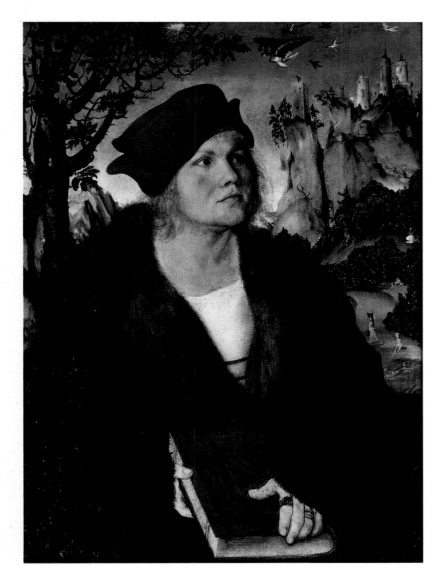

While influenced by Dürer, Cranach's portraits seem to make a subtle progression in crystallizing the atmosphere of a world still changing from Gothic ideas to the Renaissance. Cranach's remarkable adaptability, however, is displayed by his complete adoption of mid-century means of expression in his powerful *Self Portrait* of 1550 (Uffizi, Florence). This portrait marked the end of his career as court painter at Wittenberg, first to Frederick the Wise, Elector of Saxony. Having served there for forty-five years, Cranach followed the last Saxon Elector of that line – John Frederick – into exile at Augsburg. His most innovative portraits are full-length, and lovingly delineate costume, as in *Henry the Pious* of 1514 (Gemäldegalerie, Dresden). The sitters included a remarkable cross-section of the German aristocracy and intelligentsia (see plate 272). Cranach was the archetypal court artist of his period in Germany, creating images of aristocratic elegance even within biblical themes. This ensured a high demand for his work, of which the many contemporary copies and versions are an indication. Something of the nervous elegance of Mannerism pervades Cranach's figures, and this was exploited by his son Lucas the Younger (1515–86) who led the Cranach workshop and completed his father's last painting, the moving *Allegory of Redemption* (Stadtkirche, Weimar).

Highly honoured in Wittenberg, (Luther was godfather to one of his children), Cranach evolved a sophisticated and witty visual language, especially in paintings of the nude. He appears to have kept himself informed on painting elsewhere, travelling in 1509 to the Netherlands and adopting some Flemish ideas in his *Holy Kinship Altarpiece* (Stadelsches Kunstinstitut, Frankfurt), with its striking floor tiles, contemporary fashion and anecdotal detail. His woodcuts are influenced by both Dürer and Flemish artists and include secular and religious themes.

Mathis Grünewald

A court painter of a very different stamp from Cranach was Mathis Gothardt or Neithart (*c.*1470/80–1528). He was mistakenly called Grünewald by his first biographer, Joachim Sandrart, in his study of German art, the *Teutsche Akademie*, published in 1675. Grünewald is, however, a rediscovery of the twentieth century, and has proved very much to its taste. German Expressionist painters strongly identified with his angst. His long neglect seems surprising when we now rank him second only to Dürer, but his melancholy nature and unapproachable painting may explain it to some extent. Like Dürer, he is mentioned by only one contemporary, Melanchthon, after his death.

Grünewald's particular strength lies in his marriage of the spiritual world of the Middle Ages with new and unique imagery, colour and drama.

His departure from Albrecht von Brandenburg's service because of his sympathies with the Peasants' War, the loss of a major altarpiece at sea, the romance of his rediscovery and his painting style itself combine to create a fascinating figure. A further oddity is that he was documented as a waterwork designer in 1510. Grünewald, a convinced Lutheran, seems to have studied in Nuremberg in the early years of the century, where Dürer's influence was unavoidable. He moved to Mainz where he worked for Archbishop Uriel von Gemmingen from 1508–14, and for his successor, Albrecht von Brandenburg. Grünewald met Dürer in 1520 when he accompanied Albrecht to Aix-la-Chapelle for Charles V's coronation.

His first known work is the *Lindenhardt Altarpiece* of 1503 (Lindenhardt Parish Church) whose mixture of disturbing, angular figures meticulously rendered in strong contrasts of light and dark, looks forward to his major work, the *Isenheim Altarpiece* (see plate 282). There is none of Dürer's optimism here, and already in a slightly later chalk drawing, *Christ on the Cross* (Staatliche Kunsthalle, Karlsruhe) the agonized angularity of the Christ and a realism of detail appear that characterizes subsequent works, such as the *Small Crucifixion* (see plate 281). The multiple visual and psychological possibilities of the Crucifixion scene repeatedly drew Grünewald to express himself most fully with this theme.

Working independently, Grünewald painted the four healing saints for the (now lost) central panel of the *Heller Altarpiece* of 1508–10 (Städelsches Kunstinstitut, Frankfurt and Fürstenber Collection, Donaueschingen). Costume dominates these slightly contorted figures, with heavy, tangible drapery. The whole effect is somewhat eerie, suggesting the mystical world they inhabit.

The *Isenheim Altarpiece* (see plate 282) contains all the artist's most important statements, and although it was followed immediately by a painting of real charm, the heavily symbolic *Virgin in the Garden* (Stuppach Parish Church), his later work reveals the desire for increasing profundity. This did not exclude, however, an apparent concession to High Renaissance principles of proportion and composition in the *Meeting of Saints Erasmus and Maurice* of the early 1520s (Alte Pinakothek, Munich). He then reverted to an intense, pessimistic world in his later works. His last years seem to have been spent in penury in Frankfurt. He apparently suffered from paranoia, and in 1527 he fled to Halle where he died of plague. Of the few artists attracted to him, Baldung Grien derived superficial elements from his style.

Hans Baldung Grien

The extensive output of Hans Baldung Grien (1484/5–1545) included religious and mythological paintings, tapestry, stained glass, book illustration and drawings. There is a strongly erotic (sometimes obscene) element in his renderings of women and death, and in woodcuts like the *Fall*. The epicene contrasts between voluptuous female figures and voracious skeletons are particularly memorable. These were made as a result of his training with Dürer, but early in his career he manifested

273 HANS BALDUNG GRIEN The Three Ages of Woman and Death 1509-11
This allegory of earthly vanity may have been part of a series of the Dance of Death. While the Düreresque woman admires herself unknowingly in the mirror, Death waves an hourglass above her and traps her by her veil. Below, a child also plays with a veil - probably a reference to the medieval idea of a veiled cupid symbolizing lust. The old woman at the left attempts to forestall Death's action. Typical of Germanic humanist taste, such allegories were virtually unknown in Italy at this time.

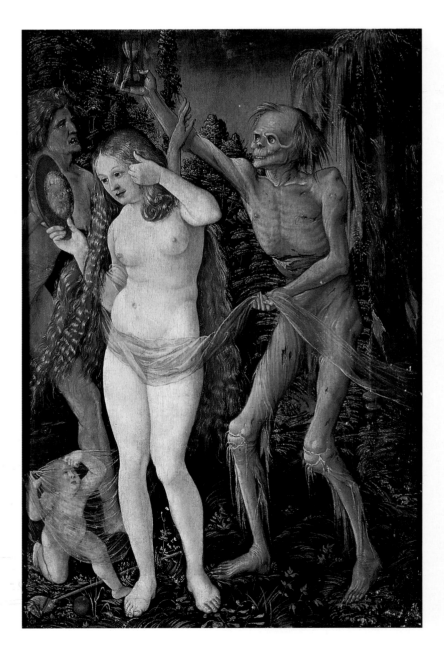

a love of the grotesque, supernatural or gruesome (see plate 273). Born in Schwäbisch-Tremünd in southern Germany, of an academic family, he studied in Strasburg at the turn of the century before entering Dürer's studio about 1503. His *Adoration of the Magi Altarpiece* of 1507 (Gemäldegalerie, Berlin) clearly shows Dürer's influence. Strasburg was later to be Baldung's adopted city.

An interest in witchcraft and the supernatural emerged throughout European art in the later Renaissance (for example, in Rosso Fiorentino) and Baldung's *chiaroscuro* woodcut, *The Witches* (1510), shows superficial similarities to figures in Altdorfer. Although not obviously connected with such themes, his later woodcuts, such as *Wild Horses* (1534) and *The Bewitched Groom* (1544), possibly an allegory of lust, often suggest sinister overtones, which were taken up with some relish by the eighteenth-century Swiss artist Fuseli. Baldung borrows from the medieval Dance of Death, but combines it with the more contemporary Italianate theme of *vanitas*.

Baldung's masterpiece was the high altar (1512–16) for Freiburg Minster. The central panel, showing the *Coronation of the Virgin*, radiates colour and light, and its crowded composition placed closely parallel to the picture plane recalls that he was working at the same time on the Emperor Maximilian's prayer book. It is one of the rare works reflecting aspects of Grünewald's *Isenheim Altarpiece* and its *Nativity* is one of the finest night-pieces of the period.

His portraiture is distinguished, the most famous example being his 1521 woodcut of Luther, shown in the light of the Holy Ghost, with distinctly Gothic drapery folds to his monk's habit. The likenesses of his Freiburg period are possibly his most penetrating, the best example showing *Count Palatine Philip the Warlike* in 1517 (Alte Pinakothek, Munich) with an acuity worthy of Holbein.

A postscript on Swiss painting, closely linked with German developments, must include Urs Graf (*c.*1485–1527/8), who spent time as a mercenary in Italy and is best known for his engravings, and many drawings of soldiers and fashionably attired prostitutes.

Painting in Augsburg: the Holbeins, Burgkmair and Amberger

Much grandeur remains today to show how wealthy was the city-republic of Augsburg, Nuremberg's principal Renaissance rival. The great banking and merchant families, such as the Fuggers, Peutingers and Welsers, not only built lavishly but were important patrons of painting and sculpture. This flourishing culture was furthered by the Emperor Maximilian, whose favourite city Augsburg became. Here Italianate ideas were encouraged, culminating in the distinguished portraits of Christoph Amberger. Its most famous citizens were the Holbeins, father and son, followed by Hans Burgkmair. Hans Holbein the Elder (*c.*1465–1524) attained considerable fame in Germany, while his son became one of Europe's greatest portraitists. Holbein the Elder probably went to the Netherlands before establishing himself in Augsburg, since he shows the influence of Van der Weyden and Gerard David in his elongated figures and certain poses. This can all be seen in his *Saint Sebastian Altarpiece* of 1515–17 (Alte Pinakothek, Munich) one of his most elegant mature works. His accomplished and sensitive portraiture and drawings must have been immensely influential on his son.

Hans Holbein the Younger (1497/8–1543) matured into a completely different world from that of his father, and proved to be Germany's last major Renaissance painter. He trained with his father, and this, coupled with his father's reputation, certainly furthered his career. Holbein belongs to the reign of Charles V, whose court painter he might easily have become. Perhaps fortunately for posterity, instead of the religious commissions which had occupied his father and his workshop, the Reformation forced Holbein to specialize almost exclusively in portraiture. He went with his brother Ambrosius to Basle in 1514–15, where he worked mainly in graphics and printing, but was in Lucerne in 1517–18, collaborating with his father on the decoration (now destroyed) of a house belonging to the Von Hertenstein family. In 1516 he painted a diptych showing the mayor of Basle, *Jakob Meyer and his Wife*, set against a Renaissance arch (Öffentliche Kunstsammlung, Basle). In using tempera and oil on lindenwood for these, he established the technique he preferred throughout his portraits.

His superbly dramatic – and suddenly mature – portrait of *Bonifacius Amerbach* of 1519 (see plate 290) suggests that he had travelled to Italy, for it already has the breadth of vision and softer style of his best later work. He was certainly in France in 1524, where he saw the work of Raphael in the royal collection. This is probably reflected in his *Madonna of Burgomaster Meyer* of 1526 (Schlossmuseum, Darmstadt) and in his *Dance of Death* series of prints, which were not published until 1538 in Lyons because of their Reformation ideas.

It was obvious by now that Holbein was drawn to portraiture, since even his bust-length *Adam and Eve* of 1517 (Öffentliche Kunstsammlung, Basle) is clearly based on actual people influenced by figures in Dürer and Baldung Grien. Italy is also recalled by his *Christ in the*

Sepulchre (see plate 274). In addition Holbein made nearly 1200 woodcut and metalcut engravings, stained glass designs and painted house façade decorations.

In 1520, Holbein became a citizen of Basle and married the widow Elsbeth Schmid, by whom he had four children. At this time, he painted the impressive *Oberreid Altarpiece* in Freiburg Minster followed by a portrait of *Erasmus* (see plate 14), for whom he also provided marginal illustrations to *In Praise of Folly*. He went to England in 1526, having been recommended by Erasmus to Thomas More. After returning to Basle, he witnessed the iconoclasm unleashed there, and in spite of considerable official patronage, may have decided to seek work elsewhere. Finally, in 1532, he left to work permanently in England (see Chapter VI). Germany had lost its greatest portraitist to a foreign court. His magnificent likeness of *Georg Gisze* (see plate 291) spans the transition from his old to his new life, looking forward to the richness of his English style.

The third artist of note in Augsburg in this period was Hans Burgkmair the Elder (1473–1531), who trained with Schongauer at Colmar and probably visited Milan and Venice, prior to establishing himself in his native town by 1498. He married Holbein the Elder's sister in that year. A second visit to Italy is possible since echoes of Leonardo and even Michelangelo's influence are perceptible in his work. He also went to Bruges, which gave him a wider vision than his brother-in-law, and, like Dürer, collaborated on Maximilian's triumphal arch. His finest (and most Italianate) work is the *Saint John Altarpiece*, and it was he rather than Holbein the Elder who made significant steps forward in Augsburg's adoption of Italian colour and sensuousness.

274 HANS HOLBEIN THE YOUNGER Christ in the Sepulchre 1521–2
This probably formed an unusual predella to the two wings of Holbein's Oberreid Altar, saved from iconoclastic destruction in 1529 and now in Freiburg Cathedral. It may refer to sculpted figures of this type which were only exposed during Holy Week, and shows the deep religious feeling which the Reformation forced painters like Holbein to stifle. The harrowing intensity of the image remains unique in his work.

Innovations in Italian Mannerist court portraiture were certainly becoming known in northern Europe, and Charles V's employment of Titian as a portraitist must have spurred on German painters to update their styles. In Augsburg, which was so in touch with Imperial tastes, the one portraitist who achieved something of the international court style of the mid-century was a pupil of Burgkmair, Christoph Amberger (c.1505–61). Amberger had met Titian in Augsburg in 1548, and consciously aimed for Venetian grandeur of form, which he achieved in his *Charles V* (Staatliche Museen, Berlin) and *Christoph Fugger* of 1541 (see plate 9), which resembles Bronzino. There is little of Holbein's directness in his stylized depiction of his sitters.

The Netherlands

Through the Empire the artistic fortunes of the Netherlands and Germany in the sixteenth century were interlinked and painters from both areas knew their contemporaries' work. Moderately peaceful conditions during the first half of the century favoured the arts, but this situation did not continue. Philip II was brutal in his repression of Protestantism in the Netherlands, and the more the Netherlands rebelled, the harsher he became. His main tool was the Inquisition, which butchered thousands of people. In 1566, a decision was taken among Netherlandish rebels to rid themselves of the dreaded Inquisition, and destroy Catholic works of art throughout their country. The so-called 'Spanish Fury' followed, in which Philip violently quelled the uprising. Bruegel may have painted the *Crippled Beggars* of 1568 (Musée du Louvre, Paris) as a direct result of this.

Antwerp, which had been of slight artistic importance in the fifteenth century, supplanted Bruges (whose estuary had silted up) as a trading centre and became a leading international port. Many of the great Flemish paintings now in Spain and Portugal were collected by Iberian merchants in Antwerp at this time. Such collectors may also have developed a sophisticated taste for much earlier painting, which resulted in a revival of elements of Van Eyck's style: even Holbein partook of

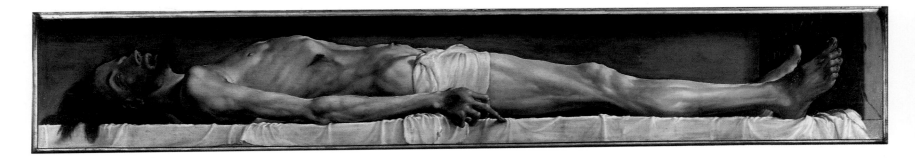

this. Antwerp's growing artistic and economic reputation attracted increasing numbers of painters. Painters' guild records are an important source of dates, and we owe a great debt to the writings of the Netherlandish painter Karel van Mander (1548–1606), who worked mainly in Haarlem. His three-part *Het schilderboeck* (The Book of Painters) published in 1604, provides over 170 biographies of German and Netherlandish artists since Van Eyck, lives of Italian painters since Cimabue (derived from Vasari) and practical advice on technique and theory. Van Mander came to be known as the 'Dutch Vasari'.

Metsys, Patinir, Joos van Cleve and Mabuse all distinguished the first decades of the century in the Netherlands. Flemish painting did not, however, attain the greatness of the fifteenth century, and with the exception of Pieter Bruegel, failed to produce a genius of Dürer's standing. Gradually, various cities became known as centres in which accomplished painters could be found: Antwerp, Haarlem, Leiden, Bruges and Strasburg. Court art was centred in Brussels and Malines, where the Emperor's regent was based.

The most remarkable single feature of Netherlandish painting in this period was its interest in Italy and eager adoption of Italianate ideas, which eventually culminated in the Northern Caravaggesque artists in the next century. One of the most important events in the early years of the century was the presence, until 1519, of Raphael's Sistine Chapel tapestry cartoons in the Brussels weaving studios (see plate 205). This major masterpiece suddenly exposed painters to the latest High Renaissance style and, along with the influx of Italian prints, helped to form the 'Antwerp Mannerist' style. Those painters in the northern Netherlands who adopted Italian ideas without the exaggerations of early Mannerism, came to be known as Romanists. Jan van Scorel (1495–1562) was the most important of these. He travelled widely to Italy, Jerusalem and Cyprus, and returned to Utrecht in 1524, where he achieved a balanced Classicism influenced by Raphael, Michelangelo and the Venetians. Most of his major altarpieces are lost, but his influence was immense, notably on his pupils Maerten van Heemskerck and the internationally successful Anthonis Mor (see plate 297).

Quinten Metsys

Quinten Metsys (or Matsys or Massys, 1465/6–1530) was born in Louvain. By about 1510, he was Antwerp's principal painter, giving the city a new artistic importance with his versatility. He knew Erasmus, and painted him in 1517 with the philosopher Petrus Aegidius in a

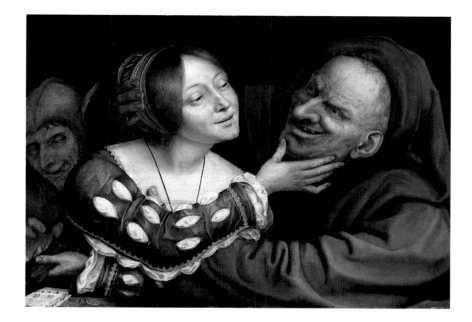

275 QUINTEN METSYS Ill-Matched Lovers *c.*1520–5
This is an early example of a genre scene with the type of moral found in the writings of Erasmus. The old man is duped into imagining the girl's attentions to be genuine, while in fact she is robbing him, thus illustrating the saying that a fool is soon parted from his money. This was a very popular theme in the art of the time, and the long ears on the hat of the background accomplice may also refer to the writings of Sebastian Brunt. Such subjects were soon adopted in Italian painting. The combination of the grotesque with the beautiful culminates in the paintings of Marinus van Reymerswaele (see plate 298).

'Friendship Diptych' for Sir Thomas More in England. His career seems to have been entirely successful and uncomplicated, and he had twelve children from two marriages, two of whom became painters.

Compared with that of his contemporary Dürer, Metsys' style is firmly rooted in the fifteenth century and his first dated work, the *Saint Anne Altarpiece* of 1507–9 (Musées Royaux des Beaux-Arts, Brussels), continues that tradition. His delightful *Saint Christopher*, probably painted about 1504–5 (Musée Royal des Beaux-Arts, Antwerp), shows originality in the use of light and *chiaroscuro* (perhaps gained from Leonardo) and psychological perception. Metsys began to demonstrate an increasing awareness of Italian ideas – notably Leonardo's – which indicate that he made an Italian journey. He seems also to have felt Dürer's influence, but in his natural eclecticism selected devices as they suited him. He happily mixed fifteenth-century ideas with newer concepts, as in his *Madonna and Child with Angels* (Courtauld Institute, London), and *The Banker and his Wife* (Musée du Louvre, Paris), whose sophisticated evocation of earlier Flemish art appealed to a subsequent owner, Rubens.

Metsys was primarily concerned with the human figure, which he often depicted with disarming directness

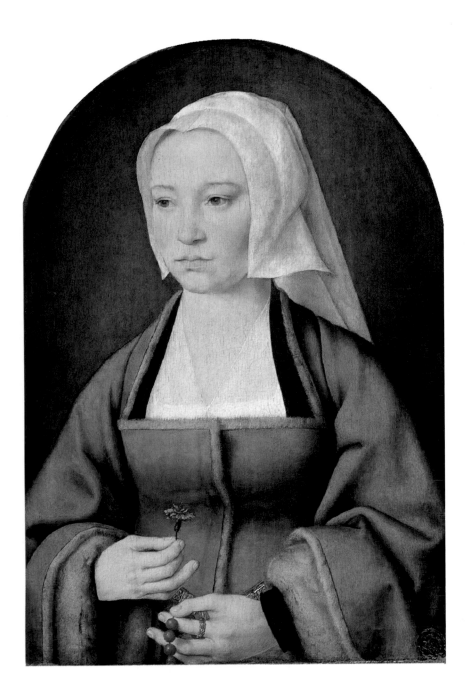

277 JOOS VAN CLEVE Margaretha Boghe *c.*1518
This is the companion portrait to that of Joris Vezeler, and
commemorates the sitter's marriage to him. She is holding a pink, a
symbol of betrothal, and a rosary. Its clarity and directness, and the
way in which the figure fills the picture space, are typical of Van
Cleve's portraiture, and support the possibility that he visited Italy
and saw High Renaissance portraits there.

Eleanore, in an enamelled French manner with overtones
of Leonardo's *sfumato* technique, which was popular there
(see Chapter VI). These are now in the Johnson
Collection, Philadelphia and the Royal Collection,
Hampton Court.

Other painters of note in Antwerp were Pieter Coecke
van Aelst (1502–50) and Jan Sanders van Hemessen
(*c.*1500–*c.*1575). Van Aelst visited Constantinople and his
interest in Italian painting, particularly Leonardo's, made
him adopt 'Antwerp Mannerist' exaggerations, and look
forward to a more rational style. Van Hemessen's paintings often illustrate parables and proverbs, and his satirical
portraits parallel those of Metsys.

Painting in Brussels

Court taste at Brussels is best represented by Bernard (or
Bernaert or Barend) van Orley (*c.*1490–1541). He fulfilled
a wide range of court duties throughout his career, painting portraits, altarpieces, and designing tapestries (influenced by the Raphael cartoons whose weaving he
supervised) and stained glass. His meeting with Dürer in
1520–21 had a strong impact on his painting, but he combined this with Italianate elements (see plate 283). Van
Orley retained many features of 'Antwerp Mannerism',
especially his love of fantastic architectural backgrounds,
as in his *Job Altarpiece* of 1521 (Musées Royaux, Brussels).
In about 1516, he painted one of the most memorable
images of Charles V (Museum of Fine Arts, Budapest).

Other artists who worked for the court include Jan
Mostaert, (*c.*1475–1555/6) who was employed by the
Regent, Margaret of Austria, before 1519. He introduced
the southern Netherlandish courtly style into his native
Haarlem, where much of his work was lost in the Great
Fire of Haarlem in 1576. Jacob Cornelisz van Oostsanen
(1470–1533) preferred crowded compositions whose
figures fill the foreground with colourful activity. His style
is close to that of Cornelis Engelbrechtsz, the leading
painter of Leiden, in the northern Netherlands.

Painting in Leiden

At the turn of the fifteenth century, Leiden was beginning
to assume the importance it was later to enjoy fully in
Dutch painting. Its leading painter was Cornelis
Engelbrechtsz (1468–1533), who had been an apprentice
in Brussels, where he must have absorbed the sophistication of the court. It seems that he returned to Leiden by
way of Antwerp, and the 'Antwerp Mannerist' interest in
elongated forms, startling colour effects and bizarre detail
clearly intrigued him. The jewel-like quality of his smaller
panels enabled him to achieve some images of remarkable
concentration (see plate 278), which have been described
as showing 'Late Gothic Mannerism'.

Engelbrechtsz was the master of Lucas van Leyden
(1494–1533), who was said to have been active as a successful engraver by the age of nine. He was only fourteen
when he made his first known print, *Mohammed and the*
Murdered Monk Sergius, which has genre overtones.
During his brief life, he was a highly successful painter,
as is shown in his vibrant *Last Judgement* triptych of 1526–7
(Stedelijk Museum, Leiden). However, he was more
occupied as a prolific engraver, and was influenced by
Dürer, whom Vasari says he bettered. His prints (which

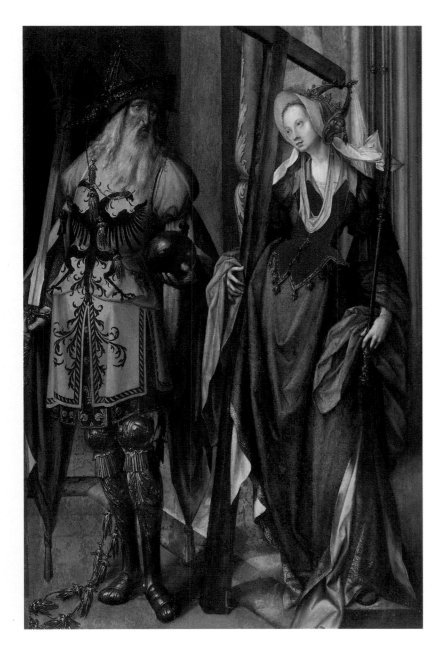

278 CORNELIS ENGELBRECHTSZ Emperor Constantine (?) and Saint Helena, after 1517
The Emperor Constantine the Great allegedly defeated his enemy Maxentius 'under the sign of the Cross', and his mother St Helena supposedly found the True Cross and had it transported to Constantinople. Probably a fragment of an altarpiece, it may have been connected with the supposed relic of the Cross which arrived in Leiden in 1517. Its high degree of stylization suggests both Gothic and Mannerist types.

sometimes include extensive and rationally presented architecture, as in the *Ecce Homo* of 1510) were influential even in Italy.

Lucas's travels took him to Antwerp in 1521 and he met Gossaert in Middleburg in 1527. Van Mander's endearing portrait of him (which agrees with Vasari) says that he often worked from his bed, and gives a slightly misleading picture of his superficiality – possibly a misinterpretation of the welcome lightness which is often found in his work. Apart from his woodcuts, etchings, engravings and drawings, Lucas's lasting contribution may have been his pioneering enthusiasm for genre painting

bearing no religious or allegorical implication (see plate 279). This was soon to be adopted with unparalleled interest as a Dutch speciality, for example by Pieter Aertsen (see plate 296). There is a strong genre element in Lucas's *Worship of the Golden Calf* of the mid-1520s (see plate 280), coupled with an unusual ability to link figures and mountainous landscape which looks forward fifty years to developments which were to lead to the Baroque.

The transition between the paintings of Lucas van Leyden and Jan van Scorel and the next generation, who were to open the way for the great developments of seventeenth-century Dutch art, is seen in the work of Maerten van Heemskerck, Pieter Aertsen and Frans Floris. Heemskerck (1498–1574) made an Italian journey in 1532–5 which was dominated by his encounter with Michelangelo, whom he emulated on his return to Haarlem. The transformation which thereby occurred in his work is evident from a comparison of pre-Italian portraits, such as *A Family Group* probably of *c.*1530 (Staatliche Kunstsammlungen, Kassel), which still recalls Scorel, and his finest post-Italian painting, the *Self Portrait* (see plate 305). The latter is a milestone in the attitude of Northern painters to Italy and the antique, leaving behind all 'Antwerp Mannerist' and 'Romanist' pretensions to Mediterranean culture. Heemskerck's two Italian sketchbooks provide insight into this absorption with Roman art and architecture, and single him out as an antiquarian more in the manner of eighteenth-century artists.

279 LUCAS VAN LEYDEN The Card Players *c.*1514
Van Leyden had already experimented with a similar novel genre theme in his Chess Players *of around 1510, and such subjects indicate an increasing interest in everyday life, since they almost certainly carry no meanings deeper than a warning of the dangers of gambling. It was from such experiments that the taste for this type of genre picture filtered into northern Italy during subsequent decades.*

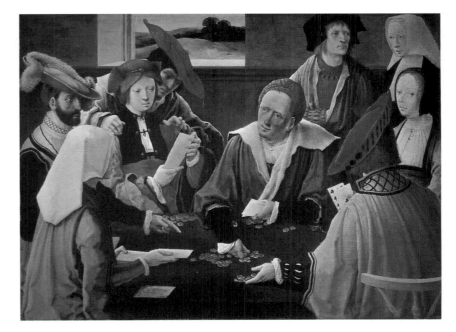

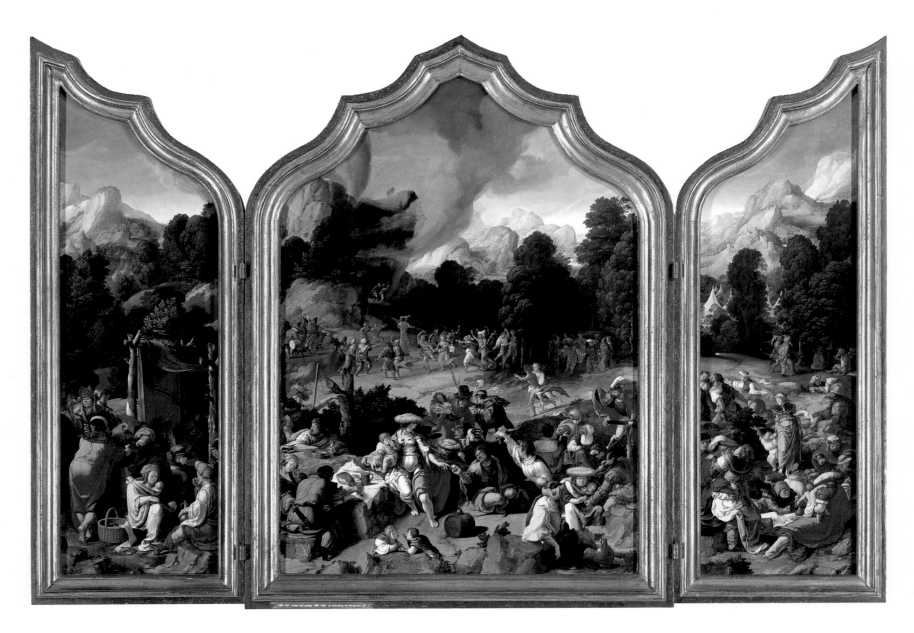

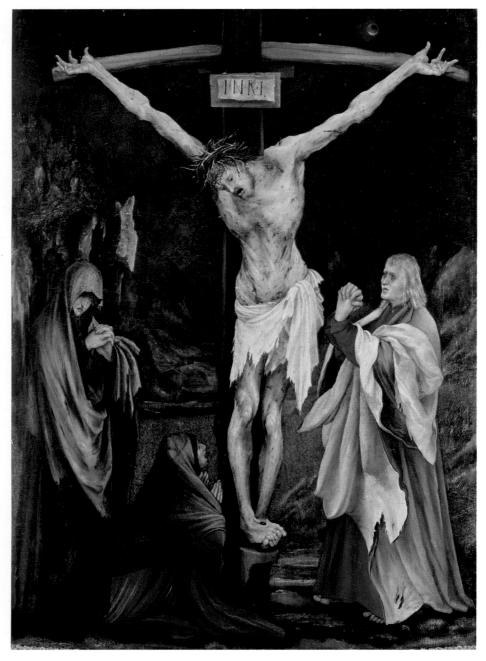

280 LUCAS VAN LEYDEN Worship of the Golden Calf
c.1525–8
(Above) Vasari rated Van Leyden above Dürer. Here he
achieves a rare balance between spacious landscape and crowds of
figures. Typically Mannerist is his placing of the main theme in
the middle distance, while the genre groups in the foreground
carry moral and symbolic overtones. The detail and rich colour in
the costumes emulate the Italian High Renaissance.

281 MATHIS GRÜNEWALD The Small Crucifixion, c.1511–20
(Left) The anguish of all three figures here is carefully
differentiated, and the crisp drapery folds, hand gestures and
brilliant colour are offset by the dark background, which
accentuates the terrible drama.

282 MATHIS GRÜNEWALD The Isenheim Altarpiece,
completed 1515
(Right) Painted for the Antonite chapel at Isenheim, this was
Grünewald's major work. Its original arrangement was
dominated by the Crucifixion on the outside, and Sts
Anthony and Sebastian in the wings. The first opening conceals
the fixed wings and shows a concert of angels before the Virgin,
flanked by the Annunciation and Resurrection. The second
opening shows Sts Athanasius, Anthony and Jerome, with the
meeting of Sts Anthony and Paul and the Temptation of St
Anthony in the wings. The painting is permeated by a sense of
terrible suffering, offset by the beauty of the angels' concert and
the hope of the Resurrection. Such emotional intensity, achieved
by gesture, dramatic outline, quasi-hallucinatory light effects and
gruesome detail, had no precedent in European art.

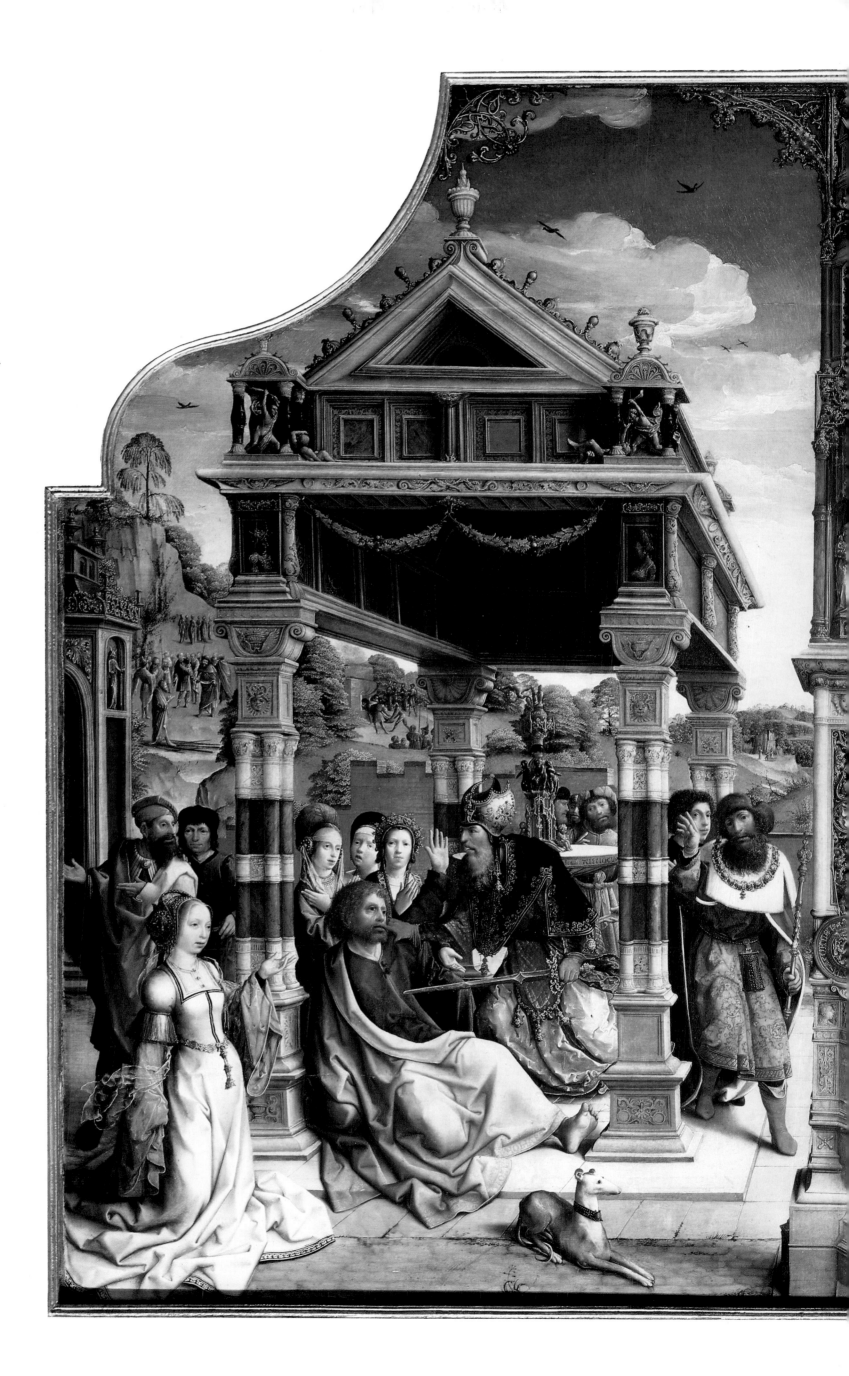

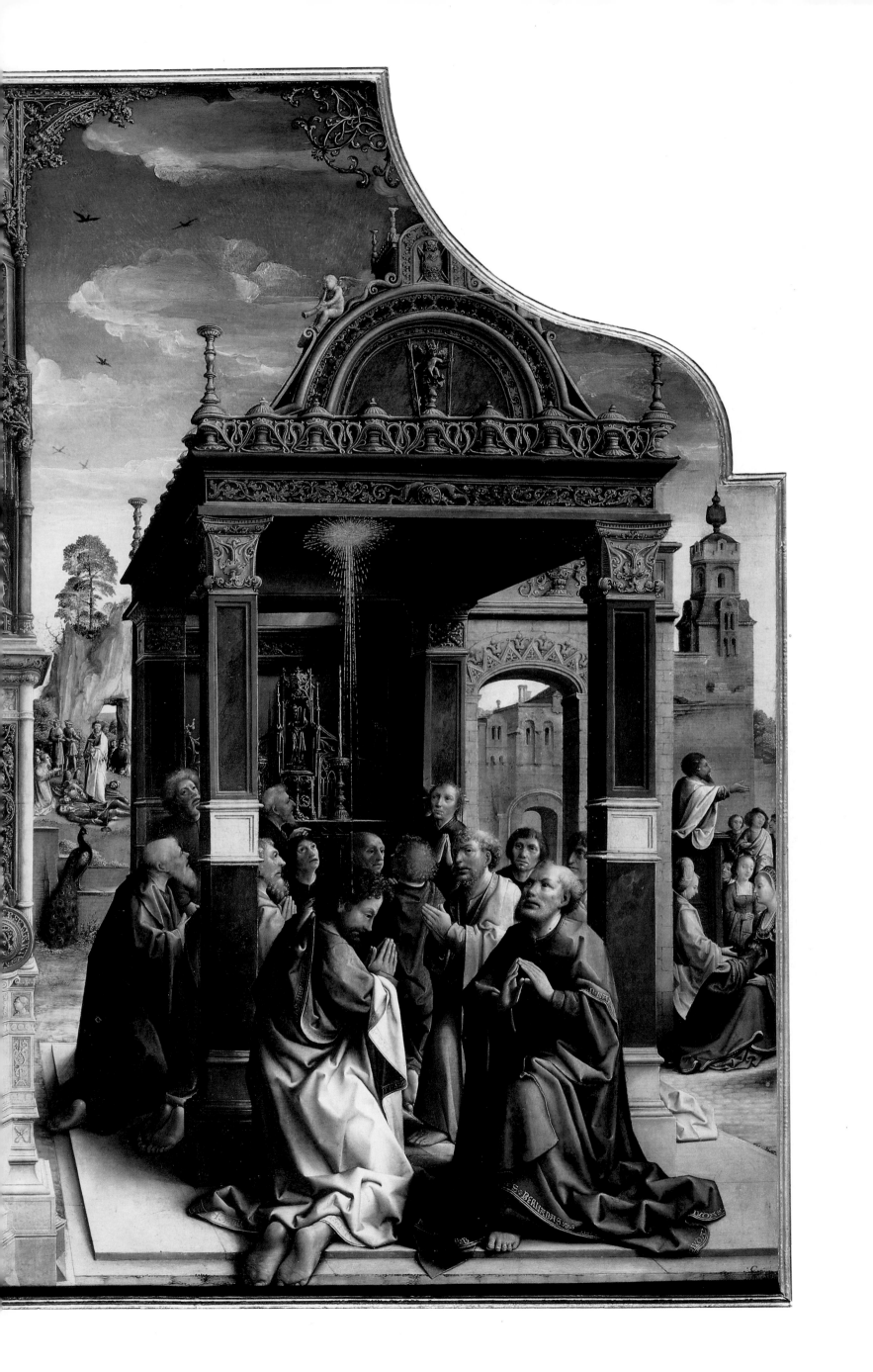

The increasing interest in genre (as an advance on the symbolic still-life detail which proliferates in fifteenth-century painting) is one of the most unexpected aspects of mid-sixteenth century painting in Europe, particularly in the Netherlands, but also in Italy. As such scenes were most common in a mercantile society, it was natural they should become popular initially with that same bourgeois public. Transition to pure genre was not rapid and ostensibly genre scenes continued to contain religious or allegorical undertones, as in Aertsen's famous *Egg Dance* of 1557 (Rijksmuseum, Amsterdam). Pieter Aertsen (1508/9–75) was the leading painter in both his native Amsterdam and Antwerp, and his mature style is robust, full of realistic detail and vigorously composed. Unlike many of the Northern realists of the early Baroque period, his figures retain immense dignity (see plate 296), a legacy of the Renaissance.

The Netherlandish-German portrait tradition of the sixteenth century came to a close with the leading international portraitist, Anthonis Mor (*c.*1517/20–76/7). Mor achieved a perfect balance between Italian Mannerist *hauteur* and lavish if restrained detail, and an ability to render character. He travelled all over the Holy Roman Empire, and to England in 1554, where he painted one of the outstanding court likenesses of the century, *Mary Tudor* (Museo del Prado, Madrid). His *Self Portrait* (see plate 297) shows the grandeur of which he was capable, combining a Venetian atmosphere with a Northern attention to detail.

The portraits of Frans Floris exhibit a restrained naturalism that anticipates the work of later Dutch painters, such as Frans Hals. This can be seen most clearly in his *Portrait of an Elderly Woman* (*The Falconer's Wife*) of 1558 (Musée des Beaux-Arts, Caen). Floris, like Heemskerck before him, was overwhelmed by Rome, where he was present in 1541 at the unveiling of Michelangelo's *Last Judgement* in the Vatican's Sistine Chapel. His wide experience outside Antwerp appears to have drawn many pupils to his studio after his return. Particularly in his later pictures, his brushwork frees itself from the meticulousness still sought by many of his contemporaries. His pupil Martin de Vos (1531/2–1603) who also studied in Rome, Florence and Venice, became Antwerp's leading Italianate painter after Floris's death.

283 BERNARD VAN ORLEY Saint Matthew *c.*1512

As one of the leading court painters to adopt Mannerist ideas in his maturity, Van Orley developed a style of some sophistication in which decorative architecture and other details are occasionally overwhelming. This altarpiece shows him uniting Italianate ideas with Northern prototypes.

Pieter Bruegel the Elder

Netherlandish painting in the sixteenth century comes to its natural conclusion with the great art of Pieter Bruegel (or Breughel, *c.*1525–69). Although firmly linked to many Netherlandish traditions in painting, he also stands alone. Known as Bruegel the Elder since he was the founder of a dynasty of painters, he has been described as a great comic illustrator (Van Mander) or a populist painter – 'Peasant Bruegel'. Modern studies, however, reveal him as a sensitive and cultured figure in touch with the leading intellectual and political events of his day. Van Mander's story of Bruegel dressing up as a peasant to observe rural life at close quarters is indicative of a sophisticated approach to his subject matter, as his delightful late drawing, *Artist and Connoisseur* (Albertina, Vienna), proves. His work has struck a deep note in twentieth-century consciousness, and certain of his pictures rank among the most popular images in European art.

Our information on Bruegel is limited to Van Mander's account and suppositions from dated paintings, so that he is one of the few major painters of his age who remains largely mysterious. The one area which he – alone among his contemporaries – appears to have avoided is painted portraiture. This seems odd, given his illustrious and discriminating patrons. These included Cardinal de Granvelle (Philip II's advisor who was more concerned about the loss of his Bruegels than anything else when his palace was sacked in 1572), and Niclaes Jonghelinck of Antwerp who owned sixteen of his pictures and in 1565 commissioned the *Months* series. Bruegel was equally gifted as a draughtsman, engraver and painter. Van Mander says he was born in Brueghel near Breda, but this is uncertain, and he studied under Pieter Coecke van Aelst whose daughter he married. In 1551–3 he travelled to France, Italy and Sicily, but was back in Antwerp after 1555.

Curiously, he seems to have remained impervious to the lure of Italy and the antique (as early critics rightly noted), which suggests that his art was intensely spontaneous and not susceptible to dramatic artistic changes elsewhere. Only in later life did he produce large-scale figure subjects. Since he collaborated in Rome with one of the greatest artists of his day, the miniaturist Giulio Clovio (see plate 258), who is known to have owned several of Bruegel's works, some influence from this source might have been expected. But Bruegel never depicted a Classical figure, and his drawings show only peasants and the grotesque underdogs of society, and were largely done for their own sake, not preparatory for other works.

Only drawings or engravings after drawings survive from 1552–5. As with Dürer, Breugel's return journey

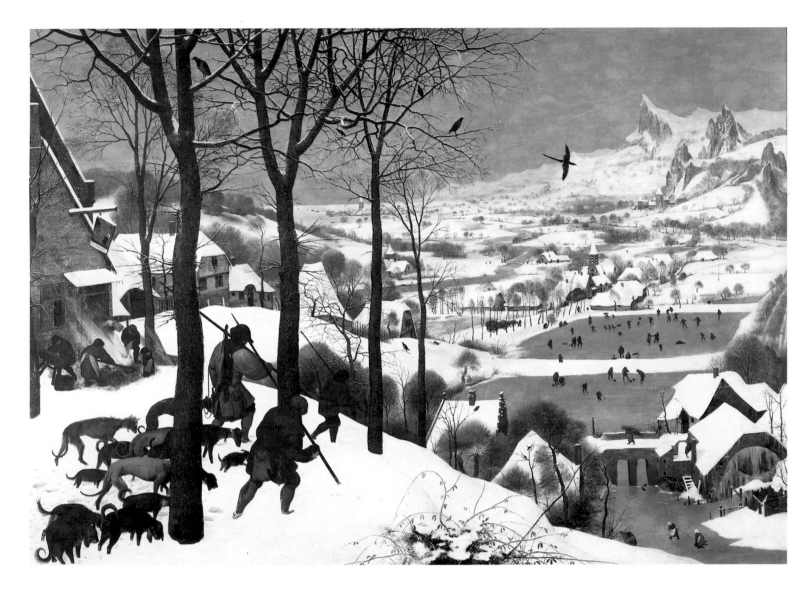

from Italy through the Alps proved of incomparable inspiration for many deeply felt landscape drawings. He designed for the engraver Hieronymous Cock, producing *Big Fish Eat Little Fish* in 1556. His *Seven Deadly Sins* (1558) established his public reputation for engraved work, and he otherwise worked for private patrons.

Bruegel's first known paintings are landscapes and seascapes recalling Patinir's high viewpoint. *The Fall of Icarus* of *c*.1555 (Musées Royaux des Beaux-Arts, Brussels) is already full of a unique magic and uses ideas he explored in his landscape drawings of the Alps. Much influenced by Bosch, paintings from the end of third decade feature multi-figure scenes illustrating popular proverbs about humanity's folly, such as *Netherlandish Proverbs* of 1559 (Gemäldegalerie, Berlin), where the sadness of human existence underlies the comic. From the same year, the *Combat between Carnival and Lent* and *Children's Games* of 1560 (both Kunsthistorisches Museum Vienna) have high viewpoints which suggest our remoteness even from scenes which might normally seem familiar. They tell us much about Bruegel's purpose in future paintings.

The period of Bruegel's most intense and original images now followed. After his move to Brussels and his marriage in 1563, human beings occupy a smaller position

284 PIETER BRUEGEL THE ELDER Hunters in the Snow 1565
This is one of five paintings from an incomplete decorative scheme for Niclaes Jonghelinck's Antwerp house, in which the painter Frans Floris also participated. The whole year may have been represented by one painting for each two-month period. Hunters in the Snow was probably the first in the series to be completed, and it has become the classic representation of winter. Its high viewpoint, restrained colour and receding silhouetted trees, reveal Bruegel's direct observation of nature, based on his own sketches of Alpine scenery.

in nature which has become all-embracing. This is seen in his series of *Months* (the five surviving panels are now in New York, Vienna and Prague), which brings them closer to modern landscape than any previous landscapes. In *Two Monkeys* of 1562 (Gemäldegalerie, Berlin), the futility of man's effort is perhaps the real subject, as it certainly is in the *Tower of Babel* (see plate 286), one of the Renaissance's most moving images.

Bruegel brought to religious themes immense pathos and originality. In 1564, he painted the *Road to Calvary* (Kunsthistorisches Museum, Vienna) and the *Adoration of the Magi* (National Gallery, London). Compared with Dürer's painting of the latter subject (see plate 287), with its Renaissance humanist optimism, Bruegel's is heavy with pessimism, the scene craggy, the background crowd threatening. From about the same date, his grisaille *Death of the Virgin* (Upton House, Banbury) is a night scene which, using an exaggerated Mannerist perspective, gives the impression of an event taking place in some indefinable distance, from which we are separated by darkness.

Bruegel is best known for his scenes of peasant life – wedding dances, peasant feasts, hay-making, herding, hunts and parables current in everyday life. In his last years, he alternated between his large-figure style, as in the *Peasant Wedding Feast* (Kunsthistorisches Museum, Vienna) or the *Land of Cockaigne* (Alte Pinakothek, Munich) and single figure themes such as the *Parable of the Bird's Nest* of 1568 (Kunsthistorisches Museum, Vienna). In both types, figures have all the solidity and volume of High Renaissance art, but their 'idealization' consists in an unvarnished depiction of peasant models, which in itself assumes a kind of dignity. The subtlety of his inclusion of popular philosophies is such that only close observation of the figures reveals that they partake not in genre, but in what might be termed 'natural allegory'. It is this concern with a universal topicality which sets Bruegel apart from his contemporaries, and places his work in a modern context, deriving from Renaissance ideals but transcending them.

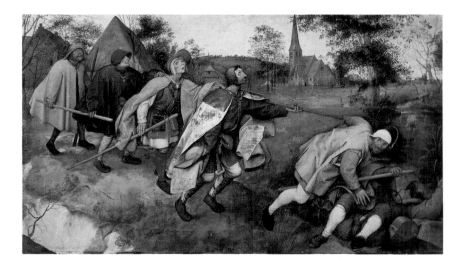

285 PIETER BRUEGEL THE ELDER Parable of the Blind 1568
This illustrates the words in the Gospel of St Matthew, 'If the blind lead the blind, both shall fall into the ditch.' The parable refers to the blindness of the soul closed to the truths of religion, symbolized by the church set in a closely-observed landscape.

286 PIETER BRUEGEL THE ELDER Tower of Babel 1563
Niclaes Jonghelinck owned sixteen paintings by Bruegel, among which was a painting of this theme, probably this version. Two years later, he commissioned the Months series from Bruegel. The tower is probably modelled in part on the Colosseum.

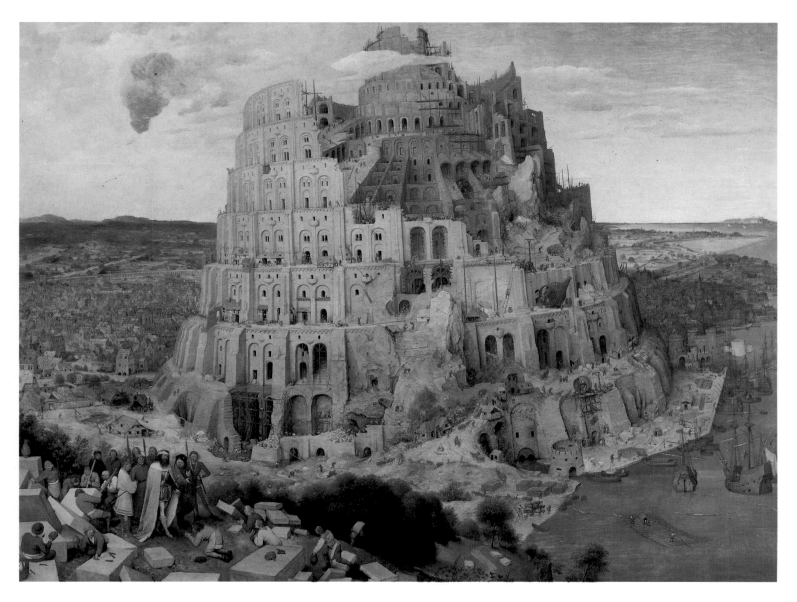

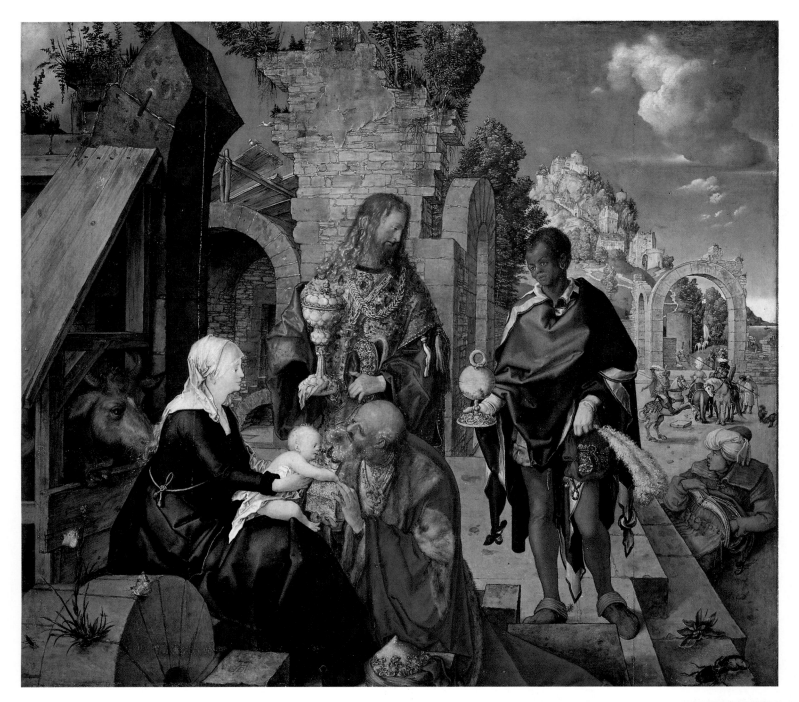

287 ALBRECHT DÜRER Adoration of the Magi 1504
*This composition was painted for Frederick the Wise, and the
figures, the perspective and the ruined Classical architecture,
indicate that Dürer knew the Leonardo da Vinci rendering of
the theme. It ends the period immediately prior to Dürer's
second Italian visit. Frederick was among the most respected
and pious of the German Electors, and is portrayed in prints
by both Dürer and Cranach.*

288 ALBRECHT ALTDORFER Birth of the Virgin
*c.*1520–1
*It is unusual to set this theme in a church, and St Anne's
bed at the left almost recalls an altar. The figure entering at
the right is cut off in a way that later became a frequent
visual device in German Mannerism. Altdorfer's inspiration
for the great ring of angels may come from Cranach. Strong
colour and contrasts of light and shade intensify the drama.*

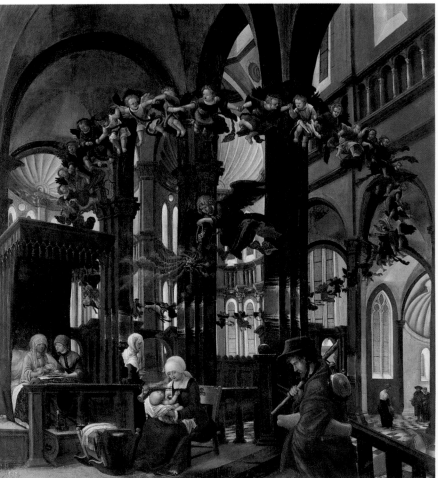

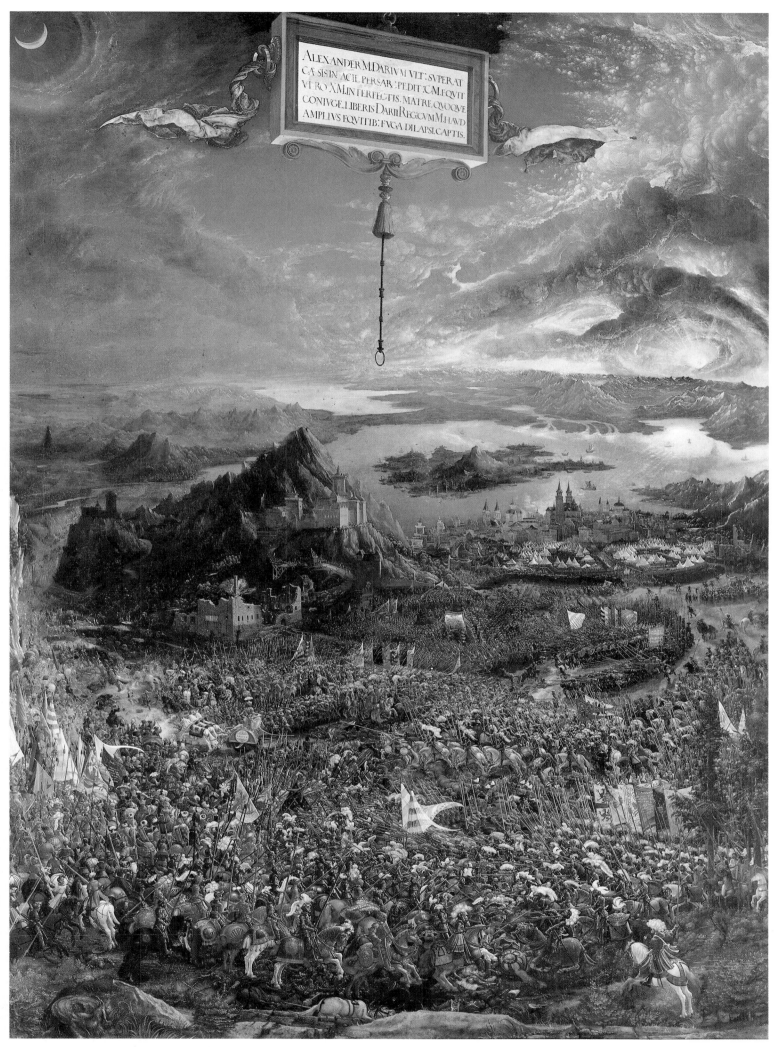

289 ALBRECHT ALTDORFER Battle of Issus 1529
The painting shows the Battle of Issus of 333 B.C., but is also an
allegory of the conflict of human forces compared with the dynamism
of the universe. The figure of Alexander the Great can be clearly seen
under the vertical line of the hanging cord, forcing the Persian King
Darius to flee in his three-horse chariot.

290 HANS HOLBEIN THE YOUNGER
Bonifacius Amerbach 1519

*Holbein painted this portrait in the year of
his Italian visit. Amerbach was the son of
the Basle printer, and later became
Professor of Law at Basle University. He
was the close friend and heir of Erasmus
and a great admirer of Holbein, several of
whose paintings he saved from destruction
by the iconoclasts. The portrait is uniquely
intense for Holbein, and may have been
his first work after his admission as a
master to the painter's guild on 25
September 1519.*

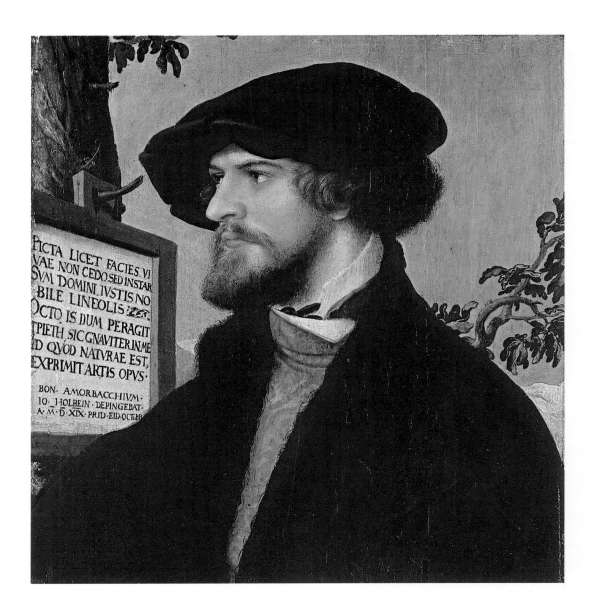

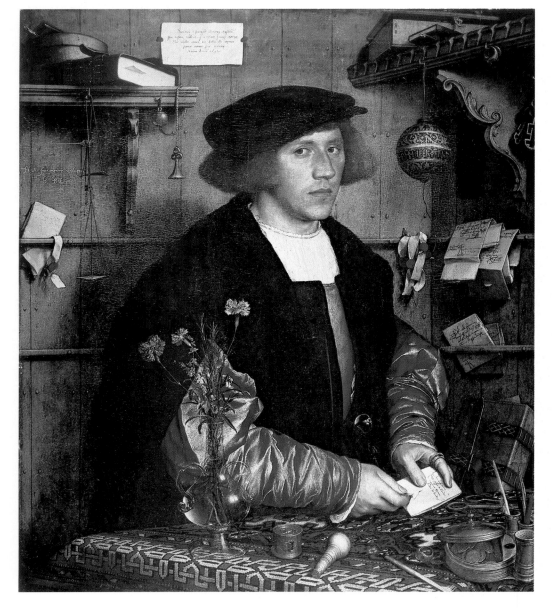

291 HANS HOLBEIN THE YOUNGER Portrait of
Georg Gisze 1532

*(Left) The merchant is portrayed at the age of thirty-
four, behind a work table in his office. He probably
spent much of his life in London, where he is
documented in the London Steelyard with which
Holbein had connections. He is surrounded by a
superb still life of objects connected with his
profession; sealing-wax, a pewter writing case, quill
pens, a gold balance and other luxurious items such
as a table-carpet, a gold clock and a Venetian glass
vase with carnations and other flowers referring to
Gisze's qualities. As carnations symbolize love and
fidelity, the portrait commission may date from the
time of his betrothal to Kristine Krüger.*

292 LUCAS CRANACH THE ELDER Judith with
the Head of Holofernes *c.*1530

*(Right) Cranach was the most successful purveyor of
the female nude in the Northern European
Renaissance. He also had considerable success with
elaborately dressed and coiffed female figures, who
wear the latest fashion in spite of their biblical or
Classical identity. Here, the beautiful Old Testament
heroine wears the type of large-brimmed hat with
feathers which occurs in many Cranach paintings.*

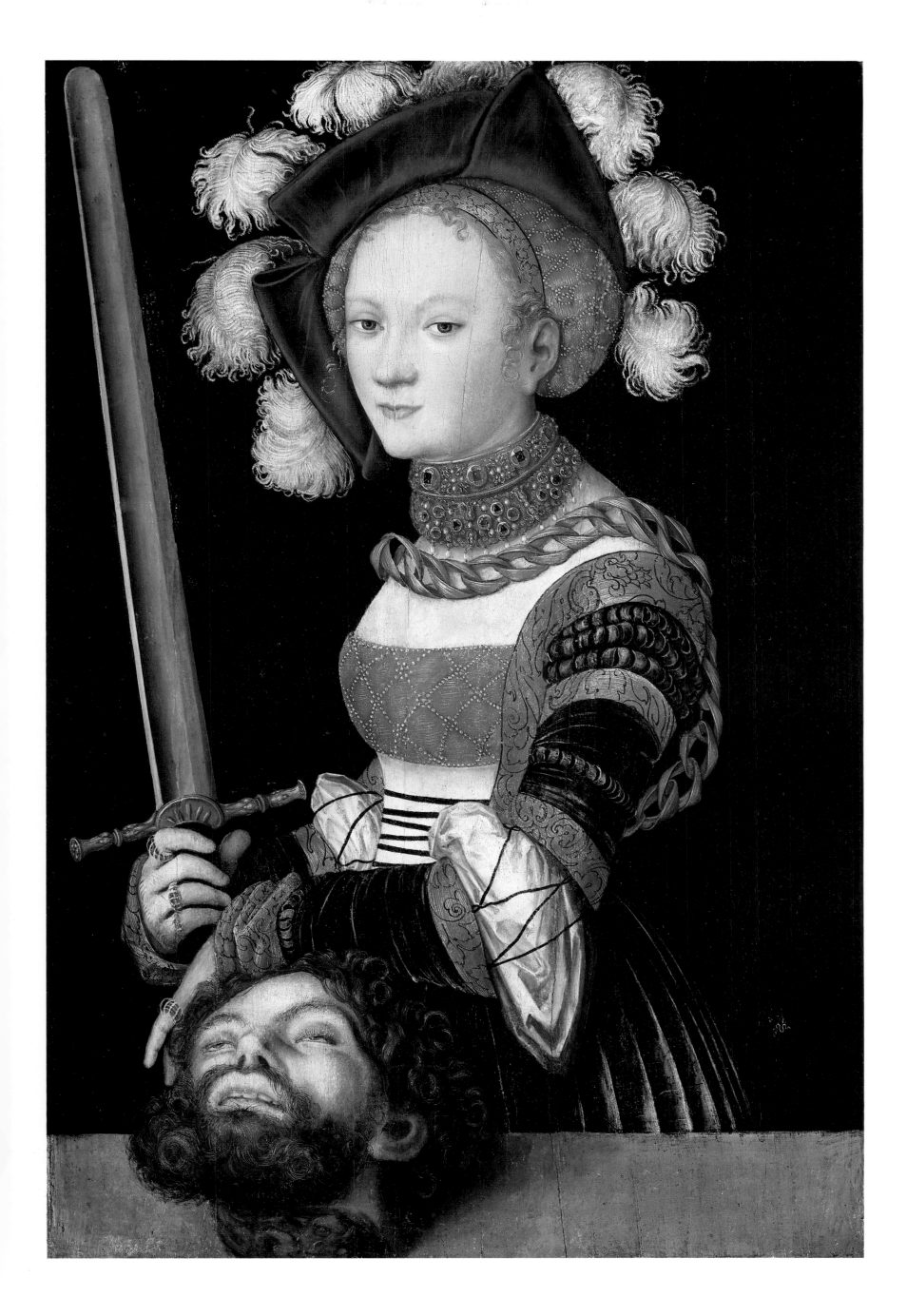

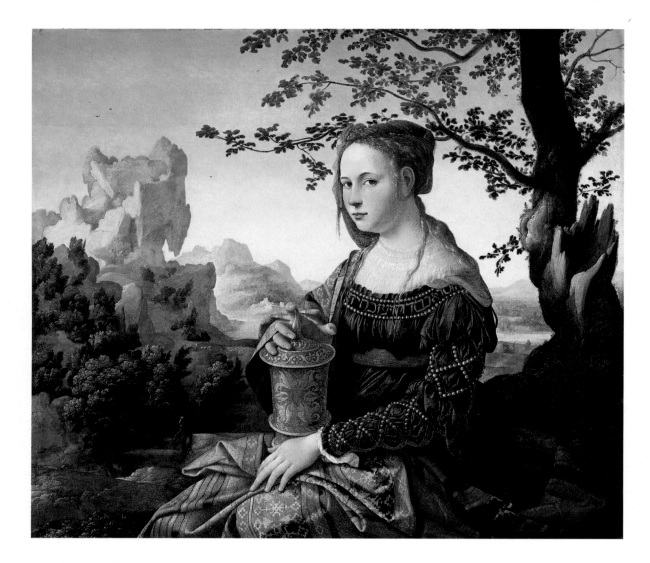

293 JAN VAN SCOREL Saint Mary Magdalen *c.*1529
(Above) One of the most delightful representations of the Magdalen
in Northern painting, it conforms to the oblong format more usually
associated with Venetian figure compositions set in landscape. This
feature, coupled with the saint's lavish clothes, her somewhat
ambiguous expression and the prevailing sense of calm, create an
almost Italianate Classical effect.

294 JOACHIM PATINIR and QUINTEN METSYS Temptation of
Saint Anthony *c.*1520–4
(Below) Both masters are documented as working on this, one of the
most dramatic landscapes of the period. It shows many signs of the
work of Patinir, such as the carefully differentiated foreground, middle
distance and background. Its high, tilted viewpoint and varied scenery
and cloudscape are unique.

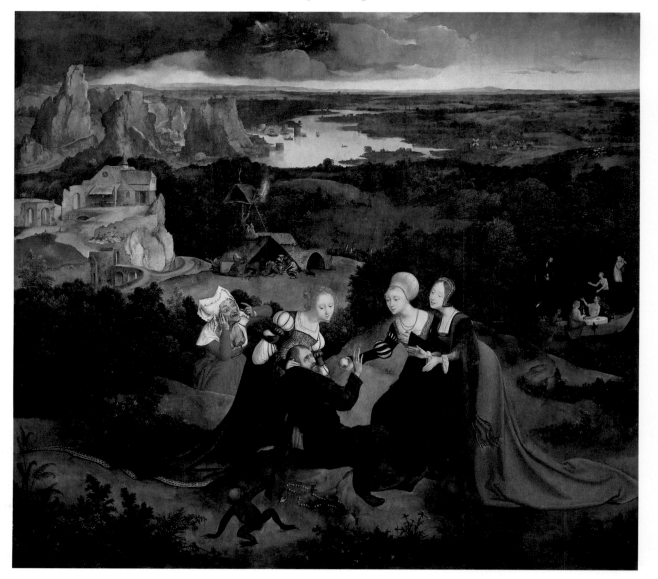

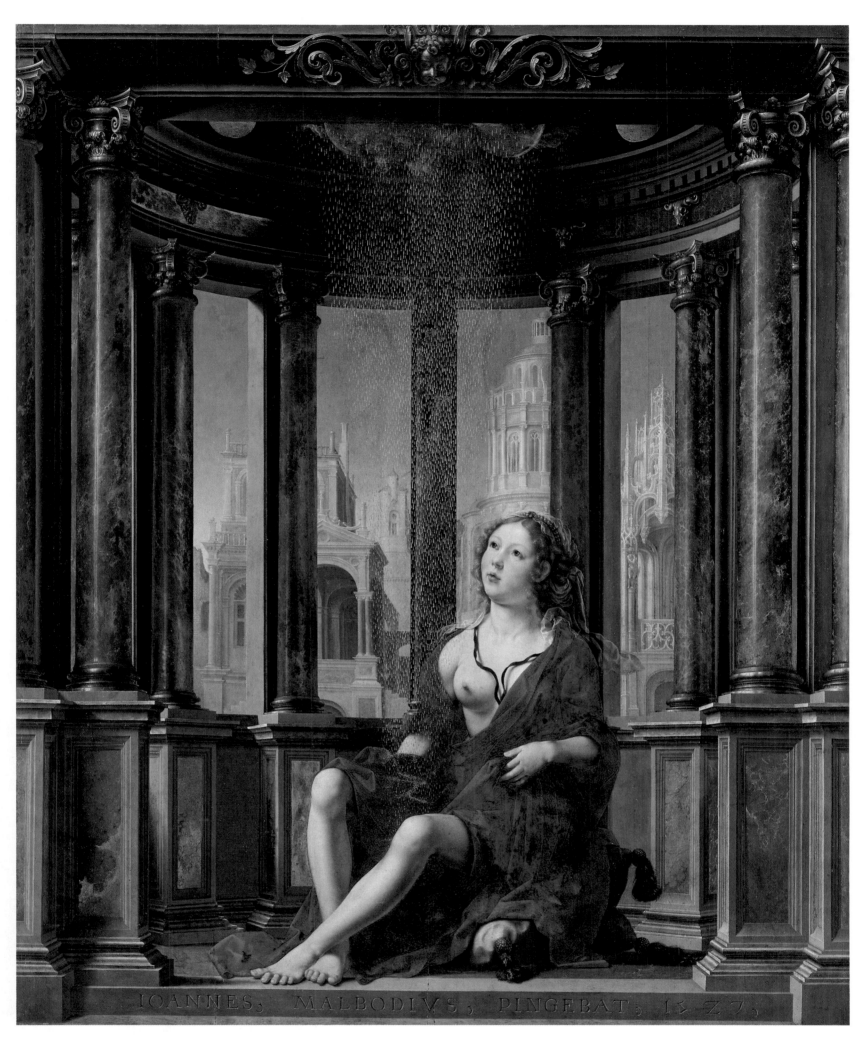

IOANNES, MALBODIVS, PINGEBAT, 15 Z7,

295 JAN GOSSAERT Danaë 1527

Danaë was locked by her father Acrisius of Argos in a 'chamber of brass' to prevent the prophesy of the Delphic Oracle that he would die at the hand of his daughter's son. Zeus, however, penetrated the chamber in a shower of gold, and their offspring was Perseus. Correggio and Titian both painted the theme with a nude reclining Danaë, while Gossaert shows her dressed (if provocatively), probably

as an allegory of Chastity tempted by gold. Set in a glittering marble semicircle of columns, with fantastic background architecture of different periods, Danaë's rich blue robe is offset by the surrounding colours and her marmoreal flesh. Gossaert's late masterpiece, this probably belonged to Emperor Rudolph II in Prague, to whose rarefied taste it would have appealed.

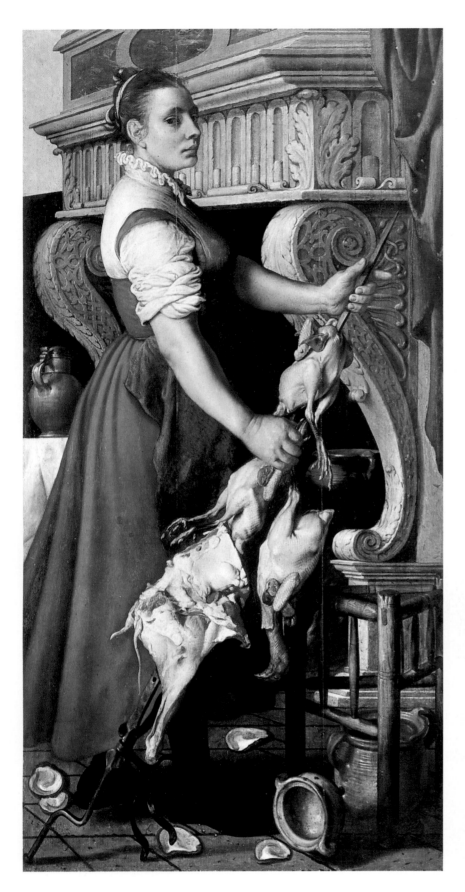

296 PIETER AERTSEN The Cook 1559
(Left) Aertsen's life spans the Mannerist period, and he created genre pictures whose innate dignity harks back to the High Renaissance but which also foretell the vigour of Baroque realism. Many of his genre scenes also contain moral lessons and Christian symbolism in the fashion of the time, but incorporated with great subtlety and often humour. There is rarely any of the grotesque element found in his contemporaries. This remarkable image is one of many such striking scenes ostensibly from everyday life but imbued with a unique drama, created not only by the strong female figure but also by the superb Classical chimneypiece.

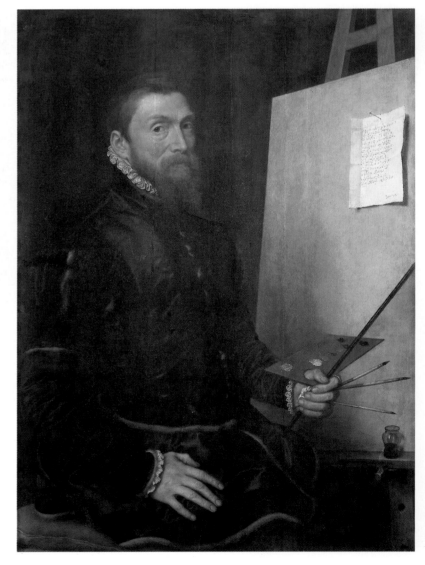

297 ANTHONIS MOR Self Portrait 1558
(Right) Mor met Charles V and his son Philip II in Brussels in 1550, and during the following four years he acted as royal portraitist for Spain in Rome, Lisbon, Madrid and London. He shared his court appointment with Titian and Coello. Mor's was a distinctly Northern manner, with forceful line, striking presence and a love of surface realism in flesh and costume. The austere grandeur of his images attracted the Spanish court. His sitters included Mary Tudor, whom he painted in 1554, for which he was apparently knighted.

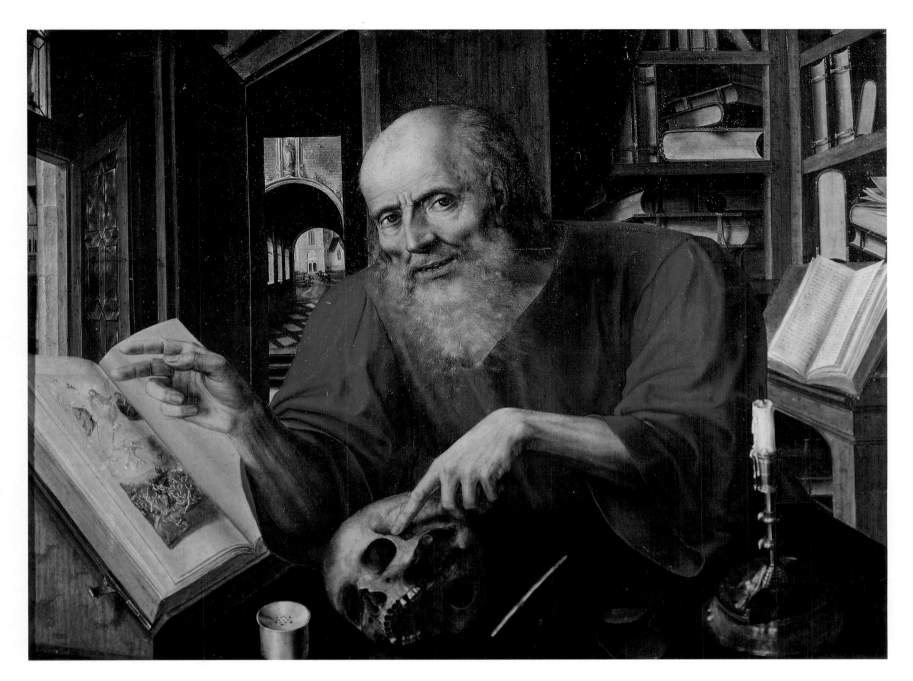

298 MARINUS VAN REYMERSWAELE Saint Jerome 1521
*Reymerswaele remains unique for the quirky angularity of his quasi-
caricatural style, seen here to perfection with his passion for
meticulous genre-like detail and still life.*

*One of the four Fathers of the Church, St Jerome is shown seated
at work in his study. The book open on his reading stand contains an
illumination of the Last Judgement, and the skull and candle on the
desk reinforce the memento mori theme.*

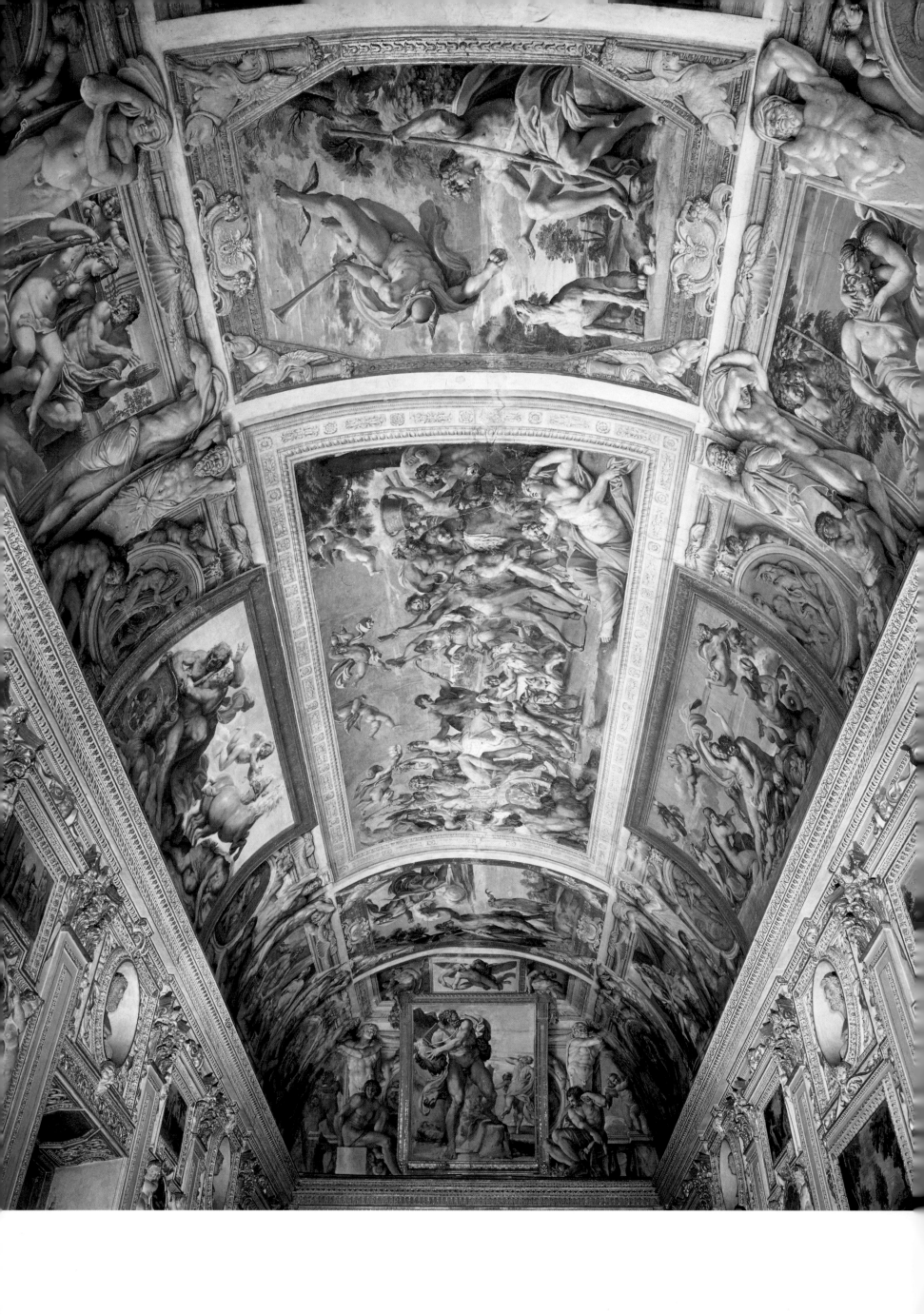

CHAPTER X

The End of Mannerism and the Dawn of the Baroque

The Renaissance began in Italy, and it was there that its demise was first and most clearly visible. Having filtered into the rest of Europe in widely differing forms and created many more variations, often being grafted on to irrepressible local traditions, Renaissance ideas lingered on in the North long after the Baroque had swept through Italy. This was nowhere more true than in Central Europe, while the French and Dutch, having been awakened to Italy's supremacy in art, clung longer to many aspects of Mannerism.

It has been argued that the Renaissance in Italy ended with the deaths of such major painters as Raphael (1520) and Correggio (1534), and that Michelangelo (died 1564) and Titian (died 1576) were survivors from a previous age who maintained Renaissance ideals while all around succumbed to the sophistries of Mannerism. Dürer's death

299 ANNIBALE CARRACCI The Farnese Gallery, Rome
c.1597–1600

Annibale Carracci was commissioned by Cardinal Odoardo Farnese to fresco the barrel vault of the Gallery, probably in honour of the marriage of Ranuccio Farnese and Margherita Aldobrandi in 1600. The central fresco, the Triumph of Bacchus and Ariadne, *is the culmination of the whole scheme, which illustrates the transforming effects of love on the gods (Venus, Mars and others), monsters (such as Polyphemus) and mankind. Inspired partly by the Sistine Ceiling, Annibale combined scenes frescoed to resemble canvases set against the vault surface, fictive bronze roundels, 'sculpted' and naturally painted youths and fighting* putti, *possibly representing Eros and Anteros (in the corners). Annibale's biographer Bellori defined the theme as 'the war and the peace between celestial and earthly Love as instituted by Plato'. By combining countless drawings from the model with Classical and other sources, and a rich palette derived in part from Venetian art, Annibale created the liveliest work of art to bridge the transition from Renaissance ideas to the early Baroque.*

in 1528, however, had no comparable significance, since it was only with his maturity that many true Renaissance concepts became current in Germany. It is therefore erroneous to impose on the period a notion of the Renaissance as representing certain inflexible ideas and clearly definable characteristics. While this approach remains more valid for the Baroque, Rococo and Neo-classical styles, it is difficult to apply convincingly to the Renaissance. Vasari's analysis of what we now call Mannerism, and his insistence on certain artistic 'codes of behaviour' led partly to an idea that Mannerism had little to do with Renaissance principles. But as we have seen, the style grew naturally out of elements present in the earlier Renaissance and had matured long before he set pen to paper on the subject.

In Italy, the transition from the late Renaissance and Mannerism to the Baroque was in many ways more perceptible and self-conscious than elsewhere, and partly resulted from a reaction against Mannerism on the part of both artists and theorists.

Italy led the way into the new style as it had throughout the development of the Renaissance in the fifteenth and sixteenth centuries. Vasari believed that there could be no real development from the art of Michelangelo, which for him and many of his contemporaries meant that the only possible way forward was Michelangelism. In terms of the Mannerist style, he was correct, but what he did not envisage was what actually happened for some later sixteenth-century artists – they reverted to the art of the High Renaissance itself for their inspiration.

Reactions to the demands of the Counter-Reformation and the 'Church Militant' for more comprehensible religious imagery in public settings varied widely in Italy and the other Catholic countries. Contrary to general belief, 'Jesuit art' (a term wrongly used as synonymous with the Baroque) was initially restrained

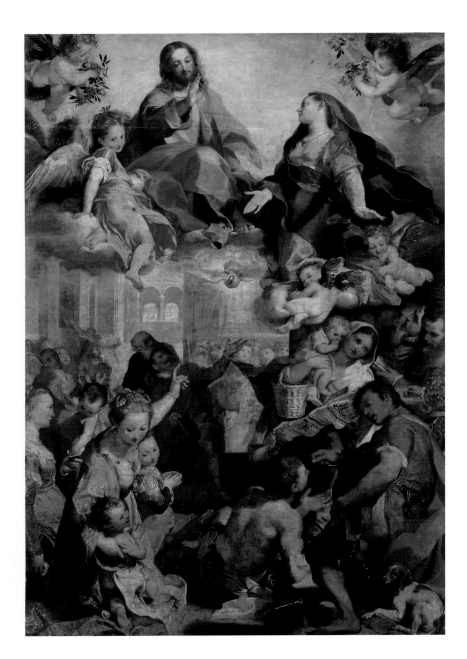

300 FEDERICO BAROCCI Madonna of the People 1576–9
The Urbino painter Barocci combined his study of Correggio with
many drawings from live models, resulting in a highly sensitive
reaction to the artificiality of Mannerism. He also made use of small
oil sketches, bozzetti, *which prepared both artist and patron for the*
appearance of the finished work and became normal practice during
the Baroque period. Barocci's ability to render miraculous events
tangibly real is seen to perfection here, where the heavenly and
earthly figures are barely distinguishable. This links earlier
Renaissance compositional approaches to those of the nascent Baroque
style. It was precisely this accessibility of sacred events to the ordinary
man which Counter-Reformation theoreticians demanded, in order to
counteract the alienating effects of so much Mannerist imagery.

Barocci painted this great altarpiece for the Pia Confraternità dei
Laici della Madonna della Misericordia at Arezzo, together with a
lunette showing God the Father. *A large number of preparatory*
drawings document Barocci's meticulous preparation for the picture.
This practice of his returned to High Renaissance principles, and
ensured the importance of each gesture and expression in his pictures.
Barocci was a brilliant colourist, using colour to heighten his innate
genius for drama. He was among the first painters to perfect the use
of pastel as a medium.

and didactic, in keeping with the Jesuits' rational and
intellectual aproach to Catholic propaganda. The interior
of the Jesuit mother church in Rome, the Gesù
(1568–75), today one of the richest examples of lavish
Baroque decoration, was planned to be bare of ornament
so as to create no distraction to the faithful.

In Florence itself, under Vasari's own nose as it were,
the decoration of the tiny *studiolo* of the Grand Duke
Francis I de' Medici in the Palazzo Vecchio (1570–2),
which Vasari supervised, included paintings by Santi di
Tito (1536–1603) which already encompassed a partial
rejection of the *maniera* extremes dear to Vasari in favour
of a new directness and naturalism. This was rapidly
followed by the early activities in the Medici capital of
Jacopo da Empoli (1551–1640) and Lodovico Cigoli
(1559–1613), now both seen as seminal 'reformers' of
painting there. Cigoli turned for inspiration not to the
masters of the mid-century but to Correggio, Titian and
the Venetians. His precursor in many of his aims was
Federico Barocci (*c*.1535–1612, see plate 300), a great,
influential and seriously underestimated painter who was
somewhat outside the mainstream of Italian art of the
sixteenth century.

They too were the sources for the greatest reforming
painters of the later years of the century, Annibale
Carracci (1560–1609) and Michelangelo Merisi da
Caravaggio (1571–1610). Both Caravaggio and Annibale
are associated with the earliest manifestations of the
Baroque, and indeed from their respective innovations
sprang many features of the new style. However, in their
different ways, they reverted to Renaissance prototypes
forming the strongest link between the first and the last
years of the sixteenth century. Annibale's superb *Pietà with*
Saints (Galleria Nazionale, Parma) painted in 1585 has
rightly been called 'the first Baroque picture', and is a
remarkable reassessment of the century's great masters.

In addition to Correggio and the Venetians, Annibale
also studied Raphael, Andrea del Sarto and the more classical aspects of Michelangelo. Annibale and his brother
Agostino (1557–1602) and cousin Lodovico (1555–1619)
were from Bologna and were influenced by the reforming theories of Cardinal Gabriele Paleotti (1522–97).
They probably read his 1582 treatise on painting, the
Discourse Concerning Sacred and Profane Imagery. It is important to realize that the tone of this and other such manuals
was fundamentally different from the exploratory writings
of the fifteenth century, of Alberti and his contemporaries. Counter-Reformation writing was didactic, not
theoretical, intent on instigating change, not proposing an
example. In Milan, parallels exist with the activities of
Cardinal Federico Borromeo (1564–1631).

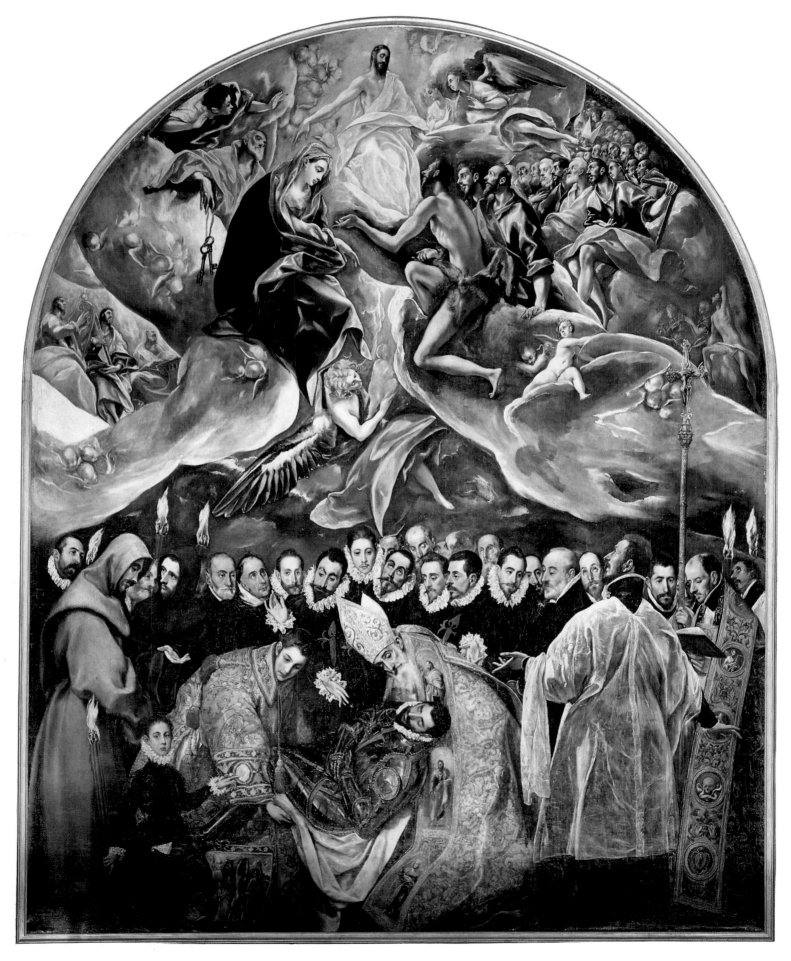

301 EL GRECO Burial of the Count of Orgaz 1586–8

This picture, painted for the parish church of Santo Tomé in Toledo, commemorates a supposed miracle in 1323 when Sts Stephen and Augustine appeared at the funeral of Gonzalo de Ruiz, Lord of Orgaz, and lowered his corpse into the tomb in acknowledgement of his charitable life. Royal recognition of the miracle was granted in 1583. While a priest chants a hymn the body is lowered, and an

angel guides Orgaz's soul to judgement before Christ. The Virgin and St John are shown interceding for him. Typical of the Counter-Reformation is the glorification of the saints in the role of intercessors; El Greco's familiarity with contemporary Catholic iconography is found in all his pictures. He owned and annotated copies of Vasari's Lives *and Vitruvius's* On Architecture.

The Carracci were long known as the 'Eclectics' and it was their conscious borrowing of style, colour, paint handling and even poses and compositions from earlier painters, coupled with a deliberate naturalism, which liberated them and their followers from the constraints of Mannerism. Annibale helped to found the tradition of Classical landscape painting which was to culminate in Claude Lorraine in the seventeenth century. This innovatory interest in nature also led him to experiment with caricature and genre. His earliest works are astonishingly direct in handling and subject matter such as the *Butcher's Shop* (see plate 302), and recall similar initiatives in Netherlandish art by Pieter Aertsen (see plate 296) and his pupil Joachim Bueckelaer (*c*.1535–74), which Annibale almost certainly knew through imports into Italy.

302 Annibale Carracci Butcher's Shop *c*.1582–3
This, one of Annibale's earliest paintings, shows his passion for earthy, carefully observed detail verging on the caricature, which he also practised in drawings. Together with his Crucifixion with Saints *in Bologna's Santa Maria della Carità of the same period, this shows how Annibale applied his close observation of nature with a directness forgotten during the Mannerist period. Most of his early work was in this vein, but was soon supplemented with conscious borrowings from High Renaissance masters which led to the Carracci family's being termed 'Eclectics'.*

In complete contrast to such realism, which remained largely a Northern prerogative, Annibale's greatest legacy was the incomparable vault fresco of the Farnese Gallery (see plate 299). While announcing all the joyful exuberance of the Baroque, it is also a conscious homage to the finest achievements of mature Renaissance painting, and a fitting culmination to the sixteenth century.

Caravaggio, from Lombardy, was Annibale's near-contemporary and shared the ability to escape prevailing conventions. He too studied and understood his Classical predecessors, along with the style of Giorgione and his followers, notably Lotto and Savoldo. From them, he derived his dominant passion for light, whose dramatic and mysterious effects he turned to unique account. Although like Annibale, he went early to Rome, it was not with the aid of august patrons (Annibale's were the Farnese family). After very humble beginnings there, he rose gradually to a position of dubious fame, based on his startlingly novel pictures and his violent nature, which led to his committing a murder in 1606.

Even in his first paintings of fortune-tellers, melancholy, erotic youths and decaying still life (see plate 306), Caravaggio evolved a new pictorial language from his north Italian sources. About 1600 he achieved a maturity in his paintings evident in the Contarelli Chapel (San Luigi dei Francesi, Rome), the Cerasi Chapel in Santa

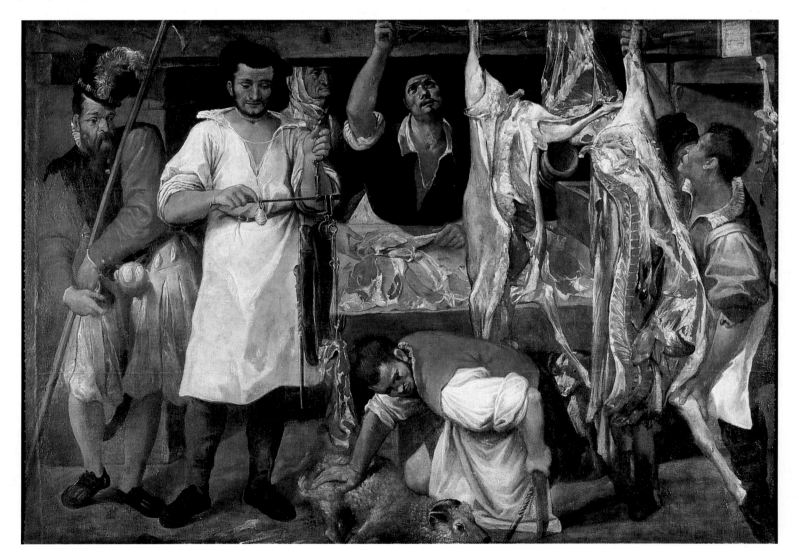

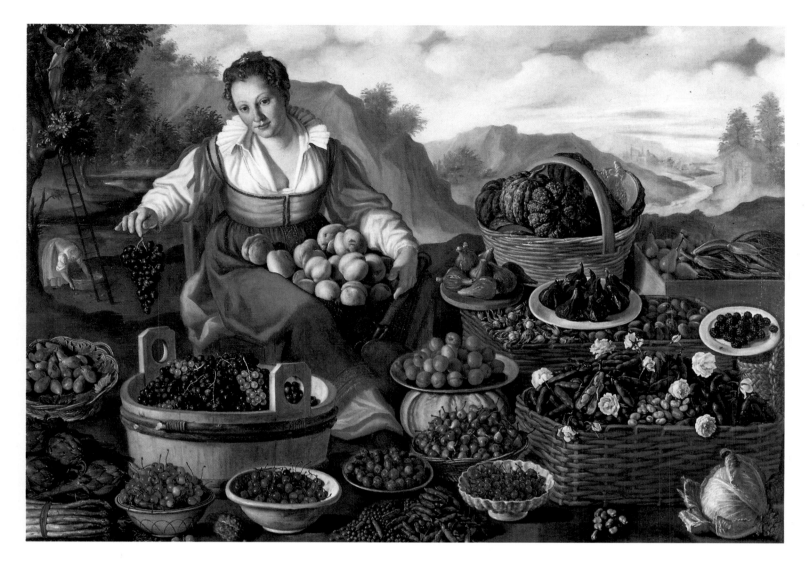

303 VINCENZO CAMPI The Fruit Vendor *c.1580*
Taking as his models such painters as Aertsen and Bueckelaer, Campi appears to have painted his earliest still life scenes with human figures during the later 1570s. The closest contemporary parallels to this are in the Venetian works of the Bassani: their interest in such still life for its own sake is new and totally different from the work of a painter such as Arcimboldo in Milan, who combined natural forms to create fantastic images. Thus was born one of the greatest preoccupations of seventeenth-century Italian art.

Maria del Popolo, and grand altarpieces like the *Death of the Virgin* (Musée du Louvre, Paris). In these, he used forms and figure groups as imposing as Annibale's, although imbued with a brutal physical realism which led to their rejection, particularly by clerics. Like Annibale's compositions of the same years, these recall the magnificent approach to the human figure so typical of High Renaissance altarpieces. Interestingly, this was one feature of Caravaggio's art which found little favour with his imitators. As great innovators, both he and Annibale were fully aware of the importance of the past, perceiving in the pictorial clarity of Raphael and Michelangelo the route to an art which could directly and unselfconsciously touch the soul. But while it was Annibale's influence which was most lasting and far-reaching in Italy itself, Caravaggism extended rapidly throughout Europe,

particularly to Spain and the Netherlands. Caravaggio may be held responsible for the break with late Mannerism in Spain and the Netherlands, and, ultimately, for the emergence of the intensely national manifestations of Baroque ideas perfected in Rembrandt and Velazquez.

With the papacy of Clement VIII, Rome saw a sudden restoration of the position it had held during the High Renaissance, and the visual arts began to enjoy the resurgence which endured throughout the next two centuries. The glorious period of Julius II and Leo X's papacies became idealized during the century's last years. Foreign painters flocked to 'the city of saints', which celebrated them with fervour. Although they had been lured to Rome in increasing numbers from the fifteenth century onwards, the wealth of the great frescoes and altarpieces, ancient architecture and sculpture, made Rome even more attractive to painters during the sixteenth century.

Many Northern painters of the mid to late century lingered or settled there, including the Flemish landscapist Paul Brill (1554–1626), who, with the German Adam Elsheimer (1578–1610) played a vital role in the evolution of landscape painting. These were artists who were building on the achievements of Bruegel, German landscape painters and Flemish Mannerists, but finding direct inspiration from Italian art and nature. Thus, paradoxically, they brought the wheel of Italianate inspiration full circle.

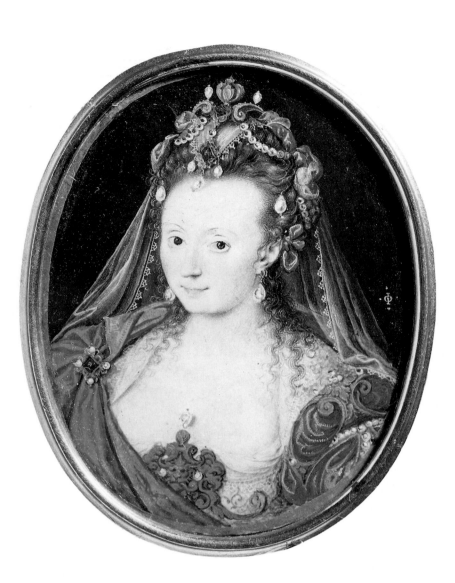

by Spanish critics as 'capricious' and 'extravagant'.

In Venice, the quasi-expressionist aspects of Tintoretto's style were what most attracted El Greco, but he professed to disdain Michelangelo. Two versions of the *Purification of the Temple* (National Gallery of Art, Washington, and Minneapolis Institute of Arts,) together with his portrait of *Giulio Clovio* (see plate 258) typify his style while he was in Italy. Their elongated figures and novel, chilly palette are already fully his own, however, and this was the original manner which he further developed in Toledo. The German Expressionist painters of the early twentieth century claimed him as their precursor.

In Spain, he painted several very grandiose pictures, notably the *Martyrdom of Saint Maurice* of 1580–82 (El Escorial, Madrid). Nearly fifteen feet high, its composition unites High Renaissance monumentality with Mannerist spatial effects, but emulates neither. The *Burial of the Count of Orgaz* of 1586–8 (see plate 301) echoes Renaissance compositional ideas but is somewhat mundane in its figure grouping in spite of its bustling heavenly activity. What most distinguishes it and the best of El Greco's painting is a searing spirituality, which reminds us that his contemporaries were religious writers

304 ISAAC OLIVER A Lady in Masque Costume 1610
Isaac Oliver was the most international miniaturist of his period. He was of French origin, and he had gained direct experience of European art on his visit to Venice in 1596. He is also known to have made direct miniature copies of the Old Masters. This portrait of a woman wearing a costume in Ben Jonson's 'Masque of Queens' reveals an awareness of the international trends implicit in the masque, which traced its origins back to entertainments such as those for the Medici in Florence.

Of all the painters who came to Italy from abroad and gained training and inspiration there, El Greco was perhaps the most notable in this period. His art belongs neither fully to the Mannerist nor to the early Baroque styles, yet he certainly must be classified as a 'Renaissance' artist, particularly in the light of the recent discovery of his extensive writings. He stands as an atypical product of the late Renaissance period, and particularly of extreme Counter-Reformation fervour.

We may think of El Greco (Domenikos Theotocopoulos, 1541–1614) as Spanish – 'El Greco of Toledo' – but he was born in Crete, a key Venetian possession since 1204. By 1568 he was in Venice, moving on to Rome, but he settled permanently in Toledo in 1577. The truth was probably that he had little success in Italy, and both during and after his lifetime he was regarded

305 MAERTEN VAN HEEMSKERCK Self Portrait with the Colosseum, Rome 1553
From 1532 Heemskerck spent four years in Rome, familiarizing himself with the ancient and modern monuments of the city through sketches. Those of the rebuilding of St Peter's are of particular interest. In contrast to the Mannerism of much of his religious work, this picture is surprisingly naturalistic, as if to indicate his admiration for the great Roman ruins. Although it seems to look forward to the souvenir portraits of the Grand Tour two centuries later, its intention is more scholarly, linking the artist directly with the inspiration to be derived from antiquity.

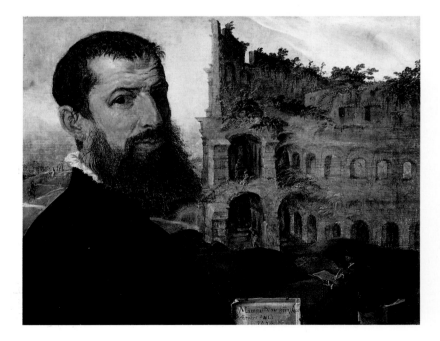

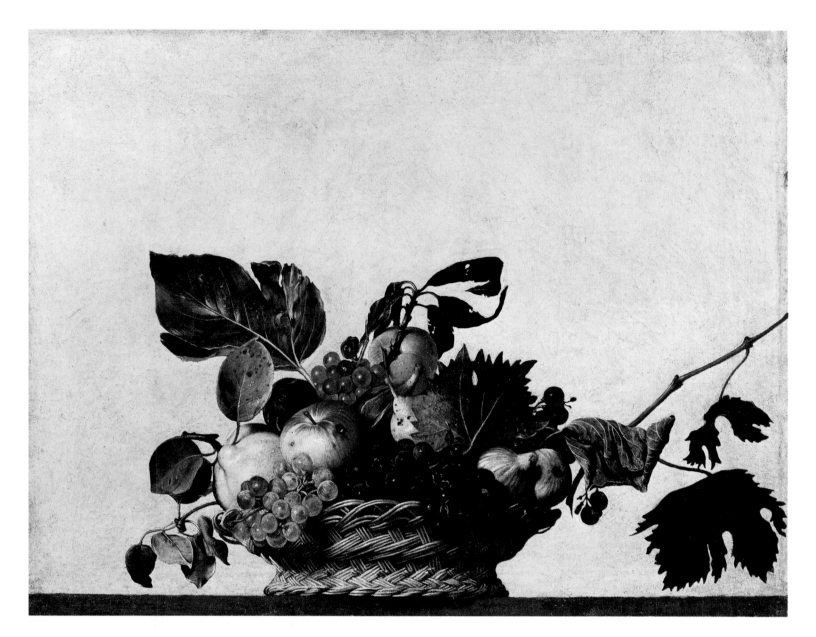

306 CARAVAGGIO Basket of Fruit *c*.1596

This is Caravaggio's only pure still life painting. It shows his ability with texture, light and even illusionism, since the basket overhangs its ledge as if to intrude into our space, much as later Baroque illusionism was to do on a larger scale. The picture encapsulates the sixteenth century's developing interest in still life painting as an expressive means, in which mundane objects could be imbued with symbolic associations: here the rotting fruit may suggest the transitoriness of life.

and visionaries such as St Theresa of Avila and St John of the Cross. As one of El Greco's finest critics, Paul Guinard, writes: '. . . the problems that haunted El Greco fall into a distinctly liberal order of meditation – that of a man of the Renaissance – embracing poetry, science and the purely technical side of the painter's art.'

The preoccupation of the sixteenth-century Northern Renaissance with questions of realism never impinged on El Greco in spite of its effects on Italian painting. Neither did it disturb the dream world of the so-called Elizabethan Renaissance in England, from which Spanish spiritual convulsions were firmly excluded, and where ideas promulgated in the 1540s remained current well into the

sixteenth century (see plate 304). It has even been said that while the Renaissance flowered in English literature, the 'discovery of man' so characteristic of humanist ideals was totally absent from most painting of the period in England, which was dominated by traditional and rigidly imposed court criteria.

Ultimately, the period described under the general heading 'the Renaissance' can only be truly perceived as the sum of its parts. Even then, conclusions are bound to be different according to national and historical perspectives. Given that our perception of the Renaissance is historically comparatively modern, dating from the mid-nineteenth-century studies of Jakob Burckhardt and others, it follows that constant shifts of emphasis are not only inevitable, but to be hoped for. If, however, the term Renaissance may be used to describe the aspects of civilization of the fifteenth and sixteenth centuries which broke the mould of the Middle Ages and established modern man's place in a shrinking universe, then our critical task is simplified. By this standard, it may be accepted that many of the paintings reproduced in this book will vindicate – at least in part – Vasari's understanding of the Renaissance as a continuing progress towards perfection.

Bibliography

EXHIBITION CATALOGUES
(Listed Chronologically)

Baudoin, F. and Boon, K.G. *Dieric Bouts*, Musées royaux des Beaux-Arts, Brussels, 1958.

de Smet, (ed.) *Bruegel, une dynastie de peintres*, Musées royaux des Beaux-Arts, Brussels, 1980.

Chambers, D. and Martineau, J. (eds). *The Splendours of the Gonzaga*, Victoria and Albert Museum, London, 1981.

Ames-Lewis, F. and Wright, J. *Drawing in the Italian Renaissance Workshop*, British Museum, London, 1983.

The Genius of Venice 1500–1600, Royal Academy of Arts, London, 1983.

Spike, J.T. *Italian Still Life Paintings from Three Centuries*, National Academy of Design, New York, 1983.

From Borso to Cesare d'Este. The School of Ferrara 1450–1628, Matthiesen Fine Art, London, 1984.

Andrea del Sarto, Dipinti e Disegni a Firenze, Pitti Palace, Florence, 1986.

Roberts, J. *Drawings by Holbein from the Court of Henry VIII*, Orlando, 1987.

Goddard, S. (ed.) *The World in Miniature: Engravings by the German Little Masters, 1500–1550*, University of Kansas, Lawrence, 1988.

Martineau, J. (ed). *Mantegna*, Royal Academy, London, 1992.

BOOKS
(Listed alphabetically under author)

Alberti, L.B. *On Painting and Sculpture*, ed. G. Grayson, London. 1972.

Ames-Lewis. F. *Drawing in Early Renaissance Italy*, New Haven and London, 1981.

Antal, F. *Florentine Painting and its Social Background*, London, 1947.

Anzelewsky, F. *Dürer. His Art and Life*, trans. H. Grieve, New York, 1981.

Arentino, P. *Selected Letters*, trans. G. Bull, London, 1976.

Baldini, U. and Casazza, O. *The Brancacci Chapel Frescoes*, London, 1992.

Baldwin Brown, G. (ed.) *Vasari on Technique*, New York, 1960.

Bartsch, A. *Le peintre-graveur*, Vienna, 1803–21.

Baxendall, M. *Painting and Experience in Fifteenth-century Italy*, Oxford, 1972.

Benesch, O. *The Art of the Renaissance in Northern Europe*, Cambridge, Mass., 1947, repr. 1967.

Berenson, B. *The Drawings of the Florentine Painters*, 3 vols., Chicago, 1938.

Bergstrom, I. *Dutch Still-Life Painting*, New York, 1956.

Blunt, A. *Art and Architecture in France 1500–1700*, London, 1982.

———— *Artistic Theory in Italy 1450–1600*, Oxford, 1978.

Borsook, E. *The Mural Painters of Tuscany*, Oxford, 1980.

Briganti, G. (ed.) *La Pittura in Italia. Il Cinquecento*, 2 vols., Milan, 1988.

Brown, P.F. *Venetian Narrative Painting in the Age of Carpaccio*, London, 1988.

Burckhardt, J. *The Civilization of the Renaissance in Italy*, trans. S.G.C. Middlemore, London, 1944.

Burke, P. *The Italian Renaissance. Culture and Society in Italy*, London, 1986.

Campbell, L. *Van der Weyden*, New York, 1980.

———— *Renaissance Portraits. European Portrait Painting in the 14th, 15th and 16th Centuries*, New Haven, 1990.

Castiglione, B. *The Book of the Courtier*, trans. G. Bull, London, 1967.

Cellini, B. *Autobiography*, ed. J. Pope-Hennessy, London, 1960.

Cennini, C. *The Craftsman's Handbook: 'Il Libro dell'Arte'*, trans. D.V. Thompson, New Haven, 1993.

Chambers, D. *The Imperial Age of Venice 1380–1580*, London, 1970.

———— *Painters and Artists in the Italian Renaissance*, Columbia, 1971.

Chatelet, A. *Early Dutch Painting. Painting in the Northern Netherlands in the Fifteenth Century*, trans. C. Brown and A. Turner, Seacaucus N.J., 1980.

Christensen, C.C. *Art and the Reformation in Germany*, Athens, 1979.

Clarke, K. *Leonardo da Vinci*, rev. ed. Harmondsworth, 1988.

Cole, B. *Giotto and Florentine Painting*, London, 1969.

———— *The Renaissance Artists at Work: from Pisano to Titian*, New York, 1983.

Cox-Rearick, J. *Dynasty and Destiny. Pontormo, Leo X and the two Cosimos*, Princeton, 1984.

Cuttler, C.D. *Northern Painting from Pucelle to Bruegel*, Fort Worth, 1991.

Davies, M. *Rogier van der Weyden*, London and New York, 1972.

Delaisse, L.M.J. *A Century of Dutch Manuscript Illuminations*, Berkeley, 1968.

Deusch, W. *German Painting of the 16th Century*, London, 1936.

Dhanens, E. *Hubert and Jan van Eyck*, Antwerp, 1980.

Dickens, A.G. *The Counter-Reformation*, London, 1968.

———— (ed.) *The Courts of Europe: Politics, Patronage and Royalty 1400–1800*, London, 1977.

Durrieu, P. *La miniature flamande aux temps de la cour de Bourgogne*, 2nd ed. Paris and Brussels, 1927.

Edgerton, S.Y. *The Renaissance Rediscovery of Linear Perspective*, New York, 1975.

Elton, G.R. *Reformation Europe 1517–1559*, London, 1963.

Ettlinger, L.D. *Antonio and Piero Pollaiuolo*, Oxford, 1978.

Fermor, S. *Piero di Cosimo*, London, 1993.

Fierens, P. and Gevaert, *Histoire de la Peinture Flamande*, Paris, 1927–9.

Freedberg, S.J. *Painting of the High Renaissance in Rome and Florence*, 2 vols., Cambridge, Mass., 1961.

———— *Painting in Italy 1500–1600*, Harmondsworth, 1979.

Friedlander, M.J. *From Van Eyck to Bruegel*, London, 1956.

Friedlander, M.J. and Rosenberg, J. *The Paintings of Lucas Cranach*, rev. ed. Secaucus, N.J. 1978.

Friedlander, W. *Mannerism and Anti-Mannerism in Italian Painting*, New York, 1976.

Ganz, P. *The Paintings of Hans Holbein*, London, 1956.

Geisberg, M. *The German Single-Leaf Woodcut, 1500–1550*, rev. ed. W.L. Strauss, New York, 1974.

Gombrich, E.H. *Symbolic Images: Studies in the Art of the Renaissance*, London, 1985.

Gombrich, E.H. *Norm and Form: Studies in the Art of the Renaissance*, London, 1966.

Gould, C. *The Paintings of Correggio*, London, 1971.

Grossman, F. *Bruegel, the Paintings: Complete Edition*, London, 3rd ed., 1973.

Gudiol, J. *Spanish Painting*, Toledo, 1941.

Hale, J. *The Civilization of Europe in the Renaissance*, London, 1993.

———————— (ed.) *A Concise Encyclopedia of the Renaissance*, London, 1981.

Hall, M. *Color and Meaning. Practice and Theory in Renaissance Painting*, Cambridge, 1992.

Hartt, F. *A History of Italian Renaissance Art*, London, 1994.

Hauser, A. *Mannerism. The Crisis of the Renaissance and the Origin of Modern Art*, London, 1965.

Hibbard, H. *Michelangelo*, London, 1975.

Hind, A.M. *Early Italian Engraving*, 5 vols., London, 1938–48.

Hirst, M. *Sebastiano del Piombo*, Oxford, 1981.

Hope, C. *Titian*, London, 1980.

Huillet d'Istria, M. *La peinture française de la fin du moyen age (1480–1530)*, Paris, 1961.

Joannides, P. *Masaccio and Masolino. A Complete Catalogue*, London, 1993.

Jones, R. and Penny, N. *Raphael*, New Haven, 1983.

Kemp, M. *Leonardo da Vinci, The Marvellous Works of Nature and Man*, London, 1981.

Kristeller, P.O. *Renaissance Thought*, New York, 1965.

Landau, D. and Parshall, P. *The Renaissance Print*, New Haven and London, 1994.

Lassaigne, J. *Spanish Painting I*. Geneva, 1952.

Lassaigne, J. and Delevoy, R. *Flemish Painting II: From Bosch to Rubens*, Geneva, 1958.

Lavalleye, J. *Le Palais Ducal d'Urbin*, Brussels, 1964.

Leonardo da Vinci, *Treatise on Painting*, trans. A.P. McMahon. 2 vols., Princeton, N.J. 1956.

Lightbown, R. *Mantegna*, Oxford, 1986.
———————— *Piero della Francesca*, London, 1992.

———————— *Sandro Botticelli*, 2 vols., Berkeley, Ca., 1978.

Linfert, K. *Bosch*, London, 1989.

van Mander, C. *Dutch and Flemish Painters*, trans. C. van der Wall, New York, 1936.

Marijnissen, R. and Ruysselare, P. *Hieronymus Bosch. The Complete Works*, trans. T. Alkins et al., Antwerp, 1987.

———————— *Bruegel: Tout l'oeuvre peint et dessiné*, Antwerp and Paris, 1988.

Meiss, M. *Painting in Florence and Siena after the Black Death*, New York, 1964.

———————— *The Painter's Choice. Problems in the Interpretation of Renaissance Art*, New York, 1976.

Mellen, P. *Jean Clouet, Complete Edition of the Drawings, Miniatures and Paintings*, London and New York, 1971.

McCorquodale, C. *Bronzino*, London, 1981.

Miegroet, H.J. *Gerard David, his Life, his Oeuvre*, Antwerp, 1989.

Murray, P. and Murray, L. *The Art of the Renaissance*, London, 1963.

von der Osten, G. and Vey, H. *Painting and Sculpture in Germany and the Netherlands: 1500–1600*, Harmondsworth and Baltimore, 1969.

Panofsky, E. *Early Netherlandish Painting: its Origins and Character*, Cambridge, Mass., 1953.

———————— *The Life and Art of Albrecht Dürer*, 4th ed. Princeton, N.J. 1955.

———————— *Studies in Iconology*, Evanston and London, 1962.

———————— *Renaissance and Renascences in Western Art*, 2nd ed., Stockholm, 1965.

Pedretti, C. *Leonardo, a Study in Chronology and Style*, Berkeley, Ca., 1973.

Pevsner, N. *Academies of Art*, London, 1940.

Philip, L.B. *The Ghent Altarpiece and the Art of Jan van Eyck*, Princeton, N.J., 1971.

Pope-Hennessy, J. *The Portrait in the Renaissance*, New York, 1966.

———————— *Fra Angelico*, 2nd ed., 1974.

Popham, A.E. *The Drawings of Leonardo da Vinci*, London, 1956.

Post, C.R. *History of Spanish Painting, II-XII*, Cambridge, Mass., 1930–58.

van Puyvelde, L. *La peinture flamande, au siècle des Van Eyck*, Paris, 1953.

———————— *The Flemish Primitives*, Brussels, 1958.

Ragghianti, C. and dalli Regoli, G.G. *Firenze, 1470–1480, Disegni dal Modello*, Pisa, 1975.

Rosand, D. *Painting in Cinquecento Venice: Titian, Veronese, Tintoretto*, New Haven, 1986.

Rowlands, J. *Holbein. The Paintings of Hans Holbein the Younger, Complete Edition*, Oxford, 1985.

Ruda, J. *Fra Filippo Lippi. Life and Work with a Complete Catalogue*, London, 1993.

Schade, W. *Cranach. A Family of Painters*, trans. H. Sebba, New York, 1980.

Seznec, J. *The Survival of the Pagan Gods*, New York, 1953.

Shearman, J. *Mannerism*, Harmondsworth, 1967.

———————— *Andrea del Sarto*, 2 vols, Oxford, 1965.

Silver, L. *The Paintings of Quinten Massys with catalogue raisonné*, Oxford, 1984.

Smart, A. *The Dawn of Italian Painting 1200–1400*, Oxford, 1978.

Smith, J.C. (ed.) *Nuremberg, a Renaissance City, 1500–1618*, Austin, Tx., 1983.

Snyder, J. *Northern Renaissance Art*, New York, 1985.

Stechow, W. *Bruegel*, London, 1990.

Steer, J.A. *A Concise History of Venetian Painting*, London, 1970.

Steinberg, L. *Michelangelo's Last Paintings*, London 1975.

Strauss, W.L. *The Complete Drawings of Albrecht Dürer*, 6 vols., New York, 1974.

———————— *Albrecht Dürer: Woodcuts and Woodblocks*, New York, 1980.

———————— *The Intaglio Prints of Albrecht Dürer: Engravings, etchings and dry-points*, 3rd ed., New York, 1981.

Strong, R. *The English Renaissance Miniature*, London, 1993.

Summers, D. *Michelangelo and the Language of Art*, Princeton, N.J. 1981.

de Tolnay, C. *Le maître de Flemalle et les frères Van Eyck*, Brussels, 1939.

———————— *Hieronymus Bosch*, rev. ed. Baden-Baden, 1966.

———————— *Michelangelo*, 5 vols., Princeton, 1943–60.

Thompson, C. and Campbell, L. *Hugo van der Goes and the Trinity Panels in Edinburgh*, Edinburgh, 1974.

Vasari, G. *Lives of the Artists*, trans. G. Bull, Harmondsworth, 1987.

Vedman, I. *Maarten van Heemskerck and Dutch Humanism in the Sixteenth Century*, Maarsen, 1977.

Wasserman, J. *Leonardo da Vinci*, London, 1987.

Wethey, H. *Titian*, 3 vols., London, 1969–75.

White, J. *The Birth and Rebirth of Pictorial Space*, London, 1957.

———————— *Art and Architecture in Italy 1250–1400*, London, 1966.

Wilde, J. *Venetian Art from Bellini to Titian*, Oxford, 1974.

Winzinger, F. *Albrecht Altdorfer, Die Gemälde*, Munich and Zurich, 1975.

Wolfflin, H. *Classic Art*, Oxford, 1986.

Zeri, F. (ed.) *La Pittura in Italia. Il Quattrocento*, Milan, 1987.

Picture Acknowledgements

The author and publishers would like to thank the following collectors, galleries and picture archives for permission to reproduce their illustrations:

1 RAPHAEL: *Pope Julius II*, *c.*1512
oil on panel 108 × 80 cm
The National Gallery, London

2 AGNOLO BRONZINO: *Duke Cosimo I de' Medici in Armour*, *c.*1545
panel 86 × 67 cm
Uffizi, Florence (Scala, Florence)

3 JUSTUS VAN UTENS: *The Villa Medici at Poggio a Caiano*, after 1598
tempera on panel 141 × 237 cm
Museo di Firenze com'era (Scala, Florence)

4 UNKNOWN TUSCAN PAINTER: *The Martyrdom of Savonarola*, 1498
tempera on panel 100 × 115 cm
Museo di S. Marco, Florence (Scala, Florence)

5 LEONARDO DA VINCI: *Isabella d'Este*, 1500
black chalk, charcoal & pastel 63 × 46 cm
Musée du Louvre, Paris (Réunion des musées nationaux, Paris)

6 ANTONIO PISANELLO: *Lionello d'Este*, 1441–4
tempera on panel 28 × 19 cm
Galleria dell'Accademia Carrara, Bergamo (Scala, Florence)

7 TITIAN: *Emperor Charles V at Muhlberg*, 1548
Oil on canvas 332 × 279 cm
Prado, Madrid (Arxiu Mas, Madrid)

8 JEAN FOUQUET: *Charles VII*, *c.*1447
panel 86 × 71 cm
Musée du Louvre, Paris (Réunion des musées nationaux, Paris)

9 CHRISTOPH AMBERGER: *Christoph Fugger*, 1540
panel 97.5 × 80 cm
Alte Pinakothek, Munich (Artothek, Munich)

10 LUCAS CRANACH: *Martin Luther as Junker Jorg*, after 1521
woodcut 28.3 × 20.4 cm
British Museum, London

11 AGNOLO BRONZINO: *Eleonora of Toledo*, *c.*1545
oil on panel 115 × 95 cm
Uffizi, Florence (Scala, Florence)

12 RAPHAEL: *Baldassare Castiglione*, 1514-15
oil on canvas 82 × 66 cm
Musée du Louvre, Paris (Réunion des musées nationaux, Paris)

13 SEBASTIANO DEL PIOMBO: *Christopher Columbus*, 1519
oil on canvas 106.7 × 88.3 cm
The Metropolitan Museum of Art, New York, gift of J. Pierpont Morgan, 1900(00.18.2)

14 HANS HOLBEIN THE YOUNGER: *Erasmus of Rotterdam*, 1523
panel 42 × 32 cm
Musée du Louvre, Paris (Réunion des musées nationaux, Paris)

15 PEDRO BERRUGUETE: *Federico da Montefeltro and his Son Guidobaldo*, undated
oil on canvas 134.5 × 75.5 cm
Palazzo Ducale, Urbino (Scala, Florence)

16 JEAN CLOUET: *Francis I*, undated
panel 96 × 74 cm
Musée du Louvre, Paris (Réunion des musées nationaux, Paris)

17 ATTRIBUTED TO ROBERT PEAKE: *Eliza Triumphans*, *c.*1600
oil on canvas 132 × 190.5 cm
Private Collection

18 HENDRICK GOLTZIUS: *Sine Cerere et Libero friget Venus (Without Ceres and Bacchus Venus is A-Chill)* 1599–1602
oil on linen 106.5 × 80 cm
Philadelphia Museum of Art: Purchased: The Mr. and Mrs. Walter H. Annenberg Fund for Major Acquisitions, The Henry P. McIlhenny fund in memory of Frances P. McIlhenny bequest (by exchange) of Mr. and Mrs. Herbert C. Morris, and gift (by exchange) of Frank and Alice Osborn

19 ALBRECHT DÜRER: *Self Portrait as a Journeyman*, 1491-2
pen and ink on paper 20.4 × 20.8 cm
Universitätsbibliothek Erlangen-Nürnberg

20 FRANÇOIS CLOUET: *Francis II c.*1553
black, red and white chalk on off-white paper 30.9 × 21.5 cm
The Harvard University Art Museums. Loan from the Houghton Library (2.1968)

21 LEONARDO DA VINCI: *The Anatomy of a Shoulder*, *c.*1510
pen and ink with wash over black chalk 28.9 × 19.9 cm
Royal Collection © 1994 Her Majesty the Queen

22 AGOSTINO VENEZIANO: *Baccio Bandinelli's Studio c.*1531
copper plate line engraving 27 × 29.5 cm
The Courtald Institute Galleries, London, Witt Print Collection

23 FOLLOWER OF ANTONELLO DA MESSINA: *Five compositional studies*, undated
pen and brown ink on paper tinted pink 24.5 × 12.3 cm
British Museum, London

24 WORKSHOP OF MASO FINIGUERRA: *Seated Youth Drawing*, *c.*1450?
pen, ink and watercolour on paper 19.2 × 11.4 cm
British Museum, London

25 CIMA DA CONEGLIANO: *Virgin and Child with Saint Andrew and Saint Peter*, 1490s
panel 55.6 × 47.2 cm
The National Gallery of Scotland, Edinburgh

26 ANDREA DEL VERROCCHIO: *Head of a Woman*, undated
black chalk, heightened with white, on paper pricked for transfer 40.8 × 32.7 cm
The Governing Body, Christ Church, Oxford

27 HANS HOLBEIN THE YOUNGER: *Sir Thomas More, his Father and his Household*, 1527-8
pen and ink on paper 38.7 × 52.4 cm
Kunstmuseum, Basle (Colorphoto Hans Hinz, Allschwil)

28 GIOVANNI DA MILANO: *Detail from the Rinuccini Chapel*, *c.*1365
fresco
Santa Croce, Florence (Scala, Florence)

29 LUCA SIGNORELLI: *The Damned in Hell*, detail, 1499-1504
fresco
Duomo, Orvieto (Scala, Florence)

30 LUCA SIGNORELLI: *Three Horsemen*, undated
black chalk on paper pricked for transfer 34.2 × 27.2 cm
British Museum, London

31 STYLE OF FRANCESCO DI GIORGIO MARTINI: *Cassone with Solomon and the Queen of Sheba*, *c.* 1470–80
wood decorated with gilt and gesso H.99 W.190. D.66 cm
The Trustees of the Victoria & Albert Museum, London

32 MICHELANGELO: *Head of Cleopatra*, *c.*1533
lead pencil on paper 23.4 × 18.2 cm
Uffizi, Florence, Gabinetto dei Disegni e delle Stampe (Scala, Florence)

33 JAN VAN EYCK: *Cardinal Niccolò Albergati*, *c.*1431
silverpoint with white chalk on paper 21.4 × 18 cm
Staatliche Kunstsammlungen, Dresden

34 JAN VAN EYCK: *Saint Barbara*, 1437
oil on panel 32.2 × 18.6 cm
Musée des Beaux-Arts, Antwerp (Giraudon, Paris)

35 ALBRECHT DÜRER: *View in the Val d'Arco*, 1495
watercolour, pen and ink and gouache 22.3 × 22.2 cm
Musée du Louvre, Paris (Réunion des musées nationaux, Paris)

36 PAOLO VERONESE: *Battle of Lepanto*, 1572-81
oil over grey chalk on paper coloured red, squared in grey chalk 30 × 40.7 cm
British Mueum, London

37 GIORGIO VASARI: *Page from the 'Libro de' Disegni'*, undated
metalpoint heightened with white bodycolour 56.2 × 12.3 cm overall
Private Collection (Christie's Images, London)

38 ANDREA DEL CASTAGNO: *Sinopia for 'The Resurrection,'* detail, *c.*1445
chalk on paper
S. Apollonia, Florence (Scala, Florence)

39 ANDREA DEL CASTAGNO: *The Resurrection*, 1445-50
fresco
S. Apollonia, Florence (Scala, Florence)

40 MICHELANGELO: *The Deluge*, 1508
fresco
Sistine Chapel, The Vatican (Scala, Florence)

41 LEONARDO DA VINCI: *Last Supper*, 1495-7
oil on plaster
S. Maria delle Grazie, Milan (Scala, Florence)

42 ROGIER VAN DER WEYDEN: *The Saint Columba Altarpiece*, *c.* 1435
middle panel 138 × 153 cm
Bayerische Staatsgemaldesammlungen, Alte Pinakothek, Munich

43 ALBRECHT DÜRER: *Knight, Death and the Devil*, 1513-14
copperplate engraving 24.4 × 18.9 cm
British Museum, London

44 PIETRO CAVALLINI: *Angels*, before 1308
fresco
S. Cecilia in Trastevere, Rome (Scala, Florence)

45 GIOTTO: *The Stigmatization of St. Francis*, *c.*1325
fresco
Bardi Chapel, S. Croce, Florence (Scala, Florence)

46 CIMABUE: *Crucifixion* (before flood damage), undated
panel 448 × 390 cm
S. Croce, Florence (Scala, Florence)

47 GIOTTO: *Enrico Scrovegni Offering his Chapel to the Virgin*, 1306
fresco
Arena Chapel, Padua (Scala, Florence)

48 General view of the upper church, *c.*1290-1307
S. Francesco, Assisi (Scala, Florence)

49 GIOTTO: *The Stefaneschi Altarpiece, c.*1300?
tempera on panel front 220 × 245 cm
Pinacoteca, The Vatican (Scala, Florence)

50 TADDEO GADDI: *The Life of the Virgin,* 1332-8
fresco
Baroncelli Chapel, S. Croce, Florence (Scala,
Florence)

51 DUCCIO: *The Rucellai Madonna, c.* 1285
panel 450 × 290 cm
Uffizi, Florence (Scala, Florence)

52 DUCCIO: *Christ's Entry into Jerusalem* (detail of
the *Maestà*) 1308-11
panel 102 × 53.5 cm
Museo dell'Opera Metropolitana, Siena (Scala,
Florence)

53 SIMONE MARTINI: *The Apotheosis of Virgil,* 1340
vellum 29.5 × 20 cm
Pinacoteca Ambrosiana, Milan (Scala, Florence)

54 AMBROGIO LORENZETTI: *Allegories of Good and
Bad Government,* 1338-9
fresco
Sala della Pace, Palazzo Pubblico, Siena (Scala,
Florence)

55 AMBROGIO LORENZETTI: *Presentation in the
Temple,* 1342
panel 257 × 168 cm
Uffizi, Florence (The Bridgeman Art Library,
London)

56 GIOTTO: *Interior of the Arena Chapel, Padua,* 1303-6
fresco
(Scala, Florence)

57 GIOTTO: *The Ognissanti Madonna, c.*1305-10
panel 325 × 204 cm
Uffizi, Florence (Scala, Florence)

58 CIMABUE: *Santa Trinità Madonna,* early 1280s
panel 353 × 223.5 cm
Uffizi, Florence (Scala, Florence)

59 DUCCIO: *Madonna and Child with Saints and
Angels,* 1308-11
front panel 213.5 × 396 cm
Museo dell'Opera Metropolitana, Siena (Scala,
Florence)

60 BERNARDO DADDI: *Madonna and Child,* 1346-7
panel 250 × 180 cm
Orsanmichele, Florence (Scala, Florence)

61 SIMONE MARTINI: *Maestà,* 1317
fresco
Palazzo Pubblico, Siena (Scala, Florence)

62 PIETRO LORENZETTI: *Birth of the Virgin,* 1342
panel 186.5 × 181.5 cm
Museo dell'Opera Metropolitana, Siena (Scala,
Florence)

63 MASTER OF THE TRIUMPH OF DEATH: *Music-
making in a Garden,* pre-1348
fresco
Camposanto, Pisa (Scala, Florence)

64 AMBROGIO LORENZETTI: *The Effects of Good
Government in the City,* 1338-9
fresco
Palazzo Pubblico, Siena (The Bridgeman Art
Library, London)

65 ALTICHIERO: *The Crucifixion, c.*1379
fresco
S. Antonio, Padua (Scala, Florence)

66 ANDREA BONAIUTI: *Triumph of the Church,* 1365-7
fresco
Spanish Chapel, S. Maria Novella, Florence
(Scala, Florence)

67 PAOLO VENEZIANO: *St. Mark's Body Carried to
Venice,* undated
panel 58 × 42 cm
Museo S. Marco, Venice (Scala, Florence)

68 PINTURICCHIO: *Scenes from the Life of Pio II,*
detail of *Aeneas Silvius Piccolomini,* 1502-9
fresco
Piccolomini Library, Duomo, Siena (Scala,
Florence)

69 GENTILE DA FABRIANO: *Adoration of the Magi,*
1423
panel 300 × 282 cm
Uffizi, Florence (Scala, Florence)

70 MASACCIO, MASOLINO AND FILIPPINO LIPPI: *The
Brancacci Chapel* general view, 1425-7 and 1481-83
fresco
Church of the Carmine, Florence (Scala,
Florence)

71 MASOLINO DA PANICALE: *Feast of Herod,* 1435
fresco
Baptistry, Castiglione Olona (Scala, Florence)

72 FRA ANGELICO: *The San Marco Altarpiece,*
1438-40
panel 220 × 227 cm
Museo di S. Marco, Florence (Scala, Florence)

73 FILIPPINO LIPPO: *The Virgin Appearing to Saint
Bernardo, c.* 1482-6
panel 208.5 × 195.5 cm
Badia, Florence (Scala, Florence)

74 PAOLO UCCELLO: *The Flood and the Recession of
the Waters,* 1446-8
fresco
S. Maria Novella, Florence (The Bridgeman Art
Library, London)

75 PAOLO UCCELLO: *Cenotaph to Sir John
Hawkwood,* 1436
fresco transferred to canvas 820 × 515 cm
Duomo, Florence (Scala, Florence)

76 ANDREA DEL CASTAGNO: *Last Supper,* 1447-50
fresco
S. Apollonia, Florence (Scala, Florence)

77 ANTONIO DEL POLLAIUOLO: *Battle of the Ten
Nudes,* after 1483?
engraving 40.4 × 59 cm
British Museum, London

78 SANDRO BOTTICELLI: *Adoration of the Magi,
c.* 1475
panel 111 × 134 cm
Uffizi, Florence (Scala, Florence)

79 SANDRO BOTTICELLI: *Lamentation of Christ,*
after 1490
tempera on panel 140 × 207 cm
Alte Pinakothek, Munich (Artothek, Munich)

80 VITTORE CARPACCIO: *The Arrival of the
Ambassadors,* 1490-4
oil on canvas 275 × 589 cm
Accademia, Venice (Scala, Florence)

81 PIERO DI COSIMO: *Cleopatra* (so-called *Simonetta
Vespucci*)
c. 1485-90
panel 57 × 42 cm
Musée Condé, Chantilly (Giraudon, Paris)

82 LEONARDO DA VINCI: *Adoration of the Magi,*
1481-2
panel 244 × 246 cm
Uffizi, Florence (The Bridgeman Art Library,
London)

83 ANDREA DEL VERROCCHIO: *Baptism of Christ,*
1472-5
panel 176.5 × 151 cm
Uffizi, Florence (Scala, Florence)

84 BARTOLOMMEO DELLA GATTA: *Stigmatization of
Saint Francis,* 1486
panel 186 × 172 cm
Pinacoteca, Castelfiorentino (Electa, Milan)

85 CIRCLE OF PIERO DELLA FRANCESCA: *View of an
Ideal City, c.* 1470
panel 60 × 200 cm
Palazzo Ducale, Urbino (Scala, Florence)

86 PIERO DELLA FRANCESCA: *Dream of Constantine,*
1455
fresco
S. Francesco, Arezzo (Scala, Florence)

87 ANDREA MANTEGNA: *Pallas Expelling the Vices
from the Garden of Virtue, c.* 1499-1500
oil on canvas 160 × 192 cm
Musée du Louvre, Paris (Giraudon/Bridgeman
Art Library, London)

88 ANDREA MANTEGNA: *Men of Sorrows with Two
Angels, c.* 1500
oil on canvas 70 × 49.5 cm
Statens Museum for Kunst, Copenhagen

89 ANTONELLO DA MESSINA: *Virgin Annunciate,*
1474
panel 45 × 34 cm
Galleria Nazionale della Sicilia, Palermo (Scala,
Florence)

90 GIOVANNI BELLINI: *The San Giobbe Altarpiece,*
before 1490
panel 471 × 258 cm
Accademia, Venice (Scala, Florence)

91 COSMÈ TURA: *Virgin and Child Enthroned, c.* 1480
panel 239 × 101 cm
The National Gallery, London

92 ANTONIO PISANELLO: *Saint George and the
Princess,* 1437-8
fresco
S. Anastasia, Verona (Scala, Florence)

93 MASACCIO: *Trinity,* 1425-8
fresco
S. Maria Novella, Florence (Scala, Florence)

94 FRA ANGELICO: *Saint Dominic Adoring the
Crucifix,* after 1442
fresco
Museo di S. Marco, Florence (Scala, Florence)

95 FRA ANGELICO: *Annunciation, c.* 1450
fresco
Museo di S. Marco, Florence (Scala, Florence)

96 LUCA SIGNORELLI: *Calling of the Elect,* 1500-4
fresco
Duomo, Orvieto (Scala, Florence)

97 FILIPPO LIPPI: *Dance of Salomé (Herod's Feast),*
1452-66
fresco
Duomo, Prato (Scala, Florence)

98 DOMENICO GHIRLANDAIO: *The Birth of Saint John
the Baptist,* 1485-90
fresco
S. Maria Novella, Florence (Scala, Florence)

99 PIERO DELLA FRANCESCA: *The Brera Altarpiece,*
1472-4
tempera on panel 248 × 170 cm
Pinacoteca di Brera, Milan (Scala, Florence)

100 PIERO DELLA FRANCESCA: *Flagellation of Christ,*
1455
tempera on panel 59 × 81.5 cm
Palazzo Ducale, Urbino (Scala, Florence)

101 & 102 PIERO DELLA FRANCESCA: *Federico II da
Montefeltro and Battista Sforza,* 1465
tempera on panel each 47 × 33 cm
Uffizi, Florence (Scala, Florence)

103 DOMENICO GHIRLANDAIO: *An Old Man with a Young Boy*, c. 1480
panel 63 × 46 cm
Musée du Louvre, Paris (The Bridgeman Art Library, London)

104 ANDREA MANTEGNA: *The Ceiling Oculus of the Camera degli Sposi*, 1465-73
fresco
Palazzo Ducale, Mantua (Scala, Florence)

105 ANDREA MANTEGNA: *The Gonzaga Court*, 1465-74
fresco
Palazzo Ducale, Mantua (Scala, Florence)

106 GIOVANNI BELLINI: *Doge Leonardo Loredan*, c. 1501
panel 61.6 × 45.1 cm
The National Gallery, London

107 GIOVANNI BELLINI: *Giovanni Emo*, c.1475-80
tempera and oil on panel 48.9 × 32.2 cm
National Gallery of Art, Washington D.C., Samuel H. Kress Collection (1939.1.224)

108 ANTONELLO DA MESSINA: *Saint Jerome in his Study*, 1474
panel 45.7 × 36.2 cm
The National Gallery, London

109 VITTORE CARPACCIO: *Hunting on the Lagoon*, c. 1490-6
oil on panel 75.4 × 63.8 cm
Collection of the J. Paul Getty Museum, Malibu, California

110 VITTORE CARPACCIO: *Two Women seated on a Balcony*, c. 1490-6
oil on panel 94 × 64 cm
Civico Museo Correr, Venice (The Bridgeman Art Library, London)

111 VITTORE CARPACCIO: *Young Knight in a Landscape*, 1510
oil on canvas 218.5 × 151.5 cm
Museo Thyssen Bornemisza, Madrid

112 PIERO DI COSIMO: *The Building of a Palace*, c. 1515-20
oil on panel 82.6 × 196.9 cm
The John and Mable Ringling Museum of Art, Sarasota

113 PIETRO PERUGINO: *Christ Handing the Keys to Saint Peter*, 1482
fresco
Sistine Chapel, The Vatican (Scala, Florence)

114 BENOZZO GOZZOLI: *Journey of the Magi*, 1459
fresco
Palazzo Medici Riccardi, Florence (Scala, Florence)

115 SANDRO BOTTICELLI: *Primavera*, c.1478
panel 203 × 315 cm
Uffizi, Florence (Scala, Florence)

116 SANDRO BOTTICELLI: *Birth of Venus*, 1484-6
oil on canvas 175 × 279.5 cm
Uffizi, Florence (The Bridgeman Art Library, London)

117 SANDRO BOTTICELLI: *Minerva and the Centaur*, c. 1480
oil on canvas 207 × 148 cm
Uffizi, Florence (The Bridgeman Art Library, London)

118 LEONARDO DA VINCI: *A Lady with an Ermine*, 1485-90
tempera on panel 55 × 40.4 cm
Czartorysky Museum, Cracow (Scala, Florence)

119 LORENZO COSTA: *A Concert*, 1487-1500
panel 95.3 × 75.6 cm
The National Gallery, London

120 MELOZZO DA FORLÌ: *Musical Angel*, 1478-80
fresco
Pinacoteca, The Vatican (Scala, Florence)

121 GENTILE BELLINI: *A Procession in Piazza San Marco*, 1496
oil on canvas 367 × 745 cm
Accademia, Venice (Scala, Florence)

122 CARLO CRIVELLI: *The Annunciation with Saint Emidius*, 1486
panel transferred to canvas 207 × 146.7 cm
The National Gallery, London

123 JAN VAN EYCK: *Man in a Turban*, 1433
panel 25.7 × 19 cm
The National Gallery, London

124 THE MASTER OF FLÉMALLE: *Saint Veronica*, c.1430-34
panel 151.5 × 61 cm
Stadelsches Kunstinstitut, Frankfurt (Artothek, Munich)

125 JAN VAN EYCK: *The Madonna in the Church*, c.1425
panel 31 × 14 cm
Staatliche Gemäldegalerie, Berlin (Artothek, Munich)

126 JAN VAN EYCK: *Madonna and Child with Canon van der Paele*, 1434-6
oil on panel 141 × 176.5 cm
Groeningemuseum, Bruges (The Bridgeman Art Library, London)

127 PETRUS CHRISTUS: *Portrait of a Young Woman*, c. 1460-73
panel 29 × 22.5 cm
Gemäldegalerie Staatliche Museen Preussischer Kulturbesitz, Berlin (Jorg P. Anders, Berlin)

128 ROGIER VAN DER WEYDEN: *Portrait of a Lady*, c. 1450-60
panel 36.2 × 27.6 cm
The National Gallery, London

129 ROGIER VAN DER WEYDEN: *Last Judgement Altarpiece*, c. 1444-8
panel 215 × 110 cm
Hôtel-Dieu, Beaune (Giraudon, Paris)

130 DIERIC BOUTS: *Deposition Altarpiece*, c.1450-55
oil on panel central panel 191 × 145 cm
Capilla Real, Granada (Arxiu Mas, Madrid)

131 HUGO VAN DER GOES: *Adam and Eve (The Fall of Man)*, c. 1468-70
panel 33.8 × 23 cm
Kunsthistorisches Museum, Vienna

132 GEERTGEN TOT SINT JANS: *The Baptist in the Wilderness*, c. 1490-95
panel 42 × 28 cm
National Galerie, Berlin (Artothek, Munich)

133 HUGO VAN DER GOES: *The Trinity Altarpiece, King James III*, c.1478-9
panel 78 × 38 cm
The Royal Collection © 1994 Her Majesty the Queen. On loan to the National Gallery of Scotland, Edinburgh

134 HUGO VAN DER GOES: *The Trinity Altarpiece, Queen Margaret*, c. 1478-9
panel 78 × 38 cm
The Royal Collection © 1994 Her Majesty the Queen. On loan to the National Gallery of Scotland, Edinburgh

135 HANS MEMLINC: *Saint Christopher Altarpiece*, 1484
panel 123 × 156 cm
Groeningemuseum, Bruges (The Bridgeman Art Library, London)

136 GERARD DAVID: *Christ Nailed to the Cross*, c.1480-85
panel 48.3 × 94 cm
The National Gallery, London

137 HIERONYMUS BOSCH: *Christ Carrying the Cross*, c.1501-2
oil on panel 74 × 81 cm
Museum voor Schone Kunsten, Ghent (Scala, Florence)

138 HIERONYMUS BOSCH: *Garden of Earthly Delights*, c.1505-10
panel 220 × 389 cm
Prado, Madrid (Arxiu Mas, Madrid)

139 MARTIN SCHONGAUER: *Christ Carrying the Cross*, c. 1480
engraving 28.4 × 43.4 cm
Christie's, New York

140 ROGIER VAN DER WEYDEN: *Annunciation*, c.1433
panel 86 × 93 cm
Musée du Louvre, Paris (Réunion des musées nationaux, Paris)

141 ROGIER VAN DER WEYDEN: *Deposition*, c.1438
panel 220 × 262 cm
Prado, Madrid (Arxiu Mas, Madrid)

142 JAN VAN EYCK: *Madonna of the Chancellor Nicolas Rolin*, c. 1434
central panel 66 × 62 cm
Musée du Louvre, Paris (Giraudon-Bridgeman Art Library, London)

143 ROGIER VAN DER WEYDEN: *Saint Luke Drawing the Virgin*, c.1435-7
oil on tempera on panel 137.5 × 110.8 cm
Museum of Fine Arts, Boston. Gift of Mr. and Mrs. Henry Lee Higginson

144 JAN VAN EYCK: *The Marriage of Giovanni Arnolfini and Giovanna Cenami*, 1434
panel 81.8 × 59.7 cm
The National Gallery, London

145 PETRUS CHRISTUS: *Saint Eligius and the Lovers*, 1449
oil on panel 99 × 85 cm
The Metropolitan Museum of Art, New York, Robert Lehman Collection 1975 (1975.1.10)

146 HIERONYMUS BOSCH: *Haywain*, 1495-1500
oil on panel 135 × 200 cm
Prado, Madrid (Arxiu Mas)

147 HIERONYMUS BOSCH: *Death and the Miser*, c. 1485-90
oil on panel 93 × 31 cm
National Gallery of Art, Washington D.C. Samuel H. Kress Collection

148 DIERIC BOUTS: *Last Supper Altarpiece*, 1464-7
central panel 180 × 151 cm
St. Peter's, Louvain (The Bridgeman Art Library, London)

149 JAN VAN EYCK: *The Ghent Altarpiece*, completed 1432
exterior panels 375 × 260 cm interior panels 365 × 520 cm
St. Bavo Cathedral Ghent (Giraudon, Paris)

150 THE MASTER OF FLÉMALLE: *Triptych of the Annunciation (The Mérode Altarpiece)*, c. 1426
oil on panel central panel 64.1 × 63.2 cm
The Metropolitan Museum of Art, New York. The Cloisters Collection 1956 (56.70)

151 HUGO VAN DER GOES: *The Portinari Altarpiece*, 1474-6
central panel 253 × 304 cm
Uffizi, Florence (Scala, Florence)

152 GERARD DAVID: *Annunciation*, undated
panel 40 × 32 cm
Stadelsches Kunstinstitut, Frankfurt (The Bridgeman Art Library, London)

202 JACOPO DE'BARBARI: *Still Life*, 1504
panel 52 × 42.5 cm
Alte Pinakothek, Munich (Artothek, Munich)

203 PALMA VECCHIO: *Venus and Cupid*, 1522-4
oil on canvas 118.1 × 208.9 cm
Fitzwilliam Museum, Cambridge

204 CORREGGIO: *Nativity*, 1529-30
panel 256.5 × 188 cm
Gemäldegalerie, Dresden (The Bridgeman Art
Library, London)

205 RAPHAEL: *Christ's Charge to Saint Peter*, 1515-16
gouache on paper 343 × 532 cm
The Trustees of the Victoria & Albert Museum,
London (The Bridgeman Art Library, London)

206 FRA BARTOLOMMEO: *Carandolet Altarpiece*, c. 1511
panel 260 × 230 cm
Besançon Cathedral, (Giraudon, Paris)

207 GIOVANNI ANTONIO BOLTRAFFIO: *Virgin and
Child*, late 1490s
panel 83 × 63.5 cm
Museum of Art, Budapest (Artothek, Munich)

208 LEONARDO DA VINCI: *Virgin with Child with
Saint Anne and Saint John the Baptist*, late 1490s
black chalk heightened with white on paper
141.5 × 104.6 cm
The National Gallery, London

209 ARISTOTILE DA SANGALLO AFTER MICHELANGELO:
Battle of Cascina, c. 1542
grisaille on paper 76 × 132 cm
Holkham Hall, Norfolk (The Bridgeman Art
Library, London)

210 MICHELANGELO: *Holy Family with Saint John the
Baptist (Doni Tondo)*, 1504
panel 120 cm diameter
Uffizi, Florence (Scala, Florence)

211 RAPHAEL: *Madonna Alba*, 1511
oil on panel transferred to canvas 94.5 cm diameter
National Gallery of Art, Washington D.C.,
Andrew W. Mellon Collection

212 GIOVANNI BELLINI: *Madonna in the Meadow*,
c. 1505
oil on panel transferred to canvas 67.3 × 86.4 cm
The National Gallery, London

213 ANDREA DEL SARTO: *Holy Family with the
Youthful Saint John*, c.1530
oil on panel 135.9 × 100.6 cm
The Metropolitan Museum of Art, New York,
Maria DeWitt Jesup Fund, 1922 (22.75)

214 RAPHAEL: *Triumph of Galatea*, 1511
fresco
Palazzo della Farnesina, Rome (Scala, Florence)

215 GIOVANNI BELLINI: *Lady at her Toilet*, 1515
panel 62 × 79 cm
Kunsthistorisches Museum, Vienna

216 SEBASTIANO DEL PIOMBO: *Death of Adonis*,
c. 1512
oil on canvas 189 × 295 cm
Uffizi, Florence (Scala, Florence)

217 MICHELANGELO: *Lybian Sybil*, 1511
fresco
Sistine Chapel, The Vatican (Scala, Florence)

218 MICHELANGELO: *Sistine Chapel Ceiling*, 1508-12
(since cleaning)
fresco
Sistine Chapel, The Vatican (© Nippon
Television Network Corporation Tokyo 1991)

219 TITIAN: *Sacred and Profane Love*, c. 1514
oil on canvas 120 × 280 cm
Galleria Borghese, Rome (Scala, Rome)

220 GIORGIONE: *Sleeping Venus*, c. 1510
oil on canvas 108.5 × 175 cm
Gemäldegalerie, Dresden (Artothek, Munich)

221 TITIAN: *The Three Ages of Man*, 1516
oil on canvas 90 × 150.7 cm
Duke of Sutherland Collection, on loan to the
National Gallery of Scotland, Edinburgh

222 CORREGGIO: *Assumption of the Virgin*, 1526-8
fresco
Duomo, Parma (Scala, Florence)

223 CORREGGIO: *Martrydom of Four Saints*, 1524-6
oil on canvas 158.5 × 184.3 cm
Galleria Nazionale, Parma (Scala, Florence)

224 CORREGGIO: *Io*, 1531
oil on canvas 162 × 73.5 cm
Kunsthistorisches Museum, Vienna

225 MORETTO DA BRESCIA: *Count Sciarra Martinengo
Cesaresco*, c. 1545-50
oil on canvas 113.7 × 94 cm
The National Gallery, London

226 GIAN GIROLAMO SAVOLDO: *Saint Mary
Magdalene Approaching the Sepulchre*, c. 1528-30
oil on canvas 86.4 × 79.4 cm
The National Gallery, London

227 SODOMA: *Marriage of Alexander with Roxana*,
1516-17
fresco
Palazzo della Farnesina, Rome (Scala, Florence)

228 AGNOLO BRONZINO: *Allegory of Venus, Folly and
Time*, c. 1545
panel 146.1 × 116.2 cm
The National Gallery, London

229 MICHELANGELO: *Last Judgement*, 1535-41
fresco
Sistine Chapel, The Vatican (Scala, Florence)

230 MICHELANGELO: *Conversion of Saint Paul*, 1542-5
fresco
Pauline Chapel, The Vatican (Scala, Florence)

231 JACOPO PONTORMO: *Pietà*, c. 1526-8
panel 313 × 192 cm
S. Felicità, Florence (Scala, Florence)

232 PARMIGIANINO: *Madonna of the Long Neck*,
c. 1535
panel 216 × 132 cm
Uffizi, Florence (Scala, Florence)

233 PERINO DEL VAGA: *Martyrdom of the Ten
Thousand*, 1522-3
pen and brown ink heightened with white and
watercolour on paper 36.4 × 33.9 cm
Albertina, Vienna

234 ROSSO FIORENTINO: *Dead Christ supported by
Angels*, c.1525-6
oil on paper 135.5 104.1 cm
Museum of Fine Arts, Boston, Charles Potter
Kling Fund

235 AGNOLO BRONZINO: *Deposition*, 1545
oil on panel 268 × 173 cm
Musée des Beaux Arts, Besançon (Scala,
Florence)

236 TITIAN: *Bacchanal of the Andrians*, completed
1522
oil on canvas 175 × 193 cm
Prado, Madrid (The Bridgeman Art Library,
London)

237 TITIAN: *Diana and Callisto*, 1556-9
oil on canvas 187 × 204.5 cm
Duke of Sutherland Collection, on loan to the
National Gallery of Scotland, Edinburgh

238 TITIAN: *Diana and Actaeon*, 1556-9
oil on canvas 184.5 × 202.2 cm
Duke of Sutherland Collection, on loan to the
National Gallery of Scotland, Edinburgh

239 JACOPO TINTORETTO: *Miracle of Saint Mark*, 1548
oil on canvas 415 × 541 cm
Accademia, Venice (Scala, Florence)

240 PAOLO VERONESE: *Interior View of the Villa
Barbaro, Maser*, 1561
Fresco
Villa Barbaro, Maser (Scala, Florence)

241 PAOLO VERONESE: *Triumph of Venice*, 1583
oil on canvas 904 × 580 cm
Palazzo Ducale, Venice (Scala, Florence)

242 JACOPO BASSANO: *Adoration of the Magi*, early
1540s
oil on canvas 183 × 235 cm
The National Gallery of Scotland, Edinburgh

243 NICCOLÒ DELL'ABATE: *A Concert*, 1548-52
fresco
Palazzo Poggi, Bologna (Scala, Florence)

244 PELLEGRINO TIBALDI: *Adoration of the Shepherds*,
1548-9
oil on canvas 157 × 105 cm
Galleria Borghese, Rome (Scala, Florence)

245 PARMIGIANINO: *A Lady 'The Turkish Slave'*,
c. 1522
panel 67 × 53 cm
Galleria Nazionale, Parma (Scala, Florence)

246 LORENZO LOTTO: *Andrea Odoni*, 1527
oil on canvas 104 × 101 cm
The Royal Collection © 1994 Her Majesty the
Queen

247 LORENZO LOTTO: *Brother Gregorio Belo of
Vicenza*, 1547
oil on canvas 87.3 × 71.1 cm
The Metropolitan Museum of Art, New York,
Rogers Fund 1965 (65.117)

248 RAPHAEL: *Transfiguration*, 1518-20
oil on panel 405 × 278 cm
Pinacoteca, The Vatican (Scala, Florence)

249 JACOPO PONTORMO: *Joseph in Egypt*, 1517-18
panel 96 × 109 cm
The National Gallery, London

250 RAPHAEL: *The Road to Calvary (Lo Spasimo di
Sicilia)*, c. 1517
oil on canvas 318 × 229 cm
Prado, Madrid (Arxiu Mas, Madrid)

251 ROSSO FIORENTINO: *A Young Man*, c. 1528
panel 120 × 86 cm
Museo di Capodimonte, Naples (Scala, Florence)

252 AGNOLO BRONZINO: *Giovanni de'Medici as a
Baby*, 1545
panel 58 × 45 cm
Uffizi, Florence (Scala, Florence)

253 AGNOLO BRONZINO: *Laura Battiferi*, late 1550s
oil on panel 83 × 60 cm
Palazzo Vecchio, Florence (Scala, Florence)

254 TITIAN: *Assumption of the Virgin*, 1516-18
panel 686 × 361 cm
S. Maria Gloriosa dei Frari, Venice (The
Bridgeman Art Library, London)

255 TITIAN: *Pietro Aretino*, 1545
oil on canvas 98 × 78 cm
Galleria Palatina, Florence (Scala, Florence)

256 TITIAN: *Pietà*, 1576
oil on canvas 352 × 349 cm
Accademia, Venice (Scala, Florence)

257 FRANCESCO SALVIATI: *Triumph of Camillus*, 1543-5
fresco
Palazzo Vecchio, Florence (Scala, Florence)

258 EL GRECO: *Giulio Clovio holding the Farnese Hours*, 1570-2
oil on canvas 58 × 86 cm
Museo di Capodimonte, Naples (Scala, Florence)

259 GIULIO CLOVIO: *Pages from the Farnese Hours*, completed 1546
vellum 17.3 × 11 cm
© The Pierpont Morgan Library 1994, New York (Ms. M.69 f.59v-60)

260 SEBASTIANO DEL PIOMBO: *Ferry Carandolet and his Secretaries*, 1511-12
oil on canvas 112.5 × 87 cm
Museo Thyssen-Bornemisza, Madrid

261 PAOLO VERONESE: *Marriage Feast at Cana*, 1562-3
oil on canvas 666 × 990 cm
Musée du Louvre, Paris (Réunion des musées nationaux, Paris)

262 JACOPO TINTORETTO: *Susanna and the Elders*, 1557
oil on canvas 146 × 199.6 cm
Kunsthistorisches Museum, Vienna

263 GIULIO ROMANO: The Sala dei Giganti, Palazzo del Tè, 1532-4
fresco
Palazzo del Tè, Mantua (Scala, Florence)

264 LORENZO LOTTO: *Triumph of Chastity, c.* 1531
oil on canvas 76 × 118 cm
Private Collection, Rome (Scala, Florence)

265 PARMIGIANINO: *Conversion of Saint Paul*, 1527-8
oil on canvas 117.5 × 128.5 cm
Kunsthistorisches Museum, Vienna

266 DOSSO DOSSI: *Jupiter, Mercury and Virtue, c.* 1529
oil on canvas 112 × 150 cm
Kunsthistorisches Museum, Vienna

267 ALESSANDRO ALLORI: *The Pearl Fishers*, 1570-2
oil on canvas 115.5 × 86.5 cm
Palazzo Vecchio, Florence (Scala, Florence)

268 ALBRECHT DURER: *Self Portrait with a Fur-Trimmed Robe*, 1500
panel 67 × 49 cm
Alte Pinakothek, Munich (Blauel/Ghamm Artothek, Munich)

269 ALBRECHT DURER: *The Hare*, 1502
watercolour and bodycolour on paper 25.1 × 22.6 cm
Albertina, Vienna (The Bridgeman Art Library, London)

270 ALBRECHT DURER: *A Young Woman*, 1506
panel 28.5 × 21.5 cm
Staatliche Gemäldegalerie, Berlin (Artothek, Munich)

271 ALBRECHT ALTDORFER: *Landscape with a Footbridge, c.* 1518-20
parchment on panel 41.2 × 35.5 cm
The National Gallery, London

272 LUCAS CRANACH THE ELDER: *Johannes Cuspinian, c.* 1502
panel 59 × 45 cm
Reinhart Collection, Winterthur (Colorphoto Hans Hinz, Allschwil)

273 HANS BALDUNG GRIEN: *The Three Ages of Woman and Death*, 1509-11
panel 48.2 × 32.7 cm
Kunsthistorisches Museum, Vienna

274 HANS HOLBEIN THE YOUNGER: *Christ in the Sepulchre*, 1521-2
tempera on panel 30.5 × 200 cm
Offentliche Sammlung, Basle (Colorphoto Hans Hinz, Allschwil)

275 QUINTEN METSYS: *Ill-Matched Lovers, c.* 1520-25
oil on panel 43.2 × 63 cm
National Gallery of Art, Washington D.C., Ailsa Mellon Bruce Fund

276 JAN GOSSAERT: *The Malvagna Triptych*, 1510-11.
oil on panel central panel 45.5 × 35 cm side panel 45.5 × 17.5 cm
Galleria Nazionale della Sicilia, Palermo (Scala, Florence)

277 JOOS VAN CLEVE: *Margaretha Boghe, c.* 1518
panel 57.1 × 39.6 cm
National Gallery of Art, Washington D.C., Andrew W. Mellon fund

278 CORNELIS ENGELBRECHTSZ: *Emperor Constantine (?) and Saint Helena*, after 1517
panel 87.5 × 56.5 cm
Alte Pinakothek, Munich (Joachim Blauel/Artothek, Munich)

279 LUCAS VAN LEYDEN: *The Card Players, c.* 1514
oil on panel 33.5 × 47.5 cm
Wilton House, Wiltshire (The Bridgeman Art Library, London)

280 LUCAS VAN LEYDEN: *Worship of the Golden Calf, c.* 1525-8
central panels 93 × 67 cm side panels 91 × 30 cm
Rijksmuseum, Amsterdam

281 MATHIS GRÜNEWALD: *The Small Crucifixion, c.* 1511-20
oil on panel 61.6 × 46 cm
National Gallery of Art, Washington D.C., Samuel H. Kress Collection

282 MATHIS GRÜNEWALD: *The Isenheim Altarpiece*, completed 1515
central panel 269 × 307 cm
Unterlinden Museum, Colmar (The Bridgeman Art Library, London)

283 BERNARD VAN ORLEY: *Saint Matthew, c.* 1512
panel 140 × 180 cm
Kunsthistorisches Museum, Vienna

284 PIETER BRUEGEL THE ELDER: *Hunters in the Snow*, 1565
panel 117 × 162 cm
Kunsthistorisches Museum, Vienna

285 PIETER BRUEGEL THE ELDER: *Parable of the Blind*, 1568
distemper on canvas 86 × 154 cm
Museo di Capodimonte, Naples (The Bridgeman Art Library, London)

286 PIETER BRUEGEL THE ELDER: *Tower of Babel*, 1563
panel 114 × 155 cm
Kunsthistorisches Museum, Vienna

287 ALBRECHT DÜRER: *Adoration of the Magi*, 1504
panel 100 × 114 cm
Uffizi, Florence (Scala, Florence)

288 ALBRECHT ALTDORFER: *Birth of the Virgin, c.* 1520-1
panel 140.7 × 130 cm
Alte Pinakothek, Munich (Joachim Blauel/Artothek, Munich)

289 ALBRECHT ALTDORFER: *Battle of Issus*, 1529
panel 158.4 × 120.3 cm
Alte Pinakothek, Munich (Joachim Blauel/Artothek, Munich)

290 HANS HOLBEIN THE YOUNGER: *Bonifacius Amerbach*, 1519
tempera on panel 28.5 × 27.5 cm
Kunstmuseum, Basle (Colorphoto Hans Hinz, Allschwil)

291 HANS HOLBEIN THE YOUNGER: *George Gisze*, 1532
panel 96.3 × 85.7 cm
Staatliche Gemäldegalerie, Berlin (The Bridgeman Art Library, London)

292 LUCAS CRANACH THE ELDER: *Judith with the Head of Holofernes, c.* 1530
tempera and oil on panel 89.6 × 62 cm
The Metropolitan Museum of Art, New York, Rogers Fund 1911 (11.15)

293 JAN VAN SCOREL: *Saint Mary Magdalen, c.* 1529
panel 67 × 76.5 cm
Rijksmuseum, Amsterdam

294 JOACHIM PATINIR AND QUINTEN METSYS: *Temptation of Saint Anthony, c.* 1520-4
oil on canvas 155 × 173 cm
Prado, Madrid (Arxiu Mas, Madrid)

295 JAN GOSSAERT: *Danaë* 1527
panel 113.5 × 95 cm
Alte Pinakothek, Munich (Joachim Blauel/Artothek, Munich)

296 PIETER AERTSEN: *The Cook*, 1559
panel 161 × 79 cm
Palazzo Biano, Genoa (Scala, Florence)

297 ANTONIS MOR: *Self Portrait*, 1528
panel 113 × 87 cm
Uffizi, Florence (Scala, Florence)

298 MARINUS VAN REYMERSWAELE: *Saint Jerome*, 1521
oil on canvas 75 × 101 cm
Prado, Madrid (Arxiu Mas, Madrid)

299 ANNIBALE CARRACCI: *The Farnese Gallery, Rome, c.* 1597-1600
fresco
Palazzo Farnese, Rome (Scala, Florence)

300 FEDERICO BAROCCI: *Madonna of the People*, 1576-9
panel 359 × 252 cm
Uffizi, Florence (Scala, Florence)

301 EL GRECO: *Burial of the Count of Orgaz*, 1586-8
oil on canvas 487.5 × 360 cm
Sto. Tome, Toledo (Arxiu Mas, Madrid)

302 ANNIBALE CARRACCI: *The Butcher's Shop, c.* 1582-3
oil on canvas 190 × 271 cm
The Governing Body, Christ Church, Oxford

303 VINCENZO CAMPI: *The Fruit Vendor, c.* 1580
oil on canvas 143 × 213 cm
Pinacoteca di Brera, Milan (Scala, Florence)

304 ISAAC OLIVER: *A Lady in Masque Costume*, 1610
vellum 6.4 × 5.1 cm
The Trustees of the Victoria & Albert Museum, London

305 MAERTEN VAN HEEMSKERCK: *Self Portrait with the Colosseum*, Rome, 1553
panel 42.2 × 54 cm
Fitzwilliam Museum, Cambridge

306 CARAVAGGIO: *Basket of Fruit, c.* 1596
oil on canvas 46 × 64.5 cm
Pinacoteca Ambrosiana, Milan (Scala, Florence)

Index